GEORGE FRIDERIC HANDEL

Also by Paul Henry Lang

MUSIC IN WESTERN CIVILIZATION

MUSIC AND HISTORY

A PICTORIAL HISTORY OF MUSIC (WITH OTTO L. BETTMANN)

PROBLEMS OF MODERN MUSIC (EDITOR)

THE CREATIVE WORLD OF MOZART (EDITOR)

STRAVINSKY: A NEW APPRAISAL OF HIS WORK (EDITOR)

ONE HUNDRED YEARS OF MUSIC IN AMERICA (EDITOR)

CONTEMPORARY MUSIC IN EUROPE (EDITOR WITH NATHAN BRODER)

THE SYMPHONY: 1800-1900 (EDITOR)

THE CONCERTO: 1800-1900 (EDITOR)

GEORGE FRIDERIC

HANDEL

by

Paul Henry Lang

The Norton Library

W · W · NORTON & COMPANY · INC · New York

Books That Live
The Norton imprint on a book means that in the publisher's
estimation it is a book not for a single season but for the years.
W. W. Norton & Company, Inc.

ISBN 0 393 00815 0

1 2 3 4 5 6 7 8 9 0

TO MY DAUGHTER

Stephanie Lang Martin

CONTENTS

XII (1737–1741)   295

XIII (1741–1742)   332

XIV   357

XV (1742–1744)   394

XVI (1744–1745)   421

suspension of concerts — Handel vacates Haymarket Theatre — Suffers another
physical collapse

summer of 1758 — Last oratorio season ends, April 6, 1759 — Final codicil — Handel dies on April 14, 1759, and is buried in Westminster Abbey

XXVII

ILLUSTRATIONS

THE VIGNETTE on the binding is taken from an engraving by James
Stow (1825), based on a silver token designed by William
Hogarth, issued as a "season ticket" to regular visitors to
Vauxhall Gardens. It shows Roubiliac's statue of Handel, with
the inscription "Blandius Orpheo" (Horace, *Odes,* I. xxiv. 13).

FOREWORD

EXPLANATION OF THE METHOD FOLLOWED IN AN ESSAY IS usually the enumeration of extenuating circumstances; here it is perhaps unnecessary because this study should not be judged for what it avoids or omits. It is neither my intention, nor is it possible within the framework of such a volume, to give a comprehensive, elaborate biographical portrait or a detailed analysis of the genesis and execution of every composition in the hundred volumes of Handel's collected works. Nor shall I attempt, with the aid of dark, pithy sentences, to explain the inexplicable, any more than I wish to reduce to a comfortable format the art of an immense genius. What I have done is to endeavor to examine matters that influenced Handel's development and art and that may explain how this man, whose life was so much of a piece, could touch the extremes of obloquy and veneration, and how the German immigrant became England's national composer. Perhaps the reader will find this interesting.

This book was not written yesterday but is the result of ideas carried in the literary valise from place to place for years. While I am much beholden to the critical work of others, I make little use of the usual form of documentation; wherever I have recourse to conjecture this is not concealed and is obvious to the reader. Such conjecture, when clearly indicated as such, has its necessary place in biography. The alternative, when documents are lacking that could fill the silences, is to present a mere skeleton of facts, which is only a caricature of reality. I have permitted myself to digress and to repeat, to select and omit, elaborate and wander as the spirit moved me. But I did not absolve myself of the responsibilities of the historian, remembering that the cause is as important to learn as the event, that all human history is one, and that though there is nothing new under the sun, the essence of history is asking questions. Others may have different ideas, but perhaps they will have patience with my view. I do not mind if some reject these thoughts as being "unscientific," but hope that there will be others who may not find them foreign to their own thoughts. They may feel, as I do, that no biography can be "definitive"; there is always something for us to add from another angle. Finally, I hope that I may not be censured for attacking the venerable bulwarks of Handelian lore and for offending the accustomed attitude of piety.

One is always indebted to colleagues, students, friends, and institutions. Among the latter I am especially grateful to the Guggenheim Foundation for its grant that enabled me to follow Handel's tracks in Italy and study his original manuscripts in England. I should really cite the entire membership of Columbia University's Seminar on the Eighteenth Century, for the deliberations of that admirable group of scholars, covering the whole range of 18th-century thought and history, helped me immeasurably to clarify many an obscure problem. Then there is the amiable crew that makes up W. W. Norton & Co., my publishers. Year after year I disappointed them (the book was planned for the Handel bicentennial in 1959!), but their patience and good will never gave out. Far from using pressure, they just urged me to continue in peace.

And I have three large private creditors who must be publicly acknowledged. My literary vessel has a navigator, my wife, without whose guidance I would not venture beyond the breakwaters. In all fairness she should be named co-author, for there is not one paragraph in what follows that did not benefit from her discerning scrutiny. The vessel also has an able engineer, Nathan Broder, my old friend and comrade in arms for over twenty years as Associate Editor of *The Musical Quarterly*. He keeps everything in good running order. Finally, my daughter Stephanie typed the whole manuscript, appending to every batch perceptive and useful comments that were not disregarded. In the end, however, even this powerful support cannot prevent *faux pas,* and they are my sole responsibility. Perhaps I may be permitted to quote Foulke Robartes, author of the *Revenue of the Gospel,* who so nicely apportions blame for mistakes:

Who faulteth not, liveth not; who mendeth faults is commended: The Printer hath faulted a little: it may be the author oversighted more. Thy paine Reader is the least; then erre thou not most by misconstruing or sharpe censuring; least thou be more charitable than either of them hath been heedlesse.

                                                                                P.H.L.

GEORGE FRIDERIC HANDEL

INTRODUCTION

F AME," SAYS RILKE, "IS NOTHING BUT THE SUM TOTAL OF MIS-
understandings that cling to a name." There is no more misunderstood
and misrepresented composer in the history of music than Handel. With a
few laudable exceptions the Handelian literature is selective, and the selection is not history and esthetics so much as edification, therefore his
name has become a religious monument. But behind that name is the man
and the musician who is the object of this study. I shall attempt to speak
about Handel, not impartially, but with the objectivity of a faith that rests
on firm conviction.

How does one approach such a veiled and distant figure? Weighted
down with a historical sense and obsessed with the idea of evolution and
progress, we tend to see the past exclusively in the light of later development. We think that it is more important to know how the artist stands in
relation to us than to himself. He becomes for us a bit of history. But his
history cannot be understood, nor his relationship either to his own time
or to ours, without knowing the man, his nature, his spirit. We like to proceed in inverse order, often mistaking results for intentions; and the out-
sider approaching a long-lost cultural era inclines to take the features he
first perceives as the most important. Indeed, the farther removed we are
from a period the less we separate material from spirit. We can hardly
view Palestrina or Bach purely historically; we are compelled to see them
immediately as the creators of works of art, their personality retreats behind their work and can be seen only through it.

If one enters such an immense territory as Handel's he must be careful to state at the outset what part of it he intends to traverse. The occasion does not permit a visit to every obscure corner, for, two hundred
years after Handel's death, only what is lasting is important. We propose
to resort to that old-fashioned method of art criticism which seeks to understand not only the man from his works, but the works from the man.
This does not entail a scientific case history. We shall never see the inner
picture of the whole man, that could be divulged to us only by the artist

himself or by a faithful Horatio. But Handel said very little about himself and had false, self-appointed Horatios. The regrettable and incredible fact is that the magnitude of Handel's genius and the avalanche of great music he wrote is scarcely suspected today. True, he is always bracketed with Bach, but once we remove the brackets and omit *Messiah* and two or three other works, we have precious little left. We know that his was a purposeful life, that he went through heroic and incessant struggles, and that he finally came to rest with Britain's great in Westminster Abbey. Little was accidental in his life, for Handel virtually controlled his fate. Yet, by merely following external criteria, using them for the measuring of personality, we can never arrive at a true appreciation of Handel.

The central fact of a musician's life is his music, and here the biographer is confronted with an obstacle unknown to his colleagues in other fields. It is extremely difficult to convey to the reader, instructed or uninstructed, just what constitutes the essential and particular quality of the musician's thoughts, methods, speculations, and inventions. Yet his musical *thought* is the very core of his life story. Something may be made of tales of musical precocity, of the early struggles of genius, of the triumphs of the master, but the great man's thought remains the root of his life, and an effort must be made to bring home to the reader a notion, however partial, however resistant to verbalization, of what lies behind the external events in the life of so colorful a man of action as Handel.

Hero worship has dominated our musical outlook for over a century. It has caused untold damage, making the contemplation of the work of art in all its aspects virtually impossible. Fortunately, there are some who realize that even the work of genius can be viewed and examined with scholarly detachment—witness Winton Dean's magnificent *Handel's Dramatic Oratorios and Masques* and Otto Erich Deutsch's invaluable *Handel, a Documentary Biography*.

Sir Newman Flower has rightly said: "It is questionable whether any music, composed in England or imported into it, has reached the heart of the people so truly as Handel's." Yet, familiar as the picture of Handel is, some of its most vital aspects elude us. He has always been before us; we know his consummate confidence in himself; we know he had no illusions about either himself or his works; he chose his part and played it to perfection. It is his silence that is so baffling. No family doctor or lawyer, no father confessor was ever more close-mouthed about the confidences entrusted to him than Handel was about his own person and private life.

We do not know the real reason for artistic creativity—and probably never shall know. We can find some similarities in the manifestations of creative force, which we then attempt to range into types, but the reasons for their differentiation are still largely unknown. It can be seen, then, that creative power itself cannot be espied in its secret functioning by any known method or science, yet we are always trying to do just that. This naive belief falsifies esthetics and musicological thought alike, while the psychologists have their own merry time by themselves. All we can do is to endeavor to follow the development of thought and technique, placing them in their proper environment, so that the image of the artist will appear before us. And since the scholar recognizes that this great musician's portrait is covered by countless layers of overpainting, like a very old canvas, his true features indistinct and even distorted, the layers will have to be peeled off one by one.

In the English-speaking Protestant world Handel is known by a portrait distinct, indeed, but painted in a later age without first-hand acquaintance with its subject. Here Handel is universally and uniquely known as the composer of *Messiah*. But it was not with *Messiah* that Handel first entered the ranks of the very great, though it was this work that made his name a household word. No matter what came before or after—and the masterpieces are legion—it is always *Messiah* that is immediately associated with his name whenever it is mentioned. For generations we have known the oratorio by heart, and *Messiah* is perhaps the only major work about which public sentiment is unanimous. Its freshness, its warmth, its beautifully rounded forms and sculptured melodies offer universal experience to men of all walks of life and all shades of faith. Handel achieved with this work the most widespread critical recognition ever accorded a composer, for among his acclaimers are not only every English-speaking church congregation, small or large, but also Mozart, Haydn, Beethoven, Brahms, and every musician who ever tried his hand at choral writing.

Still, for all we know, Bacon may have composed the rest of the hundred volumes of the old Händelgesellschaft edition. No other great master is so narrowly known. His works have to be uncovered and washed free of the prejudices and falsifications that cling to them. Granted, no one can go through the entire work of Handel without admitting that a good deal of it has faded away, perhaps forever, and it is easy to suppose that he always owed his fame to one oratorio and half a dozen opera tunes that were turned into "sacred" songs. But we know that much contained in these volumes possesses real life, and it is shocking how reluctant the musical world is to investigate. (Anatole France says somewhere that the best way to travel to the land of immortality is with a small suitcase. This is hardly true: Bach, Mozart, and many others prove the contrary.)

One of the important reasons for this regrettable situation is that the principal musical representatives of Handel's generation were not primarily composers of suites, sonatas, and concertos—though they wrote them too—but of works for the lyric theatre and of concerted church music, which then was part of the great field of dramatic music. But both Baroque opera and concerted church music have long since faded from our world, and with a few exceptions their creators have either disappeared from the annals or, if like Vivaldi they also composed fine sonatas and concertos, they are remembered only for their instrumental works, which seem to stand for the whole era. As we look at this vast amount of music we seem to behold historical ruins, which one contemplates with a curiosity mingled with pity. Handel composed operas, dozens of them, for thirty-six years. To succeeding generations they appeared to have been composed in an idiom not only dead but quite safely buried. Surely, there must be more than a few among them that need only be excavated and cleaned to radiate that life we seek in a work of art. Unfortunately, those few operas that have been revived have been so badly mutilated that they were only a shadow of their original state. It is a pity that the "restorers" of these operas come either from the ranks of practicing musicians without adequate stylistic insight or from among men of letters unschooled in music. Oskar Hagen, the person who had the taste and foresight to start the Handelian opera renaissance in the 1920s in Göttingen, was an eminent art historian but an amateur in musicology, as the scores he edited prove conclusively. All these men have had the best intentions, but they worked under the terrible handicap of the cumulative force of prejudice and prohibition which made them helpless, panicky, and ruthless. Their fatal error was that they saw in Handel's operas not things resurrected but things renovated.

A study of Handel's operas and other dramatic works in addition to the undramatic and hence atypical *Messiah* will disclose a Handel largely unknown: a composer with a remarkable sense for dramatic human character. He saw men and women where others have seen only historical-mythical busts. There are artists to whom the demands of one genre remain a priori for their entire life, whose soul is so filled by these demands that they see them everywhere, no matter what the occasion, or the setting, or even the material. Michelangelo divined in every block of stone the statue hidden in it, and even his paintings were envisaged with the eye of the sculptor. It was the same with Beethoven the symphonist, and it was the same with Handel the dramatist.

If so important a part of Handel's life work as the operas must remain unknown to the public (they cannot be resuscitated without a renaissance of Baroque opera in general), there is no excuse for the neglect of the oratorios—more properly, the English music dramas—and the other vocal works. They are modern and accessible and can be made wonderfully viable with intelligent and knowledgeable editorial work. We have been misled and have been deprived of these great works because they are divested—the few that are heard—of their true nature, forcibly removed from their true home, the theatre, and made to present religion as a rather athletic system of health and happiness. It was from Handel's personal struggle that the English oratorio was born. Under the gradual impact of the ideological, rational pressure of English middle-class attitudes his long-held faith in the future of opera in England had to succumb. But we should never forget what Arnold Schering wisely said: "Handel's operas are to his life work as Beethoven's quartets are to the symphonies."

There are few instances in the history of music in which an immigrant has so completely assimilated himself with his new surroundings as Handel; perhaps Lully is the only other example. Handel became an English subject not only *de jure* but even more so *de facto*, and remained one to the end of his life. We can see how he was gradually enveloped by the particular qualities, tenets, and problems of his adopted country, and how he tied himself ever more strongly to England. This assimilation must be borne in mind if we want to understand why the imagination of one who so strenuously lived in the present turned to the Old Testament and the oratorio.

Handel recognized no artistic absolutes; he wrote a great deal out of necessity, for money, or because he wanted to beat the opposition. And much of this he did rather loosely and with a careless hand. Like all Baroque masters he was the purveyor of musical entertainment for everyday use, but he was never a hypocrite and was absolutely free of false refinement. His confidence in his vocation had not only the objective strength of genius but the profound conviction that he must reach his aim no matter what might happen, no matter what he must do to himself or to anyone else. His ruthlessness and boundless courage are awe-inspiring, his audacious speculative temper and passion for business extraordinary. For such a temper competition is a challenge that must be met at any cost. That he was a good businessman and an impresario in the grand style did not bother anyone until the Romantic era, when this proclivity became embarrassing. In the eyes of the Romantics this conflicted with the ordinary habits of both the genius and the dedicated "religious" composer. But Handel was serious about his art; he demands understanding and respect, not uncritical adulation or righteous censure.

The man and artist form a unity, though with various points of gravity. Since these points of gravity are not always clear to us, we must study the man and the artist separately, though never losing sight of one when we are dealing with the other. This is what I propose to do in the following pages, fully realizing that it is difficult to catalogue a man's virtues without appearing to freeze him into a statue.

I

EVERYTHING GREAT MEN ACHIEVE DURING THEIR RECORDED
public lives is the transformation into negotiable currency of forces and
capabilities they gathered when they were as yet neither great nor famous. If we want to judge the individuality of great men without the
images their greatness and fame thrust upon them, so far as this is possible, we must begin our investigation in that period of their lives when
in the darkness of anonymity they prepared themselves, consciously or
unconsciously, for their future vocations.

If an artist could live to read his biography, he would recognize not
so much himself as the mask that covered his face. Where is his true face?
We see it in his works, which testify to the gifts he was endowed with,
which made him what he is. Here we discover that humility, that patience, that disinterestedness and love to which are opposed the many rivalries of life. It is for these reasons the artist's creative work is called a
confession, for in the work of art he is purely himself. To write a biography of a great composer without constantly exploring the music that accompanies the stations of his life is an idle undertaking; it is one of the
chief reasons Handel is so little understood in the English-speaking world.
But biography presents problems that become all the more acute if it is
attempted in an unorthodox and unsystematic way. Where is the emphasis to be thrown? On the personality of the subject or on the measure of
his work? There is the biographical thrill of demonstrating how personality gradually broadens out into the event. Yet there is the danger that a

biographer may attempt to organize and arrange history.

Handel steps into history suddenly, already full-grown, in the first decade of the 18th century. To the average lover of music this date must be advanced farther, to the time of the successful oratorios, but even some of the well-informed Handelian authors in England and America deal perfunctorily with the youthful experiences that were vital to his future career. The twenty-five-year-old Handel who arrived in England was a mature master, but even the twenty-one-year-old who ventured into Italy was an accomplished composer capable of plunging immediately into the thick of the highly competitive Italian musical life and holding his own. And now we must turn the clock back still farther: the eighteen-year-old Handel, scarcely more than an adolescent, who left his home town to seek his fortune in the Hanseatic metropolis was a superbly trained, confident musician and virtuoso player with far more practical experience, knowledge, and assurance than most professionals many years his senior. He is never spoken of as a child prodigy, but in fact he was one, and at eighteen had all the assurance and savoir-faire of that miraculous youngster in the second half of the century: Mozart.

How had this style, already so mature, been formed? Surely this compels the historian to take a much more searching look at Handel's "German phase" than is customary among our English and American authors. Hitherto, for English readers, the period of Handel's apprenticeship as a composer has been shrouded in a certain mystery. They had a vague knowledge of his studies with Zachow and of his years of wandering in Italy, where he made the acquaintance of great musicians, but for them the curtain really rose on Handel's career with his arrival in England.

[2]

GEORG FRIEDRICH HÄNDEL was born February 23, 1685, in Halle, the second issue of his father's second marriage, to a pastor's daughter thirty years his junior. The family and surroundings into which he was born were conservative, steady, thrifty, unadventurous, and unimaginative, a typical provincial Saxon petit bourgeois existence. But his father, Georg, a barber-surgeon, was a man of strength, if lacking in warmth. Iron self-discipline, force of character, robust health, pugnacious will to fight for a cause, courage, infinite capacity for work, as well as an astute business sense, the son inherited from the father, though fortunately not his morose, misanthropic disposition. His mother came from a dynasty of Lutheran pastors. Equally sturdy and courageous, she was a good and pious woman whom Handel remembered with warm affection, even though he saw very little of her after leaving Halle in his early youth. Obviously, his kind and hearty nature came from the maternal stock. His musical abilities must have been noticed at an early age, but the dour surgeon paid no attention to such frivolities as music; that sort of thing was not encouraged in a solid professional family, and he preferred a lawyer's career for his son.

The boy must have taken part in the singing at grammar school and heard the Sunday music in Our Lady's Lutheran church where the family worshipped, but where and in what manner he acquired his early proficiency at the keyboard is unknown. There are many romantic stories, such as one about a clavichord hidden in the attic, but none of them can be proved. One important fact is known: the barber-surgeon held a court appointment, and therefore often journeyed to nearby Weissenfels, where the duke had established his residence after Prussia annexed the city of Halle. Georg Händel undoubtedly took his son with him on many occasions, because a relative of his first wife was employed at the court and could look after the youngster while the father made his professional rounds. On one of these occasions when young Handel was permitted to play the postlude to a service, the duke happened to be lingering and was impressed that an eight- or nine-year-old child should play with such ease and fluency. His Serene Highness summoned the elder Händel, suggesting he encourage such a manifest talent. Ducal hints are not to be disregarded, especially by such a hard-bitten status seeker as the court surgeon, so upon their return to Halle the boy was turned over for musical instruction to the organist of the Händels' parish church. Here we have arrived at the first important turn in the future great composer's life but also at the first crucial biographical, artistic, and historical lacuna in the Handel literature.

Friedrich Wilhelm Zachow (1663–1712), Handel's first and only teacher, was still a young man of about thirty when the new student was entrusted to him, but he was already widely known as a fine organist and a rather original composer in the "new style." This man, who is referred to as "lacking in imagination," whose music, "innocuous and trifling," "never rose to great heights," whom even Friedrich Chrysander, the editor of Handel's collected works, held in low esteem, was actually one of the most cultivated, learned, and imaginative musicians in Germany at the end of the century. Nor was Zachow an ordinary cantor, for he enthusiastically embraced the new concerted, dramatic style. His cantatas, often highly dramatic, are distinguished by very imaginative choral writing, colorful orchestration, and skilful handling of the concerted element. Many traits we consider typically Handelian are present in Zachow's music; [1] it is spacious, euphonious, its melody sturdily designed yet sensuous, it can be suave but also monumental. Above all, this music is healthy and communicative; Zachow too had the ability—and the power—to be simple yet effective. He understood the Italians and managed to unite their art felicitously with his German heritage.

This distinguished musician was also an excellent, understanding, and solicitous teacher of both composition and performance. He taught the boy harpsichord and organ (as well as other instruments), which Handel played so capably that by his eleventh year he was able to substitute for Zachow on the organ when the need arose. Handel's first compositions date from this same year, 1696. He received from his master a solid grounding in harmony, counterpoint, and choral writing, as well as in very imaginative orchestration. This consisted not only in writing for a full ensemble with all the winds but also in the subtle art of coaxing varied effects from a simple string orchestra. More than that, Zachow inculcated in his young pupil an intellectual curiosity, a desire to know all styles of music in all countries, an interest he always retained. And there was something else he received from Zachow that became his for the rest of his life: the cool discipline, the artistic brakes to tame the wayward flights of a rich imagination. It is amusing to read in a popular Handel biography that "Zachow had taught him the rudiments of counterpoint and harmony," as if the instruction had been something like a college course for freshmen. The thorough training he received at Zachow's hand formed the boy's musical nature for life.

These studies were copious and severe, but the disciple could not get too much of them and composed steadily. "I used to write like the devil in those days," reminisced Handel many years later, and in view of the enormous productivity of the years of his full maturity, reams of note paper must have been covered for daily exercises with Zachow. Handel's admiration for his teacher was boundless and reverential. After Zachow's death in 1712, Handel, famous London composer, sent "frequent remittances" to his widow.

The manner in which Zachow dealt with Handel shows that he recognized the child's exceptional musical talents. There was a system in this

---

[1] See Vols. 21 and 22 of the *Denkmäler deutscher Tonkunst*. It was Max Seiffert who changed the unfavorable picture of Zachow painted by Chrysander. Later Hugo Leichtentritt in his biography recognized Zachow's pervasive influence on Handel, not only as composer but also as organist.

instruction as rare as it was enlightened and thorough. Zachow possessed an unusually well-stocked library of music that reflected both the catholicity of his taste and the inquisitive turn of his mind. During the years of his apprenticeship, Handel became methodically acquainted with the contents of this library, thus acquiring as comprehensive a knowledge of styles and techniques as possible. Apparently, besides strenuous exercises in the *strenger Satz*, the cantor's traditional art in fugue and cantus firmus work, the master made the pupil copy what he considered significant and instructive scores by all manner of composers. Here we are dealing with actual documents, particularly with a notebook dating from 1698, which Handel kept all his life. While unfortunately lost, the book was sufficiently well described so that we know whose airs, choruses, fugues, and other works it contained.

Now let us examine the panorama offered by the notebook, which is in fact the panorama of music Handel beheld in the most impressionable years of his life. There were, of course, the works of his teacher, but we also encounter some of the key figures in German musical history.

There is Johann Krieger (1652–1735), who, according to Mattheson, excelled all the "brave old masters" in fugues. Indeed, Handel took a copy of Krieger's *Clavier-Übung* with him to England, later presenting it to his friend Bernard Granville. Granville wrote on the flyleaf: "The printed book is by one of the celebrated Organ players of Germany; Mr. Handel in his youth formed himself a good deal on his plan, and said that Krieger was one of the best writers of his time for the organ." Krieger's counterpoint is smooth and fluent, the handling of the themes, especially countersubjects, individual and incisive, and he shows considerable inventiveness and originality in the devising of fugal episodes. Unfortunately, his harmonic sense was not venturesome. Handel was undoubtedly also acquainted with Krieger's cantatas, of which there were over two hundred, though scarcely three dozen survive. However, at least one, *Geliebet sei der Herr* (printed in the Bavarian *Denkmäler*, VI/1), was preserved in a copy made by Zachow. Handel did not miss the remarkable triple fugue contained in this work.

Johann Caspar Kerll (1627–1693), the much-travelled disciple of Valentini, Carissimi, and Frescobaldi, is another significant German master represented in the notebook who looms large in Handel's initial musical formation. With him Handel was introduced to the southern style and manner, for Kerll, though born a Saxon, spent ten years in Italy and was so thoroughly converted to the southern way that he even became a Catholic. Kerll's keyboard works were highly regarded and soon became known in the north, where Zachow and Handel studied them avidly. Handel remembered this music for a long time, borrowing not only bits but an entire movement, which he used in *Israel in Egypt*. Kerll's bold, even romantic, treatment of dissonance fascinated Bach too, who not only studied Kerll's works but, like Handel, borrowed from them.

Still another keyboard composer who appears in the notebook is Johann Jakob Froberger (1616–1667). In his works, Handel, who later became a past master of the art, could observe the working of the mind of an internationally oriented musician who, like himself, was receptive to ideas, no matter what source they came from, that he could reconcile and fuse in a logical and well-balanced style. Once more, both Handel and Bach (together with Zachow and Buxtehude, whose wondrous preludes and toccatas cannot be imagined without Froberger's example) studied this music closely and with considerable profit. Another southerner appearing in the notebook was Froberger's Viennese colleague Wolfgang Ebner (1612–1665). But Ebner, though less well known than Froberger, surely must be considered co-founder of this 17th-century Viennese keyboard school; besides, he was the originator of Viennese ballet music.

Vocal composers were not neglected. Handel was introduced to Heinrich Albert (1604–1651),[2] the most popular and admired song composer of his time, virtually the founder of the modern German song. Albert's songs and arias appeared in practically every anthology, were printed and pirated for two centuries, and many of them are still alive as folksongs. Handel must have been attracted by the irregular period structure, the highly expressive and free recitative encountered in Albert's works, all of which became part and parcel of his own style.

Adam Krieger (1634–1666), a disciple of Samuel Scheidt, was one of the most engaging song composers of the German Baroque. Handel studied his so-called ritornel constructions and later used them in the formal articulation of some of his choral movements. Johann Philipp Krieger (1649–1725), who in the seventies was active in Halle and later in nearby Weissenfels where he stayed for forty-five years until his death, was a prolific opera and cantata composer. He impressed Handel both as an instrumental and as a vocal composer. Aside from studying his works with Zachow, Handel must have heard—even met—the court conductor in Weissenfels; it is hard to believe that the duke did not consult his court

---

[2] The list of composers in the copy book includes an "Alberti," who could have been Johann Friedrich Alberti (1642–1710), a fairly well known church musician, but he was not sufficiently distinguished to have attracted Zachow's attention. Nor could it be the Bolognese Giuseppe Matteo Alberti, who was of Handel's own age.

musician before summoning the elder Händel to that memorable audience. The fugal Amens or Hallelujah choruses in Krieger's cantatas (of which he wrote at least six times as many as Bach), simple but solid and very effective, lingered in Handel's capacious memory. Krieger was an experienced, worldly-wise musician quite different from his home-bred colleagues. This could not have escaped Handel, no matter how young. Also, Krieger had the "Handelian" characteristic of dominating the musical scene around him.

The notebook also contained music by Georg Muffat (1653–1704), in whose works the young student could observe the entire formative process of the age he was about to enter. Muffat, whose distant ancestors were Catholic Scots who fled from Elizabethan Britain, was born (of a French mother) in Savoy, but always professed himself a German, and indeed, aside from his years of study, his professional life was spent within the German orbit. Since he studied with Lully, Corelli, and Pasquini, his music is as many-sided as his ancestry, a remarkable combination of Italian, French, and German elements that made him a style builder of the rank of a Froberger. It seems that the French accents we encounter in Handel owe their inception to Muffat's works, which abound in them. Muffat's easy and imaginative synthesis of suite, sonata, and fugue found a ready echo in the younger man.

Johann Kuhnau (1660–1722), Bach's predecessor in the cantor's chair at St. Thomas's, though represented in the book, did not seem to have impressed Handel. Kuhnau opened new doors in the history of keyboard music, but there is a certain blandness in his music that Handel may have found uncongenial. Of the others, Johann Heinrich Buttstett and Andreas Nicolaus Vetter were minor masters whose presence in the notebook does not imply any particular interest, but their teacher, Johann Pachelbel (1653–1706), did attract Handel. This Bavarian musician, who introduced the southern German strain into Saxon-Thuringian music, shows a melodiousness and intimacy quite different from the music of his northern colleagues. His easy-flowing and plastic counterpoint can be playful, and he exhibits a genial disregard for such a rule as maintenance of a stated number of parts, something that was not approved by the Northern cantors but was practiced with equal geniality by Handel. Of the foreigners represented in the notebook, we should mention Alessandro Poglietti (d. 1683), an Italian settled in Vienna. Poglietti's brilliant and witty keyboard pieces were not forgotten by Handel; Max Seiffert has pointed out borrowings, notably in the first movement of the eleventh *Grand Concerto*, Opus 6.

Handel was not a solitary disciple, for Zachow had around him a number of talented youngsters; the exchange and companionship among them must have been mutually beneficial. Of these we know of Gottfried Kirchhoff, exactly Handel's age, who later succeeded his master, upon the latter's death, as organist and choirmaster of Our Lady's Church. (Incidentally, he was almost nosed out of this position by Sebastian Bach.) While not a distinguished composer, Kirchhoff was an able and versatile musician, fairly widely known, especially for his keyboard music. Leopold Mozart appreciated him sufficiently to include one of his sonatas in the instruction book he prepared for Wolfgang in 1761.

Thus we can see that the young musician became acquainted with the entire range and tradition of German music and undoubtedly with a good deal of Italian and French music—surely a musical education as thorough, comprehensive, and enlightened as one could wish.

[3]

ZACHOW ALSO took his pupil on trips, usually to nearby places. A visit to Berlin in 1698 (without his master?) was of decisive influence upon Handel's future plans, even though its impact was not immediately in evidence. Nothing is known about the circumstances leading to the Berlin trip. Biographers set the date as 1696, in the boy's eleventh year, and wonder why the stubborn barber-surgeon permitted his son to go to a place where his objectionable musical leanings would only receive a powerful boost. Some even intimate that it was his father who took him to Berlin. Furthermore, the argument runs, this trip, of several months' duration rather than one of those short excursions taken in the company of Zachow, must have been financed by the elder Händel; surely a largesse quite out of character. We are obviously dealing here with faulty dates: the journey took place at least two years later than 1696, and the means were probably provided by Handel's kindly mother. There is absolutely no documentary proof that the visit took place in 1696, or, as is supposed, that the elder Händel refused to accede to the Berlin court's wish that his son be sent to Italy on a stipend, but there are quite plausible indications that the trip took place in 1698, after his father's death, when Handel was thirteen. Mainwaring, Handel's first biographer (1760), is often unreliable, but Mattheson, the close friend of his years in Hamburg, seldom so. In this case both agree on 1698. Since all parties accept the fact that Handel met Ariosti repeatedly in Berlin, this ought to settle the question: Ariosti did not arrive in Berlin until 1697; in 1696 he was definitely in Mantua. It is also held that Handel met Giovanni Bononcini in Berlin, which makes the date 1696 even more implausible because the Italian did not arrive in Berlin until 1702.

Though at that time a modest city, Berlin was a metropolis as far as music is concerned, mainly because of the energetic and enthusiastic Electress Sophie Charlotte, later Queen of Prussia. This lady is depicted by Sir Newman Flower as a neurotic scatterbrain and her husband, the future Frederick I of Prussia, as a henpecked nonentity who had to put up with his wife's musical prodigality while he himself did not care a whit about the art. Sophie Charlotte was anything but an empty-headed dilettante with a compulsion to throw away her money. She was extremely fond of music, not necessarily a sign of an unbalanced mind, and besides being fond of it was a well-trained and versatile musician and a highly cultivated woman, later earning the sobriquet the "Philosopher Queen." Sophie was the daughter of the Elector of Hanover (and sister of the future George I of England); she heard good music at her father's court and received excellent instruction from Agostino Steffani, with whom she remained on friendly terms all her life. She composed, and was a good harpsichord player perfectly capable of officiating as *maestra al cembalo* at chamber music and even opera performances. The Elector himself was an amateur with a good grasp of music, and his court orchestra, drilled in the French manner of Lully, was one of the best in Europe. Above all, the court was teeming with illustrious musicians: Ariosti, Steffani, Pistocchi, Bononcini, Corelli, and others, who not only visited and worked there but composed for and dedicated works to Sophie Charlotte. In 1700 Corelli published and dedicated to her his famous Opus 5, the twelve sonatas, the last of which is the *Follia*. While dedicatory prefaces in that age were of course flowery to the point of being obsequious, Corelli's specifically emphasizes that the Electress's interest in music was "not a simple divertissement; she has a sound and scientific [i.e. professional] knowledge of it."

Here was something new and exciting for Handel: flesh-and-blood Italians and their original music. According to Mainwaring and Mattheson, Handel particularly cultivated Ariosti, and, considering the sound judgment Handel exhibited from his youth, his preference is quite understandable. Notwithstanding Chrysander's and others' patronizing or derogatory estimates of this Servite friar, he is again one of those whose music exerted a powerful influence on the great composer in his formative years.

Attilio Ariosti (1666–c. 1740) was a musician who could take his place in the Scarlatti-Steffani-Caldara-Bononcini-Lotti circle at no disadvantage. He composed excellent instrumental music as well as cantatas and operas of a very dramatic hue. But there is something else in his *oeuvre* that seems to have escaped the Handel specialists, though not that able historian of the oratorio, Schering: Ariosti the composer of dramatic oratorios. *La Passione di Cristo* (1693) is described by Schering as being strong and vigorous, and its dramatically agitated choral scenes seem to have been the first modern *turbae* depicting a people in action. Unfortunately, Ariosti is one of those neglected, solitary figures to whom modern musicology owes a debt. A few instrumental pieces of his are available in modern prints, and of his dramatic works, sacred and secular, only a few arias appear in anthologies. Of the music he composed for Berlin we know nothing.

The impact of the rich secular musical life in the Brandenburg capital and of such powerful musical personalities as Ariosti's upon the impressionable and receptive youngster must have been considerable and the contrast with provincial and bourgeois Halle enlightening. But even at that tender age Handel's rocklike character was in evidence: he was not ready to abrogate an understanding reached with his late father that he continue his humanistic studies with a view to entering the law school of the university. While in Berlin he so enchanted the electoral couple by his playing that the Prince offered to send the boy to Italy with a stipend. Most biographies agree that the offer was made in a letter to the barber-surgeon, who turned it down; but no one ever seems to have seen the letter. The fact is that his father was dead by that time, and it is quite clear from Mainwaring and Mattheson that the offer was made to and declined by a sort of family council; a "trusted member" of the family actually resided in Berlin, employed at the court. Upon his return to Halle the departed father's wish was observed and music relegated to off-hours. These spare hours, however, were well utilized, and Zachow undoubtedly stood by. The boy began to acquire a reputation. In 1701 Telemann, on his way to Leipzig, stopped over in Halle and sought out the young organist about whom he had heard complimentary things. Thus began a long friendship, as half a century of correspondence shows.

In 1702 Handel was appointed probationary organist at Halle Cathedral. Though he was a Lutheran and the cathedral belonged to the Calvinists, no lovers of Lutherans, his superiority over other possible candidates was so manifest that the authorities were willing to forget about the denominational disability. The document of appointment states that "the student Georg Friedrich Händel has already at different times acted as deputy to the former [incumbent]," therefore they were familiar with his capabilities.

Now a curious and seemingly inexplicable event takes place. At the end of the probationary year, just when he was about to be confirmed as cathedral organist, Handel resigned his office and decided to move to Hamburg. The biographers are in a quandary to explain this momentous decision. Why did Handel resign from a good position? Had he not received a thorough preparation for precisely such a career at the hands of one of the most estimable practitioners in a region that could boast of many? And was this not an unusually auspicious start—cathedral organist and *regens chori* at eighteen? Since he had no visible means of making a living waiting for him in Hamburg, and his savings could not have amounted to much, the conclusion arrived at was summarized by Sir Newman Flower: "He had left Halle aimlessly to find fortune." George Frideric Handel never crossed a street aimlessly; he would certainly not have made such a fateful decision without due deliberation. Ironically, Sir Newman himself has the key to the question, though he neglects to use it: "Hamburg was the beginning of the great search." This is very nicely and accurately put. In reality, Handel faced up to a multitude of problems and questions, which his responsive and acute mind had considered and examined from every angle. In no admissible way can this decision be presented as an unmeditated caprice; but in order to explain the chain of events we must turn to the youngster standing at the bier of his strange father and then examine his life and work in Halle.

[4]

GERMAN CUSTOM, upon the death of a respected and substantial burgher, was to compose and print an obituary pamphlet containing the funeral orations as well as poems by friends and relations. Georg Händel's family observed the tradition, and among the poems that appeared in print a few days after the funeral was one by the twelve-year-old son. Though of course conventional in versification, it is a remarkably mature piece for one so young, but the most interesting part is the signature: "Georg Friedrich Händel, *dedicated to the liberal arts.*" This was at once a true statement as to his present activity and a humble filial acknowledgment of the father's will. And indeed, young Handel was devoted to the liberal arts, receiving an excellent training either in Halle's Lutheran Gymnasium or the Latin School. But he was also an autodidact who with a good mind, intuition, and sharp powers of observation learned and retained everything that came upon his horizon. It is attested that the mature Handel knew English, French, and Italian, besides his mother tongue and Latin, all of which he spoke and wrote fluently. Only a thorough humanistic grounding made this possible.

A little while ago we remarked on the contrast between the brilliant court in Berlin and the provincial milieu in Halle—but that contrast concerned secular music only. Halle was an old seat of culture, and its church music was always on a high level. Though once considered one of the most Catholic cities in Germany, Halle became a stronghold of Lutheranism in the Reformer's lifetime. Its rich cultural traditions continued, and at the opening of the 17th century arts and letters were cultivated on a remarkably high and progressive level. The theatre performed Shakespeare early in the 17th century. Samuel Scheidt played the organ in the Moritzkirche, and all other churches had able organists and fair choirs. The humanistic schools also had their musical establishments, notably choirs. The ravages of the Thirty Years' War did not leave the cultural life of Halle untouched, but recovery was remarkably swift. It is interesting to note that the city had good resident organ-builders, and in fact, the church elders complained about the cost of maintaining the several large instruments in the city's churches. (After Zachow's death in 1712, Bach himself put in a bid for the vacant position of organist at Our Lady's Church. He must have been attracted by the fine instrument in the church, for the emoluments were not enticing. In the end he went to Weimar.)

Halle's university was founded in 1694 by the Elector for the express purpose of accommodating the great jurist Christian Thomasius, who had been expelled from Leipzig for his liberal views. Many of his students followed him to Halle. The university was one of the principal seats of Protestant theology, though at times rather prominently tinged with Pietism. It was at this institution that Handel matriculated in 1702 after finishing his secondary education. *Grove's Dictionary* (1954), like biographical sketches of Handel elsewhere, is satisfied with the simple statement: "In February 1702 he entered the University and finished the study of law, to which his father set him." While Handel did not actually matriculate in the faculty of law—the students' roster is extant—he undoubtedly attended the courses given by the famous professor of law, the guiding light of the university. But what was this "study of law" in the 17th and 18th centuries, particularly in Halle?

It was not a study of the empirical-analytical practice of jurisprudence, though of course then as now lawyers had to learn the requirements of everyday law practice, but an examination of the great philosophical, moral, and ethical problems of the social organization of human affairs. That is, "law" was still closely allied with the humanities, a good deal of it consisting in reflections on human conduct, and it was not far different from the philosophy of history. Somewhat weighted down with metaphysical thought, German philosophy of law as professed in Halle was nevertheless distinctly liberal and progressive. The dominant figure in the university was Rector Christian Thomasius (1655–1728), a true pioneer of the Enlightenment and a most influential thinker and teacher. Handel of course heard the distinguished professor of law, the first academician to dare to lecture in German. The great liberal's ideas as well as his lectures went far beyond law, embracing literature, theology, and social science. This courageous man made Halle into the most enlightened place in Germany. Much has been said about his valiant crusade against witch hunts and the unspeakable cruelties connected with them, but his principal aim was larger. He wanted to free statecraft, politics, and law from theology. It was here, indeed, that Handel first encountered respect for the dignity and freedom of man's mind and for the solemn majesty of the law, principles under which he was to live for almost half a century in England. It is very important to realize that these ideals were acquired in his youth, in his home town, and not in England, otherwise his subsequent moves and decisions will make little sense.

He encountered another remarkable man at the university in Halle, August Hermann Francke (1663–1727), Professor of Greek, Oriental Languages, and Theology. Francke was particularly devoted to the welfare of wayward children and orphans and established an orphanage, a foundlings' hospital, that became a model for all Germany. He passionately proclaimed the duty of society and of the state to look after these poor children; this made a deep impression on Handel, a charitable man and very fond of children. All his life he remembered Francke and his solicitous care for these unfortunates, and when Handel found a similar institution in London, at a time when he had the means to lend a helping hand, he gave unstintingly of his time and money. As is well known, the rights to *Messiah* were vested in the London Foundling Hospital, bringing the institution a handsome revenue.

It was from this atmosphere that the young man emerged at the age of eighteen with an independent, well-stocked, clear, tough brain, and a spirit touched with something of prophetic fire. He was altogether self-sufficient, and though good-natured, even gregarious, he accepted rather than gave friendship: he had no need of others to complement himself. He was now ready to make decisions that no one else could make for him.

[5]

ABOUT THE COMPOSITIONS of the Halle period we know very little, but Mattheson, a reliable witness, analyzed them succinctly in his *Ehrenpforte.* "Handel in those days set very, very long arias and sheerly unending cantatas which, while not possessing the proper knack or correct taste, were perfect so far as harmony is concerned." Then he adds: "Handel was a stranger to melody, but knew far more about fugue and counterpoint than Kuhnau." This criticism is most interesting and reveals a great deal of the character of both young men. Mattheson accepts the fact that Handel is a superbly trained composer—in the cantor's art. Why, he even declares the youngster superior to Sebastian Bach's famous predecessor at St. Thomas's. But the adverse comments are significant: Handel did not have the "knack" to use his excellent training to write "modern" music. This is obviously the judgment of a progressive musician well acquainted with the new Italian dramatic style. Unfortunately, few of these early compositions—cantatas, German arias, etc.—can be reliably dated.[3]

The "perfect" knowledge of the métier is much more in evidence in Handel's early instrumental music. The six trio sonatas for two oboes and basso continuo in Vol. 27 of the old Handel edition are generally dated as the earliest of Handel's extant compositions; Chrysander assigns them to his eleventh year. Many years later when Handel was the much-admired London composer, they were discovered in Germany by Lord Polwarth, who purchased them and brought them to London. The statement quoted on page 12 ("I used to write like the devil in those days") is supposed to have been made when Lord Polwarth showed the old manuscript to Handel. It is known that Handel was very fond of the oboe, and so was Zachow, whose way with wind instruments was far more modern than contemporary usage in Germany. Both of them acquired their taste for the

[3] Some chamber music undoubtedly originated in this period, as well as perhaps three of the German lieder, but the harpsichord pieces published by Chrysander (Vol. 48) and assigned to Halle are certainly later. Nor is there any proof that the cantata *Ach Herr, mich armen Sünder (Organum,* No. 12) is an authentic work. Handel must have composed a great deal while holding the position of probationary organist, for it was the organist's duty to supply new music for the various services, but none of it is now identifiable.

instrument from Michael Hyntzsch and his son, Johann Georg, who introduced the oboe in Halle. One of Zachow's trio sonatas for flute, bassoon, and basso continuo is available; it is a very fine work and makes us regret the more that this is the only piece of chamber music preserved from his output. So the circumstances favor Chrysander's dating; the only thing that contradicts it is the music itself, and on the basis of the score it is impossible to accept Chrysander's assumption. These are very good compositions, showing a maturity that no eleven-year-old child ever possessed. No autograph is known, but the copy brought to England bears the date 1700. Some of the other chamber music pieces, assigned to the Hamburg period (in Vol. 48), supposedly composed by the twenty-year-old Handel, would then represent an incomprehensible regression. Whatever the situation, and assuming that 1700 is the correct date on the copy (which I have not seen) and that the sonatas were not reworked at a later date, always a possibility with Handel, these are remarkable works that show thorough acquaintance with the distilled sonata style of the Corelli school. Handel's typically active and sensitive bass line is there, and the pathos of the slow movements is pervasive. But what would be most disconcerting—if these works were indeed composed by an eleven-year-old—is the concentration, the formal security, and the cleanness of the texture.

A collection of chamber music brought out in Amsterdam in 1724 as Handel's Opus 1 contains much superb music along with routine stuff, but of course these compositions do not represent his first published work; in fact, this disorderly cupboard contains works thrown into it for at least a couple of decades. Every once in a while Handel would reach into it and pull out a piece for use elsewhere and in a different medium; it is quite impossible here for us to single out the early works. As we shall see later, some of these sonatas represent Baroque chamber music at its best.

[6]

LIKE ALMOST ALL composers in the Saxon-Thuringian cultural area, Handel grew up in the humble surroundings of the organ bench and choir loft. Among his contemporaries there were other gifted musicians, but their talents were of a different nature, and they were ready to retire before a stronger god. These were the cantors, born professionals to whom music was bread and office. The German cantor, organist, and conductor was a hard-working, honest, well-trained musician and public servant, not as a rule interested in worldly affairs. His entire education was practical, tradition-bound, and he took great pride in his knowledge of the métier. Throughout his life Handel retained this characteristic German command of the métier. To the cantors, a work of art could not be merely the result of spontaneous eruption, and to these fine musicians the Romantic ideal of the "God-given artist" who is an untutored genius would have been inconceivable. They observed severe "rules" and condemned all eccentrics who offended the discipline of the craft. What they expected of the creative artist was the presentation of something original within the accepted style and with known ingredients, the principal one of which was the chorale.

This was the *Zeitgeist*, which was considered binding and which certainly permeated the organ loft in the cathedral where Handel was scheduled to take up permanent residence; it should have been in his bones. But the *Zeitgeist* is not an absolute, extra-human force; it is formed by men, by their ideas about the sense and value of life. Life itself is independent of what in any given time is thought of it; life is the origin, not the result, of the *Zeitgeist*. No modern historian would concede that an artist can be rooted outside the *Zeitgeist*, but we cannot insist on the axiom that his time must be his measure. It is often the exact opposite, that man gives dimension to his times.

Handel, with all his love for the organ, refused to continue the cantor's art and was altogether free of the latter's inherited mentality. He did not want to be a musician learned in the ways of the *strenger Satz*. He did not want to address the intellect within the accepted frames of cantata, chorale, and fugue, but to appeal to the senses and the imagination; he wanted the hearer's soul to vibrate with his. In Handel's time German music still harbored a good deal of the "Gothic"; its architecture was severe yet insisted on the arbitrary juxtaposition of details that, though well worked out and well understood, can be very strange to us. The contours are firm, the invention magnificent, and order reigns everywhere, but the elements are often disparate, for they are, to use the very graphic term of the period, *gearbeitet*, that is, tooled and toiled over.

Handel desired to become a free and independent artist, something unheard of in Germany, but familiar to the travelling Italians whom he first encountered in Berlin. Once more he wanted to convince himself of the rightness of his decision. When he eventually did arrive in Hamburg he set out within a month with his new friend, Mattheson, to visit Buxtehude in Lübeck. The aged master wanted to retire and the coveted position at St. Mary's was available to the right bidder. It is perhaps easy to explain Handel's refusal to apply for the position: the future master of the magnificent organ was required to take unto himself the old organist's daughter as his wife; Buxtehude had married Franz Tunder's daughter, and this arrangement was a traditional procedure of succession. The human dowry that went with the deal was a dozen years older than Handel, and though Georg Händel the elder founded his solid existence under exactly such circumstances when he married a surgeon's widow ten years his senior, and inherited the departed surgeon's practice, the son flatly refused. So did Mattheson, and so would Sebastian Bach, who was also to inspect the "job." But that in itself does not tell the full story. There was in Handel an eagerness that could not tolerate such a restricted future. His original gifts, the quality of his mind, predestined him for a more strenuous and adventurous life.

The decision to change his course and go to Hamburg went much deeper than the problems of a musical career. The many large and small, more or less independent German states, kingdoms, electorates, and principalities lived in eternal intrigue and compromise. On one hand they wanted to preserve their independence, on the other they had to reconcile this with the concept of the Empire. Shadowy as the latter was, it was nevertheless a potential reality, though in the first half of the 18th century the relationship of the individual states within its boundaries was altogether chaotic. Able politicians such as Agostino Steffani, the prelate-ambassador-composer, could carry out diplomatic coups of astounding consequences with relative ease. The picture was really incredible in its colorful—and disorderly—magnitude. There were the marches of the Holy Roman Empire, which "included" such distant domains as the proud young kingdom of Prussia or, at the other end, Naples and later Tuscany. The maintenance of the Italian, Neapolitan, Sicilian, and Hungarian territories saddled the Viennese Imperial headquarters with tasks that inevitably weakened its hold on the western provinces, especially those that were predominantly Protestant. However, the Viennese politicians, well trained in the art of patriarchal absolutism and highly cultivated men of the Enlightenment, knew that if princes and electors were left to enjoy their privileges they would not meddle unduly in the affairs of the Empire. Since the political sagacity and savoir-faire of the Germans was notoriously of a low order—Goethe still bewails it—their understanding for this type of statecraft, which was already centuries old in other parts of Europe, was practically nil.

How well Handel appraised this situation is of course pure conjecture, and I shall not attempt to make an estimate, but that he, a student of Thomasius, was occupied with it is beyond doubt. This was part of the "great search," and at least one aspect of Handel's politico-social thought is clear: he did not want to be restricted to one class, and he realized that in the Germany of his day he could not escape this. Culture flourished only in the higher strata of society, to which he was not admitted except as a paid performer. And yet Handel was born a "gentleman." It would be irrelevant to say this of a Constable or a Sir Christopher Wren, but in the case of a musician coming from the social milieu of the German cantor it is of considerable importance. Opera, which became Handel's chief concern for decades, and in a way was his chief concern throughout his life, had, and still has, a social connotation to Germans and Englishmen entirely different from that of church music. The 18th-century term "polite art" fits opera admirably. What Handel craved was personal freedom to raise himself out of his provincial milieu to a life of culture. What he understood by this may be difficult to analyze, but when nothing of the sense of social inferiority so characteristic of the early 18th-century German artisan remains, then something is achieved that the German biographers who bracket Handel with Bach fail to appreciate. Handel was as unaffected by the prejudices of the higher society he frequented in England as he was by upstart envies—he was a free man. The first step in acquiring this freedom from constricting social inhibitions was migration to a "free city," to the quasi-republic of Hamburg.

Then there was the question of religious orthodoxy. To Handel's active, imperious nature religion was not a mystical concept but one that rested on rational consciousness, a theism based on the harmony of the universe, a universe that, however, emphatically included the secular kingdom on earth. He must have been familiar with the tenets, poetry, and songs of Pietism, for at Halle University the disciples of Philip Jakob Spener, the founder of Pietism, were strongly entrenched. Spener's *Pia Desiderata* (1675) became the literary beacon of the movement, which was almost immediately opposed by orthodox Lutheranism. Spener himself was a staunch believer in the articles of Lutheran faith, and there is nothing in this man's character of the extreme sentimentality later associated with Pietism. It was the disciples who distorted Spener's aims and methods, and though its exaggerated phase came after Handel had left Germany, he did not want any part of Pietism. The Pietists, like Calvin, differed sharply with Luther on the role of music in worship, and in this Spener agreed with them. Elaborate music was not welcome in the church; only simple songs with equally simple organ accompaniment were considered churchly and proper. This led to a prodigious output of such songs, though these were intended mainly for domestic religious devotions rather than for church use. To Handel, who was not only a confirmed Lutheran but by nature and artistic instinct devoted to elaborate ritual, all this must have been anathema.

It is quite apparent that at an early age Handel showed an independent mind when it came to religion, and we shall see that this independence was pointedly asserted a few years later in Italy when it was tested from an entirely different quarter. Handel believed more deeply than any of his German colleagues of the time not only in eternal law, eternal values, and eternal being, but in change, development, and progress. His was a consciously unmetaphysical concept of life and therefore markedly different from that of the typical German. He firmly believed that life's problems are capable of being resolved without recourse to metaphysics. An earnest and convinced Christian he remained all his life but henceforth largely without denominational and cultic restrictions.

The aggregate of these ideas, forces, and developments steered Handel away from collective Christian prayer towards the accents that can be found only in the individual—and that meant dramatic music, opera. An early incentive must have come from Telemann, on the occasion of his stopover in Halle in 1701. It is significant that the principal subject of their discussions and in their correspondence was melody, its construction, use, and application. In his autobiographical sketch for Mattheson's *Ehrenpforte*, Telemann names Steffani as his model; therefore the Italian master who influenced so many German composers must have been brought to Handel's attention at an early date. But it is inconceivable that he did not hear an occasional opera performance in Weissenfels, and of course Zachow early inculcated in him a love for the dramatic. All this was beckoning in Hamburg, the famous operatic center of Germany. So we see that what is called an "aimless quest to find fortune" was in reality a step dictated by inexorable logic. The psalmist comes much closer to the truth: "He rejoiceth like a giant in running his course."

II

1703–1706

Hamburg—Music in Hamburg—Handel arrives in 1703—Friendship with Mattheson—Handel joins opera orchestra—Keiser, his influence on Handel—First attempt at opera, *Almira* (1705)—Handel-Keiser relationship—Altercation and reconciliation with Mattheson—Debacle of *Nero*—Handel resigns from Hamburg opera—Composes *St. John Passion*—State of oratorio-Passion in Germany—The Passion in Handel's life work—Handel leaves for Italy

H AMBURG, THE NORTH GERMAN METROPOLIS OF COM- merce, was an old seat of culture. Independent and rich, and spared most of the horrors of the Thirty Years' War, it was a unique city-state, international and progressive, though ruled by a hard-headed plutocracy (the quotations from the Hamburg stock exchange were distributed in church even during services!). An early convert to Protestantism and little touched by the Counter-Reformation, Hamburg developed a distinct intellectual life of its own. While the political situation there was tense during Handel's stay (1703–1706), the burghers hotly contesting the autocratic power of the Senate made up of the very wealthy, the city's musical life was not affected. Her well-to-do citizenry was cultivated and very fond of music. Because of far-flung commercial relations and the habit of engaging well-paid foreign artists who brought with them Netherlandish, English, Venetian, and all manner of other music, Hamburg was in the forefront of modern tendencies, and soon after the opening of the 17th century concerted music made its appearance in her principal churches.

Towards the middle of the century, the cantor of the Johanneum, and hence the music director of the city's five principal churches (for the Johanneum was the Hamburg counterpart of Leipzig's Thomasschule), was Thomas Selle (1599–1663), an able and progressive musician whose *St. John Passion* (1643) was the first such work to use large choral movements. There were many other distinguished musicians engaged in church music. Christoph Bernhard (1627–1692), a disciple of Schütz and Carissimi, held the cantorship at St. James's from 1664 to 1674, and in nearby Lübeck was Buxtehude. The city had magnificent organs, built by the great North German organ builder, Arp Schnitger. They were new when Handel arrived, and he did not lose time in getting acquainted with them. The Hamburg organists had been famous since the early Baroque. There was the Praetorius clan, as well as Heinrich Scheidemann (d. 1663), an outstanding composer and teacher of Jan Adams Reinken; Matthias Weckmann (1619–1674), fine keyboard and very expressive vocal composer; and others. Most of these able musicians were natives of the city and products, directly or indirectly, of Sweelinck's school. The tradition continued with Jan Adams Reinken (1623–1722), who bridges three generations and was so admired by Bach, and with the brilliant, original, and highly imaginative Vincent Lübeck (1654–1740). Lübeck was organist at St. Nicholas's from 1702 to his death and so was in Hamburg when Handel was there. Whether Handel met him and Reinken cannot be proved, but it stands to reason that he must have known them; he was too fond of organ playing and too interested in other men's music, always, to ignore such prominent and original masters. Hamburg was musically so eminent and positions there were so desirable that Schütz sent his pupils to the city. In his old age he would have liked to retire there himself.

Nor were Hamburg cantors ill-disposed toward secular music—even opera. In 1660 the Collegium Musicum was founded and weekly concerts were offered. And Hamburg was full of song. Pastor Johann Rist, the leading poet of the North, gathered around him composers who have become known as members of the Hamburg Song School. There were a large number of municipal musicians (*Ratsmusikanten*), often employed for private festivities, and they too were abreast of the times. English influence from across the narrow seas was ever present. William Brade (1560–1630), celebrated English violist and composer, joined the municipal musicians in 1608 and became their director in 1613. After holding various other positions, he returned to Hamburg and died there in 1630. His instrumental suites served as models for the North German style; both Schein and Scheidt are indebted to him. Nikolaus Adam Strungk (1640–1700), a violin virtuoso, organist, and good composer (also represented in Handel's notebook), was the director of municipal music in 1678.

Finally, Hamburg was the most important seat of early German opera from the foundation of its lyric theatre in 1678. The Hamburg bourgeoisie was fond of the theatre in all its forms, and being socially a democracy of sorts, the stage, both non-musical and lyric, was a popular institution, accessible and catering to all. As a matter of fact the opera was called "public and popular opera theatre." The clergy did not look upon this with favor and tried to suppress the "opera theatre" which, to tell the truth, attracted all kinds of ruffians and ladies of easy virtue. Sir Newman Flower also finds it abhorrent, but neither he nor the good pastors could have stopped opera, and as time passed a more liberal Hamburg divine, Heinrich Elmenhorst, admitted that opera is permissible to Christians as one of those "intermediate things." His liberality was perhaps somewhat colored by the fact that he was a librettist.

Opera in Hamburg started with "sacred"—that is, biblical—song plays. German Protestant thought still steadfastly sought its values in religious sources. The sturdy Hamburg musicians, organized in their municipal and church groups and institutions, were acquainted with the new trends and introduced them into their chamber, orchestral, and church music; but they were lacking in the operatic experience needed to build up the genre in an original way. The first requisite, literary ability to provide the librettos, was sadly missing, and the Germans were not endowed with the sort of temperament that is capable of fusing theatre and music into a convincing whole, an organic emanation of public life, as was opera in Italy. They could not leave the framework of religious subjects presented in simple dialogues, for it was only in this type of music that they had some experience. The works of the first opera composer in Hamburg, Johann Theile (1646–1724), if we may judge from the remnants of his second opera, *Orontes* (the music for the first, *Adam and Eve, or the Created, Fallen, and Redeemed Man*, is unfortunately lost), give no indication of the fact that Theile, a pupil of Schütz and the teacher of Zachow, was a very able church-music composer and a master contrapuntist whose activity leads straight to Bach himself. Probably it was the unfamiliar medium and the wretched libretto that thwarted him. This early musical drama demonstrated that the German middle classes had a limited understanding for this particular form of the theatre and could not rise to the stylistic requirements of the genre except with outside help. This primitive "opera," badly written, dramatically inept, poorly sung, and offering a hodgepodge of religious, mythological, historical, and local elements, failed to leave the ground.

Gradually the freer technique of the Latin countries began to make itself felt, and composers better equipped for opera appeared. By the time Johann Sigismund Kusser (1660–1727), a pupil of Lully (or at least a close follower) and an experienced opera man, took over the management, probably in 1694, nothing was left of the old sacred panache. Kusser, a quarrelsome fellow and a mediocre composer, was nevertheless an able musician and obviously an expert conductor and orchestral coach who brought to Germany the highly developed French style of string playing. Moreover, he was a skilful administrator who raised the Hamburg opera to the position of chief lyric stage in the North. He himself furnished several operas and saw to it that works of the leading composers were performed. Three years later, Kusser, always at odds with everyone, was succeeded by Reinhard Keiser (1674–1739), who represents the high point reached by the Hamburg opera, with the ablest operatic composition by a German before Gluck and Mozart.[1]

This was, then, the musical situation in Hamburg when Handel arrived in 1703. It must be made clear that by this time opera had altered the hierarchy of musical genres. The fact that the Hamburg opera collapsed a quarter of a century later does not alter the circumstances at the opening of the century.

[2]

Soon after his arrival in Hamburg, Handel met Johann Mattheson, and they became inseparable companions. The two young men exchanged their experiences, Handel teaching Mattheson the finer aspects of counterpoint while Mattheson, at twenty-two a veteran of the stage as singer, composer, and conductor, introduced Handel to the mysteries of opera. We mentioned that in his *Ehrenpforte* Mattheson states that when Handel arrived in Hamburg he was "strong" in harmony and counterpoint but a "poor melodist." This may have appeared to be true —for the moment—because Handel was trained in the German cantoral tradition of functional-constructive counterpoint. (Even the young Sebastian Bach, rambling and exuberant, was deficient in this regard when compared to the Italians. Realizing this shortcoming, he improved himself by applying his superior contrapuntal ability to materials, especially themes, borrowed from Corelli, Legrenzi, and Albinoni. It was thus that he acquired his incomparable conciseness and plasticity of melodic design.) But neither Mattheson's opinion nor that of Romain Rolland (who accepts the idea that Handel was originally a "feeble melodist") can stand in the light of the subsequent rapid development of the arch-melodist. It is obvious that Handel was a born melodist and all he needed was an opportunity to exercise this gift.

The new Hamburg resident was not "aimless" for long; he became a

---

[1] It is interesting to observe that the restless Kusser eventually migrated to the British Isles, dying in Dublin in 1727.

member of the violin section in Keiser's opera orchestra. Mattheson, a habitué of the Hamburg opera since his sixteenth year, must have stood by with help, though he rated Handel's violin playing rather low. He also introduced Handel to the "English Resident," i.e. consul, in Hamburg, John Wyche, a cultivated man with literary leanings, very fond of music, and the possessor of a fine library.[2] Handel was engaged as harpsichord tutor to the diplomat's son and was thus introduced into higher society, where he quickly gained acceptance, a facility that never left him. Within a matter of months the barrier he resented at Halle and from which he was fleeing was eliminated. He soon had a number of pupils, thus acquiring, together with the pay from the opera, a not uncomfortable, though frugal, livelihood.

The English-language biographies of Handel make short shrift of Mattheson, whom they really do not know. Even so distinguished a scholar as Edward J. Dent calls Mattheson "a voluminous pedant and an embittered critic." A popular biographer calls Mattheson's *Das Neu-Eröffnete Orchestre* (1713) "a book on the contemporary orchestra"! This book—and it shares its subject with all the others whether called "orchestra" or "honor portal"—represents the most enlightened and advanced treatise on musical esthetics of the age. Yet Rolland's fine work on Handel was available to all these authors, having been published in 1910.[3] In it Rolland, that great connoisseur of the 17th and 18th centuries, ranks Mattheson with Boileau and Lessing—and justly so. Indeed, Mattheson's *oeuvre* provided modern musical esthetics and criticism as well as musicology with its point of departure and not a little of its subject matter. His influence on German musical thought was paramount for half a century, and it is unthinkable that Handel did not profit from his intercourse with this man, perhaps vain and egotistical, but challenging and inspiring. And besides his valuable esthetic and philosophical writings, he is our best and most trustworthy source for the musical history of the first half of the 18th century, a storehouse of information, delightfully written, on individuals and institutions as well as on the practice of music.

Mattheson was a man thoroughly versed in the classics as well as in French and English literature and philosophy, an experienced diplomat, a fine all-round musician—composer, singer, conductor, and player. If his

[2] John Wyche came from a distinguished family. His grandfather and father, Sir Peter Wyche, Sr. and Jr., were both ambassadors and scholars as well as privy councillors. The younger Sir Peter, a noted geographer and man of letters, preceded his son, John, in the post of English envoy in Hamburg.

[3] More recent authors could have profitably read Beekman Cannon's excellent book, *Johann Mattheson* (New Haven, 1947).

critics among writers on Handel disdained his music, they should have inquired into his English connections, and would have seen that Mattheson
must have played a part in Handel's ultimate decision to settle in England. In Mattheson's own words he was well acquainted with "English
humour & witt," but as a matter of fact he was one of the chief intermediaries between English and German letters in the North. Translator of
Richardson, Defoe, and others, of many large historical, legal, and political tracts, he was also the founder, on English models, of the German periodical literature. Later he became so prominent and expert in diplomatic affairs that when the English Resident was in London Mattheson
was left in charge of the Embassy. He was very much interested in this
position and devoted to England, a sentiment that in Hamburg was easily
understandable, the great German port being vitally dependent on that
seafaring nation's political and economic policies. These policies Mattheson made it his business to study closely. While of course all this was yet
in the future, his connections with the English legation and his interest in
English letters and institutions were already well formed when Handel
was in Hamburg.

This versatile man also had a keen business sense and a great liking
for wealth—he died a rich man; perhaps Handel picked up a few pointers
from him. Careful reading of Mattheson's many books discloses a wide
range of ideas and incentives that must have influenced Handel. When in
his *Ehrenpforte* Mattheson says that he "envisaged being something else
than an organist," refusing advantageous positions offered in Amsterdam,
Hamburg, and other places, we may be sure that Handel not only was
aware of these sentiments but shared them; his somewhat older and far
more experienced friend surely contributed to his decision to abandon the
cantor's career. But finally we must not forget that Mattheson was the first
thoroughly "modern" musician Handel got to know and know intimately.
From his early youth Mattheson was an enthusiastic champion of new
music, which of course meant opera and dramatic, concerted church
music, as opposed to the Lutheran musical tradition; and at the time of
their association in Hamburg his experience in this modern music was
very considerable. Like his great senior contemporary in Vienna, Johann
Joseph Fux, Mattheson is far better known as an author than as a composer, yet this one-sided view is unjust. Brahms, always poking around in
old scores, accumulating in his quiet way a wide variety of interesting
music, copied parts of one of Mattheson's oratorios, but otherwise his
many works are largely unexplored.

[3]

THE SEASON WAS long at the Hamburg opera and the experience varied and concentrated, if also a little bewildering. The organists and church musicians little adept at writing for the stage had left, and the direction was in the hands of able professionals, but the librettists were still poor, and all sorts of questionable elements crept into this German opera. The business gentry visiting in Hamburg had to be entertained, and it should be remembered that this was a "commercial," not a court, opera. As the religious subjects were supplanted by worldly ones, the literary quality of the librettos, primitive before, now became coarse, often violating the standards of decency, while the rhymes in the lyrics defy description. Beheadings, with amply flowing artificial blood, were particularly popular, and live animals, even camels and monkeys, appeared to the delight of the audience. The opera house itself was a real Baroque theatre, with elaborate machinery and spectacular staging. The influence of the English theatre, especially the figure of the English clown, considerably vulgarized, was strong, and soon low comedy was mixed with local history, mythology, and Italian arias sung in the original language. This created a distinct if unsavory Hamburg opera type, the combination of elements being unique and not a little disconcerting. But there was also pure German and Italian opera and, what most intrigued Handel, there was an active German composer of extraordinary abilities whose work he could observe at close range.

Reinhard Keiser, a passionate, undisciplined, and profligate man of genius, began his career with church music, like the young man from Halle who was to annoy him presently, but he was irresistibly attracted to the stage. Keiser had a good schooling at St Thomas's School in Leipzig under Cantor Schelle, but at the age of eighteen or nineteen absconded, turning up two or three years later (all his moves are conjectural) in Hamburg. Keiser was a bohemian who alternately created and caroused, always thirsting for success and money, but he was a prodigious worker and a born entrepreneur, two traits that Handel observed with interest. Of Keiser's well over a hundred operas only twenty-six are preserved in manuscript, four of these being available in modern editions.[4] These

---

[4] *Octavia,* in the Supplement to the Händelgesellschaft edition; *Croesus* and *L'Inganno fedele* (incomplete), in *Denkmäler deutscher Tonkunst,* Vols. 37, 38; and *Jodelet,* a comic opera, in *Publikationen der Gesellschaft für Musikforschung,* Vols. 20–22.

scores disclose a starkly dramatic talent that can penetrate to truly tragic depths and a tender, sensuous, and enchanting melodic invention that must have been a revelation to Handel. It is unfortunate that Chrysander, who knew these works, failed to recognize their exceptional qualities. His low opinion of Keiser has been unquestioningly accepted in the general Handel literature.

Handel was tremendously impressed by Keiser's music and soon set about trying his hand at opera. *Almira* (1705), his very first venture, in which Mattheson sang the lead, met with success. It was one of those mixed affairs with a nondescript libretto, the recitatives in German, and some of the arias in Italian. The stiff German cantata style, noticeable especially in the recitatives which were quite "churchly," was not yet eliminated. Handel was still inexperienced but could easily hold his own among German opera composers, with the exception of Keiser. This first, youthful opera was a remarkable achievement. One is particularly impressed by Handel's already developed aural imagination—the music sounds well because it was planned for sound values. The fine set of Lullian dances is still fresh and elegant. Sebastian Bach knew and admired *Almira,* he even borrowed from it; traces show up in his cantatas and even in the Passions.

In a way that became characteristic of him, Handel immediately followed his success with another opera, *Nero,* once more with Mattheson in the lead role. This second opera was a resounding failure, being dropped after three performances. As a matter of fact, it disappeared altogether, for the score is lost. Only the libretto is preserved in a few copies; its miserable quality may well explain the debacle.

Now Keiser swings into action. According to biographers he was piqued by the young man's success and was determined to take him down a peg or two. He set to music the same *Almira* libretto, but the text was so leaden and undramatic that the veteran maestro's work did not meet with success. The story of Keiser's jealousy is questionable, even though a modicum of truth may attach to it. All Handel biographers belabor poor Keiser, and Flower cannot conceal his righteous scorn. Like so many Handel legends, this one also goes back to Chrysander. When Handel left for Italy he took with him a copy of Keiser's *Octavia,* from which he borrowed rather copiously for his *Agrippina.* Even much later, Keiser's memory was vivid enough for Handel to use material from the latter's *La Forza della Virtù* in his *Joshua.* Surely the extremely successful Keiser did not have to fear competition from the young ripienist in his orchestra. Setting the same libretto was a widespread custom, and in this instance both Keiser and Handel actually had an earlier *Almira* before them. Ruggiero Fedeli (c. 1655–1722), a Venetian who spent many years in Germany, had his opera *Almira* performed in Brunswick in 1703. A restless, quarrelsome, and unpredictable fellow who shared many traits with Kusser and Keiser, Fedeli was active in practically all operatic centers in Germany from Dresden to Berlin, and since he was a good composer he was well known. There is documentary proof that both Handel and Keiser were familiar with his *Almira* and that Handel actually built his own work on the Italian's model. In all likelihood, Keiser, who was, after all, manager of the opera house, simply did not like Handel's *Almira*. Its awkward, instrumentally conceived melodies did not suit his taste, so he set the libretto, which was originally intended for him and which, for that matter, he himself gave to Handel, in his own way.

As late as 1737, Keiser remembered Handel and gladly wrote the connecting recitatives for the latter's *Partenope*, produced in Hamburg. Nor was he such an ogre and so dissolute as biographers describe him. Once more this characterization goes back to Chrysander and the Victorians, but no document supports the contention. Chrysander called him a man completely devoid of moral sense, while Flower notes with satisfaction that he "was to disappear in the slough of vice that enthralled him." If so, why did the Hamburg cathedral appoint him minor canon and cantor as late as 1728, by which time his libertine life should have been common knowledge? That he liked luxury, good food, and women and was a spendthrift is scarcely a "vice"; men of the theatre, and even biographers, often exhibit such traits without being moral degenerates. Keiser was considered one of the top musicians of his time; the city fathers always treated him with respect, and Mattheson, who later may have become estranged from him, praised him highly and so did Telemann. Hasse, a pupil of Keiser, considered his master the greatest living composer. Long after Keiser's death, Scheibe called him perhaps the most original genius German music had ever produced, and Burney heard similar opinions from various musicians.[5]

Keiser's felicity in the musical setting of words, his observance of natural inflections, the rise and fall of the prosody, his deft use of recitation, in which he had no peer, and his colorful orchestration influenced not

---

[5] Since Keiser came from the Weissenfels district, Handel may have heard about his spectacular career from mutual acquaintances and may actually have been in contact with him before going to Hamburg. Keiser was a friendly man, and Handel's almost instantaneous entry into the Hamburg opera may have been at least partly due to the older composer, who was also director-manager of the theatre.

only Handel but Bach. The Leipzig cantor possessed a copy of Keiser's *Passion According to St. Mark,* which he performed repeatedly. But what impressed Handel most was undoubtedly the older composer's delicate and expressive lyricism, the tender pastoral scenes, and the delightfully sensuous, even erotic, melody. Keiser's *Croesus* alone furnished Handel with a number of models; this score, readily available as we have seen, deserves to be better known. And there was another thing composers, notably Handel, learned from this enigmatic musician: the architectural use of key relationships. It is unfortunate that when the Italian tidal wave became irresistible, Keiser abandoned his original style, mixing Italian songs with German, a mixture that withered the budding German opera in general and his own congenial style in particular. A great deal remains to be done by historians to rescue this important and gifted composer, whom Dent was willing to place "beside Purcell," from undeserved neglect.

In the meantime the friendship between Handel and Mattheson underwent a crisis, moves and countermoves coming swiftly. Mattheson's opera *Cleopatra* was very successful, the composer himself taking the leading role of Antonius. By this time the ripieno violinist Handel was also acting as *maestro al cembalo,* lending a firm helping hand to his composer friend. Mattheson, however, had displaced Handel in the favor of John Wyche and had become tutor to his son, Handel's first pupil. But Handel was not vindictive; only in professional matters was he stubborn, and it was a professional offense that precipitated the crisis between the two friends. At the performance of *Cleopatra* Mattheson, vain and footlight-conscious, wanted to take over the conductor's post at the harpsichord (occupied by Handel) as soon as his role ended on the stage, thus not only keeping himself in the public eye from beginning to end (half an act remained to be played), but also demonstrating his comprehensive talents as composer, singer, and conductor. Handel refused to yield the harpsichord. An altercation ensued; the two repaired to the Goosemarket and with drawn swords had at each other, with the opera audience that followed heckling and egging them on. "The duel might have ended very badly for us both," says Mattheson in his *Ehrenpforte,* "if by God's mercy my sword had not broken on a metal button of my adversary's coat." He is gracious about the affair: "It was the result of a misunderstanding such as with young and ambitious people is nothing new . . . we became better friends than ever." The two hotheads reconciled, Mattheson immediately lent a hand with Handel's next opera, and the two continued friends for the rest of their lives, through correspondence; after Handel left Hamburg they never again saw each other.

After the debacle of *Nero* (1705), Handel once more took stock, and his acts may once more seem aimless unless one considers his deliberate way of dealing with every phase of his life. Surprisingly enough, he resigned from the opera but stayed on in Hamburg, quickening the pace of his creative activity. Keiser's successor commissioned him to write an opera, the memory of the eighteen or twenty performances of *Almira* having made him forget *Nero*. This new opera turned out to be an enormously sprawling affair that in the end had to be broken into two separate pieces named *Florinda* and *Daphne*. The unwieldy work must have caused all sorts of difficulties to the management, resulting in repeated postponements; the two operas were not produced until after Handel had left Hamburg; he never heard them, and the scores perished.

[4]

ABOUT HALFWAY BETWEEN his arrival in Hamburg in 1703 and his departure in 1706, Handel set to music the *Passion According to St. John*. There is so much ill-conceived speculation about this work that we must examine it in some detail.

It is a mistake to see here either any wavering of his artistic intentions or even a return to tradition. On the contrary, there was a new trend in Germany (though familiar in Italy), in which opera composers *also* wrote oratorios and cantatas, the latter having become dramatic genres no longer exclusively intended for church use. This is attested to by the fact that Christian Postel, the author of the book of the Passion, was an opera librettist attached to the Hamburg theatre. As such Hamburg literature went, he was a relatively skilful man of letters (Chrysander modestly calls him "the German Metastasio," and he is known to have had some influence on Klopstock); Keiser thought highly of him and set his texts by preference. As a matter of fact, it may well have been Keiser's example that prompted the composition of the Passion, for the admired master was a successful oratorio composer.

At the opening of the century the German cantata and oratorio were still largely a distinctly German genre and quite different either from what Handel ultimately created under the name of "oratorio," or even from the German variety composed in the twenties and thirties by German masters already reconciled with the opera seria. By the century's beginning the Passion was no longer a liturgical composition, a role it had originally filled in both the Catholic and the Lutheran rites; it had long since left the orbit of liturgical *Gebrauchsmusik* for the realm of quasi-independent dramatic art.

The reading of the Gospel of the Passion of Our Lord, according to Matthew on Palm Sunday, Mark on Tuesday, Luke on Wednesday, and John on Good Friday, was an integral part of both liturgies during Holy Week. Even in its earliest form, when it was but a simple recitation with very few musical inflections, the Passion was dramatized, different types of voices being assigned for the dramatis personae. The designation of tenor for the role of the Evangelist, bass for that of Christ, and so on, with which we are familiar from the Passions of Bach, is a tradition of very long standing. By the 15th century the polyphonic Passion made its appearance, gradually supplanting the old monophonic variety, and the style employed was altogether within the spirit and technique of the motet. The attraction of the dramatic was so strong that even the old Gregorian Passion, which continued to live side by side with the polyphonic type throughout the 15th and 16th centuries, called on a many-voiced chorus in the *turbae*, the scenes representing the "multitude," or "crowd." But now the liturgical role of the musical setting of the Passion begins to diminish. Schütz opens the way for "free" Passion composition, and Theile (1673), with his arias and ritornels, definitely forsakes the liturgy. When Handel tried his hand at the genre, composers no longer dealt with Scripture but with a libretto *fashioned* on a scriptural subject.

Handel knew all this literature. The motet-madrigal mixture combined with instrumental obbligatos he encountered in the works of Andreas Hammerschmidt (1611–1675), which were widely distributed and known. This fine composer was a great lyricist and a fastidious craftsman. His contemporaries attest the popularity of his works, which could be heard in the smallest village churches. He was indeed the most popular German church composer in the Middle Baroque and next to Schütz the most distinguished. But Hammerschmidt was a modern composer who exploited the affective implications of the text.

There was still another kind of cantata (the oratorio being only an extended cantata or a string of cantatas even in Bach's works) that Handel must have known intimately. Zachow, who had an independent mind and knew a great deal about Italian music, created a type of his own. He used scriptural texts in a distinctly dramatic manner, with recitatives and arias—da capo arias; the texture is often fugal, and obbligato instruments are given important roles. This was a far grander style than that of the German cantata of the closing decades of the 17th century and was not really matched until Bach came on the scene. Another composer who showed a similar bent was Johann Philipp Krieger, of whose approximately two thousand cantatas about sixty are extant. Krieger, the Weissenfels resident maestro, an opera composer, was more than conversant with the dramatic style, and he was, of course, well known to Handel, who was undoubtedly familiar with his *historiae,* of which we have a list from Krieger himself. *Die Historia des Leidens und Sterbens unsers Herrn Jesu Christi* was presented in the Weissenfels palace chapel from 1685 onward, enjoying a reputation not unlike that of *Messiah* at the Foundling Hospital many years later. Finally, we must count upon the profound influence of Schütz, who, it should be remembered, used to be *Kapellmeister* in Weissenfels. Though it is impossible to ascertain whether Handel knew Schütz's music, he could not have been unaware that the Halle order of service in his day still prescribed that the Resurrection be sung to Schütz's music. In general, it is noteworthy that the Passion, or *historia,* was especially well cultivated in the Saxon-Thuringian region.

This, then, was the state of the German Lutheran Passion when Handel undertook the setting of Postel's libretto. The indecision that Handel shows in his *St. John Passion,* poor timing, stiff and archaic recitation, and so on, is surprising in view of his already considerable experience, his already highly developed expressive powers, and his innate ability to appropriate styles practically overnight. To be sure, there are some very respectable, even beautiful, numbers in the Passion, but on the whole one feels that something is amiss here. Scriptural passages and the narrating Evangelist were retained by Postel, but he also added a good deal of original "poetry," some of it scarcely conducive to lyric expression. When the soldiers are casting dice for Christ's coat, they repeat the ludicrous line "you must lose your coat" again and again. These poems could not fire the mind of a composer so dependent on imagery as was Handel's, and indeed with few exceptions the arias fashioned on them are rather drab and static, and most of the choral numbers are also lacking in life. But there are flashes of the real Handel even in this early work, for when Pilate contends with the people one feels a rising dramatic excitement that immediately affects the chorus. While Christ's lines are set with dignity, it is perhaps significant that what characterization and dramatic ingenuity there is in the Passion is conspicuously vested in Pilate. He was a man, and Handel could deal with men. The final chorus, "Schlafe wohl nach deinen Leiden" (Sleep well after your sufferings), is Handel the future great master of the choral commentary, and if any proof is needed that he possessed this mastery to a remarkable degree while still a German composer in his homeland, this epilogue provides it eloquently.

That Handel was thoroughly familiar with the Hammerschmidt-

Zachow-Krieger style and capable of utilizing it to some degree even at this early stage in his career cannot be doubted. Everything we mentioned above that characterizes the work of these able composers is to be found later in Handel's "English" music. While a little uneasy about this Passion, most biographers praise it, or if they admit weak points they blame the librettist, Postel, for it, as they blame Brockes for the failure of the next work in this genre. But the quality of the librettos was misjudged by writers unfamiliar with German literary and religious history as well as with the musical esthetics that were a corollary to the former. As Friedrich Blume ably summarized in his history of Protestant music in the Bücken series, this represented not so much a low literary level as a certain positive concept aimed at providing the composer with opportunities for affective representation, the text being distinctly subordinated to the music.

The curious mingling of archaic with modern elements in the *St. John Passion* cannot be ascribed solely to youthful inexperience. In fact, the hesitations represent a conflict in Handel's mind that we fail to recognize because our evaluation of this work is based partly on Bach's tremendous settings of the Passion, partly on *Messiah* and the other great works of the later Handel. A glance at the German Passion in the decade following the turn of the century should explain the dilemma in Handel's mind, and we shall see that even in 1716, when for the second and last time he addressed himself to the setting of a German religious text, the dilemma still inhibited the mature composer.

Hamburg had many churches, fine organists, and must have offered the highest type of traditional North German Protestant church music, with which Handel was thoroughly familiar. Yet the antiliturgical, even secular, tendency was unmistakable. In nearby Lübeck the grand master, Buxtehude, admired and revered by all, composed a very large number of cantatas on religious texts, conducting his famed *Abendmusiken*, which were the pride of St. Mary's. But while the texts were religious, this was altogether "concert" music; only the locale where it was performed was churchly. Buxtehude and all the other "modern" composers mentioned above were no longer interested, or at least only intermittently, in the chorale; they wrote dramatic concerted music. It may seem strange that Pietism should have neglected the chorale, which was considered virtually the revealed word of God, possessing a spiritual strength and liturgical fitness almost equalling that of the Bible. Clearly, Pietism changed the point of gravity from formal religion to private, familial piety at home, preferring the naive ditties that were composed by the thousands to the

sturdy old hymns of the Lutherans. The tendency in the Passions was toward *explicatio,* that is, interpretation of the scriptural story, which gradually eliminated the Gospels in favor of "poetic-meditative" songs. This
did not appeal to Handel, who was attracted by the solemnity of a formal
liturgy. Trained as a professional church musician, proud of the calling
and of the métier, and fond of the artistic realization of the stated articles
of faith, he wanted to be no party to the sing-song that had invaded the
cantata and turned the Passion into sentimental—and even gory—"sacred" opera. A man of powerful instincts and with an innate feeling for
style, he deliberately avoided what must have appeared to him an incongruity. Nowhere does he show a real interest in the cornerstone of German Protestant church music: congregational singing; therefore the Passion's sole link with the liturgy, the chorale, is missing. In this connection
it is significant that true to this attitude, and even though Handel was a
passionate lover of the organ, he totally abstained from the Protestant art
par excellence, which was the chorale prelude and chorale variation. Nor
did he compose choral music for the Lutheran liturgy.

The indecision evident in his Passion rests on this conflict. He tried to
reconcile it but was unsuccessful; reversion to more archaic practices did
not help. If we refer to Bach for comparison we are using an inadmissible
yardstick. By the time Bach composed his Passions the genre was in irrevocable decline, and indeed, its history ends with him forever. However, it must be borne in mind that Bach's Passions, which raised the musical rendition of the Gospels to its unsurpassable peak, were deliberately
archaic and in contradiction of the prevailing trend and style. At a time
when Keiser and others composed Passion-oratorios that no longer had any
connections with the liturgy, with the scriptures, or even with the church,
Bach put together gigantic works consisting of strings of cantatas. He utilized all the secular means that had come to dominate church music—
recitative, arioso, da capo aria—but every one of the cantatas that makes
up the oratorio *ends with a chorale.* No one but this immense genius, profoundly rooted in Lutheran tradition, could have achieved this blend
without risking utter failure—*vide* Graun and his almost ludicrous *Der
Tod Jesu.* Granted, there are moments, especially in the great *St. Matthew Passion,* where the contemplative, Pietistic libretto misleads Bach,
and the drama comes to a temporary halt, but the music reflects such genuine faith, is so overwhelmingly beautiful, that it overcomes the stylistic
and dramatic pitfalls. In the first chorus of the *St. Matthew Passion,* a
tonal mural of incredible vastness and grandeur, which is not scriptural
and clearly takes a dramatic turn with the two choruses thundering ques-

tions and answers, every churchly tradition is flouted; this is pure music drama. But then, at the height of the tumultuous scene, the treble choir intones the chorale "O Lamb of God," which floats serenely over the animated choruses, suddenly investing the scene with the strength of the old Lutheran profession of faith. This was the work of a sturdy, unflinching, and seasoned composer for whom the outside world scarcely existed, who held the fort all by himself with rocklike conviction in traditional beliefs and ideas that were being assaulted all around him. Handel was a very young man when he composed his Passion, a man to whom the outside world meant a great deal. The born dramatist in him rebelled at any thought of compromise, and it is for this reason that this first essay of the future great oratorio composer remains an inconclusive and insignificant episode in his life work.

The Passion was ready for performance for Holy Week in 1704, and Handel wanted his friend Mattheson, who had departed for Holland, to be present. The younger man valued the more experienced Mattheson's judgment, and the latter, though bound for England, changed his plans to oblige his friend. Handel's letter (in Mattheson's *Ehrenpforte*) is one of the few, and one of the three in German, that have been preserved at least indirectly. Mattheson did not arrive in time to witness the performance, but subsequently examined the score, which he censured rather severely. We are told that this "vicious" review was written a quarter of a century after the event and was the result of hindsight, poor memory, and jealousy; but Mattheson's critique, even though published later (perhaps even for the second time), was certainly written soon after his return. The review is no flippant treatment from memory. It analyzes everything, from text declamation to part-writing, demonstrating careful study of the score, which he could no longer have possessed nor examined in 1725. It is unreasonable, moreover, to see in the review a retrospective attack on Handel, for had it been written years after the event, the possible original motive of jealousy would long since have ceased to influence Mattheson; and by that time Handel had not only given up this type of sacred music but had become a pronouncedly secular composer, a master acclaimed in England. In any case the critique was not "vicious." It was perhaps severe, but certainly not unreasonable, for aside from a few impressive numbers, especially in the choruses, there is little of value when measured in Handelian terms. As late as 1760, Marpurg, the most respected musical scholar and critic of the 18th century, declared this "review" the first competent musical criticism of vocal music.

While not particularly successful, the Passion raised Handel's professional standing in the community, and the young musician seems to have been on the threshold of a career similar to that which Keiser had carved for himself in Hamburg. As mentioned earlier, *Almira* and the *St. John Passion* have been cited by almost all biographers as having been regarded by Keiser as the works of an incipient dangerous rival. But Handel now abandoned Hamburg and left for Italy.

[5]

THE CIRCUMSTANCES surrounding his departure are once more shrouded in conjecture. Biographers wonder who made the decision and who provided the funds. In all his life Handel always made his own decisions and nothing and no one could change them. As to funds, the frugal and astute businessman who had collected the allowance for his lodging while cathedral organist in Halle but who had lived in the family house undoubtedly was saving money throughout his stay in Hamburg for precisely this purpose. That Handel's earning and husbanding of money started early is demonstrated by the fact that in 1703 he had already returned to his mother the money she had sent him and began to support her with modest remittances. From every account it appears that the young harpsichord instructor was well paid for the lessons he gave to well-to-do pupils. Mattheson mentions a saving of two hundred ducats, a respectable sum, if not sufficient for the journey. But this was merely an estimate on Mattheson's part; Handel was just as close-mouthed about his business affairs as he was about his religion or his love affairs. He undoubtedly had the necessary means for the journey, for there was no one else who could have provided it for him.

There is, however, an indistinct figure in the background who has given rise to speculation. The reader will remember that through Mattheson and John Wyche Handel found entrée into high intellectual and social circles. It was thus that he made the acquaintance of Prince Gastone de' Medici. It is possible that this prince extended an invitation to Handel to come to Florence, though it is very unlikely that he had the means to support the invitation or any authority to place the Medici court at Handel's disposal. Gastone was in fact a black-sheep Medici, the sickly, dissolute second son of Grand Duke Cosimo III of Tuscany. The wastrel was practically exiled from Florence and heartily despised by the reigning family and the court. When Cosimo's first-born son died childless, the aged Duke was so loath to permit Gastone to succeed him that he seriously entertained the idea of reconstituting the Florentine Republic; but the leading European powers, perfectly aware of the vulnerability of Tuscany if Gastone ascended the throne, would not hear of that. Eventually Gastone did succeed Cosimo III, but that was in 1723, long after Handel's visit to Italy. Nor could Gastone have held out hopes to Handel about a career at the Medici court, for the undisputed ruler in artistic matters at the court was the Crown Prince, Ferdinando, especially devoted to music. It was in the latter's palace that Bartolomeo Cristofori, in charge of the Prince's collection of musical instruments, built the first pianoforte (c. 1710). Ferdinando, who died in 1713, thus throwing the succession to Gastone, was very unlikely to have accepted suggestions from his despised brother concerning a totally unknown young German musician. We must dismiss this poor wretch, whose reign gave the *coup de grâce* to Tuscany's independence when Spanish and Austrian troops occupied the duchy; he could have had very little influence on Handel, though he may have contributed to the idea of an Italian sojourn. As usual it was Handel's powers of observation and his purposeful planning that led to the decision. As Mainwaring quaintly says, he chose to go to Italy "on his own bottom."

From his early youth Handel was aware that many of the composers he admired and whose works he copied in the sketchbook had worked in Italy before achieving fame, and of course he well knew that Italy was the land of opera. This was not a perilous leap into uncharted regions. Hamburg could not offer him further advancement; besides, he clearly sensed the debacle toward which Keiser and even the Hamburg theatre itself were headed. The composer who could not compromise in the Passion could not accept the ungainly hybrid that was German opera in Hamburg, with Italian arias inserted at random into the body of a German stage work. Italy was the answer, and to Italy he went in the fall of 1706, quietly but determinedly, without even taking leave of Mattheson.

III

ALL LIGHT, IT IS SAID, COMES FROM THE EAST, BUT
surely all beauty comes from the south. Musicians, painters, poets, and
architects have always known this, and for a long time foreign artists could
be found all over the Italian peninsula. This boundless, and in a way inexplicable, love of the Mediterranean has drawn many a musician to Italy,
but few of them found it as congenial as did certain German Protestants,
born and raised in a totally different milieu. The situation was altogether
different with the southern Germans; they were Catholics and lived in a
region for centuries either contiguous to Italy or strongly under her influence. (Salzburg is a bit of Italy nestled in the Austrian mountains.) But it
must be borne in mind that many a northern pine transplanted to the
Mediterranean did not change its needles to broad leaves. Dürer and
Goethe, Keats and Handel became what they were in Italy, but for the
Germans and the English, not the Italians. Italy became an apocalyptic
dream to Handel, which remained with him to the end of his life—but it
always remained a dream.

Ruskin, who recognized four types of landscape, calls Italy a blue region, and the Mediterranean blue is indeed irresistible. Nature adorns
herself under this blue sky with multicolored flowers and fruits, inducing
man to adorn himself and his possessions with bright colors. The farther
south the traveller goes the more colorful the garments, the more profuse
the ornaments, the more lighthearted the decorations. When Goethe vis-

ited Italy, he still travelled in a coach painted Pompeian red, the harness gilded, the horses wearing enormous bouquets on their heads, while in their manes were woven many tiny flags that fluttered. To northern taste this riot of color seems almost barbarous—as indeed it would be in the north—but under the azure of the Italian skies nothing is too colorful for nothing can outdo the sun's fire.

But there is another attraction to the Italian countryside, whether in Sicily or Tuscany, that fascinates the northern visitor. The Italians are closer to plants and animals than it is ever possible for Germans, or even for other Latins to be. It is the supreme virtue of the Italian nation that it can afford to let Nature be a full partner in life. Foreigners could only watch this partnership with worshipful amazement. While Goethe with all his perceptive admiration and enjoyment remained mostly a spectator (the impressions gained in Italy came to creative fruition through a complicated process of metathesis), in Handel Italians found a German who could live their life, play their own game—and beat them at it. And he discovered what at home he only divined: worldly values that see the earth not as a vale of tears but as the rich treasury of life's beauties. What in the Latin school in Halle he studied as monuments of a long-departed civilization he found to be a living tradition—the pagan world was always alive in Italy. Another thing he discovered was pathos. In Italian pathos there seems to the northerner an element of pose, but since pathos is almost always the expression of a sincere passion, it must be accepted as serious, even if the proportion between passion and expression does not seem natural. The Italian spirit can represent its ideas with great energy and immediacy; it is moving and "showy" as no other.

There was Handel, in this Italian world, in Venice, the city rich with the creations of a phenomenal school of music, which sat in judgment over the foreigners who came to the promised land of opera to try their hand right at the source. Most of the pilgrims appeared in vain; whether respected mature masters or fiery youths, the Transalpines could not quite win their case before the court, for few are among the elect. But this young Saxon, whom they will call *il caro Sassone,* settled among the legion of the obscure with secure calm and confidence, and when Venice judged the court found in his favor. Then one day, without hesitation, Handel sat down on the throne in the royal palace of opera and, almost before anyone was aware of it, put on the king's robe. Now the robe was his and could have been for life, but as we shall see, for some mysterious reason he laid it down soon after his possession of it was recognized all over Italy, to return to the Germanic world.

Earlier, when he arrived in Rome, Handel went to the great churches. He knew churches at home: the sturdy and cool Calvinist cathedral, Our Lady's Lutheran Church in Halle, and the many in Hamburg and other North German cities. But in these Roman churches he again discovered what was all round him in Italy: color—red, white, green, and black slabs of marble lining the walls, the golden altars, the mosaics, the statues and pictures, and the hundreds of candles. He had a good eye for such things, and all his life he was interested in paintings, roaming the galleries and even indulging in a bit of collecting himself—he was very proud of the pictures he later owned in London. To the German cantor uniform, quiet colors, uninterrupted lines, and well-filled surfaces stood for monumentality. Handel was searching for something else and found it in Italy in the sharp delineation of colors, in the concentrated energy of the lines, in the absolute clarity of the expression. He saw that the paintings represented not only the gentle embossing of the surfaces of the human body but also the energetic and immediately perceptible plasticity of the forms, the clear and pure disclosure of the structure of those bodies. He realized that there is disciplined passion in the great Renaissance paintings, the resolution of powerful conflicts, but he also noted that the Baroque liberated this suppressed drama—the figures step out of their suggestive immobility—and that all this could be expressed in music. At first his figures do not move, they have only static gestures, but before long he begins to animate them, and the illusion of a third dimension materializes.

Among the rising national styles of music the Italian was most capable of representing clearly the aspirations of the age. Italy's ancient culture, her vivacious and susceptible mentality, early assured her a more developed social life than could be found elsewhere in Europe. Her numerous small states with their independent and competitive intellectual lives made her culture many-sided, rich, and decentralized. The Italian sense of form combined with an instinct for basic artistic expression to achieve the ideally beautiful. Europe became her vassal, followed her lead, imitated her music with feverish joy, and tried to derive from her the laws of beauty. Thus Italy's goals and inclinations became of international validity. The primordial instinct of Latin-Italian society, unlike the German, is individualistic, an instinct that early raised political and artistic life in the small states to a high level. Italian musical sense is by nature individualistic; more precisely, it is more suited to the conveying of individual passions than of permanent, collective feelings. Besides this, Italy is the home of singing, of homophony, of melody. Musicians from all over

Europe journeyed to Italy to learn the secrets of this magic, and Italian musicians carried all over Europe their warm and sensuous art. Since the Italian genius is not contemplative, since its ability to shape is pronounced and facile, and since it always seeks out the essential, the guiding lines, it tends to found schools and methods of wide adaptability and acceptability.

This was the reason for Italy's musical hegemony, and it was her art that largely determined a manner of music and music making that best fitted the demands of the times. On the other hand, the insecure political conditions, the frequent domination of parts of the country by foreign powers, made it difficult for the Italian musician to do work of a consistently national character, and his frequent subjection to foreign interests developed in him a certain unrestrained, adventurous trait for which he had a penchant anyway. In the face of the lameness of national policies, Italy became the site of an unreal world basking in the light and warmth of artistic life. Although all northerners and westerners felt the irresistible attraction of this fairy world, so far as music is concerned the interesting fact remains that of all peoples it was the Germans who proved capable of assimilating that spirit and that art most felicitously—Handel, John Christian Bach, Mozart. (Just as interestingly, the Germans who remained at home steadfastly insisted on the frivolity and low value of Italian music, and in the north even the Viennese, obviously tainted by *welscher Tand,* were scarcely less derided.)

With her erstwhile far-flung commerce in decline, the economy of Italy failed to support this overflowing artistic productivity; as a result she became an artistic export nation furnishing all of Europe with music and musicians, and by the 17th century their language had become the international language of music. The magnificent sonority of the Italian language, its pliable and easily pronounced constellation of vowels and consonants that never form harsh and grating clusters, was born for music, and this smoothness is quite characteristic both of the Italian's music and his nature in general. The Italian seeks external light and a responsive public, always aiming at the most advantageous and prominent display of his personality. He loves pomp, festivities, elaborate services, all of which show in his music, which insinuates itself into our favor, is easy to understand, effective, and particularly suitable for public representation. The most original and important phenomena of the musical Baroque, opera and concerted music, are altogether Italian inventions; starting in the 17th century, these new genres embarked on a world conquest, captivating all and sundry with their sensuous charm.

The Germans' musical style was also determined to a considerable extent by their language, but this was not a brilliant language, and its rather heavy, thoughtful manner of construction is characteristic of the music itself. Since this music was not colorful it preferred to remain in smaller circles; it is inward in character and until the 18th century did not find its most personal expression in soaring melody but rather in artful construction. It was the German masters who preserved the medieval tradition of polyphony and, especially in the Protestant north and center, remained quite faithful to their conservative chorale-based art even when it diligently assimilated the progressive currents coming from Italy and France. The Italians were the leaders in music; they never attempted to rival German music, which to the Catholic south was strange and remote. But the greatness and independence of German music were built precisely on its chorale-born polyphonic art.

The remarkable proclivity of the Germans for synthesis, the manner in which they accept, filter, and assimilate foreign influences, led, when combined with their innate intimacy of feeling, to the incomparable art of a Schütz and a Bach, but the most essential ingredient in this great music, the counterpoint born of a profound religious feeling, was not transferable; it was too deeply rooted in the hymns of German Protestantism to become a conquering force beyond that specific cultural territory. In their sequestered, intimate life, the Germans guarded a secret treasure without wanting to claim a part of the glory of the international world of music. Italian music—like Italian religion—was a community affair, whereas German music and faith were, so to speak, a family matter, though the influence radiating from Italy, notably opera and the concerto, eventually changed this—Buxtehude's famous *Abendmusiken* were already concerts, not service music. By the time a successor to Kuhnau was to be chosen in Leipzig, the authorities at the Thomasschule wanted a "modern" cantor; it was only because they could not secure the services of a more fashionable musician that, somewhat reluctantly, they settled on Sebastian Bach, considered a good but conservative musician of the old school.

[2]

HANDEL WENT TO Italy in quest of this modern music. Nothing is known about the circumstances of his departure or arrival, nor are we well informed about his wanderings through Italy from the autumn of 1706 till the spring of 1710. Having made up his mind in his usual taciturn but positive way, he simply turned his back on Hamburg and the next thing we know of is his appearance in Florence. So, the "great search" continued, initially under circumstances even more insecure than when he abandoned Halle for Hamburg. The times were bad. The War of the Spanish Succession was at its height, and as usual, Italy was one of the battlegrounds. Soon Handel was to learn that even St. Peter's See could be besieged and sacked, for the Holy Roman Emperor or his underlings were wont periodically to remind the Pope that he reigned not so much by the grace of God as by the political convenience of the Catholic monarchs.

All Handel brought with him were a few scores—some of his own, some of Keiser's—and of course his phenomenal performing ability, which was the only negotiable currency he possessed at that time. He arrived in the promised land a totally unknown German musician, though he had one "contact," the black-sheep Medici, Prince Gastone, whom, as we have seen, he met in Hamburg. He may have revived the acquaintance, because a visit in Florence is the first station of his journey where the historian catches up with the elusive traveller. But as we noted earlier, that noble's influence with Prince Ferdinand was negligible. Moreover, the court was literally teeming with excellent musicians, so that an unknown German Protestant musician had very little to recommend him, even though where artists were concerned the Italians were always far more liberal towards religious deviation than other nations. There was not much room for Handel, and he soon left Florence for Rome.

Nevertheless, the first stopover in Italy was of considerable importance. It was here that he got his first taste of the reigning musical tendencies, and of the culture, the nobility of life, and the intellectual and social graces of the highest stratum of Italian society. The brief experience in Florence prepared him for the resplendent gatherings of Roman aristocracy, the hierarchy, the great Maecenases, poets, artists, and adventurers, for the academies with their highly selective membership, the bucolic and classicistic delights of the High Baroque, statues and fountains, elaborate feasts and festivities, masquerades—all saturated with music. André Pirro's wonderfully succinct characterization of the attraction of this music, though written about the impact of the Italian concerto on Bach, is equally valid when applied to Handel. For he too was overwhelmed by the Italian

fecundity, by the magnificence of the ideas and the indefatigable energy. In these Italian works one finds the fluent prattling, the ability to say nothing, inexhaustible eloquence, the plenitude of the rhetoricians of antiquity. The

smallest idea is amplified, transformed, ennobled, everything radiating and
whirling in a grand splendor of sonority.

The three and a half years spent in this environment had a decisive influence on the rest of Handel's life. And of course he met the men who made
this music. Almost all of them were helpful, and some of them became his
friends.

[3]

HANDEL UNDOUBTEDLY arrived in Rome with some recommendations from Prince Ferdinand and others, but his great performing skill
would have opened the doors in any case. All he had to do was to go to a
church and play the organ, and he became known. Newman Flower
found a Roman diary entry for January 14, 1707, stating that "a Saxon
played the organ at San Giovanni di Laterano to universal admiration."
The picture that greeted him in Rome must have been confusing. On the
one hand, the spirit of the Counter-Reformation ruled the Vatican,
though it also had a Pietism of its own. On the other, some of the very
persons who embraced this spirit with fervor indulged in the most extravagant secular, humanistic, social-artistic cult. Thus while opera was prohibited in Rome by the Pope on grounds not materially different from
those the Fundamentalist clergy professed in Germany, oratorio, almost
entirely patterned on opera, flourished. Innocent XI, who in 1697 ordered
the Roman opera house, Tor di Nona, demolished in the name of morality, actually encouraged oratorio though he must have known that it was
a form of subterfuge. A visiting cardinal attending a performance of Colonna's *Caduta di Gerusalemme* was so outraged by the violation of the
spirit of Lent, the presence of women in the cast, and the eating, drink-
ing, and dancing at the close of the performance that though the event
took place in a private residence he demanded that Colonna be thrown
into jail. However, the cardinal was a Pole and while his indignation was
shared, he could not get his Italian colleagues too much excited about it.
Giovanni Paolo Colonna (1637–1695), a pupil of Benevoli and Carissimi,
was a widely known and admired composer of oratorios (which, incidentally, Handel surely encountered), and no Italian prelate would have
wanted to harm him.

In spite of the ambiguous situation, both Innocent XI and Innocent
XII, whose reforms were still felt when Handel lived in Rome, earnestly
strove to cleanse the moral atmosphere that enveloped the Holy See and

the Eternal City, abolishing nepotism and in general ruling the Church in exemplary fashion, but not even a new Savonarola could have interfered with the Italians' love of music. Clement XI, during whose pontificate the Holy See suffered grave political reverses, was the Pope during Handel's Italian visit. Another one of those high churchmen of blameless life, and a man of vast learning and culture, a great patron of the arts and letters, he nevertheless saw the prestige of the papacy sink to the lowest level in centuries. In the Treaty of Utrecht (1713), which Handel was to memorialize in a splendid Te Deum in London, the Pope was completely ignored by both the Protestant and the Catholic parties.

In contradistinction, the humanistic societies, led by cardinals and princes, were flourishing, and Handel saw them in their most extraordinary splendor. The principal circle of cultivated intellectuals met in the academy called *Accademia Poetico-Musicale,* usually in the palace of Cardinal Pietro Ottoboni, and occasionally at the residence of the Marquess Francesco Maria Ruspoli, later Prince of Cerveteri. The Academy was founded in memory of Queen Christina of Sweden. This daughter of the great Protestant warrior Gustavus Adolphus abdicated, embraced Catholicism, and moved to Rome in 1659, becoming alternately the despair and the laughing stock of European diplomacy. Her life was beset by scandals, and in the end, the Pope, who had hailed her conversion and her advent to Rome, was making every effort to get rid of this embarrassing and ill-behaved guest with her questionable retinue. But her influence on Roman arts and letters was considerable, and she was especially fond of music. The queen died in 1689, and the Academy was founded the following year by her friends and protégés as a tribute to her.

The eccentric queen's role as high patron of the arts fell to Cardinal Ottoboni, but ten years after the death of Christina another exiled queen, a member of the Academy, claimed the vacant throne of patroness, though without success. Queen Maria Casimira of Poland, a woman of very ordinary intellectual capabilities, nevertheless managed to recruit a distinguished coterie. For a brief period Alessandro Scarlatti was her court maestro, and after Alessandro's departure to Naples, his son Domenico inherited the post early in 1709. Handel undoubtedly watched the exiled queen's moves to restore opera. Maria Casimira petitioned the Pope to permit her to produce musical plays in her palace, assuring him that they would be altogether free of frivolity. Permission granted, the first such musical plays were innocent serenatas for very small ensembles. Emboldened, by 1708 she built herself a tiny theatre, engaged a full-time librettist, and actually advanced to opera, the first production being, naturally, by Alessandro Scarlatti. But the move was abortive, and during Handel's stay the interdict was enforced.

Giovanni Maria Crescimbeni (1663–1728), critic, poet, and historian, for thirty-eight years "custodian general" of the Academy, remembered for his great chronicle of Italian poets and poetry (*Dell' Istoria della volgar poesia*, 1698), an able and observant man of letters, is our reliable witness for the meetings and concerts held in the Academy. His interesting descriptions are detailed and inform us of the paramount role music played in the sessions. Though Handel was not a member, perhaps because he was under the minimum age requirement or because he was a foreigner, he was nevertheless often present as a guest, and thus came to know at first hand the three coryphaei of Italian music, who were honored members of the Academy: Corelli, Scarlatti, Pasquini. Their acquaintance gave new directions to Handel's entire concept of music.

Arcangelo Corelli (1653–1713) was the undisputed and universally admired leader of instrumental music in Italy. A patrician, he lived honored like a prince in a private apartment in Cardinal Ottoboni's palace. Corelli was a very slow, meticulous, and highly critical worker who corrected and polished eternally. Moreover, the great master of the sonata and the concerto apparently never wrote a single piece of vocal music. His distilled classicism, based on tradition yet advancing into the future, was new to Handel, as was the clarity of form, the logical yet imaginative exploitation of ideas, the pathos, and the beauty of the noble string tone that was never beclouded by empty virtuosity or reckless adventures. Corelli sums up everything that a century of instrumental music had produced; his influence was tremendous. Handel, like everyone else, was deeply indebted to Corelli, and his own concertos were a direct continuation of the Italian's work. But the significance of the concerto as form and principle was not restricted to the genre itself: this most original "invention" of the Italian Baroque affected all music to the marrow. The concerto invaded and reformed everything, reaching even such seemingly unrelated fields as fugue, cantata, and opera. As in Sebastian Bach, where the spirit of the concerto touches his very fugue themes and the choruses of his cantatas, in Handel we must proceed beyond his concertos and realize that essential stylistic features in his operas and oratorios are governed by ideas coming from that form. We shall see how fond he was of shaping his orchestral accompaniments to arias in the concerto grosso manner. The type we might call "concerto grosso aria" is already present in some of the Italian cantatas Handel composed in Rome. The flowing concerto style is likewise present in Bach's da capo arias, but even some of his great organ fugues are veritable concertos, and not a few of the chorale preludes are "concerted." No one could resist the appeal of this invigorating musical principle, least of all Handel; the meeting with Corelli was an overwhelming experience.

Alessandro Scarlatti (1660–1725), a lineal descendant of the great Roman and Venetian masters of the 17th century and the real founder of the Neapolitan school, was a Fra Filippo Lippi let loose on the walls of Prato Cathedral. It is impossible to enumerate his works—operas, oratorios, cantatas, Masses, instrumental music—all of them glowing with a resilient yet gentle and wonderfully arching melody expressing the accents of warm and passionate lyricism. This prodigal inventor, who must have been composing every waking hour of his life, was also an incomparable musical thinker who reformed almost every aspect of music, creating an operatic ideal that for a long time was accepted as the musical ten commandments by the whole world. As Frank Walker puts it, Mozart, who never knew Scarlatti's music, "was yet his best pupil"; but we can safely go beyond the limits of the 18th century and affirm that Scarlatti was one of those on whose broad shoulders our music is still uneasily poised. It was Scarlatti who ensconced the da capo aria in its position as the principal element of the pure "music opera," who brought life and variety to the orchestral accompaniment of arias by placing the concerted style into a new perspective in the opera pit, who established the Italian overture, reversing Lully's sequence of slow-fast-slow and thereby giving impetus to a type that was to play a capital role in the symphonic style of the Classic era.

Bernardo Pasquini (1637–1710), the third of the distinguished musical Arcadians, is one of the great unknowns. A Handelian figure, robust yet at the same time gentle, his works show Tuscan nobility, exquisite taste, and marvelous knowledge of all facets of music. He was so famous that Emperor Leopold automatically sent his protégés to Rome to his school, and indeed the roster of his pupils is most impressive, from the Germans, Kerll, Krieger, and Muffat, to Durante, Gasparini, Della Ciaia, and Domenico Scarlatti. In his old age he was proclaimed "Organist to the Senate and to the People of Rome." His craftsmanship had a quality of its own, a sort of quiet incandescence, but he also had practical gifts of a high order, such as extraordinary skill at the keyboard and above all a power of actively directing and inspiring others. Scarlatti was greatly indebted to him, and it stands to reason that Handel, observing him at close range, could not escape the attraction of this great musician. Pasquini is known as a pioneer keyboard composer, but he was much more than that.

His dramatic and other vocal works are numerous—the Italian libraries are full of his manuscript cantatas—and they were at least as famous and influential as his keyboard works.

When we speak of Scarlatti and of his influence on Handel, we are really indulging in a little game of historical anachronism. At the time Handel met Scarlatti in Rome, the musician in the Italian master was far superior to the dramatist, and what made his opera stylistically consistent was his pure musicality, not dramatic insight. He was of course considerably restricted by the interdict in Rome, while in Naples he had to cater to the rather shallow tastes of the viceroys. Even Prince Ferdinand in Florence demanded a "light" style, constantly criticizing Scarlatti for the "severity" of his music and finally replacing him with Perti. It is for this reason that his most remarkable works up to about 1710 are his cantatas, of which there are hundreds. Though he had some very fine operas to his credit by 1707, the great dramatist first appears before us in *Tigrane* (1715), years after Handel's departure. Here the orchestra is large and elaborate, the continuo aria disappears, the characterization is highly dramatic, and Scarlatti pays particular attention to delicately worked ensembles that are simultaneous and not dialogued, as in the earlier operas. Therefore, the operas had little to do with Handel's immediate Italian impressions, but the influence of the cantatas was permanent and pervasive. Scarlatti's cantatas are composed with conspicuous delicacy, freshness, and a delightful suggestiveness of detail. There is often a capricious flitting from one little oddity to another, bold modulations, and astringent dissonances. But his whimsicalities are never forced, and his trifling is often significant; the profusion of the attractive detail work is subordinated to the classical clarity of outline and to discipline. These cantatas were the first overwhelming experience for Handel, and the validity of the experience he proceeded to test scrupulously.

Handel knew Protestant church music, and he knew opera, and he must have been acquainted with the Italian cantata, either from Zachow —which seems very likely, for Zachow surely possessed in his fine library the scores of such older cantata composers as Luigi Rossi and Marcantonio Cesti—or, if not, at least from the Hamburg period. Kusser was a friend and admirer of Steffani, and so were Telemann and Mattheson, and Steffani's duets and other vocal chamber music were even better known and admired than his operas. Throughout much of the 17th and 18th centuries the *cantata a voce sola* was the principal form of serious music for polite entertainment in courts and cultivated homes. But the cantata acquired new meaning when Handel heard it in its natural habitat, performed by Italian singers. He came to Italy because of opera, but with his sound judgment he realized that opera is a country that can be travelled in only if one learns the language spoken there. The key to that language was the cantata.

[4]

CANTATA, SERENATA, PASTORAL PLAY, ORATORIO, OPERA—they seem to be inseparable and indistinguishable; they overlap and merge and at first glance it is difficult to establish categorical genres, but we can start our analysis by recognizing the outer boundaries. These are the solo cantata with basso continuo and the opera; all the rest lies between these two. Handel's judgment of the situation was clear: in order to learn the finer aspects of the Italian musical and linguistic idiom he must start with the chamber cantata, and since Alessandro Scarlatti was in Prince Ferdinand's service, composing countless cantatas, he began his studies right then and there, using the master's works as models. He undoubtedly heard many cantatas by other composers, not only in Florence and Rome but also in Naples and Venice, for all composers were devoted to this delightful form of miniature opera, on which they usually cut their operatic teeth. While Scarlatti was the sun of this planetary system, the demand for cantatas was so enormous that even the copious output of practically all active composers was not sufficient to satisfy it, and a good many older composers' works were still in circulation and widely performed. Of these composers, Florence and Rome, and even the south, showed particular interest in Giovanni Battista Mazzaferrata (d. 1691), a Ferrarese of very advanced and adventurous bent; the lilting tone of his chamber cantatas kept him popular long after his death.

Considerable influence came from the Bolognese school, one of the prominent regional centers of music. Pietro degli Antonii (c. 1645–1720), whose solo cantatas were composed in the nineties, was uncommonly popular. Giacomo Antonio Perti (1661–1756) was so highly regarded that he was five times elected "Prince" of the Bolognese *Accademia filarmonica*. Over six hundred manuscript compositions of Perti are preserved in San Petronio (whose maestro he was), among them many Masses for double choir whose choral writing is magnificent, but his hundred-odd cantatas, duets, and serenatas were staples at musical gatherings.

Francesco Antonio Pistocchi (1659–1726), though a Sicilian by birth, was another member of the Bolognese school, a pupil of Perti, and a member of the Oratorian order. A fine connoisseur of singing and vocal

style, Pistocchi was the founder of what might be described as the first
methodical school of bel canto (around 1700). He wrote operas and oratorios, of course, but what surely came to Handel's attention was the
Duetti e terzetti, a collection published in 1700. From this circle also came
Giovanni Carlo Maria Clari (1677–1754), a good all-round composer.
Handel later borrowed from Clari's very fine vocal duets and trios for
Theodora. To be sure, this was a later event and the borrowed music of
much later composition,[1] but Handel must have discovered Clari while
still in Italy.

Most certainly Handel knew some of Giovanni Bononcini's beautifully turned cantatas, for they were famous all over Europe. Giovanni
Bononcini (1670–1747), who also came from the Bolognese school, having studied with its famous founder, Colonna, became in the 1720s Handel's rival in London, a real rival, for he was half a generation his senior,
an experienced, original, and highly gifted musician who left his mark
wherever he worked—Vienna, Venice, London. Unfortunately, his portrait is as distorted as Handel's own, except that Handelian biographers
were not willing to permit him even an equivalent to a "Largo." Chrysander, who responded with automatic deprecation to any challenge to
Handel's categorical pre-eminence, is once more at the bottom of this lopsided appraisal, for many subsequent writers accepted his views without
investigating Bononcini's music. English opinions show the typical mistrust of the Italian melodist. Even Burney hedges a little. He acknowledges the beauty of Bononcini's melodies but mentions, with implicit
approval, the judgment of those who found this melody pleasing but
lightweight. Bononcini was a bold, inventive, and resourceful composer,
with a very personal melodic and dramatic talent. His expressive musical
declamation was noticed even by Sebastian Bach. Handel could not have
failed to see some of his cantatas in Halle, Berlin, or Hamburg, because
Raguenet in his comparative essay on the merits of French and Italian
music (1702) speaks of him as universally known and admired in Europe, and his *Duetti da camera* of 1691 were widely disseminated. Judging from Handel's subsequent acts in London, he must have kept a
weather eye on this excellent musician. The borrowings from Bononcini's
Cantate e duetti (1721) are known, but no one has yet investigated how
many borrowings from Bononcini there are in Handel's operas.

Another place of particular importance must be given to Alessandro
Stradella (1642–1688), whose cantatas show, along with gentle and ele-

---

[1] Published by Chrysander in the supplementary volumes of the Händelgesellschaft
edition.

gant lyricism and beautifully turned melody, dramatic power and a fine
theatrical sense. Of his nearly two hundred cantatas only a handful are
available, but the serenatas especially served as models for Handel, who
admired them so much that he implanted some in his own music. With
Stradella the trend to separate recitatives from arias solidifies into a custom. The aria becomes the most important element in all dramatic genres,
and as it grows in size and artfulness so does the obbligato accompaniment.

It is here, in the cantata, of which Handel composed seventy-two for
solo voice with basso continuo and twenty-eight with orchestral accompaniment,[2] that we can observe for the first time his extraordinary ability
to fuse various styles—Venetian, Roman, Neapolitan, Bolognese; he used
them all, but soon with his own personal stamp. These hundred compositions not only form an important and as yet very largely unexplored part
of his *oeuvre,* they also contain many masterpieces, some of which were
later embedded in his oratorios. The cantata played such an important
role in the formation of Handel's style and whole musical view that we
must take a closer look at its nature. The cantata was not only the proving
ground for his melodic skills; it was there that he began to experiment
with descriptive music and with the delightful bucolic tone we shall encounter in such mature works as *Acis and Galatea.*

To most of us the term "cantata" usually means a piece of sacred
music and we have a very firm idea when we mention it, but to the historian it is one of the vaguest and most troublesome of genres. From the
early 17th century the Baroque produced the cantata in profusion, yet
neither its form, nor its text, nor its medium is sufficiently well defined to
permit us to present a categorical opposition to the "cantata" as we know
it—which is to say, from Bach. At any rate, the cantata Handel encountered in Italy was a form of vocal chamber music, more inclined towards
lyricism than towards drama, usually being *a voce sola* with thoroughbass
accompaniment. However, the more elaborate varieties such as the
serenata used an orchestral accompaniment and obbligato concerted instruments, as well as a choral number or two. The dividing line between
this and the Italian oratorio is only faintly, if at all, visible. The secular
variety of cantata we know fairly well, and while the manuscript sources
are close to inexhaustible, the few printed anthologies, among them Riemann's *Kantaten Frühling* and Jeppesen's *La Flora,* nevertheless give us a
very good idea of this engaging species, and Eugen Schmitz's monograph
devoted to it is a reliable guide. Unfortunately no such work exists in the

[2] A few of these were composed later, in London.

realm of the Italian sacred cantata, and here our information is very sketchy indeed. Yet from what little is available,[3] it is clear that neither in style nor in form do the two species differ materially, the recitative-aria scheme being followed by both, though in the sacred cantata the order is often unaccountably reversed: aria-recitative.

The secular cantata, the result of a merger of madrigal and aria, actually developed from the magnificently flourishing monodic "concert" songs as a natural result of the introduction of narrative-dramatic elements. The earliest known example of this type is a set by Alessandro Grandi, *Cantate e arie a voce sola* (1620), while Sigismondo d'India published a remarkable collection of chamber duets as early as 1615. Monteverdi's *Scherzi Musicali* (1632) and his solo madrigals also belong in this category. These songs are expressive, at times powerfully dramatic, at others so dainty and diminutive that only the most intimate surroundings would be appropriate for them; "a dulcet and luscious form of verbosity," as Swinburne said of his own poetry. Many were undoubtedly sung in the evening, out in a meadow or on a riverbank, with a lute or *chitarrone*. There are many paintings from the period that preserve the memory of these outdoor concerts. At first often called *scena di camera,* the monodic song had a bucolic, idyllic nature that was very popular, and the poets were the old poets of the madrigalian era. In Italy the poets stay alive forever. Dante's language is still a living language, not like medieval English, French, or German, which must be deciphered for the modern reader. Handel, like Montaigne and Goethe, could have heard even simple people recite Tasso and Ariosto. This language, which Handel obviously studied closely, judging from his steadily improving musical prosody, is music itself. But while the language was a new experience—after the miserable concoctions he set to music in Hamburg this polished poetry was a revelation—the melody must have been of even greater fascination. It is no exaggeration to state that it was the Italian cantata that enabled Handel to deploy his latent melodic gifts, and it was the cantata that gave him the sense for the carrying power of a theme or melody and the knowledge of when to break off lest it lose its strength by being overdrawn.

[5]

It will be remembered that while Mattheson had praised Handel's skill in harmony and counterpoint, he had found the young

[3] A recent anthology containing a number of Italian sacred cantatas is Rudolf Ewerhart's *Kantate.*

man's melody mediocre. Though not exactly mediocre, it was the German cantor's somewhat abstract and instrumentally inspired melody. Italian melody, which Handel now observed at first hand, does not concern itself with mysticism, it is very much of this world, in the foreground, an experience that takes place once and will never again happen in exactly the same way. This experience is sentiment, feeling, the purest form of lyricism. In the final analysis this is the root of all music, and music could never altogether cut itself off from this root, that is, not until it became willing to entrust its creation to the machine. But that does not concern us here.

Melody evokes mood, and mood is the expression of a fusion of emotions and images, an inward state of soul. We feel each mood to be individual and unique. Since it forms a bridge between conscious beings, its every emanation has its own individuality.

It is unfortunate that the German word *Stimmung* is untranslatable. Neither the Italian *tonalità* or *sfumatura*, nor the French *état d'âme*, nor the English *mood* expresses quite the same thing, for the German word virtually suggests the striking of a tuning fork or the plucking of a chord and thus indicates the relationship that is established among men's souls by mood. Mood spreads like sound. (Regrettably, in English the word has also acquired the secondary meaning of an unstable, even morbid, temper —"a man of moods"—for which the Germans again have a special word: *Laune.*)

In the mood created by a composer there is often concentrated an immense culture, the distillation of a style, for creation of mood has a great tradition. If there is considerable distance in time between the originator of a mood and the listener, the latter may be unable to identify himself with the mood, unless by study he acquires an understanding of the style. This is why most operagoers have difficulty in adjusting to Baroque opera and why they are often unable to penetrate into the infinitely complicated moods of, say, Mozart's *Così fan tutte*. Nevertheless, at the bottom of every artistically created mood there is hidden secret and miracle. This is true even when a very conscious artist such as Handel deliberately and with consummate skill mixes the perfumes of mood. He is successful because he is working with the instinctive arcanum that characterizes the master. A great composer may create a mood instinctively, projecting an idea beyond his conscious grasp. It is perhaps somewhat disconcerting to realize that an artist often "feels" how to create a religious mood and thus without faith achieves a state only faith illuminates. Many a worldly Renaissance artist painted famous courtesans, transforming them into Madonnas of unearthly tenderness, and many a composer transmuted a salacious chanson into a Mass or motet of true spirituality.

It was through the Italian cantata that Handel acquired his incomparable art of creating mood without the help of scenic representation. The flood of his poetic imagination, imprisoned in the cantor's tradition, was released. What drew him to Italy—what drew all foreign composers to Italy—was to learn how a mood can be created by melody. In the cantata it is accomplished with the illumination of a dream, without marching a crowd on the stage or presenting heartbreaking scenes; moreover, cantata composers knew that the night can harbor far more mood than a sun-drenched day. A tragedy is not necessarily more intense than a quiet, ballad-like cantata.

At first there was perhaps danger that Italian melodic euphony would beguile Handel as it did many another northern pilgrim, only to submerge him in the Italian-colored international style. Among other transalpine composers only Christian Bach and Mozart were able to escape unscathed. It is very easy to say that these two simply became Italianized. Perhaps this was the case with the type represented by Hasse, but with Handel, Christian Bach, and Mozart innate affinity with the radiant Italian melody enriched and enhanced their art without doing violence to its essential nature. To us they may seem altogether Italianized, but the Italians detected the difference. The mature Mozart never became really popular in Italy, even though his operas were pure Italian operas composed on Italian librettos, and the "English" Handel was a closed book to the great musical cities that once had resounded with admiration for *il caro Sassone*. Though Handel held fast to old Italian forms and procedures, more so than did Christian Bach and Mozart, he arrived at a more condensed simplicity of music than Venice and Naples offered. What was at first expansive and suave became later weighty, its tensile strength tremendous. Italian cantata and opera did not have that strength; they had to yield to euphony, the supreme Latin ideal. Handel retained this ideal learned in Italy all his life, never permitting construction or symbolism to interfere with euphony, but he always insisted that euphony should conform to the idea, must clearly mirror the mood and the feeling of the characters and not shine in abstract beauty. The rapidity with which Handel managed to acquire his own tone in this old art, in which countless fine composers had preceded him, is amazing, for the form of the language of art is governed by solid conventions and the composer's personality normally can impinge on the style of the period only gradually. In his cantata *La Lucretia* and in his very first original and full-fledged Italian opera, *Agrippina*, Handel has already hit his stride.

Several cantatas may be traced to Handel's first Florentine visit, among them *O numi eterni; Sarai contenta un dì; Clori, degl' occhi miei* (Händelgesellschaft, Vol. 50). *O numi*, better known as *La Lucretia* (or *Lucrezia*), is a masterpiece difficult to account for. Mattheson, in his *Grosse Generalbass-Schule*, discusses it in 1731 in enthusiastic terms, praising in particular Handel's bold modulations. While some of his biographers are very much pleased that no love affair can be ascribed to Handel with absolute certainty—a pious man does not trifle with women—one notices that from Hamburg to London there are entr'actes in Handel's busy and studious life where many signs point to the comforting fact that he was an ordinary healthy mortal. Among the cantatas of this period *La Lucretia* is by far the most accomplished—and ardent—which lends some credence to the rumored love affair with Lucrezia d'André, a diva at the court, for whom it was composed. One wonders why this admirable piece is not heard, for it is surely one of the most impressive *scene*, and it is available in a good modern edition by Schering. Interestingly, in spite of its ardor, the cantata is full of elaborate contrapuntal devices. There is another early cantata that seems to echo personal experience—*Parti l'idolo mio*, about a forsaken maiden. (*Partenza*, too, sounds like a romantic farewell.)

In Rome, Handel advanced to more elaborate cantatas of the serenata variety, which we shall discuss presently, not, however, before claiming the reader's indulgence for dealing somewhat cavalierly with chronology. While we know the main dates and stations of Handel's peregrinations in Italy, the details are fuzzy. There is, for instance, the mention of a first, fleeting visit to Venice somewhere in 1708, during Handel's stay in Rome. It cannot be proved and is very unlikely. Then there is the uncertainty of the dates of some of the compositions; accordingly, we shall observe chronology as well as possible, but deal with the various genres in groups. Handel's Roman sojourn was extremely fruitful for his future development, and it is far more useful to deal with cantata, oratorio, and Latin sacred music in one place than to try to pin down each work according to Handel's temporary presence in or absence from Rome.

The larger cantatas, such as the serenatas, are really small operas; moreover, they can hardly be distinguished from the secular oratorios. By the middle of the 17th century when Carissimi turned to the orchestrally accompanied cantata, it was a rich and flexible genre, often highly dramatic in tone, studded with hardy chromaticism and altered harmonies, with coloratura as elaborate as in opera, and with a differentiated orchestral accompaniment that is often independent and thematically signifi-

cant. Recitative, both secco and *stromentato,* arioso, ostinato basses, miniature concertos, sinfonias and ritornels—the whole arsenal of dramatic
music was present. Nor were these cantatas restricted to languorous unrequited love or noble allegorical philosophizing about the merits of
beauty and valor; Carissimi himself wrote alongside his grandly elevated
biblical works comical cantatas of a buffo character, even mixing the two,
as was done in the 17th-century Roman opera. This did not escape Handel, ordinarily little interested in the buffo element in spite of his well-
known sense of humor: his *Dalla guerra amorosa* is a perfect opera buffa
scena. In other works, such as *Venne voglia ad Amore,* the comic is light
and airy; it could grace any fine opera buffa; and *Nel dolce dell' oblio,*
with its gentle humor, is already close to Pergolesi's style. Also, many of
the works, whether cantata, festa, or oratorio, clearly demand staged performance; there is documentary proof that the oratorio *La Resurrezione*
was staged in the Ruspoli palace. While some of the larger cantatas are
satisfied with a single obbligato instrument and thoroughbass, there are
others that are very elaborate, with impressive ensembles. Some of the
orchestral cantatas are for two voices, and there are even instances of
trios.

By this time Handel was very highly regarded in Rome, not only as a
performer but as a composer. Cardinal Ottoboni, issue of an old Venetian
patrician family that gave the Church a pope and himself a nephew of
the reigning pope, was an uncommonly cultivated patron of the arts and a
poet of no mean ability who wrote librettos for Scarlatti. His reputation
was international—even Dryden praised him—and contemporaries found
him a very charming person. (There were some detractors, however.
Montesquieu and de Brosses called him a lecher and a man without
morals, though *grand musicien.*) The cardinal, a sound judge of men and
music, who counted Corelli among his closest friends, now took an interest in the young German, shepherding him in the Academy where he met
some of the outstanding personalities of the Roman aristocracy, such as
the Marquess Ruspoli and Cardinals Colonna and Panfili, the latter another poet-humanist of distinction. That Handel was fully appreciated is
demonstrated by the libretto Cardinal Panfili wrote in his honor—to be
set to music by Handel himself for performance in the Academy. *Hendel,
non può mia musa,* discovered some years ago by Dent, compares the
young musician with Orpheus—to the latter's detriment. However, to
judge by the music, Handel did not find his own person a particularly
rousing subject.

Cardinal Panfili was also the author of the libretto of Handel's next venture: *Il Trionfo del Tempo e del Disinganno,* completed in May 1707, an allegorical poem in which Beauty, Pleasure, Time, and Truth are engaged in rivalry. This is a fresh and poetic work in which the Italian style and manner are assimilated, and to which Handel was to return repeatedly many years later. Schering demonstrated that Handel here had already put his Italian studies to good use, basing some of the tone and construction of *Il Trionfo* on Perti's *Nerone* (1693). *Il Trionfo* is classified as an oratorio, but it is clearly a serenata which, though eminently vocal in conception, nevertheless allots a considerable share in the proceedings to the orchestra. For Handel had also absorbed the lessons learned from Corelli, and the extraordinary experience of repeatedly hearing the orchestra under Corelli's direction could not but affect his own orchestral technique. Indeed, Handel had never before indulged in such an elaborate accompaniment; in the arias the instruments do not simply merge with the voices into one unit but "concertize" with them. The overture itself is a fine concerto grosso in Corelli's style but more advanced and venturesome, using oboes and trumpets. Several of the instruments, such as the organ (presumably played by Handel), are given tiny concertos, while "Come nembo che fugge," an elaborate vocal number, is accompanied by a full-fledged concerto grosso. The arias are lovely, in Handel's "gentle" manner that we know so little, and the ensembles, though not in the dramatic vein, are enchanting.

Several other large cantatas were composed about this time; one of them, *Lungi dal mio bel Nume,* is dated March 1708. *Apollo e Dafne* is another very fine serenata, and the two trios, *Se tu non lasci amore,* and *Quel fior che all' alba ride,* also from 1708, are on the same high level. *Apollo e Dafne* is a neglected gem, charmingly characterized by Anthony Lewis as Handel's *Entführung.* The finely spun arias are accompanied by an imaginative orchestra full of delectable surprises, the whole breathing a ravishing bucolic air. This work fairly demands staging. *Udite il mio consiglio* is also an elaborate composition, but the most ambitious of the large cantatas is *Aci, Galatea, e Polifemo,* which must have been composed somewhat later in the same year in Naples or brought there from Rome to be finished. Once more, this work is catalogued as an "oratorio," but it is palpably a large cantata or serenata, for action and plot are rudimentary; yet at the same time *Aci, Galatea, e Polifemo* goes far beyond the previous cantatas, trespassing into the genuinely operatic: Handel draws characters in music. Polifemo is a flesh-and-blood figure, and the giant comes to life almost graphically in the outrageously wide intervals he sings. The other two protagonists are not so vividly drawn, though

Galatea's grief is very moving, but their music is of a consistently fine quality. The orchestral part is brilliant and carefully worked, and Handel took particular pains with the ensembles, in which the three characters stand out as individuals—we are in the presence of the modern and truly dramatic ensemble, such as we shall hear much later in *Solomon*. Handel himself was fond of this piece.

The emotional range in the cantatas, even in the basso continuo cantatas, is very wide. They are pensive, elegiac, delicate, at times slightly ironical, often tinged with gentle eroticism. Handel can be gay and he can be tempestuous and ardent. Several of the cantatas are flower pieces, elegant and dainty, but *Nell' Africane selve,* in which the composer depicts the terrors of the jungle, is at the opposite extreme—almost bizarre in its pictorialism. The solo cantata with basso continuo is the source of his life-long love of intimate lyricism; the serenata laid the foundations for his larger-scale dramatic music.

Perhaps the most remarkable feature of these cantatas and serenatas is Handel's ability to vary the routine. The simple solo cantata, especially, was pretty well standardized, but he found ways to impress his individuality on the old pattern: here changing the sequence of recitative–arioso or aria, there modifying the da capo, interrupting the vocal line with a ritornel—or vice versa—but above all by internal manipulation of the melodic line, playing out symmetry against asymmetry. The basso continuo should not be taken for a perfunctory harmonic support. Anthony Lewis characterizes the colorfully worked bass lines aptly, for indeed the bass is a full partner in these cantatas and not merely "the good listener in a one-sided conversation." That Handel rapidly learned the finer points of Italian diction is shown in the alternate versions of some of the cantatas. At times he had to transpose or otherwise rearrange a cantata for a different singer; usually on such occasions he tightened the declamation to accord with the natural rhythm and inflection of the text. We notice that in many instances Handel painstakingly wrote out the embellishments, as if to exercise himself in the art of the professional Italian singer whose skill was new to him.

Some of the orchestrally accompanied cantatas are miniature operas, or at least amount to a substantial portion of an act. *Arresta il passo,* to mention one, has nine numbers and many recitatives. These orchestral accompaniments are deft and full of happy invention. At times they are preceded by a fine overture or long ritornel. Handel now experiments with a far more complicated orchestra than the one to which he was accustomed. He uses gamba, the transverse flute, large lute, oboe, and even trumpet, and while most of the time the tone is that of chamber music, the full concerto grosso appears in the dramatic scenes.

There are many authentic masterpieces among these secular cantatas; they should be much better known, for they show Handel a master in the true sense of the word, a master doubly attractive because of his youthful ebullience. And they should be known not only for their intrinsic beauty, but because they represent an idea bank in which Handel deposited funds that lasted for the remaining half century of his life. Throughout his active career the depositor withdrew from his ample hoard, here little sums in the form of a theme or motif, there whole arias or even entire works to be used and elaborated in a new context. Chrysander was altogether wrong in assigning some of these cantatas to the Halle period; Handel could not have written any of them before he heard Italian singers in their own habitat. Very annoyingly, Chrysander often abbreviated the cantatas; like most other biographers and editors, he wanted to have done with what he considered youthful aberrations and move on to the "sacred works."

[6]

As a matter of fact, Handel also composed some sacred cantatas, though with few exceptions these do not compare with the secular ones either in quality or quantity. They are often in the old busy contrapuntal style, and their vocal line is instrumentally conceived. Moreover, Handel fails to reconcile the polyphonic with the homophonic, which results in a somewhat awkward mixture of heterogeneous elements. Some, however, are on the level of the fine secular cantatas; indeed, *Silete venti*, for soprano with orchestra, is placed by some in the Cannons period. This cantata obviously belongs among the Roman works, but with its French overture and secure workmanship it could be shifted a whole decade without suffering from the journey. The unusual feature of *Silete venti* is that it ends with an Alleluia, a long florid piece in the pastoral meter of 12/8. There are several others that end with an Alleluia, betraying the presence of old Protestant elements. Not that the Alleluia was unknown to the Italians; it often appears as the concluding da capo aria in sacred cantatas, and usually in the pastoral meter and vein. A number of such cantatas were published in the 1690s and also during Handel's stay in Italy. But Buxtehude, Zachow, Bruhns, Krieger, and others whose works Handel knew well also composed rather elaborate Alleluia cantatas, which while showing Italian influence and differing markedly from the chorale cantata, are nevertheless within the orbit of the German cantata.

When examining Handel's works of this type, one's first impression is that perhaps they were brought with him from Germany, but his Alleluia cantatas were found in the Santini collection and therefore definitely were written in Italy. Handel entitled them "motets," but this is of no particular significance; they are in fact solo cantatas. The concerted solo motet can be followed all the way to Mozart's *Exsultate jubilate*. The terminology in the 17th and 18th centuries was flexible, motet being applied simply to call attention to their sacred nature. One cannot escape the conclusion that, as with the German Passion, Handel felt in some way inhibited by the conflict between his ambitions and desires and the traditions of his early youth; the spirit of his surroundings did not accord with the spirit of his heritage. As usual, he turned from what was problematic to what was congenial, and in his Latin-Catholic sacred music once more met the Italians successfully on their own territory.

The traditions and practice of Italian church music that Handel found in Rome was altogether new to him and must have astounded him. Such southern Catholics as the Austrian Mozart took to it naturally; but to the Protestant from the north it was a matter fundamentally affecting not only his music but his entire view of life. It is here, we think, that Handel's eventual decision to leave Italy must be sought, and we cannot agree with Percy Young that had Handel stayed for another few years he would have become a Catholic. On the contrary, the more he penetrated into the spirit of this Latin-Catholic world—and with his marvelous ability to assimilate he indeed went to the core of this world—the more he stood by his ancestral faith. Nevertheless, the experience had vital consequences for his entire future, musically, humanly, and, we think, religiously.

There have always been very important cultural energies that cannot be distilled into the other-worldly. The Italian-Latin loves life, not only in its nobler aspects, but even in its vulgarity, and he sees it whole, not arranged in tight compartments. When Handel first visited Italy he found church music, opera, and instrumental music all mingling together. In Baroque Italy, church and opera house were the focal points of musical life; the difference between liturgical and nonliturgical music was slight and often nonexistent. Instrumental music itself was often used for liturgical purposes; hostility towards instrumental music in the church, so pronounced in our time, was unknown. Throughout its history, the Church wisely compromised with such irresistible artistic tendencies, for she knew that a religion unrelated to culture, language, or national ethos would experience great difficulties, if it survived at all. In the case of instrumental music, Benedict XIV officially recognized in 1749 a situation that had been tacitly sanctioned for a long time.

In large measure this secular tendency was not restricted to Italy, for the national spirit had been gaining ground in church music in Germany and France for a long time, but the incentive and the model came from Italy. The innate, original characteristics of the European peoples, bolstered by the new, free philosophy and literature of the Renaissance, introduced elements that hitherto had been considered alien in the church. Secular modes supplant the ecclesiastic and the original melodic treasures of various regions overcome the remnants of Gregorianism in secular music. The materials and precepts of national-secular music making intrude more and more into the music of the church, and the great and celebrated masters build their successes increasingly on secular grounds. Though church music retains its tremendous importance, the reigning taste converts it to its own image, to a style substantially identical with the secular. Whatever is composed in the codified church style of old is indeed so labelled: *stile antico, stylus gravis,* or *stylus ecclesiasticus.* Therefore, while its importance in its own sphere remains unimpaired, church music is no longer the focal point from which everything else derives its guidance; rather church art becomes assimilated to secular art and secular art now represents the central force.

Since Handel knew all this from Buxtehude, Zachow, and the other German masters, a mere regional-stylistic difference should not have created any difficulty for him, especially since as we have seen he was a well-trained and experienced composer, acquainted with Italian music even before his trip to Italy. Nevertheless, the age-old spirit of this Italian church music, bound with a thousand threads to life as it is lived on earth, must have been to him an experience of revelatory force.

The religious poetry of the Franciscans, the laudi, faithfully expresses the spirit of Italian church music as early as the 13th century. The laudi are not simple conventional hymns like the religious folksongs of other nations, but rhapsodic and personal. In them we find an important clue to the spirit of Italian sacred music that never left it across the centuries, for this music, singing of heavenly love, was in reality love poetry in the most sensuous meaning of the term, only its symbolism covering its true nature. And we must not think that because the industrious ants of the Renaissance, the humanists, severely separated themselves from this ardently popular tone, even shunning the vernacular for Latin, this spirit had departed; all we have to do is to look at the music, for the music of the frottola, which even the somber Netherlanders found irresistible, this fresh, popular, earthbound music, is interchangeable with that of the laude. Even Lorenzo de' Medici, head of one of the most aristocratic courts the world has ever known, which was filled with the learned pedants of humanism, and himself fully conversant with that learning, was a poet nurtured on this popular song. In the elaborate carnival festivities he gave back to the people in *rispetti, strambotti,* and *canti carnascialeschi* what he had taken from them. Savonarola could, for a moment, freeze this secular orgy; he cast fear into the people, and it seemed as if Italy would do penance and turn to the fanatical mystic dreamer's Republic of Christ. But the new prophet failed, and the people's zeal and fire began to subside even before the real flames consumed Savonarola.

Then the *sacra rappresentazione* appeared and, though church drama, soon was suffused with popular music, worldly music, and with romantic decoration. With this we are in the vicinity of Italian church and sacred music as it was constituted in Handel's time, a church music inextricably tied to the dramatic-concerted music of cantata, oratorio, and opera. But at this point we find a most bewildering contradiction, or at least what appears to us a categorical contradiction: the survival and warm appreciation of the Palestrinian ideal of music.

It is not the infinitely suave, balanced, and crystalline counterpoint of Palestrina that we find in the concerted works of Handel's Italian contemporaries, for that had disappeared; what remained was only the suavity and the crystallinity: euphony is the key to this art. But while the Palestrinian counterpoint was not employed in the current dramatic and concerted vocal music, it was ever present in most composers' minds and was diligently taught in the conservatories in the later 18th century by the very maestros of the frivolous opera buffa.

The Baroque concern with the *stile antico* was quite different from the historicism of the 19th century, as it is from that of our age. This vocal music was the Italians' very own territory; they knew that in true vocal music the text, no matter how great the poetry, is completely turned into song, drowned in melody. This is what they associated with the Palestrinian spirit, music that is pure song, that sublimates the conceptual text. Or, as Prunières eloquently summarized it in Lavignac's *Encyclopédie:* "elle est le symbol de la revanche que la musique prit sur la littérature, à laquelle les florentins avaient prétendu l'asservir." These Italian musicians simply became "bilingual," to use Bukofzer's felicitous term: able to speak with equal fluency the language of classical polyphony and that of modern concerted music.

What the Italian Palestrinians worshipped was not so much the letter of this marvelously logical system, as the spirit that animated it, the effort-less part-writing and the wondrous euphony of choral sound. At first both the letter and the spirit were observed by the great Palestrina disciples and descendants: Nanino, the two Anerios, Soriano, Allegri, Cifra, and others, but the "bilingual" composers of the next generation were also thoroughly familiar with the essence of this art. Under the influence of the "Colossal Baroque" they increased their choirs to double, triple, and quadruple tiers: even the Roman opera was rich in choruses, Rossi and Landi already liking opulent eight-part ensembles at the end of acts.

Pasquini, in the preface to one of his volumes of motets, calls any musician who does not know the works of Palestrina "a miserable wretch," and even Domenico Scarlatti (as Kirkpatrick reports) was de-voted to the Palestrina ideal, though his own activity was far removed from it. The others, the bilingual composers, form an impressive chain: Vitali, Legrenzi, Bassani, Lotti, Pitoni. Handel heard their music every-where. The great Venetians we shall meet presently, but a word must be said about Bassani and Pitoni.

Giovanni Battista Bassani (1657–1716) was a composer of the stature of the Roman and Venetian leaders, a magnificent choral composer whose freely moving but seldom "strict" counterpoint should have had particular appeal for Handel. Though he was more famous outside Italy for his fine cantatas and instrumental music, he is definitely one of the imposing fig-ures in the main line of choral art. Giuseppe Ottavio Pitoni (1657–1743) was for a while the resident composer at the Collegium Germanicum in Rome but moved around a great deal. He composed a fantastic amount of a cappella music, Masses, motets, Psalms, and so on, for from four to six-teen parts. This music is distinguished by a wonderful clarity of choral texture and sound, and virtuoso counterpoint, yet everything in it is song, pure, even popular, song, and the tonality is modern.

Practically all the composers just enumerated, with whom Handel came in contact either personally or through their music, are known to us as composers of operas and concerted vocal and instrumental music; it is perhaps difficult to imagine them as worshippers of the "emotionless" and "other-worldly" Palestrina ideal. Once we look at their melody we will understand, however, why Verdi still claimed descent from Palestrina. In-deed, a Stradella was but an early Bellini, and a vocal quality is present even in the great instrumental composers, for the Palestrinian ideal was not only choral sound but sculptured vocal melody. Coloratura writing, with its breathless runs, scales, arpeggios, and sequences, is definitely an instrumental element within this vocal art, brought about by the phe-

nomenal virtuosity of the castratos, which drove composers to bravura
even in ensemble music. Yet, even if in a very restricted sense, the Palestrinian melody was also partial to scalelike melodic runs; "l'esthétique de
la gamme," André Pirro used to say in his class. Rapprochement between
vocal and instrumental melody under the suzerainty of the former was
one of the characteristics of the Italian Baroque.[4]

The Italian language's large proportion of open vowels and terminal
vowels encouraged a free, melismatic extension of phrases flowing into
each other without undue caesuras. This "long melody" favored the aria
over the chorus but could also be employed in part-writing if the treble
assumed the unquestioned leading role. This songlike quality infused Italian choral style, giving it its particular charm. But there is also polyphony
in this Italian choral music of the Baroque, and it can be elaborate, but it
wants to sound well; its very point of departure is that of sound. This is
still the "Palestrina" ideal and tradition, even if latent and considerably
modified. Handel immediately tried his hand at it in *La Resurrezione*, for
as can be seen, in contrast to his German choruses, the lower voices here
merely support the treble.

Although Handel was used to good choral music, it was in Italy that
he first came to know really great singers and singing. The German Protestant church choir was mostly a school choir, it came from the *Kantorei*,
which was not specifically a church body; throughout the Baroque professional choirs were unknown in the Protestant churches in Germany.
Bach's *Thomaner* were students, treble and alto from the secondary
school, tenor and bass from the university or from the public. It was only
a few years before Handel's time in Hamburg that Kusser began to train
German singers—coming from the cantors' schools and having absolutely
no experience with opera—in the expressive Italian manner, and coloratura made its first appearance in German works. Still, this was a rather
awkward superimposition of an altogether foreign musical style upon the
German song idiom, and it was not until Keiser that a German composer
was able to handle with skill and imagination the new manner of vocal

[4] Many of the German students in Italy, not only Schütz, became bilingual and
took home with them the Italian love of Palestrina's art. Thus Kerll cultivated it by
writing, besides his concerted pieces and operas, church music *alla* Palestrina, that
is, a cappella. In the Germanic countries the Palestrina cult was notably observed in
Vienna where the great Baroque master, Johann Joseph Fux, was its most admired
guardian. His a cappella Masses are masterpieces, but Fux was also a full-blooded
dramatist, wholly at home both in opera and concerted church music. Yet, a "bilingual
composer," he separated the two styles quite distinctly, whereas the Italians were able
to reconcile them.

writing; he was the first German to write real arias. Another vast difference between the Italian and the German singer in the early 18th century was the systematic professional training the former received, not only in voice production but in musical theory and composition. He was expected to, and usually could, improvise with the skill of a composer. Handel also discovered that the great Italian singer was often a tyrannical potentate who ruled both librettist and composer and whose whims had to be respected.

All this was new, but we must not forget the very considerable experience in choral composition that Handel brought with him to Italy. He knew not only the involved cantus firmus work of his German colleagues and predecessors, but also the dramatic choral declamation, offset or contrasted by running orchestral accompaniment. This form of German choral music owes a debt to the chorale prelude, and at times the similarity to the organ species is so obvious that one is tempted to call such works choral chorale preludes. He also knew the old German imitative motet style with its phrases interwoven in a continuous polyphonic pattern, with motifs varied and broken up, inverted, augmented, diminished, and so on, the choral fugues, and the choral recitative. The marked tendency towards concerted choral writing that we see in his Italian works was also known in Germany; Zachow and others used it, often with felicity, and even the "choral aria" we see in some of the Roman compositions he must have encountered in the works of Nicolaus Bruhns (1665–1697). Bruhns, a Schleswig-Holstein composer of great repute and a disciple of Buxtehude, was an early German exponent of the choral aria. Handel may have encountered him personally in Zachow's circle, and certainly knew his works. Mattheson cites Bruhns's amusing ability to play two parts on a violin while seated on the organ bench playing the bass of the trio on the pedals. But that sort of instrumental virtuosity does not negate the fact that Bruhns's cantatas belong among the finest before Bach's works in the genre and show a lyric quality unusual in the German cantata.[5] In addition, there is the interesting fact that around 1700 much more choral music was composed in Germany than in Italy.[6]

But choral composition took on an entirely new hue and meaning when Handel faced vocal music in Italy and felt the pervasive spirit of the "Palestrina ideal." His problem was the reconciliation of the German

[5] See *Das Erbe deutscher Musik*, Schleswig-Holstein, Vols. 1, 2.

[6] In this a cappella literature Schütz's incomparable choruses in his Passion-oratorios stand all by themselves. They may have been influenced by Venetian choral music but are unique in their truly biblical majesty and essentially Protestant tone.

cantus firmus style with Italian choral lyricism. That this choral lyricism, of which an excellent example is Stradella's *Serenata,* later quoted in *Israel in Egypt,* profoundly affected him is demonstrated not so much by what he immediately did in Italy as by his use of it decades later in his English oratorios.

The church music he composed in Rome consisted of Latin Psalm settings: *Laudate pueri; Nisi Dominus; Dixit Dominus.* There is furthermore a *Gloria Patri* for double choir and double orchestra, discovered and published in Japan, of all places, in 1930. (Whether a certain Magnificat was written by Handel or by one Erba, or whether a Te Deum is by Handel or by Urio should not worry us nearly so much as it did Chrysander and some other biographers; they are not very important works considered either way.) Some think that the first version of *Laudate pueri* dates from Handel's earliest and most youthful period, while others see in *Nisi Dominus* and *Dixit Dominus* portions that antedate the Italian journey. Possibly, but it seems to us that these analysts are simply seeing the reminiscences of the German cantor's art, which of course would not have disappeared overnight. Thus *Dixit Dominus* still has a cantus-firmus-like treble, but the counterpoint is definitely subordinate to the planned choral sound, and even the fourth verse, where the texture is fugal, has a new transparency. Handel has become euphony conscious, the antithesis of his Eisenach neighbor, to whom linear logic took precedence over euphony. He also begins to experiment with the splendid and rich-sounding multipart writing of the Italian Baroque, first with five-part chorus, then with eight-part double chorus. A fine *Salve Regina* is dated later by some, but it surely comes from the Roman period. In the first place, there was no conceivable occasion for setting such a text in England, in the second, the "mature Handel" seen here could be encountered at any period in his life after his twentieth year.

All these works are usually mentioned in passing, yet they are of crucial importance to Handel's future career. They are not youthful essays; they show that Handel had become aware of certain stabilizing virtues in choral music, virtues he adapted to his own creed as a composer and never forswore. In this connection *Dixit Dominus* is the diploma of Handel's Italian studies. There are remarkable things in the Italian oratorio-serenatas and in *Agrippina,* and of course the cantatas include genuine masterpieces, but *Dixit Dominus* has power and grandeur, the qualities we associate with the English oratorios. The choral drama is here in this astonishing piece, for Handel already knows how to lead his choral forces to cumulative heights. He did not forget the Latin church music composed in Rome; we shall meet with portions of it decades later, they fit admirably in the great historical choral dramas and the ceremonial anthems.

The final chorus in the second part of Handel's *St. John Passion*, "Schlafe wohl," is the most accomplished choral piece from his pre-Italian period. It shows a mature and well-schooled technique; moreover, as we must remind ourselves again and again, it shows acquaintance with the Italian style. Yet Jens Peter Larsen, one of the few scholars fully aware of the exceptional importance of Handel's Latin church music composed in Italy, is fully justified when he states in his study of *Messiah* that the road from the choral writing in the Latin Psalms to the Hallelujah Chorus in *Messiah* seems short in comparison with the road traversed from "Schlafe wohl" to the Latin choruses.

IV

AND NOW WE REACH A VARIETY OF SACRED MUSIC THAT
was to become a symbol of Handel's art, the oratorio. Today we are familiar only with the Protestant oratorio of the late Baroque. The century-old
Romantic cult of *Messiah* in the English-speaking world and of the two
Bach Passions both here and in Central Europe has established a pattern
and an attitude toward the genre that converts and swallows up everything
within its orbit. These three works, though quite different even among
themselves, have established the "sacred oratorio" tone that is applied to
every large choral work, from the 17th century to the 19th. It is no wonder,
then, that the Italian oratorio of the Middle Baroque presents such a bewildering spectacle: oratorio, cantata, opera all seemingly interchangeable and practically inseparable.

The short solo cantata was the operatic composer's training ground.
It became so popular that with the spread of the "solo opera" (the "commercial" opera houses in Venice having abandoned the chorus for reasons
of economy), Carissimi's magnificent choral art had to give way. This sacred music became the counterpart of the sentimental-romantic Baroque
painting of a Guido Reni or a Carlo Dolci, and was not without influence
in Germany. Buxtehude, Johann Christoph Bach, Johann Michael Bach,
and others show it unmistakably, but there was also the great German
sentinel, the chorale, which kept them within bounds—at least temporarily. By the time we reach Graun (1755) the restraint is gone; the cho-

rale is little more than a poorly harmonized and perfunctory reminder of the glorious past of Lutheran music.

Because of the exceptional importance of the oratorio in Handel's lifework, we should delve somewhat into its history, for while there is no comparison and little connection between the English oratorio created by Handel and the Italian oratorio he learned to know while in that country, he gained from it impressions that, as we have said, stayed with him for the rest of his life. But before doing this, an important postulate must be made without which the gradual development and transformation of this music cannot be clarified: what constitutes "sacred music" as opposed to liturgical music is not a theological, not even an artistic, but a sociological determination, altogether dependent on the surroundings, the milieu in which it is expressed. And even liturgical music proper is vastly dependent on socio-artistic factors.

[2]

ALL THREE churches we are concerned with in this study, the Lutheran in Germany, the Catholic in Italy, and the Anglican in England, were state churches in the sense that all of them had temporal powers, which in many instances tended to dominate the religious. In all cases there was a distinct desire on the part of religious persons, especially the less affluent and socially inferior, for emotional fulfillment beyond what they received within the formal church. In Italy this began with St. Francis of Assisi, gaining momentum, as we have seen, with the popular movement of the *laudesi.* How tenacious this movement was is well illustrated by the fact that some of the *Compagnie de' laudesi,* to be found in every Italian city from the Middle Ages onward, survived as late as the 19th century. In conformity with the prevailing tendency all over Europe, in the latter part of the 16th century the laudi assumed a pietistic character —the Counter-Reformation had strong pietist leanings—especially in St. Philip Neri's circle. As is well known, it was from the music of the gatherings in the oratory of his church that the oratorio derived its name. The simple services of devotion soon established a relationship with the higher realms of art music, the culminating point being reached with Animuccia's and Palestrina's spiritual madrigals. However, the connection between the popular and the artistic is even more apparent in music where the simple declamation in lessons or litanies, dear to the people, were set by the greatest composers. Thus the famous litanies sung during processions in Loreto, the *Litaniae Lauretanae,* were set in a simple choral style by Palestrina and others. As can be seen, the almost mythical *princeps musicae,* Palestrina, does appear in this Italian music wherever we probe into it.

From here to the oratorio proper there is only one step, but that step also coincides with the birth of the *seconda prattica,* the new musical style of the early Baroque, and the main body of this sacred music gradually turns altogether to the secular sources of the new dramatic-monodic movement. Paralleling this gradual shift towards the secular was an even earlier shift from Latin to the vernacular. The first Petrucci print of laudi (1508) contains sixty-six numbers, of which fifty-one are in the vernacular. Almost all of its composers are known as frottola composers, that is, secular masters, and, indeed, the resemblance to the simple, uncomplicated frottola, with its homophony and love of the chordal, is manifest. It is noteworthy that the treble part in these compositions is always the leader, for essentially these are harmonized melodies.

The early Christian Church adopted the Hebrew custom of reading from the Scriptures during services, the singing of the Psalms forming part of the primitive liturgy. Many of the Jewish lessons were, of course, soon replaced by selections from the New Testament, but a Psalm, usually shortened to a verse or two, continued to be used as the Introit. These lessons were originally a very simple form of the chant where the principal role of the music was to facilitate articulation and enhance the expressive recitation of the text. There were no melodies, only certain musical formulas centered around a given pitch, but the melodic element soon grew in importance, as did a tendency towards dramatization. Extrabiblical elements appear in the form of refrains and exclamations, and they were also used to "introduce" the Gospel itself in the quasi dialogue between reader and congregation. Eventually all this followed the general trend in music as polyphony gained in acceptance; on the other hand, the other inevitable trend, the theatrical, led to the liturgical play. The scriptural lessons, then, gave rise to a large motet literature which in the Lutheran rite was liturgical and leads directly to the "dialogues" of Scheidt and Schütz—that is, to the German cantata. In Italy the development was quite different, for the pantomimic element almost immediately accompanied the musical development. The visual-theatrical sense of the Italian is so strong that sooner or later it takes hold of every genre. The laudi too were first dialogued, then dramatized. These dramatized laudi were called *devozioni,* and later *rappresentazioni,* and most of them were sung, often after Mass, in the church.

The modern term "liturgical play" (or "drama") is nevertheless not a very accurate one, because while the musical material may have come from liturgical sources, the play itself was altogether nonliturgical even if the language was Latin. Moreover, plays in the vernacular, if they had a "sacred" subject, were also placed under this classification. The distinction should not worry us, however, for we are mainly interested in the appearance of the dramatic-theatrical element as it bears on the rise of the oratorio. As we shall see, confusing classifications accompany the Handelian oratorio to this day.

Before proceeding with the dramatized lessons, a word must be said about a famous musico-historical landmark that can easily cause confusion. Emilio de' Cavalieri's *Rappresentazione di Anima e di Corpo* (1602), long considered the "first" oratorio, does not really belong in this category. Though produced at St. Philip Neri's oratory, it is clearly a sacred opera: it was indeed "produced"—staged with costumes and dances —as were many similar works. Cavalieri's allegorical *rappresentazione* should not therefore be considered a point of departure for the history of the oratorio but should be regarded as a branch of early Roman opera. The 17th-century historians do not mention Cavalieri among the founders of the oratorio; Doni simply refers to this celebrated work as "a monk's comedy."

While the liturgical play was known and practiced all over the Christian world, it is in Italy that we find the first traces of an element we recognize as particularly characteristic of the oratorio: the *testo,* or narrator —the Evangelist in Bach's Passions. The subjects of these plays were prevailingly from the New Testament, though in the second half of the 17th century, for reasons we shall discuss presently, plays based on the Old Testament are more frequent. The Old Testament subjects were regarded as prefigurations of the events in the New Testament and usually ended with a Magnificat or Te Deum.

We must now turn to the very important question of the role of the Scriptures in all this music, a question that we shall find once more entwined with the history of the Handelian oratorio in England. This is the more necessary to investigate because of the repeated attempts that have been made to connect the English with the Italian oratorio.

"The Bible, and the Bible alone is the religion of Protestants," whereas St. Augustine had stated emphatically "I should not believe the Gospel except on the authority of the Catholic Church." The Catholic Church has always considered herself the divinely appointed custodian and interpreter of Holy Writ, never permitting "private interpretation"; moreover, the Church has always held that Holy Scripture alone is insufficient to equip the faithful with a sure knowledge of faith and morals. Indeed, the history of the Catholic Church's attitude toward the Bible was for a long time virtually a negative one as regards its use by laymen. In earlier times it was considered that reading the Bible in the vernacular without ecclesiastical counsel and supervision was "dangerous" for persons not trained in doctrine (Innocent III), while during the century of the Reformation the Holy See (Pius IV) held that the Old Testament may be read by learned and pious men in the vernacular, but for the New Testament permission from the pastor was required. One of the serious offenses of the Jansenists was their emphasis on the necessity of reading the Bible unaided by ecclesiastical supervision, and Catholic authorities still insist that scriptural reading be restricted to texts annotated by approved scholars, in an edition sanctioned by the Church. It was only at the turn of this century, when Dom Guéranger and his devoted monks began their noble work for a revival of the liturgy, that a new interest in the Bible arose among Catholics. Indeed, the Catholic Church always made selective use of the Bible, in the case of the Old Testament a highly selective use, usually balanced by juxtaposition with passages from the New, for liturgical purposes. It is in the light of these historical facts that we must weigh the oratorios, especially the Old Testament oratorios, that Handel heard in Italy.

Oratorio, Passion, and *historia* are just as difficult to unravel as oratorio, cantata, and opera. The Easter *historiae* and Passions are far more numerous than the Christmas oratorios and Resurrection *historiae*, because the dramatic motif was stronger. Their connections with the medieval spiritual play are obvious, even though the historical evolution has not yet been sufficiently investigated. To the Lutherans the *historia*, i.e. the musical setting of the Gospel, acquired a deep theological-liturgical significance, but even with them it was from the very beginning a dramatic "reading." They were quite conscious of its specifically Protestant nature, for as early as 1565 we find Joachim à Burck entitling his work *Die deutsche Passion.* Though the term itself is of theological-liturgical origin, from the 16th century onward the biblical *historiae* did not serve purely cultic purposes; the dramatic intent, the exploitation of the dramatic content, is almost immediately present. With the advent of opera the dramatic treatment—recitative opposed to chorus, and so on—grew rapidly in importance, and under humanistic influence its secularization was well under way by the time Schütz brought to Germany the new Italian style. By the middle of the century the Roman "chorus opera" and the oratorio are practically indistinguishable. However, after Carissimi the importance

of the chorus declined, precisely because the oratorio was so closely patterned after the opera; thus while in Germany the chorus remained the
dominant element in Passion and cantata, in Italy the leadership passed
to the solo parts. The ratio of choruses to arias that Handel used in
his later oratorios was the exact opposite of that in the species he encountered in Italy. Still, Carissimi's music was not forgotten and it left an indelible impression on Handel.

It is with Giacomo Carissimi (1605–1694) that we reach the true oratorio. While Schütz created from the impressions gained at home and in
Italy his severely magnificent mixed style, Carissimi reached for the popular, the public-conquering cantata, to express in it what was most characteristic of his day. Mattheson called him the creator of the modern cantata. Carissimi divorced music from the last vestiges of the older churchly
technique, distilled the aria form, made the dull recitative attractive and
expressive, thus altogether turning his back on the Florentine tradition.
This earnest musician, whose Latin prosody was a marvel of musical diction and who often brilliantly exploited his ability in word painting, could
be uproariously funny. In his *Requiem jocosum* (!) he takes the old chanson text that Lasso once made famous, *Quant mon mari vient de dehors,*
and then sets under the piquant text ("pots and pans are thrown at me,"
etc.) a solemn *Requiem aeternam.* Clearly, far from espousing antiquarianism, Carissimi offered a unified, transparent, and rounded form based
on "popular" melodies. He was modern, bold, and secure, a kindred soul
to Handel.

And now a seemingly new and curious tone appears in Catholic and
classical Italy: the Old Testament oratorio, with dramatically agitated
choruses that were part of the dramatis personae, indeed at times assuming the role of chief protagonist. Carissimi sets to music the Latin version
of the Old Testament; *Jephtha, Solomon, Jonah, Balthasar,* and so on,
with their dramatic splendor became the perfect musical counterpart of
that new Catholic spirit which created the Jesuit style of architecture. In
fact Carissimi was attached to the Jesuit Collegium Germanicum for,
though initially opposed to music, by the 17th century the Society of
Jesus, with its sure instinct for success, was an ardent supporter both of
church music and the theatre, including the musical stage. The College
was one of the best places in Rome for music; it always had good organists and excellent resident composers, from Victoria to Carissimi and Pitoni. Carissimi, their illustrious master of music, was so highly regarded
that after his death Clement X forbade the sale or even the loan of his
manuscripts. Unfortunately, in the 18th century, when the Jesuit order

was suspended, everything was stolen and the manuscripts disappeared.

There were other composers who set to music Old Testament librettos, and there is a *rappresentazione* entitled *Abramo e Isacco* that is considerably earlier than any of those we are concerned with here, but the works Handel heard all came from the Carissimi circle. Among those he certainly heard we might mention Gasparini's *Joseph in Egypt,* G. Bononcini's *David,* Ferrari's *Samson,* and Perti's *Moses,* but lest irrelevant comparisons be made between these and Handel's Old Testament oratorios, it must be borne in mind that in Italy there was only one reason for turning to the Old Testament: a provision in the liturgy. In the Catholic liturgy during Lent all weekday Lessons in the Mass are taken from the Old Testament, in place of the usual Epistles. Since during Lent opera was forbidden and oratorio substituted as a subterfuge, decorum was even better observed—or camouflaged—by hewing to the subjects of the liturgy special to the season. No one was deceived and no one was indignant. At practically all other times they preferred the New Testament, the lives of the saints, or allegorical subjects.

Like Handel, Carissimi was a religious man; nevertheless, his oratorio was clearly operatic in nature. Indeed there could not have been different sacred and secular techniques when recitative, aria, arioso, ensemble, and chorus—that is, the forms and means of dramatic music—were used in oratorio as well as opera. The *historicus* or *testo* was not different from the narrator in Monteverdi's *Il Combattimento di Tancredi e Clorinda.* Indeed, as the recitative gradually turns into expressive singing, the *historicus* begins to sing arias and then disappears from the Italian oratorio. After 1690 he is seldom encountered. Even closer to opera was the *oratorio volgare,* the oratorio in the vernacular, whose principal seats were Bologna, Modena, Ferrara, Naples, and Venice, and which became so popular that it all but eliminated the Latin variety. The particularly Italian twist in the development of sacred music is again in evidence, and perplexes the historian, for while the Italian Latin oratorio descended from the dialogue-motet and the *historia*-Passion, it has scarcely any connections with Catholic liturgy. Its counterpart, the popular oratorio in the vernacular, which owed its existence to religious practices, descending as it were from the dramatized laude, shows even more decided operatic influences. If we glance at the historical precedents, this turn of events will be seen to be quite natural.

As early as in the second decade of the 17th century we find such works as Antonio Cifra's *Scherzi sacri* (1616) or Paolo Quagliati's *Affetti amorosi spirituali* (1617), in the *stile misto,* the "mixed style," and even the circle around St. Philip Neri insisted that the music performed in their oratory should be popular in tone and agreeable in melody, defending the principle of *travestimento spirituale*, a notion incomprehensible to the northerner. The secular tendencies towards what we may call the "concert oratorio" received an even stronger impetus with Carissimi's works, which united Roman moral-allegorical opera with the concerted motet and cantata. Here we have a first synthesis of dramatic and church styles, in which is at work the same sensuous sorcery we see in opera. The southern Germans—Catholic—immediately accepted this new art (Kerll was a pupil of Carissimi) but the Protestant North was cautious. Handel watched and absorbed. There was no immediate need for the genre—he came to Italy to compose opera—and his Lutheran training must have made him somewhat apprehensive at seeing the Bible put to such use. But that incredible storehouse that was his brain preserved the impressions intact, ready for use at an instant's notice.

Among other oratorio composers whose influence was far-reaching we must mention Francesco Foggia (1604–1688), a Roman, who next to Carissimi was the outstanding master. His son Antonio (1650–1707) was also well regarded, and since he worked with Alessandro Scarlatti at Santa Maria Maggiore, Handel must have met him during his first Roman visit. At any rate, Scarlatti surely brought the works of father and son to Handel's attention.

Neither the old "liturgical" plays, nor the 17th–18th-century oratorios were inhibited, and they often abound in comical scenes and characters. The buffo elements were used as in the Roman opera. The secularization and the turning to the purely operatic ended by eliminating any distinction between the Latin and the vernacular oratorio; when Handel arrived in Italy this was a *fait accompli*. In Rome and everywhere else he could not help hearing a great many oratorios, and of course he realized that the road to oratorio led through cantata and opera. Like a sculptor who becomes a painter and retains a good many sculptural elements in the new medium, the oratorio composer never lost his dramatic bent and secular origins. Italian oratorio in the vernacular was definitely a form of entertainment that accompanied opera everywhere—in the Catholic world. In the Catholic courts abroad, such as Vienna or Dresden, it fulfilled the same function as in Rome: a substitute for opera during Lent.

We have said that Handel watched and observed; actually he did compose one work that was clearly neither a festa nor a cantata but an oratorio. A little of the mature Handel shows even in this early work, for a certain psychological insight penetrates behind the allegory—in a word, he tries to characterize in music. The contemporary trend is shown in that *La Resurrezione* has only two choruses, and they are a bit perfunctory, but the rest, notably the imaginative orchestration, demonstrates that Handel was a good student.

Handel, used to the grammar-school poetry of Postel, was now given a libretto in the elegant language of an able and cultivated poet. The story of the Resurrection is, however, complicated, in the operatic manner, by the introduction of the extraneous figure of Lucifer. Here we encounter the ancestor of Polyphemus, for the Prince of Hell is a vigorous and malevolent basso whose extremely difficult and virtuoso lines are already wholly Italianate and full of picturesque word-painting. Also, as Percy Young shrewdly observed, in this very first of Handel's oratorios "the angel who admonishes Lucifer . . . exhibits delicious femininity," and he justly laments that "Handel's gentle courtesy and his chivalry" are not properly appreciated. Outstanding is the work's orchestral part, the muted violins creating a convincing mood, the violas often divided into several parts, gamba arpeggios combined with flute, and many other happy and very modern touches; a real genre piece cast in a nocturnal mood. While Handel's reorientation is manifest and deliberate and the Italian influence marked, *La Resurrezione* still shows counterpoint and canonic writing that come from the cantor's art, though all this is considerably attenuated. *La Resurrezione* is altogether secular and in keeping with the prevailing Roman conception of subterfuge opera. Some of this music appears in *Agrippina* also. Handel remembered *La Resurrezione* for a long time and borrowed from it for *Alexander Balus* and *Joshua*.

The performance of this oratorio (which followed Scarlatti's *Oratorio della santissima Annunziata* by two weeks) took place in the Ruspoli palace in a sumptuous production and with a large orchestra under Corelli's direction. The operatic nature of the production was enhanced by the presence of a prima donna who took the role of Mary Magdalene. Ruspoli was severely reprimanded by the Pope for his violation of the edict forbidding undisguised opera. Handel moved into the Ruspoli residence to be close at hand, and was rewarded with a resounding success. Still, he must have decided that the Roman scene had yielded enough for his purposes, and it was time to explore the other musical centers of Italy. Accordingly, he left Rome in May of 1708, arriving in Naples in June. His departure was hastened by the impending siege of Rome by the imperial forces, which he must have watched with anxiety as the city's gates were sealed one by one.

[3]

BEFORE FOLLOWING Handel on his trip to Naples, we must re-trace our steps and examine an entr'acte in Handel's Roman adventure —a second visit to Florence, which took place in July 1707. There must have been some reason for this interruption of his Roman explorations, and it is usually ascribed to the production of his opera *Rodrigo*. While opera was proscribed in Rome, and Handel was occupied with cantata, church music, and oratorio, in the privacy of his quarters he did not forget the main purpose of his Italian tour, making his first experiment since Hamburg in the genre by refurbishing his *Almira* with the aid of newly acquired techniques. *Rodrigo* was scarcely more than an experiment, since the body of the work, especially the arias, was taken from the score he had brought with him from Hamburg; but there are changes. The arias in *Rodrigo* remained somewhat ungainly, rather conspicuously instrumental in conception, but the recitatives, which in *Almira* have a perfunctory church flavor, show considerable gains in dramatic awareness and expression. Some biographers think that *Rodrigo* was produced during Handel's first visit to Florence; there is little likelihood that this is so. Most others place it during this second visit; however, Otto Erich Deutsch, whose knowledge of the documents relating to Handel's life is unexcelled, states that "whether this opera was really performed in Florence has not yet been established." [1] So here our musicological sources end; not, however, the human documents, for apparently Lucrezia d'André was not the only Florentine musical belle in whom Handel became interested. Vittoria Tarquini, called La Bombace, was the singer to whom Mainwaring assigns the partnership in the second Florentine love affair; she sang at the opera house. Where the English biographer obtained his story is not known, but since he was writing in 1760 he could have had access to sources the modern historian can no longer hunt down. Although Mainwaring was not the most reliable of researchers, he spent some time and effort collecting his data before composing his biography, which was published one year after Handel's death. It was immediately translated into German by one who knew Handel very well and would be expected to object to the story, if unfounded, or at least to question its authenticity; Mattheson never hesitated to correct another author. In addition, a decorous and solemn Englishman of Mainwaring's cast would have preferred to do without the love story; most modern Handel biographers are

[1] See his fine volume, *Handel, a Documentary Biography*.

still nervous about such earthy things. It seems, therefore, that we have both an affirmation of the performance of *Rodrigo* and a little chink in the Handelian armor through which we can see a portion of the man.

Mainwaring describes La Bombace charmingly:

She was a fine woman, and had for some time been much in the good graces of his Serene Highness. But, from the natural restlessness of certain hearts, so little sensible was she of her exalted situation, that she conceived a design of transferring her affections to another person. Handel's youth and comeliness, joined with his fame and abilities in Music, had made impressions on her heart.

But La Bombace was ruled out by Handel's best-known modern English biographer, Sir Newman Flower, as a most unlikely object of his love— she was of middle age! Our eminent and strait-laced historian could not have been familiar with the traditional role middle-aged women have always played in the introduction of young men, especially artists, to the mysteries and delights of love. It is rather well known that they were successful in their noble endeavor even when smoking big black cigars and wearing men's trousers. As a matter of fact, it seems that La Bombace's charms were still sufficient to attract the attention of Prince Ferdinand himself. On this pleasant note the second Florentine visit ended and Handel returned to Rome, where we have already seen him engaged in more profitable pursuits.

[4]

Naples in 1708 presented a rather fantastic political-artistic picture. Though of course an ancient Italian city-state, it was then a Spanish colony ruled by a viceroy who, in the admirable custom of international politics of the day, did not have to be a Spaniard if his allegiance and executive abilities were satisfactory. When Handel stayed in Naples the viceroy was Cardinal Vincenzo Grimani, a Venetian, whose wealthy family owned several opera houses, a circumstance that was to benefit Handel. Armed with recommendations from Roman Arcadians, Handel immediately found himself at home, settling down for a stay of nearly a whole year. His sojourn in Naples is a complete mystery. He had no position yet lived well, and though we get an occasional fleeting glimpse of his doings, all we know is that he composed and presumably watched the scene, which was well worth watching.

Mainwaring is positive that while in Naples Handel had at his disposal "a palazzo and was provided with table, coach, and all other accommodations." In the absence of any visible means of livelihood, considering the mores of the times (as well as Handel's still unbeatified status), the known passion of many of the great and wealthy for music and musicians, especially if the musician was a heroic-sized young man who when seated at the keyboard bowled over everyone within hearing, he should have had no difficulty obtaining his table, coach, and palazzo. In the circles Handel frequented this sort of largesse was not unusual. A life of lettered ease, of enlightened dilettantism, of refined luxury, of discreet libertinage, was characteristic of Baroque aristocracy, especially in Naples, where the per capita density of nobility was exceptionally high.

Although Handel's sojourn in Naples consumed nearly a third of his time in Italy, it is usually dealt with in a few paragraphs. While it is true that we know next to nothing about his activity there, it is noteworthy that his first—and phenomenally successful—original Italian opera, *Agrippina,* was composed in Naples and not in Venice where it was produced. The serenata *Aci, Galatea, e Polifemo* was written in Naples too. There were a multitude of things to be observed, studied, and assimilated in a city that had rich and ancient musical traditions. In 1708 Naples was not yet the famous seat of opera it became shortly after Handel's departure, though it already had an operatic tradition of its own. Here we should recall Henry Prunières's pertinent observation that in the second half of the 17th century opera was not so much regional as it was "pan-Italian." Undoubtedly Handel learned a great deal in Naples, his later works show this on every page. Once we probe into the state of music in St. Januarius's city at the turn of the century it will be seen that the year Handel spent there must have yielded very profitable experiences.

The long Spanish reign left its mark on Naples. The territory was practically bilingual, and the combination of Italian with Spanish Catholicism resulted in an extraordinary number of religious institutions. With the influx of Spanish officials the already numerous Neapolitan nobility was doubled, and since in those days churches, monasteries, and noble houses all cultivated music, Naples was by nature a musical center. There was another regional feature that was to determine the course of the Neapolitan School: the presence of the *commedia dell' arte* and of the highly developed and popular Spanish spoken theatre, both of which eventually called forth musical prototypes. The famous orphanages, called conservatories, founded in the 16th century, became much-admired musical institutions in the 17th, especially beginning with the activity of Francesco Provenzale. It was here that Handel first learned about the prowess of the castratos; Naples, particularly the Conservatorio dei

Poveri di Gesù Cristo, trained singers who were sought for all over the country.

Francesco Provenzale, a native Neapolitan, must be considered the "founder" of the school. His was a disappointing career, for after finally rising to the post of royal conductor, he was twice displaced by Alessandro Scarlatti (1680, 1684). Finally, in 1690 he was made honorary maestro, whose obligation was to assist and substitute for the titular conductor. Since Scarlatti was often absent or ill, Provenzale was largely responsible for the office, which he fulfilled with fine musicianship. When he assumed his duties as master of the Conservatorio de' Turchini, after having successfully taught at the Loreto, the number of students who wanted to work under his guidance was so large that they had to be limited by law—to a hundred and fifty! Provenzale not only taught his students but saw to it that their operas were performed, a system emulated by all other conservatories in the country. Similarly influential as a teacher was Gaetano Greco (c. 1657–c. 1728), himself a pupil of Scarlatti and the teacher of Domenico Scarlatti and Nicola Porpora, and probably also of Durante, Vinci, Pergolesi, and many other future masters of the Neapolitan school. This lively and imaginative composer attracted disciples and colleagues alike. Handel could also observe a procedure of no mean significance to him: Greco was an extremely skilful master at borrowing a popular motif and working it into a poetic and very personal composition.

During Handel's stay an impressive number of Neapolitan masters were active, and whenever he ventured out of his palazzo he ran into music and musicians. The principal opera composer of the older generation besides Provenzale was Pietro Andrea Ziani (c. 1620–1684), whose operas Handel must have heard. Though a native of Venice, from 1678 to his death he taught in Naples at the Conservatorio di Sant' Onofrio and was master of the Royal Chapel, where Alessandro Scarlatti succeeded him at his death. A many-sided and prolific composer of operas, cantatas, and church music, a colleague and friend of Cazzati and Cavalli, he was well known and much performed both in Naples and in Venice.

Opera in Naples started in the middle of the 17th century, first with performances of Monteverdi, Cavalli, and other Venetians; but soon the Neapolitans Coppola, Provenzale, Ziani, and others were represented. In the eighties Scarlatti took command of the scene, but the Teatro San Bartolomeo continued a remarkable repertory of works by Pasquini, Legrenzi, Pallavicino, Gasparini—that is, the leading lights of Venetian opera. However, we must bear in mind that Naples had a very pronounced spirit of its own, that Scarlatti, though he eventually became synonymous with Neapolitan opera, was only a "naturalized" Neapolitan, himself being vastly influenced by this spirit. Perhaps nowhere else is there the same intimate blending of sobriety with softness of line, of crude drama with delicacy, of scrupulous observation of realistic and humorous detail with spiritual intensity.

Among the native composers of note was Francesco Mancini (1672–1737), an orphan educated at the Conservatorio di Santa Maria di Loreto, and a pupil of Provenzale. In January 1708 he became conductor, but by the end of the year had to cede his post to the returning Scarlatti. He had to wait until Scarlatti's death in 1725 before his "right to succession" could be exercised. Mancini, intimately bound to local traditions, was actually Scarlatti's competitor; his fame spread all over Italy and then to England. Compared to Scarlatti's, his music is less carefully worked; his part-writing, especially, was inferior to the great Sicilian's, but in noble Neapolitan pathos he matched his formidable rival. Mancini, whom Handel could not miss in Naples, will come within our purview as soon as we follow Handel to England; his *Idaspe* was among the very first Italian operas performed in their entirety in England. He also composed a great deal of other music, and how highly he was esteemed can be seen from the fact that some of his chamber music was edited for London by Geminiani.

Among other important local musicians mention should be made of Gaetano Veneziano (d. 1716), a Provenzale disciple, who succeeded Scarlatti in the post of royal conductor in 1704, holding the position until 1707. He was particularly known for his oratorios, of which *Il Sacrifizio di Elia*, composed in 1704, was still a favorite when Handel was in Naples. Another notable figure was Domenico Sarri (1679–1744), whose many operas, oratorios, and Masses were all produced for Naples.

Since the Oratorians had a branch in Naples that was at least as active as the original Philippine group in Rome, the oratorio flourished in the viceregal city. Unfortunately, very little is known about it before Mancini's time. In particular, it is difficult to differentiate between the very popular *dramma sacro,* a "sacred opera" fully staged, and the ordinary opera seria and oratorio, especially since Oratorians, conservatories, and other groups and institutions cultivated the various genres. These sacred operas abound in buffo scenes that show a kinship with the older Roman opera and with their pronounced naturalism laid the foundation for the Neapolitan opera buffa, which was shortly to conquer the world. Sumptuous choral music was heard in the churches, and Handel, always eager to try out church organs—there were dozens of them to be tried in

Naples—must have heard much sacred music by contemporary composers.

Then we come to Handel's own generation of Neapolitans, just beginning to make themselves felt on the contemporary scene. Among these early ripening southerners special attention is due to Nicola Porpora (1686–1768), who entered the conservatory at the age of ten to study with Greco. His *Agrippina,* produced in 1708, was lost neither on Cardinal Grimani nor on Handel. We shall meet Porpora again in London, where, next to Bononcini, he was Handel's most troublesome rival.

Naples had two opera houses, San Bartolomeo and the Teatro dei Fiorentini, but operas were also produced in the great hall of the royal palace, in the conservatories, the convents, and the monasteries. This brisk operatic life was enhanced by a merry rivalry caused by Scarlatti's rather capricious coming and going. Whenever he was away, legally or illegally, the capable—and impatient—resident musicians jockeyed for a favorable position to capture the coveted post of royal conductor, but so great was Scarlatti's prestige that whenever he was willing to return, even after years of unauthorized absence, the position was immediately restored to him; and this in spite of some very questionable intrigues by his family, in particular by one of his sisters of somewhat liberal moral views and easy virtue. When Cardinal Grimani became viceroy, the merry-go-round was once more arrested by Scarlatti's reinstatement.

The opera houses, the churches, and the great private residences loom large in the historian's view; their accomplishments are recorded in word and picture. But the Neapolitan countryside too was full of music, not the 19th-century commercial Neapolitan "folksong" the modern tourist hears but age-old genuine folk music. Handel's fondness for southern Italian dance patterns and tunes, for the "pastoral symphony" and the siciliana, is well known. Though he must have heard most of these in Rome—Corelli, Scarlatti, Pasquini, and all the others frequently used them —once more the spirit of the place had attractions that could not be apprehended from a distance.

Having composed the cantata *Partenza* as a farewell to Rome in May 1708, Handel must have left immediately for Naples, because on June 16 he records the completion of the serenata *Aci, Galatea, e Polifemo,* written for a princely wedding in Naples on the nineteenth of July. July also yielded the fine vocal trio, *Se tu non lasci amore.* From this point onward we have no accurate information about Handel's activity until he reappears at the Ottoboni palace in the spring of 1709, but various facts can be established from circumstantial evidence.

Cardinal Grimani, an able diplomat who had to step gingerly between Spain, Austria, and the Papal States, was a passionate lover and patron of music, as well as a good judge of talent. He recognized not only the genius of the mature and celebrated elder Scarlatti but also that of young Domenico and Handel. (Handel's friend from Rome, Alessandro Scarlatti, had also returned to Naples soon after Handel's arrival, and he undoubtedly stood by his young colleague.) The Cardinal presented to his German protégé the libretto of *Agrippina,* which Handel set to music in Naples, and the churchman-diplomat was obviously paving the way for the production of their joint work in Venice, in the family-owned theatre of San Grisostomo. Why the work had not been produced in Naples, where there were ample facilities for even the most lavish production and where Cardinal Grimani had even more power than in Venice, is not clear. However, Naples was still far behind Venice in prestige and the shrewd and experienced Cardinal must have justly concluded that even a modest success in Venice was to be preferred to a triumph in "provincial" Naples.

An unexplained and curious interlude of the Neapolitan days is represented by a set of French chansons Handel composed for a solo voice with accompaniment. It is rather puzzling that he suddenly took to the writing of chansons. While his ability to express himself in a strange idiom is once more astounding, it is difficult to account for the occasion that prompted the young man, avidly assimilating Italian music, to set to music French texts, and of all places in Naples. Rolland suggests the presence of a French singer, which is not implausible. Another oddity is the only cantata Handel wrote on a Spanish text, with guitar accompaniment.

[5]

THE VENETIAN CHAPTER IN Handel's Italian journey is, if anything, even more barren of documents than the Neapolitan. He arrived in the fall of 1709 and left in the spring of 1710. We do not even know what he composed there, for *Agrippina* originated in Naples and was ready for performance when Handel arrived in the Adriatic metropolis of opera. We are therefore reduced to the one known fact of the period, the production and tremendous success of *Agrippina,* and to a few conjectures on such matters as the whereabouts of the Scarlattis, the presence or absence of Agostino Steffani, and the reasons for Handel's leaving Italy for

Hanover.

With *Agrippina* Cardinal Grimani gave Handel a typically Venetian plot of intrigue: a number of lovers furnished opportunity for dozens of arias and permutations of love interest that were particularly appreciated by the public, who also liked the deft satire on lust for political power. Considering Handel's subsequent career as an opera composer, it is perhaps surprising that this firstling was not a heroic opera seria; it has buffo scenes, even buffo ensembles, among them a fine trio. Though *Agrippina* still has a large number of basso continuo arias, it also contains several great concerted arias and in general shows a very good knowledge of Venetian opera, especially the works of Pollarolo and Legrenzi, some of which of course he heard in Naples. The opera also shows acquaintance with the advanced Venetian orchestral accompaniment. This is a remarkable and prophetic score despite certain shortcomings. It stayed with Handel all his life, and some of its engaging melodies reappear even in his last work, *The Triumph of Time and Truth.*

Agrippina was first presented in San Giovanni Grisostomo December 26, 1709, and ran for twenty-seven nights—an unusual success not only in Venice but in all the annals of Italian opera for an initial run. The Venetians were bowled over and Handel became their darling. Such a triumph, of course, brought world fame, because any successful Venetian production immediately made the rounds of the Italian operatic dependencies abroad. Cardinal Grimani's calculations had proved to be correct. Between *Rodrigo* and *Agrippina* there had been less than two years and no other opera, yet during those months Handel rose from apprentice to master of opera.

With this memorable première Handel's Venetian sojourn, indeed the Italian journey, ends, and biographers immediately turn their attention to Hanover and London. But surely several months' residence in what was then the hub of both operatic and instrumental music of the most progressive kind should not be ignored in the life of a composer who shows the Venetian influence from *Rinaldo* (1711) to *Serse* (1738). However, before taking a look at the Venetian scene there are a few loose ends that must be tied.

Mainwaring insists that La Bombace was in Venice during Handel's visit, singing in one of the other opera houses, and if so Handel had a tried companion to seek solace with. A somewhat younger friend was Domenico Scarlatti. There is a story, hotly disputed, that Handel travelled to Venice in the company of one or both of the Scarlattis or of Steffani— or all three. It really does not matter; he knew all three of them well and since the elder Scarlatti and the distinguished Titular Bishop Steffani were great travellers—and opera composers—they must have been in and out of Venice, while Domenico had been domiciled there for some time. The younger Scarlatti, who was of his own age, became Handel's boon companion. An experienced musician, he had already held several positions of responsibility and was a successful composer of not particularly accomplished operas. This very attractive young man blossomed into a great master much later than Handel, and when he did, he forsook opera for the keyboard; therefore as a composer his influence on Handel was nil. It has been suggested that Handel profited from Scarlatti's keyboard music, but Scarlatti's magnificent "sonatas" or "exercises" are from a much later period. Nor is there any Handelian influence to be found in Scarlatti. Both young men were experimenting and taking in the scene. Different as they were, they found each other's company very congenial. Domenico was the exact opposite of Handel: an introvert who shunned publicity, and though a fabulous virtuoso (which undoubtedly was the quality in him that fascinated Handel), he never played in public. But two things they had in common: Domenico was just as uncommunicative about himself as Handel, and his travels are as difficult to follow as Handel's.

We know that during Lent, 1709, Domenico was in Rome, but there can be no question that a good deal of 1709 was spent in Venice, where his knowledge of the place and the people must have been a great help to Handel. After Handel left Italy the two friends never met again, for the story of Domenico's London journey is pure fabrication. It is very difficult to ascertain when they were together in Venice. The fleeting visit Handel was supposed to have made to Venice in 1708 is improbable though not to be ruled out. Domenico Scarlatti was then definitely in Venice studying with Gasparini. Every biographer delights in telling an anecdote supposed to have taken place on the occasion of the "first" Venetian visit. Handel, though disguised at a masked ball, was recognized when he sat down at the harpsichord: "If this is not the Saxon," exclaimed Domenico, "it can only be the devil"—or something like that. Unfortunately, variants of the engaging story are so many, and applied to so many musicians, that the anecdote must be considered a biographical ostinato. Though Scarlatti was in Rome during Lent of 1708 too, that is, during the "season," when the great residences had their private performances (he was then music master to Maria Casimira), the whole year is by no means accounted for; given the Scarlattis' very mobile inclinations and the great attraction of Venice for all opera composers, we should think that several months of 1709–10 were spent there, and that it was on Handel's "second" journey that the two young men roamed the town together.

In connection with Domenico we must mention the two Marcello brothers, Alessandro (1684–1750) and Benedetto (1686–1739), Venetian patricians and amateurs of Handel's age. Though they called themselves amateurs (*Nobile Veneto dilettante di contrappunto* was Benedetto's phrase), the sole reason for this modesty was the fact that, being wealthy, they did not have to make a living from music. As composers and men of letters they were both first-class professionals. One of Alessandro's oboe concertos was long held to be by Sebastian Bach, who transcribed it for harpsichord (it has also been assigned to Vivaldi and to Benedetto). Although Benedetto's Psalm settings, which were still admired by Verdi, and other excellent compositions date from later years, performances of his works in Venice began in 1707. Alessandro's cantatas appeared in print in 1708. Both of these cultivated humanists were to make their impress on music history, but what interests us here is their "salon," the meeting place of Venice's artistic and literary elite, where concerts were frequently given. Although nothing is known about Handel's relationship to them, Domenico was a frequent visitor and must have taken along his bosom friend.

[6]

HANDEL FOUND A musical life in Venice that for splendor, intensity, and variety far surpassed anything he had so far seen, and of course here he finally found the mainstream of opera, his chief reason for leaving Hamburg. Always a progressive center of music, Venice had been in the forefront since the early 16th century. It was the home of the inception of the music-printing industry, of the madrigal, of the brilliant instrumental music that arose at the end of the Renaissance, and of the colorful polychoral art. By 1637 Venice became indisputable leader in the new art of opera, harboring among its local composers none other than Monteverdi. While Venice later lost this position to Naples, it was still held by her when Handel arrived. Even in that incredibly rich musical life of Italy, with great regional centers such as Rome, Bologna, Brescia, Ferrara, and Naples, Venice occupied a special place of honor. The Venetians, clear-sighted, adaptable, and artistic, learned from all and were blind followers of none. Musicians from everywhere came to the city and settled down, the second generation becoming native in more than one sense. From there they colonized the European operatic world: Vienna, Dresden, Munich, Berlin, and even London. Many of the qualities and techniques ascribed to Neapolitan opera were really developed in Venice, and we should beware of using the term "Neapolitan opera" without qualification.

Venice had as many opera houses as it had parishes, and several of them were active at the same time. Almost all of the theatres, though open to the public and operated for profit, belonged to Venetian patricians who, like the Grimanis, liked to run them personally, though they also rented them to entrepreneurs. The Grimanis actually owned two other theatres besides San Grisostomo. The production of operas proceeded at a fantastic rate—at least a hundred new operas during the first decades of the 18th century—and this in spite of the fluctuation of fad and fashion. Important changes had taken place in the development of Venetian opera since the days of Cavalli and Cesti, changes due partly to economic, partly to literary and artistic causes. The public opera house was a commercial undertaking, and managers began to cut corners to make the enterprise profitable, eliminating such expensive factors as the professional chorus and reducing the large cast to a handful of principals. Cavalli's magnificent choral scenes disappeared. Then the mythical-pastoral world of the Renaissance from which the librettos were derived gradually changed into the historical-political.[2]

Handel of course heard the operas of the contemporary masters, but many of the previous generation's works were still being sung. That he studied Venetian opera from the ground up is shown by his borrowing from the opening "sonata" of Cesti's *Il Pomo d'oro*. Legrenzi's memory was still very much alive and his music performed when Handel surveyed the Venetian scene. Handel was acquainted with and already used the da capo aria in Hamburg, but Legrenzi's arias must have surprised him. Here Handel could study at first hand the reconciliation of musical with dramatic logic, for while Legrenzi was the first champion of the da capo aria as the main lyric frame in opera, he did not adhere to a pattern; many of his arias are through-composed, and he set the text with great fidelity while retaining a remarkable flexibility. Legrenzi's operas are of heroic Baroque proportions, and like his contemporaries he indulged in comic scenes within the opera seria. His fine church and instrumental music was also heard everywhere. Handel copied one of his six-part motets and later used it in *Samson*. This great Venetian was among the first masters of the trio sonata, which prepared for the classic synthesis of Corelli, and his motets and Psalm settings testify to a mastery of the

---

[2] Only in the elaborate court theatres such as were maintained in Vienna and Dresden did the "imperial" style of the earlier Venetian opera survive.

Palestrina style. Handel was not the only one to be fascinated by this music; next to Vivaldi, Legrenzi was Bach's favorite Italian.

Within a year or two before Handel's arrival, several highly successful operas were produced, such as Ziani's *Meleagro* and Alessandro Scarlatti's *Mitridate Eupatore;* Ariosti and Caldara too were in and out of Venice with several works, and all these operas were still in the repertory. Ziani's bold and virtuoso use of winds and strings opened new horizons; its lessons were later brilliantly utilized in the *Water Music.*

Antonio Caldara (c. 1670–1736), who later became an ornament of the Viennese court as co-regent with Fux of the capital's musical life, was a Venetian, a disciple of Legrenzi. He was a restless traveller before settling in Vienna in 1716, and his path presumably crossed Handel's repeatedly. This prolific composer of operas, oratorios, and a great deal of excellent church and instrumental music had a particularly felicitous sense for spacious, euphonious sound—again the Palestrinian legacy—which made him famous all over Italy.[3] Handel met him in Rome, where Caldara was one of Cardinal Ottoboni's favorites, or in Venice, probably in both places.

Another celebrity was Carlo Francesco Pollarolo (1653–1722), a pupil and colleague of Legrenzi, who was attached to St. Mark's Cathedral from 1692 until his death. Some of his many operas (we know seventy-three titles) were always in the repertory and enjoyed great popularity. Tomaso Albinoni (1671–1750), another native Venetian who is slowly beginning to reach modern audiences, was a highly regarded opera and instrumental composer from whom Bach borrowed fugue themes. Handel could not have overlooked this inventive and progressive composer. There were many others, but the commanding personality of Venetian music was Antonio Lotti (1667–1740), a Venetian by birth and the incarnation of Venetian High Baroque by accomplishment.

Chrysander is positive that Handel met Lotti in Venice, and if Lotti was there at the time—which, although he travelled a good deal, seems extremely likely because of his position as organist and choirmaster at St. Mark's—they could not have failed to meet: Handel never missed a good organist. At the time of Handel's visit Lotti was already a highly admired composer and his works were heard all over Italy. Even though his international reputation dates from later years, his remarkable church music in the noblest choral traditions coming after 1719 when he had abandoned opera, the admirable qualities of his music were fully in evi-

---

[3] See his magnificent choruses, among them an eight-part Te Deum and a sixteen-part *Crucifixus,* in the Austrian *Denkmäler,* XIII, 1.

dence in 1709–10 when Handel met him.

The regal pathos of this admirable musician who was the final link in the chain formed by Monteverdi, Cavalli, and Cesti, his superb dramatic choruses and penetrating characterizations confronted Handel with the ideal he had travelled so far to find. Lotti was a kindred soul, among the few composer-dramatists who avoided the *parti buffe*, being solely interested in darkly pessimistic subjects. A most versatile musician, he was equally at home in the late madrigal or in smoothly flowing contrapuntal choral music. Incidentally, while *Agrippina* ran at San Grisostomo, other opera houses, presided over by Gasparini and Lotti, were in session. Here Handel could observe performed on a competent professional level what he had seen done in Hamburg in the most haphazard way: both Gasparini and Lotti were composer-producers, which was to become Handel's status in England.

The famous Venetian conservatories—Mendicanti, Pietà, Incurabili, SS. Giovanni e Paolo—all had distinguished resident maestros and superbly trained orchestras. Visitors from foreign lands expressed unstinted admiration of the excellence of the performances of these orphaned children. The students were not restricted to the convent-conservatory, and an orchestra made up of girls and conducted by one of the maestros was often hired for private concerts and festivities. Handel surely visited them, especially the Pietà, because his friend Domenico Scarlatti was a frequent caller there. Francesco Gasparini, maestro at the Pietà, a close friend of Alessandro Scarlatti's, was Domenico's principal teacher. The numerous churches also had well-appointed music at their services composed in both styles of the "bilingual" masters.

There was still another form of vocal music, not yet sufficiently investigated, that undoubtedly contributed to Handel's exceptionally light and flexible choral idiom: the post-Renaissance madrigal, which was particularly admired in Venice. The refined miniature work in the madrigals of Steffani, Bononcini, Lotti, Caldara, and others did not go unnoticed by Handel; the delicate, fragrant, and very modern madrigal, "Bid the maids the youths provoke to join the dance," in *Hercules,* is a good example of the type. The idiom is also in evidence in those of his choral numbers in which he expanded a smaller to a larger ensemble, such as the duets that were converted into full four-part movements.

Little, if any, attention has been paid to the effect upon Handel of the instrumental music he heard in Venice, both at the church concerts and at the opera, where concerted arias displayed writing for the strings that went even beyond the requirements of the older concerto. In fact,

though the influence was mutual, we must conclude that opera contributed a great deal to the subsequent development of the concerto. The
"motto aria" (it was Riemann who established the notion, calling it
Devisenarie), in which the opening of the principal theme in the da capo
aria is "inscribed" in advance, was clearly the origin of the initial tutti
in the concerto. Though the device was not unknown in Hamburg, Handel's frequent use of it in opera dates from his Italian sojourn.

Among the famous conservatory maestros one in particular must be
mentioned, though he does not seem to have made a particular impression
on Handel. Marc Pincherle, in his great monograph devoted to Vivaldi,
definitely established that Vivaldi was active at the Pietà when Handel
was in Venice. Wherever Vivaldi was there was abundant music making.
Handel could not have avoided the Red Priest, yet, strangely, there is
scarcely a trace in his music of the very personal style of Vivaldi. This is
puzzling, the more so because it was precisely the young Vivaldi who attracted Bach so much, whereas Handel seems to have ignored the fiery
Italian's vigorous and adventurous music. With his good eye for "usable"
material he must have spotted many a sharply profiled theme in Vivaldi's
works, especially since both Opus 1 and the fine Opus 2 were available in
print, published in 1705 and early in 1709, respectively. Moreover, Walsh
began publishing Vivaldi as early as 1712, and Matthew Dubourg,
Handel's violinist friend, and other English virtuosos played his concertos
not infrequently. Throughout his life Handel remained faithful to the line
that culminated in Corelli's distilled and classically poised works. There
were others, such as Albinoni, from whom he learned a great deal, but the
arch master of the late Italian Baroque does not figure among them.[4]

This instrumental music of the High Baroque was not empty virtuosity or mere playful romping, as Stravinsky, Dallapiccola, and some
other modern masters so contemptuously regard it. In the first place,
church sonata and church concerto were not casual designations. It is
perhaps difficult for us, accustomed as we are to a noncommittal, standardized, and mushy organ sound, to the atrocious preludizing of the average organist, to the anemic voluntaries and offertories of that anomaly of
modern times, the professional church composer who certainly is *not* "bilingual," to imagine the noble and vibrant sound played on exquisite instruments *during the service*. For indeed, some of the choir's functions
were taken from it and assigned to the instruments. Such instrumental

[4] Another great composer of whose markedly personal style there is no trace in
Handel is Frescobaldi. This is the more surprising because Frescobaldi's music was
ever present and his influence affected generations of musicians.

compositions may appear at various places during Mass, not only during the Offertory. Mazzaferrata, Vitali, Bassani, Ruggieri, Legrenzi, Albinoni, Torelli, Caldara, and a host of others may be mere names to us (though Corelli and Vivaldi are beginning to take their rightful place in the repertory), but to Handel their music was a deeply satisfying experience. It was here that he learned the true handling of the four-part string orchestra, no longer basically a trio with the tenor part hobbling along between alto and bass; the viola part was made a full partner and the setting was genuine quartet writing. The forms were classically clear, the harmony opulent, the melody wide-ranging, and the sound always rich and "filling." A glance at Handel's E minor Concerto Grosso will show what he learned from the Italians, for this glowing pathos, this cantability, this elevated tone was their creation.

How little this great art is known and appreciated can be seen from a statement in one of the English-language Handel biographies to the effect that the overture to *Agrippina* must have been a revelation to the Venetians, whose *sinfonie* the author judges vastly inferior to Handel's prelude. It was this music, the stately church sonatas, suites, concertos, and *sinfonie* which that indefatigable and shrewd researcher, Dr. Burney, no antiquarian but a champion of living music, characterized as being of "great dignity" and "mellifluous voice." He was so intrigued by the music of such masters as Bassani that he visited the eminent Padre Martini, "who was old enough to have formed his opinion from those who had often heard him [Bassani] perform," to get more information about these little-known composers. And it was of one of them that Prunières, great connoisseur of Venetian music, made the significant statement that is valid for the whole school. What emerges from this music, he says, is "une âme d'une noblesse, d'une serenité, d'une gravité religieuse qui n'est pas sans rapport avec celle d'un Palestrina."

The remark about the startling novelty and superiority of Handel's overture to *Agrippina* is utterly naive. To cite one example, the magnificent *Sinfonia avanti l'opera* in Antonio Maria Bononcini's *Il Trionfo di Camilla* (1696), later famous even in London, is a rousing concert symphony, modern, brilliant, and gloriously euphonious. Moreover, it clearly operates with form-defining tonal relations. Scarlatti's fine Italian overtures were also fully developed by the opening of the 18th century. Indeed, it was in Venice that Handel learned that *brio insolito* which is so attractive in his own concertos and which he introduced, as did the Venetians, into his opera orchestra. It was here too (though he had a foretaste of it in Naples) that he learned about orchestral accompaniment with independent motifs as opposed to the largely *colla parte* manner, not only in overtures and ritornels, but in arias and accompanied recitatives, thus acquiring rich new means of expressing dramatic commentary. The mighty tuttis falling upon a monodic scene, the brilliant "trumpet arias" in which the voice is pitted against a concertante trumpet, similar ones with oboe or violin, and many other modern instrumental devices were all derived from Venetian instrumental music.

One would think that, having acquired mastery of Italian music and the admiration of Italians, Handel would have rested content. His mind and his music are organized and settled, the Italian pattern absorbed and utilized. Already in *Agrippina,* which still shows some elements of the erstwhile cantor's art, the conversion is nevertheless achieved. Even the recitative is no mere inorganic parlando; the melodic substance is formed, the phrases are complemented lineally and metrically, the basso continuo accompaniment often giving way to a differentiated and expressive orchestra. But above all, Handel had made the *suavità,* the *dolcezza,* the *durezze* of this beguiling musical language of Italy completely his own. The road was open to a career that was surely to place even Lotti in the shadow. Yet Handel abandoned Italy.

[7]

As we have said, there are a number of conflicting reports and interpretations concerning Handel's relationship with Steffani, the most amazing of these being Handel's own statement as reported by Sir John Hawkins. "When I first arrived in Hanover, I was a young man under twenty; I was acquainted with the merits of Steffani and he had heard of me." Did Hawkins misquote Handel or did Handel's memory play him tricks? One would very much hesitate to mistrust that marvelous apparatus which was Handel's memory, and Hawkins was a conscientious scholar; but then this suggests that Handel first met Steffani on a hitherto unrecorded and undocumented visit to Hanover during the Hamburg period, that is, before he went to Italy. The possibility of such a "residence" in Hanover in 1704 or 1705 cannot be ruled out. Whatever the situation, the two certainly met in the Ottoboni circle, and in 1709–10 Steffani was in Venice, where he heard *Agrippina.*

This enigmatic person played a decisive role in Handel's life, both artistically and personally. Of obscure origin, and possessed of an insatiable *Wanderlust* and great ambitions, Steffani actually received his first musical education in Germany. At an early age he turned up in Munich, where he studied with Kerll, later continuing his apprenticeship in Rome with Ercole Bernabei, the excellent Benevoli disciple who, incidentally, also resided in Munich. Subsequently court organist in Munich (1675), in 1678–79 the inquisitive Steffani repaired to Paris, where he lost no time in getting thoroughly acquainted with Lully's art. Then begins the other aspect of his career: the Italian musician is ordained a priest in 1680.

At first we see only the not unfamiliar figure of the opera-composing cleric, producing operas by the half dozen, but also some very fine church music and cantatas. In 1688 Steffani went to Hanover as court conductor, raising the musical establishment to considerable excellence. By this time he was a famous man, equally renowned for his music and his intellect. He was the third member of that extraordinary intellectual triumvirate that included the Electress Sophia and the philosopher Leibniz. His very personal and refined style exerted a wide influence on German composers—we have seen that both Mattheson and Telemann considered him the most accomplished melodist of the day—but Zachow, Keiser, and Handel were also strongly affected by this suave melody. At the time Handel met him in Venice, Steffani was, with Legrenzi, Lotti, and Fux, among the great Baroque classicists who preserved the traditions of polyphony while belonging to the dramatic avant-garde. In spite of his long residence in Germany, his early education there, and his many connections with German musicians, Steffani's music is Venetian of a somewhat earlier cast. There are an uncommon number of arias in his operas—fifty, sixty, and even seventy in a single work—but they are mostly continuo arias, and his recitative is perfunctory. There are, however, many attractive melodies, especially in the duets. His chamber duets, which far surpass even those in the operas, are, indeed, together with his very elevated church music, his main contribution to the style of the period. Haas rightly considers them "the pinnacle of three-part Baroque counterpoint." Steffani was a born lyricist with little sense for the truly dramatic.

In spite of his extensive musical output and his remarkable ability as conductor and organizer, Steffani's main business and vocation was politics and diplomacy; he was passionately interested in it, and intrigue was in his bones. The high and mighty, while appreciative of his musical talents, favored him because of his political shrewdness and savoir-faire. As Papal envoy, he was constantly on the move from one German court to another, and if not on a mission he occupied high political posts, such as administrative head of the government of the Palatinate, or Apostolic Vicar for the North of Germany, with his seat in Hanover. Wherever he could combine these functions with a resident court musician's office he did so, for his love of music was as genuine as his gifts, but diplomacy always ranked ahead of the musician's career—his real ambition was to become a cardinal. That these political tasks were of extraordinary magnitude is well indicated by his diplomatic papers, filling dozens of as yet unexplored dossiers in the Vatican.

Steffani may have been a lover of political intrigue, but as a musician and man of the world he was all amiability. Though thirty years Handel's senior and a very famous composer, Steffani had nothing but praise for the young Saxon and it was he who warmly recommended Handel for the position in Hanover that he was about to vacate. This brings us to what is perhaps the most perplexing question in a life that is full of them: why did Handel decide to leave Italy?

The external circumstances are very simple. Prince Ernest of Hanover, a passionate amateur of music, was residing at this time in Venice. The Prince not only heard *Agrippina* but was so enchanted by it that he attended the performances at San Grisostomo practically every night throughout its long run. Convinced that this German who could outdo the Italians in their very own field was the ideal replacement for Steffani, he extended to Handel an invitation to come to Hanover. Baron Kielmansegg, the Elector's Master of the Horse, who accompanied Prince Ernest, concurred, and so did the illustrious court maestro, Steffani. The invitation was accepted, and Handel departed for Hanover. But surely this decision hides very serious deliberations and inner struggles, though as usual the imperturbable Saxon shows no outward sign of it.

The Italian triumphs had begun to reverberate beyond the Alps. In 1708 the twenty-three-year-old was already spoken of in Hamburg as "the famous Monsieur Händel, loved by all Italy," and the tremendous success of *Agrippina* carried his name all over Europe. Every Italian opera house would have been at his feet, every noble house glad to receive him, for did he not triumph in the very bailiwick of Gasparini and Lotti? Clearly, Cardinal Panfili's cantata was prophetic: Handel was about to become *Orpheus aetatis*. Yet he left Italy. Why?

No one really knows. No historical scholar nowadays can pretend to that immanent and infallible sense of knowledge that infuses Carlyle's writings with their dogmatic charm. The usual explanations of restlessness, or whim, or patriotism are once more inadequate. To understand this immigrant to England, who for nearly half a century thereafter was not "restless," and whose "patriotism" became altogether English, it is necessary to understand the forces that made him forsake Italy, and in these matters there is a large array of such interesting inferences as we may choose to draw, two of which seem to dominate.

It seems to us that one of the keys to Handel's decision is to be found in a brief statement he made to Sir John Hawkins. Reminiscing on his animated career, he said to the historian that what he particularly appreciated in England was that there a man's religious views were his private affair.[5] It is an extraordinary statement, coming as it does from a German Lutheran, but we are convinced that religious-moral reasons strongly influenced his decision to leave Italy. This is altogether in harmony with his previous and subsequent acts.

That Handel remained a steadfast Protestant is supported by the fact that although while in Italy he wrote works that were within the orbit of Italian Catholic music, he never did anything to identify himself other than musically with Italy and her religion. We can go farther than that. Handel not only composed Italian Catholic music, he penetrated to its most intimate and characteristic region: the Marian cult, surely the most remote to Protestants. Such a work as his hymn to the Virgin, *Ah! Che troppo ineguali* (among the accompanied sacred cantatas), is a direct descendant of the laudi, and his tender *Salve Regina* shows that he might have followed the example of John Christian Bach, Kerll, and Froberger, who found this spirit irresistible. Percy Young, in his brief but perceptive biographical sketch in Gerald Abraham's *Handel, a Symposium,* noted this "unmistakable chivalrous devotion before the Queen of Heaven," but, as we have said above, we cannot agree with his conclusions that this was an indication of Catholic leanings on the part of Handel that might have led to a conversion had he stayed a while longer. That Handel was attracted to the elaborate Catholic ritual cannot be doubted; but he also had unshakable convictions, which no amount of proselytizing could overcome.

We have noted that the Italians were—and still are—remarkably tolerant of the religious convictions of artists; they accepted nonbelievers even in Vatican circles without the slightest hindrance. This does not mean, though, that they did not attempt conversion, and often with suc-

---

[5] The statement needs qualification, however, for obviously it is valid only so far as Protestants were concerned. Though a great man of letters such as Dryden was not molested by the government, he lost his office and pension as laureate and historiographer royal when he became a Catholic. The great poet of the Handelian era, Pope, never enjoyed a regular education because as a Catholic the public schools and the universities were closed to him. Indeed, Catholics were discriminated against well into the 19th century, and their religious faith was not their "private affair." But there can be no doubt that Handel's statement refers to the situation in which he found himself in Italy.

cess. Handel's case was no exception. Mainwaring, though using no documents, states this rather convincingly—and rather movingly.

As he was familiar with so many of the Sacred Order, and of a persuasion so totally repugnant to theirs, it is natural to imagine that some of them would expostulate with him on that subject . . . . Being pressed very closely on this article by one of these exalted Ecclesiastics, he replied, that he was neither qualified, nor disposed to enter into enquiries of this sort, but was resolved to die a member of the communion, whether true or false, in which he was born and bred. No hopes appearing of a real conversion, the next attempt was to win him over to outward conformity. But neither arguments, nor offers had any effect, unless it were of confirming him still more in the principles of protestantism. These applications were made only by a few persons. The generality looked upon him as a man of honest, though mistaken principles, and therefore concluded that he would not easily be induced to change them.

He withstood all the Italians' eloquence, for he was of a different temperament from the Milan Bach or any other of the German pilgrims in Italy with the exception of Schütz. But the most redoubtable and experienced Catholic apologist was yet to be encountered, and that one appears, interestingly enough, just when the decision to leave was about to be made. One cannot help wondering how much Steffani's efforts contributed to this decision.

Steffani, the churchman-diplomat-composer extraordinary, had still another passion, even more ambitious than his bold political operations: he wanted to regain the German Protestant princes for Catholicism. He did not succeed, though not for lack of effort, for he used every means at his disposal. He went so far as to tackle the dour soldier-king of Prussia, an attempt that led to a hasty retreat. This belated exponent of the Counter-Reformation, always eager to save souls, particularly souls of stature, must have worked hard to convert Handel, but to no avail. Once more, it is a pleasure to record that Handel's intransigeance did not in the least affect the cordial relations between him and the crusading bishop; the elder man warmly supported his fellow musician.

The exact value that Handel attached to this privacy of religious belief is impossible to ascertain. But we may note that in all his years in England, he never publicly affiliated himself with the Anglican Church, although he was a frequent churchgoer, and we may be sure that the remark to Hawkins reflected the thoughts of a naturally reticent man who was very much in earnest and completely sincere with himself before God, for his independence was not synonymous with irreligion.

The other paramount reason for Handel's departure we see in opera itself, a view not at all contradictory to the facts when we are familiar with Handel's operas after *Agrippina*.

Handel was not a "bilingual" composer; everything he learned in Italy was blended into a single, personal language. In the basic contours of his forms he depended, equally with his colleagues, on the period, but in his artistic means and aims he was far more independent. The creations resulting from his plastic force of characterization were different from the often statuesque Venetian operatic figures, and in this as in many other aspects of his art Handel reaches far into modern times. The question he posed was similar to Verdi's: not whether the libretto gives the composer opportunity to create a broad, unified, all-encompassing picture—the Venetians could do that masterfully—but whether he could build musical scenes based on the inner dramatic qualities of the dramatis personae. To him every line of thought was a path of access to the actual life of man. At the age of twenty-one he had clearly assessed the future of opera in Hamburg, and now, after years of rich experience among the masters of opera, he once more must have sensed a tendency that was contrary to his ideals. Seventeenth-century Italian opera was pure music drama, but in the first half of the 18th it turned into a poetry of the senses, often without intellectual or emotional depth, effete, and luxurious. This could not have been to his liking, for the true dramatist is in action with the very first chords; the curtain rises and he is fully engaged. Some of the great masters of the music drama were still alive, and both Scarlatti and Lotti were yet to write their mature masterpieces, but the tendency was already discernible.

True, the history of opera in the first half of the 18th century is not yet sufficiently explored, and it is quite possible that our present view concerning the decline and schematic nature of the seria and the corresponding exaltation of the buffa may change when more works are known. The production of *opere serie* was enormous, but we know only an infinitely small portion of it since so little is available in print; but the opera buffa was bound to be victorious over the seria, for when tragedy and comedy collide, it is usually comedy that wins. The realistic and practical sense of the Italians has always overcome abstractions; they love the good story, the amusing situations, the *double-entendre*. In recent operatic history even Puccini, essentially a composer of *comédie larmoyante*, turned to the opera buffa towards the end of his career. But Handel was not a composer of comedy, in which he again resembles Verdi, although like Verdi he too composed a comic masterpiece. Even in *Serse*, however, the humor and the satire consist not at all in the situations but in the character portrayal. It is conveyed by the curl of a musical phrase in the ear, by speed, or by stillness.

Having explored the whole range of Italian music, having learned the trade, supremely confident in his power to create a world of his own, he was looking for a place where he could build this world, where he could establish his own laws, where both a man's religious and artistic views were his private affair; and all this he hoped to find, as we shall see, in England.

The decision made, Handel packed his belongings, the considerable number of scores he had composed in Italy—as well as some by Stradella, Scarlatti, Lotti, and others—and left Venice, where he had become world famous and the idol of a spoiled and knowledgeable audience.

V

ANDEL'S APPOINTMENT AS COURT CONDUCTOR IN HAN-
over took effect on June 16, 1710. One would think that for a man of
twenty-five such a position, occupied before him by no less distinguished
a figure than Steffani, would represent a very desirable station in his
career. Hanover was not a negligible provincial residence; the court under
the energetic and cultivated Electress Sophie was intellectually far above
the average (though this brilliance was not transferred to the Court of St.
James when after the death of the Electress her son became George I of
England). Nor was Hanover's musical past, though fairly recent, inconsiderable. From 1639 to 1641 Schütz was *Hofkapellmeister,* and later,
along with a bevy of excellent French and Italian musicians, the court
establishment counted among its members Nicolaus Adam Strungk. Opera
was first produced there in 1672, and in 1688 Elector Ernst Augustus (who
spent most of his time in Venice and worshipped everything Italian) erected a 1300-seat theatre that was considered the most beautiful opera house
in Germany. It was inaugurated with one of Steffani's operas and continued
under the diplomat-composer's direction until the death of Ernst Augustus in 1698. Although in 1710 there was no longer an active opera
company in existence, Hanover still had several good instrumentalists
and some able singers. But once more matters are not so simple as documents and circumstances would indicate. Handel stayed in Hanover for

little more than the summer of 1710. In October or November he appears in London.

We know nothing about the compositions Handel produced during this brief sojourn in Hanover, though he must have done some works for the court musicales, as he certainly did during a second stay. Some of his numerous chamber compositions may well fall into this period; such works, however, are very difficult to date because they were usually re-worked years later. Perhaps the most important result of this stay lay in the friendships and acquaintances made among the electoral family and some of the electoral musicians, all of whom figure prominently in his subsequent career in England.

Georg Ludwig was a dull and unambitious country squire, but he in-herited his father's pleasure in wine, women, and song. While Ernst Au-gustus maintained a box in five Venetian opera houses and, as we have seen, built a magnificent theatre of his own in Hanover (to which his sub-jects gladly contributed in order to keep him at home), the son liked opera only when it did not cost him money, and therefore disbanded the fine company, though plays, especially French comedies, continued to be performed in the theatre. The Elector liked and admired Handel, as the latter must have been aware; otherwise his conduct during a second leave from Hanover cannot be explained.

The real friend was Georg Ludwig's daughter-in-law, Caroline (1683–1737), the future Princess of Wales and Queen of England. Caro-line, the daughter of the Margrave of Brandenburg-Ansbach, was married in 1705 to the electoral prince, later George II. This was in all probability her second meeting with Handel, because Caroline spent her youth in Berlin and was at the court when Handel visited it from Halle. Growing up in a highly artistic environment in the court dominated by the brilliant Sophie Charlotte, she received a good musical training, reputedly study-ing with Pistocchi, and most certainly with Steffani after she moved to Hanover. She was a good harpsichordist, and Leibniz, with whom she was on intimate terms, praised her voice. Archduke Charles of Austria, the future Emperor, also admired her singing and liked to accompany her on the harpsichord. In fact, Charles was so taken with her that she could have become German Empress, instead of becoming, in a roundabout way, Queen of England. As Princess of Wales she was the one popular member of the new dynasty, mediating between the Hanoverians and the English. Her popularity and her loyalty to her unstable husband, the Prince of Wales, eventually embroiled her with King George I. Of about the same age as Handel, she was devoted to him, and he reciprocated her feelings, treasuring her friendship and memorializing her death in one of his finest compositions, the magnificent *Funeral Ode.*

One might conclude that Handel missed the opportunities for opera in Hanover and moved to London, as the young Mozart left Salzburg for Vienna; but then why was a magnificent opportunity to become associated with a fine opera house in Düsseldorf rejected?

The Elector Palatine, Johann Wilhelm, came from a branch of the Wittelsbach family that had a tradition of close relations with Italy and a fondness for Italian art and music. Indeed, his wife was a Medici, sister of our old acquaintance, Prince Gastone. The Elector, a fervent lover of music, heard glowing reports about Handel's great success in Venice, and Steffani is once more in the picture, for he must have recommended Handel to the Elector while the former was still in Venice. The peregrinating Bishop had been in the Elector's service since the dissolution of the opera company in Hanover. Steffani had come as usual on a diplomatic mission, but finding the musical situation ripe for positive intervention, soon took charge and brought the Düsseldorf opera to that peak of excellence that seems always to have crowned his efforts. Under Johann Wilhelm's rule some of the most notable musicians resided in or visited Düsseldorf; Corelli dedicated his last work, Opus VI, the great set of Concerti Grossi, to the Elector Palatine. The theatre, built in 1659, was modern, the troupe excellent, and the Elector's largesse considerable. Düsseldorf therefore offered everything that Handel missed in Hanover; moreover, he could have remained in Germany rather than try his fortune in a strange land where opera was just beginning to take root, and where the language was totally foreign to him. Yet he firmly declined the appointment. In truth he never considered either Hanover or Düsseldorf at all.

A forceful argument may be advanced by those who have observed that at no time in his life did Handel show any interest in a fixed position; an inveterate free-lancer, he was by constitution fiercely independent. There is undoubtedly some validity in this point, but once more the trip to London was the result of his own decision made while still in Italy, and adhered to with his usual tenacity. This decision has been discussed in the previous chapter, and although the ultimate reasons that prompted it must necessarily remain speculative, the circumstances require further examination.

In accepting the post of court conductor in Hanover, Handel made the unusual stipulation that leaves of absence of considerable duration should be an essential part of the contract. All appearances point to the fact that a journey to England was planned even before the offer from

Prince Ernst was accepted. Perhaps the prudent businessman merely wanted a safe berth in case the London expedition proved a failure. There can be no question that the Düsseldorf offer also was known before the acceptance of the Hanover call, and many biographers take it for granted that so was a definite invitation to England, though agreement here is not unanimous. Mainwaring, however, is quite explicit on all these points.

[Handel] expressed his apprehensions [to Baron Kielmansegg] that the favour intended him would hardly be consistent either with the promise he had actually made to visit the court of the Elector Palatine, or with the resolution he had long taken to pass over into England. . . . Upon this objection . . . [he had obtained] leave to be absent for a twelve-month or more, if he chose it; and to go whithersoever he pleased.

Mainwaring further believed that Handel was invited to England by the Earl of Manchester, whom we met in Venice as British Ambassador. Possibly, but there are no documents to support the assumption. Charles Montagu, Earl of Manchester, was a cultivated soldier-diplomat, who occupied several important posts before becoming attached in 1714 to the household of King George I, the king subsequently creating him first Duke of Manchester. He was fond of music, appreciated Handel, and we find his name among the original subscribers to the Royal Academy of Music (1719); he seems to have been one of the moving spirits of the institution, and its deputy governor.

Flower says: "No call had come to Handel from England, no invitation from high quarters." In contradiction, Rolland maintains that "Handel asked and obtained leave to go to England, from whence proposals had been made to him." However, none of the biographers comes forward with documentary proof. Manchester may have voiced the desire of those who wanted to establish Italian opera—the nobility on their grand tours were impressed with the social and artistic role of opera—and felt that a likely leader, a "winner," must be secured who would produce such works on the spot. Handel's success in Venice pointed clearly to the likelihood of a brilliant career, an estimate that was shared by the maestros in London, judging from their hostility to the newcomer. (Of course, the smartest of the lot soon elected to join the conqueror rather than to oppose him.) Another possible source for the "invitation" may be sought in the Wyche family. We have seen that John Wyche, the English diplomatic representative in Hamburg, was much interested in music and appreciative of Handel's talents. Son of a rather celebrated father, our diplo-

mat does not rate an entry in the *Dictionary of National Biography* beyond a bare identification as his father's son, but he was connected with
many in the world of the great and in the world of arts and letters. It is
clear that if we postulate that Handel moved in this circle he would also
be familiar with these people. And he must have gathered a certain
amount of knowledge about England elsewhere in Hamburg, a city where
English influence was considerable. There was also the indefatigable
champion of English thought, Mattheson, Handel's bosom friend and
mentor in Hamburg, who must have transmitted at least some of his
ardent Anglophile sentiments to his junior companion. So, all of this may
have contributed to Handel's departure for England, but the strongest
beckoning was from his own past—the "great search" continued.

On his way to what was to become his home, Handel stopped in
Halle to visit his family. His mother lived quietly with Handel's kindly
aunt, Anna, unable to understand why her son, a solid German middle-
class artisan, must roam the world. His younger sister, Johanna Christi-
ana, had died the year before, while the other, Dorothea Sophia, had married Dr. Michael Michaelsen, a civil servant of some standing, thereby
stepping into a higher social stratum. And of course, as Mainwaring
points out, his revered "old Master Zackaw was by no means forgot" by
the now famous pupil. The visit was very short and was followed by an
even shorter stop in Düsseldorf, where Handel stayed merely long enough
to collect a present from the Elector Palatine. The man of the world
bowed out of a flattering offer gracefully in person, and "the Elector Palatine was much pleased with the punctual performance of his promise [of
a visit] but much disappointed to find that he was engaged elsewhere."
With his gift, "a fine set of wrought plate," says Mainwaring, and his
usual hoard of scores, he once more took to the road, arriving in London
sometime in October or November 1710.[1]

[2]

BRITAIN'S CAPITAL is not usually regarded as a colorful city; it
has neither the crisp sea breeze of Hamburg nor the azure of Naples, yet
Turner and later Whistler painted the banks of the Thames, shrouded in
fog, seeing not the dull mist but the many shades of color that filtered
through its curtain. In 1710 London was a great metropolis, the hub of an

---

[1] This was the second set of tableware Handel received and one wonders what
a travelling bachelor could have done with such a cumbersome collection of household goods.

empire, almost entirely rebuilt after the Great Fire of 1666, and distinguished by many stately public edifices and aristocratic mansions, a number of them designed by Sir Christopher Wren, as well as handsome and capacious middle-class houses. This was not the entire picture, however, for it must be admitted that London was, so to speak, picturesquely clothed in silk and satin, covering almost incredible squalor, misery, and crime. But between the aristocracy, grown rich and dissolute from the wealth of the colonies, and the many living in abject poverty, there was the large stratum of the bourgeoisie, industrious, religious, and moral.

At the opening of the 18th century censorship had been abolished in England, and there were a dozen or more political newspapers, the *Daily Courant* being the first daily to appear in Europe. By the time of Handel's arrival these publications served not merely for the dissemination of news; they printed serious writings on law, economics, social and political questions, and literary problems. One could read contributions by William Temple, North, Davenant, Locke, Steele, Addison, Defoe, Swift, and many others. The *Spectator* was just coming into its own in 1711, and though it did not last long, it established a tone that was to remain a characteristic aspect of intellectual life in Britain. Since the creation of the Habeas Corpus Act and the Bill of Rights the middle classes had gained constantly, their position improving with the skills acquired in parliamentary battles. They were conscious of their power and guarded it jealously. The aristocracy still played a leading role, but the bourgeoisie was rapidly gaining under the new mass psyche, which gave birth to the ideas and principles of rational business and the amassing of wealth, resulting in the gradual secularization of the middle classes. It was this spirit that made England a parliamentary state with free institutions alongside a Europe ruled by absolutism, and it was this spirit of political freedom that brought with it the triumph of individualism. Germany still largely followed the world of the Middle Ages, a world divided into little units, the distinctions being made on the basis of occupation; the individual was only a molecule in his occupation's entity. In England these units gradually became more comprehensive, the principal unit, to which the individual owed direct allegiance, becoming the national state.

Any newly arrived stranger would be in danger of foundering in the "omnivorous ocean" of London life, especially if he came, as did Handel, from an environment and society having quite different traditions. Unable to speak the language, Handel could not immediately feel the distinctive atmosphere of this great city. At first he failed to make contact with the middle-class urban intelligentsia, thereby missing what was undoubtedly the most novel aspect of English life to a German: the position of the artist. The artist's situation was ambiguous in this new society, and in reality the middle-class artist led a double life. While he was still a purveyor of music to the aristocracy, he had become a factor in the furthering of the intellectual aspirations of the bourgeoisie. This role the English artist, especially the musician, had to fulfill under difficult conditions, for he was subjected to crushing competition imposed upon him by the very freedom that a modern capitalist society assured.

England achieved a political and commercial hegemony that was as world-wide as was Italy's artistic conquest. Her national forces were occupied to such a degree with the building of an empire, a modern state, and the ruling of the seas, that her artistic life declined. Her tremendous musical heritage was still strong enough to supply the needs of society, but it no longer had the power to uphold a high level of productivity. England gradually became a market place for foreign talent, and her developing business and industry provided a living—often lucrative—for visiting foreign celebrities, some of whom, like Handel, settled down to become British subjects. No other nation until the advent of the modern United States could offer such opportunities to foreign artists. Though Handel must have watched this scene unfolding before him, his customary systematic study had to wait until he had the necessary leisure; his immediate aim was to strike a blow with opera.

Basic differences will arise in a composer's creative style according to whether he is really part of his social surroundings, taking part in its battles, or merely observes what is taking place around him. These differences play a part in selecting creative processes, and the very experience that calls forth the work may require a particular structure. Whether a creative artist is active in his society or is an observer is not always dependent on his psychological make-up; it is often determined by circumstances. More than one contemplatively inclined composer has been carried away by the intensity of contemporary events, becoming involved in them. Verdi is a good example, and so would Handel become within a short time. But for the moment he was exclusively interested in obtaining a foothold in England with his opera, and this he did at his very first attempt. The triumph of *Rinaldo*, his first opera composed for London, rivalled his success in Venice. How he managed to find his way to the right persons and to obtain their backing is still largely a matter of conjecture, but in the light of his known character these conjectures appear quite plausible.

[3]

WHEN HANDEL burst upon the London scene there was already a respectable repertory of Italian opera, even though the genre had been introduced in England only in the previous half decade. "At this time Operas were a sort of new acquaintance, but began to be established in the affections of the Nobility," says Mainwaring. Opposition was not wanting, yet Steele's and Addison's murderous satire notwithstanding, by the time Handel arrived opera was not only accepted, at least by the higher strata of society; it had already assumed its future pre-eminence as an instrument of state entertainment and diplomacy.[2] A trio of rather interesting if dissimilar musical entrepreneurs was responsible for the first attempts at transplanting Italian opera onto English soil.

The first of these, Nicola Haym (1679–1729), was born of German parents in Italy, where he must have received a sound musical and humanistic education. He was a composer, cellist, adapter and arranger, librettist, man of letters, and archaeologist, an expert on numismatics and on rare books. On all these subjects he wrote and published elaborate monographs. Settling in England in 1702, Haym eventually joined forces with Charles Dieupart and Thomas Clayton, the other members of the trio, and had a hand in all productions at the Drury Lane Theatre until Handel's arrival. The great success of *Rinaldo* at the Haymarket hurt their undertaking, and at first Haym joined the detractors who protested the "new style" of Handel's opera; but shrewdly evaluating the Saxon's talents and probable future, instead of sulking and opposing him like Pepusch and others, he soon formed an association with him that lasted, on and off, for some fifteen years. Haym was responsible for the librettos of some of Handel's greatest operas, among them *Radamisto, Giulio Cesare, Tamerlano,* and *Rodelinda.* He also wrote librettos for Ariosti and Bononcini. Hawkins considered him a great composer, though one wonders why the composer, whom the bemused historian ranked above Alessandro Scarlatti, should remain so obstinately obscured by the librettist. Incidentally, Haym himself planned the writing of a large history of music.

Charles Dieupart (d. c. 1740), a French composer-harpsichordist-

[2] Upon the coronation of George I, in 1714, Sir Cyril Wyche, the British Resident in Hamburg, Handel's erstwhile pupil, reported to the Secretary of State that besides dining and wining the diplomatic corps, fifty strong, he entertained them by taking them to the opera, the work having been expressly commissioned for the occasion. This, as Beekman Cannon tells us, was a serenata by the legation secretary, Mattheson.

violinist, was known from about 1700 in London as an excellent and most versatile performer, among the first great interpreters of Corelli. When Handel practically annihilated the Drury Lane corporation with his initial try at opera in England, Dieupart, a very able musician but no entrepreneur at heart, soon gave up opera and returned to his safe teaching and concertizing activity. He was a composer of international repute, one of the best clavecin masters next to the great Couperin. His works must have been well known because Sebastian Bach himself liked them sufficiently to copy and study them closely, even borrowing here and there.[3]

Thomas Clayton, the third partner (of uncertain dates), was an Englishman and member of the King's band from 1692 to 1702, after which he went to Italy to perfect himself in composition. Having been impressed, like all the others, by Italian opera, he joined forces with Haym and Dieupart to see whether they could not profitably acclimatize this exciting form of the lyric theatre in England.

Their first production, in 1705, was *Arsinoe, Queen of Cyprus*, which they called "an opera after the Italian manner: All sung," Clayton supplying the bulk of the music. The critics derided *Arsinoe*, but the public liked the novelty well enough to support thirty-six performances in less than two years. There is a long-standing mystification about Clayton's true role in the venture: everyone says that he merely used airs collected in Italy, but no one has as yet been able to disprove his authorship by positive identification of the allegedly borrowed airs. It does not make any difference, because the music does not amount to much.

After this promising start, Clayton associated himself with a "Person of Quality," Joseph Addison, whose libretto served as vehicle for the second opera, *Rosamond,* performed March 15, 1707.[4] This time the reward was a resounding failure which finished Clayton as an opera composer and Addison as a librettist, turning the eminent man of letters into a bitter enemy of opera. The Drury Lane enterprise had reaped its greatest success with Antonio Maria Bononcini's *Camilla* on April 10, 1706; the work was done in an English version, the music arranged, but apparently not substantially altered, by Haym. It was the most successful Italian opera presented in England in the 18th century—but of course it was sung in

---

[3] An unsubstantiated legend has it that Bach's study of Dieupart was the reason for calling the set of suites in which he pays this oblique homage to Dieupart, "English Suites."

[4] All dates follow the "Old Style," or Julian, calendar in use in England before the adoption in 1752 of the "New Style," that is, the Gregorian calendar. This procedure seemed to us preferable to either the double listing of dates or the summary elimination of the eleven-day differential.

English, though later some arias were presented in the original Italian. One notices at this stage of opera in London a similarity to the Hamburg opera at the time of Handel's stay in that city: the public preferred performances in their native tongue and it was only gradually that Italian supplanted the vernacular.

Pepusch's *Thomyris, Queen of Scythia* (April 12, 1707) can hardly be said to be a composition by that veteran German. It was a pasticcio consisting of airs by half a dozen famous Italian composers; Pepusch only arranged and fitted them together and wrote the perfunctory recitatives. With some songs in English and others in Italian, it was also very successful. After another such medley, the Drury Lane company proceeded to a far more ambitious work on December 25, 1708. *Pyrrhus and Demetrius,* an English version of Alessandro Scarlatti's *Pirro e Demetrio* (Naples, 1694), again sung partly in English, partly in Italian, was arranged by Haym. How faithful Haym remained to the original—this is one of Scarlatti's fine earlier operas—is an open question; the presence of some numbers from Scarlatti's *Rosaura* indicates at least some "arranging," but the opera was highly successful, and it served for the début of the great Italian castrato, Nicolo Grimaldi, better known as Nicolini.

In the meantime the Haymarket Theatre also caught the operatic fervor. The management, under Aaron Hill, assisted by still another continental musical speculator, Johann Jakob Heidegger, meant to capture the business from Drury Lane. Aaron Hill (1685–1750) was of the same age as Handel, and like him was precocious, much-travelled, good-natured, ready to help, and enamored of the theatre. The difference was in their talents, for Hill was a minor literary figure and a hapless businessman. Pope's harsh picture of Hill in *The Dunciad* does injustice to the man, who may have had some foolish business escapades but was not without merit. Hill, first at Drury Lane and from 1710 at the Haymarket, had many literary friends and undoubtedly was of great help to Handel, especially at the beginning of his career in England.

Heidegger was a German whose family hailed from Bavaria, eventually settling in Switzerland, whence Johann Jakob came to London in 1707. The purpose of the trip was a nebulous business affair that did not materialize, for we find him enlisting in the Queen's Life Guards as an ordinary private. In the life of an adventurer this seemingly desperate measure simply indicates a lack of funds, providing a needed pause to reconnoiter the possibilities. Evidently Heidegger did his scouting so well that soon after shedding his uniform the one-time private was moving in high society circles, where he was well liked, for he was a man of good manners and a certain charm which compensated for features famous for their ugliness all over London. They called him the "Swiss Count." Presently, Heidegger entered the world of the theatre, partly because it offered good business opportunities, partly because he was a man with excellent theatrical instincts and, as his subsequent acts proved, of considerable knowledge of the theatre. Where he acquired this knowledge remains a mystery. Like Hill and Haym, Heidegger was instantly to realize Handel's true stature and to lose no time in associating himself with the coming monarch of opera in London.

After producing a pasticcio or two, on January 21, 1710 the Haymarket Theatre proceeded to bona fide opera: *Almahide*. Burney positively states that this work by (presumably) Giovanni Bononcini "was the first opera performed in England *wholly in Italian* and by Italian singers." Nevertheless, *Almahide* still had intermezzi in English.[5] Mancini's *Hydaspes* (*L'Idaspe fedele*) and Giovanni Bononcini's *Etearco* followed —it can be seen that Handel would be pitting his talents not against a Clayton but against some world-famous masters of Italian opera. Now the Haymarket Theatre became the principal opera house in London, and for some time the only one.

How did the newcomer, unable to speak English, find his way into this milieu and almost instantly persuade the Haymarket administration to mount his opera? First he must have made contact with the resident German musicians. Among these there was John Ernest (Johann Ernst) Galliard, a few years Handel's senior, originally from Celle, who received his early education in the excellent French court orchestra there. He was a good oboe player, and also a well-trained composer, who had studied with Steffani in Hanover. Galliard (evidently a distortion of Gaillard) settled in London in the first decade of the century. One of the founders of the Academy of Ancient Music, he was a versatile musician and apparently a cultivated one, for he translated Tosi's celebrated *Opinioni de' cantori* into excellent English. In 1712 his *Calypso and Telemachus*, the last all-English opera for decades, closed the season of opera. Later at the performances of Handel's *Teseo* he played the oboe in the orchestra. Handel and Galliard stayed on friendly terms, as can be seen from their mutual subscriptions to their respective works.

[5] Alfred Loewenberg, in his *Annals of Opera,* proves that *The Loves of Ergasto* (*Gli amori piacevole d'Ergasto*) by a certain Greber, presented at the inauguration of the Haymarket Theatre five years before, was the first opera sung wholly in Italian. This obscure composer is identifiable as Johann Jakob Greber (d. c. 1723), a German who went to London with the singer Margherita L'Épine, Pepusch's future wife. *Ergasto,* which had two performances in London, was later produced in Vienna.

Then there was Andrew (Andreas) Roner, well regarded in London and very friendly to Handel. We know next to nothing about him, but he was at home in both musical and literary circles and acted as an intermediary between Handel and the poet Hughes. Both Roner and Galliard had direct connections with the theatre. There were also some professional acquaintances from Italy and Hanover, singers who preceded Handel to London. Boschi, the prodigious basso, and his wife Francesca, both of whom sang in *Agrippina* in Venice, surely delighted Handel, whose Italian was fluent; they furthered his career at the opera house, where they were employed and had a considerable reputation. It is a matter of record that Francesca introduced Handel to an unaware English public scarcely a month after his arrival, by inserting an aria from *Agrippina* into Scarlatti's *Pyrrhus* on December 6, 1710. Valeriano Pellegrini, an old acquaintance from the original cast of *Agrippina,* sang in Handel's *Pastor fido* in 1712, but it is not known whether he was already in London in 1710. Still another professional friend about whom we have information was Elisabetta Pilotti, a court singer from Hanover who, since she was billed as being in the service of the Elector of Hanover, was also presumably on a leave of absence. She sang in *Rinaldo,* and one surmises that the two Hanoverians vacationing in London must have exchanged ideas about the art of staying away from their employer.

These intermediaries undoubtedly were of substantial assistance to Handel, but it is the manager who decides whether or not to mount a new opera. Aaron Hill was a shrewd man, and biographers credit him with helping Handel to orient himself in the strange country, but then Handel always found his way to a good organ and to a likely theatre wherever he was, and the Haymarket Theatre was a likely place. It had a manager whose adventurous spirit and willingness to gamble were akin to Handel's, and they found each other congenial right from the beginning. And of course Handel was no risk; he was known in professional circles and among the high-born amateurs; a record-breaking success in Venice such as *Agrippina* achieved becomes known wherever opera is cultivated. When, in the preface to *Rinaldo,* Hill referred to "Mr. Hendel" as a composer "whom the world justly celebrates," he was not merely writing the customary encomium. It seems likely that it was Handel who sought out the manager rather than vice versa, and the latter, seeing that the German was champing at the bit, scented an excellent opportunity for himself and his theatre. A librettist was quickly produced, and about three months after his arrival Handel affixed his name to the annals of English music, from which it was never to be erased.

[4]

THE LIBRETTIST, Giacomo Rossi, is universally condemned as a miserable poetaster, but perhaps he deserves some grace—at least for *Rinaldo*, his first libretto for Handel. In his preface the poor man, who had never faced anything like the imperious Saxon, defends himself for the unseemly haste forced upon him in the preparation of the libretto. "Mr. Hendel, the *Orpheus* of our century, while composing the music, scarcely gave me the time to write, and to my great wonder I saw an entire opera put to music by that surprising genius, with the greatest degree of perfection, in only two weeks." Indeed, Handel could outpace any librettist, but of course in addition he also had a fistful of numbers culled from earlier works ready for transplantation, about which Rossi was ignorant. The impatient Handel could not even wait for the verses; on at least one occasion when he was ahead of the librettist, as in Almirena's aria, "Bel piacere," he simply used words from *Agrippina*.

Rinaldo was first performed on February 24, 1711. The cast consisted of the Boschi couple, Isabella Girardeau, Nicolini, Valentini, Elisabetta Pilotti, and Giuseppe Cassani—a star assembly. The success was tremendous, and rightfully so, because in spite of the hasty composition and the many borrowings, *Rinaldo* is one of Handel's great operas; from the overture, a spacious piece, the music flows beguilingly. Such airs as "Lascia ch'io pianga" and "Cara sposa" belong among his finest melodies, and, while this level is not maintained throughout, the emotional and descriptive passages are managed with a fine evocative economy. The orchestra is also treated with a skill never before heard in London; notably the imaginative use of the brass was an innovation. The staging was lavish, though perhaps a little too realistic, for in Almirena's "Bird Song," "Augelletti che canto," a flock of live sparrows was let loose, creating a sensation and providing the satirists with a theme they utilized with relish. In his very first opera in England Handel set a precedent that he was to follow throughout his career in opera and oratorio: he assigned himself virtuoso tasks on the conductor's harpsichord (in the oratorios he was to play organ concertos between the acts). These improvisations were highly appreciated by the public, constituting a drawing card that almost equalled the works themselves. In the score of *Rinaldo* these passages are only indicated, not written out, Handel obviously improvising as only he could, but Walsh, the publisher, aware of the admiration for Handel's virtuoso improvisations, found someone who remembered them—after a fashion

—and in his 1711 edition of the keyboard score of the airs from *Rinaldo* had them reconstructed by William Babell. Chrysander printed two of Babell's more ambitious Handel fantasias in Vols. 48 and 58 of the Händelgesellschaft edition. Babell, who died young in 1723, was a pupil of Pepusch, a good organist and violinist, but especially skilful at the harpsichord. He must have been the Liszt of the age, for he was celebrated for his opera transcriptions and fantasies not only in England but all over the Continent.

Rinaldo ran for fifteen nights to full houses. It was frequently revived in subsequent seasons, invariably with great success, and London still talked about it in the thirties. Dublin heard the opera on March 11, 1711, the first Italian opera to be sung there; Hamburg in 1715, in German; Milan in 1718. Perhaps the best sign of Handel's victory and "arrival" was the appearance on the scene of a publisher willing to invest in the printing of *Rinaldo*'s music. John Walsh, proprietor of "The Golden Harp and Hoboy," was the dominant figure in English music publishing. A hardbitten, ruthless, piratical businessman for whom no one seems to have a good word to say, he was an able publisher, probably the ablest of the whole age. Walsh lost no time when the first opera reached England, and no sooner had Clayton's *Arsinoe* started the genre on its English career than he was on the spot, publishing all the "songs" of the Drury Lane productions. A *succès fou* such as *Rinaldo* naturally attracted him, and in no time there appeared the first printed volume of Handel's music: *Song's in the Opera of Rinaldo Compos'd by Mr Hendel*. Walsh's mean business practices did not appeal to Handel, and the publisher had to wait a long time before again doing business with this composer. Needless to say, in those days the composer's refusal was not an absolute deterrent to publication; piracy was always possible and John Walsh was an expert at it.

Overnight *Rinaldo* had established the unquestioned supremacy of the Haymarket Theatre over the Drury Lane Theatre, or over any other form of public music-making. It was quite clear that this newcomer was not only a celebrity but a power and hence a menace to those who had vested interests in the musical theatre; they therefore lost no time in trying to whittle him down. In addition, when Handel arrived in London there was an articulate opposition to Italian opera in certain literary circles. This is a natural phenomenon in any country where the spoken theatre is highly developed; the same literary opposition greeted opera in France.[6] The first salvo, from Addison's pen, appeared in the *Spectator* on

[6] The leading spirit in France among those disputing the *raison d'être* of opera was Saint-Évremond, one of the earliest critical essayists. A political refugee for

March 6, 1711, followed ten days later by one from Richard Steele. Both these critics nurtured grievances; Addison was embittered by the failure of his *Rosamond,* while Steele was angry with the intruder who lured away audiences from his concerts in York Buildings. At the end of Steele's piece one detects the first signs of some of the arguments opponents of opera were to become fond of marshalling against the genre. "I shall only observe one thing further, in which both Dramas agree; which is, that by the Squeak of their Voices the Heroes of each are Eunuchs; and as the Wit in both Pieces are equal, I must prefer the Performance of Mr. *Powell,* because it is in our Language." It must be conceded, though, that Addison did appreciate good singing and praised Nicolini highly. Even if Handel was apprised of the critics' views, it is not likely that he was disturbed—he had seen worse before. The critical literature in Germany in the age of the Enlightenment was rough, sarcastic, and offensive, with no holds barred, and Handel had got a good taste of it from the violent and coarse pamphleteering that had raged about the libretto of his *Almira* in Hamburg.

Rinaldo's success was both artistic and social. It made Handel's name known, and now he began to move out of the precincts of the theatre, seeking the intellectual and social circles that were his natural habitat. Very little is known about his life during 1711, though it is plain that Hill, Heidegger, Roner, and others gradually introduced him to a number of persons who were instrumental in facilitating his gradual rise in social level. He may already, as Flower suggests, have made his way to the Piccadilly residence of the Dowager Countess Juliana and her son Richard, Earl of Burlington, but Hawkins and others do not say anything about Burlington House before the second London visit. All biographers agree that throughout 1711 Handel was a frequent visitor at the musical gatherings organized by Thomas Britton, the musical "Small Coal Man." As a characteristic middle-class phenomenon Britton can be imagined only in

over forty years in London, where he died in 1703, he lies buried in Westminster Abbey. Saint-Évremond was in particular favor with Charles II and his two immediate successors, and was well acquainted with Dryden and other literary figures even though he never learned even the rudiments of the English language. That too-little-appreciated lover of wine, women, and Montaigne had considerable influence on operatic criticism. I have seen a number of his sentences—even whole paragraphs—quoted (without acknowledgment) in the works of Italian critics such as Algarotti, but some are present in Addison's writings; John Lockman still quotes him in 1740, as does Henry Home in his *Elements of Criticism* (1762). Though not complete, a three-volume edition of his works, entitled *Oeuvres meslées,* was published in London in 1705, and translated in 1714. Perhaps someone will address himself to the not unrewarding task of tracing the French satirist's influence on his English colleagues.

England. By trade a coal merchant, in his spare time a bibliophile and good gamba player, he fitted out the low-ceilinged room over his coal bins as a "concert hall," with a harpsichord and a small organ. The finest musicians of the day, leading literary men, earls and duchesses climbed the rickety stairs to the uncomfortable loft to hear and make music. Handel's presence at these meetings seems inevitable; he knew many of the persons who were regular participants at Britton's concerts, yet, strangely, even Otto Erich Deutsch was unable to run down a single positive document attesting such attendance. It would seem perverse to question the accuracy of the assumption that he did attend, and it was undoubtedly at Britton's that he met Pepusch and others, among them John Hughes.

Hughes (1677–1720) was a not inconsiderable literary figure; his tragedy, *The Siege of Damascus,* became a long-time favorite in the theatre later in the century. Author of librettos for Pepusch and Galliard, Hughes was an advocate of opera, in particular of English opera, and as a frequent contributor to the *Spectator,* the *Tatler,* and the *Guardian,* he was well known in the literary world (Johnson wrote his biography), very likely introducing Handel to a number of influential persons. But as we know from past experience, all that Handel needed for making his way was a harpsichord or an organ and an audience, and since there was a harpsichord in many well-appointed London drawing rooms, this was a simple matter. We shall see him ranging far and wide in these drawing rooms upon his return from Hanover in 1712, but it is noteworthy that apparently even during his first visit he managed to gain entry to the court itself. Mainwaring states that before returning to Hanover, Handel paid his respects to Queen Anne, who gave him "large presents and [intimated] her desire of seeing him again." He adds that Handel promised to return "the moment he could obtain permission from the Prince," and although there is no other evidence that the visit to the court, the Queen's invitation, and Handel's promise actually took place, subsequent events seem to lend credibility to the story.

At the end of the opera season the exciting London days came abruptly to an end. Handel had to remember that he was not a free agent, but a musician under contract to the Elector of Hanover; he must have left soon after the June 2 closing of the Haymarket Theatre, because his presence in Düsseldorf is recorded on June 17. Apparently Handel was somewhat uneasy about his reception at the hands of Georg Ludwig, perhaps expecting a reprimand, though he had not exceeded the "twelvemonth" permitted by the contract. At any rate, he conveyed his misgivings to his great admirer, the Elector Palatine, who graciously gave him a letter to his "cousin," Hanover, begging leniency. Handel, being a thorough man, and knowing who was most influential at the Hanover court, wheedled a second letter from Johann Wilhelm to the Dowager Electress Sophie. The Hanoverian court conductor resumed his post without any untoward unpleasantness.

[5]

AFTER THE animated days in London, Hanover must have seemed a very dull place to Handel, but it is obvious that he considered his return a tactical move within a much larger strategy—he did not have the slightest intention of staying in Hanover. The position of dependency that he had resumed in Hanover grated, however well treated he was or how light his duties. Almost immediately upon his arrival he wrote to Andrew Roner requesting him to procure from John Hughes some of his *charmantes poésies en Anglois* (Handel preferred to correspond in French), significantly adding that he is studying English and has "made some progress in that language." The intention is clear; we see the moves of a man who knows very well what he is about. Anyway, there was little for him to do; there was no opera in Hanover, the theatre was given over to a French troupe of comedians, the handful of musicians in residence needed only chamber music, which Handel undoubtedly supplied, and he also composed vocal chamber music for the ladies of the court. The uneventful stay was interrupted by a visit to Halle, where Handel attended the baptism of his niece, Johanna Friderike Michaelsen, who became his favorite and the principal beneficiary of his estate. It was again a short visit, and upon his return he applied for another substantial leave of absence, which was granted. In October 1712, almost two years to the day after his first setting foot on English soil, Handel was back in London—this time forever.

The only significant compositions that positively originated during the brief second residence in Hanover are a remarkable set of chamber duets. In composing them Handel followed a tradition established by Steffani, whose superb duets were created for use at court musicales, probably sung by ladies-in-waiting, though occasioned by the interest of Princess Caroline. The twelve duets, numbered 3–14 in the Händelgesellschaft edition, composed on texts by Ortensio Mauro, Hanoverian court poet, are quite different from such other vocal chamber music as, for instance, the solo cantata with basso continuo. They are indeed chamber music, the vocal version of the trio sonata: the upper parts are imitative, deploying their counterpoint in the manner of the church sonata, the bass is active but nonthematic, and the harmonic support is furnished by the harpsichord. Since they are prevailingly contrapuntal—some of them vocal fugues with accompaniment—the da capo aria form is infrequently used, and of course recitative and ritornel are absent. Although Steffani's influence was inescapable (some of the duets, like "Che vai pensando," actually borrow material from Steffani), Handel was by this time not only vastly experienced, but so sure of his own way that he was able to assert his personality even in a genre for which Steffani was the universally admired model of all musicians—Italian, German, and even French. Perhaps the most interesting aspect of this independence is reflected in Handel's conduct of the linear element. He can be "strict" with his imitation, even though at times the imitative voice enters at the astonishingly wide distance of twelve or sixteen measures, but just as often this part writing is unpredictable and full of surprises; linear logic is never permitted to harm melodic euphony. The writing is very careful, the curves of the various melodic figures are consciously balanced to create a deliberately sculptured pattern in which controlled tensions are resolved. The number of movements within the duets ranges from one to four, the majority of them having either two or three. Only No. 9 is a true one-movement piece. The sections are always tonally related, often forming a harmonic da capo.

These duets (as well as the others Handel composed earlier in Italy and later in London) deserve considerable attention because Handel found them a particularly congenial medium. Even in his four-part fugues he often operates with two sets of "duets," since he was very fond of pairing his vocal parts. We shall see, furthermore, that some of the chamber duets formed the basis for four-part choral pieces; in so enlarging them Handel revealed a musical imagination of the most felicitous sort. Finally, these exquisite works represent a facet of Handel's musical personality that is often overlooked. The duets differ markedly from his better-known choral works and arias. There is no accent on drama, no brilliant contrast, none of the pomp, solemnity, and grandeur usually associated with the composer of anthems and oratorios. This is music for the drawing room, transparent, intricate, and elegant; chamber music for the elite.

We are fortunate in possessing most of the great duets—in a fine edition by Johannes Brahms. His realization of the figured bass is a model of taste, scholarship, and of course musicianship. Even where the editor is carried away and actually adds a complementary obbligato part, this is done with such thorough understanding of the style that one is tempted to believe that Handel himself would have realized the figured bass in like manner.

Other works attributed to the second Hanover stay are German songs, harpsichord music, chamber music, and an oboe concerto or two, but none of them can be confidently assigned to this period—or even to any period before about 1720; our only witness, Chrysander, is not reliable. The German songs are really arias on German texts. Max Seiffert in the *Liliencron Festschrift* proved that three of the set of twelve must be assigned to the Halle period, not unconvincingly arguing that their text had the same author who in early youth wrote a funeral poem for his late father. The remaining nine songs could not have been composed in Hanover, as Chrysander claimed, for among Handel's few compositions on German texts they are by far the most mature. Seiffert offers the convincing suggestion that they were composed in Hamburg in 1729, when Handel stopped there on his way back from Italy, where he had gone to recruit singers for his opera company. Handel for some reason took the opportunity to pay homage to the local literary celebrity, Brockes. Though the pietistic moralizing of the eminent Hamburg senator must have been difficult to swallow, Handel, in his usual way when he did not care for a text, concentrated on the texture. These arias have concertante parts for a solo instrument in addition to the voice, and are thus a sort of duet; but the keyboard part can also be elaborate, so that the listener's attention is engaged by the ensemble as a whole. Portions from these fine songs appear in *Acis and Galatea* and in *Messiah*.

VI

R ETURNED TO LONDON, HANDEL IMMEDIATELY ACTED TO
realize two ambitions that were important to him: to take the helm of
London's operatic life, and to secure a *pied à terre* where he could live and
work in undisturbed comfort. His luck with high society held good, and we
see him in his usual role, being admired—and maintained. First he lodged
in Surrey in the home of a wealthy amateur musician, a Mr. Andrews,
about whom nothing is known. Apparently he moved to the Andrews
residence immediately upon arrival, which suggests an arrangement made
beforehand. Soon Handel found his accustomed level, when he took up his
abode in Burlington House, the Piccadilly palace of the Earl of Burlington and his mother, the Dowager Countess Juliana.

The third Earl of Burlington was an English Arcadian, the counterpart of Roman aristocrats and prelates, and in spite of his tender age—he
was only about seventeen at that time—Burlington House was already
one of the great "salons" of the early 18th century where "men of first
eminence for genius" gathered. One must allow a role in this to the Dowager Countess; nevertheless, that Burlington was a known and respected

patron of music is clear from the dedications addressed to him. Both Hei-degger and Haym emphasized in their dedications of librettos that his "Lordship has always shown generous concern for the promoting of The-atrical Musick." Moreover, Burlington House and its master pass even Sir Newman Flower's closest scrutiny; he could not find any trace of "loose living" that would have made the place and the company unfit for the future composer of *Messiah*. Handel lived there not unlike Corelli in the Ottoboni palace, in his own apartment; he was altogether independent and left undisturbed even when the Earl was away on extended trips. Just when the move to Burlington House was made is not recorded. It seems to this writer, however, that there must be some connection between Handel's first settings of ceremonial music to English texts and his resi-dence at Burlington House.

The *Ode for Queen Anne's Birthday* was surely composed there, which would date his residence from 1713, while his opera *Teseo* was still running. Indeed, now begins the acclimatization, the conversion of the German into the Briton, a process that will be discussed in detail below.

We also see him at his favorite pastime, playing the organ. Hawkins relates that the fine new instrument in St. Paul's Cathedral had a particu-lar attraction for Handel. The organist, Richard Brind, and especially the latter's youthful pupil, Maurice Greene (1695–1755), who later achieved a distinguished career, were full of admiration for Handel's playing, and for a while Greene and Handel became fast friends. Handel played after evening services, staying long after the delighted congregation as well as the bellows boys had left. Greene obligingly trod the bellows, and Burney reports that on several occasions they had themselves locked in for the night. St. Paul's Churchyard was the center, the stock exchange of music in London, for both professionals and amateurs. A number of taverns, cafés, and music shops were located nearby, and it was here that persons interested in music (and in the fine services conducted in the Cathedral since 1712) gathered for business and pleasure. Hawkins speaks of Han-del's custom of frequenting Queen Anne's Tavern in the Churchyard, which was the gathering place of the choristers, and thus becoming better acquainted with these able English musicians. The tavern was equipped with a harpsichord, and there was much music-making as well as gossip-ing. All these new territories conquered and acquaintances made were to have far-reaching consequences in Handel's future career, but for the moment the foremost matter of interest to him was opera.

Handel's return to London found the operatic situation considera-bly changed. Most of the great Italian singers were gone; so was Aaron

Hill, who had yielded the management of the Haymarket Theatre to a shady operator by the name of Owen Swiney, though Haym was still connected with the enterprise. As if affected by this general deterioration, Handel permitted himself a *faux pas:* a somewhat careless and hasty new opera, *Il Pastor fido.* The manuscript states "finished Oct 24," which has been interpreted to mean that the opera was largely if not entirely composed in Hanover, which is possible but not probable. The unusually haphazard—for Handel—nature of *The Faithful Shepherd* indicates rather that it was a *pièce d'occasion,* the response to a chance for a quick production, which actually took place on November 22. Handel probably threw it together in a few days. The opera did not pass muster, to the great delight of Addison and Steele, who saw a chance to eliminate this troublesome intruder and turned their fire on the German with renewed vigor. After six performances the opera was given up as a failure. Opinions were almost unanimously low, and the production must have been of the "shoestring" variety, for one critic scornfully remarked that "ye Habits were old.—ye Opera Short." *Pastor fido* was a pasticcio, very Italian, and reverted to a somewhat older style, but the work is not so poor as first reactions would indicate, and in the second version of 1734 proved to be a very appealing piece. To be sure, Rossi's libretto is silly, it fearfully mangles Guarini's original, and the librettist failed to provide any dramatic interest, but *Pastor fido* is in Handel's pastoral, bucolic vein, which always means delightful music, charming dances, and delicate orchestral writing. The original version also had an extended and very impressive overture, which may have been a concerto composed for Hanover.

Handel learned his lesson, and on his next work, which he undertook immediately, he spent three weeks—probably three times what he had needed for *Pastor fido.* As his enemies were to learn, a failure acted on him as a stimulant that usually led to a superior sequel. The new opera was finished on December 19, 1712, and first performed on January 10, 1713. Giving up the hapless Rossi, Handel had turned to Haym, who, like da Ponte with Mozart, studied his composer, carefully estimating his gifts and leanings. The libretto he prepared, *Teseo,* was a "heroick" piece designed to bring out the best in Handel. Haym's sagacity was rewarded with a resounding success. This time "ye Habits" were "new & richer" than in the earlier work, and Handel regained his commanding position on the London operatic scene. Unfortunately, he almost immediately met with a painful financial setback. Swiney decamped with the box-office receipts of the first two full houses of *Teseo* without paying anyone— librettist, composer, stage designer, or singers. The situation was catastrophic, but Heidegger persuaded all parties to continue. *Teseo* was maintained in the repertory, and, while the participants' loss was irreplaceable, everyone shared in the proceeds of the remaining performances. Although a fine work, *Teseo* is inevitably made colorless by the total absence of natural men's voices: none of the six roles is lower than alto.

[2]

IN THE MEANTIME, Handel took the first steps in the direction that was to make him England's national composer. While the announcements of *Pastor fido* and *Teseo* still proclaimed him as being in the service of his Electoral Highness of Hanover, two events actually made him into an English court musician, if not *de jure* certainly *de facto,* for with his *Utrecht Te Deum* and *Jubilate* Handel virtually assumed Purcell's legacy as purveyor of ceremonial music for state occasions at St. Paul's. The Te Deum was performed at the Cathedral on July 7, 1713. Its success was instantaneous and the work became a "repertory piece" rivalling Purcell's hallowed "St. Cecilia" Te Deum, the presentation of which for such festivities had been considered *de rigueur* since 1694. Thereafter the *Utrecht Te Deum* alternated with Purcell's for three decades until Handel's own *Dettingen Te Deum* replaced both. Yet neither the success nor the timely appearance of the Te Deum was a simple matter of offering such a work for performance; the whole affair had to be carefully planned.

As a German, Handel could not have had the slightest reason for celebrating a peace treaty disadvantageous to his fatherland, nor, indeed, were such works composed in the 18th century out of personal impulse. Handel was perfectly aware of the custom, fortified by statutory restrictions, of not allowing foreigners to compose ceremonial music for state occasions. Characteristically, he set about circumventing the prohibition. That Handel quietly but deliberately planned his moves is attested by all known facts. The coming peace treaty was "in the air" for some time; it was finally concluded on March 31 and proclaimed in London on May 5. Handel, privy to the political developments, composed the Te Deum in January and put it aside to be used at the right moment; only the *Jubilate* was composed at or about the time of the official celebration. The *Jubilate* did not take long to write because Handel used his fine *Laudate pueri* of Roman memory. We have no document to show that the Te Deum was ordered or commissioned, but no work presented at such an official celebration, with Parliament attending, could have been sung without the Queen's consent, and in this particular case only royal command could have set aside the legal restrictions.

While Mainwaring's statement that Handel had already been introduced to the Queen during his first visit to England remains conjectural,
there can be no doubt that by his second visit he was well known and
respected by Queen Anne. The circumstances are easy to reconstruct.
Handel's hostess, the Dowager Countess of Burlington, was one of the
Ladies of the Bedchamber, and thus had easy access to the sovereign's
ear, but there was another, even more influential intimate of the Queen
who, as an habitué of Burlington House, took a great liking to Handel. Dr.
John Arbuthnot, the Royal Physician in Ordinary and a close friend of the
literary great of the day, was described by Samuel Johnson as "the most
universal genius, being an excellent physician, a man of deep learning,
and a man of humours." Since the Queen was almost constantly ailing,
Dr. Arbuthnot was frequently at her side, and could scarcely have failed
to communicate to her his admiration for Handel. So it came about that
in January 1713 Handel composed an *Ode for the Birthday of Queen
Anne,* performed at court February 6 by an all-English cast from the
Chapel Royal. In so doing, Handel trespassed on the domain long and
honorably occupied by John Eccles, who furnished such odes annually ex
officio. Handel's tactics worked to perfection, for the delighted Queen undoubtedly commanded him to write the Te Deum.

The *Utrecht Te Deum* was modelled on Purcell's "St. Cecilia" Te
Deum, then the outstanding ceremonial piece, well known and much admired; nevertheless, to say that Handel's work is altogether indebted to
Purcell is vastly to oversimplify the case. It was of course natural that
Handel should have studied Purcell's Te Deum, and have followed its
general outline, but Chrysander and others are surely mistaken when they
claim intimate correspondences. Handel espied the specifically English
tone but not Purcell's essential and very personal qualities. This English
tone was new to him—and congenial—but it took some time to penetrate
underneath the pomp and panoply; that insight into Purcell's delicately
refined art came much later.

Indisposed, Queen Anne did not attend the July 7 festivities at St.
Paul's, but heard the Te Deum later at St. James's Palace and as a consequence settled on the composer an annual pension of £200. This created
a curious and awkward situation. The law was explicit on such matters:
"No foreigner shall receive a grant from the Crown, or hold office, civil or
military," yet Handel received a grant and was virtually assuming the position of a court composer. Mainwaring, closest among biographers to the
events, takes pains to remark on this fact, which must have been apparent

to observers: "This act of the royal bounty was the more extraordinary as [Handel's] foreign engagements were not unknown." Given the Queen's distaste for her heirs presumptive, it is quite likely that aside from her genuine appreciation of Handel we are also dealing with a subtle insult to the Hanoverians that could not have been lost either on Sophie or on Georg Ludwig.

If the situation created by these events was awkward, it was as nothing compared to what was to follow in the aftermath of Queen Anne's death on August 1, 1714. None of Anne's numerous offspring having survived, the Crown, by virtue of the Act of Succession, descended to the Protestant House of Hanover, the Catholic line of Anne's half-brother James Stuart having been excluded. Anne disliked the Hanoverians, especially the clever and intelligent Dowager Electress Sophie, while for Georg Ludwig she had nothing but contempt. After many entreaties by her ministers to demonstrate her attachment to the Protestant succession and thus silence the rumors of Jacobite sympathies, she made a gesture towards her heirs by creating Georg Ludwig's son Duke of Cambridge in 1706, but she remained adamant about permitting the Elector himself to visit England. Although she never disavowed James as a brother, she considered him a "popish pretender" and never wavered in her constitutional duty as head of the Church, and for this reason supported the Succession Act. Anne was of very mediocre intelligence and small ability, not greatly interested in culture though she liked music and played the harpsichord with some fluency. But the Queen had homely virtues; she was devoted to the Established Church (disliking both Catholics and Nonconformists), maintained strict standards of moral conduct at court, was generous and kind, "never loved to do anything that looked like an affected contraint" —hence her sobriquet: "Good Queen Anne." Her reign, which saw the union of Scotland and England, was one of the most brilliant periods in English history.

Upon the death in 1714 of the Duke of Gloucester, last of the English line of Protestant princes, Ernst Augustus's widow, Sophie, the youngest daughter of Elizabeth, the daughter of James I of England, was the next Protestant heir to Anne. Since the Act of Settlement of 1701 secured the succession to her and her descendants, the Dowager Electress suddenly found herself in line for the throne of England. Considering her age, she was under no illusions as to her probable assumption of the crown, but to his discomfort Georg Ludwig, no man to shoulder responsibilities, realized that he might well have to give up his comfortable and carefree existence to rule as king in a strange country. The death within three months of both Sophie and Anne opened the way for Georg Ludwig (1660–1727), a German prince who did not speak English and had no understanding of anything English. On the very day of the Queen's death, Georg Ludwig of Hanover was proclaimed King George I of England; he landed on English soil with an impressively large German retinue on September 18, 1714, arrived in London on the 20th, and was crowned a month later in Westminster Abbey.

All the King saw in his new position was an opportunity to improve the situation of Hanover, of his family, and of his retainers, among whom there was always a covey of mistresses. The personal union between England and Hanover remained until 1837. George's only desire was to leave these unfathomable islanders as often and for as long as possible, to spend his time in the familiar surroundings of Hanover. The King's frequent visits to Hanover (like George II's, too) caused a good deal of resentment in England. George simply let the Whigs run the country while he attended to his own pleasures, chief among which, next to his two favorite mistresses, was music. The two ladies in question, Baroness von der Schulenburg and Baroness von Kielmansegg (the latter, an illegitimate daughter of Ernst Augustus, was therefore George's illegitimate half-sister as well as his paramour) were prodigiously bulky and unattractive, long past the flower of youth, which at that court was not a necessary qualification for a royal mistress. When in 1722 Sir Robert Walpole, the first true Prime Minister, took over the government from such minor Whigs as Stanhope, Townshend, and Sunderland (derisively called "the German ministry"), George left matters entirely in the great statesman's hands. Since he could not speak English, he did not attend the cabinet meetings, and his frequent absences from the country permitted his ministers to have their own way. The power of the King, as exercised by William and by Anne, all but passed from his hands. Yet it is a mistake to regard George I as totally uninterested in his new domain. He took a direct hand in external affairs, and on the whole the country benefitted from his rule.

The arrival of George caused a delicate dilemma for Handel. His employer, whom he had certainly slighted by ignoring the terms of his contract, now became the sovereign of the land where he resided. His biographers seem to be embarrassed by the situation. Mainwaring gently remarks that "the promise he had given [to the Elector] had somehow slipt out of his memory," ruefully adding that Handel "did not dare to shew himself at court." For once, even Chrysander exhibits some annoyance with his hero, for his patriotic and sentimental nature did not approve of such an affront to a German prince who in good faith permitted his servant a leave of absence of a stipulated length. But while the biographers are embarrassed, Handel surely was not, nor does the Elector-King seem to have shown anger or disappointment. In the first place, there was no sign from Hanover that the Elector resented Handel's absence or ordered his return. Rolland may not be far from the truth when he says that it behooved the aspirant to the throne of England to be on good terms with Queen Anne, and since the Queen showed interest in Handel, Georg Ludwig could not very well order him home without displeasing her. In the second place, it is inconceivable that Handel, who moved in circles where he could observe political developments at first hand, was not aware of the imminence of the succession; the Queen was visibly in bad health. Moreover, he had a lively sense of legal and contractual niceties as well as a very good idea of George's turn of mind and of the measures he was likely to take.

As it happened, after his succession George showed no interest in calling his truant Hanoverian court conductor on the carpet, and Handel attended to his own affairs, sure of his case, simply waiting for a move from his sovereign. Whether the King was angry or not is hard to tell; the story about the "reconciliation" on the occasion of the famous barge party on the Thames when the *Water Music* was played is fictitious, and so, probably, are all the others.[1] On the other hand, the King could not have missed the fact that his sometime music master was a famous man in London; since he had as little taste for the English as Queen Anne had had for the Hanoverians, and since he remained a German to the end of his life, he probably concluded that he might just as well hold on to this German musician. The chances are that both were sensible enough to rationalize the situation, and that there was no falling out between them, only a situation that was best solved by ignoring it and refraining from meeting in public until the dust had settled. At any rate, it is positively known that the King attended, albeit incognito, the revival of *Rinaldo* in 1714, as well as the new opera *Amadigi* a few months later and eventually confirmed Anne's pension, adding another £200 to it. Handel received still another £200 from the Princess of Wales, Caroline, as music master to her daughters, and together these payments amply compensated for the loss of the Hanoverian emoluments. It will be noted that upon George's first visit to Hanover as King of England (July, 1716), his "es-

---

[1] Hawkins tells a reconciliation story according to which the great Italian violinist Geminiani, when invited to play his sonatas for the King, insisted that the accompaniment be entrusted to Handel, who thereby gained readmittance to the court.

tranged" erstwhile court conductor accompanied him, closely following
the King's schedule. This raises the question whether the personal union
of Britain and Hanover extended to the King's Master of Musick and the
Elector's *Hofkapellmeister*. There is nothing to indicate such an arrangement. Handel had no stated duties, was not in attendance, and soon went
his own way and the King his. They remained on good terms, for the
King really liked music, especially opera.

[3]

THE OPERA SEASON commenced soon after the dynastic change
took place, and Handel was of course fully engaged in its vagaries. *Rinaldo* was revived on December 30, 1714, eleven other performances following; both the King and the Prince of Wales attended several evenings.
For the moment this took care of the situation in the public theatre, and
in the meantime Handel wrote an opera for the private stage of his host,
the Earl of Burlington. *Silla* was a slight work, designed for amateur performers, but it contained a good deal of fine music, which of course was
not wasted but was immediately transferred to his next opera, composed
for the Haymarket Theatre.

Amadis of Gaul, or *Amadigi di Gaula,* the third opera fashioned on
the successful pattern of *Rinaldo*—plot and characters as well as tone are
all similar—saw its first night on May 25, 1715. It is not clear who the
librettist was; to judge from the similarity, the old partnership of Rossi
and Haym had a hand in it, but it was Heidegger who assumed responsibility for the book, and in all probability his was the lion's share. Handel
rose to the occasion and the success was tremendous, for the libretto was
good and the music spirited. The production, too, was lavish; "All the
Coaths and Scenes were entirely new," and the stage and its machinery,
with its wings, shutters, pulleys, candles, lanterns, torches, and other
paraphernalia rivalled those of the most elaborate European Baroque
theatres. The bubbling fountain, bathed in colored lights, was the talk of
the town, but what mattered above all was that Nicolini was back, and
the popular Anastasia Robinson had her second role. Now Handel rode
on the crest of the wave; *Rinaldo* and *Amadigi* alternated, constituting
the core of the repertory; the composer was a celebrity, the opposition
was silenced, and the King himself attended several performances. Handel's financial situation must also have improved materially, for we see
him invest £500 in the hottest stock of the day, the South Sea Company,
collecting—for the time being—a nice dividend from this hazardous ven-

ture. As can be seen, it did not take long for the provincial German musician to become a "capitalist," a free middle-class citizen running his own business.

The opera season, interrupted by "ye Rebellion of ye Tories and Papists," ended late. It was a troublesome year, indeed. The Jacobites, among them prominent Tories, though losing a powerful backer in the death of Louis XIV, had not given up hope of installing "James III" on the throne; a rebellion started in Scotland in September and threw London into a fright, but it was put down within a month. The Old Pretender himself landed in England at the end of December, but by February 1716 he too was routed and everyone breathed freely. George, not quite *au courant*, was bored and could not even wait for the end of the opera season. He left on July 7 for Hanover to get away from high politics and the tedium of the monarchy; he longed for the carefree life of the country squire he was at heart. Handel is supposed to have followed the King within a day or two, but it seems that this was more likely a week. On July 12 Handel's youthful idol, Attilio Ariosti, newly arrived in London, played the viola d'amore between the acts of *Amadigi;* it is difficult to imagine that Handel would have been absent on the occasion.

[4]

Back in Hanover, Handel was as much out of his element as the King was genially in his. Having no duties at court, he took the opportunity to travel. The family seat came first, but we know of no particular event connected with the visit; Handel's mother was by now an aged lady, and her famous son a rather distant figure to the household in Halle. His old master Zachow was dead, and Handel found his widow in straitened circumstances. With his innate generosity—which kept pace with his improved means—he eased the financial distress of the poor woman. Nor was this the only time he paid homage to the memory of his teacher by helping the widow; Frau Zachow was the recipient of several remittances from London. Another trip took Handel to Ansbach. This might very well have been a diplomatic errand on behalf of Caroline, Princess of Wales, whose family resided there—at least no other purpose is apparent. While in Ansbach, Handel was reunited with an old companion from Halle University days, Johann Christoph Schmidt. Schmidt, a wool merchant, but a lover of music, was eking out a less than modest living, once more touching the generous heart of Handel. The old friend was persuaded to come to London where Handel promised to look after him, and he arrived there with his small son soon after Handel's return in the fall. The rest of Schmidt's family was left behind while he reconnoitered; then rejoined him when Schmidt saw that Handel was capable of providing a safe existence for him. We shall meet in each John Christopher Smith, senior and junior, as devoted a combination of friend, servant, secretary, major domo, and business manager as any man has ever had.

Handel also made a mysterious visit to Hamburg, which interests us particularly because the one major work composed during this period, a Passion, is supposed to have been written there. The circumstances of this trip to Hamburg are a riddle. True, Handel had been famous there for years, his operas were in the repertory—only a year before, *Rinaldo* had been presented with great acclaim—and he had several acquaintances residing there, but not a single document exists to show that the visit to Hamburg, mentioned by everyone, actually took place. Mattheson, writing in his *Ehrenpforte* (1740), explicitly states that he *corresponded* with Handel while the latter was in Hanover in 1716, but says nothing about a visit to Hamburg, which could not have escaped him. Nor was the Passion performed at that time, and it is a matter of record that Handel sent a fair score of the work to Hamburg *after* his return to London, the performance taking place in 1719. Nor have we any sign of Handel having visited Germany between the two documented trips of 1716 and 1719. We do lose track of him for about a year and a half after July 1717, but the chances are that he stayed at Cannons.

But why then did he compose a German Passion? He had few ties left with Germany besides his family, the Hanover post, kept up for the sake of appearance only, was obviously abandoned after his trip in 1716, and we have seen that except for the early *St. John Passion* he consistently refused to compose liturgical or "sacred" music for the Lutheran service. Though Handel was always ready to accept a challenge, it is a little tenuous to surmise that he composed Brockes's Passion because it was famous and had been set to music by the leading musicians of the day; but in the absence of other explanations, and given Brockes's eminence, perhaps there is something to this motive. At any rate, while Handel made use of the good parts of his Passion in different contexts— among them *Giulio Cesare!*—he never made any attempt to present it in its original form, which of course was unsuitable for England anyway. It is only fair, though, to add that the Passion itself is indebted to the *Utrecht Te Deum* and other works.

Barthold Heinrich Brockes, a member of the Hamburg Senate and one of the famous literary men of the age, was no stranger to Handel. He

studied at the University of Halle in 1700–02, where they must have met,
especially since Brockes was fond of music. In his autobiography, the
Senator speaks of concerts held "several times a week" in his little flat, the
thrifty bourgeois adding that "it did not cost much." Handel, who though
scarcely more than an adolescent was by that time a well regarded local
musician, could not have missed these soirées. Brockes was a widely travelled, highly educated, learned man, a diplomat, lawyer, man of letters,
and legislator. But he had a strong streak of Pietism in him, aggravated
by a very offensive religious hypocrisy, and his was a most unpleasant,
grasping, and devious character. On the other hand, having come in contact with English thought in Hamburg (he translated Pope and Thomson),
he was also touched by the Enlightenment. Some biographers writing in
English dismiss him as a nonentity and call his Passion text "preposterous,"
but that is historiography based on ignorance of German history and
literature. We must look at the state of the German Passion-oratorio at
the time of Handel's composition of his second so-called *St. John Passion*.

By 1716 Pietism and the early Enlightenment had made considerable
inroads into the concept of the Passion; the serene and severe biblical
tone of a Schütz was long since forgotten. The influence of Christian Friedrich Hunold (1681–1721), also known by his pseudonym, Menantes, and
Erdmann Neumeister (1671–1756) changed the German cantata and Passion considerably. Both of these literary men insisted on infusing poetry
and a theatrical element into concerted sacred music, but while Hunold's
Passion text, *The Bleeding and Dying Jesus,* obviously reflected Pietist
leanings, Neumeister, the orthodox Lutheran clergyman, preferred to
embrace warmly all the new dramatic means coming from Italy. It was he
who established the free, "madrigalian" style of cantata construction,
based on recitative and da capo aria, and it is well known that Bach composed music for several of his "reform cantata" texts.

Brockes's place in this picture is somewhere between Hunold and
Neumeister, and his great influence can be explained by his attempt to
animate the biblical story with dramatic elements of a more personal nature. To be sure, he diluted the strength of the Gospel with his sentimental and wordy poetry, but in the absence of an abler poet he naturally
became the most admired model for those who wanted to move with the
spirit of the times. It was Brockes who restored to the Passion the biblical
element that distinguishes it from the purely operatic. In particular it was
to his credit to have restored the role of the Evangelist as narrator of
scriptural paraphrases (a figure that provided Bach with a most important vehicle for dramatic expression), and it was he who gave the chief

characters a recognizable dramatic personality by attempting to probe into their thoughts. By assigning definite places for the chorales, and by clearly dividing the action into self-contained scenes and numbers, he greatly facilitated the composer's task. Even though full of verbose allegories, tasteless pictorialism, and overelaborated word play, Brockes's passion libretto was so highly regarded that it was translated into French and Swedish, besides being circulated all over Germany. Incidentally, it was this "preposterous" litterateur who introduced into German letters the contemplation of nature, and even though today his poetry strikes us as a sort of watery pantheism, its significance cannot be belittled, because Brockes's influence on the future of German poetry was considerable.

As we look at Handel's score, or rather at its copies, because to complete the mystery the original manuscript is lost, the first thing we notice is the title. The work is always referred to as the *Brockes,* or *St. John Passion,* but the original full title is *The Story of Jesus, suffering and dying for the sins of the world, presented according to the narrative as related by the four* [!] *Evangelists.* Clearly, this is the Pietist approach, and that was anathema to Handel. Accordingly, the music is only too often the routine work of an experienced craftsman, and surprisingly enough, this quality extends even to some of the choruses, of which there are few. But where dramatic interest is present Handel is roused.[2] Several numbers are very remarkable. We may single out Christ's noble aria, "My Father," while among the many numbers given to the Daughter of Zion the one where she pleads with Pilate is superb, and so is Mary's song, "O God! My Son is dragged away and torn from me." The entire scene from the prayer in Gethsemane to the denial of Peter is major Handel, and a particularly magnificent scene is the ensemble "Awake!" which later was used in *Esther.*

Yet, as in his first setting of the Passion, we once more find Handel strangely embarrassed by the tradition, style, and tone into which he was born and for which he was originally trained. He could not compose such quasi-liturgical, churchly music, nor could he really unfold his natural dramatic talents because of this inhibiting tradition. Chrysander is far out of line when he calls this work a giant step toward the final peaks of German Protestant church music. True, Handel used chorales and used them well, but he also used the old rage and revenge arias from the Hamburg opera and all manner of other incongruous elements that do not accord with the more elevated moments. It is possible that he was thinking along

[2] It is interesting to note that there are some superscriptions in the score that amount to stage directions.

the lines of Keiser's setting of the same text, a similarly uneven work. Up to the Last Supper scene Keiser often rises to engaging serenity, but thereafter he descends to a tone that is sheer low comic opera. These extravaganzas mix strangely with the "liturgical" elements. When Handel composed the anthem *The King shall rejoice* he was not inhibited; he wrote for the entire populace, from King to commoner, music that was so simple—yet grand—that everyone could understand and enjoy it. But when he wrote a German Passion he was not at ease. As to the chorales, it is interesting to compare the Passion with the great *Funeral Ode for Queen Caroline*. In both works Handel uses the chorale, and in both of them he plainly intends to conjure up a churchly tone and attitude, but while in 1737 he warmly and pensively reminisced of his youth, which was also the beloved Queen's youth, in 1716–17 he tried to conform to a tradition. As a "sacred" composition, the Passion pales before the tremendous opening number, "The Ways of Zion mourn," of the *Ode*.

Comparisons with Bach and his Passions are also futile. Everyone hastens to remark that Bach copied out Handel's *Brockes Passion*, as he assuredly did—more precisely, half of it; the rest was done by Anna Magdalena. More than that, he studied the score rather carefully, for Handel was a famous man and Bach was a student of famous men's works. Nevertheless, it is difficult to imagine what he saw in Handel's Passion beyond the fact that here was the most widely admired Passion text (a text he himself was to use in part), which had been set to music by Keiser, Mattheson, Telemann, and now by the famous dramatic composer, Handel. Bach did actually make use of his study of Handel's score in his *St. Matthew Passion*, but the two composers were worlds apart; what was a casual effort for the great London dramatic composer was the life work of his erstwhile compatriot in Leipzig.[3] Winton Dean sums up the difference most convincingly when he says that, unlike Keiser and Handel in their Passions, Bach "created an artistic and spiritual unity. It was left to Handel to achieve this later in his English oratorios."

[5]

HANDEL PRECEDED THE King by a few weeks in his return to London, arriving towards the end of the year. The opera season opened on

[3] That Handel the dramatist had a certain fascination for Bach has been pointed out by Percy Robinson in his *Handel and His Orbit*. He calls attention to Bach's strange fondness for Handel's first and rather primitive operatic essay, *Almira*, which haunted Bach all the way to the *St. Matthew Passion*.

December 8, and by January 5, 1717, *Rinaldo* was back in the repertory, followed in a month by *Amadigi,* both of them successfully running until the closing of the theatre on June 29, 1717. Now a curious silence descends around Handel. After the Haymarket Theatre closed in June, Italian opera seemed to be extinct in London; three years were to elapse before the Haymarket resumed operatic production. Then it was again Handel who gave it new life, and an altogether new epoch of opera, both for Handel and for London, was to begin. There had already been a hiatus between the *Utrecht Te Deum* (July 1713) and *Amadigi* (May 1715), but at least we know what Handel was doing during those years. The year 1718 and much of 1719 are barren of notices and records. There was no opera at the King's Theatre, only dances, masquerades, concerts, and comedies. Heidegger would have preferred opera, but being a rational businessman made the most of "Subscription Masquerades." Handel's silence can be explained, for he undoubtedly watched and studied the scene—as he had in Italy—to acquire its feeling, taste, and tone. As Rolland so aptly and graphically says, "Handel was waiting without hurry to be saturated by the English atmosphere."

After the close of the season Handel left Burlington House and is supposed to have taken up residence at Cannons, remaining there for two years. James Brydges, Earl of Carnarvon, later Duke of Chandos (1673–1744), had built himself a magnificent residence at Cannons. As paymaster general of the English forces in Queen Anne's reign, and hence throughout the turbulent War of the Spanish Succession, he had made an immense fortune which caused him to be generally regarded as an embezzler on a royal scale, but he manipulated his malfeasance with such skill that the Royal Commission, appointed to investigate the many angry accusations, could not pin him down on any point. Since Brydges was "tolerably moral" as far as women were concerned, even Sir Newman Flower speaks rather gently about this rogue. The Duke was vain and ostentatious; Swift called him "a great complier with every court," and Pope also scorned him, though more guardedly, but all of them sat at his table, a bountiful table at which the Burlington group was often augmented by other literary, artistic, and political lights.

Whether the Duke really cared for music is not known, but no sumptuous princely household could be called complete without a permanent musical establishment; therefore Chandos founded for himself a ducal chapel with all the necessary appurtenances. It was placed under John Christopher Pepusch, who occupied the post of director of music at Cannons from 1712 to 1732. It is therefore clear that Handel was not engaged in the capacity of music director or master, as is usually stated, but as resident composer—that is, in the largely independent role he always preferred. Mainwaring was aware of the rather unusual situation, because he remarked that "having such a Composer, was an instance of *real* magnificence, such as no private person or subject; nay, such as no prince or potentate on earth could at that time pretend to." This accords well with the character of the Duke, who was given to such exhibitionism as to take some mustered-out veterans of Marlborough's army and dress them up as Swiss palace guards. To him Handel was another emblem of power and possession: he had the most talked-about musician of the day attached to his court.[4]

Handel's actual residence at Cannons is somewhat uncertain though quite plausible. The Duke spent a great deal of his time in his London house, and since Handel surely did not interrupt the music lessons given to the royal princesses (he may have had other noble pupils also), he could not have stayed away from London for the entire two years he is supposed to have spent at Cannons. He did move out of Burlington House and undoubtedly entered the "services" of Chandos, but probably lived most of the time, working and studying quietly, at the Duke's house in Albemarle Street in London, with seasonal visits to Cannons, or whenever the Duke had his famous parties.[5] The Duke was not the kind of man who listened to anthems in private. The numerous stories connected with Cannons, such as the romantic tale about *The Harmonious Blacksmith*, or the organ "on" which Handel composed, now suitably marked with a tablet, are all canards invented long after the composer's death. It is clear that by the spring of 1719, if not earlier, Handel reverted to his independent status and may very well have gone back to Burlington House; he remained on cordial terms with the Earl, whom he liked and esteemed.

As resident composer, Handel turned out music carefully tailored to suit the forces available at Cannons: anthems, a masque, and a pastoral.

[4] Upon the death of the Duke, who fell into serious financial straits after the bursting of the South Sea Bubble, the little Versailles at Cannons came to an ignominious end: it was sold for the marble, stone, and iron it contained.

[5] If we examine the career of the titular music director at Cannons it becomes clear that even he was not tied to the place and had plenty of time to pursue his many other activities in London. While administering the Duke of Chandos's musical establishment, Pepusch was concurrently director of the Lincoln's Inn Fields Theatre, for which he composed and arranged many masques and pasticcios, attended with close interest to the business of his favorite antiquarian institution, the Academy of Ancient Music, spent a great deal of time on research for which the London and Oxford libraries were indispensable (he was England's first musicologist), and had numerous pupils.

This was *English* music, and in order to be able to deal with this momentous change in the life and work of the composer of Italian opera, we
shall once more deviate from strict chronology, making a fresh start
after pursuing Handel's other activities that round out this period.

During the late summer of 1718 Handel's only remaining sister,
Dorothea Michaelsen, died in Halle. Handel was very fond of her and
deeply grieved by her premature death—she was barely thirty. Characteristically, he thanked his brother-in-law Michaelsen for his kindness to
Dorothea. Later, in November, another death, that of Kielmansegg, though
not, of course, one that touched Handel so personally, nevertheless deprived him of a person always friendly to him. Both the King and Handel
lost "a great Encourager of Arts and Sciences," for, while little more than
an ordinary courtier, the Baron really liked and understood music.

Aside from the Chandos works, which we shall presently discuss in
detail, Handel composed a good deal of instrumental music during 1717–
20. Of the harpsichord pieces we shall speak later, but we must return to
the much-disputed *Water Music*, because it definitely belongs to these
years and it represents a first peak in Handel's orchestral music. Gerald
Abraham and others have conclusively proved that the final version of the
Water Music unites two suites written at different times. One, the larger
of the two, was composed for the positively documented barge party in
1717, the other probably a couple of years earlier, in which case it could
have been the music performed at the water-borne "reconciliation" party
—if that episode actually took place. At any rate, today we usually perform
the two suites as one set. This lengthy suite is fragrant, expansive, and
unflaggingly inspired outdoor music, written for a large orchestra manipulated with sovereign skill. The silly "modernizations" and arrangements we
usually hear instead of the original distort these qualities; when this music
is heard out of doors Sir Hamilton Harty is not needed to realize its
full charm. The variety is very great because concerto and dance suite are
combined in a colorful blend; the continuity is well planned, for while the
music grows in grandeur, this rising amplitude is suitably interrupted by
the most delicate, meditative—indeed, *galant*—pieces. A close inspection
of the score will reveal that the writing very carefully avoids "holes" in
the harmony—there was not likely to be a continuo atop a barge.

The six concertos, Opus 3, also known as the "Oboe Concertos," were
probably composed at Cannons. They are really concerti grossi with winds,
and while less remarkable than the later set, Opus 6, they offer very fine
and very enjoyable music. Handel borrowed and reworked several instrumental pieces from the *Brockes Passion*, from *Amadigi*, and from his earlier

chamber music, but most of the rest is not only new but attractively fresh material. In his orchestral music Handel remained faithful to the Corelli-Albinoni-Locatelli lineage, and none of his concertos should be compared with the altogether differently oriented *Brandenburg Concertos* of Bach. This is popular music in the best sense of the word; simple, fluent, clearly articulated, and gloriously euphonious. The contrast between tutti and concertino is usually very sharp, the tuttis being robust, while the solos are gentle and at times even unaccompanied. Though one of the greatest contrapuntists of the time, Handel was not interested in intricate part writing but in plasticity of representation and expression, in melodiousness, and in differentiated orchestral sound. The concertos do contain some very fine fugues, but they would cause despair to any theorist attempting to analyze them according to the "rules," for Handel is always ready to drop linear logic for the sake of a nice turn or rich sound.

[6]

ON FEBRUARY 20, 1719, Handel wrote to his brother-in-law Michaelsen apologizing for his inability to undertake a family visit, which he apparently had promised upon learning of the death of his sister. The affairs unavoidably keeping him in London are of such importance, says Handel, that his entire future may depend on them. The business he referred to was the intense preparation for what amounted to a genuine permanent opera society to be called the Royal Academy of Music. This was not really a court opera on the Continental model, though the King was the chief patron and contributed a thousand pounds yearly; rather it was like the Metropolitan Opera House in New York before the World Wars and before income taxes: a plaything for the nobility. As a matter of fact, the similarity between the two institutions is striking. Neither showed the least interest in native art, each wanted the best singers procurable from abroad, and the directors of each felt that since they were footing the bill they had the right to dictate the policies and run the show. If the reader will substitute "Mr. Gatti-Casazza" for "Mr. Hendel, Master of Musick," all he has to do is to modernize the spelling of the "Instructions" issued to the latter on May 24, 1719 by the governor of the Royal Academy of Music, the Duke of Newcastle, to obtain a document that could have been issued in New York in 1910. Similarly, "Caruso" could replace the name of the great castrato in this passage: "Mr. Hendel shall engage Senezino as soon as possible to Serve the said Company and for as many years as may be."

The plan was to issue joint stock for £10,000, each of the share-holders subscribing £200, but the issue was heavily oversubscribed by an illustrious group of some seventy of Britain's great families. The Duke of Chandos and the Earl of Burlington, Handel's particular patrons, pledged five shares each. The comparison with New York's Metropolitan Opera ends, however, when we examine the business structure of the enterprise; these English aristocrats were indeed modern businessmen. The Royal Academy of Music was a corporation whose stocks were listed on the Stock Exchange, and a number of shareholders joined the enterprise for investment and speculation, not for music. This was a time of "easy money" and hazardous gambling, as exemplified by the South Sea Company. Indeed, the satirists never failed to quote the Academy's stocks in the same breath with the South Sea Company's to emphasize its precarious stability.[6]

The Governors' instructions directed Handel to proceed abroad—undoubtedly referring to Italy—to recruit a company of singers. Handel must have responded immediately, for within two weeks we can trace him to Düsseldorf, to the court of the Elector Palatine. But he was no longer quite the same welcome visitor, the admired maestro of former years; his relationship with the Elector, as indeed with all ruling heads who maintained opera houses, must have undergone a certain change. Handel had become a threat, an impresario who with plenty of money behind him could entice singers to leave their employ and go to London. But Handel was careful and urbane; everyone treated him with respect if with a little nervousness. There was of course a visit to Halle. The big old house had become a sad, depopulated place occupied by two old and helpless women, Mother Händel and Aunt Anna. Handel always dropped into his home town whenever he was on the Continent, but by that time his world had become incomprehensible to them.[7]

The most important stop on this trip was Dresden, a business call to see which of the fine singers at the splendid Dresden opera he could

---

[6] *The Theatre*, edited by Sir Richard Steele, made a practice of "quoting" the Royal Academy of Music stocks, usually distorting names and titles with sarcastic wit, though in such a manner that they remained identifiable. On March 8, 1720, the notice took this form: "At the Rehearsal on *Friday* last, Signior Nihilini Beneditti [Nicolini] rose half a Note above his Pitch formerly known. Opera stock from 83 and a half, when he began; at 90 when he ended."

[7] There is an unconfirmed story that upon hearing of Handel's arrival, Bach, then residing in Cöthen, set out for nearby Halle to meet his famous erstwhile compatriot and fellow musician, but missed him by a day. Though the only witnesses to the story are Forkel and Chrysander, it is plausible enough. The two greatest musical figures of the waning Baroque were destined never to meet.

lure away to London. Dresden was one of the most brilliant centers of music in Germany, and its opera rivalled the best in the world. During the 17th century the capital of Saxony established a remarkable tradition both for lavish *Festspiele* of all sorts, which would put to shame anything seen today, and for Italian opera. The electoral palace boasted a gigantic hall, a combination of ballroom and theatre, for the festivities, and there was a magnificent opera house (replacing an equally magnificent older building), the largest in Germany, which was to open its doors in September 1719, soon after Handel's arrival in the city. Antonio Lotti was the resident composer and conductor, and both the singers and the orchestra were of the best. It was into this magnificent operatic plenty that Handel walked with ulterior motives; he knew exactly what he wanted, and I am convinced that he knew why he should seek it in this particular spot.

Historians have wondered why Handel went so far east in Germany when his obvious destination should have been Italy. True, Senesino, his main quarry, was at that time in Dresden, but his task was to recruit a whole company, and it is difficult to see how he could have hoped to denude a wealthy, flourishing opera house of its members. This rich display of resources in Dresden hid, however, a potentially catastrophic situation: the profligate King-Elector's treasury was empty, and the extensive operatic establishment was on the verge of tottering. Handel must have had an inkling of the situation, or in any case it could not have taken him long to find out once he talked to those closely involved in Dresden. He concluded that it was not necessary to go to Italy, for even if Senesino received six times the salary of the local German music director, it clearly would not be forthcoming much longer—the Italian opera in Dresden did in fact collapse in the following year. It took more than a decade to piece it together once more, to start the second glorious chapter of its history under Hasse.

Handel arrived in Dresden probably in late June, that is, before the grand opening of the new opera house, but the singers were there, and so was his old friend of the Venetian days, Antonio Lotti. The first "situation report" was dispatched to the Earl of Burlington, one of the directors of the Royal Academy of Music, on July 15. Handel advises the Earl of his negotiations with Senesino, Matteo Berselli, and another, a singer by the name of Guicciardi; the outlook is favorable. Later, matters turned a little sour, the negotiations with Senesino falling through, though he duly arrived in London in the fall of 1720, when Dresden could no longer pay him his fee. Nor was Handel able to sign Guicciardi, but Berselli agreed to come, and he also engaged a second old acquaintance, Margherita Durastanti, his first Agrippina of a decade before, as well as another soprano, Maddalena Salvai. Since he had some very fine singers, such as Boschi, already spoken for, Handel could feel satisfied with the troupe at his disposal. Just when the engagements were concluded is difficult to verify—instructions from London were still arriving in November. Handel stayed on, attended the festivities, gave a concert at court in September (though his fee was not collected for several months; it was eventually remitted to London), and finally, towards the end of the year, began the return journey to London.

In the meantime Heidegger was made manager of the Academy, Rolli staff librettist, and Roberto Clerici master of décor and machines. The board of directors made further important decisions. Handel was named "Master of the Orchestra," i.e. music director, and Giovanni Bononcini was invited "for composing & performing in the Orchestra" (as was later Ariosti in a similar capacity). Heidegger as manager also engaged a few singers, among them Mrs. Robinson, and Senesino was finally brought into the fold through the intermediation of one of the Italian diplomats stationed in London. When Handel returned and 1720 dawned, everything was ready for a spectacular rebirth of opera in London: three of the leading composers of Italian opera in residence (Giovanni Porta was there), all of them also redoubtable conductors, a fine group of singers, a good and experienced manager, and seemingly inexhaustible funds. But before we proceed to the opening of the Royal Academy of Music, we must examine this Baroque opera, than which there is no more misunderstood and misinterpreted genre in the entire history of music.

VII

MANY OF THOSE WHO HAVE VISITED THE GREAT MU-
seums of the world would be surprised to hear that the magnificent Greek
statues, which they always see in their pristine white, were once colored
with paint. This could not have been otherwise, for ancient Hellas, no less
than its modern offspring, was bathed in sunshine under a blue sky; the
southern sun gives even the bare rocks a radiant coat of color. Cold white
is unthinkable in such surroundings; the white of Greek sculpture and
architecture, which we look upon as the embodiment of the spirit of antiquity, is the barbarous handiwork of time. Archaeologists have proved
that once the halls of the Acropolis glowed with colors as deep and dazzling as the landscape. Perhaps the Venus of Milo smiled with blue eyes,
and her now snow-white breasts and shoulders were softened by wax or oil
enamel. Now she looks at us with deathly pallor from a room in the
Louvre; living, conquering beauty bare and imprisoned. The cruelty of
time could not ruin the perfection of her figure, nor wrinkle the smoothness of her face, but in her millennial dream among the earth's debris the
moisture of the soil sucked away the life-giving colors, bleached her garment, robbed her of a measure of her charm. After many centuries, those
of the classical statues that escaped the rough blows of the barbarians
arose from their graves, and in their colorless whiteness weighed, like
ghosts, on the sculpture of the Renaissance and on that of subsequent ages.
These ages saw only the distilled forms, which they managed to resurrect
and at times rival with their own, but the pulsating life, the hypnotic sor-

cery cannot be conjured up without color. Those who have seen the purple, the red, and the blue on Augustus's statue in the Vatican will have an idea what the Romans learned from their masters.

Just so are we suffering from a misconception of Baroque opera, in which we see nothing but pure white melodies. It will take several more decades before musical archaeologists will convince the public and the musicians that these musical statues also had colors. Music being the most perishable of the arts, it did not take millennia for this old opera to lose its colors, only a couple of generations of composers, singers, and audiences, but the distance that separates us from a Scarlatti, a Bononcini, or a Handel is in effect greater than that which separates us from a Myron, a Praxiteles, or a Lysippus. Handel's operas were already completely strange to musicians and audiences at the end of the 18th century, when the composer of *Messiah* was already venerated as an English institution. In 1787 *Giulio Cesare* was revived, but the libretto states that "the original offering a great number of incongruities, both in the language and the conduct, several material alterations have been thought absolutely necessary, to give the piece a dramatic consistency, *and to suit it to the refinement of a modern audience.*" Variants of this refrain can be followed up to Sir Thomas Beecham and other notable musicians of our day. Still, is it not only fashions that change while passions remain? One would think that love and hatred, heroism and sacrifice are the same from Agamemnon to Mario Cavaradossi.

The theatre does not operate with durable materials, it must form its public night after night. The poet and the composer can address an imaginary, future public, but over the theatre the judge is Today, and there is no Court of Appeal; a theatre not understood is nonexistent. The theatre is entirely dependent on the age and on its disposition.

If the spoken theatre is perishable, its lyric counterpart is far more so; opera does not grow naturally out of "the boards"; there is something in it that is actually hostile to the stage. In fact, opera is a paradox, it cannot be justified intellectually. Drama in the theatre attempts to render life, to conjure up in a small place, in a short time, with a limited number of figures, the illusion of the whole world. It is in the nature of the spoken drama that the conflicts of its figures must be treated in a form that is opposed to stylization. It demands a certain logical construction, and necessity reigns in it with more consequence than in life itself. The construction rests on a chain of cause and effect, on a causal procedure. Opera cannot express the fullness and richness of life in the manner of the spoken theatre; its expressive possibilities are not on the same plane with reality but are stylized abbreviations of it. Therefore, completeness of content is replaced by formal completeness, the empirical by the symbolical, the expansive by the intensive. Dialectical exposition and causal reason are merely a sketchy basic frame, for the decisive element will be the constructive, formal, expressive power of music.

The constant intellectual procedure followed in the drama hampers immediate sensuous expression, an inhibition missing in opera. What the music offers in a good opera is something that comes from a region that precedes the concrete concept of drama and, strictly speaking, stands outside the world of drama. Opera does not permit men to appear in nakedly logical acts, for the music dissolves feelings and thoughts into melodies and rhythms, harmonies and counterpoints, which in themselves have no conceptual meaning. Thus in opera objective situations may very well become entirely subjective expressions. Because of its paradoxical nature opera is capable of paradoxical effects; it can express purely sensuously the most profound abstractions, and the musical drama, exerting a mass effect far more than does the spoken drama, is much more primitive as drama than the spoken theatre; it must render conflict and character in immediate symbols. If it departs from this, as in the "philosophical" operas, it immediately sacrifices its naive security, for it can convey intellectual theses only to a very limited degree.

This paradox of the merger of the concrete and the abstract that characterizes opera is present in all its components. At first glance everything in an opera is the same as in the ordinary theatre: dramatic personalities appear, act, and give the illusion of life, except that they present their lines in song. But this in itself is the chief paradox, for living, spontaneously acting persons do not normally sing, yet here music represents and conveys life and the concrete, and it is the music that is charged with the creation of the illusion of life.

In an opera, character and action can be disparate. The sketching of character in a spoken drama demands time, in opera it is almost instantaneous; the action in a play requires a certain movement, in opera action is constantly suspended; in drama plot and action can be both detailed and extensive, opera aims at comprehensive summary. Scale is different too, and while 19th-century grand opera has accustomed us to decorative monumentality, essentially opera is near and intimate.

There can be no question that in a composite art such as opera we must accept the fact (which also influences the form) that in its contemplation the energy of the individual senses is divided. The spoken theatre unites the spatial and the temporal; opera in addition unites the conceptual, the text, with the nonconceptual, music. Obviously, therefore, in this complicated symbiosis form must be achieved by certain inevitable concessions and compromises. Take an operatic duet or ensemble: it is both theme and its elaboration, material and form simultaneously, once more something that is difficult to reconcile intellectually. Such a piece is largely—and in Baroque opera almost entirely—determined by its material and not by the logic of its text. The musico-formal requirements determine its extent and progression. An aria may be superfluous and dispensable from the point of view of dramatic structure, but may have considerable relevance in terms of tonal symmetry and logic. If the text in these older operas is too short for the form dictated by musical logic, individual lines or even words will be repeated arbitrarily. Thus the aria or ensemble becomes an almost total stylization—but it can also become a concentrated symbolic expression of a man and of his entire fate. Universality rises here to such heights, mood and communication become so elevated, that they can no longer contain anything concrete and real. And this is the very power of opera, it is through this extraordinary ability of music that opera can rise far above the finite world into a mystic atmosphere.

Ever since the Romantic era the theatre has satisfied its adventurous desires by means of exact observation of the most varied relations, the most different circumstances, the most picturesque and interesting surroundings, while the early lyric theatre fulfilled its temperament in the Baroque excesses of its formal classical heritage. The latter-day opera house was unwilling to be left behind its supposed rival, the theatre; it engaged a barker who, standing at the main entrance, harangued the passers-by: "Do enter, ladies and gentlemen! What you will see here is no make-believe but life itself, life with all its shades and tones as you see it every day."

To say that an artist takes his figures from life is a truism; everyone takes everything from life, for even the boldest imagination receives its materials from life. Such statements hide from us not only the truth but also the problems to be solved. The dramatist's subjects and figures are the result of the work of centuries, in some cases of millennia. They are developed and changed but slowly, and we are closer to the truth when we say that the dramatist receives his figures not from life but from tradition. The dramatic figure is the offspring of culture, nourished by the soul of generations, from which the impress of the too capricious individual has been eliminated to make way for the type, for the universal. The great creative artist only seizes these types with greater force and effect than the ordinary talent, because genius is precisely the interpreter of the universal. The genius has a better eye with which to see truth, a more generously endowed heart to feel values, and a stronger voice to proclaim what he has seen and felt and understood.

The old individualism was naive, the new is conscious. Our modern concept rejects any conformity that it finds hobbling, but it has created an entirely new set of conformities. This again leads to a paradox, for in the new opera individual character is vastly more important than in the old; character is everything because the struggle is about it and for it, therefore character has become *the* problem of style. Unfortunately, while the dissection of "cases" can be interesting, it seldom succeeds in opera. In the old opera there were gigantic individual characters—Alexander, Julius Caesar—but they were part of a mysticism that was the direct opposite of our rationalism and which saturated the dramatic psychology as it did the composition itself. The technique, the musical representation itself, was rational, often excessively so, but character appeared within a logical musical form. What made this Baroque operatic hero a "real" man was beyond the drama: he was entirely dissolved in music; the action does not claim the entire man, and he reveals himself in his actions only to a limited extent. The situation is not unlike that in Leonardo's *Holy Family*, where the mathematical infallibility of the triangle, which is the frame of composition, is nevertheless reconciled with the mystic view of the figures without actually fully merging with them.

This mode of composition demands a broad foundation for characterization, a broadness that turns the accidental nature of the happenings in the drama into a necessity, because in the drama there are either no accidents or they are placed at the proper spot, whereas in life they often occur quite *mal à propos*. This poetic nullification of accident, the classical method, is "old-fashioned" and is no longer appreciated in our day. Our dramatists believe that mere accident ceases to be accident if its immediate reasons can be causally established. But artistic motivation gains little by this method. The crudely carpentered and barely explained accidents in the catastrophe of Romeo and Juliet do not impress at all as accidents. And so we judge Baroque librettos from an inadmissible angle. They were not bona fide dramas but literary texts that provided the composer with the opportunity for lyric effusion. They were "literary" because in general they were impeccably written if seemingly cool and often stereotyped poetry, but the librettists knew perfectly well what would happen to the words once they were clothed in music. Fundamentally these operas were not dramatic; they stressed nobility of tone and attitude, classical restraint, which is what the public liked, hence the demand for the same subjects—even the same librettos—set by different composers to see how the familiar subject would be treated by a different hand. As a matter of fact, arias were often so general in tone that they could be shifted from one opera to another when situations were at all similar.

The 19th and 20th centuries liberated the operatic stage, its form and language, from every accustomed fetter, and as the old conventions disappeared so did understanding for all opera before Gluck. Except for the Italians, opera as a genre departed from its ancient nature and began to decline. The crown passed from the stage to the orchestra pit, the aria yielded to the "endless melody," the orchestral symphonic ecstasy. Opera's territory was widened until it became almost limitless, the composers and librettists became philosophers, sociologists, psychologists, reformers—even politicians. Then came naturalism, which in turn was rejected as more recent composers found it a limiting factor. Still, a great deal of *Weltanschauung* remains attached to the lyric stage. It would never have occurred to a Baroque dramatist to say that the German spirit would be purified and renewed by the magic fire of the music drama, as Nietzsche and Wagner maintained. Perhaps the most noteworthy difference between the Baroque composer and the Romantic and post-Romantic musico-dramatist is that the latter intensifies or "dynamizes" the elements of his conflicts, while the former on the contrary tends to tone them down. The Baroque *operista* is not a psychologist; his portraits of men are not made up from analytical observation, the reconstruction of a character from observed states of mind. Rather his characterization is deductive and formal. The thread is formed not so much by events as by the lyric stream and *élan*. Nevertheless, he did understand, only he wanted not to paint his figures in action but rather to interpret their reactions to events.

W. H. Auden maintains that "drama is not suited to the analysis of character, which is the province of the novel. Dramatic characters are simplified, easily recognizable and over life-size." The simplified creatures of a single mood in Baroque opera carry out this definition to the letter; they are the natural vehicles of the Baroque composer's emotions and thought. They are also likely to disturb the ordinary plausibilities of the "normal" theatre, even though there can be no question that Auden's postulate has a great deal to recommend it. True drama does not involve minutiae of "characterization," the petty naturalistic surface of minor habit. It is the representative aspect of character that we, used to naturalism, no longer recognize and experience, though it must be added that by trying to avoid minutiae, Baroque opera often ran too far in the other direction. The dramatic composer, as opposed to the playwright or the novelist, feels a single mood, observes a single aspect of life with extreme intensity, and it is inevitable that he should wish to exclude everything else as irrelevant. Thus in an opera a character may represent no more than jealousy or innocence, a single quality detached and intensified, the figure made complete only by the music. And often there is even less realism than is implied by such a procedure; a single mood may be expressed not only in one character but in a large part of an opera. For this reason ordinary methods of telling a story can be neglected in an opera while the attention of the audience is still held.

The Baroque opera composer is invisible, and to most modern lovers of music—as well as to many music historians—nameless as well. True, there is a fine *Scarlatti* by Dent, a fascinating *Lully* by Prunières, and a valuable *Jommelli* by Abert, but judging by the continued obscurity of these composers, few in a position of artistic leadership have read them. Furthermore, almost all this Baroque opera is in manuscript or rare early editions; of the entire 17th century all we have at our disposal in modern printed editions, if we do not count Lully, are less than a dozen works. As to the first half of the 18th century, Handel's and Rameau's operas are available in antiquated editions badly in need of thoroughgoing revision, but otherwise we have nothing but samples before Gluck. It is almost incredible that of Scarlatti we should have nothing in print but fragments. With so mysterious a medium as that of the stage it is impossible without trial to know what will "play," but surely many of these operas would prove viable with very little editorial work. We know from our experience with Cammarano, Piave, and all the other grand-opera librettists that music can lend magic to worn and leaden platitudes.

The historian's difficulties with this buried treasure are endless. We can seldom date the individual works, cannot pull them out of the current of musical history to the safe banks where they can be examined. To us there are in these works no individual traits by which the composer stakes his claim and avoids being confused with others. There were hundreds upon hundreds of operas, and the Baroque opera became so well constructed and polished that it could belong to anyone and everyone. But this collective character is not purely negative, for this opera expressed with steadily growing confidence and force what the public liked and wanted.

It looks then as though in Baroque opera music was victorious over the composer, and in certain measure music is here indeed the only essential thing, yet the great composers of Baroque opera did not surrender their rights, they only adjusted to the peculiar circumstances of the times. This is what Mozart did, and half a century ago we completely misunderstood him, berating the conventions he felt it necessary to follow. We took away his secco recitatives, reworked his librettos, helped out here and there with the orchestration, and reshuffled the numbers within the acts. A Richard Strauss did not find it objectionable to perform such collegial service for Mozart, as Wagner and Berlioz had done for Gluck and Weber, and indeed, Mozart himself before them for Handel. But today the enlightened musician knows that such editing can be done only with a historical sense and with loyalty toward original conceptions.

The greatest obstacle to the understanding of "old" opera is our over-rating of the value of realism. The classic maxim of esthetics is that the real is what we feel as real, what the artist can compel us to accept as real. Improbabilities, illogical time sequences, loose plots are nothing, for the powerful creative mind can make us forget our objections. Or does anyone doubt the reality of the Queen of the Night, sitting on the edge of the moon and singing hair-raising coloraturas? It is impossible and it is absolutely true and real. What we do not feel today is the synthesis of the external and the internal in the Handelian Baroque opera; his inwardness is not yet so morbidly intensive as that of the Romantic composers, there is not yet present the desire, the necessity, to follow every mood to its final psychological roots. The Baroque dramatist—though not the choral composer—usually stops before the ultimate door, nor does he see external events in all their hard brutality and strong sensuality. As a consequence, the two extremes are not so far removed from each other that they cannot be held in an organic whole. To us the heroes of this old opera seem more passive than active; they are acted upon rather than acting, and their heroism often seems prescribed rather than achieved. It can be said of any one of them that he acts as that kind of man would act, but seldom as he, a significant individual, would act; he is a type. But there is still in them much of the spirit of that great cradle of our civilization which supplied the favorite subject of these operas, even if the characters often indulge in long-winded exegesis and in cryptic or allusive dissertations about the riddles of ancient history and mythology.

The modern opera public demands variety and a lively pace, but in Baroque opera variety of moods and rapidity of action would impede the aim, which is the depiction of single moods requiring little action. Metastasio, the "Sophocles of Italy," knew this, and while he has often been reproached for being frosty and formal, in reality his fine librettos present the quintessence of Baroque dramaturgy: the more the center of motivation moves away—that is, the more the external, visible factors gain in their determining force upon the drama—the more the affective struggle moves inward. In opera this is expressed in pure lyricism; the means become the end, wherefore (to us) the hierarchy of things becomes uncertain. Yet this is still the drama of idealism, powerful and intense, but we no longer recognize it as such, for individualism as a problem of life dates for us from the advent of middle-class culture following the French Revolution—and the Handelian opera is purely aristocratic.

What makes it very difficult for the modern operagoer to assimilate Baroque opera is that movement and action are more in the style than in the drama; the music does not need constant attachment to the libretto. Moreover, the struggle for expression in the old Baroque composer is not easily perceptible to the uninitiated; to us it seems smooth, subdued, and equalized, whereas in the Romantic works the smoke of the battle always hangs over the scene. Critics of Baroque opera say that the weight of its "eternal pathos" renders it monotonous, but this weight is the lead on the sole of the cothurnus, and to the Baroque audience it was congenial, for it appealed to a well-developed collective understanding for style. This collective feeling was not something vague or fluid—the jury can have a much more characteristic profile than the single judge. The Baroque composer may be less powerful than the collectivity that created the style, but he possesses muscles that he can flex under beautifully cut garments. He does have originality; since this originality, however, was within the boundaries of the collectivity it is no longer apparent to us who have no such sense of stylistic oneness and cannot conjure up the spirit that animated the Baroque audience, to whom "originality" meant not new songs but characteristic variants of eternal themes. The Baroque composer—and often his public—knew the previous musical settings of the libretto upon which he was engaged, as did his librettist who reworked older models sometimes with little or no change, or used plot and characters approximately in the same spirit. They knew them well, even if the material was fifty or seventy years old.

It would be a great mistake to assume that this 18th-century public was naive, ready to accept any cliché; nor was it a mere consumer to whom the publisher or impresario sold goods made by a stranger; it was a federation dedicated to music and including within its own ranks composer, performer, and audience. We are speaking, of course, of the Italian public, for Baroque opera was thoroughly Italian, but the same is true of the Italian "islands" such as those in Dresden, Vienna, and London. We might add that the fate of this Baroque opera was not so dependent as our own on the brilliance or failure of the composer, for the public riveted its attention on the artistic conditions of the genre rather than on what happened to the individual contribution.

There is a parallel to Baroque opera in the Elizabethan theatre. Indeed, one often stops when reading Shakespeare to enjoy an unexpected association, the gait of a line or two, to consume it in sips, like good brandy. The action, even the story, is of little importance, often conventional; Shakespeare himself cared neither where he found his stories nor how he manipulated them. What is great in the plays, the philosophical heights, the wondrous art of characterization, the imponderable beauty of language and verse, the lyricism, the imagery, the lavish description of nature, the epic certainty of the milieu, and the profoundly felt moods —all these are independent of the quality of the action. But it is far more difficult to recapture Baroque opera than Baroque dramatic poetry; the music is much more elusive than the words. Handel, the opera composer, seems to the modern opera public a ghost coming from the remote past, of which practically all traces have vanished. The textbooks all pay homage to the operas, whose titles are listed like the clubs in a substantial citizen's obituary, and they deplore these operas' unsuitability for our time, while praising their melodies. Even the great musicologists of the last century, from Chrysander onward, seem to have acquiesced in the general opinion that these operas are lost forever, that they cannot be resuscitated for modern audiences. Of all Handelian scholars of the older generation, Hugo Leichtentritt approached this problem most intelligently when he refused to accept the various operatic reforms as necessarily constituting progress. "The Handelian opera is neither rationalistic nor sentimental but fantastic storytelling. Those who do not like fairy tales will of necessity regard these operas as childlike, flat, and lacking content." Then he spells out his opinion with precision by saying that the Handelian opera is pure *Gefühlsmusik*, not weighted down with psychological complications. This was said a good many years ago, and has since been ably seconded by Hermann Abert, Donald Grout, and a few others, yet most critics and historians still cannot see anything in Handel's operas beyond a stubborn insistence on forcing upon the English public something it did not want: a genre doomed to almost aimless struggle, conflict, failure.

[2]

WHEN WE SPEAK of Baroque opera we must distinguish between opera of the second half of the 17th century and that of the early 18th. The older opera, though often bizarre and unconscionably complicated as well as heterogeneous, was nevertheless true music drama. It often abounded in pointless episodes and comic incidents, but in the great scenes it rose to true tragic eloquence.[1] In Handel's time the older opera turned into the "concert opera," enthusiastically abandoning itself to the sensuous attraction of the human voice. Beautiful melody and ravishing singing became the principal aims; the melting arias not only changed opera but vitally influenced all music. The reflective arias tended to convey not the personal feelings of the protagonists but generalized feelings themselves, thus adjusting the independent life of sensuous music more or less externally to the drama. This made it possible to put together the many pasticcios, in which composers took successful numbers from earlier operas and tacked them onto more or less new scores for the gratification of both singers and public. In a word, what was being said became less and less important than how it was said.

Most Transalpine musicians and literary men regarded this Italian opera with contempt, a residue of which can still be felt to this very day, especially in the English-speaking world; but within the last two or three decades a notable *rapprochement* has become perceptible, a realization that technical terms such as "concert opera," "aria opera," and the like do not cover the whole situation. Granted all the abuses, we must still recognize a real and serious esthetic, dramaturgical, and psychological contribution made by these "concert arias." The Italians knew that it is difficult to express wholly inward emotions in concretely articulated words; the all-embracing power of music is far more suited to do so. The spoken theatre's monologue or soliloquy can be bent to this purpose, but the aria is made for it—the unutterable reigns over the absolute meaning of the words. Opera has wrestled with the problem of the aria's relevance and function ever since the 17th century—various "reforms" were all aimed at solving it—but the Italians and the Italian-oriented Germans and Frenchmen, from Gluck to Verdi, never really gave up the much-maligned "formal" aria, recognizing it as the pillar of opera, its essential element. Those

---

[1] Handel knew this vanished old Venetian type of opera and even used it on occasion. Medea's part in his *Teseo* is clearly modelled after Medea in Cavalli's *Giasone* (1649).

who concede the triumph of Wagnerian esthetics in Verdi's *Otello* simply do not hear this music properly; the arias are there, and in fact they can be found, not even fully concealed, in Wagner himself.[2]

Unfortunately, the great advantages of the aria were considerably limited by the rigid conventions established by the opera seria; arias were only too often not organically fused but merely linked, here successfully, there not. The difficulties of the bravura pieces are notorious and many of them unnecessary; for, we feel, they could have sprung only from a desire for technical triumph for its own sake. In particular, the coloratura arias devised for the castratos seem almost a wanton trial of strength, a burden added to the already difficult task the composer set himself. In many an opera human relationships were forced into a pattern to mark entry upon and withdrawal from the stage.[3] But naturalness in an entrance or exit aria was not an essential consideration in Baroque opera, though it can coincide with, or serve, genuine dramatic ends.

The overabundance of the da capo aria also contributed to a distressing uniformity, making the opera continually revolve around its own axis. The 19th century, with its ingrained rationalistic view, found the da capo aria the most objectionable part of Baroque opera, though devoutly accepting it in Bach's cantatas and Passions. Having lost this idiom from our musical and intellectual equipment and therefore failing to understand what the da capo aria conveyed to a Baroque audience, we readily reach the conclusion that it is meaningless. But, unless employed exclusively or too frequently, it is far from being the result of the "tyranny of the singers." It owes its existence to purely musical, formal instincts, for the Baroque composer was seeking not what we call "dramatic truth" but a musical stylization of the "basic affection"—that is, of one exclusive and undisturbed mood, though he was not unfamiliar with the *affetti misti*. The da capo aria was an elaborate and carefully composed piece of music. Its often purely musical logic could make it undramatic, but just as often it did not want to be dramatic but lyric-expressive instead; the dramatic expression was left to the recitative. The recitative carried the narrative, preparing for and building up to the aria, which discharges the function of what the Germans so graphically call *Affektenentladung*, the "unloading" of the affective content.

The objection to the da capo aria usually revolves around the "de-

[3] The custom of entrance and exit arias, carefully designed to accommodate applause, is clearly followed in grand opera, including the verismo of the beginning of our century.

struction" of the logic of the text, which cannot be so symmetrically set and still retain its meaning and dramatic function. But a close examination of da capo arias will disclose that even in the most stereotyped of them a certain accommodation to the text is evident. Charges of "senseless repetition" of portions or single words of the text have frequently been made, but these too yield to scholarly analysis. "One of the most important aspects of aria construction is the indissoluble connection between the formal layout of the text (repetitions and recurrences) and the formal and tonal layout of the composition. Textual repetitions match musical extensions, textual recurrences match musical returns." [4] Those who object to these beautifully designed arias forget that the opera aria was the ancestor of most of our present organized, tonally defined, and logically articulated musical forms, vocal and instrumental, as well as the breeding ground for all new means of musical expression from Monteverdi to Wagner.

Handel did not object to the da capo aria as did Gluck and some even before Gluck. In fact, it seems that for a long time he considered it the indispensable foundation of operatic style. We must remember that Handel was a "conservative" composer, if in the noblest sense of the word. On the other hand, how little conservative he was in dealing with the custom, how varied his arias are, how many different ways he could find to color them and give them dramatic validity! In *Floridante*, the aria "Dimmi o speme" uses for the middle section a dialogue in recitative; in Cleopatra's great aria in *Giulio Cesare*, "Venere bella," the ending of the first part defies all symmetry and orderliness as Handel plays with the A major cadence, delaying its finality for two dozen measures in a constant chain of surprises. There is scarcely an opera without such unusual aria construction, for the Handelian formal design is simple only if the face of a clock is simple. It is better to think of it as complicated but candid. The other great composers also knew how to minimize the sameness of the da capo aria, or, if they adhered to the routine, we often find the correct and formal da capo next to the most imaginative "free" forms. It may, of course, be said by objectors that the crux of the matter lies precisely at this point, and the theory of value advanced by such authors as the writer of these lines must at least partake of the undemonstrability that attends reconstructions, but the proof rests on the demonstrable fact that there are innumerable instances when form in the aria, by virtue of its beauty

[4] Harold Powers, in *The Musical Quarterly*, January 1962. Though his findings are restricted to Handel, they are equally valid for most of the great Baroque opera composers.

and perfection, becomes content.

The emergence of the aria as the mainstay of opera caused many difficulties in an era that showed a growing tendency to subjectivity, thus colliding with the rigid organization of the seria. The more individual interest is lavished on the hero the more the rules and conventions are threatened. Thus, while many arias were either actionless elegies or ballads, there were others that clearly transcended the limitations. The finely drawn characterizations, the many little refinements in the parts of accessory figures that are frequently to be found in Handel's and the great Italians' operas, disturb the "orderly" continuity of the opera.

Yet it would be idle to claim that Handel did not have a full share in the routine. In many of his arias the singer donned the ample gown of the rhetorician, but underneath the gown there was only a mannikin, and at times the composer seems more interested in beautiful sound than in the drama. The hero could be so pathetically heroic that there was no genuine pathos left for the rest of the cast, and for certain situations we see two exact copies of the same character type in the same opera. There is a very real danger that the modern listener will find this pathos not touching but comical. These heroes are halfway between action and reflection, always wanting to pass from one state to the other, moving among conflicts that fail to develop into dramatic dissonances. The relationship of ideal and reality is uncertain; the idea is strong enough to create real values, but even as it appears to be victorious, the compulsory order, number, and distribution of the arias turns victory into defeat. The protagonists were compelled by tradition to leave after a big aria or, what is worse, to remain on the stage as spectators, reclining on a couch and in many instances actually going to sleep. Double action—that is, two pairs of lovers—was almost a law in Baroque opera; the pairs took turns on the stage and, remaining in a certain equilibrium, provided a more or less orderly alternation of the two principal moods. The arrangement of the contents of the acts was also well regulated, as were correspondences of the grand scenes in the various parts of the opera.

To recapitulate, the aria constituted a stationary pause having consequences that seem flatly contradictory to dramatic requirements. The most personal utterances, the intimate confessions—the arias—suspend the drama, while the emotion-free and often perfunctory recitatives restore the temporal continuity. It is easy to see that an art so dependent on formal beauty cannot speak to us until we manage to perceive its expressive power. The key to this appreciation is vocal lyricism, melody. After the Baroque, the lyric, epic, and dramatic forms of music gradually yielded before "absolute" music—symphony, quartet, sonata, and kindred species—just as poetry was overshadowed by the novel. (The entr'acte provided by the German Romantic *Lied* does not change this trend either qualitatively or quantitatively.) Who would say that lyric poetry is a less significant genre than the novel? Could English literature be envisaged without a Shelley? And could we appreciate a Shelley from prose transcriptions? Yet this parallels exactly what we are trying to do with Baroque opera in general and Handelian opera in particular.

Let us remember that such words and notions as "incantation" or "enchantment" come from music and express the power of music, and they all refer to melody, the most powerful means for creating a mood, which in turn creates the sorcery. The composer may begin with something to which we listen with polite indifference, then his pathos forces us to fall in with him, his intensity vanquishes us. There is an empathy factor even in the shortest piece, for the mood created can reach far beyond the duration of the music. In a song there is no time to prepare and create empathy—it must be almost instantaneous—but an operatic aria is another matter. In spite of all the paradoxes in opera, this lyricism is drama, therefore the poet does not reveal himself the way a song-lyricist does; he is portraying a dramatic figure.

All just criticisms notwithstanding, we cannot gloss over the fact that composers of great talent turned out operas by the hundreds, that they lavished the most beautiful melodies on the verses. The applause that accompanied a well-turned delivery of this intoxicating melody came from the bottom of the heart of the people—and not only in Italy.[5] Thus, while Baroque opera was a singers' economy, a restricted and one-sided art, marred by abuses, arbitrary acts, intrigue, nonsense, and disappointment, over it shone the unsurpassable radiance of Italian melody, which no other branch of music could match. At the turn of the 17th century there appeared a musician who raised this sensuous art to such heights that for a hundred years it dominated musical thought. His melodies brought to opera a freshness, amplitude, and nobility, an unerring sense for rounded form, and his ability to create and paint a mood made his music irresistible. The sweet, long-breathed melodies, the beautifully proportioned arias of Alessandro Scarlatti became the model for all composers for generations.

Melodic construction is the most difficult component of composition,

---

[5] As early as 1715, when Handel's *Amadigi* obtained a tremendous success, the management of the King's Theatre prohibited the repetition of arias, which the public clamored to hear over and over.

the bold, broad, widely arching melody, the one with the "long breath," being of particular difficulty. Aside from the rise and fall of the line, there are the structure and the punctuation—periods, commas, and colons—which give it clarity. And this melody must have that "divine simplicity" which the Italians valued so much, and which half a century ago was found tiresome—even laughable. It is well known that Verdi's great tunes were called hurdy-gurdy music by the ardent Wagnerians, who also maintained that such melodies as Bellini's could be invented by any moderately competent musician. But the Wagnerians failed to consult Wagner himself, who, in an uncharacteristically sincere moment, wrote in an album for Bellini that the Italian was one of his favorite composers because his music is all mood, "innig und genau mit dem Text verbunden." Now this statement is most interesting, because according to the Wagnerian standards of vocal composition, Bellini's is certainly loose and often slights the text. But there can be no question about the mood, and this mood is entirely dominated by the melody, as in Scarlatti and Handel. The drama takes place within the melodies, for to the Baroque composer the external happenings are too "coarse" to be noticed and represented.

Handel the melodist is fascinatingly powerful, usually from the beginning of a melody, if not from the very upbeat. His melodic language is bold and free in an era that regarded the Alexandrine as the ideal in both poetry and music; it is full of the most unexpected and subtle elisions, abbreviations, and elongations. Very often a single line of this melody affects us with the finality of a complete masterpiece. His wondrous melodies, refined as though passed through fire a thousand times, give the impression of simple improvisation, but their simplicity hides an artfully magnificent structure that cannot be improvised. Handel wrote many melodies that came from the public domain of the Baroque, many more that represent the beguiling best of all ages. The study of their repeated palingenesis in different works, sometimes decades apart, will disclose the extraordinary rejuvenation one changed interval or dot can accomplish.

[3]

SOME CRITICS MAINTAIN that the German, inclined to polyphony and the symphonic, is too somber and heavy to take to opera naturally, and explain that Mozart was a southerner with an Italian background, while Handel, Hasse, and John Christian Bach became completely Italianized. This is true, of course, but the very fact that these northerners could so completely absorb the spirit and essence of opera that they were able to beat the Italians at their own game shows that inherently the German is perfectly capable of true lyric drama. Why its realization was restricted to the Italian-oriented Germans is explained by the most German of opera composers, Richard Wagner, for it is not that the German is "heavy," but that drama in Germany always runs parallel with philosophy. This is not so elsewhere, and it is totally otherwise in Italy. In France, Corneille and Descartes were contemporaries, yet they had little in common, and in the 18th century, when philosophy proliferated in that country, there was no significant playwright until the end of the century. The times of Hume and Mill produced no outstanding dramatist in England, but Kant is present in every drama in Germany.

In the Handelian theatre maxims and philosophical contemplation have no place; Handel neither formulated nor employed theories. And what is, of course, of decisive importance in an opera composer, he was a dramatist of the first water and at the same time a lyric poet, as well as a stylist, a storyteller, and an architect. All of these qualities are far removed from the world of philosophy. At times this clear, truly "classic" style warms to rhetoric in constantly rising, beautifully articulated musical sentences, for Handel is the master of musical characterization in melody. Stylistic problems did not exist for him. His artistic world existed a priori and it was largely the verbal material that came to hand which determined whether a work was more or less successful, although, as we shall see, even that was not a necessary criterion, for Handel could overcome the limitations of poor materials. His musical language was capable of expressing thought and emotion entwined, but also, and with equal assurance, emotion almost divorced from thought. At times his music may be imaginatively so condensed as to tax the listener's intuition, but the difficulty is never that of willful experiment, for while the texture is fastidiously wrought, it is quick with the insight that has discovered the meaning of beauty.

The general form of the Handelian opera is largely a faithful copy of the classic Venetian-Neapolitan prototype. For a long time he must have felt that since in the works of the Scarlatti circle the modus vivendi was well formulated, he could live by their ten commandments; it was only later that he decided to add an eleventh of his own devising. The conventions were strong (they are equally strong in the fashionable grand opera), and they were respected, but while the frame is the same, and so are the subjects, Handel's music is not rigid and does not follow pattern and etiquette unconditionally. His opera is no longer merely the old court opera; it is music drama whose figures are often snatched by force from the strait jacket of classicist make-believe.

Nevertheless, there were many dramaturgical rules of the opera seria that he accepted unquestioningly—and even welcomed. Thus the relegation off stage of many incidents of the plot permitted him to concentrate on the state of mind of the protagonists, disclosing surprisingly romantic traits. He was romantic because against the abstract types of the seria he could oppose real individuals. These are not always altogether real in our sense, but perhaps more than that, they are ideals of men, which Plato considered the true reality. To actuality they are still tied by a few strands: we see ancient Greeks and Romans, Scythians, Parthians, Visigothic kings and Egyptian queens. They all lived long, long ago, and could be freely elaborated, but all of them recognize ideals, the ideal of patriotism, sacrifice, honor, loyalty, fidelity, love, filial duty. All of them are filled with consciousness and the will to carry these ideals to victory despite the conventions of the opera seria. The point of gravity in the drama is not so much in the great clashes, but in their preparation and lyric aftermath. One or two figures remain on stage and bare their souls. This is Handel's favorite moment, which can rise into the monumental.

The monumental impression is due to the fact that the musical forms have saturated themselves with content and impress of themselves, though they do not detach themselves from plot and figures. This is the moment in Baroque opera that causes the greatest difficulty to musician and layman alike brought up on the heritage of the Romantic era; they ask, "What can one, what *must* one give up for the sake of form? Or is it necessary at all to make this sacrifice?" The answer is that here pure art fills with its own life and raises above time and the possibility of change what actual life has offered. There is perhaps a false touch here and there, for at times the relationship of these perfect forms is merely tonal, constantly gaining in detail but also weakening continuity, and at times the material is so breathtakingly beautiful that its meaning is outshone. Such objections are not unjustified. As a rule Handel subjected the feelings to be expressed in an aria to the closest scrutiny in his determination to purify it of all questionable emotional alloy. Yet it appears that his impressions were occasionally so intense as to overshadow his vigilant intellect.

There was in this powerful, highly trained, intelligent, and virtuoso artist a genuine and unconscious naiveté that was one of the principal strengths of his art, but at times it betrayed him. It is somewhat ironical that this appealing naiveté can become the most refined means whereby a true dramatic continuity and development are diluted, drawing attention to sheer musical attraction at the expense of the drama. This presents a real obstacle to the modern hearer, though to Handel it was a well-respected tradition inherited from Scarlatti. The composers of the old opera seria tended to neglect the dramatic-human element—they could not do otherwise—because in their period every musical act that did not seek the purely aural-esthetic, the sensuous sound value, was bound to turn into allegory; it became a symbol rather than characterization. The development from this stage of opera to the Mozartean is a most complicated process in which the opera buffa was the catalyst. In Handel the purely "acoustic"—that is, the purely abstract—musical concordances between the dramatis personae are still very much within the spirit of the Baroque, and we must learn to understand it, to hear in the Baroque manner. This should not be too difficult: the musical-formal concept is fresh and interesting; precisely because the characters are essentially musical visions, nothing impedes the powerful effect of the music; through the sheer beauty of the aural impression the whole sensory apparatus of the listener is engaged. Perhaps a close parallel illustrative of this unusual phenomenon is to be found in Fra Angelico's celestial landscapes, where the meadows clad in vernal ornament are not landscapes at all but optic impressions solely serving the purpose of providing a background for the beatified who disport themselves in it.

In climactic moments the forces employed are of such intensity that at times the lyric beauty of the melody makes the situation seem almost grotesque, even undramatic, for the characters do not act but tell about the motives of their action. This was the original sin of the opera seria and was difficult to overcome. In such moments the confrontation of two human beings in extraordinary circumstances is transmuted into the expression of a profound and very human relationship, but it avoids the conflict of two points of view. Eloquence, lyric melody become the rulers over dramatic gesture. It is the form of the seria that forced Handel to this stylization, even though his own inclinations were against it. Thus in many of his operas there are uneven and irreconcilable contradictions which are jarring, yet just where objective expression overpowers the subjective the greatest beauties are revealed as pulsating life fills the most abstractly formulated da capo aria.

Handel felt the incongruity between what was available to him and what he was striving for. He was to resolve all his doubts and problems in the oratorio, but in his operas this dichotomy created a certain vacillation and very personal problems of style not even remotely understood until recent times. He constantly struggled for equilibrium, and this had many consequences for his art. Characterization is sometimes developed to the neglect of dramatic relationships, or vice versa, and there is often disparity between the feelings of his dramatic figures and their expression. There are many wondrously intimate and delicate scenes where sensitive men and women insist on explaining their state of mind, but they keep on defining matters whose nature is precisely that they cannot fit any definition. When Handel does overcome this impediment it is usually despite the words rather than with their aid. This ability to override the libretto and compel it to disappear under the power of music is his most personal characteristic, particularly in the oratorios. The love all lyricists feel for the many-keyed instrument that is language explains a Handelian trait that to us appears to be a dramatic weakness: his sharp ear for the quality of the single, isolated word. Occasionally one is amazed to discover that Handel actually abandons the librettist's lines; disliking them, he proceeds to set them in such a manner that they lose their meaning. He will concentrate on isolated words, lift them out of context by pouring significant music over them. This may altogether change the librettist's intentions —which is the object—but satisfy his own, with the result that the poor libretto may turn into a fine opera. He is also capable of a feat that seems equally impossible and for which his librettists were totally unprepared: endowing a secondary figure with life even though that figure, as conveyed by the text, virtually excludes any semblance of character, his entire role being accessory and without influence or significance for the drama.

When all such means fail to reconcile loose dramatic threads in a bad libretto, Handel's phenomenal ability to create an atmosphere comes to the rescue. A persuasive atmosphere can bring disparate elements together, can lend the whole a tone and substance that reconcile even the sharp divergences and dissonances. True drama is built on dissonance and its resolution, therefore the gains achieved by atmospheric unity also harbor fatal weaknesses for the drama: it tends to dissolve the conflicts, the drama disintegrating into idyllic and elegiac lyricism. The dichotomy we have mentioned then causes Handel to struggle powerfully, for his instincts were severely and exclusively dramatic, and he saw his heroes essentially free of the atmosphere surrounding them. Thus he once more tends to a monumentality that does not tolerate accessories of any kind, and when this point is reached everything else—the rest of the cast and even the drama itself—disappears. It can be awe-inspiring and a little ridiculous at the same time. Also, in many instances tragedy occurs before the drama really gets under way, for the power of imagination, the creative urge, is impatient. In others he explodes the drama prematurely because of pragmatic reasons his librettist may have forced upon him. But when this eager and glowing capacity for creative work was under full critical control, his dramatic instinct could work wonders even while obeying restrictions and conventions. Passion was restrained until the way had been carefully chosen and defined in his mind—then it was released.

Those who meet this opera taken out of its historical context, and out of Handel's own musical development, are surprised by his genuine respect and love for classical antiquity, his constant recourse to this heritage, for they see all this as a mere residue of a post-Renaissance cult, a fad that from Rinuccini to Metastasio was kept alive and made into a convention that no longer had connections with the spirit of classicism, a virtual caricature of a faded and no longer understood culture. But in Handel this classical heritage does not signify an arbitrary or a literal return to the past, it is rather an esthetic kinship, a recognition of the power of a concept of art that sees man as a whole.

Seen from this angle, Handel's opera is clearly the antithesis of naturalism and realism. Today's naturalism and psychologism make it difficult to see in this opera anything but a type, both in the dramatis personae and in the dramatic situations—nothing but endless repetitions, whereas naturalism represents the unique, the never recurring. Modern naturalism demands easily followed and effective plots; the story has independent strength, the figures of the drama lean on it. In Handel the story leans on the figures of the drama, for his shaping force is guided and nourished by lyricism. He was a lyric dramatist like Aeschylus. It is the force of this lyricism, its tremendous scale, that breathes life into the sketches provided by his librettists, and it is the expression that creates dramatic figures, compelling them to act dramatically. The Handelian opera does not deny the values of the Baroque world even though it purports to represent antiquity, nor does it deny the plasticity of human relations or the dynamism of mood and mind. But it does oppose chaos of mood and ecstasy of color, because to the Baroque mind the cult of constantly varying color and mood destroys the oneness of man. Swinburne thought that "the fusion of lyric with dramatic form gives the highest type of poetry"; this is particularly true in music, and this is, indeed, what a *Rodelinda* and a *Giulio Cesare* offer. But they also give us a vision of life that a modern audience, its imagination kept within bounds by exposure to realistic scenery, lighting, and various effects and techniques of the spoken theatre, finds hard to apprehend.

The undeniable anomalies in the old Baroque opera have been judged so overwhelming that its revival has been thought practically impossible. These anomalies can be made bearable once they are recognized and once their causes are understood. Perhaps we of the second half of the 20th century can approach these problems and resolve them—the 19th could not; but then we must completely cleanse our mind of 19th-century ideals of dramaturgy. First of all we must realize that the "classicism" of the Handelian stage was the vehicle for a thoroughly Baroque spirit. Archaeologically, Handel's Greek or Roman heroes and heroines, bewigged and crinoline-clad, are undoubtedly false, but as noble patriots or lovers they are true and compelling figures. Historical accuracy and authenticity of décor and costumes neither add to nor detract from their integrity. The view that verisimilitude is the aim of art is no longer what it once was, though it is not yet extinct. Art strives to create illusion, to convince that this illusion is of the essence, that it can only be this way and no other way. We do not interrupt the storyteller when he says "Once upon a time there was a wicked old witch . . ." to say that there is no such thing. Rather, supposing that there might be such a thing, we wonder what he knows about it. Baroque opera does not depend on verisimilitude; we should not confuse its musical logic of structure with the verbal logic of the spoken theatre. With suitable changes that remove the nonesthetic limitations, the seemingly inevitable conceptual blocks, and with careful editing of the score, we should be able to present many of these operas in such a manner that our musical imagination will recognize the reality of the esthetic sphere. The ignoring of the "realities of life" in the re-creation of Handel's operas would enable us to hear resonances of such subtlety as the realistic stage is incapable of. Naturalism with its marvelous analyses does present human documents—but this is not necessarily art; the copying of life can be a criticism of life, but not necessarily the solution of its problems.

This does not mean, however, that we should neglect the theatre in the Baroque opera. A knowledge of the technique of the lyric theatre, by which we understand the sum total of the means and procedures peculiar to this particular art, is neither the supreme requirement it is considered to be by theatrical people not conversant with opera nor is it the negligible matter so many musicians think. Every true opera composer has his own technique peculiar to himself. The musico-dramatist must know the contours of the stage and stagecraft in general—how to make appearances telling, how to make his figures communicate, how to articulate the action, and where to place accent and emphasis. But the stage director must always make his dispositions with the score in hand; if he proceeds from the point of view of the spoken theatre he is lost, and so is the opera he is directing. When dealing with Italian opera, the director must remember the maxim: "What is truth this side of the Alps may be error beyond them."

The proponents of the illusionist stage, with its scientific-historical exactitude and sobriety, flatly maintain that Handel's operas present insurmountable staging difficulties, but these cannot be accepted as constituting a serious hazard any more than those presented by Shakespeare's plays. As with Shakespeare, Handel does not need much in the way of décor; the work has the décor in itself. It is unnecessary to recreate Rome or Carthage or any other ancient city, its houses and courtyards and yellow lamps, and tack them down onto the stage with nails. It is in Handel's musical diction that we must seek the lyric stage, not in ethnographic and historical accuracy but in the intelligent manipulation of singing actors with a fine sense for balance and plasticity.

[4]

THERE REMAINS THE serious question of the castrato parts, opinions about which remind one of the boat in the fairy tale to which were harnessed an eagle, a pike, and a lobster; the one pulling up, the other down, and the third sideways. Dent and others maintain that it is "fatal" to assign castrato roles to tenors or baritones to sing them in transposition. I cannot agree to that. It is perfectly true that in so doing we are "destroying" a very special quality, but since this quality was entirely artificial in the first place and can never again be recaptured, there is no use championing it. Unquestionably, in this complete reversal of the natural function of voices there must have been a very sophisticated aural refinement, but to us it has become an extravagance no longer realizable. It is also true that the Baroque did associate heroic stature with high tessitura and coloratura. This the castrato supplied in full measure, but by the end of the 18th century the heroic conception was transferred to the tenor. Both the Italian heroic tenor, as exemplified in Verdi, and the Wagnerian *Heldentenor* still represent it.

We no longer have any sense for the older conception. Ever since the opera buffa and the "reformed" opera seria of the latter half of the 18th century we have identified operatic roles with vocal timbres belonging to and representing the sexes; this makes it permanently unsatisfactory to hear a man sing with a woman's voice. Once we have established inseparable union of voice timbre and sex there is no turning back, for they cannot be sundered. The opera buffa was a natural rebellion against the unnatural; musicians and the public alike felt a profound and intimate relationship between voice and sex, vocal color and character; between the masculinity of the male voice and the femininity of the female there is no middle ground, and even less a neutral ground. The Encyclopedists had already castigated the Italians for their "blunder of having Alexander, Caesar, and Pompey settle the destiny of the world with women's voices." Even the countertenor is strange to us and will gain only limited acceptance. The handful of very fine countertenors active at present sing delicate Elizabethan music delightfully but in dramatic music, including the Handelian opera and oratorio, the ambiguous quality of the voice makes them only characterless puppets no matter how sensitively musical their phrasing and delivery.

The singing voice is a direct expression of a personality. The castrato had neither sex nor natural personality; he was an instrument of prodigious versatility and perfection, but still a musical instrument and not a living human character. He destroyed the efficacy of the female voice by duplicating its register without the passion and the expressivity of the woman incarnate in her voice. Correspondingly, he could not truly express the instincts and desires of a man in the vocal range of a woman.[6] It is generally assumed that sex as a distinction between singers did not matter very much in the age of the castrato. This is true to a certain extent; it is also true, however, that Handel was not unaffected by the sexless quality of the castrato voice. In any number of operas we find that while he did compose elaborate and very fine arias for the castrato hero, these arias seldom compare in warmth and passionate expression with those composed for women, for the bass, and later, in the oratorios, for the tenor. The indignant, or rollicking, or raging, or grieving bass part was one of Handel's favorites and was seldom transposed; its register and the masculinity of the singer were positive attributes. Even the tenor, in those days almost always assigned to minor roles, received heroic tasks from Handel in a number of operas. In fact, Handel was among the first to establish the present role of the tenor in the dramatic scheme, though this took place in the oratorios. We may go even further and observe that if there is merely conventional music for the principal characters in a Handelian

---

[6] The bass was early associated with kings, tyrants, high priests, and fathers, but never with principal heroes. The baritone was a newcomer, especially favored by Mozart, to whom even the tenor was not manly enough for a principal character. He used the tenor mainly for youthful lovers (Belmonte, Tamino) or for characters somewhat lacking in forcefulness (Don Ottavio).

opera—and even some of the best contain such music—it is usually allotted to the castrato. Handel's imagination was not as a rule fired by them; he had to put up with a convention he could not question in Italian opera, but which he eventually discarded in the English oratorio.

In general, the Baroque composer often regarded the castrato as a virtuoso rather than a dramatic figure, belonging more to the décor than to the drama itself. This should be borne in mind when considering the shifting of coloratura arias written for soprano or alto to the tenor or baritone range, where they may be idiomatically strange. But since the castrato part was in many instances "concert music," it could be simplified by removing excessive roulades and ornaments. Sung by a man, these arias would gain in compatibility with the fine "sex-conscious" songs written for natural voices. "There are two causes for Beauty," says Sir Christopher Wren, "natural and customary. Natural is from Geometry consisting of Uniformity (that is Equality) and Proportion. Customary Beauty is begotten by the use of our senses to those objects which are usually pleasing to us from other causes, as particular Inclination breeds Love of Things not in themselves lovely." It would be well if this important distinction were borne in mind whenever the question of preservation or reconstruction of a work of art arises, clearing the issue from the "woodsman, spare that tree" kind of argument. In sum, this loyalty to the original register of the castrato part is a lost cause. An able and historically schooled musician can always adjust the score with tact and taste to accommodate men to sing the parts of the "Italian capons." Unless we are willing to accept the early 18th-century taste that ranked virtuosity above drama—and that is impossible to a public used to the modern opera theatre—we cannot resuscitate this Baroque opera in its original form.

The makeshift subterfuge of giving the castrato part to a female soprano only aggravates a bad situation. A woman wearing the armor or toga of a man appears ridiculous to us. Orpheus, in Gluck's opera, is about the only such principal role in the standard operatic repertory, and it concerns an alto castrato's part. Although the female alto who these days sings the role has acquired a certain sanctioned musical quality, she has lost her personality in the bargain. Gluck, who lived at the time when the castrato was beginning to pass into limbo, was aware of the need of saving from oblivion a good opera designed for one, nor was he unmindful of the merciless satire he would draw from the French, who looked upon the castrato with scorn. His *Orphée,* the French version of *Orfeo,* in which the castrato part was altered to fit a tenor, is a far better opera—a least for us—than the original.

At this point it may be asked where such reasoning would leave Cherubino or the Knight of the Rose. Everyone of course adores Cherubino, but this wondrous creature is a special case; he is an adolescent just discovering the attraction of women. Mozart's uncanny sense for the psychology of characterization seized upon a moment in the boy's life when he was about to emerge from the pupal stage: no longer an innocent, but not yet fully awakened. What better way to represent this than by the delightful *ambiguity* of having the part sung by a mezzo-soprano? And make no mistake, no Valkyrie can sing this part either; a quality boyish yet at the same time feminine is indispensable. The Knight of the Rose, as well as all other characters of this sort in modern opera, are descended from Cherubino, though none of them can remotely re-create the delicious ambiguity of this Mozartean miracle.

If we accept the point of view of those who insist on replacing the castrato with female soprano or alto, we should logically go the whole way: replace the choral trebles and altos with boys and falsettists. The result would be the loss of the last vestiges of drama and excitement, antiquarianism overwhelming life. By the same reasoning we should employ boys for women's roles as was done on the English stage, where women were not permitted to appear until the Restoration. Juliet played by a rosy-cheeked choirboy would be as strangely unreal as Julius Caesar sung by a comely soprano.

We must also bear in mind that until the first half of the 19th century, and especially in the Baroque era, most operas were composed for performance by certain singers, in a certain theatre, before certain spectators, at a certain time. This fact, which is largely true also of the oratorio, makes it doubly difficult to approximate the original conception and conditions. But we know that when an opera or oratorio was revived from season to season the original parts were often altered to fit new singers. We are not advocating here the acceptance of the often wanton disregard Handel showed toward his own creations when tossing off a hasty revision; that was the act of the entrepreneur, not the composer. But he often made vital changes as the result of second thoughts, greatly improving an original role or scene. It is true that in the majority of cases Handel's transpositions were upward whereas what we are suggesting is the opposite; nevertheless the principle is the same. In a world that had a topsy-turvy attitude toward the quality, nature, and range of the human voice, Handel had many more good high voices at his disposal than low ones.

The castrato voice has disappeared forever, but the music is still here. We can never recapture the fantastic unreality of that voice, but we can salvage the music. This music can only be salvaged, however, if we substitute for the impersonal instrument a human character. The contrast between men and women is vital, there can be no drama without it—not to us. But this restoration cannot be done—as it has been done—by uninformed conductors and amateur musicologists lacking historial and theatrical insight. There is a phonograph recording of *Giulio Cesare* in which so much plastic surgery was practiced on the score that even the Bertillon method would be no help in tracing the original features of the work. Cuts are not only permissible but in many instances mandatory, but the utmost discretion is needed to avoid wanton dislocation of delicate tonal and other concordances. The orchestration is another matter: it must not be touched beyond the few alterations necessitated by the transposition of the castrato parts. To modernize Handel's extraordinarily supple and imaginative orchestra would indeed "destroy" something that is neither artificial nor archaic. Finally, our custom of making earlier 18th-century opera palatable by forcing upon it ballet and choreography is completely without foundation or reason. There are some fine short ballets in several of Handel's operas, but they are all incidental; to shift the accent from the aural to the visual violates the spirit of this opera.

The recent successful revival of Bellini's and other early 19th-century Italian bel canto operas shows that the sense for pure melodic expression as well as the singing skill needed for their execution can be reacquired. Handel's infallible and profound musicality, which can catch a mood with unparalleled eloquence yet which holds fast with the utmost tenacity to the boundaries of the songlike, can also be recaptured. It would be an exaggeration to say that this melodiousness, this vocal, euphony-determined form is all there is to his dramatic lyricism, but it is the main factor in the representative summation of a long development and tradition.

VIII

O N HIS RETURN FROM THE RECRUITING TRIP TO DRESDEN,
Handel threw his immense energies into the affairs of the Royal Academy
of Music. He attended the meetings of the board and concerned himself
with every aspect of the enterprise: general administration, the engagement of the singers, scenery and staging, arrangement of other composers'
music, and drilling of the orchestra and the singers. Whether these manifold activities left insufficient time for composing, or for some other reason, his new opera was not ready for the grand opening of the Academy,
and the first season began on April 2, 1720, with Giovanni Porta's *Numi-
tore*, libretto by Rolli. Since the libretto states that Porta was in the service of the Duke of Wharton, he apparently was in London at that time.
Porta was a good musician, but as an opera composer was altogether beholden to the routine aria opera, which he handled with ease and with an
eye for pleasing the public.

Then, on April 27, *Radamisto,* Handel's first opera for the Academy,
was presented to a full house, the King and "his ladies," as well as the
Prince of Wales, being in the audience. Mainwaring says that "several
gentlemen were turned back, who had offered forty shillings for a seat in
the gallery" (usually selling for two shillings and sixpence). The success
was tremendous, and indeed *Radamisto* is one of Handel's great operas. It

has a good libretto, and the work is well and tightly composed even though the proportions are large. *Radamisto* contains elaborate instrumental numbers, ritornels and preludes, in addition to a wealth of great arias. Hawkins reports that Handel considered "Ombra cara" his finest melody next to "Cara sposa" from *Rinaldo*. As was frequent in Handel's works, the outstanding character portrayed in the opera is that of a woman, Zenobia, Radamisto's wife. It is quite obvious that this score was composed with minute care and elaboration and was intended to be a knockout—which in fact it was. Also, almost all of it is new music; only one of his Italian cantatas and a little from the *Brockes Passion* were used for fillers. The cast, consisting of Durastanti, Galerati, Anastasia Robinson, the lesser known Mrs. Turner Robinson, Lagarde, Gordon, and Baldassari, immediately attracts attention for two reasons: the absence of castratos, and the presence of English singers. Of the latter, only Anastasia Robinson, for a long time a faithful Handelian, could to some degree compete with the Italians.

At the end of April, Domenico Scarlatti's *Narciso* joined the repertory. It has been proved by Frank Walker that this opera was a considerably altered version of Scarlatti's *Amor d'un ombra e gelosia d'un' aura,* with additional music by Thomas Roseingrave, Carlo Capece's original libretto having been adapted by the Academy's resident dramatic poet, Rolli. The long-held belief that Domenico was present and thus reunited with his old friend of the happy Venetian days is now discredited.

On the whole, the first season of the Royal Academy of Music was a success, and at thirty-five Handel could feel that with *Rinaldo, Teseo, Amadigi,* and now *Radamisto* he had reached the commanding position he sought. In the meantime, however, the directorate of the Academy was not willing to stake everything on Handel. It was, after all, a business enterprise that had to be made profitable—there were stockholders. Accordingly, Lord Burlington was dispatched to Italy to scout for another resident composer of stature. As we have seen, the choice fell on Giovanni Bononcini (1670–1747), with whose arrival in London in the fall of 1720 the scene changed and Handel found himself facing a formidable rival.

Bononcini was a member of a distinguished family of musicians. Giovanni Maria (1642–1678), the father, was a versatile composer and writer, whose fine cantatas and church music Handel had heard in Italy. His younger son, Antonio Maria (1675–1726), was considered by Padre Martini, the most widely influential teacher of the age, superior to the famous Giovanni. Padre Martini was a good judge, but we cannot weigh the validity of his view because, aside from some "favorite songs" from

Camilla, nothing of Antonio has been printed. His *Trionfo di Camilla,* composed at the age of twenty, was one of the most successful operas in the Baroque era, and it undoubtedly paved the way for his brother's engagement in London. The two Bononcinis are a musicologist's nightmare. Several librettos were set by both of them, both were fine musicians, and at times it is most difficult to distinguish between them when the ascription refers to "Signor Bononcini." Also, they were both excellent instrumentalists and often served together in the same place, playing, as in Berlin and Vienna, in the same orchestra.

Giovanni had a thorough education in the Bolognese school of Colonna, and at the opening of the 18th century was one of the most famous composers in Europe, regarded as second only to Scarlatti, but he was equally admired for his sensitive and expressive cello playing. There is a little-known province of his art which nevertheless is significant to us: Bononcini was a much-admired composer of oratorios, works that Handel knew. While his charming cavatinas and little arias captivated the London public, Bononcini's talent was by no means restricted to bonbons; he was capable of much more substantial accomplishments. Even Chrysander, who is responsible for posterity's low opinion of this able composer, has nothing but respect for his church music (naturally, Catholic church music did not compete with any of Handel's mature works). Indeed, Bononcini cannot be so summarily dismissed as Chrysander and some other Handel biographers are wont to do. The success of the Academy's third season was due to his operas, and an invitation for the Royal Academy to play in Paris (which came to naught) was also largely due to his fame. Although Schering has convincingly corrected Chrysander's misleading judgment, this worthy composer still awaits rehabilitation. Though a rather proud and restless man, he was not the intrigant and faker he was reported to be. The exact facts in the celebrated case of plagiarism that ruined his career in London have by no means been satisfactorily established. The Academy of Ancient Music investigated the affair, addressing itself directly to Antonio Lotti, whose madrigal was allegedly plagiarized in toto by Bononcini. The assembled evidence was published in a multilingual document entitled: *Letters from the Academy of Ancient Music at London to Signor Antonio Lotti of Venice, with answers and testimonies,* London, 1732. This was a devastating document, yet Bononcini haughtily refused to defend himself.

The last word has not yet been said about this curious and sad affair. There are good reasons to suspect that Bononcini was the innocent victim of a vendetta raging around him. It does not seem at all probable that a composer as gifted and facile as Bononcini, who could compose a madrigal in half an afternoon, should resort to so questionable a maneuver when a deadline was not involved. The score from which the music was sung at the Academy bears no signature, and nowhere did Bononcini himself claim authorship. Maurice Greene, who became a sworn enemy of Handel and who lost no opportunity to make trouble for his erstwhile friend and idol, appears to be the culprit who caused Bononcini's embarrassment. "No one was as industrious as [Greene] in decrying the compositions of Handel," says Hawkins; and at another point the historian furnishes what seems to be the key to this riddle. "[Greene] was a member of the Academy of Ancient Music, and, with a view to exalt the character of Bononcini, produced in the year 1728 the madrigal 'In una siepe ombrosa,' which gave rise to a dispute that terminated in the disgrace of his friend." (It must be admitted, though, that this was not the first time that a Bononcini was accused of plagiarism. The father, Giovanni Maria, published a *Discorso musicale* in which he defends himself against the accusation of having put together his Opus 3 from other composers' works.) In the long run Bononcini could not stand up to Handel, and the aggregate of his misfortunes eventually drove him from London. Falling into the hands of an unscrupulous adventurer, an "alchemist," who fleeced him of all his possessions, he wandered around in France, Italy, Portugal, and Austria, dying in Vienna, forgotten and destitute, in 1747.[1]

The directors congratulated themselves on Lord Burlington's coup in persuading Bononcini to accept the post of artistic co-regent with Handel (Ariosti joined the group later), but soon they began to wonder whether this clever move had not hatched a rivalry that, by getting out of hand, might hurt rather than help them. Bononcini's success created a schism, though in the beginning it was among the Academy's patrons rather than between the composers themselves. As was to happen later in the century when two honorable composers, Gluck and Piccinni, became objects of an ardent rivalry despite their mutual esteem, the Bononcini-Handel rivalry was not founded on personal envy or hostility but was the work of self-appointed partisans, though eventually the two men became personally involved. Given the clientele of the Academy, it was inevitable that politics should intrude even into its artistic policies, and since Handel was a German and a former court musician to the unpopular Hanoverian king, the Tories immediately espoused Bononcini's cause as a form of indirect affront to the dynasty and to its chief political agent, Prime Minister Wal-

---

[1] While his scores are not easily available, a pair of very fine arias from *Griselda* and *Erminia* were published by Landshoff in *Alte Meister des Bel Canto*.

pole. This being the case, the Whigs came to Handel's defense—and the war was on. The Prince of Wales, though well disposed toward Handel, joined the Bononcini camp out of hatred for his father, a move that surely created a curious alliance, since the Tories' real target was the royal family.

The second season of the Academy opened at the Haymarket Theatre on November 19, 1720, with Bononcini's *Astarto,* the libretto fashioned by Rolli after Zeno. Its great success is attested to by its many performances. Bononcini also had the advantage of a fine, experienced, all-Italian cast, headed by Senesino (Boschi was also back in London). Handel made use of the same outstanding cast when *Radamisto,* reworked and enlarged, was revived at the end of December.

In April a new opera, *Muzio Scevola,* was produced with a top cast. A story has it that the directors, hoping to stimulate public interest, organized a sort of tournament in which the three acts of a libretto were set by three rival composers: Filippo Amadei, Bononcini, and Handel. Amadei (also known as Mattei), of about Handel's age, was a very good cellist and a composer of sorts, who had joined the orchestra at the time of the founding of the Royal Academy of Music. He was a popular figure and recognized as a good "arranger," which may account for his selection as one of the co-composers of *Muzio Scevola,* but it seems more plausible that he was only substituting for the logical choice, Ariosti, who was reluctant to enter into competition with Handel and Bononcini. Ariosti was in a difficult position. He had known Bononcini from the days when both were in Berlin, when he wrote the libretto for Bononcini's successful opera *Polifemo* (1702), but he also felt an affection, which lasted to the end of his life, for the considerably younger Handel. *Muzio Scevola* did not entirely realize the hoped-for results. Amadei's first act was poor, Bononcini's second fair, and Handel's third clearly far superior to either. Regrettably, Handel put a good deal of fine music into this mélange, from which at least the sparkling overture to the third act should be salvaged. While there was undoubtedly an element of contest intended in the commissioning of *Muzio Scevola,* this sort of thing was by no means unknown throughout the century. It would have been quite natural for the management to court a quick success by displaying its collective hoard of talent. Bononcini's *Ciro* added to the Italian's conquest, and on this note and with this opera, the season closed on July first.

The third season saw another revival of *Radamisto,* and then, on December 9, Handel presented his new opera, *Floridante.* This is not one of his great works, nor did Rolli's libretto contribute to Handel's inspiration.

His plot, with its multiple concealed identity *cum* womanly faithfulness, was hard to manage, but Handel found some dramatic opportunities even in this concoction. It is again the women who emerge as true dramatic characters. Elmira, sung by Mrs. Robinson, is sad and lofty, Rossane (Signora Salvai) gay and friendly. The general aspects of the opera aside, it does contain much very fine music. "Notte cara" is one of Handel's ravishing "night pieces," a wonderful arioso in B minor full of the mystery of the night. The duets, notably "Fuor di periglio," are idyllic pieces, in which woodwinds, strings, and harpsichord concertize in happy abandonment with the voices. In general, the accompaniments are marked by delicacy and refinement, attributes surely wasted on Handel's audience. Handel here fell back on older practices, with the difference that he raised the old instrumental obbligato of the 17th century to the level of a flexible, capricious, and tender art. It seems as if he wanted to show in *Floridante* that he could ascend to the higher regions of art as well as meet Bononcini on his own ground, because some other numbers are in Bononcini's light, easy, and elegant manner. Though given fifteen times, *Floridante* was not a real success, and Bononcini immediately followed up this unexpected tactical gain with two operas: *Crispo,* in January 1722, and *Griselda,* in February, both of which were enthusiastically received, especially *Griselda.* This, the third season of the Academy, was definitely Bononcini's round, and he was equally successful outside the theatre. His collection of chamber duets (which Handel studied to advantage) were dedicated to the King. The set sold a number of copies unheard of in those days, in addition fetching the equally unusual price of two guineas. Handel's answer to the situation was a strategic retreat and reorganization of his resources. He withdrew from circulation, and, realizing that new operas alone would not redress the balance, he and Heidegger engaged the famous Italian soprano, Francesca Cuzzoni.

The fourth season opened October 27, 1722, with revivals of *Muzio Scevola* and *Floridante;* then on January 12, 1723, in the King's presence, Handel's new opera, *Ottone,* was first performed, with the new prima donna in the cast. Haym's rather wordy and complicated libretto did not prevent Handel from composing an opera that clearly showed who was master in the King's Theatre on the Haymarket. The success was resounding, and rightfully so—*Ottone* is a great opera. Everyone spoke of "Mr. Hendel's new opera," and the final piece in the fine overture became the "C-sharp minor Prelude" of the age, played in every English drawing room where there was a harpsichord, though as Burney said, it was also played on "every imaginable instrument." The title role was sung by

Senesino, to whom Handel allotted some exquisitely turned romances, of which "Ritorna, o dolce amore," is one of his most beguiling melodies; whenever he turns to the siciliana this special inspiration is bound to result. There are a number of these wonderful elegies (as well as some commonplace arias), and the admired castrato must have overwhelmed his public with them, but the best dramatic music again goes to the women, Teofane, Matilda, and Gismonda. Teofane's role, designed for La Cuzzoni, is always in the highest sphere of the art of bel canto, and the little, squat, and homely soprano conquered her audience to the last man. In "Falsa imagine" Handel composed for her one of his greatest arias, embellished by a fine cello obbligato, and she also sings one of those bewitching sicilianas, "Affani del penser." While Teofane is gentle and maidenly, Matilda (Mrs. Robinson) vacillates between despair and hatred, an entirely different type of woman who sings entirely different music. The third woman, Gismonda (Durastanti), is one of those imperious matriarchs and devoted mothers whom we shall meet in Handel's oratorios. Emireno, a pirate, sung by Boschi, is a robust bass part—he is a man, not an *evirato*. *Ottone* is delicately polyphonic in structure and often displays romantic-sounding chromaticism.

This opera was a blow to Bononcini, but Handel was not satisfied with one blow. When Bononcini's *Erminia* could not measure up to the success of *Ottone*, Handel immediately followed with his *Flavio* (May 14, 1723), which, though a mediocre work, kept alive the favorable impression created by *Ottone*, further undermining Bononcini's position. The extreme passions and dramatic scenes of Haym's libretto are uneasily yoked with Handel's attempted imitation of Bononcini's light manner. What the public liked about Bononcini was that his arias did not tax their musical sensibilities; they were songs, short and dainty, easily assimilated and retained. *Flavio* has some good music here and there, but on the whole it must be placed low in the list of Handel's dramatic works. The fourth season ended with it, a season that also offered Ariosti's first London opera, *Cajo Marzio Coriolano*.

The fifth season opened on November 27, 1723, with Bononcini's new *Farnace*, followed by a revival of *Ottone*, and Ariosti's *Vespasiano*. Then, on February 20, 1724, came the *coup de grâce*, Handel's *Giulio Cesare*, with the remarkable cast headed by Senesino, Cuzzoni, and Boschi. The impact of this masterpiece proved to be too much for Bononcini. His *Calfurnia* was produced in April, but by that time he had withdrawn from the Academy's artistic triumvirate, leaving Ariosti and Handel in charge, and as Handel became the unquestioned master of the operatic roost, the

Italian began to fade away, for the time being satisfied with the position of master of music in the household of the Duchess of Marlborough. He still had his champions, however, and the cabal was by no means at an end. There were other casualties stemming from the éclat of the great productions. Durastanti, unable to stand the competition offered by the much younger Cuzzoni, left England, and Anastasia Robinson also withdrew from the stage. Mrs. Robinson was an intelligent, well-educated, and pleasant woman (she gets a clean bill of health even from Sir Newman, who found that "her morals from first to last were above reproach"), a good actress, and a fair singer, but her voice could not nearly equal that of any of the Italians, let alone Cuzzoni's. Though a veteran Handelian, upon her withdrawal she joined the Bononcini camp.

Giulio Cesare, composed on a very good libretto by Haym, is one of Handel's outstanding operas. This time Handel created a true heroic role, even though it was for a castrato. Caesar is in turn contemplative (his superb arioso as he stands before Pompey's urn—in G-sharp minor!), bold (the mighty aria "Al lampo dell'armi"), and amorous (when he awakens the sleeping Cleopatra). Cleopatra is an enchantress, her rich coloratura part giving her a dazzling countenance. Handel's characterization of this flaming woman is one of the miracles of the operatic literature. Intending to use Caesar as a tool against Ptolemy, she beseeches Venus, in the spacious aria "Venere bella"—one of those pieces with Handel's long-breathed melodies—to give her charms to attract the Roman, yet she is always confident of her inborn power over men. But when she really falls in love with Caesar, Handel changes the revengeful schemer into a woman despairing of the safety of her beloved, begging the gods not for charms but for his protection. "Se pietà di me non sente" is one of the great moments in the history of opera. Then when this fascinating creature is captured by Ptolemy and brought before him in shackles, she seethes with rage and vindictiveness, matching the violence of her temporary master. Finally, defeated, desperate, and forlorn, she sings to herself the ineffable song "Piangerò la sorte mia." The other parts are also most ably characterized. Cornelia is noble and restrained, Sextus ardent with youth, Ptolemy a brutal egotist, and Achilla a cold opportunist. The contrast between the sophisticated love music of Caesar and Cleopatra and the direct and coarse approach of Ptolemy to Cornelia is striking.

Giulio Cesare is full of vivid dramatic scenes, some of them of the festive "grand opera" type that would make this great work especially suitable for modern audiences. The opening chorus of Egyptians foreshadows similar scenes in the oratorios, and the ending of the opera is equally spectacular. Those who consider secco recitative an antiquated and makeshift convention should study the scene where Caesar is trapped. The whole scene, in which the emperor goes to a tryst only to find himself ambushed, is in secco (which leads to the great aria "Al lampo"), creating the most vivid tension. Elsewhere, the orchestral accompaniment is rich, since in addition to the usual complement Handel calls on harp, gamba, theorbo, and virtuoso French horn parts; obviously he wanted to create a lush "oriental" climate. Cleopatra's aria "V'adoro pupille," one of those aromatic night pieces with muted strings, is as modern as late Verdi.

Handel kept the fires going as the sixth season, opening on October 31, 1724, got under way with a new opera, *Tamerlano.* Haym's libretto is quite good, though its theme, that nobility of spirit will win over pride, is difficult to realize in opera. Here the principal role, that of Bajazet, is given to a tenor, hence it has force. This is the first great tenor role in opera. Handel was entirely successful in portraying Bajazet, a noble hero who dominates the opera; his antagonist, Tamerlano, sung by a new alto castrato, Pacini, is not nearly so convincing. On the other hand, Asteria (Cuzzoni) is a woman of flesh and blood. By and large *Tamerlano* is dramatically miscalculated. The final scene, Bajazet's farewell and Asteria's lament, is extraordinarily beautiful and poignant, but the love story is weak; Asteria is more convincing as the distraught daughter than as the lover. Andronico, sung by Senesino, is once more the Don Ottavio type; he sings beautiful music but is a puppet.

After a new opera by Ariosti (*Artaserse*), *Giulio Cesare* was revived with much success in January 1725, and on February 13 Handel produced the second masterpiece of the season, *Rodelinda.* Presented with the same cast, it was an instant success; in fact, next to *Giulio Cesare,* this was Handel's most popular opera. Haym once more delivered a fair libretto of somewhat mysterious origin, but what mattered was that the plot was workable.[2] *Rodelinda* deals with a subject destined to become a favorite: steadfastness of "conjugal love," to quote the subtitle of several late 18th-century operas that were to inspire Beethoven. Haym rightly spotted a special sympathy for such loyalty and fortitude in the bachelor Handel and lost no time in exploiting it. Rodelinda is a strong and finely drawn

[2] Much has been made by certain writers of Haym's "silence" concerning the sources of his librettos, but this was not owing to any nefarious practices; in the 18th century everyone looked at the finished product without bothering about its provenance. Haym was an able man of the theatre and when he borrowed a plot or an entire libretto which he—like all other librettists—had to adapt to the requirements of a particular theatre, he usually performed his task acceptably.

character from the opening scene. Cuzzoni shone to great advantage in the role because Handel lavished warm and expressive music on the heroine, but the other characters are no less well conceived. Those who are puzzled by Handel's attitude towards women should listen to Bertarido's longing song, "Dove sei amato bene." Even though written for Senesino, it expresses all the nuances a man pining for his beloved experiences. Similarly ardent and magnificent is the duet betwn Rodelinda and Bertarido, "Io t'abraccio." The third act, with the prison scene, the wounding of Bertarido's faithful servant, Rodelinda's fainting, all this taking place at dusk, is romantic opera of a very modern cast. Unfortunately, the dénouement is very weak, though this does not inhibit the music, which remains on a high plane throughout the opera. There is also some discrepancy in the otherwise well-designed character of Grimoaldo (Borosini), whose eventual magnanimity is not quite convincing. *Rodelinda* abounds in the most exquisite nature scenes, with marvels of delicate orchestral coloring. This is one of Handel's great operas that could be restored to the repertory by intelligent editing.

After these mighty exertions Handel rested for the moment, letting the season run its course. *Rodelinda* ran for fourteen nights and he could afford to let his old friend Ariosti try his fortunes with *Dario,* produced in April. *Tamerlano* was revived but had only three performances; the public was no longer satisfied with Handel's lesser efforts. He also busied himself with the music director's duties, writing the recitatives to *Elpindia,* a pasticcio of music by Leonardo Vinci and others. So the sixth season ended in June.

In the meantime Handel's domestic situation had changed. Somewhere between July and December 1723 he acquired a house in Lower Brook Street, near Hanover Square, which remained his abode to the end of his life. Several of his scores had been published, and a number of his operas performed on the Continent.[3] As his own situation solidified, the Academy's deteriorated. When the South Sea Bubble had burst in the summer of 1720, the Academy's stocks went with the rest. Rolli, in a letter to Giuseppe Riva that year, says that "our subscription [shares] could not fetch 30% cash value."[4] Already in 1721 the Academy began to experi-

---

[3] Among the subscribers for Handel's opera scores in the mid-twenties (more precisely, song "scores," because full scores were seldom published, to avoid piracy), one notices old Sigismund Kusser, who at that time lived in Dublin, and a "Mr. Cook of New York," probably the first American Handelian. Both Newburgh Hamilton and Charles Jennens, Handel's future oratorio librettists, were faithful subscribers.

[4] Rolli's delightfully entertaining, malicious, and informative correspondence with Riva, the Modenese diplomat who secured Senesino's services for the Academy, can

ence financial difficulties, issuing calls for five per cent levies or assess-
ments. Presently, to bolster the institution's fortunes, the directors decided
to provide a foil for Cuzzoni in the person of Faustina Bordoni, then a
rising young soprano much admired in Italy and Germany. That Faustina
was engaged with the idea of creating a rivalry, and hence some *réclame*
for the Academy, is clear from the press notices that appeared months before her arrival, the *London Journal* plainly announcing that "a famous
Italian Lady is coming over to rival Signiora Cuzzoni." Since Faustina
was not only a remarkable singer but a personable young woman,
whereas La Cuzzoni was rotund and homely, a conflict was inevitable.
The directors had not learned to avoid such rivalries and soon found that
the two singers inspired warring factions similar to those figuring in the
Handel-Bononcini contretemps, and in fact they became involved in that
affair too. Quantz, the oracle of musical wisdom of the day, and Tosi, the
greatest living authority on singing, both expressed themselves in terms of
the highest admiration for the two sopranos, but both gave the edge to
Faustina. Tosi could not forbear speculating on what would happen if
Cuzzoni's legato and portamento could be combined with Bordoni's
agility.

The seventh season, 1725–26, introduced two new Handel operas,
Paolo Rolli reappearing in the role of staff librettist with less than felicitous results. His *Scipione* (March 12, 1726) is steeped in grave pathos
which could not be sustained for long stretches, compelling Handel to indulge in distracting episodes. The heroine, Berenice, does come to life,
and the opera, rather polyphonic in texture, has excellent instrumental
pieces, among them the famous march that was parodied in *Polly* as
"Brave boys, prepare."

The next production, *Alessandro* (May 5), was performed eleven
times in the month of May—an unheard-of record then as now for a new
serious opera—but there was a good reason for it. Handel had been given
the special task of catering to two prima donnas in the same opera (this
was Faustina's début), for both he and the directors hoped that the combination would so overwhelm the public that the Academy's future would
be assured. Dramaturgically the plan was very vulnerable, because equal
favor had to be shown to both temperamental and jealous artists, but
Rolli and Handel skilfully walked this tightrope by the careful planning
of minutely balanced roles and correspondingly impartial dosage of good
music for each of the stars. In addition, the two women's situation vis-à-

be found in excellent selections in Otto Erich Deutsch's *Handel, a Documentary Biography.*

vis Senesino had to be equalized, and there was the fourth member of the Academy's top quartet, Boschi. Accordingly, at first Alexander inclines to Rossana (Bordoni), whereupon Lisaura (Cuzzoni) is very much disappointed. The love music in the second act when Rossana awaits Alexander is Handel at his idyllic-pastoral best and the orchestration is an absolute delight. But now Lisaura has her moment (Rossana having conveniently gone to sleep) and, her love music being equally beguiling, it is the wakened Rossana's turn to feel slighted. The great warrior is in a dilemma, upon which he expatiates in a sumptuous aria, "Vano amore"; it is a typical castrato aria, wondrous bel canto but not convincing drama. Finally, the Macedonian comes to the conclusion that the solution is to give up love altogether and concentrate on being king. However, before doing so he has another round with each of the songstresses in the form of finely wrought duets. The ladies also sing magnificent arias, every one of them carefully tailored to suit the particular voice. Now the librettist is in a dilemma of his own, because while the king's noble and practical resolution may have saved a delicate situation, it fails to lead to the mandatory happy ending; therefore Alexander changes his mind and finally settles on Rossana, while Lisaura is compensated by a lesser king, Tassile of India. Thus was satisfied a cast whose aggregate emoluments amounted to many thousands of pounds per annum. Surprisingly enough, this tour de force of an opera is full of music of very high quality, of spectacular and animated scenes, and martial strains. Any opera house that could assemble the extraordinary cast demanded by *Alessandro* would create a stampede with this work even today.

The eighth season, which began on January 7, 1727, saw the three leading London opera composers in competition for the last time. Ariosti's *Lucio Vero*, indifferently received, was followed by Handel's *Admeto* (January 31), which once more filled the Haymarket Theatre, and at the end of the season Bononcini's *Astianatte* closed the cycle. *Admeto*, putting in the field the incomparable quartet of stars, was greeted with unstinted admiration: eight performances within a month, and ten more during the rest of the season. Since, in addition, *Ottone* and *Floridante* were in the active repertory, Handel certainly had another profitable and prestigious year. The libretto, by either Rolli or Haym—or both—has potentially good theatrical qualities, but the drama itself is poorly constructed. Still, Handel's now-dead, now-alive Alceste is not materially different from Gluck's Eurydice, who also goes through such metamorphoses to no one's objection. What is carried to a ridiculous extent in this libretto is the favorite Baroque opera trick of the "picture," i.e. the likeness of the heroine (or less frequently of the hero) carried around for identification—and trouble; in this instance the game is complicated by inadvertently exchanged pictures. These weaknesses, added to a dénouement that is moral instead of dramatic, are near fatal for the play. Nevertheless, Handel made a great opera out of this farrago; the music is powerful and the individual scenes impressive. The very first scene, with the king raving on his sickbed surrounded by the furies, is uncommonly powerful, far surpassing the memorable scene in Gluck's *Orfeo* with which it is often compared. Once more the women are masterfully characterized; they are in turn passionate, gentle, and jealous, and Handel is notably successful in deepening their conflict. *Admeto* contains so much surpassing music that it should be salvaged.

As the season ended, with Bononcini's *Astianatte,* the rivalry of the two *prime donne* reached a climax in a noisy and vulgar scandal that rocked the Academy, London society, and even the court. The Princess of Wales was a pained spectator as the two women, incited by the audience, fell upon each other with pummeling and hair pulling. The disorderly spectacle was brought about by the partisans who greeted the singing of their respective champion's rival with catcalls, which of course infuriated the two women.

The year was marked by two important events. Handel became a naturalized British subject on February 20, and George I died on June 11 in Osnabrück, on his way to his beloved Hanover. The Prince of Wales was immediately proclaimed King George II. Handel and the Prince were not on the best of terms, but this was because George I was a staunch supporter of the composer, and since the Prince loathed everything about his father, the animosity was extended to Handel, even though he liked his music and had nothing against him personally. Handel, who knew the son as well as he did the father, had paid no attention to the Prince's moodiness, and there was of course his great friend, Caroline, on whom he could always count. The object of George II's hatred having been eliminated by Providence, the new King lost no time in reinstating Handel in his good graces, immediately commissioning him to compose the anthems for the coronation, a commission duly and magnificently executed. George II proved to be a steady patron, and the Queen, and especially the princesses, went often to the opera.

But for the moment Handel's interest could not be diverted for any length of time from opera, as the ninth season of the Royal Academy of Music opened on September 30, 1727, with a revival of *Admeto*. The new contribution to the repertory was Handel's *Riccardo I, Re d'Inghilterra,* presented on November 11, 1727. Rolli's libretto owed its existence to the recent dynastic events. The English subject, craftily selected by the Italian librettist and dedicated with a flourish to the new sovereign, is rather transparently opportunistic. The heroic tone is fortified with a good deal of warlike music, and the nobility of England is proclaimed in dithyrambs. A few good numbers were buried with this *pièce d'occasion.*

After a revival of *Alessandro, Siroe* was produced on February 17, 1728, again with the top cast—the employment of two *prime donne* having become a standard practice. Eighteen performances indicate a favored work, but *Siroe* is not a great opera. This was Handel's first Metastasian libretto, and though *Siroe* is early Metastasio—the great Italian poet's second lyric drama—superior literary qualities are already in evidence. The language is clear, poetic, and easy to set. Nor is the dramatic construction so poor as Dent would have it, though Haym did mangle the original by excessive condensation. After all, practically every representative composer of the earlier part of the 18th century set *Siroe* to music, and it was this libretto that started Metastasio on his spectacular career. The clear and forceful lines prompted Handel to write many recitatives that are dramatic and imaginative; in fact, the dramatic tone, as opposed to the lyric, dominates in this opera. But on the whole it contains much conventional music. The entire royal family attended the first night.

The last new Handelian opera of the season—and of the sinking Academy—was also Haym's last libretto; he died in the following year. *Tolomeo* is a strange opera, coming as it does after *Siroe:* it is altogether undramatic, episodic, lacking recitatives, an almost pure aria opera of the old Scarlatti cast. Many of these arias are very beautiful, and since Haym made the contending lovers fall into slumber to get them out of the way, there are many fine elegiac and pastoral scenes; nevertheless, as a whole the opera is only a collection of grateful concert numbers.

The season ended prematurely on June 1, 1728, ostensibly because of Senesino's indisposition. Actually, sensing the demise of the Academy, the singers began to melt away as they had from Dresden when Handel was there on his first recruiting trip. The signs were plain enough for anyone to notice. Mrs. Pendarves (Mary Granville), better known after her second marriage as Mrs. Patrick Delany, who was a devoted Handelian and a keen observer, had written to her sister on November 25, 1727: "I doubt operas will not survive longer than this winter, they are now at their last gasp; the subscription is expired and nobody will renew it." The staff itself saw the handwriting on the wall. In his dedication of the libretto of *Tolomeo* to the Earl of Albemarle, Haym speaks of opera "now fast declining." But the most ominous warning came from the directors of the Academy, who by that time had exacted their twentieth five per cent assessment from the subscribers. A notice in the *Daily Courant* for May 31, 1728, summons the General Court of the Royal Academy of Musick "in order to consider of proper Measures for recovering the Debts due to the Academy, and discharging what is due to Performers, Tradesmen, and others; and also to determine how the Scenes, Cloaths, etc. are to be disposed of, if the Operas cannot be continued." They could not be continued, at least not by this association.

The collapse was due partly to extravagant expenditures in an extravagant age but largely to opera itself, and not least to the Handelian operas. Chrysander, with his infinite zeal and patience, made a careful audit of the nine years of the Academy's existence; his figures should be pretty close to the actual facts. There were 487 performances of opera: 245 by Handel, 108 by Bononcini, 55 by Ariosti, and 79 by all others—thus Handel's operas constituted half the total. In general his operas were far above the level of the Academy audiences; they were weightier, more elaborate, worked with more sophistication than the usual run of Venetian-Neapolitan opera. The dimensions were large, the orchestra used with a skill and imagination no one in those days could match, and the stereotyped and obvious instrumental obbligatos turned into delicate counterpoint set against the voice.

[2]

ONE WOULD THINK THAT A country with ancient musical traditions—"the English are a singing people"—would naturally take to the mellifluous art of the Italians. Was it not in England that the Italian madrigal had its greatest flowering in the north? There were songs in Shakespeare's plays, in Stuart drama, and the first quarter century following the Restoration was brimming with theatrical productions that made copious use of music. Nor was the spirit of the Baroque that created opera missing in England; the stage was elaborate, the machines rivalling those of the best French and Italian theatres, the productions sumptuous, and there were many good instrumentalists available for the pit orchestras. Music at the court of the first two Stuart kings was lavish, the productions with their music and dancing resembling the French *ballet de cour,* the stage and décors designed by such great architects as Inigo Jones. The ravages suffered by theatrical life under the Commonwealth were rapidly forgotten, and by the end of the century, when Samuel Chappuzeau, a French traveller-critic, visited London he found that not only was the court "no less polished nor less elegant than the French court, but the people of London liked their pleasures no less than the people of Paris." He mentions three theatres in commission, with "superb decorations and change of scenery, the music is excellent and the ballet magnificent." [5] It has been proved that the English theatre orchestras were well developed in the latter 17th century [6] (though Pepys did not think that the orchestra's disposition in the Drury Lane Theatre was well conceived). But the failure of Italian opera had causes other than musical; they were deeply imbedded in English character and thought.

The tradition and living force of the theatre in England did not permit the development of an alien form of the stage; the only concession English taste made was to music as an incidental ornament. The playwrights of this highly developed and experienced theatre held views concerning the drama that created an unbridgeable cleft between the spoken theatre and opera. They saw life from close proximity, in its specifically modern, contemporary aspects, which they considered completely lost and ignored in opera. In sum, they perceived in opera an abandonment of all the values they cherished, without adequate compensation by the music. Fond as they were of music, nevertheless they saw in opera not only an irrational play, but a perversion of the nature of music, or, as the Beggar says in the introduction of the ballad opera by Gay and Pepusch: "I hope that I have not made my Opera throughout unnatural, like those in vogue." All that Handel's audiences expected was to see the singer get set for his aria, step in front of the footlights, sing an enjoyable but unintelligible song in a foreign tongue, reap the applause, and depart. Thomas Shadwell, the industrious playwright and connoisseur of Restoration mores, who was a pioneer in "English opera," had already perceived this attitude of the public and had no illusions about the musical sensibilities of the audiences that flocked to the public theatres. In his preface to the libretto of *Psyche* he gives unstinted praise to the composer, Matthew Locke, but remarks ruefully that "the unskilful in Musick will not like the more solemn [i.e. elaborate] part of it," which he recommends "to the judgment of able Musicians." For those who are unable to comprehend the finer points of music "there are light and airy things to please them."

In the last decades of the 17th century interest in Italian art reached a considerable pitch of intensity in England. Hundreds of agents scoured Italy (and to a lesser extent the Low Countries) buying up everything

[5] *L'Europe vivant*, Paris, 1707, reprint 1876.
[6] William J. Lawrence, in *The Musical Quarterly*, January 1917.

they could. It was then that the foundations were laid for England's great galleries, as the mansions of the rich were filled with these imported treasures. Interest in importing and acclimatizing Italian and French music was also very real, even antedating the preoccupation with art. Thomas Killegrew, playwright, adventurer, wit, builder of the original Drury Lane Theatre, and theatrical producer, observed operatic productions on his frequent trips to France and Italy. After the Restoration he planned to import companies with the purpose of establishing regular seasons of opera—but nothing came of the plan. Charles II, familiar with French music and an admirer of Lully, sent Pelham Humphrey abroad to study music, and since he there learned about opera at first hand one would have expected him to return eager to transplant this new and glamorous genre to England. Humphrey was an able, literate, and highly talented musician with a decided gift for the lyric-theatrical; the results of his studies abroad are in evidence everywhere in his music, yet he did not attempt the composition of a genuine opera. Nor did his great pupil, Henry Purcell, even though a staunch admirer of French and Italian music, make any effort to establish English opera. *Dido and Aeneas,* his one true opera, was significantly not written for the public theatre but for a young ladies' school in Chelsea. If we add to this that English playwrights definitely knew and appreciated the fact that lyricism in song affords a direct communication between author and audience and that there was a keen understanding of the practical psychology of music both by theatrical people and the public, our puzzlement at their failure to create opera increases.

As was remarked above, the plays were generously dotted with songs, and while incidental, these were not used at random but had a structural function in the play that the audience understood and relished. Preparation was always carefully made for their appearance so that they should seem natural. The songs identified character, created and depicted moods, offered genre scenes such as slumber songs, processionals, and so forth, but they were sung *to* the characters, in the form of serenades or other entertainment or commentary; self-expression in music by the protagonists was consistently avoided. Edward Dent, in his *Foundations of English Opera,* makes the important and perceptive qualification that "Shakespeare and his contemporaries never show us speech intensified into song under stress of emotion, but only the emotional effect produced by music on the characters represented." This is the attitude that governs the role of music in the English theatre throughout the 17th century and the Handelian era, and it is the crux of the problem of opera. The increased use of music in plays does not signify a changed esthetic doctrine; the public demanded song and dance for entertainment, but everyone was agreed that this musical entertainment must not intrude upon the drama itself. "To an English audience," says Hawkins, "music joined to poetry was not an entertainment for an evening, something that had the appearance of a plot or fable was necessary to keep their attention awake." They wanted the spoken dialogue—that is, the self-expression of the principals of the play—left intact; not made *in* music but at most *with* music, thus excluding the possibility of the rise of a true native opera.

As we examine these songs we discover that they were used with skill and deliberation. The brilliant exchange of wit and epigrams in the comedy of the Restoration theatre could not be set to music, while in the tragedies music was assigned to the illusory figures, supernatural spirits, or to solemn announcements such as prophecies. While in the comedies the use of songs, and of music in general, was not so carefully regulated as in the tragedies, the conventions and the patterns are similiar. Whereas in the tragedy it is the supernatural beings who sing, in the comedy the songs are given to eccentric characters, to fools or drunkards who, unlike normal men, are permitted to express themselves in such an "unrealistic" manner directly in song rather than in speech. In both types of play the most natural spot for music was where an entertainment takes place, at which point popular tunes universally known were parodied or even a whole brief masque inserted.

This dramaturgical concept is similar to that held by contemporary French critics, and since in both countries the esthetics of the musical stage were dictated by the men of letters, one wonders whether there were not some close ties between the two literary camps. Molière was the first to advance the theory that in a play songs are particularly suitable to the *personnages accessoires* or *de fantaisie*—that is, to supernatural figures that are only accessory to the drama. Dryden, in the preface to *Albion and Albanius,* faithfully echoes this concept (even though he does not follow it strictly in the work itself). Wherever we look in 17th-century English plays, we see that it is indeed the *personnages accessoires* who sing. The literary men rejected the principles of the *stile rappresentativo,* and Dryden took care to point out that his *Albion and Albanius* is not an opera because the music is incidental, at the same time averring that it is not a genuine play either, because the entire story is supernatural; whichever way they viewed it, "opera" was a troublesome proposition.

Attention has already been called to Saint-Évremond, the father of hostile French operatic criticism, who as a long-time resident in England could not have failed to influence his English colleagues and whose influence in fact extended even to Italy. His definition of opera is a classic example of French logic which, inadmissible as it is in this particular case, was generally shared by most English men of letters. "An opera is an odd combination of poetry and music in which the poet and musician, equally hindered by each other, take great pains to produce a wretched work."[7] Any English writer could have been the author of Saint-Évremond's statement that "opera is so contrary to nature that my imagination is shocked by it; that is, to sing the whole piece from beginning to end." Again, "There are some things which ought to be sung, and some which may be sung without offending decency and reason." Similarly, and even before Saint-Évremond, the Abbé François Hédelin d'Aubignac in his *Pratique du théâtre* (1657) says that "the theatre can undoubtedly tolerate some music, but it must be to awaken the appetite, not to satiate it." The question cannot be avoided: given this startling similarity of views, why was it that opera triumphed in France though Lully was its solitary musical champion of note, whereas in England two far superior musicians of genius, Purcell and Handel, were unable to breach the opposition?[8]

The answer is in the attitude of the *grand siècle* towards the libretto, for if the latter had merit the intrusion of music was grudgingly forgiven. Philippe Quinault, Lully's principal collaborator, was a mediocre playwright but stood head and shoulders above the average librettist. His librettos were *read* as literature, and even a century later, La Harpe, the keenest and most merciless critic of 17th-century drama, still regarded Quinault as far superior to Lully: "The one is no longer sung, but the other is always read." The very fact that Lully's works were never referred to as operas but as "lyric tragedies" shows that the French considered their opera "une espèce de tragédie avec musique."

In contradistinction, the term "opera" was frequently used in England in the 17th century, but we must beware of regarding these works as examples of the musical drama as we understand it. To the English of the Restoration, "opera" simply meant an elaborate spectacle enhanced by music and dancing. Matthew Locke called his setting of *Psyche* an opera

---

[7] *Sur les operas,* in *Oeuvres,* IV, Paris, 1753.

[8] It is interesting to note that there is a remarkable similarity between Lully and Purcell in that each succeeded in paralleling the Italian recitative with one that admirably reflects the genius of his own language. No one to this day has surpassed either of them in the faithful musical declamation of the French or English language. The recitative, which Saint-Évremond called *un méchant usage du chant et de la parole,* was one of the chief stumbling blocks to opera beyond the Alps, and the most consistently attacked.

but felt constrained to defend the validity of the title because "all the tragedy be not in music." He correctly reflects the prevailing literary opinion when, continuing, he ventures that "though Italy was and is the greatest academy of the world for that science [opera], England is not; and therefore [we] mix [the music] with interlocutions, as more proper to our genius." Nothing positive can be said about Sir William Davenant's *Siege of Rhodes,* usually considered "the first English opera"; the music is lost but it is significant that Pepys called it more a piece of literature than an opera. Purcell himself (Preface to *Dioclesian*) makes a distinction between opera and "English opera," defining the latter as "a play of which music forms a frequent, necessary, and integrated part, but of which the dialogue is spoken."

Among the popular features of the Restoration theatre were the revivals of Shakespeare's plays, which, as a rule roughly handled by the producers and arrangers, often fall within the category of "English opera." *The Tempest,* rewritten by John Dryden with the collaboration of Sir William Davenant, was one of the most admired of these. Produced in 1670 with added characters, it had become almost a new creation. But when *The Tempest* is mentioned as the cornerstone of English dramatic music, it is usually Shadwell's version that is meant. John Downes, the Théophile Gautier of the 17th-century English theatre, expressly says in his *Roscius Anglicanus* (1702) that *The Tempest* was "made into an opera by Mr. Shadwell." His description shows that "opera" was used in the sense that this was a spectacular *comédie à machines* with music and was not a true opera even though the historians always point out that the production boasted an unusually large orchestra. This is no criterion, however; Purcell's *Dioclesian* employed an orchestra larger than the Haymarket Theatre's—yet *Dioclesian* is not an opera.

The score of *The Tempest* contains very good instrumental music by Matthew Locke. The vocal numbers, composed by John Banister, Pelham Humphrey, and James Hart, are songs, many of them very fine, with well-contrasted and flowing lines, but they too were "insertions" and once more assigned to supernatural beings. Indeed, *The Tempest* was particularly suited for treatment as an "English opera"; its arrangers could observe the cardinal tenet of English dramaturgy: the music may be concerned with the principal characters, but is not sung by them as an act of lyric self-revelation. Shadwell himself was an ardent amateur musician, and it seems that he consciously strove towards the establishment of some sort of English counterpart to Italian opera, a view supported by the many satires, similar to those later aimed at Handel and the Haymarket

Theatre, that were directed against him. In his preface to *Psyche* he made a statement such as could have been made—and indeed was made a century later—by Goldoni. "In all the words which are sung, I did not so much take care of the Wit or Fancy of 'em, as the making of 'em proper for Musick." This is the attitude of the true librettist.[9]

It is obvious, then, that before the advent of Handel and Italian opera, music had become an integral part of the English theatre. This theatre, whose musical worth cannot be lightly dismissed, did create a specific esthetic, as well as authentic masterpieces in the works of Purcell, to which we shall return when discussing Handel's contributions to the English lyric stage. It is equally obvious in the light of these historical developments that when Addison wrote his celebrated pieces in the *Spectator* his irony hid a good deal of deep conviction and full agreement with his French literary colleagues. Fundamentally, the core of the opposition to opera rests on Boileau's maxim: *On ne peut jamais faire un bon opéra, parce que la musique ne sait narrer.* This was interpreted by the critics, both French and English, to mean that since music is "unable to narrate," to tell a story, opera is a drama in which essentials have little relation to the permanent realities of human conduct. In Addison's words: "Our countrymen could not forbear laughing when they heard a Lover chanting out a Billet-doux, and even the Superscription of a Letter set to a Tune." His description of an opera as "extravagantly lavish in its Decorations, as its only Design is to gratify the Senses, and keep up an indolent Attention in the Audience," is similar to that given by Chappuzeau somewhat earlier: "But, after all, these fine spectacles are only for the eyes and ears; they do not touch the soul and one may say afterwards that one has seen and heard, but not that one has been edified." This tone of criticism continued throughout Handel's activity and far into the late 18th century. In a letter to his son, Lord Chesterfield said: "Whenever I go to an Opera, I leave my sense and reason at the door with my half guinea, and deliver myself up to my eyes and ears." Johnson, in his *Life of Hughes,* also believed that opera was "an exotick and irrational entertainment." [10]

All this should not reflect adversely on Addison's keen insight into the nature of the relationship of music to a cultural circle. "A Composer should fit his Musick to the Genius of the People, and consider that the

[9] Goldoni, in the preface to his *Statira*, 1756: "When I write for music the last person I think of is myself."

[10] Sir Isaac Newton is quoted by the Reverend William Stukely as having said that "he never was at more than one Opera. The first Act he heard with pleasure, the second stretch'd his patience, at the third he ran away."

Delicacy of Hearing, and the Taste of Harmony, has been founded upon those Sounds which every Country abounds with: in short, that Musick is of a relative Nature." This Handel's opera totally disregarded, and while in the meantime, at Cannons, Handel found "those sounds which abounded" in England, it took him a long time to realize that they could not be found in Italian opera.

There were additional weighty reasons for the failure of the Royal Academy of Music and for Italian opera in general. First of all, the language barrier was not only insuperable but caused effects totally unexpected by the foreign staff running the King's Theatre. In Vienna or Dresden, opera in Italian was accepted without any objection, and if there was any objection later in the 18th century, it was on nationalistic or patriotic grounds—the foreign language did not irritate those audiences. Frederick the Great would not let an Italian composer into his Berlin opera house, not because of his language—he himself preferred French to his native tongue, and liked Italian opera—but because he wanted to help German opera. Not so in England, where songs in a foreign language, or even in Welsh, or English with a strong accent, invariably created a comic effect and were deliberately used in plays for this purpose. When Addison scornfully refers to the Haymarket Theatre audience as preferring "High Dutch" to English he is using a term that has frequently been applied to comic songs in Stuart drama and, quite logically, it seemed to him that if a whole piece is presented in "High Dutch," not only is the realistic effect of a comic interlude lost, but the entire work makes no sense. Another reason for popular dislike of Italian operas was their subject matter. Caesar, Scipio, and all the other Romans were to the Italians their ancestors, but beyond the Alps they became boring historical figures with whom the public felt no kinship. English letters may have been steeped in classical antiquity, but the man in the street was not.

We have seen the political connotation attached to the events at the Academy, but the middle-class public also saw in opera foreign popery that affronted their sturdy English Protestantism. Furthermore, the middle-class Englishman, aware of the corruption and immorality rife in aristocratic circles, equated Italian opera, the plaything of aristocrats, with the wily, unscrupulous, pleasure-seeking, and dagger-wielding Italians, the most frivolous and ungodly race on earth. Then there was the castrato, upon whom this Italian opera was largely built. Since the castratos were prominent in the papal choir from the 16th century onward (as they were in other church choirs) and were mostly Italians, they were associated—not without some justification—with Catholicism. The

Church recognized them and it took a long time before indignation—not missing in Italy either—forced their abandonment. It must be acknowledged, though, that while in the young Mozart's time the opera buffa evicted the "unnatural ones" from the opera theatre, church choirs retained them for another century, and castration of promising young singers continued, though infrequently, far into the 19th century. In Italy these male sopranos and altos were so highly regarded—and highly paid —that there are authenticated records of natural sopranos—that is, women—making a career by masquerading as *evirati.* The English, who on their trips to the peninsula could see on the shields of veterinarians and barber-surgeons the legend: *Qui si castrano ragazzi,* found the practice repulsive and a gross violation of morality. They were also disgusted by the physical appearance of the castratos. Some of these were merely feminine looking, with marked feminine characteristics, but many became huge and grotesquely misshapen. The *beau monde* did not share in this revulsion and welcomed them into their homes as chic and exciting foreign specialties. Wild accusations were hurled at the castratos by the public, though mostly without foundation. They were vain and demanding, but so were natural sopranos, and so are our natural tenors today. On the whole, their probity matched that of other human beings. Dr. Burney, gentleman and scholar, came to the castrato's rescue to remove, "in justice, as well as humanity," the contempt in which they were held, denying that they were "cowards and illiterates," and praising them highly for their incomparable singing.

If all this militated against Italian opera in England, the *coup de grâce* to the Academy was administered by that irony which is so engaging in English letters. On January 29, 1728, at Lincoln's Inn Fields, the *Beggar's Opera,* a glittering, full-blooded epic of roguery triumphant, full of wit and bitter cynicism, was first performed to "a prodigious Concourse of Nobility and Gentry." Its run of over sixty performances topped all existing theatrical records. John Gay's spirited farce was accompanied by a garland of popular tunes, cleverly selected, arranged, and prefaced with an original overture by Handel's erstwhile compatriot, present fellow-Briton, and old competitor, Dr. Pepusch. The *Beggar's Opera* won lavish praise not only for being English theatre, but for what it was: musical comedy in the modern sense. This was a thoroughly English form of the theatre, a challenge to Italian opera both as to native wit and language, and as to masculinity. Dean Swift confirmed the challenge plainly in the *Intelligencer:* "This comedy likewise exposes, with good justice, that unnatural taste for Italian music among us which is wholly unsuitable to our

northern climate, and the genius of the people, whereby we are over-run
with Italian effeminacy, and Italian nonsense." There is scarcely a creature in this magnificent farce who is not, if seriously considered, corrupt
and despicable, yet every spectator took the characters to his heart. While
ballad operas and satires were a popular entertainment, called by historians a "democratic art" and "low-life opera," it is incorrect to consider
them merely an entertainment for the populace; all classes of society enjoyed them, not least some of the outstanding literary figures of the age as
well as the nobility. Underneath the cynicism there is a wealth of theatrical skill, good writing, and wisdom; Pope and Swift were not only interested in the *Beggar's Opera* but had some part in its preparation, and Dr.
Johnson also thought highly of it. Furthermore, the ballad opera was a
potent political weapon, something always relished by Englishmen. Its
merciless satire hastened the retirement of more than one political potentate, among them Walpole.

The ballad opera is generally dated from 1728, though Gay's masterpiece is only the most successful specimen of the genre. Some historians
carry its origins back to Richard Brome and even Ben Jonson, properly
considering also the French *comédie en vaudeville*, which could be heard
at the Haymarket Theatre, where visiting French troupes played. These
are reasonable historical reconstructions, but the very fact that by the
middle of the century the ballad opera had practically disappeared shows
that it owed a great deal to the English reaction to Italian opera in general and the Handelian in particular. There can be no doubt that the most
important ingredient in its make-up was the direct—and immediate—
parody of every successful "serious" opera, the parody being accentuated
by the borrowing of famous arias from the very opera that was the subject of the satire, which were then sung with bawdy lyrics. The satirical
and often riotous take-offs started with the first Italian operas performed
in London, *Arsinoe* and *Camilla*, and not a few of Handel's new offerings
were immediately greeted with a hilarious travesty at Drury Lane or some
other place. The intended ridiculing of Italian opera is manifest in such
titles as *Tragi-Comic-Farcical Ballad Opera*, and so on.

The ballad opera is a genre by itself, different from both the masque
and the "English opera," or the "semi-opera." While the flavor of its wit
was so English as to refuse transplantation to foreign languages, its influence was nevertheless considerable. On its way southward on the Continent it merged with kindred French types, eventually calling to life the
German *Singspiel*, its most notable distant progeny.

The *Beggar's Opera* drove the biggest nail in the coffin of the Royal

Academy of Music, but the collapse of the Academy did not mean "ruin" and "bankruptcy" for Handel; his personal fortunes were not at all threatened, nor was his reputation as a composer, which was international. He was not even in straitened circumstances. Percy M. Young, who in his biography made an interesting study of Handel's numerous financial dealings, shows that at the end of the final season of the Academy Handel purchased £700 worth of annuities of the reorganized South Sea Company, followed within a month by a further £400. He must have accumulated a tidy investment of several thousand pounds and was ready, willing, and able to launch his next venture. However, before following him on his further operatic quest we must retrace our steps to Burlington House and Cannons to investigate the beginnings of the "English" Handel.

IX

ALTHOUGH HANDEL'S EARLIER STAY AT BURLINGTON
house and at Cannons, viewed from the perspective of the Royal Academy
of Music, seems to be a mere interlude, it represents the period of gestation for Handel as we know him. The newspapers might refer to him for
years to come as "Mr. Handell, the famous composer of Italian Musick,"
but with the anthems, the Te Deums, pastoral, and masque composed
during these years, there began the decisive change that was to turn the
purveyor of exotic entertainment for the aristocracy into a national
English composer.

The anthem plays an important part in this change and is a constituent element in the oratorio, though it must be remembered that the
anthem was ceremonial music while the oratorio was music drama. It is
the extrovert, festive—even "official"—tone and manner of the anthems
that reappear in the oratorios at places appropriate for such tone and
manner, not the "churchly" quality that is so often emphasized. Even
Messiah really culminates on a heroic-triumphal tone that is distinctly
secular, for the Hallelujah Chorus is a "coronation anthem," one of the
many Handel composed. It is true, however, that in instances where there
is no dramatic construction and characterization, as in *Judas Maccabaeus,*
the anthem style may dominate the whole work. With the very first of
these "English" compositions, the *Birthday Ode for Queen Anne* and the
Utrecht Te Deum, Handel was seeking the formula for a music that
would express the collectivity of the nation; henceforth the problem was

to make this also a personal art. Many of Handel's biographers see him almost apart from his environment and experience, yet the influence of the climate of English civilization and culture is inevitably present in his works as the decisive constructive force determining perspective, subject, and expression. Perhaps it will not be superfluous, then, to meditate a little on English thought and history, some of which we take so much for granted that its significance is lost. The England of green lawns, cottages, manors, old family retainers, porridge, and high tea, all presenting an appearance of flawless cleanliness and freshness, may be the impression the tourist gains, but the tourist of history must go far beyond this Sunday heritage of Victorian England. For this is also a nation that can get along comfortably with a statue of Cromwell at one end of a short street and a statue of Charles I at the other.

The arts of the Augustan age expressed the standards of the dominant aristocracy, who, well placed, well poised, secure in the possession of power, and untroubled, were free to concentrate upon formal perfection in their way of life, their intellectual no less than their social manners. The principle of aristocratic superiority in politics found its analogy in literature and music, in the attention paid to correctness and solemnity of style. This clarity of view, which differs from the Italian's because of the Englishman's calm, is the enemy of all obscurity; the mystic and metaphysical that is characteristic of the German is far removed from the Englishman. His aversion to abstract speculation, rejection of mysticism, love of liberty, of tolerance, of free inquiry, delight in the attainable and in the exercising of reason are all summed up in John Locke, who was as characteristic of the English mind as were Descartes of the French and Kant of the German.

The monarchy was the apex of society, but it was the craftsmen and the tradesmen, and also the highest stratum of the middle classes, the literary men, who in airing their views evolved the ideals of liberty and order, the principle that none should have too much power and none too little, ideals developed in the spirit of reasonable compromise that made Britain's institutions possible. All this was palpable reality even though political morality was very low in Georgian England, following a tradition well established by Charles II, though, of course, neither English invention nor monopoly. What the non-Briton must remember is that despite lax political morals there was an abiding respect for the rule of law and that constitutional practices rest on the rule of the spirit of the law rather than on its letter. Constitutional rigidity is alien to the English political genius.

The richness of the Elizabethan age and its immediate sequel was bound to create a reaction against its irrational profligacy, a reaction of sobriety and of the rational mind. With Mind there appears its pretty sister, Cleverness, to take over from Genius the governing of thought. On the Continent, prestige and authority still ruled, the authority of the monarch and of God; this was the age of the Habsburgs, of the Jesuits, of Louis XIV, the *grand siècle*. But England proved that divinely sanctioned royal prestige can be in conflict with popular authority, and a revolution took place in the name of the Puritan God, eliminating that frivolous and superfluous pomp which is called the monarchy.

Milton, the great poet of the Puritans, defends the revolution—though in Latin tracts; he even defends the execution of the sinful King: *Pro populo Anglicano defensio.* The religious background was of course very real, yet the new, utilitarian conception of life, for which ample sanction was found in the Hebrew Scriptures, is an important point that must not be overlooked. The Lord Protector of the Commonwealth was a "conservative" dictator; there is evidence that he would have been willing to go farther in the direction of religious tolerance. It was another matter when Parliament threatened private property; here he would not yield. One recalls his famous words to Parliament in 1654 in which he protested the "Levelling Principle" that would "make a Tenant as liberal a fortune as the Landlord." Indeed, some historians call him, with right, "the guardian of private property." Here is the beginning of what the Puritans, though unwittingly, assuredly helped to develop: "Class consciousness superseding chapel consciousness," to quote Trevelyan. Religion in practice is inevitably affected by social and economic ideas. It had its role to play in the development of the idea of human unity, but the class society prevailed and used religion for its own ends—that is, to maintain itself.

The sparkling world of the English Renaissance gave way to new moral tenets, a new art, and a new science: a civilization based on industry, finance, and commerce, on the building of an empire; the primary fact of human life had become economic and political well-being. Roger Boyle, a Restoration dramatist, expressed the frame of mind of this rising capitalist, empire-building society:

> *That Prince, whose Flags are bow'd to on the Seas,*
> *Of all Kings shores keeps in his hands the Keys:*
> *No King can him, he may all Kings invade,*
> *And on his Will depends their Peace and Trade.*
> *Trade, which does Kings and Subjects Wealth increase;*
> *Trade, which more necessary is than Peace.*

Trade and finance did, indeed, expand, and by Handel's time there was no limit to the profits that capitalist adventurers, triggered by personal greed and untrammelled ambition, could acquire. The scramble for wealth resulted in the rise to power of new men, like the Earl of Carnarvon, later Duke of Chandos, Handel's patron, who carried the looting of the nation's treasury to enormous lengths. But even to the vast majority of virtuous Englishmen, those of the middle classes, the 18th century was an age when luxury was the prize to be obtained from life.

The gradual process of democratization also created powerful opposition to the spirit of the Renaissance; at the same time it de-emphasized everything superhuman, though this denial appeared in a proper religious guise. This is the most paradoxical feature of English Protestantism, for, while always quoting Scripture, this increasingly democratic society reformed its functioning according to human power and institutions—English institutions.[1] Thus man once more became the measure of all things. Catholic dogma set limits to his powers and, from a somewhat different point of view, so did Lutheranism, but the Englishman of the Church of England had no doubt of his abilities. It was man's business to deal with the world, and he considered himself to be dealing with it quite adequately. The consequence of this proud and positive attitude was an obsession with material and political achievement that siphoned away the energies of the artistic creativity so profusely present in the Englishman of the Renaissance; the new Englishman gained political liberty but his creative individuality became considerably circumscribed.

The religion of the Church of England in Handel's time faithfully reflected socio-economic developments; the cultic elements descended from Catholicism remained, but in reality this religion was a system of organized life that under its theocratic exterior was essentially political. The contrast with the absolutist monarchies on the Continent was startling. Louis XIV's France was a monarchy, humanistic, allowing creative freedom to the individual, and characterized by an esthetic awareness unrivalled in the English or German courts—but allowing no personal-political freedom. As the French Revolution proved, this humanistic monarchy was not durable; the democratic monarchy, however, prevailed.

Imperialism brought with it a will for rule and power, as well as a

---

[1] Such terms as "democracy" and "democratization" must not be taken in our sense, for the main qualifications, universal suffrage and a free party system, were still missing. The electorate was small, uneven, manipulated, even if with much freedom and often for the nation's good, by an oligarchy.

new form of collectivism. Besides bringing material advantages, empire for the British was stimulus to idealistic experiment, for this imperialism was just as much a cultural dream as it was an economic one. It is not an accident that so many of Britain's statesmen and public servants were—and still are—accomplished writers. The English character, its conservatism notwithstanding, is revolutionary, for a realistic spirit is the quickest to perceive new realities. It also soon discovers when old realities are no longer valid, and then, as is true nowhere but in England, it uses them for their decorative values. English philosophy has for centuries dispensed with such authoritarian tenets and ideas as hindered free thought. Hobbes, Locke, and Berkeley follow one another, and then Hume. This was also the age when Newton, himself a religious man, proved the miraculous events in the Old Testament to be untenable, for by now there was a new conception of the "laws of nature." Dean Swift, though a churchman, had doubts about everything; his *A Tale of a Tub* is one of the most radical books of all time. Gibbon, too, in his gigantic historical work, magnificent not only in workmanship but also in style, can curl his lip like Voltaire. Nor does he, when speaking of Christianity, hide the ironic manifestations of his religious skepticism. And in Lord Chesterfield's letters we see a catechism of how to succeed in the world without any moral scruples.

The audience of these flagbearers of culture was the educated bourgeoisie. The men of letters were members of the same class—a broad one—to which their audience belonged. The middle classes constituted not only the reading public but also the theatrical and musical; it was for them and about them that the writers and composers created.

The novel, rising from the national character and dealing with everyday life, with the English family, was about to become the preferred literary form in England. Essay and novel often merge; Steele's and Addison's essays contain the materials of novels. Unfortunately, as sober mind takes over, poetry becomes boring and tragedy rigid because everything is governed by cool reason and logic. The qualities the Englishman appreciated in the novel he also sought in the theatre. The play came to resemble the much-admired novel, only the playwrights' talents were considerably below those of the novelists. Nevertheless, the London merchants sent their clerks and apprentices to see Lillo's *George Barnwell* to learn to appreciate the rewards for faithfulness, and for thievery. The angry—and justified—attacks on the vulgarity of the Restoration theatre (even Congreve is not free of it) do not change the fact of its popularity. Besides, the most uncompromising and articulate foe of the theatre, Jeremy Collier, was totally devoid of any artistic sense. Those who read only the title of his famous tract, *Short View of the Immorality and Profaneness of the English Stage* (1698), ascribe his attitude to Puritanism, but Collier was no Puritan, rather a Tory and a High Churchman, one of the first of those new divines for whom esthetics ceased to exist. But even the Puritans' objection to the theatre was more social and hygienic than religious and moral.

To this middle-class audience opera was not congenial; the literary world immediately challenged its justification vis-à-vis the spoken theatre and, forgetting that the English were once a "singing people," they even questioned the validity of music's place among the humanities. Upon hearing that Scarlatti's *Pirro e Demetrio* had been performed with great success at the Haymarket Theatre, Steele expressed his displeasure in the *Tatler* (1709):

> This intelligence is not very acceptable to us Friends of the Theatre; for the Stage being an Entertainment of the Reason, and all the Faculties, this Way of being pleased with the suspense of them for three Hours together, and being given up to the shallow satisfaction of Eyes and Ears only, seems to arise rather from the Degeneracy of our Understanding than an Improvement of our Diversions.

Two years later Addison in the *Spectator* makes a more direct comparison. "If the Italians have a Genius for Musick above the English, the English have a Genius for other Performances of a much higher Nature, and capable of giving the Mind a much nobler Entertainment." Continuing, he spells out precisely the English fear that if music "would take the entire Possession of our Ears, it would make us incapable of hearing Sense . . . it would exclude Arts that have a much greater Tendency to the Refinement of Human Nature." The *London Journal* of February 24, 1722 stated what the average Englishman considered the proper role of music: "It should chase away ennui, and relieve clever men from the trouble of thinking." The success of the Royal Academy of Music was observed with similar alarm. In the *London Journal* of February 5, 1726, a writer who signs himself "Philomuses" expresses surprise at the "reigning taste" for music at the expense of letters, "the pleasures of the Ear having prevailed over those of the Understanding." He finally ventures the hope that "when Apollo's Harp ceases to be valued more than his Head . . . then, and not till then, may we begin to hope for an Augustan Age."

The Burlington circle (substantially the same that gathered at Cannons) counted among its members Pope, Hughes, Arbuthnot, perhaps

Swift, and a little later Gay. Gay, whose *Beggar's Opera* hastened the first debacle in Handel's operatic career, also launched Handel on his ultimate triumph by being the principal librettist of his first English pastoral, *Acis and Galatea*. Handel met all these men, and thus in this crucial period of acclimatization he had the opportunity to experience at first hand the agility that is perhaps the most characteristic trait of the educated English mind. Given his association with the leading men of letters, Handel, an enthusiastic reader, must have become acquainted with such works as Arbuthnot's *John Bull* (1713), and by the time Defoe's *Robinson Crusoe* appeared (1719) his understanding of English was considerable, in spite of his wayward command of the spoken language.[2] In this novel, Robinson Crusoe recreates the entire history of civilization in miniature, and in his isolation he practically discovers culture anew. Here Handel could not escape pondering a question that would not have presented itself to an artisan-cantor in Germany: the value of mind and culture. But while there are unmistakable signs that all this made a profound impression on his inquisitive mind, for the time being Handel was not willing to draw the consequences, and even misread the many signs that did not augur well for the future of opera, to which he continued to cling with unshakable tenacity. It is the more surprising that the English Handel is now before us practically fully developed in two genres that are directly attributable to his intercourse with the literary men and to his observations of the English character: the pastoral-masque and the anthem.

The poets of the age of Dryden and Pope concurred that, in the words of the latter, "the proper study of mankind is man." Whatever else they spoke of, it was with man as stated reference. They understood the splendors of nature, yet they did not find the proper accents to describe them—this remained for Ambrose Philips and especially Thomson. Dryden and Pope's treatment of nature pictures was a sophisticated intellectual play; their regard for man made them indifferent towards nature, which interested them only as it was controlled by man. In the spirit of the age the theme of the pastoral was still man, though he is here a handsome creature provided with harmless emotions which last only to the end of the piece. And the writers of pastoral verse, like the cultivators of formal English gardens, controlled their material with a firm hand. They knew that the pastoral was deception, a literary plaything, and everything had to be simple, gentle, fragrant, and elegant—nature should really imi-

[2] In 1720 we find Handel's name among the subscribers for John Gay's *Poems on several occasions*. Throughout his life in England he stayed abreast of literary events.

tate art. We shall see what consequences this association with the classical poets was to have on Handel's poetic and dramatic muse. Absorbing this English pastoral poetry, he yet transcended the conventions of the genre in his very first English pastoral. *Acis and Galatea,* written at Cannons, is an incomparable masterpiece saturated with exquisite musical poetry. However, we must once more abandon chronology to permit an uninterrupted study of Handel's pastorals and masques at a later point. Our present concern is with Handel's church music, the result of his residence at Burlington House and at Cannons, and the bulk of it composed there. In this music we first see clearly that the impact of English society and its Church is making an English composer of the immigrant.

[*2*]

DIVINE SERVICE IS worship by a congregation; the music on such an occasion should serve this congregation by binding it into one body. There can be no question that the Handelian anthem or Te Deum achieves this community to the highest degree, but is its spirit that of a churchly or religious community? The question immediately raises another and most important query: are churchly and religious values necessarily one and the same? Now we shall add a new complication to an already involved problem by asking whether religious music is at the same time churchly music, and whether churchly music is always religious?

The power of a musical personality expressed through religious texts can create a strong religious atmosphere, but we must be careful because altogether profane music in a concert hall can produce a similar effect; the slow movement in a symphony may have been intended to serve as a contrasting movement, no more, but we may hear in it a prayer. What is it that made the melting sensuousness of "Ombra mai fù" into a piece of "sacred" music, or the second movement of Beethoven's *Emperor Concerto* into a hymn? *Contrafacta* (literally, counterfeits), the substitutions of religious texts for the originals in secular compositions, were of course always practiced and accepted, often enriching church music, but after all, the music remains exactly the same as it was before, when it conveyed amorous languor, or, as in the case of the Beethoven concerto, nothing in particular beyond a magnificent composition in the unusual key of B major. Among other things that confuse the issue one might mention the ingrained feeling that polyphonic texture serves to heighten the churchly quality; a choral fugue usually creates a vaguely solemn or devotional sensation, effectively neutralizing the inner tension of the parts. The time-honored conception of religious music is so firmly entrenched that it is difficult for us to think in terms of personal expressiveness, for to the untrained ear only the generalized "religious" feeling is accessible. Of course the language, especially if it is archaic, has a great deal to do with making music "religious." The sturdy old English spoken in the Bible by the prophets, kings, and psalmists of Israel when associated with almost any suitably stately music will produce a devotional impression.

The artist's desire is to communicate and affect; this desire is already implicit in the concept of form. The important point here is the personal aim, and the degree to which the artist achieves it is, in a large measure, responsible for the work of art. Even so, it is clear that the social element must be considered, for it matters greatly what stratum of the "public" is involved, what are its feelings, thoughts, and convictions, what are the values it cherishes. Nevertheless, the beauties of an individual work can be recognized and described without calling on sociological ramifications, though its particular development, purpose, and connotations cannot. At any rate, while the difference between the two extremes, the socio-cultural and the purely esthetic concept, is probably less than their respective champions maintain, the fact remains that while Handel's church music affects us strongly, if we lack a good knowledge of Georgian times in England much of its significance escapes us.

Though it is perhaps less apparent to the observer from afar, in another state church of the 18th century, the Evangelical-Lutheran, we are also dealing with a spirit of national life. This church, before being undermined by Pietism, was a comprehensive cultural force. In both state churches, connections with the paramount interests of the nation are so strong that artistic aims and principles are palpably influenced by them. Bach and Handel both composed Protestant music, but one is thoroughly German while the other is unmistakably English. We must proceed with care, for the socio-cultural is so entwined with the musical that either alone will surely lead us astray.

German music of the Baroque shows a tremendous capacity for absorption and development but little interest in creating its own forms. The German composer of the age does not show particular inventiveness when new modes are required for the adequate expression of the period's feelings, but he is infinitely versatile in carrying forward the acquired, often far beyond the boundaries of the original inventors. This was recognized by the Germans themselves, witness Quantz in his *Versuch:* "Even if it cannot be said that the Germans have produced an individual style entirely different from that of other nations, they are all the more capable of taking whatever they like from another style, and they know how to make use of the good things in all types of foreign music." The music of the Bach era is the result of French and, even more, of Italian inventiveness; it was the Italians who gave the world music that captivated all nations. In accepting French and Italian musical forms, idioms, and techniques, the Germans not only proved to be excellent pupils, they created from the imported cultural goods a great German art which in turn became the guiding light for generations to come. The Italians are dramatists and ravishing melodists, the French lead in the dance, but the Germans of the Baroque blended all this into what is principally a religious art of breadth and profundity. The outstanding heroes of this great art are the German composers from Schein to Bach. As we have seen, the Germans complacently add Handel to the list, though of course their sole justification is the composer's birth certificate. It must be emphatically repeated again and again that Handel's art was *not* German music composed on English soil.

To Bach and to other earnest Lutherans, God and the world were separate entities; to English Protestants, the world was a very real and comprehensive entity that included God. This latter is a religion oriented towards the external world, while the orthodox Lutheran represented the old German Christian mysticism that turns away from the external world and seeks the soul, seen as independent of the body. The Englishman no longer sought grace alone, he wanted to work out his destiny through a reasonable religion which paid proper attention to life on this earth. What to the Lutheran, and presumably to the young Handel too, was the blessing of grace, assumed to the English the character of laudable virtue. It was in music that the Lutheran spirit reached its warmest and highest human fulfillment, but to the Church of England, once it passed beyond the last remnants of the Elizabethan-Jacobean heritage, music became an accessory.

The Evangelical *Kirchenlied*, the Lutheran chorale, is the core of German Protestant music. The chorale was (and, though to a lesser degree, still is) far more than a musical accessory to worship; to a large section of Germany it represented a culture, a religious consciousness. The spirit of the chorale dominated not only their church music but their organ music and, to a degree, even other instrumental music. Even after the inevitable intrusion of aria and recitative from Italian opera into the German cantata and oratorio, the chorale was ever-present, lending the music an unmistakably German Protestant cast. This dependence on the chorale, the constant use of cantus firmi derived from chorales even in contexts uncongenial to such use,[3] had its drawbacks, to which even Bach was not immune. To the average cantor the old art of polyphonic architecture was imposed from above, out of cultic tradition and learning, instead of arising in response to a creative desire or an instinct for shapeliness, as with the Italians. The German *gearbeiteter Stil* describes this very graphically. Thus for the Lutheran cantors there was a compulsion that at times limited them artistically; they were often more dutiful craftsmen than creative artists whose music coursed through their being.

It is most interesting and instructive to consider the case of Schütz. He developed in his *Geistliche Konzerte* a German musical diction, a German melodic speech previously unknown. The German prose of Luther's Bible translation was as decisive in the formation of a German Protestant style as was the King James Version in the English. But to a dramatically inclined composer—and Schütz was a dramatist of the first water—the rich, descriptive, narrative language is an incentive to "free" composition; Schütz used the chorale very sparingly. A hundred years later we see the same reluctance in another dramatist, Handel, though his exact contemporary Bach was devoted to the hymns. When Handel does use the chorale (there are fewer than a handful of such occasions), one gets the impression that he is remembering his youth, his sturdy Lutheran upbringing. What he elaborates is a musical quotation without dogmatic or particularly churchly significance.

The two opposing elements of the age, polyphony on one side, aria and recitative on the other, were destined for a showdown, and under the impact of social developments the latter eventually became victorious. The settlement between the churchly and secular spirit in music also ended with the victory of the secular, and music enters into the service of free European art, definitely and irrevocably, even in the field of church music. The Italian cantata was the chief agent in this change; its gold-dust texts and sweet music had completely left the domain of the "sacred." Yet once more, the noble traditions were not lost. Such composers as Antonio Lotti still wrote genuine church music, and to object to their passionate dramatic accents is to deny to great artists the right to be living human beings saturated with the spirit of their times. The German cantors were not eager to accept the Italian cantata style, preferring the carefully worked out motet style. Their addiction to abstract ideals, their symbolism and Protestant mysticism searched for the inner life, the attraction of a beautifully shaped external form being secondary. At the

[3] Reger still uses the chorale in such an unlikely surrounding as his Piano Concerto.

same time, the German cantata and oratorio could not have developed into the type cultivated by Buxtehude, Zachow, and Bach without incorporating such basically secular elements as recitative, arioso, and aria, all of which came from opera. It was in the choruses that the old polyphonic art was preserved.

[3]

IN ENGLAND, as religion moved from the center to the peripheries, the transition from the old to the new faith was strongly affected by political-cultural considerations; indeed, English nationalism made the Church of England as Roman Catholicism made the Irish nation. This linking of the spiritual with the political institutions of England gradually became stronger during the centuries following the Reformation. The national state with the monarch at its head as symbol became the visible Church, and in Handel's time that Church was an almost secular institution, its dignitaries only too often spiritual opportunists who acknowledged their God but exploited this acknowledgment. The critics of the era were outspoken in their condemnation of the Lords Spiritual. Horace Walpole, commending Archbishop Cornwallis as "a good sort of man," says "he was free from hypocrisy" and "without the abject soul of most of his brethren." When the Primacy was offered to Joseph Butler in 1747, he declined it, so it is said, on the ground that it was too late for him "to try to support a failing Church." We read that in the last decade of Handel's life Archbishop Herring conducted a thriving business by selling the bones of his Canterbury saints. Apparently this traffic in bones and other relics, a custom in southern Catholicism and violently opposed by the Reformation, was sometimes found useful in the Protestant stronghold of England.

It must be acknowledged, of course, that there is a religious overtone in all political loyalties; the State has always made an explicit claim to at least semidivine authority, a claim that in modern no less than ancient times has sometimes emerged in a quasi deification of the political head of the state. The Christian priest who functions in the king's chapel has in practice been too often indistinguishable from the courtier who functions in the king's court. The English did indeed read into the words of Holy Writ a conception of the "nation" that is entirely modern. The cause for the distortion is plain: religion *is* politics. After all, kings acquired the habit of relying on lawyers instead of ecclesiastics long before the Reformation, and were opposed to the theory of a papally controlled internationalism even in overwhelmingly Catholic countries. History is full of edifying episodes in which religious decorum was observed while rapacious kings fought poltroon popes.

There can be no question that the Church of England in Handel's time was bereft of the spirit of any holy tradition. It had abandoned the mysteries of religion, and its real *raison d'être* was a form of materialism couched in biblical words. All that was left was Holy Scripture, and it must be admitted that some of the Bible's teachings can be as contorted as a chapter in *Das Kapital*. The fact is that the Church was an arm of Government, of the social system, and everything else was of secondary importance.

There is another reality in English history we must recognize in order to understand the spirit of English Protestantism: a historical consciousness that represents a particular form of living, influenced by tradition and continuity. English thought is dependent on this tradition. For the rationalistic English Protestant theology the Bible furnished dramatic raw material that eminently suited English tastes and desires. The victorious battles and advantageous peace treaties, the king's triumphs and anniversaries were celebrated not with the cantatas and motets of the Lutherans, but with great and festive musical murals that actually had an almost scenic grandeur. English composers (and of course this goes back to before Handel's time, for Purcell was the incarnation of this style) did not suffer and lament with resignation the errors of human insensibility. They were entirely taken with the great dramatic pictures of the Bible, and the Bible to them usually meant the Old Testament; the vast majority of Purcell's and all of Handel's anthems were composed on Old Testament texts. Purcell dealt with the biblical texts on purely artistic-ceremonial grounds; their religious meaning was altogether secondary, and in most instances there is not a shred of Christian spirit or attitude. What appears as spiritual content in these magnificent works is not the manifestation of a religious mood but the infinitely subtle and artistic expression of a creative soul inspired by the grandeur and poetry of religious themes. Nor must we overlook the English love for historical precedent, for ancient techniques and manners.

The state Church presented, then, a cultural-political religion whose connections with Christian spirituality became tenuous until the great revival of spirituality in English Protestantism beginning with John Wesley and culminating in the mid-19th century. When every allowance for exaggeration has been made, the fact is inescapable that Wesley found the vast masses of the people mainly without any religious guidance and

eager to hear him. Had the Church of England even remotely approxi-
mated what it should have been, the Methodist movement would not
have taken place. The alliance of English Protestantism with rising capi-
talism, with commerce, industry, and finance, and with the modern political organization of the state that governed all this, was a move with far-
reaching consequences. Only in more recent times, after the emergence of
the Kingdom of Prussia as a modern power, do we find a similar phenomenon in the Lutheran state Church. *Gott mit uns* parallels the English belief that Providence has arranged matters so that the Established Church
and the state should be victorious and immune from harm as long as they
were synonymous with the nation. This English ideal, while observing the
formalities of Protestant thought, asserted the principle of man's individual personality and rights, a principle that in fact represented values and
aims unknown to Lutheran doctrine. It is a reaffirmation of the belief that
man is sufficient, that his mission can be carried out by immanent human
forces, and that divine powers are needed only to ratify the human act.
Thus the state and the Church were mutually dependent, for they were in
reality two different exponents of the same principles. Their collaboration
produced that uniquely English situation in which the spirit of the modern politico-legal, humanistic state determined the form of its religious
tenets. It was a religion of blood, soil, and nation, Christianity accommodated to the prevailing mode, making a compromise with humanism.

But despite the "system," the worldliness, acumen, and opportunism
of the bishops, and a society riddled with avarice and sensuality, the English people were not merely nominal Christians. They believed in God
and the Thirty-nine Articles and subscribed to severe moral standards.
They were not, however, disposed to delay the coming of Heaven to
Earth.

Now we must turn to the peculiar but in many ways cardinal factor
in the development of English national life, Nonconformism. What distinguished the Nonconformist was his insistence on his right to "religious
freedom." He sought to create a state in the image of his religious tenets,
but it must at once be recalled that when he had power under Cromwell,
liberty did not extend even to the Anglican episcopacy, let alone the
Roman.

Puritan morals appear to hold enjoyment bad, or at least suspect, but
the Puritan does not consider suffering good; therefore to escape suffering
and sorrow he removes everything that may cause it. The Puritan ethic is
the negation of life, therefore the whole Puritan morality is the soul's
compulsion to oppose life, which serves to make life, seen as sin, even
more exciting, the way modesty makes nakedness more exciting. One

must come to the conclusion that virtue is surely here to give sin its value, but of course the choice between the two is not quite similar to a choice between two systems of geometry.

Yet the influence of Nonconformism upon social and economic life was great and in many ways salutary. While mitigating the severity of the system of laissez faire then dominant in politics and society, it also emphasized the doctrine of personal responsibility, a doctrine that found expression in the inculcation of diligence and thrift, thereby opening the way to prosperity for many Nonconformist laymen. On the other hand, the puritanical mentality created standards of ruthless materialism, the setting up of self-assertion rather than self-fulfillment as the purpose of life, and the relegation of idealism, of spiritual aspirations, to a point of unreality, thus making a full human existence impossible and preventing creative development.

And what a curious world was the Puritans' ideal when they had the power to enforce it: the theatres closed, literature and music frowned upon, professional actors persecuted. But Puritans of all hues and in all ages often have double standards, something that did not escape Handel's sharp eyes when he wrote operas on biblical texts and called them "sacred oratorios." The Puritans and Nonconformists, whose influence remained an important factor in the thinking of the lower and middle classes, were also convinced that theirs was the only way to salvation. But in the 18th century we witness a curious meeting of the minds that is uniquely English. While loudly denouncing the popish vanity of the Established Church, the Nonconformists in fact had dual church citizenship: in matters of faith they were indeed nonconforming, but for national-patriotic affairs they gladly joined all other Britons in St. Paul's Cathedral to hear an anthem or Te Deum by "Mr. Handell." These solemn services were the visible manifestations of sentiments that transcend all party strife and all discussions in a single devotion to the national interest. Hawkins is our witness that this was well understood. "Many of the anthems were made on the most joyful occasions, that is to say, thanksgivings for victories obtained over our enemies during a war in which the interests of all Europe were concerned: upon the celebration of which solemnities it was usual for Queen Anne to go in state to St. Paul's Cathedral."

[4]

THE NEW capitalistic civilization of post-Restoration Britain did not discard religion; it recognized its pragmatic usefulness, even necessity. But this God whose sanction is sought for the achievement of an industrial or merchant civilization, the God whom Handel memorialized in his music for his new compatriots, could not be the same God Bach worshipped; therefore the music Handel composed for the official English divine service must also be quite different from the Lutheran. Indeed, these are not songs wrung from man's soul as he contemplates God. Once more Addison is a reliable witness whom we can quote. His definition of the nature of English church music of the Age of Reason is most characteristic:

> Church music based on Holy Writ has its foundation in Reason, and would impose our Virtue in proportion as it raised our Delight . . . the Fear, the Love, the Sorrow, the Indignation that are awakened in the Mind by Hymns and Anthems, make the Heart better, and proceed from such Causes as are altogether reasonable and praiseworthy. Pleasure and Duty go hand in hand, and the greater our Satisfaction is, the greater is our Religion. (*Spectator*, June 14, 1712.)

Handel's church music comprises a small part of his total output. Aside from the Latin pieces composed in Italy (see p. 74) it consists of the twelve Chandos Anthems, four Coronation Anthems, one Funeral and two Wedding Anthems, the Foundling Hospital Anthem, and five Te Deums. That is, aside from the Te Deums they are all anthems, but actually there is no basic difference between anthem and Te Deum. Posterity's evaluation of them shows an astonishing range of diversity, owing to vague conceptions of the nature and purpose of church music in general and English church music in particular, from the ever-present—and inadmissible—comparisons with Bach to the mistaken notion, at the other end of the spectrum, that the Enlightenment is synonymous with atheism. The simple truth is that Handel recognized both the monarchy and the Church as necessary and useful institutions and was always ready to praise them in music appropriate to the occasion. The bold and spacious metaphors of the choral language of this church music are so persuasive that subsequent composers who tried their hand at choral writing could hardly liberate themselves from its overwhelming influence. Yet they habitually ignore the many intimate features this music contains, for they did not perceive the difference between some of the chamber-music-like Chandos Anthems and the robust and proclamatory Coronation Anthems and Te Deums. Composers and choral societies have been taught for generations that the Handelian chorus always sings in gun emplacements. Even Elgar turned the intimate anthem *In the Lord put I my trust* into a bloated choral symphony.

Kretzschmar was of the opinion that Handel developed a basic form established by Schütz without materially changing it—a view that is untenable even though Schütz is in a way an interesting counterpart to Handel since he, too, absorbed and acclimatized an alien musical idiom. But while emulating the Italian style, Schütz remained altogether faithful to his German Lutheran heritage. No one would consider him anything but a German, whereas Handel became a British institution. As Basil Lam (in *Handel, a Symposium*) correctly points out, the church works are "impeccably Anglican in tone." Yet confusion is compounded when Lam ventures that "had Handel remained in Germany he would doubtless have produced many cantatas in the style he must have learned from Zachow," while Dent categorically states in his little Handel biography that the Chandos Anthems are "works of a character new both to England and to Handel." As we have seen in Chapter I, Handel did not compose for his own church beyond a few youthful student works, nor did the devoted and enthusiastic organist compose a single "liturgical" organ piece, such as a chorale prelude. The decision not to seek the cantor's career was early and irrevocable. Nor can one agree with Dent's statement that the Chandos Anthems are "the only representatives of the Protestant cantata in Handel's output." Perhaps in function they fulfilled the role of the cantata, as in general did the anthem, but surely neither in tone, substance, nor thought do they resemble the German Protestant cantata.

Lam shows true insight into another group of this church music when he states that "the Coronation music belongs to a class of compositions not designed to promote meditation or reflection, activities usually inappropriate at such functions." He is, of course, altogether right, because these anthems have nothing to do with the religion that Whitehead epitomized with his epigram: "Religion is what a man does with his solitariness." As usual, the Germans have a proper word for the services for which these anthems were composed: *Staatsakten*, which is exactly what they were, solemn state occasions. The Church was an essential part of the state constitution, and its services, especially on solemn occasions, always had an element of political demonstration. It is for this reason that Handel's "church music" is not suitable for ordinary services. Except for some of the Chandos Anthems, these works call for a large apparatus, choral, orchestral, and ceremonial, such as even the great cathedrals can muster only for exceptional occasions. Finally, the fact must be considered that there are some able critics who consider the Chandos Anthems "good" but not "great" Handel. This judgment can only be the result of unfamiliarity with the nature of the species. What these critics see is that Handel's voluminous sentences and choral proclamations are measured with a ruler to fit the stated purpose of the occasion; what they do not see is that they also billow like sails. The anthems become more closely patterned the more expansive they become. Besides, these anthems contain some of Handel's finest choruses, among them magnificent fugues.

Perhaps we should take as a starting point for discussion the "propriety" of the music and the presence or absence of the "promotion of meditation or reflection." As was remarked above, the anthems represent in a nutshell much of Handel's formal and expressive range, from intimate pastoral scenes to jubilant Hallelujah choruses. This diversity would indicate an equally wide range of textual sources, but in fact the anthems are almost exclusively Psalm settings, a circumstance of considerable significance in view of English attitudes towards church music in general and Handel's personal preferences in particular. The Psalms have always played a very important part in the liturgy of the Christian Church, but with the exception of churches that follow a high and elaborate liturgy, this position has long since been lost in most Protestant denominations. Handel, a great connoisseur of the Bible, was attracted to the Psalms because they were not dogmatic statements but affirmations of religion expressed with the poet's vividness and perception and an intensity of conviction that gives them eternal value. Handel was always attracted to good poetry, especially the kind rich in pictorial imagery. In their turn the English people, who achieved a domestication of the Old Testament unknown to other Christian nations and whose admiration for it should not be confused with the attitude of the more extreme forms of Protestantism, also loved this fine poetry, and they appreciated that the references in the Psalms are for the most part to real personalities, to the present world rather than to a future salvation.

To the English it was not necessary to explain the tenets of the Old Testament as "pre-," "sub-," or "proto-Christian"; they regarded the ancient Hebrews of the Old Testament as the Italians regarded the Romans of antiquity—as their own past.[4] As literature the King James Version of the Bible is superior to the original, and it surely is incomparably superior to any translation into any other language. The affinity felt with the Old Testament was so strong that kinship was claimed between Hebrew and

[4] In some quarters there was even a belief that the English were representatives of the Ten Tribes, which did not return from the captivity to assist in the building of the Second Temple, and ingenious arguments can be found in popular theological literature that point out that the Lion and Unicorn that support the Royal Arms can be regarded as the Lion of Judah and the Unicorn of Ephraim.

the sturdy English of King James's time. "It happens very luckily," says Addision in the *Spectator,*

> that the Hebrew Idiom run into the English Tongue with a particular Grace and Beauty. Our Language has received innumerable Elegancies and Improvements, from that infusion of Hebraism, which are derived to it from out of the Poetical Passages in Holy Writ. They give a Force and Energy to our expressions, warm and animate our Language, and convey our Thoughts in more ardent and intense Phrases, than any that are to be met with in our own Tongue.[5]

Almost all commentators agree on the tone of this church music, and the terms "monumental," *Kolossalstil,* and so on, are freely used. To the modern musician and music lover monumentality implies mass and dynamics. But it is impossible to explain monumentality in utilitarian, i.e. spatial, terms alone. No single recipe brings about such a style, only the powerful ideal of a people, their belief in their righteousness, their optimism, their conviction of their own moral strength. The people and the composers did not get together to agree on a specific tone and manner, rather the spirit of the time and place, like all living organisms, arose naturally and developed its own proper idiom.

Some of the earlier scholars did perceive something unusual in these festive "cantatas." Kretzschmar, who did not share the opinions still held by many of his colleagues (and not only in Germany) that the Chandos Anthems are minor works, was surprised by the nature painting so prominent in some of them, considering this *Schilderung der Natur* a somewhat one-sided if "grand" concept of the lordly Psalms. This refers of course to their often pastoral quality, which was found incongruous in the midst of the splendor of the other anthems. But the pastoral is as much in Handel's poetic make-up as it is characteristic of the Psalmists'; moreover, the musical forces at Cannons were modest and some of the Chandos Anthems were written with a small ensemble in mind and are therefore gentle and intimate in texture. That Handel reworked some of them for the full complement of the Baroque "colossal style" does not change their original role. These intimate anthems point to the works of Colonna, Gasparini, Scarlatti, and Lotti, which may have led Dent to consider them "new" to England. Consciously or unconsciously, Dent must also have been swayed by the secular-Italianate quality of the pastoral scenes in the anthems, which cannot be sung in the grand style or in what Luther called the "roaring of the priests of Baal." They are not the variety that

[5] There is evidence of the teaching of Hebrew in leading grammar schools, at least up to the Restoration.

induces "meditation," for they are distinguished by charm, delicacy, and a pantheistic joy in nature. There is a world of difference between this intimate chamber music, with its three-part choruses and small orchestra, the chamber-music quality emphasized by frequent borrowings from Handel's trio sonatas, and the mighty choruses of the Coronation Anthems, though what unites all of them is a quality of ceremonial solemnity that was mistaken for religious fervor.

[5]

HANDEL SAW A good deal of history enacted in his own time that he was called upon to commemorate in festive, ceremonial music. These were the "political" compositions, patriotic, or patriotic in a religious garb, which, though the type has been practiced everywhere since time immemorial, are a very special product of English social-moral conditions, with a tone all their own. Whether ode, anthem, or Te Deum—there are even entire oratorios that come under this heading—such a commemorative composition seldom misses a chance to testify to a moral, i.e. religious, world order, to be shared by the audience. The reader will notice that anthems and Te Deums are included here, but we are still dealing with political-patriotic compositions—indeed no patriotic text can be set to music in England or America without reference to God.

The official ceremonial art (though not the music) of the Louis XIV era is well known to everyone. It was a regal art, classically calm, frosty. The King placed it under a veritable dictator, Charles Le Brun, who carried out the mandate received from his sovereign: noble and elegant display of pomp. Louis also had a "superintendent of music" whom he valued highly, the Florentine Giovanni Battista Lulli, an immigrant in France like Handel in England, who as Jean Baptiste Lully became the embodiment of French music and of the spirit of the *grand siècle*. A good deal of Versailles's ceremonial coldness is present in Lully too, yet among his "display" pieces, that is in his royal-official church music, are to be found some of his best works. The monotony of the solemn pathos of his lyric tragedies is largely absent in his ceremonial church pieces, which show a wonderful feeling for choral setting and brilliant orchestration, the trumpets blaring and the drums rolling. The particularly solemn ceremonial nature of this music was not lost on Pelham Humphrey, Master of the Children in the Chapel Royal, who had studied in France, and he did not fail to communicate his impressions to one of his wards at the

Chapel Royal, Henry Purcell.[6] Lully was bold, grandiose, and noble in the best sense of the word. Like Mansart, the great architect, he managed to combine the royal and the comfortable, the pompous and the idyllic, in a blend as attractive as it was superior to the prevailing style.

This palace art of Louis XIV eventually became the whole age's ceremonial court art, a European style. The Baroque palace, the levees, the great assemblies and parades were repeated in every princely court, small and large, all over Europe. The ballets, plays, and operas, the odes, Te Deums, and festival "motets," the fireworks, statues, and even the very park of Versailles were borrowed or imitated everywhere with worshipful admiration. Yet, as in every style, a particular national character makes itself felt even in this international style. England too had her *grand siècle*—but in her own version, one much less exclusively royal and courtly, for it rested on the middle classes as well as on the King and the aristocracy. Though a class-conscious society, the English aristocracy was not in conflict with the conditions of life of the middle classes like the French feudal aristocracy. Purcell was born and reared in this society and represented it in music that is rightfully considered among the finest manifestations of its spirit. But Handel, the immigrant, also made that spirit his own, becoming the unsurpassed master in the representation of the great forces and trends that formed his adopted country's ideologies. But this was not a religious ideology, rather an unshakable faith in humanity and in the righteousness of English aims and progress. Handel as church musician speaks not as a private person but as the embodiment of a historical-national consciousness.

Ceremonial compositions are often on the peripheries of art, but they decidedly belong within its orbit, just as the political poem or drama does. Those who want to divorce art from everything else will come a cropper when they approach this genre. They profess that in art the subject is immaterial, the realization is everything. It is true of course that the subject is meaningless if its artistic representation is poor, for in itself a subject is not artistic. But we are dealing here with the expression of a national consciousness that permeates English music with a unique blend of the national, moral, religious, and historical and that largely determined the tone and substance of Handel's music; therefore the "subject" cannot be ignored. And of course the moral effect is a corollary of the artistic effect —"effect" because moral value in art is never absolute. In its time a work of ephemeral artistic importance may have a tremendous moral impact,

---

[6] Pepys, who met Humphrey shortly after the latter's return from France, called him "an absolute Monsieur."

but this effect can no longer be galvanized into life generations later; it perishes with the work that caused it because it could not withstand time. Even if the esthetic effect of a work remains unimpaired across the centuries, the moral effect may have diminished or been altogether lost unless there is an uninterrupted tradition that keeps it alive.

The political-ceremonial composition is seldom quiet, dreamy contemplation. In literature it can be satirical and comical, vicious and belligerent, but also noble and hymnic. In music all the negative features disappear; ceremonial compositions are almost always elevated in tone, and the congratulatory, patriotic, and commemorative usually, somewhat monotonously, take a religious or quasi-religious turn and tone. Since commemorated events are notoriously ephemeral, the music usually accompanies them into limbo. Nevertheless, there are not a few works that have great and enduring qualities; they are artistic and human, composed with conviction and identification with the event. Great, strong, and universal convictions do not apply to small things, and the commemorative composer usually does his best when great men and events are celebrated. In addition he must have some special gifts, his music must be direct and readily understandable, and he must have warmth and a capacity for enthusiasm. Ceremonial-commemorative music must conquer at the first attack.

Patriotic-national poems and compositions are difficult to discuss and evaluate; as a rule they are notoriously low-grade when measured by artistic standards, and often it is only their subject that protects them. (Bad church music also enjoys this safe conduct.) Moreover, as soon as they are judged by persons belonging to a different generation or to a different cultural circle, they are relegated to a very slight eminence. The festive ceremonial piece usually assumes the rhetorical pose we know so well from the monumental statuary in public places: the outstretched hand or the folded arms, the bowed head or the defiant stare. Actually, simplicity, naturalness, truth, and objectivity are just as effective in the commemorative piece as in any other genre; but in this English ceremonial music we are dealing with something that cannot be expressed without the splendor, mass, and volume it provides. The massive, statically mature forms caught the psyche of a people who seek their inspiration from history and can express this in living form with modern manners and materials. The Englishman is far more of an individualist than the Continental, yet the aggregation of these individuals forms a nation with a marked sense for the community. They do not flaunt it; they do not carry placards emblazoned with *viribus unitis*; but they understand and revere Britain as a historical institution based on civil liberties. The Briton is not chauvinistic like the Frenchman and refuses to be regimented like the German. At the same time, like his American cousin, he often applies a moral point of view when no other national would feel the need for it; the rhetorician and the preacher are often close to the poet and not infrequently are one and the same, something that is very rare in other Western nations.

Ordinary patriotic songs and hymns are, with few exceptions, of very low vitality though sanctioned by usage; no one takes umbrage at their artistic poverty. And there are some really splendid pieces among them: *God Save the King, La Marseillaise,* and *Gott erhalte Franz den Kaiser* are everlasting songs. Such short pieces did not appeal to Handel; he never liked to traffic in miniatures. But once we advance to large-scale patriotic compositions, usually for chorus and orchestra, in England a "churchly" tone almost instantly makes itself felt, though with a tinge of the out-of-doors. That too is foreign to the German composer, especially to the Lutheran. It is a peculiar tone and mood, the significance of decisive historical moments pulsates in it. The idea expressed in these patriotic choruses, whether anthems or birthday greetings, is often dwarfed by the power of the mood. There is neither self-searching doubt nor bravado in this mood, nor easily flowing tears; what makes such compositions typically English is the frequent coupling of sobriety with imagination. This is not unusual in other types of music in many lands, but in the commemorative-patriotic-religious genre it is particularly English. There is a comfortable feeling that the Briton can take his place with confidence and pride in the national affairs thus commemorated, a place assigned by Providence, hence the religious exterior and form no matter what the occasion. This religious optimism is not synonymous with Christian hope, which fixes itself upon eternity and beyond the domain of history; it is based on the righteousness of the cause and is addressed to the immediate future. The English virtually believed that only those who are at the head of progress—that is, only they themselves—are worthy of divine grace. Did not Milton say in his *Areopagitica:* "What does God then but reveal Himself to His servants, and, as His Manner is, first to his Englishmen?" It is precisely this attitude that circumscribed the English National Church in Handel's time, and the large mass of Nonconformists not unreasonably wondered whether the Established Church really believed in God, who, after all, was the God not only of King and government in Britain but also of all humanity. But when the Church produced its great ceremonial services to give thanks for Utrecht, or Aix-la-Chapelle, or Culloden, all could join, for this was in reality a patriotic-political service. This is what makes this English "church music" so difficult for non-Britons to understand, for without the political-patriotic background the genre is unthinkable and incomprehensible.

The lessons derived from the Old Testament were understood in their moral-political sense by all shades of the English public, and besides the odes and anthems they also produced what Winton Dean appropriately calls the "victory oratorios." Thus *Judas Maccabaeus* was an instant success but the Christian pieces, very characteristically, were not. *Messiah* was at first barely acceptable, and *Theodora* a complete failure.

The ceremonial manner was the English "Baroque" church style par excellence; its very nature called for a large ensemble of chorus and orchestra. (Performances given with organ accompaniment, as is usual in churches nowadays, rob these works of their true physiognomy.) Ceremonial music also made its appearance in the oratorio, even though that elaborate apparatus excluded the possibility of individual characterization, the dramatist's real preserve. Yet while the positive, festive, political-ceremonial tone of the anthems and Te Deums is present in the oratorios, and is, if anything, enhanced, Handel often makes the chorus a protagonist, even the chief protagonist, and thereby achieves dramatic force, not infrequently of a violence that is still unparalleled. In many a "sacred oratorio" when the pious trimmings are forgotten, the ceremonial-political is very much in evidence, as for instance in *Solomon*. The political nature of the Queen of Sheba's visit cannot be mistaken for anything else. In fact, the entire third act of this oratorio is an apology and panegyric on the reign of George II, Handel's sovereign and patron, and on England and her institutions. The splendor of these choruses, notably the great eight-part ones, is thrilling, their spaciousness and euphony breathtaking; they show Handel at the summit of his powers.

A particularly characteristic form in the ceremonial style is the coronation anthem, a splendid example of which is the Hallelujah Chorus in *Messiah*. This particular type, the archetype of the ceremonial, had been a favorite since the anthems composed for the coronation of George II in 1727. It reappeared in the earliest oratorios and never failed to rouse the public. It came to be looked upon as a drawing card. An advertisement in the newspapers in 1732, when the performance of *Esther* was announced, stated that "There will be no Action on the Stage, but the House will be fitted up in a decent Manner, for the Audience. The Musick to be disposed after the Manner of the Coronation Service." We must understand that the Coronation Service is a parallel to ordination, partaking of both lay and spiritual character. The King is the wielder of the temporal sword for the protection of his Church. One should not assume, however, that the ceremonial tone must always confine itself to the brilliant, opulent, triumphal, the official tone of the Church. Within that confident tone Handel always has marvelous reserves from which constant surprises are drawn, though the surprises remain in harmony with the traditional attitude. And he could be profoundly moving even in the monumental style, as for instance in the magnificent *Funeral Ode for Queen Caroline*.

It is astonishing how clearly Handel recognized the nature of English ceremonial music, and how promptly he identified himself with it. Scarcely settled in his new environment, he composed the *Birthday Ode for Queen Anne* and the *Utrecht Te Deum*, both exuding unmistakable English ceremonial tone. This quality was immediately recognized by the public, and the early Te Deum became a "repertory" item at St. Paul's Cathedral for decades until displaced by the *Dettingen Te Deum*. The latter work, together with the anthem *The King shall rejoice*, both in what Burney called Handel's "big bow-wow" (i.e. grand ceremonial) manner, was received with enthusiasm and admiration at its first hearing in 1743. This music and this manner the English public felt to be the very embodiment of their feelings and beliefs.

[6]

A LITTLE INQUIRY will yield the interesting fact that while anthems set to English texts were already known in the early decades of the Reformation, even before the introduction of the Prayer Book in 1549, officially the anthem did not form part of the service until Charles II established his rubric for the Church. The anthem not only fulfilled the same role in the Anglican service as did the motet in the Roman, but obviously took its departure from it. Magnificent examples of the motet-anthem can be found in the works of Tye, Tallis, Farrant, and Gibbons, but the decisive change comes with the Restoration. The enforced pause in the practice of church music during the Commonwealth greatly minimized connections with the old choral polyphony and led to the admission of new stylistic elements from the Continent. Italian cantata and opera began to do their work in England as everywhere else, even before the Commonwealth. Among the musicians attracted to the Italian style were Walter Porter (c. 1595–1659), reputedly a personal pupil of Monteverdi, and especially William Child (1606–1697), both of whom are unjustly forgotten. The Restoration anthem, enriched with a French

strain, produced a literature that if not completely discounted by foreigners and Englishmen alike (all of whom see only Purcell) is at least consistently deprecated. Now the ceremonial tone dominant in the Louis XIV
style was fully established in the English anthem, especially after the
orchestra was substituted for the organ. The two main types of this characteristically and uniquely English form of church music, designed for the
"fully appointed" cathedral service, are before us in the 17th century: the
"verse anthem," with solo alternating with the chorus, and the "full
anthem," all choral. The orchestra was evidently introduced soon after the
Restoration, judging by Thomas Tudway's account of the King's displeasure with church music of his day. Charles II, reared in France after
his father's beheading, and accustomed to French music, "tired with the
grave and solemn way which has been established by Tallis and Byrd,
and others, ordered the composers of his Chapel to add symphonies etc.
with instruments to their anthems." Indeed, Lully's influence on the
Restoration anthem was considerable. Handel arrived on the scene when
the genre was fully developed; he carried it to its summit, but not before
a thorough study of its past and present.

Well might Queen Anne have been delighted with the *Birthday Ode*
(1714), first in the line of anthems. The text, by an unknown author, gave
Handel opportunities to indulge in pastoral descriptive music, rendering
the "gentle murmurs," the "rolling streams," and the flutter of "downy
wings," but also the glories of the Queen who "fix'd a lasting Peace on
Earth." The work was unquestionably based on the welcome and birthday odes of Purcell and other English composers, and it is quite apparent
that Handel had studied both recent and older English music.

O be joyful in the Lord, the first of the Chandos Anthems, all composed between 1717 and 1720, uses so much material from the *Utrecht
Jubilate* that we can pass over it after noting Handel's remarkable technical achievement in reducing the choruses from four and five parts to
three, and the orchestra to strings (without violas) and two oboes, all
without essential loss. The second Chandos Anthem, *In the Lord put I my
trust,* is a rather extended work with a number of choruses and tenor
solos, but though it contains some fine and elaborate fugues the tone is
prevailingly intimate, leaning toward the pastoral. Only in the chorus
"snares, fire, and brimstone" does Handel adopt the ceremonial tone. Perhaps the only Chandos Anthem that shows introspection is the third, the
penitential Psalm, *Have mercy upon me.* The solo numbers, especially, are
truly penitential in feeling, but even here the joyous triumphal tone of
"Thou shalt make me hear of joy" gains the upper hand, and the final

double fugue, "There shall I teach Thy ways," though dark, is positive in tone. The fourth, *O sing unto the Lord a new song*, is festive and proclamatory, yet midway Handel turns to the evocative—"O worship the Lord in the beauty of holiness"—only to make the bowed listener sit up startled when the chorus suddenly falls in with "Let the whole world stand in awe." *I will magnify Thee*, the fifth anthem, exists in two versions. The first is scored for the usual modest Cannons ensemble of three-part chorus, tenor and soprano solo, the second for four-part chorus and full solo quartet, the final "Glory and worship are before Him" broadening to a double chorus of eight parts. While the second version is the more artistic of the two, it borrows a great deal from other anthems, and the final ceremonial Amen chorus, while effective, is somewhat conventional.

The sixth anthem, *As pants the hart*, of which there are four versions, illustrates Handel's phenomenal skill in choral writing. The first version is in the chamber style, while the subsequent reworkings have magnificent choruses in several parts. The second version is a real tour de force. In the reworking of the opening chorus Handel wanted something more spacious and under normal circumstances would have enlarged the customary four-part chorus to eight parts. At Cannons he had only a three-part choral ensemble to work with, therefore the doubling resulted in a six-part chorus, but the whole thing is a feat of sleight of hand, for while the setting gives the impression of the richness of a double chorus *a* 6, nowhere does he employ six real parts. The opening of the anthem is suffused with the gentle melancholy of southern Italian church music. The magnificent soprano solo, "Tears are my daily food," also breathes this spirit; in its introduction the oboe and the violins emit delectable little sighs. The duet "Why so full of grief?" is also melting, but the tenor solo before the last chorus is a veritable *aria di bravura*. This is a great work, lamentably disfigured in the final version.

My song shall be alway (No. 7) is the least interesting of the anthems, but No. 8, *O come let us sing unto the Lord*, is one of the finest. This and the following five anthems use a four-part chorus; apparently the Cannons forces had been enlarged. It is a piece of general rejoicing, one of the real ceremonial works, as elaborate, powerful, and splendid as any of the great oratorios; indeed, some of this music will reappear in *Belshazzar*. Yet the pastoral interlude is not missing. In the tenor aria "We are the people of His pasture and the sheep of His hand," a delicate pastoral atmosphere is created simply by using two recorders. The ninth anthem, *O praise the Lord with one consent*, is also broad, hymnic, and full of rhetorical pathos. The tenth, *The Lord is my light,* clearly fore-shadows the great "military" scenes in the oratorios; the words allude to "hosts of men," to the "trembling of the earth," insisting that "Yet shall my heart be not afraid." In the chorus "For who is God" this anthem presents one of those mighty pieces where the Englishman looks with confidence to his constitutional God (who will shake the earth in *Joshua*); the anthem ends with a resounding choral fugue of praise. The grand manner continues enhanced in the eleventh anthem, *Let God arise.* The very first chorus, "Let his enemies be scattered," is sledge-hammer music, a quality that still echoes in the solos, which are interrupted by a fine choral sicil-iana, and the anthem ends in a majestic double fugue. The final Alleluia offers one of the few instances of cantus firmus work. The twelfth anthem, *O praise the Lord,* is routine Handel.

To carry this genre of works to its conclusion, we must mention the *Wedding Anthem for Princess Anne* (1734), a festive piece with its dou-ble choruses, but too dependent on borrowings. The second wedding anthem, for the Prince of Wales (1736), is not noteworthy, but the *Foundling Hospital Anthem* of 1749 is no routine work. "Blessed are they that consider the poor" touches deep feelings, for Handel was a charitable person with a love for children. Here, as in the *Funeral Anthem,* he remi-nisces from his own childhood, as is immediately evident from his use of the chorale *Aus tiefer Not,* set with an unusual "strictness"—for Handel—that recalls the German cantor's art. Even the final Hallelujah is more dig-nified than jubilant.

Though chronologically earlier (1737), the *Funeral Anthem* has been left until last because it is in a class by itself. Burney, usually judicious and somewhat cautious, abandons restraint when speaking of this anthem, which he places at the head of all Handel's works. There are even some sacrilegious voices—from Handel's native land—to be heard declaring that this great Psalm-cantata is "equal throughout to Bach's best efforts"!

This anthem is not pure ceremonial music, it is ceremonial music with a profound personal involvement, which gives it an altogether unique cast. Caroline as Handel knew her during a friendship of thirty-odd years—as the fairy princess of his childhood, as the Princess of Wales, and as the steadfast Queen supporting a vacillating, shallow King —passes before his mind's eye as the music recapitulates that life. The opening chorus, "The ways of Zion do mourn," brings back Handel's youth, the cantor's apprentice who from the organ led the congregation in the singing of the chorale, *Herr Jesu Christ, du höchstes Gut.* But the manner in which the cantus firmus is used is entirely Handel's own, the piece being a sort of free chorale fantasia, not an integral setting of the traditional *Kirchenlied*. The opening strains of the tune are announced in the usual even half notes, the "cantus firmus" gradually taking over the other parts, while two additional motifs are introduced. The combination of these elements creates a wondrous, ever-expanding contrapuntal tapestry ending in a great fugue. Then comes a gentle solo quartet, "When the ear heard her," a musical portrait of the noble friend, and, even more affecting, the simple choral setting of "She delivered the poor." Nevertheless, the heroic tone is not missing, and the contrast between the quietly meditative and narrative passages and the solemn and sturdy choral proclamations is maintained throughout. At "But their name liveth evermore" Handel quotes the great funeral motet, *Ecce quomodo moritur*, by his namesake, Jacobus Gallus (Handl), revered in German lands since the 16th century. The anthem does not end with the usual triumphant Hallelujahs; it dies away pianissimo.

The deliberate withholding of the expression of personal religious faith was alien to Evangelical-Lutheran church music; Anglican orthodoxy, more formal and externalized, virtually demanded it. In Georgian times the atmosphere of ceremonial splendor in the great London churches would have made the lyric confessions of a Bach totally incongruous. There is no need to search in the Te Deums for any religious sentiment; this is official music, state music, in which the appeal to the political-national consciousness of the people is so direct that one almost feels there is nothing to be gained by analysis of their musical construction. To us these splendid works appear to embody a kind of elevated religious rhetoric, but there can be no doubt that their composer intended them to fulfill a political and psychological purpose, and that is how his contemporaries saw them.

With the banishment of the Stuarts the face of England may have changed, but in John Locke's treatises the Miltonian ideas are not absent. The King receives his sovereignty from the people, and he obliges himself to use the powers vested in him for the defense of their rights and of the laws that safeguard them. Nevertheless, the sovereigns still called themselves "kings by the grace of God," a seeming violation of the basic constitutional principle but gladly supported by the English people, who knew well that it presented no threat to their institutions. For Anglican festive occasions nothing was more appropriate than the poetry of the Old Testament, since such ancient religions as the Semitic had, for the most part, no creed; they consisted rather of institutions and practices. History has demonstrated that institutions are far more lasting than their interpretations. Over these interpretations, of which the Handelian anthems are magnificent examples, the Englishman's ardent consciousness, pride, and tolerance shed a glow that obscures from us the basic ground of fact. Basil Lam wittily remarks that "Handel seems to have accepted readily the convention by which the Almighty was assumed to have special responsibility for national victories," yet whenever we encounter Handel's sumptuous ceremonial music it is subjected in our minds to an unconscious meiosis that is very difficult to correct without falling into the contrary error. We must not forget that though wholeheartedly agreeing with the English conception, and preferring the Old Testament and classical antiquity to Christian subjects, Handel's faith in divine grace, in an inner guiding voice, remained unshaken; each of his acts proves that he was filled with a peace and fortitude that could withstand every assault from without, every adversity, and every pain. But he did not compose for this God; the recognition of a spiritual order lying at the foundation of political reality displaced his early Lutheran religious faith.

The *grandezza* of the Te Deums and Coronation Anthems is well emphasized by the forces used. The Te Deums, though they have solos, are essentially choral works, the very first of them, the *Utrecht Te Deum,* consisting of eleven sections. Its constituent numbers are short, the whole being a well-constructed, compact work set for a five-part chorus and brilliant orchestra with trumpets and drums. There are some echoes of the German past, notably in the opening chorus, "We praise Thee O God," with its cantus firmus work, but also palpable memories of Roman and Venetian choral techniques and of Carissimi. Of the others, the D major Te Deum seems to be an early work composed about the time of the *Utrecht Te Deum,* and the A major was perhaps written for the coronation in 1727. Neither of these two is significant; much more important is the B-flat Te Deum from the end of the Cannons period, even though it is a partial reworking of the *Utrecht Te Deum.* This is a mature piece, though in its recasting of some of the choruses in the *Utrecht Te Deum,* their simple but telling impact lost some of its freshness.[7] The *Dettingen Te Deum,* much later than the others, is more monumental, extended, and varied in its techniques, but also somewhat more "official" in tone and substance. Very interesting composite structures provide both attractiveness and a logical building up to the culminating choruses. A fine example of this procedure is "Thou art the King of glory," where the bass solo, ac-

[7] The A major Te Deum in turn reworks the B-flat, and though it has some fine music, the compound reworking cancelled many of the qualities of the original.

companied by continuo and a concertante trumpet, leads like a precentor, followed by the chorus, until everything is swallowed up in the jubilation of the full chorus and orchestra.

The Coronation Anthems are somewhat simpler in design; their counterpoint, even their rhythm, is less elaborate, but the ceremonial-proclamatory quality is overwhelming. This is most deceptive music when studied from the score; one sees simple diatonic harmonies, but they are so placed in the voices and so timed that when heard the effect is irresistible. The first Coronation Anthem, *Zadok the Priest*, begins with a simple undulating introduction in the strings which, welling up repeatedly, leads to a veritable explosion when the chorus enters. One might say with a little exaggeration that it does not matter much what follows, the issues are settled then and there. What neither apologists nor detractors seem to understand is that in ceremonial music of this kind the ritual aspects must needs develop at the expense of the religious, even at the expense of the more subtly musical. Nor can such a piece tarry for individuals to meditate upon their feelings. Where psychology begins there are no longer deeds, only motives for deeds; the solidity offered by the unequivocal is lost.

Zadok the Priest is the supreme example of this ceremonial music, though the second Coronation Anthem, *The King shall rejoice*, is no less magnificent, even if more elaborate and polyphonic. The third, *My heart is inditing*, differs from the others. It is gentle and warm, since it served for the part of the ceremony where the Queen was crowned. Nothing massive here, but a good deal of Purcellian finesse, especially in the delicately worked "Kings' daughters were among thy honorable women," and in "Upon thy right hand did stand the Queen," whose dancelike lattice work is most attractive. Only at the end does the tone turn to the proclamatory. *Let thy hand be strengthened* is the least important of the four anthems.

Handel's ceremonial music "faithfully reproduces the tone of Anglican church music," it is true, but his means and substance are his own. A comparison with Purcell's and other English composers' works will show in Handel's a more imaginative texture as well as elements coming from German, Italian, and French sources, the presence of which may have prompted Dent's statement referred to on page 215. But neither is there any similarity to the German cantata, steeped in mysticism, to which the anthems are often compared even by English authors. Outwardly the anthem may look like a cantata because it consists of several sections or numbers, the solos alternating with chorus, but the tone and purpose exclude all comparison. The cantus firmus technique is used sparingly. In the *Utrecht Te Deum and Jubilate* it surely represents a natural employment of Handel's German training, for it appeared in the earlier *Laudate pueri* whence it was transferred to the English work. The final chorus again makes use of an old cantus firmus, paraphrased around the turn of the century by many German masters. The insistence on motivic elaboration in "Vouchsafe O Lord" in the same work also recalls German techniques and so does "O go your way to his gates." This piece, the core of the *Jubilate,* with its elaborate five-part counterpoint, is unthinkable without the old German motet style, but the independent handling of the orchestral accompaniment gives it a different coloring. When Handel transferred parts of this glorious piece to the *Brockes Passion* ("Wir alle wollen erblassen") somehow the glory was lost. It was quite natural that in the *Funeral Anthem* Handel should recall the liturgical music of his youth and quote the hallowed tunes used at funerals in Germany. Nothing of this sort was available to him in England; there was not the unbroken living tradition of church music as in Germany, for by the end of the 17th century the spirit of the Reformation had disappeared. He could not find symbolic tunes that would fit into his grand choral style and therefore returned to those he knew so well from the Liebfrauenkirche and the Calvinist cathedral in Halle.

Comparisons have also been made between the Handelian Te Deum and such of Bach's works as the opening of the *Christmas Oratorio,* quoting especially the lack of dramatic quality in the Te Deums and equating the joyous tone with Bachian religious fervor. In the first place, the dramatic quality is not absent, though it is of a special, almost static kind. As an example of the many such touches, one may quote the sudden changes at key words from minor to major, from adagio to allegro, and from solo to tutti. The ceremonial anthems have no sinfonia at the beginning, again demonstrating the conceptual difference between cantata and anthem. Only the *Funeral Anthem,* in every way an exceptional work, has one. Though some of the anthems have brief instrumental introductions, they are of the French overture type, the Lully type, as are, indeed, practically all of Handel's overtures; the Italian form is never used. But what sets these works altogether apart from the German cantata and oratorio is precisely their royal rather than their religious spirit. Te Deums were composed in the 18th century that approximate the spirit of the *1812 Overture:* cannon firing, church bells pealing, military bands blaring, but all this only amounts to a good deal of more or less harmonious noise. If we want to see the essential difference between Handel's English Te

Deums and similar works composed by Germans all we have to do is to compare the former with any of Hasse's five Te Deums. All of Hasse's are well composed, festive, and even splendid, yet basically commonplace and expressing nothing in particular. Only the aged Haydn, in his second Te Deum (1800), offers a tone and quality kindred to Handel's, undoubtedly derived from Haydn's study of Handel's music while in England. Among later composers one might mention Brahms, whose *Triumphlied* has something of the commemorative spirit of the Handelian Te Deum. On the other hand, such a "Bearbeitung" as Robert Franz's of the *Utrecht Jubilate* takes its place with Elgar's "retouching" of a Chandos Anthem mentioned above; it is a complete misreading of the spirit that animates the original.

Nor is there any parallel to the Coronation Anthems in European choral literature. It is perfectly true, as Larsen says in his book about *Messiah*, that "the tendency to exploit sonority, already so clearly seen in the Italian compositions, permeates the whole of these works." While this tendency excludes any similarity to the Bachian cantata, even the Italian influence, which is undoubtedly strong, must be qualified. No Italian composer would ever interrupt the flow of his music to nail down with hammer strokes "God save the King," or show such vastness of proportion and propulsive power. Parts of the anthems will reappear in many an oratorio and will seem perfectly natural to their new environment.

We must return once more to the role of English music in Handel's ceremonial works. Dent denies that either the Chandos Anthems or the Te Deums are indebted to Purcell, Leichtentritt insists they owe not only their outward form but essential musical features to the angelic English composer, and Larsen, while not inclined to accept Dent's categorical stand, leans toward it, considering Handel's choral style in his church music more Italian than anything else. We might say that none of them is altogether wrong and every one of them is a little right. The technical means recall the German cantor's art, and the choral style of Roman and Venetian music is palpably present together with some French elements, but form and tone are unmistakably English. Admittedly, at this stage of his career, Handel's feeling for the natural cadence and inflections of the English language was slight, he even misinterpreted some of the words he set to music, but he caught the spirit of this English music as no one since Purcell had. Purcell himself was indeed very much responsible for this. We have seen that the *Utrecht Te Deum* was modelled on Purcell's "St. Cecilia" Te Deum, and we have noticed that while the more intimate and subtle Purcellian touches eluded Handel for years to come, some are already absorbed and digested in these early English works. The anthem *Have mercy on me O God* exhibits these very positively, and *My heart is inditing* demonstrates that Handel had studied Purcell's settings of the same text. Winton Dean declares Purcell the "precipitating agent" in the formation of Handel's English style; nothing could more accurately describe the subtle yet pervasive influence of the English master upon the German. The *Funeral Anthem* shows an even more penetrating influence of English music, and of a much wider range.

Of Purcell's sixty-odd anthems Handel knew many, but since they were usually found in the company of similar works by Humphrey, Locke, and others, he had a comprehensive view of the latter-day English anthem. Pelham Humphrey, who like Purcell died tragically young, is an important link between the older anthem and that of the Restoration. He had a wonderful sense for vocal setting and an adventurous ear for harmony, as well as for grand sonorous effects. Humphrey was next to Purcell the most talented English composer of the age, and one of those who set the tone for ceremonial music. Matthew Locke (c. 1630–1677), whom we have encountered in his capacity as a composer for the stage, wrote elaborate verse-anthems that were not ignored by Handel, and there are unmistakable signs that Handel was familiar with other *fin de siècle* composers, as well as with those still active at the time he settled in England. The *Ode for St. Cecilia's Day* (1684) of John Blow (1649–1708), Blow's royal "Welcome Songs" composed from 1682 onward, and his Coronation Anthems all figure in Handel's composite style. Blow was a minor master who composed much routine music, but a master he was and English to his fingertips. This placid and hard-working musician could rise to considerable dignity and expressiveness, and his great eight-part Coronation Anthem, *God spake sometime in visions,* surely left its mark on Handel. Neither can William Croft's anthems, stately if not very original, be dismissed, as they often are. Dr. Croft (1678–1727) was a fine church composer in the Anglican vein. As we shall see later, Handel did not stop there but went all the way back to the Elizabethans, so that he had a very good idea of English music of over a century.[8]

Having taken issue with Edward J. Dent, we now must humbly hand him a large bouquet. A cardinal fact that has escaped many scholars was clear to him, and Dent, the redoubtable leader of revived English mu-

---

[8] There is a curiously archaic a cappella number in the B-flat Te Deum, "When Thou hadst overcome the sharpness of death," for treble, two tenors, and bass. It was exceptional for Handel to write unaccompanied part-music and whenever he did so, as in this particular case, the connections to Elizabethan music are unmistakable.

sicology, stated the fact so succinctly that in one sentence he gave us the key to the idea that determined the tone and quality of the full anthem as Handel received it from his predecessors. Handel's "dramatic use of the chorus came not from the English church but from the English theatre." How true! for the anthem was palpably influenced by the masque. Purcell's anthems have a theatrical quality and the solos in his verse anthems are distinctly operatic. This is not meant to disparage Handel's procedure. A great, brilliant, and solemn ritual act is theatre, and unless we still retain the Puritans' mentality we should find nothing objectionable in the terms. Does not a solemn service in a great cathedral have theatrical elements of the noblest sort? The constant search for obscure metaphysical ramifications is misplaced in the face of simple realities and can lead to ridiculous fantasies. In this connection it is amusing to note how far-fetched problem-seeking can mislead the unwary. One author, noticing that all pieces of the "coronation" type are in D major, thought that he was on the trail of a mystic bit of symbolism. "It is obvious," he says, "that for festive occasions this key was for Handel an inner necessity." The necessity was there, but it was far from "inner"; it was external and practical: the preferred tuning of the trumpets. Because of the tuning, D major actually became a sort of statutory key for ceremonial occasions. This should also warn our church musicians that performances of these works with organ accompaniment, without the trumpets, drums, and all the panoply of the orchestra, altogether rob them of their spirit.

Handel approached the anthem with a mastery of vocal writing, both solo and choral, that surely was unrivalled at that time. In his use of polyphony he was aware of the collective-universal nature of choral music, of its stability and suggestion of the spatial, of the multidimensional. And he was well aware of the English susceptibility to stirring ceremonial music, which, as we shall see, was carried over from the anthem into the oratorio.

X

T HE GENERAL COURT OF THE ROYAL ACADEMY OF MUSIC MET on January 14, 1729, "for disposing of the Effects" belonging to the institution. The Academy as such was dead, and the directors were busy "prosecuting" the delinquent shareholders, but apparently they were willing to assist Handel and Heidegger if the latter would continue on their own; the decision was reached to lend them the disposable "effects," scenery, costumes, instruments, and so forth. Handel had been quiet and seemingly inactive since the collapse of the Royal Academy the previous spring (no compositions are known from this period), but the silence, as usual, was deceiving. By the end of autumn his plan was ready: he and Heidegger forming a partnership, the two entrepreneurs undertook to finance a new opera establishment out of their own pockets. It is apparent that while the Royal Academy of Music may have been bankrupt, Handel was not, and his bank account contained enough money to yield the considerable sum needed for such a venture. Heidegger put up an equal amount, and the two partners were in business. The situation did not look too bad; the King continued his subsidy of £1,000, and, according to Mrs. Pendarves, interest in the new opera, as indicated in the rate at which the subscriptions came in, was quite satisfactory.

The first task of the managers was to recruit a new company, all of the stars having left England upon the demise of the Academy. The *Daily Post* announced on January 27, 1729, that "Mr. Handell, the famous Composer of the Italian Musick," had departed for Italy "with a Commission from the Royal Academy of Musick"; Heidegger was already there scouting the scene. The most pressing business was to secure a new castrato, and they set their sights on Carlo Broschi, called Farinelli, a singer then rising to eminence. They were unsuccessful. Since Cuzzoni was unwilling to return, and Faustina had married Hasse and was well settled in Venice, altogether new singers had to be found. There is documentary proof of Handel's presence in Rome and Venice,[1] but he undoubtedly visited other operatic centers also. One wonders how the composer felt on returning to the scene of his youthful exploits, to the places where he first received the lasting impression of Italian opera. In the meantime this opera had changed a great deal; the leading Venetian and Neapolitan musicians of twenty years before were fading and an entirely new breed was rising in Naples. We do not know what he might have heard in Italy and how he felt about this new trend, but his subsequent operas testify to his undiminished powers of observation and absorption.

When news reached him from Michaelsen that his mother was gravely ill, Handel hastened his departure from Italy, and after a short passage through Hanover, reached Halle early in June. His mother, aged and blind, was obviously in the shadow of death, and what little time Handel had was spent with her; all invitations to see other people were declined. One of these was from the indisposed Johann Sebastian Bach, who sent his eldest son, Wilhelm Friedemann, in embassy to Halle, to ask his famous colleague to visit him in Leipzig. By July first Handel was back in London, straining to get the opera venture started.

The troupe he finally recruited was a good if not superlative com-

---

[1] There is, however, no evidence whatever to support the story that while he was in Rome his old patron, Cardinal Colonna, attempted to arrange a meeting between Handel and the Old Pretender, then staying in the city. Rome was a center of Jacobite intrigue, but Vatican politicians were more realistic than to tempt a Protestant musician of German extraction on excellent terms with the Hanoverian dynasty. Moreover, Handel was altogether bent on business, and there is no indication that he renewed his acquaintanceships.

pany. Cuzzoni was replaced by another soprano, even homelier and more temperamental, Anna Strada, whom Londoners promptly nicknamed "the Pig." But she was an even better singer than Cuzzoni, and Handel would tolerate no criticism when an artist in whom he believed was concerned. It was not long before he compelled London not only to appreciate La Strada's singing but to make her welcome in high social circles. Margherita Merighi, a deep alto, was to take the male roles, and Francesca Bertolli, a mezzo, completed the female cast. The castrato, a soprano, was Antonio Bernacchi, the tenor Annibale Fabri, and Johann Gottfried Riemschneider, an old schoolmate from Halle whom he perhaps picked up in Hamburg, the bass.[2] With the exception of Bertolli and Riemschneider, these were experienced and well-trained singers. Bertolli was not unduly endowed with vocal beauty, but her physical pulchritude did not go unnoticed. Poor Riemschneider lasted only one season. Haym having died in August 1729, the post of librettist-secretary of the company was given to Giacomo Rossi. When everything was ready for the launching, Handel sat down and in a couple of weeks wrote an opera, *Lotario;* the libretto, of uncertain authorship, was an arrangement of an older Venetian book by Salvi. So the second Academy opened with this opera on December 2, 1729.

Lotario was a failure. The plot is confused and complicated, with an unusual number of attempted suicides, and form and meaning are too often diffused in mere movement, a rather stumbling movement at that. But, as usual, there is some fine music hidden in this hastily thrown-together score. It contains one of Handel's towering and implacable matriarchs, Matilda, who is superbly characterized, and the composer also succeeds here in creating a believable youthful lover, Idelbert. There are some very good arias and fine counterpoint, and the final duet between Adelaide and Lotario is a magnificent paean of love. The opera also has one of those always dramatic prison scenes that immediately induce commentators to invoke *Fidelio.*

Handel was either blind to the reigning taste or deliberately ignored it. One wonders whether the renewed contact with the universal love of opera in Italy, where all strata of society from coachmen and gondoliers to princes and cardinals enjoyed and understood it, did not fortify him in his belief that he must continue his labors to establish opera in England. But the situation had not changed; the great success of the *Beggar's Opera* still reverberated, and even though its sequel, *Polly,* was kept from

[2] As was related above (see p. 136), it was during this journey that Handel may have once more visited Hamburg.

the boards by order of the Lord Chamberlain (who remembered the merciless jibes aimed at the Prime Minister in the previous opera), many
other imitations were produced in the theatres as well as in any room that
could be made to serve the purpose.[3] Clearly the English public wanted
something else than Italian opera.

To repair the damage, Handel revived a proven success, *Giulio
Cesare* (January 17, 1730), which had a fair run. Then on February 24
the new opera of *Partenope,* libretto by Stampiglia, was presented to a
somewhat surprised audience. This was a bold new departure: an unheroic opera, not a buffa, but a rather sophisticated comedy. There is no
matriarch here but a delightfully attractive woman of many qualities.
Partenope may be a warrior—she actually leads her army—but she is a
woman through and through. This Amazon can exhibit reticent tenderness and can be inspiring, inciting, confusing, and forgiving. "Io ti levo
l'impero dell'armi" is a brilliant bravura piece, but in "Voglio amare" she
is a passionate woman. The whole opera breathes love, and the music is
remarkably original and fresh; Handel's new experiences in Italy are reflected in the remarkable, if brief, quartet.

But *Partenope* was not successful, and the repertory had to be fat-
tened with pasticcios as well as with another revival, *Tolomeo.* When the
season ended the two partners had no reason to congratulate themselves
on their enterprise; artistically, financially, and socially the season was a
near-failure. With the King away on a protracted holiday in Hanover, the
court was absent from the Haymarket Theatre; for some reason Caroline,
left behind in London as Regent, also stayed away. Heidegger, a businessman with sound instincts, saw that he must appeal to lower tastes in
order to make money; his masquerades of dubious quality were always
successful. Above all, he realized that the temper of the public was
against a foreign importation presented by foreign artists in a foreign
tongue. The *Beggar's Opera* had converted not only the populace but the
literary men and high society; obviously the musical theatre demanded
English subjects performed in the country's native language. But Handel
would not yield. There was danger of a quarrel, and Heidegger seriously
considered withdrawing his investment before all of it was in jeopardy.

There were other troubles that required urgent attention—the cast
was failing. Though a good singer, Bernacchi, the star castrato, was not
popular; he had to run the gauntlet of unfavorable comparisons with
Senesino, and Handel was compelled to dismiss him after *Partenope.* The

[3] Gay and Pepusch, by publishing *Polly* in book form, reaped a financial harvest
equal to a successful run in the theatre.

inferior German basso Riemschneider, who replaced Boschi, quit of his own accord. Only Strada, who despite her ungainly appearance captivated London by her fine singing, held her own; she became the mainstay of the company. There was no time to undertake another personal recruiting trip to Italy; therefore Handel resorted to the unusual—and risky—expedient of engaging singers through the medium of English diplomatic agents. One move was mandatory: Senesino had to be brought back at any cost even though this meant a certain humiliation for Handel; the famous castrato was not amenable to discipline and had openly defied him. The English envoy to Florence succeeded in this difficult diplomatic assignment, and when the second season of the new Academy opened on November 3, 1730, with a revival of *Scipio,* Senesino (who to Sir Newman Flower's horror "fed himself with his fingers") assumed his old role, while a new basso, Giovanni Commano, replaced Riemschneider. The till began to fill, Heidegger was satisfied for the moment; the fortunes of the Haymarket Theatre took a turn for the better.

In the meantime Handel came to terms with Walsh, who, beginning with *Partenope,* became his principal publisher, the business relationship being continued after Walsh's death by his son. Handel was forced to reach a settlement with the crafty old pirate, for he was being mercilessly plundered; whenever Cluer, Handel's publisher, put out one of his works, Walsh immediately countered with a similar or even identical publication. The Walshes grew rich on the exploitation of their captive and very productive client.

By February 1731, Handel was again riding the crest of success with his new opera, *Poro.* Fashioned from Metastasio's *Alessandro nell'Indie,* the libretto offered a historical subject that was very acceptable as a theatrical story, and in it Senesino rose to new heights of artistic triumph. The aristocracy, headed by the royal family, returned to the Haymarket Theatre, lavishing praise on Handel and his troupe, and the demand for the "songs" from *Poro* was such that Walsh could not print his editions fast enough.

Having reassembled a first-class cast, Handel had returned to the heroic style, though *Poro* is palpably different from the heroic operas of the first Academy. Everything in the new opera is elegant and sophisticated, the harmony very advanced, and in general the music is almost unfailingly imaginative and full of delectable surprises. But the new, elegant, and sophisticated Handel had not lost his ability to characterize and to overwhelm with the sensuous beauty of his melodies. Cleofide's dirge, "Se ciel mi divide," is almost too beautiful for a sad situation, while

Gandarte's aria, "Si viver non poss'io," was considered by Burney the finest of Handel's sicilianas. Another wondrous pastoral is Erissena's "Son confusa pastorella," and equally magnificent is the duet, "Caro amico complesso," sung by Poro and Cleofide. One notices Handel's increased interest in ensembles, no doubt the result of his Italian journey. He even combines two arias already sung into a duet. *Poro* was probably one of the librettos brought back from Italy and arranged in London. Unfortunately the story suffers from the overuse of magnanimity as a device to resolve dramatic situations. The drama does mount to a considerable height in the third act, until Alexander has another fit of magnanimity which robs the dénouement of its strength.

Sixteen performances testify to *Poro*'s popularity. In March *Rodelinda* was revived and "took much," followed in April by another proven success, *Rinaldo*, repeated seven times. By the time the theatre was forced to close prematurely because of the unseasonable heat, Italian opera had been re-established in its lucrative eminence; even Heidegger was convinced that Handel could make the English public eat out of his hand.

The triumph was achieved in the midst of personal grief. The news of his aged mother's death reached Handel when he was diligently working on *Poro*. Now his last tie with the land of his origin was severed, for while Handel always thought fondly of his niece he did not really know her. He continued to maintain a friendly correspondence with his erstwhile brother-in-law, Michaelsen, now a political personality of some standing, but Michaelsen, whom he had met only once, had remarried and was raising a new family. Handel was now alone. While he had seen little of his mother since his eighteenth year, his devotion to her was deep, and her spirit seems to have hovered over him wherever he was. The only living mementos of his German past were the beloved Queen Caroline and his faithful Johann Christoph Schmidt, who by this time had become an English subject, John Christopher Smith.

Throughout 1731 Handel kept to himself and did not compose any new operas. The season opened in November with *Tamerlano* and *Poro;* on January 15, 1732, *Ezio,* composed on a drastically altered libretto by Metastasio, was produced. The opera failed, though the new basso, Antonio Montagnana, engaged purely on reputation, proved to be a great success. He saved *Ezio* for at least a few performances by his excellent singing. Handel must have appreciated this second Boschi, because some of the best numbers in the opera are the bass arias. This cold reception was undeserved; *Ezio* does start slowly, even unpromisingly, but after a while Handel's imagination catches fire and soon the drama glows. The contrast between father and daughter is remarkably well drawn. Fulvia is gentle and sweet when she begs her father in her fine aria "Caro padre" not to force her into intrigue. Massimo, the father, is one of Handel's raging bassos, a compelling figure whose "I nocchier che si figura" is a powerful piece. But Massimo can be insinuating, like Iago, and Handel gives him some remarkable music whose pastoral charm and exquisite workmanship belie his ugly intentions. Both women, Fulvia and Onoria, are well characterized, and Handel is in his element when he develops their gradually rising jealousy. Ezio, though a castrato part, can also reach considerable eloquence, as when he sings "Ecco alle mie catene," a sad siciliana, before he is thrown into the dungeon. At the end, Fulvia, deeply hurt, repels her treacherous father who in turn expresses unexpected paternal love. Here there is real drama, and Handel makes the most of it; Fulvia's final scene is powerful, as this opera grows from rather tame beginnings to truly tragic accents. The happy ending dampens it a little, but it is preceded by a most vivid "mob" scene that would do honor to any grand opera.

Undaunted by this failure, Handel immediately countered with *Sosarme,* a highly involved story of dynastic intrigue, but dramatically tight. *Sosarme* is composed with a wide brush, there is no time for undue finesse in the accompaniments—these are not tender people—therefore the composer abstained from filigree work, his orchestra sounding more nearly like a pre-Classic symphony ensemble. The texture is far more homophonic than is customary with Handel; even the duets are more harmonic than linear. The music is somewhat uneven, but Erenice, one of Handel's *grandes dames,* is as admirably characterized as her music is strong, and there are many fine pieces as well as conventional ones. The chorus at the end is strikingly original; this is not a solo-ensemble but a real chorus.

Between *Sosarme* and *Orlando,* the next opera—produced in January 1733—there was a significant interlude that saw the first stirrings of pastoral and oratorio since the Cannons days. (We shall discuss these in the following chapter.) Handel was aroused by the incredible larceny whereby his *Acis and Galatea* was produced by a rival, and he retaliated with his own production of the reworked pastoral. At the same time *Haman and Mordecai,* a masque also from the Cannons days, was refurbished into *Esther,* Handel's first English oratorio. Nevertheless, his interest in opera still dominated all his activities. The interlude between operas was short and was nothing but an interlude; Handel neither recognized the significance of the warm reception of the English works nor was he inclined to give up opera for anything else. As if to take revenge on the "English party" and show the faint-hearted, among them Heidegger, that he did not propose to retire under fire, Handel produced one of his greatest operas, *Orlando*. The success was decisive; night after night the opera ran, Senesino and Strada glowing and triumphing with some of the finest arias they had ever sung.

Orlando is a Baroque opera of the first water, though one that goes back to the older Venetian grand music drama calling for the most elaborate scenic and theatrical effects. A large and well-equipped opera house could restore it to life with stunning effect. If *Sosarme* showed some pre-Classic and *galant* elements—it has some fine dance arias—*Orlando* is a romantic opera, a fairy-tale opera. The libretto, of uncertain origin, is altogether un-Metastasian, and although at times somewhat gauche, it is still a very good book. The Ariosto operas show the Italian librettists' healthy instincts and their knowledge of what happens to a libretto when music clothes the words. Popular as it was, Ariosto's great epic is a difficult source for opera. The great Italian poet, a typical late Renaissance figure, leaves the medieval world of chivalry far behind him and handles his subject with a certain amused superiority that is half mocking. What the librettists took from him were the colorful episodes that made excellent opera stories; they carefully avoided the mocking.

Because *Orlando* is a fairy opera and because of the sumptuous and solemn bass part of Zoroastro, comparisons with *The Magic Flute* have been virtually inevitable. After a fine overture, Handel presents this noble magician-priest, who immediately launches into a characteristically mystery-laden aria, "Gieroglifici eterni," soon followed by another great aria, "Lascia amor." From the warning to Orlando to mend his lascivious ways and return to heroic deeds, the change to a pastoral tone is as remarkable as the music that goes with it. Dorinda, the shepherdess, is not the traditional Arcadian ingénue; she is wonderful in her unabashed propensity for the company of men, the female of the species, untrammelled by any complexes, and her love-making is no sham formality; this is an ardent, almost violent act. The shepherdess is singing of the beauties of pastoral life when Orlando enters carrying Angelica, whom he has just saved from a monster. Angelica finds herself in a delicate situation: she loves Medoro, but this gallant rescuer of hers is obviously smitten with her. Dorinda also has her not so innocent eye on Medoro but her love remains unrequited. The difficulties are overcome for the nonce, and with very fine music, as Dorinda magnanimously helps the lovers, Medoro and Angelica, to escape. Dorinda's arias, especially "O care paroletti," in the siciliana manner, are delightful, but there is a subtle quality in the *accompagnato* that indicates that she has some ideas of her own not expressed in the song. Angelica is a different woman, passionate and purposeful though also very feminine. She can get rid of Orlando and can make Medoro feel that he is lucky to be favored by her, but she can also be genuinely distressed when Medoro is wounded. A remarkably fine trio ends the act.

Orlando, having learned of the true state of affairs, is ready to act, but Zoroastro robs him of his senses. The pastoral cooing of Dorinda, Medoro, and Angelica is an absolute delight; each one of them sings a magnificent song that is a little idyll in itself. With Zoroastro's and Orlando's ensuing numbers everything changes; Handel unburdens himself of dramatic music such as even he seldom equalled. The sorcerer is dignified, noble, and above the fray, like—well, like his namesake, Sarastro, but Orlando is indeed *furioso;* his long arioso is a masterful piece of dramatic expressiveness. The compound scene is rich in rhythmic variety; it is here that Handel employs the famous passage in 5/8, and the final gavotte is an extraordinarily telling bit of music. Composed as a passacaglia, its tone is in such contrast to the dance rhythm that it becomes fearsome.

In the third act the bewitched Orlando is singing of Dorinda's charms, but with the appearance of Angelica and Medoro his fury returns and Angelica is saved only by the intervention of Zoroastro, who puts the raging hero to sleep. Upon awakening, Orlando's senses return, and, renouncing the foibles of love, he congratulates the lovers and resumes the life of a warrior. The mandatory happy ending does not hurt the drama, because the fairy-tale atmosphere is safeguarded everywhere. Handel's ability to render in music the state of mind of a demented person is astonishing; the music is never permitted to rest, rhythm and meter are in constant disequilibrium, the da capos are unpredictable, and the contrast of the dramatic with the pastoral element very sharp. Not the least remarkable dramatic touch is the peace and quiet that return to the music when Orlando regains his mind. The quintet finale constitutes a fitting ending to a remarkable work that is also noteworthy because it begins to show more subtle Purcellian influences. In this scintillating score Handel is incessantly and joyfully aware of visual and aural and tactile beauty, of warm, solid, spontaneous human beings, of the swift and gradual interaction of character with character.

Orlando was very successful but did not equal in popular success such English works as *Acis and Galatea* and *Esther;* even Handel could

not close his eyes to this demonstrable fact (which was probably emphasized by Heidegger), and a second interlude from opera was therefore
decided upon. Samuel Humphreys, who was associated with the Academy
as second, or English, secretary to the company and who seems to have
been a biblical librettist of sorts in *Esther,* was asked to prepare a libretto
for an oratorio. *Deborah* was produced on March 17, 1733. The public did
not like anything about it. Handel raised the admission fees, xenophobia
was fanned by the King's ever-lengthening sojourns in Hanover, and
though Londoners proved again and again that they liked Handel and
were ready to rally around him, he once more found himself caught in the
crossfire of political and national sensibilities. As if to revive old spectres,
Bononcini also reappeared on the London operatic scene in 1732,
producing—in the Haymarket Theatre!—a pastoral play, undoubtedly inspired by the reception of *Acis and Galatea.* To this day the chroniclers
cannot agree whether it was magnanimity or folly, or perhaps Heidegger's
speculative wire-pulling, that caused Handel to permit Bononcini's pastoral to be produced in his own theatre. Perhaps we do not credit Handel
with the astuteness he showed on so many occasions, nor with that lack of
vindictiveness that was such an engaging trait in his character. There was
nothing to be feared from Bononcini; he had shot his bolt and could no
longer challenge Handel. Not so the formidable operatic rivals who now
appeared, for the renewed theatrical war that ensued was far more bitter
than in the days of the first Royal Academy of Music; this time people
really wanted to draw blood.

[2]

HANDEL HAD TO face the jealousy sparked by his success and the
dislike for the German dynasty and everything connected with it, including himself, the King's favorite; in addition, there were other things about
the composer that made him an unusual and baffling person. His music,
though observing most of the conventions of opera, violated the chief
convention: easy accessibility. He could throw together an opera in two
weeks, but as a rule his scores were prepared with care and refinement,
the orchestra always exquisite and sophisticated, the texture far more
polyphonic than was good for the audience. There were many complaints about the "noise" this orchestra made, thereby detracting from the
singing. Opera audiences in 18th-century London—as too often in 20th-
century New York—were interested in singers and singing, not in the
music itself. Handel alienated many singers by his uncompromising

standards, and his personal conduct was imperious and gruff; he was not a servant either to the singers or to the public. Thus, at the proper moment, a rival establishment had no difficulty in seducing his company to desert. Goupy, the designer of a number of Handel's operatic sets for the Academy, circulated cartoons that became famous all over London. Handel with the face of a pig, legs as thick as stovepipes, was seated before the organ on a wine barrel. All around him were bottles, poultry, joints of meat, alluding to his well-known gargantuan appetite, while a cannon firing in the background referred to the noise his music made. It was a devastating caricature and its effects were devastating.

The country's dislike of the dynasty was exacerbated by the unseemly hostility between the King and the Prince of Wales. There had been little love lost between George I and his Prince of Wales, but their discord was as nothing compared to the antagonism between George II and his son Frederick, who now held that title. Frederick was banished from court, his allowance was cut, and he was addressed in the crudest of terms. He in turn seized every opportunity to annoy and insult the King. The gentle Queen, staunchly supporting her worthless husband out of loyalty to tradition, went so far as to refuse to see her son when she was dying. The enmity felt towards the father was once more transferred to the King's favorite musician, but while the future George II had previously never hurt Handel and while after his father's death he was to become a firm Handelian, Frederick selected Handel as the prime target for his malevolence. The anti-Walpole faction immediately recognized the usefulness of this situation; both the Prince and Handel were considered excellent tools for political purposes. Epigrams, letters, and pamphlets excoriating Handel were circulated, some of them amusing but many scurrilous and even hateful, but part of the scheme was a convenient façade for allegorical attacks on Walpole. Since the leader in these attacks was the *Craftsman,* a radical political journal opposed to Walpole, the political intent was clear.

It was the Prince who conceived the idea of forming a rival opera society to unseat Handel; the "Opera of the Nobility" was presently established with the concurrence of such grandees as the Duke of Marlborough. How politics can sway friendship is shown by the fact that five of the directors of the first Royal Academy of Music, among them Handel's old friend and patron Burlington, joined Frederick's anti-Handel opera society. To his credit (or was he omitted?) Chandos did not join the conspiracy. The first meeting of the directors of the Opera of the Nobility was called by Frederick for June 15, 1733. They decided to lease the

Lincoln's Inn Fields Theatre, vacated by Rich when he moved to his new Covent Garden Theatre at the end of 1732. But the most important item on the agenda was a plan to persuade Handel's singers to desert him. It seems that Senesino was in touch with the Prince's men almost from the inception of the plot.

The 1733 season at the Haymarket Theatre had continued with revivals of *Tolomeo* and *Floridante*, with the interval devoted to oratorio in English: *Deborah* in March and *Esther* in April. The prices of the tickets were raised for the first night of *Deborah* but thereafter had to be dropped to normal. The royal family attended several performances of the oratorios. It was during these performances that Handel inaugurated his custom of playing the organ between the acts, which eventually attracted as many music lovers as did the oratorios themselves. The fourth season of the second Academy closed on June 9, rather surprisingly with a production of Bononcini's *Griselda*, revived May 22. Immediately upon the release from their season's contract, the singers left Handel en masse to join the new company; only Strada remained. The new association lost no time, and, since it had an almost full company, it immediately summoned the organizing committee to prepare the fall season.

The situation was catastrophic, and Handel's next move seems puzzling: he suddenly took his tattered company to Oxford for a week's stand. He still had a top performer, Strada, but for a bass we read that he had to promote his cook, Gustavus Waltz, from the kitchen to the stage. Much has been made of this "desperate" move, but Handel's single, and perhaps facetious, reference to Waltz as "my cook" is the only evidence to support it. It is possible, of course, that the hospitable and ever helpful Handel offered a "position" to Waltz, a fellow German expatriate, unemployed for the moment. Waltz, though musically trained, was more of an actor than a singer and certainly no proper replacement for Montagnana. Still, he sang a number of Handel's important bass roles to the composer's apparent satisfaction. The cast was rounded out by Mrs. Wright, soprano; Philip Rocchetti, tenor (who had sung earlier in *Acis and Galatea*); Thomas Salway, a popular tenor; and Walter Powell, countertenor, a local Oxonian worthy who joined the company for the duration of its visit. Thus all Handel's singers, with the exception of Strada, were English.[4]

The occasion for the Oxford festivities was the "Publick Act," the conferring of the degrees, and though the invitation extended to Handel seems natural and proper—Haydn was so honored later in the century—it

[4] Rocchetti may have been of Italian descent but appears to have been regarded as an English singer.

also had political undertones. The university harbored many Jacobites who, realizing that the Hanoverian dynasty was secure, decided that something had to be done to allay the rumors that the university was a hotbed of conspiracy, remove the political taint, and make peace with the court. The Vice-Chancellor, Dr. Holmes, himself a loyal subject, saw in Handel what the King's enemies saw in him, a person close to the monarch, and conceived the idea of inviting him to Oxford with his opera company, to present his music during the solemn convocations, public disputations, and orations attendant on the conferring of the degrees. Handel himself was to be awarded the degree of Doctor of Music *honoris causa*. The new Sheldonian Theatre, a capacious house, was eminently suitable for a *stagione* and Handel immediately accepted.

While Handel's success at Oxford was undisputed, he did not escape censure; xenophobia was strong as was the puritanic strain among the doctors of divinity. Dr. Thomas Hearne, the learned and irascible librarian of the Bodleian, an unregenerate Jacobite and staunch enemy of foreigners, indignantly took the Vice-Chancellor to task for permitting "one Handel, a forreigner . . . and his lowsy Crew of forreign Fiddlers" to perform. Others resented the fact that there was music making instead of "Musick Speech," i.e. a learned lecture on music, which is the proper offering at a convocation of learned men. In addition, there was great indignation at the admission prices, high for the provinces, though lower than in London. Arrived at Oxford on July 4, Handel threw himself into the venture with his old vigor. The schedule was rather severe: a performance in the morning and another one in the evening. *Acis and Galatea* and *Esther,* and a new oratorio, *Athalia,* expressly composed for Oxford and possibly intended as the doctoral offering, were presented, literally day and night. The success was tremendous, the newspapers speaking of audiences approaching 4,000, and Handel returned to London with his pockets lined.

One puzzling episode of the Oxford trip was Handel's refusal of the proffered doctoral degree. Most biographers believe that Handel was deterred by a fee of £100 asked for the degree, which is possible. Yet it is hardly believable that such a large fee would have been exacted for an honorary degree, especially in view of Dr. Holmes's avowed purpose, though some hard-bitten Jacobite may have gone over the Vice-Chancellor's head. Others, among them the Abbé Prévost, then an interested eyewitness in England, attributed Handel's refusal to modesty, which does not seem quite in character. It must be added, however, that later, in 1741 in Dublin, when he was billed as Dr. Handel, the composer publicly denied that he possessed such a degree. There is more here than meets the eye: Handel was indifferent to any recognition other than artistic, and he was not a "joiner," conspicuously staying away from any but charitable organizations. Though most of his friends and colleagues—even the Catholic Geminiani—were Freemasons, Handel refused to join them.

The warm acceptance of pastoral and oratorio at Oxford was a remarkable phenomenon that should have opened Handel's eyes. The English public was used to and fond of masques and other semi-operatic plays—*Esther* was considered a masque—and it loved the odes and commemorative pieces; St. Mary's in Oxford was filled for the performance of the *Utrecht Te Deum* and two of the Coronation Anthems. *Athalia,* however, was something new, the first mature specimen of the English oratorio as created by Handel; it was not only accepted but almost unreservedly acclaimed. This should have made Handel leave Italian opera to the Prince of Wales and his cohorts, and the composer could have rallied the vast English public round himself, but the scent of battle was in his nostrils, and, being a born competitor, Handel was not disposed to retreat. Besides, he still believed in his Italian opera and in his ability to make it triumph.

The tottering partnership with Heidegger was shored up for another try (though one wonders what could have persuaded that shrewd operator to risk what little, if any, remained of his investment), and the Haymarket Theatre opened its doors on October 30, 1733, somewhat hastily, with a pasticcio, *Semiramide.* The haste was obviously due to the Academy's desire to open ahead of the Opera of the Nobility, and indeed, Handel beat them by two months. The date was a clever choice, for, since it was the King's birthday, everyone of any standing at court was present —including the Prince of Wales! On November 13 *Ottone* was revived, again with the whole royal family in attendance. Needless to say, this type of music could not be performed without an Italian company headed by a castrato, and Handel, bereft of his company and unable to go on a personal recruiting trip with so little time at his disposal, would have been completely defeated had it not been for timely assistance from a least likely source. That vanished scoundrel, Owen Swiney, now styling himself MacSwiney, safe in Venice from prosecution for his theft of the box office receipts, did a good turn for his one-time victim by hunting up a first-class alto castrato, Giovanni Carestini. In addition Handel re-engaged Margherita Durastanti, his leading soprano who had left London nine years before, unable to bear the unfavorable comparisons with *la nuova sirena,* the youthful Faustina Bordoni. Now quite mature in years and experience, and her voice lowered to a mezzo, Durastanti apparently still could sing in the fast company of Carestini and Strada. The cast was rounded out by two lesser Italians, Maria Caterina Negri, a good contralto for the male roles, and the soprano castrato Carlo Scalzi, with Waltz taking the bass roles in the absence of a suitable Italian singer. The battle was on.

The Opera of the Nobility opened at Lincoln's Inn Fields Theatre on December 29, the company boasting Senesino, Montagnana, and all the rest of Handel's fine company except La Strada; a year later Cuzzoni rejoined this star assembly. The rival establishment also annexed Handel's secretary-librettist, Rolli, but of course the all-important person of the music director had to be sought elsewhere; the choice fell on Nicola Porpora.

Porpora (1686–1768) we have already encountered in Naples (see p. 90) where his *Agrippina* preceded Handel's opera of the same title. In the intervening time Porpora had become the most admired vocal teacher in the world, his pupils including Farinelli, Caffarelli, Salimbeni, and a host of other great singers. This curious man, who lived long enough to become Haydn's earliest teacher, was an extremely competent musician but a colorless dramatist. Some of his cantatas and, especially, a set of Latin duets show him in a very favorable light, nor is his instrumental music negligible. But fate somehow threw him into competition with the leading masters of opera, Lotti, Handel, Hasse, and Leo, whom he could not equal with his well-worked but pale operas. Nevertheless, his operas got around, being particularly highly regarded in Vienna, and the great castratos he trained made his name famous. In addition he instructed Metastasio in music, and the great court poet's recommendation carried an immense weight. Porpora's music does lack a strong personality, but it is well made and his vocal writing was second to none. He was neither the villain nor the nonentity the Handel literature often tends to make of him; Haydn always spoke of him with respect, and it was simply his misfortune to be pitted against Handel. Between 1733 and 1736 Porpora produced five operas, a serenata, and an oratorio for London. The last, *Davide e Bersabea* (Lent 1734), was supposed to best *Deborah* and *Esther* but fell far short. Thus, while the Opera of the Nobility had a superior company backed by political influence, they could not expect their redoubtable antagonist forever to temporize with pasticcios; it remained to be seen whether Porpora would be able to do what the infinitely more talented Bononcini could not.

Having got wind of Handel's plan to set to music the Ariadne legend, Porpora had quickly produced his *Arianna in Nasso* for the opening of

Lincoln's Inn Fields Theatre. Handel's new opera, *Arianna in Creta,* presented on January 26, 1734, was moderately successful but not sufficiently so to demonstrate his superiority over his rival. The libretto, originally by Pariati, was probably arranged by Francis Colman and then retranslated into Italian, for it is markedly different in spirit and tone from the conventional Italian libretto. This did not make it easy for Handel. He could set to music an English text or an Italian text, striking their respective spirits with ease, but English dramatic ideas rendered in Italian handicapped him considerably, and he strove mightily to compensate for this discrepancy. The score is worked with great care, the orchestral part as fine as Handel could make it, and there are excellent descriptive passages, slumber songs, rage arias, and so on, everything proper and skilful, yet on the whole *Arianna* is only an average opera. The Prince of Wales with his cronies applauded *Arianna in Nasso* at Lincoln's Inn Fields while the King and Queen ostentatiously attended *Arianna in Creta* at the Haymarket; the King, loathing his son, was not going to permit his favorite musician to be humbled. Humbled he was not, but even though the repeat performances testify to *Arianna in Creta*'s popularity, it left the two antagonists within their respective positions. They did not intend to stay there.

For the approaching wedding of Handel's pupil and loyal friend, Anne, the Princess Royal, and William, Prince of Orange, Handel put together a serenata called *Parnasso in Festa.* The music consisted mainly of borrowings from *Athalia,* at that time not yet heard in London. Though a pasticcio, *Parnasso in Festa* contains a good deal of new music, the whole so skilfully arranged and blended that it has every right to be considered an independent and viable piece. Also much of the music fitted very nicely into its new surroundings: "Blooming virgins" is not very far from "Verginette dotte e belle," and "Cheer her, o Baal," sounds very acceptable when sung as "Cantiamo a Bacco." This should warn those who see the oratorios as "sacred music" to be careful. The wonderfully robust and evocative hunting chorus "O quando bella gloria e quello del cacciator," with its lusty orchestral accompaniment, must have cheered the audiences. The elaborate appeal Apollo addresses to the fauns and to the flowers, "Non tardate fauni," with the following chorus, is Handel at his pastoral best. The third act contains much new music, all of it fresh and fragrant. *Parnasso in Festa* is studded with miniature concertos for oboe, bassoon, flute, and cello that offer never-ending pleasant surprises. Performed on March 13, and repeated five times, the serenata pleased the court, the bridal pair, and many Handelians, as did the Wedding Anthem (another *contrafactum;* see p. 226).

Revivals of *Sosarme, Deborah, Acis and Galatea,* and of *Il Pastor fido,* the latter a curious choice, filled out the season. By July both opera houses closed. The number of performances—even *Il Pastor fido* was repeated a dozen times—should not deceive us; the Haymarket Theatre played to nearly empty houses. But so did the Opera of the Nobility. Clearly Italian opera in London was in decline; there was not a sufficient audience for two opera houses. Heidegger, wanting to cut his losses, dissolved the partnership, and the Opera of the Nobility, taking advantage of the situation, acquired the lease of the Haymarket Theatre. Heidegger's role in the dissolution of the second Academy was not quite above board; the delivery of the Haymarket Theatre with all its appurtenances to the competitors was an underhanded affair. Now Handel had neither a theatre nor the necessary capital to invest in one. The Prince of Wales happily announced that the King's favorite musician was eliminated, and Porpora could rightly feel that the operatic crown had passed to him. This must have been the consensus, the Abbé Prévost even suggesting that nothing remained for Handel but "to return to his native land." Handel did indeed leave London, but only for a month's rest at Tunbridge Wells, whence he returned at the end of August.

All parties, from the Prince of Wales down, underestimated the will power of this magnificent opportunist. Before leaving for Tunbridge Wells, Handel unhesitatingly went to the quarter that had administered the final blow to the original Royal Academy of Music: John Rich's son. Why Rich, who was a businessman grown affluent on ballad operas and other "light" entertainment, consented to let Handel operate in his theatre is difficult to understand. Handel had little to offer. His once outstanding troupe of singers was with the competing theatre, only Strada stood by him through thick and thin; meanwhile the Haymarket Theatre considerably enhanced the lustre of its artistic personnel by adding not only Cuzzoni but also Farinelli to the roster. Opening the Haymarket season on October 29, 1734, with *Artaserse,* most of the music presumably by Hasse, with both Senesino and Farinelli in the cast, the Opera of the Nobility scored a success that dwarfed anything yet seen in London; there were twenty-eight performances of *Artaserse.* The opera played to crowded houses; for all practical purposes Handel was doomed. Nevertheless, he gathered Carestini, Strada, Waltz, Maria Negri, and her sister Rosa, completing the company with a young English tenor, John Beard, a chorister from the Chapel Royal who was to play an important part in Handel's later career, and went to work with them.

The Theatre Royal in Covent Garden, as Rich's house was now called, offered mixed fare: plays, ballets, and now with Handel's forces joining the enterprise, opera. The début of the Covent Garden opera company on November 9, 1734, was modest: they produced *Il Pastor fido,* after which *Arianna* was revived, followed by a pasticcio. Finally, on January 8, 1735, Handel presented his new opera, *Ariodante,* with two new singers added to the cast: Cecilia Young, a fine young soprano whom Burney considered superior to any female English singer of the time, and a nondescript tenor named Stoppalaer.

The libretto by Salvi (after Ariosto) was well arranged for Handel by Rolli, and Handel immediately responded, composing a magnificent opera, dramatically sound, and musically at a very high level throughout. The few moments of conventionality are reserved for some of the castrato arias. As usual, the women are outstanding. Ginevra, again, is entirely feminine but strong enough to defend herself against unwanted advances. She breaks into uninhibited joy ("Volate amori") when her father blesses her love for Ariodante, then strikes an altogether different tone when she is accused of a liaison with Polinesso. Ginevra is a remarkable personality, and all her music is equally remarkable. Dalinda does not win our entire sympathy, perhaps because she flickers a little insubstantially as a human being; she is weak in character, easily persuaded, but very pleasant and womanly. Ariodante's music is as rich as his moods are varied; seldom had Handel written such a solid, manly role for a castrato. The same is true of Polinesso, who is a cold, scheming villain whose character cannot be fully realized by a contralto. If both of these parts were arranged for male voices, *Ariodante* would be seen to be a viable and altogether modern opera. For, in addition to the fine vocal parts, this score is full of wonderful instrumental music, delectable dance tunes, and graceful ritornels. *Ariodante* represents a stylistic departure, demonstrating that Handel did not miss the new stirrings in Neapolitan opera that he must have heard during his recent trip to Italy. There is also a strong French strain in this opera, to which we shall return.

Perhaps because of its refinement and sophisticated texture, *Ariodante* did not make the impression it should have made, and we once more see Handel flirting with English works—*Esther* was revived on March 5, and ran for six performances. This, however, may have been because of Lent, the traditional oratorio season. An interesting feature of the announcement is the notice that two new concertos for the organ would be played by Handel between the acts. Apparently his playing of these concertos was beginning to be regarded as a drawing card. On March 26

Deborah followed, again interspersed with organ concertos, among them a new one. *Athalia*, "with a new concerto," joined the repertory on April 1. Thus Handel actually presented a Lenten season of oratorios as he was to do later, but he was far from capitulating. On the 16th of April he returned to Italian opera with a vengeance: *Alcina* is an absolutely beguiling masterpiece that found immediate favor.

The fairy tale from Ariosto, probably arranged by Antonio Marchi, fired Handel's imagination. This time the sorcerer is a woman, Alcina, which suited Handel better than Zoroaster, and the foil to this powerful and possessed woman, the gentle Bradamante, gave him opportunities for characterization that he particularly welcomed. Ruggiero is completely under Alcina's spell, while the faithful Bradamante tries to free her betrothed from the siren. This is the core of the story, which of course had to be suitably enlarged and complicated. Bradamante, therefore, is disguised as a fetching youth, causing complication number one: Alcina's sister, Morgana, falls in love with "him." Thereupon Morgana's lover, Oronte, is torn with jealousy. By-and-by others join the intrigue, and all the wheels of a well-appointed opera are whirling.

Handel liked his women feminine; only when they had passed the age of love-making, when they became matriarchs, did he make them forbiddingly strong and imperious. Alcina is no Turandot, she is a full-blooded and warm-hearted woman who wants to love and be loved by Ruggiero. All her arias are love music, full of desire, but there is nothing unseemly about them. Even when she sees that Ruggiero is slipping from her clutches, she is more desolated than angry. Her great arioso, "Ah, Ruggiero crudel," and especially the following aria, "Ombre pallide," are without peers in the operatic literature. Only once does she really act with vehemence, in the great aria "Ma quando tornerai," which is a rage-and-revenge piece of the type beloved by Italian composers and audiences; but womanliness returns in the ineffable siciliana, "Mi restano le lagrime." Ruggiero is not much of a man, or rather he is a ladies' man whom Handel carries to the brink of the buffo manner. But he does sing a pair of sweet and affecting love songs, of which "Verdi prati" is of extraordinary beauty. Bradamante is caught in a woman's dual existence in an enchanted world of passionate dream-surrender and an orderly world of domestic affections and duties. She is confident that her wayward lover will tire of Alcina's ardor and will return to her less unnerving charms.

Alcina is another "scenic" opera that depends on imaginative staging, good ballet, and a good chorus. As in *Ariodante,* besides the neo-Neapolitan influences, there is a French hue, and not only because of the delectable dances. Handel was obviously familiar with French opera, but just how he had acquired this familiarity it is hard to tell. Even the arias in this work often have a French tinge, and rich use is made of the chorus, a practice that is a mark of the *tragédie lyrique*. The numerous dances were inspired (as were those in *Ariodante*) by the presence at Covent Garden of Marie Sallé and her French dance company (see p. 636). *Alcina* ran till the end of the season on July 2; the Haymarket Theatre closed a month earlier. Both companies ended the season with staggering deficits.

More trouble was brewing for Handel. The Opera of the Nobility had its superb company of singers, and now its maestros were augmented by still another good composer. Francesco Maria Veracini (1690–1750), whom Burney and others considered the greatest violinist in the world, was back in London, this time in the capacity of composer. His opera, *Adriano*, was performed at the Haymarket Theatre and ran for seventeen nights. Walsh published the "favourite songs." While the opposition was growing stronger, Handel's forces diminished. Carestini, whose resentment Handel had once roused with a merciless tongue-lashing, left immediately upon the close of the season. At this time the loss of a leading castrato was considered an irreparable calamity, but even more alarming was Handel's failing health, which had to be repaired before the next artistic-political move could be risked. After another cure at Tunbridge Wells, Handel felt well enough to return to London and prepare the next season. The first and most urgent task was the rebuilding of his troupe. In *Ariodante* and *Alcina* he had already employed the excellent soprano, Cecilia Young, who was good enough to incite Strada's jealousy. The youthful tenor, John Beard, also made a favorable impression on the public. Another English singer, the bass Erard, was added to the cast, but little is known about this man, who soon disappeared from the Handelian annals. The English works Handel had produced at Oxford met with favor, and now that he had some good English singers (there was much sarcastic merriment caused by the Italian singers' English pronunciation) he decided, or was prevailed upon, to set aside opera for the moment and exploit the possibilities of oratorio and pastoral.

Alexander's Feast, composed in an incredibly short time, opened Covent Garden on February 19, 1736, a date that will remain a memorable one in English musical history. The theatre was filled and Handel's triumph was complete. The public liked the music and was especially pleased by the fine singing of native artists in their native tongue; Strada's was the only voice with a foreign accent. *Acis and Galatea* followed on March 24, and *Esther* on April 7. Thus Handel once more had a real oratorio season, something that later became an institution but in 1736 was still a novelty. Nevertheless, the omens were so clear that Handel should not have hesitated for a moment to make Covent Garden into a citadel of English music, but the oratorio season was once more a mere interlude. While the oratorios were running to general applause, Handel was getting ready for an opera season, brief though it necessarily had to be. Having acquired a replacement for Carestini in the person of a soprano castrato by the name of Gioacchino Conti, he proceeded on May 5 to revive *Ariodante*. Perhaps the return to opera was prompted by the forthcoming nuptials of the Prince of Wales which, according to the custom imported from the Continent, had to be celebrated by a festive opera. This was duly composed by Handel, while the Haymarket company celebrated the event with a festa by its director, Porpora.

Atalanta, by an unknown librettist, was first performed on May 12. It is more of a festa or large serenata, i.e. a pastoral, than an opera. The quality of its music does not falter anywhere, and those who think that Handel always hurls boulders from Mount Sinai should listen to the delectably light and aromatic pieces which, by omitting the final *licenza*, could be performed today without changing one note. The *licenza*, much used by court composers, especially in Vienna, though rather exceptional with Handel, was a transparent eulogy of the person or persons commemorated. In *Atalanta* it occurs at the end when Mercury appears to bring Jupiter's greetings to the newlyweds. *Atalanta* is an accomplished *pièce d'occasion*, not pretending to be either more or less, but it has charms adequate to compel attention.

The festa was well received, and the balance began to turn in Handel's favor. Even the Prince of Wales began to vacillate, and Porpora, a realist who was used to skulduggery, seeing that the titular head of the anti-Handelian cabal applauded his adversary, made some deductions of his own. He did not wait to be defeated like Bononcini, but departed forthwith, *nolo contendere*. The wedding anthem Handel wrote for the Prince (see p. 226) also pleased the heir to the throne, and Frederick not only abandoned the feud, inviting Handel to a tête-à-tête, but withdrew from the Opera of the Nobility. Soon we see him ostentatiously frequenting Covent Garden. Unfortunately, along with its benefits, this had its side effects: the King, displeased by these signs of amity between Handel and the despised Prince, turned his back on his favorite composer. However, since it was time to shed the affairs of state for the provincial pleasures of Hanover, for the moment the King's displeasure did little harm. George departed for Hanover a few days after the brief season of opera ended on June 9.

Handel kept on composing furiously, for he believed that, as in Bononcini's time, the opportunity for administering the *coup de grâce* to the Opera of the Nobility was nearing. A pleasant interlude in this relentless girding of loins came with the news that his favorite niece, Johanna Friderike, now twenty-five, was married to a professor of law at Halle University; the family continued to climb the social ladder. Handel, always a good family man, sent the bride and groom appropriate wedding presents. He also was appointed, or, to put it more precisely, confirmed, by the Queen as music master to the Princesses Amelia and Caroline at an annual fee of £200. As the opening day for Covent Garden drew near, the singers began to arrive, among them Domenico Annibali, the new castrato. Handel had two new operas ready, but the season opened on November 6, 1736, with *Alcina,* the Prince of Wales in attendance, followed by *Atalanta* on November 20 and *Poro* on December 8. Handel was waiting for the Opera of the Nobility to get under way (they opened with Hasse's *Siroe* late in November), and in the meantime he started work on still another new opera.

As the new year dawned, Handel judged the time ripe to throw the two new operas into the fray: *Arminio* was presented on January 12 and *Giustino* on February 16. Both were failures. *Arminio* is the work of a distraught and ailing man, one of his weakest scores. *Giustino* has somewhat better music, but the libretto was manhandled to the point where it makes little sense. Handel's fatigue is shown by his relapse into the old operatic style; the dragon and other props provided the parodists with a field day.[5] Neither of these operas yields the one or two fine arias or other numbers that one often finds in otherwise poor compositions, though the workmanship in both of them is thoroughly Handelian. What is un-Handelian in them is the absence of human characters; there are only silhouettes in these operas, and there are no deeds and conflicts, only happenings that follow in one another's wake with a degree of implausibility. Only pictures are they, and as such some of them are fine enough, but their mood is lyric, not theatrical.

With the third new opera, *Berenice,* another farrago arranged by Salvi and introduced in May, Handel returned to the Caesar and Cleopatra theme that had once covered him with glory. This time the characters are Berenice, Queen of Egypt, and Alessandro, her husband-

---

[5] *The Dragon of Wantley,* a ballad opera devoted to this purpose and produced at Covent Garden itself, was far from annoying to Handel; he is said to have found it very amusing.

designate by the Roman Senate, and the subplot consists of the usual contretemps between the heroine's sister who is in love with Demetrio, and the latter, the real object of the Queen's affections (who in turn has another admirer). There are some scenes in this work, as well as an exceptionally fine overture, that rise far above *Arminio* and *Giustino* in quality of invention. In particular, Berenice's very feminine confession of love, a minuet-aria, is extremely attractive, and Demetrio's outbursts of rage have power. But the crisis at the end of the second act, with magnanimity serving as the *deus ex machina,* is inept, and Handel did not quite know what to do with it, though the tone remains passionate. The dénouement once more sees everyone ready to forgive and forget, which leaves the heroine, otherwise well characterized, rather high and dry. Thus, while well composed and containing some fine music, *Berenice* is again one of those operas that must be excluded from the important works.

For whatever reason, another oratorio "season" relieved the operas. While, as remarked above, an oratorio season was a novelty, the performance of a serenata, festa, pastoral, or oratorio on the stage of the opera house was in Handel's time not a radical departure that would have startled the audience, in spite of the Baroque love for machines, fountains, and other spectacular staging effects. The dividing line between the genres was slight, Baroque opera was static, and its principal components, recitative and aria, were the same whether in opera, oratorio, or Passion. Nor were the costumes markedly different from the elaborate clothing worn by the rich, for even though the subjects might be taken from classical antiquity, the costumes were contemporary. One would think that the main reason for the immediate acceptance of such works as *Acis and Galatea* or *Esther* was the singing. The "oratorio singer" of grave mien and pronounced Christian humility was as yet unknown. Senesino or Strada would sing in an oratorio as they would in an opera, freely, with imagination and expression, nor would they stay riveted to one spot; there was a modicum of movement in their delivery. The English singers modelled their platform manner on the Italians', and their clear enunciation of their native tongue was much appreciated by the public.

Alexander's Feast and *Esther* were revived, and, in addition, from his vast repository of usable materials, Handel exhumed *Il Trionfo del Tempo e della Verità* of 1707, made more accessible having been translated into English and offered on March 23, 1737. The Prince of Wales, attending the performance of *Alexander's Feast,* was so taken by Handel's playing of the organ concerto that he commanded a repetition on the spot.

Still, nothing seemed to attract full houses and clearly both operatic establishments were bankrupt. The Haymarket Theatre closed on June 11, 1737, and Senesino immediately left, never to return. Covent Garden closed a fortnight later. Recent estimates prove that though hard hit, Handel was not bankrupt financially either this time or any other, but he was bankrupt in mind and health. At the end of April he was taken ill. At first the newspapers spoke of indisposition caused by rheumatism, but by the middle of May they conceded a "Paraletick Disorder," for indeed the attack was a stroke which paralyzed Handel's right arm. With super-human effort he forced himself to continue, but the ensuing reaction, after a momentary improvement, was severe, and for the first time in his variegated career Handel was forced to yield the conductor's seat at the harpsichord; he watched the première of *Berenice* from the auditorium. Presently his condition worsened, for apparently the stroke affected his mind: "his senses were disordered at intervals," says Mainwaring. While "it was with the utmost difficulty that he was prevailed on to do what was proper," continues Mainwaring, Handel finally decided to go to the famous spa of Aachen (Aix-la-Chapelle). In September 1737 the curtain seemed about to descend upon a rich and courageous artistic life.

XI

WE MUST LEAVE THE STRICKEN COMPOSER FOR THE
moment and retrace our steps to the days at Cannons, when the Handel
of the English oratorios made his first appearance.

Both the past and the future were here, and the decisive spark went
out to the future, though this was unnoticed by Handel. There can be no
question that the Handelian oratorio, the pastoral drama, and the classic-
mythological music drama all had elements and influences that came from
German, Italian, and French sources; nevertheless, what Handel produced in this line at Cannons was a direct result of his literary environment, the Burlington-Chandos circle. From our vantage point, the significance of the environment and the Cannons works is clear, but to Handel
Cannons was an episode, the works occasioned by the circumstances; for
years to come he attached no importance to them. He did his best as a
composer, as he always tried to do, with the first version of works, and he
probably would have composed an a cappella Mass or a ballet as readily
as an ode or a Te Deum if the circumstances had warranted, for he was a
true Baroque opportunist and a professional who reacted creatively to
every stimulus.

Acis and Galatea (c. 1718), the first of the Cannons dramatic pieces,
is a perfect expression of Handel's poetic vision at a moment of complete
equilibrium, every musical phrase a jewel and every turn a miracle. It is
rich in thought and perception and follows its purpose steadily from start
to finish, as without psychological frills of any kind he gets at the living

truth of his handful of characters. Yet Handel seemed ready to abandon *Acis and Galatea* forever. When after a lapse of a dozen years he returned to the English works of the Cannons period, it was once again by force of circumstance. On a superficial level, we might say that the Handelian oratorio was born of anger and the fierce competitive spirit of this artistic speculator and promoter. We might go farther and say that even the continuation of the 1732 "revivals," which produced the first master oratorio, *Athalia*—in which the true English oratorio, a *new* genre, is before us in full bloom—was the result of a chance opportunity that seemed auspicious to Handel. Because *Deborah,* a rather hasty pasticcio, was successful, Handel sat down and wrote a piece along the same lines, except that now the music was original, expressly composed for the occasion. But nothing followed, and Handel did not have the faintest intention of abandoning opera. Indeed, he unceremoniously put aside the English works until, finding himself *in extremis,* he had no choice but to return to them, having neither the physical nor the financial power to continue as composer-entrepreneur of opera. This tug of war did not end until after 1741.

Acis and Galatea and *Esther,* the two theatrical works that owe their existence to Cannons and to the men who frequented the Duke of Chandos's residence, are variously called masque, oratorio, pastoral, sacred drama, and so on. The confusion was not then so dense as it appears to us, even though all these terms, as well as "English opera," were often interchangeable. Handel's contemporaries agreed on one important point: that all this was theatre. Even *Esther* was considered a masque and was staged; it was certainly a theatrical piece, intended so and performed so. The religious connotations and the belief that Holy Writ is profaned when presented on the stage are later developments. At Cannons *Esther* was regarded as a play with a story from the Bible.

Modern literary and musical scholars, especially the former, have created the confusion. Literary critics, seeing influences converging on the English theatre from the Italian *mascherata* and *trionfo,* the French *ballet de cour,* the Elizabethan and Jacobean drama, lyric poetry and music, even the medieval mystery play, were puzzled by the music, which they took for something extraneous and irrelevant from the dramatic point of view, a mere acquiescence to the public demand for song and dance entertainment. Even the most eminent of them, such as Edward K. Chambers and Allardyce Nicoll, were looking for literary values and constructions where the emphasis was, instead, on spectacle, dance, and music. Of course, in many instances the songs were extraneous, but in general their use was structural and dramatic; the distinction between "masque," "concert Musick," "English opera" on the one hand, and "play," with or without music, on the other was fairly real. The bulk of all plays from the Stuart period contained songs and, as we have seen (p. 190 ff.), this lyricism was considered an integral and essential part of the show. The masque was different from the dramatic theatre; its appeal was spectacular rather than dramatic, it did not aim to create an illusion of life. But it had a canon of its own, highly formal and well respected, and this canon was altogether based on a well-defined program of dances, "revels," speeches, dialogues, and songs. Otto Gombosi summarized this succinctly: "The masque as a literary form is amorphous; as a form of choreographic entertainment it is highly organized." [1]

The musical scholars in their turn, with a few laudable exceptions, failed to realize that in this vacillation between music and drama there was a concept, perhaps vague but nevertheless perceptible enough, of an English opera, a concept that failed because of the insufficiency of the composers. The one towering genius, Purcell, who like Lully could have turned aspiration into reality, who with one stroke carried the masque to its pinnacle, died tragically young, and there were no native successors of even faintly comparable talent. The intentions were clear in the frequent rubric "compos'd after the Italian Manner," nor was there lack of interest in the new means of expression taken over from the Italians. Recitative was tried rather early, developing, in the works of Nicholas Lanier and Henry Lawes, into a sort of arioso, which eventually reached its finest expression in Purcell. But this too was abandoned, for while the "manner" was there, the spirit was not; the ingrained English aversion to "all sung" theatre was too strong. The concept was not unlike that of the early forms of the German *Singspiel* with spoken dialogue: at the moment of lyric effusion the song took over. Thus the songs did not merely supply a decorative element, even though the play was suspended the moment they appeared. The situation was palpably an operatic one, but the product was only half-loaf opera; the old Elizabethan tradition of "joining words and notes lovingly together" was alive, but the English theatre was not prepared to go beyond that.

Perhaps the most essential difference, subtle on the surface but in reality the key to the situation, was the unwillingness of the English composers to trespass on the rights of the words. In opera there are situations when the music must go its own way, even if it violates proper prosody, but this the English would not accept; declamatory niceties must always be observed and musical rhythm must always yield to speech rhythm. This sort of music can be theatrical but it seldom becomes operatic. Yet the incredibly rapid triumph of Italian opera in London can only be explained by the fact that the ground was prepared for it by a number of English composers. Humphrey, Blow, and Purcell all knew and used the operatic musical language, their incidental music shows many examples of it, especially in the ariosos, which are essentially operatic essays. John Blow's *Venus and Adonis* (1683), the principal musico-dramatic work of the early Restoration, turns definitely toward the operatic; the decorative mythological figures begin to be dramatic human beings. With that we have arrived at the great figure of Purcell, who could have created English opera; that, however, is a problem by itself.[2]

When the "new Italian Manner: all sung" reached England with full force in the first decade of the 18th century, a realignment took place of a swiftness unprecedented in English cultural history. Within six years opera became fully established, but was surrendered to the Italians; the English composers refused to go along and held onto their own form of musical theatre. Thomas Clayton, an insignificant composer but the first English musician to present a "full" opera, was aware of the opposition he had to face. In the preface to his *Arsinoe* (1705, see also p. 115), he tried to forestall it by the following statement:

The Musick being recitative, may not, at first, meet with that general Acceptation, as is to be hoped for, from the Audience's being better acquainted with it: but if this Attempt shall be a means of bringing this manner of Musick to be used in my native Country, I think my Study and Pains very well employed.

The only serious attempt after Purcell and before the arrival of Handel was made in 1707 by John Eccles with his *Semele*, recognized as a full-fledged opera in the "new Italian manner." But it never reached the stage.[3]

Acis and Galatea, composed sometime during 1718, though called "a

---

[2] Purcell, whose influence on Handel was of such momentous importance, we shall more conveniently discuss in the chapter on Handel's relationship to English music.

[3] Eccles was a man of the theatre, a good composer and a fine melodist, whose high reputation won him the coveted post of Master of the King's Musick. Yet, like Rossini, he retired from the arena at the height of his fame, spending the rest of his life in the placid art of angling, as Rossini busied himself with the culinary arts. There are kindred riddles in the lives of these two men, but we may note that the sudden withdrawal of each came at a time when the fortunes of opera were changing. The libretto Congreve wrote for Eccles's *Semele* was later used by Handel for his own work by that title.

masque," must have been regarded by Handel as an English version of
the serenata. Indeed, in its third reworking—that is, in its second English
version of 1732—*Acis and Galatea* was called a serenata, possibly because
it was equipped with some Italian airs. Subsequently, when it became
once more all English, "Pastoral Entertainment" was added to the title;
but at its last revival, ten years after the revision, the title reverted to the
original "masque," and the score was published in 1743 under this heading. This alone shows that the problem Handel was facing was not so
much that of a new genre as of a new language.

Nothing differentiates men's spiritual life more than language. We
can scarcely think beyond the framework that the inherited national
tongue sets up, for language is both manner and content, not only the tool
of literature but its kernel, its primeval element, its inspiration. What style
is to the individual writer, language is to the nation: *c'est l'homme, c'est le
peuple*. Those whose language refuses to be easily bent to foreign
rhythms, like for instance the French, are restricted in the possibility of
cross-fertilization and *rapprochement*. (Perhaps it is for this reason that
the French are so chauvinistic.) Italian poetic language, which Handel
had completely absorbed, was the oldest and most developed of modern
languages; Dante died more than two centuries before Ronsard and
Shakespeare were born. This language rhymes of itself, and can raise
banality and nothingness to music. English with its many one-syllable
words is as compact as Italian, but its verbal music is slower, and therefore when Italian texts are translated by anyone less than a good poet the
English version cannot keep up with the tempo of the original. That English is more varied than Italian and capable of the most unexpected turns
does not help in this regard. On the other hand, the advantages of original
English versification over that of other modern languages are obvious
when we see bilingual editions.

Had Handel approached his task, as did his compatriot Pepusch, by
simply setting English words the same way as he did Italian or German,
the results would have been altogether different, but he espied the genius
of the language of his adopted country. Contrary to popular belief,
Handel appreciated good poetry for his texts—if he could obtain it. Nor is
it true that he had little sense for the English language. He may have had
a thick German accent, and he may have mispronounced words (though
the many funny anecdotes are palpably exaggerations), and there are in
his works some awkwardly accented places, but he knew the language
well, down to the important detail of the position of single words. It is

truly remarkable how felicitously Handel sets English words to music in his early works.

[2]

IT WOULD BE foolish to attempt a full historical sketch of the masque. In the first place, it is an enormously complicated and not yet fully explored territory of English literary and theatrical history; in the second, by the time Handel arrived on the scene, the species had little in common with the original masque.

Our information concerning the period when the masque left the court and entered the theatre is scant, but we know of course that when the Italian wave of dramatic music reached England in the 17th century it found there a highly developed dramatic literature that was unique in post-classical times. The Latins have an innate sense for form and construction that led them to the creation of patterns, such as the *commedia dell'arte* or the Spanish drama. Formal patterns tend to create types: the types of the *commedia dell'arte* became treasured figures for centuries. The Italian and Spanish public, like the public of the Greek and Latin theatre, knew the pattern, the types, the characters, and their stories; what they demanded was variety in action and inventiveness in the application of the métier. The English concept was different, for the English were attached to individual character and its representation, and whenever the Mediterranean prototype took root in England it was subjected to the dictates of the national taste. In extreme cases, such as the opera seria, the differences remained irreconcilable, for to the English a drama purely in music was unnatural and a contradiction in terms. They did accept a pattern in the early masque based on a succession of dances, but eventually the pull of the national tradition proved to be stronger. The core of this tradition was the belief that however closely music, dancing, and décor may associate themselves with certain forms of the theatre, their role should not be more than adventitious. Music and the dance are external, though effective, adjuncts which, as we have seen when discussing opera in Chapter VII, can have structural importance, but which cannot usurp the primacy of brisk and vivacious dialogue, the heart of the theatre. Dryden's dictum that "the greatest pleasure of the audience is a chase of wit, kept up on both sides, and swiftly managed" is the perfect summary, the basic maxim of the English theatre. The English were not disposed to permit their spoken theatre to go the way of the Italian

Renaissance theatre, to allow it to be extinguished by (to use Voltaire's phrase) "that beautiful monster, opera." The Italians were willing and eager to create a *tabula rasa*, not so the English; they took the large step from madrigal to masque, but at the final important step, an independent musical stage, they balked.

We do have a concrete statement from Ben Jonson about a masque presented in 1617 at Lord Hayes's for the entertainment of the French Ambassador, which clearly refers to an operatic construction. "The whole Masque was sung after the Italian manner, stylo recitative [!] by Master Nicholas Lanier." This is a remarkable statement for so early a date in operatic history, and it is remarkably explicit, but if it really represents what the words say, which is doubtful,[4] it was an exception that created no school. By the time of Davenant's *Salmacida Spolia* (1640), the last and most splendid of the Stuart masques, the fate of this genre was sealed; it merged into the semi-opera long before Handel arrived on the scene.

At this point the question arises: what about Milton's *Comus*, one of the most enchanting poems in the history of English letters? It was called a masque. But *Comus* is *sui generis*, and as such exempt from any classification, for although clearly a pastoral play, in Milton's hands that genre took on a multitude of new colors from the mixture of Hellenic rhythm, Platonic philosophy, classical beauty, and the enchantment of nature.

[3]

THE RENAISSANCE rediscovered and imitated the Greek idyll and the Latin eclogue, uniting them in the pastoral play or drama, the earliest known example of which is Poliziano's *Favola di Orfeo* (1472). The humanists were, of course, not able to graft onto the living tissue of Italian culture an artificially resuscitated species—the pastoral soon turned into opera, an altogether original creation of the Baroque—but classical taste, the sense for crystalline form, which the pastoral imparted, took root and sprouted. The much admired models of this genre were Tasso's *Aminta* (1581) and Guarini's *Pastor Fido* (1590). By Guarini's time pastoral poetry was perhaps the finest branch of Italian lyricism, admired and imitated everywhere. Curiously, and in contradiction to the *rappresentazione*, the pastoral, the naive love story, while of popular origin,

---

[4] Unfortunately, very little music is available, and no complete score of any masque from the first half of the 17th century has survived, though single pieces of music were preserved in anthologies.

was less close to the people. It developed into a great literature of lyric poetry, but its artificial shepherds and nymphs, its manneristic virtuosity of style, which enraptured the connoisseurs, did not move the people.

The exquisitely artificial construction of the pastoral love poetry of the late 16th century and its stylized vocabulary, at times so dazzling and yet so often monotonous, gave little scope for original expression. But the pastorals proved to be wonderfully congenial for musical setting; they may have had little variation except in the melodious versification and in the range of allegorical invention, but they often possessed considerable beauty of poetical detail, combining fancy and artificiality in such a degree that the impression made was one of romantic caprice. The pastoral became a world genre, and its beautiful artificiality seems to have clung to it in all its national variants all the way from Sannazaro to Metastasio, from Rémy Belleau to Quinault, and from Sir Philip Sidney to Pope.

The pastoral was introduced into England during the reign of Elizabeth, Spenser's *Shepherd's Calendar* (1579) being its first example. In the beginning the English pastoral was deliberately "popular" compared to the aristocratic Italian variety, but with Sir Philip Sidney's *Arcadia* the colloquial idiom was abandoned and the spirit became rarefied. Shakespeare liked to blend elements from it into his plays, and others found it appropriate as a vehicle for lyricism. In individual instances Jonson, Fletcher, and others actually tried to rival Tasso and Guarini, as can be seen in such works as Fletcher's *The Faithful Shepherdess,* or Jonson's *The Sad Shepherd.* The neatness and symmetry of the Italian pastorals was at times opposed by the reckless extravagance of diction and rhetoric in the English ones, the flowing rhyme in the lyrics by impetuous blank verse. In Italy, after reaching its peak early in the 17th century, the pastoral declined, but in Jacobean England it continued to flourish, calling forth a rich lyric poetry whose most noted figure was Robert Herrick (1591–1674). What interests us particularly is that with Herrick we leave the spirit of abstract humanism of the Italians and enter the world of that peculiarly English appreciation and quiet worship of the countryside which so profoundly affected Handel. When Handel came to England some of the older pastorals were still known, as well as the newer ones of Ambrose Philips, Congreve, and Pope, though in Pope's pastorals artificiality overpowered the genuinely bucolic. The line of demarcation remains, however, indistinct. Fletcher's *The Faithful Shepherdess* is sometimes referred to as a masque, while *Comus,* called a masque, is closer to the pastoral drama. A variant of the pastoral drama was the "piscatorial" in which the place of the shepherds is taken by fishermen. In the next century it was Shaftesbury's philosophy as set forth in his *Characteristics* (1711) that provided the intellectual and sentimental basis for the preoccupation with nature (as Ruskin did in the 19th century), though sentimental naturalistic tendencies are, and always have been, part of the English character. Soon this renewed nature worship developed into a *furor hortensis,* a passion for landscape gardening, but it also influenced the poets just at the time when Handel joined the Chandos circle. His librettist, John Gay, was imbued with this spirit and also with the Latin classics, selecting his story from Ovid. Ovid's *Metamorphoses,* the work of a poet who said that even as a child whatever he had to say came out as poetry, was the favorite storybook of the centuries. The stories of Pyramus and Thisbe, Daedalus and Icarus, Philemon and Baucis, were all set to music, but Acis and Galatea was a special favorite.

The literary circle in which Handel moved was very much interested in the pastoral, and they knew not only their English, Italian, and Latin poets, but also Theocritus and Longus. There was nothing like this in Germany during Handel's youth, nor was there, in fact, until the Romantic era. But even the Italian serenata, glittering with a constant reproduction of the same family of stories, while elegant and charming, did not have the enchanting bucolic spirit of the English pastoral which (with Herrick) sang

> . . . *of brooks, of blossoms, birds and bowers*

but also of

> . . . *bridegrooms, brides, and their bridal cakes.*

This is the rich musical accompaniment to the natural setting of England. Little mythology is left in these pastorals, only the gods of nature and of love, and there is no empty decoration. Yet the mood of the idylls can be akin to that of tragedy—their beauty comes from the same roots. Idyll and tragedy, these are the two extremes reached by Handel's dramatic works. The tragic and majestic Handel we know, but the idyllic we do not, because those who have regarded him as a seer with a sacred mission have been embarrassed by the man of the theatre, the ardent lyricist, and the lover of pagan nature. The affection for nature that is the stamp of the Englishman only fortified in Handel an innate quality. The pastoral-bucolic is seen in his work throughout his life, beginning with *Il Trionfo del tempo e del disinganno* of his youth, and ending with its English version, *The Triumph of Time and Truth;* he could still see the beauties of nature after his eyes were darkened. The lark and the nightingale, the turtledove and the linnet sing in solos and choruses, the wind rustles and the brook bubbles, the flies buzz and the bees hum to make the "Heart the seat of soft delight." Even the dales and groves, the valleys and "shady woods" and the "barren breasts of the mountains" have their music. In the first *Acis,* the Italian serenata of 1708, there is a delicate scene in "S'agita in mezzo all'onde," where a boat rocks gently on the waves created by the violins. But the bucolic quality is not restricted to the serenata and pastoral; many of the cantatas, even the sacred ones such as *Silete venti* (see p. 67), are suffused with it.

Handel's orientation as an artist was towards man and nature. What in the eyes of the champions of the Enlightenment appeared as the speculative theses of Reason implicit in Nature, to him appeared as the divinations of a universal life pulsating in the veins of nature. His sense of the country scene and the unhurried enduring life of its uninvaded quietness was never jaded; its everlasting miracle, its inexhaustible felicity, gives radiance to his music. As an observer he sees with the perception of a poet and with the selective eye of an artist, and nearly always he convinces his hearer that he has been there and speaks truly. But nature is a dangerous and destructive force from the point of view of Christian thought, and those who profess to see in Handel Klopstock's flaming Christian fervor are still afraid of nature and are blind to her beauties conjured up by Handel with the most delicate poetic grace. They know but dare not admit that in *Acis and Galatea* that "strange God" who silenced the great Pan and the sweet eroticism of nature is nowhere to be found. Because this important and profoundly characteristic facet of Handel's genius, his ability (in Blake's words)

> To see a world in a grain of sand
> And a heaven in a wild flower

is almost completely obscured by the image of the scriptural composer, we had better take a closer look at it before we proceed.

When Taine, the philosopher and art historian, promulgated his famous doctrine that the artist is determined by his race, environment, and times, he attempted to transplant an idea from the natural sciences into the world of the spirit. The upshot of the rigorous application of a doctrine only certain elements of which hold true was that man was thought to achieve undisturbed personality and unity only in his ancestral place, being everywhere else rootless, if not entirely lost. This is a very shaky theory, amply contradicted by Handel himself, though for a time it seemed plausible.

Still, there are occasions when the environment, the attractive milieu becomes dominant, as in the pastoral. In its idealistically closed valleys, its meadows grazed by sheep with silver bells on their necks, it completely overshadows the men in the picture. This countryside has its own laws, and its inhabitants, whether nymphs and fauns and shepherdesses, or merely city folk seeking the *idylle champêtre;* see the world in different colors. Earthly worries, earthly ties, and earthly consequences are far removed from this dreamlike atmosphere; *what* happens here is not very important, only *how* it happens.

The principal attraction of the Arcady of the pastoral is untrammelled nature, the most natural though idealized milieu, into which even the most highly cultivated city dweller is attracted by atavistic instincts. In its "closedness," which is the principal characteristic of this milieu, it rivals the four walls of the artist's study. But, and this is very important and was well understood by all manner of poets and painters, the milieu is master, because it creates a unified mood which assures its particular individual effect. It affords a musical mood of a perfection seldom rivalled by any other. But it is something special that until the Romantic era no German composer understood. Bach and Mozart were untouched by nature; only the old Haydn in his oratorios found the delightfully intimate sounds for depicting the pastoral, and this, significantly, after his English sojourn.

But worship of nature cannot be taken for granted. It is the poets who deepen our consciousness of the beauties of the landscape, reflecting and enhancing a mood stemming from creation. With all its cynicism and sentimentality, the standard mixture of the period, England had an entire school of gentle nature-worshipping lyricists. In 1642 Sir John Denham published his *Cooper's Hill,* to which "landscape poets" paid homage and which they frequently imitated for two centuries. And there were the "topographical poets"—almost every hill and valley in England had its poem. Surely, few anthologies of English verse are complete without such poems as Pope's *Windsor Forest.* And this English longing for nature becomes pronounced in the Century of Reason! [5]

[4]

THE PAGAN WORLD WAS peopled with demons, man was dependent on nature and lived in fear of it, but he also felt a profound union with nature in which he saw a living organism which had a soul.

[5] We must add, though, that descriptive poems were only too often a framework for sententious drawing of "some moral truth from ev'ry scene"—and they could be atrocious.

Christianity led him out of this union, placing him in a higher sphere by making him an independent spiritual being. The regrettable part of the divorce from nature, however, was that the great Pan who brought man close to nature was banished, together with his domain. Thus the Christian liberation had a shadow. Christianity, because it is not a nature religion but a cultural-historical one in which the naive feeling for oneness with nature has been suppressed, had to frown on Pan. This is an important and characteristic attitude, especially prominent in the Middle Ages and in certain phases of Protestantism. Nature was too closely connected with the pagan world that was to be extinguished, therefore it, too, had to be condemned. The inner life of nature frightened Christian men, it smacked of commerce with the very body of paganism.

The orthodox Lutheran Bach had absolutely no interest in nature, not even noticing it, whereas Handel revelled in it and seldom missed an opportunity to set it to music; he was the greatest of musical naturalists. It is not difficult to see an almost Hellenic pantheism in his nature pictures. His conception of nature was neither naively realistic nor speculative, but purely intuitive and idealistic, a very subjective conception, a poetic conception, but differing from that of the poets and musicians of the 19th century, who made a sharp distinction between nature and culture. His musical metaphors and descriptions show him a keen and receptive observer who does not fall into sentimental ecstasy when contemplating nature's wonders but simply and openly enjoys them. His was not a systematic view, but a dramatic necessity that he seized with alacrity whenever the situation offered. Every nature scene in his works fulfills a dramatic role. The scene in *Joshua* where the sun is arrested in its orbit by the prophet's command is one of the overwhelming moments that stand out even in Handel. It is magnificently descriptive, yet not realistic, and its mighty impact rests on its dramatic effectiveness, the synthesis of the poetic, the fantastic, and the dramatic. Culture and nature were for Handel concentric forces, and he never regarded nature as a mere decoration to accompany human drama, as did the Romantics.

In studying Handel's musical language one immediately notices its pictorial quality. This language is not necessarily descriptive music, though he often uses an almost plastic "imitation." The depiction of darkness in *Israel in Egypt* and the orchestral background to the Witch's aria in *Saul* are magnificent "tone-paintings" of darkness, while the representation of the "rosy steps" of the rising sun in *Theodora* and the enchanting "crystal streams" in *Susanna* glorify the wonders of the day. The literature devoted to descriptive music, program music, and so on, abounds in nebulous terminology, of which "tone painting" and "tone poetry" (Schweitzer) seem to be applicable to Handel's nature pictures. But these authors often forget that nature and music cannot be identical; this penetration into the secrets of nature must not be thought of as the harnessing of nature for ordinary human purposes; it was purely artistic, without practical intentions. The artistically beautiful—that is, what in modern terminology is called the artistic-formal phenomena—can be examined with scholarly exactitude, but the beauty of nature can be discussed only in poetic description or by metaphysical reasoning. We too often look for naturalistic or realistic representation and forget that nature gives the artist the impulse but not the means; it cannot suggest how to arrange the notes in the score. The miracle is the artist's creative power, which transforms factual reality. The exegetes of "tone painting" and "word painting" forget that beyond and above the reality and symbolism of this "painting" there is a musical logic that must remain inviolate. Handel never attempted to use anything that is not expressable in purely musical terms. There is little imitation of natural sounds. Handel, a true Baroque composer, is more interested in "tone painting" that offers musical analogies rather than realistic imitation, and that hence is on a high artistic plane which calls for cultivated listening. Very often, in fact in most cases, he achieves his expressive ends by subtle, purely "abstract" musical means: irregular phrase building, asymmetry, displaced accents, cross rhythms, harmonic, especially modulatory operations, an imaginative subjection of the da capo principle to all manner of unexpected changes, and of course by extraordinarily sensitive orchestration.

All this was lost with the decline of the Baroque. Haydn still appreciated the "tone painting" of the Handelian era, though his wonderful little nature scenes were dismissed in the 19th century as childish tricks. But even before, Johann Georg Sulzer's famous and influential *Allgemeine Theorie der schönen Künste* (1771–1774) was already scornful of such *Mahlereyen,* singling out Handel as the worst offender. Whoever wrote the entry in this early lexicon of esthetics could not understand how a man of Handel's talents, devoted to "the highest religious aims," could so debase his art as to depict in an oratorio such "tasteless" things as the "jumping of locusts and lice."

But Sulzer mistook the occasional literal realism for the principal aim and—together with most of the more recent critics—failed to understand that Handel was concerned less with the scenes through which he strolled than with the moods and memories they evoked. In truth, the relationship of the artist with nature is not perceptual but expressive; he does not so

much want to paint the landscape he sees as to convey to us what nature
has told him. Handel's nature pictures are, like good landscape painting,
not a bit of nature within a picture frame but poetically experienced reality, the realization of the artist's dream. An esthetic phenomenon, such as
music is, clearly differs from the physical in essence; we know that an
open-air picture cannot be carried out of doors for it will immediately
pale next to the colors and lights of nature. It must be understood that
pictorialism in music is not so much imitation of physical effects as a peculiar sensibility that is able to avail itself of the most varied techniques,
not for themselves, but for lyric-dramatic appropriateness. The artist's
relationship to nature is an expressive one; he can even represent with absolute conviction such moments as nature has forgotten to create or as no
man other than he has seen. Or has there ever been a centaur? Such subjective experiences of the painter or composer cannot be turned into objective intentions.

[5]

IT IS PERHAPS significant that at this late stage of the masque its
early 18th-century librettists, led by John Hughes (see p. 122), attempted
to go beyond the "English" or "semi"-opera and create a sort of national
opera by utilizing and assimilating the principal elements and devices of
Italian opera. To their chagrin, they could not find English composers to
realize this ambitious plan—the successful composers of even the masques
were mostly foreigners, among them Germans. This is not difficult to
understand. Italian musicians would not and could not make the necessary adjustment to English and the English stage, while English musicians
had a very limited experience with Italian opera. Humphrey and Purcell
would perhaps have been successful, but both were dead. On the other
hand, the German immigrants were experienced musicians, thoroughly
acquainted with Italian opera, but since this was to them an acquired
form and style, they could adapt it to other purposes.

Thus it happened that Handel's models for his genuinely English
masque-pastoral were the works of another German, a well-trained and
well-educated musician, John Christopher Pepusch (1667–1752), whom
we have already encountered but who now looms as an important figure
in Handel's career. In some ways Pepusch was a kindred soul. He left his
native Prussia because of dissatisfaction with the lack of political freedom
and social dignity there, and he settled in London in his early thirties. He
first played in the Drury Lane theatre orchestra, as Handel had played in

the orchestra in Hamburg, advancing by 1707 to the post of staff arranger and composer. Pepusch was a learned theorist-historian, a passionate student of the writings of the authors of classical antiquity. In 1710 he was instrumental in founding the Academy of Ancient Music, the prototype of the modern collegium musicum, two years later becoming director of music at Cannons, a post he retained until 1732. In 1713 Oxford University created him Doctor of Music. When he married the celebrated and wealthy singer, Margherita de l'Épine, the affluence so acquired enabled him to devote more time to his antiquarian researches, which earned him a fellowship in the Royal Society. He was an excellent teacher and among his pupils we should mention William Boyce.

Pepusch should not be judged solely on the strength of the *Beggar's Opera*. He was a good if not highly original composer, his influence on music in the Georgian era was considerable, and he was the first English musicologist—and one of the first in modern times anywhere—whose example undoubtedly spurred Burney and Hawkins to their efforts in musical historiography. Burney said that "Handel despised the pedantry of Pepusch, and Pepusch, in return, constantly refused to join in the general chorus of Handel's praise." The two composers were not on friendly terms, but that Burney goes too far in his judgment of this relationship and that Handel esteemed Pepusch's qualities is proved by his entrusting part of the musical education of John Christopher Smith, Jr., whom he regarded almost as a son, to Dr. Pepusch. But more than that, he studied his quasi-rival's music. Pepusch's music to the English librettos was pleasant and workmanlike, but it could have served any other purpose, while *Acis and Galatea*, Handel's very first venture in the genre, carried the English pastoral to its summit. The English quality is as securely present in this first essay at dramatic music for the English stage as it was in his first ceremonial music.

As we have seen in the chapter devoted to Handel's Italian journey, he had composed an *Aci, Galatea, e Polifemo* in Italy. It was an intimate theatrical piece, the kind the Italians called a *componimento da camera* as opposed to the larger opera, the *componimento teatrale*. The English and the Italian works are not identical, though a good deal of the Italian serenata spirit as well as some thematic elements were taken over into the English pastoral. This is not to say that the early Italian work is not a delightful composition in its own right; its freshness and genuine youthfulness are as affecting as the beauty of the unsullied world of the fairy tale. But the work of the composer in his mid-thirties is not an essay; it is an incomparable masterpiece, one of the greatest he ever created, and it is also the crowning glory of a genre in both Italy and England. Upon arriving in England, Handel had discovered that the post-Renaissance flowering of the classic idyll was duplicated in English literary circles, notably among the men who gathered in Cannons, but that the particular genius of the English language and the air that flows over the English countryside endowed it with a tone of its own.

When Handel picked up the story in Italy it is very doubtful that he knew Lully's fine setting, but in England he certainly came to know John Eccles's masque. Eccles's librettist was Pierre Antoine Motteux (1663–1718), a Frenchman by birth whose command of English was extraordinary. He translated the works of Rabelais and Cervantes's *Don Quixote*, both in masterly fashion; we are dealing with a literary man of stature. But Motteux was nevertheless a wretched playwright and had no sense for the spirit of the classics. Judging from the silly farrago that is his libretto, he too was ignorant of Lully's work. Handel's libretto, like Eccles's, was a pasticcio, but it was put together from the works and classical translations of several of the able Cannons literati, among them Pope, and some use was made of "Mr. Dryden, the Poet," the chief redactor being Gay. Ovid was a facile and very elegant poet, and some of this elegance rubbed off on Gay, whose text is pleasant, full of colorful words and descriptive metaphors such as always affected and inspired Handel. Upon this text Handel created an idyll, an intimate little drama, which was once more a *componimento da camera*. Such idylls were by no means rare in England—the greatest of them undoubtedly being *As You Like It*—but Handel created from the intriguing mixture of Baroque pathos and Renaissance bucolic poetry what one might call a heroic-sentimental idyll, no longer the naive-exotic of the Renaissance and of his early Italian *Aci, Galatea, e Polifemo,* but a highly artistic stylization altogether free of the ingenuous. It gives the impression of realism but this effect is attained by pseudo-naturalistic techniques. The composer's imagination does not create a new world from reality, rather it eliminates essential conditions of the latter, for it sees the world through the glass of an artistic optimism, creating a utopian Arcadia of the past. But it is also of the present, because this kind of idyll is an artistic symbol, a picture in which the poet or composer lives out a natural desire.

The greatest difference from the early Italian setting of this pastoral theme, and one that in fact was an altogether new departure for Handel, was the use of the chorus. With "Wretched lovers" he far exceeds the boundaries of the serenata and is within the region of the choral music drama. The incentive came, of course, from English poetry and English theatre music, though the power of characterization through music he could not have received from Pepusch: it is Handel's own. Even this master of choral writing seldom achieved such a dramatically "through-composed" scene as this. The beginning, a slow dirge in which the contrapuntal parts are loath to release the suspensions, introduces something new in Handel's artistic world: this, in tone and attitude, is the chorus of the Attic tragedy. Once the contemplative and commentary part ends, the pace quickens and so does the excitement, until the intricate counterpoint is replaced by shouts. Handel charged the bucolic atmosphere with tragedy, but realizing that despite all its expressive beauty this chorus could destroy the spirit of the pastoral, with a master stroke he removed the anguish by the simple means of not taking the raging Polyphemus too seriously. In less subtle hands Polyphemus would have become a plain villain. Handel made the ungainly giant fierce but in a blustery way, and this monster is also amorous; his confession of love, "O ruddier than the cherry," restores the fairy tale atmosphere. The opening chorus, "Oh the pleasures of the plains," is the quintessence of the pastoral, the drone bass and the lightly floating recorders creating a bit of Arcadia straight from Sicily. But "Hush, ye pretty warbling choir" is English pastoral *in excelsis*. Acis's love songs are also affectingly lyrical. In the closing scene the spectators, again the Greek chorus, are seized with grief, blurting their lines between long pauses as if they cannot collect themselves. The trio "The flocks shall leave the mountains" admirably sums up the dramatic situation. It is a genuine ensemble, remarkably varied in the combination of expression, sound, rhythm, and dynamics, in which each figure retains its individuality, though as a character portrayal Polyphemus towers over the others.

The dying Acis's "Help, Galatea" was likened by Hugo Leichtentritt to Adam Krieger's *Venus and Adonis,* though he ruefully wonders whether Handel actually knew that song. It is clear beyond a doubt that it was not *Venus and Adonis* but *Dido and Aeneas* that haunted Handel; the Purcellian flavor, though subtle and anything but literal, is unmistakable throughout this work, which relies on very few borrowings. The latter are more in the nature of incipits from earlier Italian cantatas. The arias are, all but one, da capo. This has been cited as constituting a relic from the opera, but significantly, the most conspicuous feature of the seria, the castrato, is missing. It is much more likely that, considering the rather formal grace of the pastoral, Handel did not see any reason for abandoning the da capo. A close examination of the score will immediately disclose that he was aware of the freedom from the conventions of the seria offered by this unusual libretto, for he ignored the mandatory sequence of recitative and aria, proceeding with a musical line forming a wreath of idyllic fancies in an almost unbroken chain. This is what eventually made the oratorio such a different and gratifying medium for him, and it is incomprehensible why, once having tasted this freedom and having so clearly recognized the dramatic and musical possibilities, Handel failed to draw the necessary conclusion.

The story of this score, which was an immediate success with the public and continued to be so throughout Handel's life, is a sad one: after its initial performance at Cannons it was never again heard in its pristine form until our day. But even now a truly faithful performance with the original orchestration is a rarity. There were many editions of it, and among the many truncated and pirated ones is the 1743 full score by Walsh, Jr., which is one of the two full scores of a choral work published in the composer's lifetime. (The other was *Alexander's Feast.*) Since almost the entire original version is extant and most of the additions and emendations are known, an able editor should be in a position to present us with a good score.

Acis and Galatea has come to be regarded as a charming artificiality now a little remote, like *Love's Labour's Lost,* though like that play it is full of life, as well as containing some of Handel's finest tunes. The deprecation of the classic fairy tale had already begun with Dr. Johnson, for he, like the later Romantic realists, could not believe that myths and fables can live as truly as factual stories. The reigning critical world of the 19th century looked upon the fairy tale with disdain, not realizing that here was an artist who rebelled in the name of beauty against what they called "truth."

The stylization the critics found naive and unconvincing was not the result of innocent play but of very definite conceptions. Boileau, in his *L'Art poétique,* took issue with realism in the eclogue, declaring it an exaggeration to let the stylized shepherds speak in the manner of real countrymen. Whether Handel knew the "legislator of Parnassus" is doubtful, but his literary friends did; Dryden had already translated the famous treatise, and Pope wrote a magnificent imitation of it, the *Essay on Criticism,* just about the time when Handel arrived in England. The composer's friends transmitted to him the neo-classic precepts; his instinct and taste took care of the rest.

Others again made the mistake of declaring *Acis and Galatea* an oratorio. Written for stage performance, it was of course planned as a theatrical piece, and while its designations vary from serenata to masque and pastoral, it is past comprehension how it—and *Semele!*—could ever have been considered oratorios. The consequence of this was of course that *Acis* was made into a solemn piece, and all the airy gentleness, as well as the subtle humor of the giant Polyphemus stumbling and raging while singing awkwardly large intervals, is lost. Finally, the original orchestration must be restored before the work can be heard in its true pastoral charm.[6]

But though we recognize that Mozart's and all the other late 18th century musicians' views regarding the performance practice of the Handelian era were completely false, our performances, even those that actually attempt to follow at least the Händelgesellschaft score of *Acis and Galatea,* are false too. Conductors do not seem to know that when Handel specifies "flauto" he does not mean our flute but the recorder; when he wanted a flute he called for a "traverso." Flutes, but especially the shrill piccolo, completely distort the aural picture envisioned by Handel. The accompaniment for "Hush, ye pretty warbling choir" must be assigned to three recorders, one of them the *sopranino,* Handel's "flauto piccolo" (which originally may have been a flageolet). With so many recorder players available today there is no excuse for resorting to flutes in defiance of the composer's intentions.

[6]

IN THE CATALOGUE OF the music library at Cannons, drawn up August 23, 1720, there appears under Handel's name an item *O the Pleasure of the Plain,* "a masque for 5 voices and instruments in score"

---

[6] I am not referring to Mozart's reorchestration—*Acis and Galatea* was the first of Mozart's Handelian *Bearbeitungen.* Such a completely reworked edition could come only from someone in whose time neither scholarship nor a historical sense was developed. The young Viennese master loved Handel's score, but like his less naive and much less skilful colleagues Hiller, Starzer, and van Swieten (as well as the later Victorians), considered it a sketch that should be completed. The vocal and string parts were respected, in fact they were written into the new score by a copyist, unchanged; only where Handel relied on the continuo to fill out the harmony did Mozart tamper with the texture. Even the concertante wind parts were left alone, but elsewhere Mozart added the full complement of the Classic orchestra. Thus the physiognomy of the original score was completely altered. We shall discuss this procedure later; suffice it to say at this point that although Mozart professed respect for the original, the creative instinct of a great composer could not remain dormant; when "realizing" Handel's figuration, the younger master picked up thematic bits and went to work with them, making obbligato parts and inventing new counterpoints. Today we look at this as a curiosity, the pardonable fervor of an age that wanted everything modern and up-to-date, but we no longer play the Mozartean transcriptions.

(Deutsch, p. 108). Thus we know that *Acis and Galatea* was extant and must have been performed before that date. *Esther*, or *Haman and Mordecai* as it may originally have been called, was also the product of this period when Handel disappeared from view, presumably shuttling between Cannons and the Duke of Chandos's town house in London. It was, however, unquestionably written for and performed at Cannons, probably very soon after the date of the inventory of scores. *Esther* is one of those works without a resting place; it was so often manhandled for revivals that its proper shape cannot be determined. The "several new Songs," added and subtracted at each revival (of which there were at least half a dozen), finally displaced most of the material in the original score.[7] Actually this first and least significant of the English oratorios was popular in Handel's lifetime, and we see it revived as late as 1757.

Esther was called a masque, but it has little resemblance to the masques of the period or to Handel's own *Acis and Galatea*. It was also called at the first revival *Esther, an Oratorio or Sacred Drama*, but it could not originally have had any religious connotations. The libretto was based on *Esther*, a drama written by Racine in 1689, which followed classical Greek models in spite of the biblical characters; it was a didactic play, destined for Madame de Maintenon's school for daughters of the impoverished nobility. Here we have an immediate clue to the surprising decline in quality from *Acis and Galatea*; Handel could not be moved or inspired by homilies, especially when his libretto was far removed from the original work of the great French dramatist. This libretto was nothing but an amateurish medley without dramatic motivation or continuity. The authorship is once more attributable to the Cannons round table, but it is far below the capabilities that this college of men of letters exhibited in *Acis and Galatea*. Arbuthnot is the author most frequently mentioned in the various printed librettos. Judging from the poor quality of the poems, this is probable; the Doctor, though a good writer of prose, was no poet. Pope is named as the author in one of the librettos, and a few of the verses show his stamp. Apparently the absence of an editor-in-chief of Gay's stature resulted in a hopeless tangle.

Handel's music is equally half-hearted and unorganized. The score has some fine numbers, especially the closing chorus, but more than half the work consists of borrowings, and these, especially the ones taken from the *Brockes Passion*, are so haphazardly adjusted that they do not fit into their new context. For this reason *Esther* would not detain us, in view of

[7] Schoelcher describes one of these scores as "a scandalous dish of mixed vegetables."

the many masterpieces that claim attention, except that its historical importance is enormous.

The combination of the pattern of classical Greek drama with the Old Testament as communicated to the Anglo-German composer by a French dramatist, the structure of the work, the employment of the chorus as the chief protagonist, together called into life and determined the future course of the English oratorio. We shall discuss all this as soon as we encounter these Cannons theatre pieces outside the Duke's private residence; for the time being, and for twelve long years, they disappear. Handel all but forgot about them and returned to the battlefield of opera.

Bernard Gates, Master of the Children of the Chapel Royal, an early loyal Handelian, celebrated Handel's birthday on February 23, 1732, by staging a performance of *Esther* at the Crown and Anchor Tavern. How Gates came into possession of the old Cannons masque is not clear, but he had a copy of the libretto printed, for the surprise birthday performance was followed by two others for the benefit of private music clubs. All three performances were highly successful, everyone was pleased, especially Handel—and everyone returned to his accustomed routine. The children of the chapel exchanged costumes for vestments, and Handel the unaccustomed spectator's seat for the harpsichord bench in the opera pit. So far as he was concerned *Esther* could again slumber for another twelve years; he was busy with other things. Little did Gates realize what his friendly gesture was to set in motion—he deserves a statue as the foster father of the English oratorio.

There was someone in that audience who saw *Esther* in a different light, who indeed thought so highly of its possibilities that in some manner he got hold of the necessary performing material with a view to producing the masque. A few weeks later Handel was jolted when he read in the newspaper that *Esther* was to be given at York Buildings, not by the good Mr. Gates and his choirboys but by a person or persons who made a living from the theatre. The identity of the pirate is not known, but he must have been an experienced professional. The advertisement, naming Handel but not the producers of this "Oratorio or sacred Drama . . . never before Perform'd in Publick," was so equivocal that the public could not tell that this was an unauthorized invasion of the composer's private domain. Handel's reaction was instantaneous. In the absence of an enforceable copyright act he had only one recourse: to pull the rug out from under the rascals by making their *Esther* obsolete. The York Buildings performance took place on April 20, 1732; by May 2 Handel and Heidegger were ready to mount his new version in his own theatre, and for the first time we see the big trump card played: the public was informed that Handel's version had many newly composed additions and would be presented by "a great Number of the best Voices and Instruments." The skull and crossbones had to be hauled down: the pirates had no Senesino or Strada, and Handel's authority could not be challenged. The reworked score of *Esther* had indeed several additions, most of them borrowings from Handel's early Italian works as well as from his anthems and other English works, but there was also some expansion of portions of the original version and of the orchestra.

The announcement of Handel's punitive production carried a *nota bene:* "There will be no Action on the Stage, but the House will be fitted up in a decent Manner, for the Audience." We are facing for the first time the religious issue that was to accompany the Handelian oratorio seemingly forever. Those who are accustomed to hearing Handel's "sacred music" in reverent silence will be disappointed to learn that in ecclesiastical and conservative circles the "religious issue" was raised because of misgivings about the propriety of any musical and theatrical rendering of a biblical story. Had the Bishop of London the authority of the French Catholic bishops of Racine's time, Handel's first oratorio would certainly have been banned altogether, as were the original works of Racine from which the librettos for *Esther* and *Athalia* were drawn, instead of being merely deprived of staging. The oratorio was so new that most Englishmen did not even know how to spell it—"oratory," "oratoria"—but the "sacred" label was attached to it from the very beginning, both in praise and in derision. Deutsch (p. 290) quotes a 1732 excerpt from the diary of Viscount Percival, who thought that Handel's "oratory" was "composed in the Church style," yet when reporting a performance of *Esther* (May 20, 1732) the *Daily Courant* described the event as "an Entertainment of Musick." Then again in a pamphlet unearthed by Newman Flower a "Lord B . . ." commenting on the pirated *Esther,* says "This alarmed H——l, and out he brings an Oratorio, or Religious *Farce* . . . and put near 4000£ in his pocket." We must bear in mind these conflicting views and sentiments when examining the entrance of the Bishop of London into Handel's life.

Dr. Edmund Gibson, Bishop of London from 1720 to 1748, was a man of great learning and an ardent defender of the constitutional-political rights of the clergy; his *Codex juris ecclesiastici Anglicani* is a comprehensive treatise on the legal aspects of the Church of England. The Bishop may have been a dour teetotaler, a lawyer-cleric who loathed everything artistic and pleasant, but he was not the narrow-minded bigot the Handelian literature tries to make him. He knew about the slippery masquerades staged by Heidegger, which he denounced from the pulpit, and his indignation at the licentious plays was genuine. That Gibson, who had none of the moral inequity that so often accompanied the outward acts of piety, was an honest and fearless crusader is shown by his unhesitating attack on the questionable goings-on at the court, a denunciation that so enraged the King that he made his displeasure known, but to no avail. Dr. Gibson did not, however, have the faintest idea what he was attacking when his wrath descended on *Esther;* the theatre was the work of Satan, and masques were known to be frivolous and obscene. In addition this masque was "an Entertainment of Musick," and had not Jeremy Collier said that music "throws a Man off his Guard, makes way for an ill Impression, and is most commodiously planted to do Mischief"? Puritanism is never far below the surface in England, and to think that this pair of theatre people, especially the unsavory Heidegger, wanted to expose Holy Writ to such ungodly purposes gravely disturbed the Bishop. He forbade a theatrical performance. The only evidence we have of this prohibition is Dr. Burney's testimony, but there is no reason to doubt its accuracy. Thus was born the English oratorio, a *pièce de circonstance* compounded of homage, piracy, retaliation, and ecclesiastical fiat. We owe to Dr. Gibson the subsequent attitudes toward the oratorio, which thenceforth became frozen in a *tableau vivant.* Will it ever be unfrozen?

But *Esther* was a success in 1732, and Handel's top opera team, headed by Senesino, Montagnana, Strada, and Mrs. Robinson, was called upon to repeat the performance four times within three weeks. The royal family attended, and Handel bought from the proceeds quite a few shares in the South Sea Company. Though somewhat puzzled by the novelty of an operalike work presented with the singers "in their own Habits" standing still on the stage, and though amused if not annoyed by the barbarous English of the Italian singers, the public liked *Esther.*

No sooner was the unethical competition routed than Handel was once more forced to retaliate in a similar situation. Now it was *Acis and Galatea* that was advertised for an unauthorized production, which took place on May 17. This time the perpetrators were known; they did not hide their identity, because while the means employed were, to say the least, questionable, their aim was not unworthy. The company that produced English works in the Little Theatre across from Handel's opera house was headed by Thomas Arne, with John Frederick Lampe and Henry Carey rounding out the triumvirate. Henry Carey (1688–1743) was one of those minor composers who busied themselves valiantly with the English musical theatre, spoofing the Italian opera in farces, ballad operas, songs, and pamphlets. Originally a poet and playwright, he became a highly popular ballad-opera and song composer. John Frederick Lampe (1703–1751), another Saxon, born Johann Friedrich, had settled in England about 1725, playing the bassoon in theatre orchestras and composing. Unlike his more famous compatriot, he seems almost immediately to have joined the theatre party endeavoring to establish English opera "after the Italian manner." Lampe, who subsequently became Thomas Augustine Arne's brother-in-law, was a good man—Charles Wesley admired both his musical and his moral standards—and as a musician he had a flair for burlesque.[8] So far we have been dealing with musicians, perhaps of minor talent and unable to carry out the lofty aims of English opera, but professionals who left behind some works that can still be performed. The business head of the corporation, Thomas Arne, father of the composer Thomas Augustine Arne (who was better known as "Dr. Arne"), was an upholsterer by trade. But besides the piratical instincts of the businessman, he must have had more than a few drops of theatrical blood in his veins—he sired not only Dr. Arne but also Susanna, the future Mrs. Cibber. The three *compères* ran the Little Theatre and, in the spirit of the times, got their material from wherever it could be got. But they were serious about their English theatre, and one cannot but admire their pathetic efforts, pluckily carried out with their modest talent pitted against some of the best musical brains of the Continent. In the cast of the unauthorized production we see not only the young Susanna Arne but, surprisingly, Gustavus Waltz, Handel's "cook."

By June 10 Handel was ready with his answer: a revised *Acis and Galatea,* to be sung "with several Additions," and so on. It was an immediate success and was repeated seven times, causing the Little Theatre production to fold up after two performances. The price of the victory was heavy, though it did not seem so to Handel. As was usual in such cases, the hurried reworking did not result in improvement; as a matter of fact, Handel made an unholy mess of this graceful score. In order to bring to bear his heaviest weapons, the celebrated Italian singers of his troupe, he had the unfortunate idea of combining the English *Acis and Galatea* with *Aci, Galatea, e Polifemo,* the earlier Italian serenata, thus taking an unpardonable retrograde step to bilingual performances. The result of the uncritical mixing of the two versions, the haphazard transpositions and

---

[8] It was he who in collaboration with Carey produced the hilarious burlesque, *The Dragon of Wantley* (1737), which, as we have seen, Handel is said to have enjoyed even though it lampooned his own *Giustino.*

adaptations, created a fearful jumble in which all the grace of the English pastoral disappeared. (Chrysander's edition only exacerbates matters, because his compilation matches Handel's thoughtless ways.) For the Oxford performance in the following year Handel once more tortured the score, but at least this time it became somewhat more English, though the bilingual form prevailed for several years. Then in 1739, bereft of his Italian singers, Handel returned to a wholly English version, jettisoning the additions and coming much closer to the original version. The success of *Acis and Galatea* in 1732 was considerable, even though the work was maimed and grotesque in its linguistic discontinuity.

Having blundered onto something that pleased the public, Handel immediately sought to exploit the success of *Esther*. Unfortunately, *Deborah*, the new oratorio presented on March 17, 1733, was a mere pasticcio, arranged to suit the requirements of another wretched libretto. Samuel Humphreys may have been a good secretary, but he was certainly no dramatist or man of letters. On the other hand, even more than did the subsequent clergymen-librettists, he took a piously sentimental religious attitude, ill becoming the poor—even repulsive—story from the Book of Judges. The cruel tale revolves around the treacherous murder committed by Jael, the wife of Heber the Kenite. She offered asylum to Sisera, the fugitive general, who was at peace with Heber; but when he fell into an exhausted sleep, she took a hammer and a tent pin, and driving the pin through the sleeping Sisera's head, "rivetted the tyrant to the ground." This was hailed as a fine patriotic and moral act by Deborah, the judge and priestess. The virtuous Chrysander was shocked by this dastardly act, and vented his moral indignation on the score by striking out Jael's part altogether—*odi profanum vulgus*. But since there was in her part some good music that he wanted to salvage, with a remarkable scholarly sleight of hand this music was assigned—to Deborah. Thus was the core of the drama, as well as one of its main figures, eliminated; and not by a hack librettist, but by a scholar sworn to respect the truth.

Handel seems singularly uninterested in several of his figures. Jael, the murderess, is given mostly borrowings. When Handel did go to work on a portrayal of this wild woman, as in "Tyrant, now no more we dread thee," one of the typical old operatic rage-and-revenge numbers but grimmer than in the operas, he was defeated by Chrysander, who confiscated the aria and awarded it to Deborah. In general Handel placed the many borrowings in their new surroundings *ad hoc*, not even bothering to adapt them, as was his normal custom. He was in fact so casual about this work that he did not even take the trouble to write out a complete autograph; the copyist was instructed what to lift out from other scores, then the new text was superimposed on the old music. But some of the new music is very good, and while Handel still did not recognize that he was wandering on new paths, the dramatic quality of the new contributions to *Deborah* is distinctly in advance of the rest. This quality is also present in those of the borrowings that he took pains to refurbish. Above all, there is a thrust in some of the choruses that is quite different from the ceremonial majesty of the anthem choruses. The alchemy of this new quality is mysterious, because the choruses did come from anthems and from the *Brockes Passion*, and yet they sound different—timing, that important factor in drama, now appears in the Handelian chorus. Handel becomes aware of an element that was all but missing in the opera of the period: the chorus as an acting protagonist. Both this and the following oratorio, *Athalia*, have a large number of choruses, many of them in eight parts, and they are alive, active, and dramatically mobile. *Deborah* also surprises with a new and rich orchestral disposition which calls for two organs and two harpsichords besides the regular complement of instruments.

Emboldened by his success, Handel overestimated the attraction of his new stageless English works; he doubled the price of admission for *Deborah*. The move was resented, alienating a good many patrons, and the audience was scant. As we have related above, this rather bold attempt at exacting money from the regular opera subscribers, whose season tickets were suspended for the occasion, coincided with unpopular measures taken by the Walpole government, the founding of the Opera of the Nobility, and with anti-dynastic and anti-German sentiments, all of which reflected on the King's German-born favorite musician. The situation was not helped by this rather grasping move for "quick money."

Esther and *Deborah*, though the latter after its initial misfortune became popular during Handel's lifetime, are to us little more than historical documents, but as such their importance is so great that we must examine them closely before we follow Handel to Oxford to witness the first performance of *Athalia*. The step Handel made from *Deborah* to *Athalia* would be an incomprehensible vaulting over time and matter—only four months separate the two oratorios—were it not for a dramatic idea that henceforth was to rule the great masterpieces and that had already guided Handel in *Esther:* the role assigned to the chorus. This chorus is no longer the *turba* of the Passions but the acting and active *choros* of the Greek drama of antiquity. The great figure who caused this new dramatic concept to take root in Handel's art was Racine.

[7]

Racine was perhaps the only real poet in a French world distinguished by rhetoric and the stage, philosophy and literature, albeit often noble rhetoric and fine theatre, profound philosophy and spirited literature. His success, and his recognition by the supreme lawgiver, Boileau, was due to the fact that the classicizing French spirit found in him such a pliable representative. The severe law of the unities appeared to Racine natural, and not even his surprisingly restricted vocabulary, a mere fraction of Shakespeare's, could stifle his poetic force. That the severely constricted poetry burns through the cold and conventional forms accounts for the wizardry and attraction of Racine's art. He imitates Euripides, and though the erstwhile disciple of Port Royal did not dare openly and faithfully to carry the passions of antiquity onto the stage, but dressed them in the garments of the *galanterie* of the age, in the modish forms of the love intrigues of the French court, nevertheless the mysterious fluid of eroticism filters through the conventional scenes. It breaks through the elegant words of the bewigged and powdered figures, through the cadence of the verses, through the music of the Greek names: *La fille de Minos et de Pasiphaé* . . .

In these sculptured pieces, in these orderly verses, behind these conventional words, there are secret ideas, for with Racine everything is love; like Handel he is in his element when sketching women. This is not the only trait they have in common. Racine, like Handel, admires matriarchs —Andromache, Clytemnestra; he is fond of depicting jealousy, in which Handel also excelled; both of them drew an infinite variety of female characterizations, from virginal tenderness to murderous passion. Boileau divined in this supposedly polished classicist "plusieurs passions dangereuses," and Lafontaine remarked that "il aimait extrèmement les jardins, les fleurs, les ombrages"—all Handelian traits. But what was most congenial to Handel in Racine's work was the purely internal tragedy: suffering, hesitation, love, jealousy, bravery, and renunciation. The action arises from the characters in spite of external events.

Racine's concept of drama, as expressed in his various prefaces, can be summarized as the representation and characterization of human beings, showing how they are driven by their passions, in a simple action, preferably in a far-removed age and country. This analysis of character as the consequence of an already formed situation comes from Greek tragedy, especially from Euripides, though the Senecan concept of the

Pléiade is not absent. Racine knew Greek and read Attic tragedy in the original; his copy of Euripides is covered with annotations. His disposition of the chorus was decisive for the future of the oratorio.

It is of importance to note that Racine, who had renounced the mundane vanities of the stage and retired to his Jansenist Christianity, came out of retirement to write the two biblical tragedies, *Esther* (1689) and *Athalie* (1691), for Madame de Maintenon's establishment at Saint-Cyr. Though strict in matters of religion, this was not a convent but a school. Madame de Maintenon's instructions to Racine were positive: she asked him to provide something for the girl actresses that had a serious moral point presented in a historical setting, and that was so written as to make possible a musical rendition. She further specified that what today we would call "love interest" must not exceed settled conjugal affection. It was thus that this life-long devotee of dramas on classical subjects turned to the Old Testament, selecting stories of women who were more heroic than amorous.

Neither Racine nor his *Esther* was unknown in England when Handel decided to compose *Haman and Mordecai*. The French influence on Dryden and his contemporaries was pronounced and reached well into the 18th century; many English playwrights were adaptors and translators from the French. French tragedy set the example, though the comic genre in general remained more attached to the national soil. Several of Racine's plays, among them *Esther* and *Athalie*, were known in English versions, both in verse and in prose translations. One would think that if Racine's plays reached England, the music attached to them would have accompanied them—the scores were available in printed editions. Yet there does not seem to be any indication that Handel knew this music. This is puzzling, because both *Esther* and *Athalie* were planned to be furnished with music; they were in fact quasi librettos.

Racine's composer was Jean Baptiste Moreau (1656–1733), whose fame rests on this fact as Quinault's rests on the fact that he was Lully's librettist. Moreau went from the choirmaster's post at the Cathedral in Dijon to Paris, eventually becoming Madame de Maintenon's music master at Saint-Cyr. There is an interesting list of works he composed there: *Jonathas, Jephté, Judith, Absalon, Débora*. Are we on the trail of an Old Testament oratorio composer—in Catholic France? The dates will show that with the exception of *Jonathas*, all were composed after *Esther*, that is, after Racine had set the pattern. Moreau's first real success was with the performance of *Esther* in 1689, Racine himself directing it in the King's presence. *Esther* was performed as a stage work, with sumptuous

costumes lent by the King from the court ballet and with male singers
from the court chapel to sing the lower parts. Moreau was a good composer and a very good teacher (among his pupils: Montéclair, Cléram-
bault, and d'Andrieu); his music for both *Esther* and *Athalie* is available
and worth studying.[9]

Though there is no demonstrable link between Handel and Moreau,
we have touched upon the French composer not only because his music
was an essential part of Racine's final dramatic works, but also because
there is a fascinating parallel between the ways in which biblical dramas
were received in France and in England. The French clergy, like the
Bishop of London, frowned upon *Esther* and forbade performances beyond the strictly private precincts of Saint-Cyr. Puritanism was not missing in France either. Bossuet sternly denounced the theatre in general
(quoting the Church Fathers) and the "impieties" of Molière in particular. If it had not been for Madame de Maintenon's great influence, these
"sacred plays" would have been altogether suppressed. And then what do
we see? *Athalie* was not only restricted to Saint-Cyr but its performance
in 1691 was granted only upon assurance that all theatrical attributes,
such as décor and costumes, would be avoided—the drama became
oratorio in exactly the same manner as in England. *Athalie* did not reach
the Comédie Française for a quarter of a century and *Esther* not until
1720. The parallel with Handel's fate continues, for while the contemporary clergy scented blasphemy, Charles Bordes, a modern critic and
editor, like his English and German colleagues went to the other extreme.
He saw Moreau's choruses "overflowing with that spirit of the love of
charity and simplicity which is the essential trait of Christian lyricism."

Now let us examine this Christian lyricism. The principal character of
Athalie is again one of those amazons of the Old Testament who do not
shrink from bloodshed. This Queen of Judah was a particularly ferocious
female, which is perhaps understandable since she was the daughter of
Jezebel, who specialized in killing prophets. Athalia, in her turn, extermi-
nated her own son's children to clear her path to the throne and died as
violently as her mother. That is, in Racine's—and the Bible's—version, for
to the pusillanimous Humphreys this was strong meat. He considerably
weakened the dénouement by changing Racine's catastrophic and logical
ending. Athalia is not killed, she is merely deposed and retired, but her
magnificently defiant exit aria should have led to the fullness of tragedy;
a creature like that cannot live as a *pensionnaire*.

[9] Published as a musical supplement to *Oeuvres de J. Racine,* Paris, 1873; also
sizable fragments were edited by Charles Bordes in the Schola Cantorum series.

Humphreys was again at work with his dramatically unseeing eyes and his gauche pen, cutting, shifting, and in general trying to reduce Racine to Sunday sermon proportions, which was bad enough, but he had the temerity to add some poetic creations of his own. The worst feature of the English libretto—a trade mark of the philistine—is the removal of the motivations, which in this case was especially regrettable. Racine was already under a certain handicap when he had to treat carnal love in a manner fit for an innocent sorority of damsels, and therefore he very carefully developed other motifs. Fortunately, this compact and admirably constructed drama, by many considered Racine's greatest, could not be completely emasculated, and its essence reached Handel; Humphreys retained all the important characters as well as the dramatic role of the chorus. Handel found this not only sufficient but bountiful, and now that the didactic element was largely absent, he could deal with human characters.[10]

Athalia, a towering matriarch, powerful, violent, and unyielding, yet, with all her grimness, here a tragic figure, is completely before us in her first recitative. She is like Medea in Cherubini's opera, a tremendously passionate creature, the first of Handel's fully formed, overwhelming dramatic personalities. This woman no longer has any connections with the Bible, she is straight out of Euripides—her dream is pure Greek tragedy. Josabeth is a devoted mother and a tender wife, but a woman not without courage. Joad is not the usual implacable high priest but one with a heart in which loyalty and masculine force unite with compassion. It is too bad that this masculine force must be conveyed through an alto or countertenor. (In one of the subsequent revivals Handel planned to lower the part to a bass.) Joas, true to his role, is an innocent child, and Abner a staunchly honest soldier, while Mathan is the traditional intrigant. What was still somewhat tentative in *Esther* and *Deborah* is now clearly planned as a whole, with firmly delineated characters. Racine's terse construction, which was not too badly hurt by Humphreys, helped greatly; the music and the action are continuous and well connected, there are often no caesurae at all between individual numbers, and the chorus is superbly organic in its function. Handel learned from Racine the tragic responsibility of character, and now he saw the problem of individuality in two different ways: psychologically but also purely dramatically, a

[10] *Esther*, it should be added, was not only supposed to edify Madame de Maintenon's wards, but was also to serve as an object of literary studies, the famous French *explication de texte*, a quality uncongenial to Handel which he must have felt even through the botched libretto.

combination seldom achieved in opera. One notices his concern with the relationship of such a commanding figure as Athalia to the rest; he tries to match her with the background as if searching for something that would be somewhere between Shakespeare and the Greeks.

Athalia contains mostly new music, original, vigorous in invention, and often enchanting, for this violent drama also calls for "gentle airs," "melodious strains," and lulling sicilianas, not only in the solo parts but also in the chorus; "The gods who chosen blessings shed" has a quiet radiance Handel seldom duplicated. In contrast to that, the Queen's music is restless and always highly dramatic; while a murderess, in her finest moments she rises above crime. "To darkness eternal" is a defiantly moving farewell to power and pride, almost compensating for the absence of real tragedy.

What was already clear in *Esther*, the new role and importance of the chorus, which determined the oratorio as a species, is here fully developed. The number of the choruses, varying in length and tone and broadening to eight parts, is unusually large. Such sections as "Rejoice, O Judah," "Give glory," and "The clouded scene begins to clear" are Handel in his unapproachable glory. The extended choral scenes with their rich orchestra show Handel in full command of the epic-dramatic grandeur of the oratorio, which is something quite different from the expansive ceremonial tone of the anthems and Te Deums—though the spirit of the coronation anthem is not missing: the climactic chorus in the third act, a tremendous piece, shows it. The pyramidal Hallelujah Chorus in the first act, a double fugue, is actually borrowed from the Chandos Anthem, *As pants the hart*, but it is so apt for the situation that its effect is altogether new.

This imperious chorus, which interrupts the solos and forces the action, is welded into a certain unity with the solo voices and there is an admirable gradation of dramatic tension working up to the climactic third act. The recitatives are anything but perfunctory, and the accompanied ones shine with a new intensity. This integration of the arias into the whole brought about the most important dramaturgical step that characterizes the new genre and distinguishes it from opera: the da capo aria, though still present, is used sparingly. There are also two remarkable duets in *Athalia*—dramatic, not chamber duets—and many exquisite concertante parts for various instruments. Another thing we encounter here for the first time is the particular care Handel lavishes on the music of the Baalites. In the choruses of all later oratorios he made a distinction between the Hebrews and the heathen. The former are given elaborate contrapuntal settings while the latter, usually homophonically treated, are always depicted as innocent, graceful, and charming hedonists, sensuous, erotic, and addicted to dancing and merriment. The orchestra is very colorful, with recorders, flutes, oboes, bassoons, horns, trumpets, as well as organ, harpsichord, and archlute. Handel now not only had obtained his bearings but gave us a masterpiece, the first of the great English oratorios. The autograph of *Athalia* still contains stage directions, but they are reduced in the German edition, and nowhere appear in the Novello score.

[8]

WE HAVE SEEN HOW successful the English works were in Oxford. Handel now had neither a theatre nor an opera company, yet he pocketed a considerable sum from the English works, which required neither expensive décor nor the even more expensive castratos. *Athalia* was perhaps Handel's most applauded new work in the middle period, the eyewitnesses being unanimous in reporting the enthusiasm of the public, the size of which was unprecedented. The fortunes of opera were at a very low ebb even before the collapse of the Royal Academy of Music. Newman Flower's "Lord B . . ." says about these last days: "I left the *Italian* Opera [The Haymarket Theatre], the House was so thin, and cross'd over the way to the *English* one [the Little Theatre], which was so full I was forc'd to croud in upon the stage." In spite of all this, Handel still regarded the oratorio as a side show to opera; worse than that, as expendable. On the first occasion that offered itself, he dismembered *Athalia* for *Parnasso in Festa* (see p. 249). Two years later, when Handel once more tried a short season with his English works, he put them on the chopping block, as was his custom on such occasions, and a second reworking of *Athalia* in 1756 almost destroyed the work.

Though we are scarcely aware of *Athalia,* the "rediscoverers" of Handel considered it to be among the best of the oratorios; it was reorchestrated by Baron van Swieten himself for his private Handelian performances. Though a magnificent music drama, it still remains one of the least appreciated. Could it be because even the most far-fetched interpretation cannot make it "sacred"? Even Leichtentritt, one of the most enlightened of the Handelian scholars of the past generation, deplores the absence of "ethical motives" in *Athalia*. The printed editions do not help the cause. Chrysander's edition is at least serviceable, but the Novello score, the one generally in use because it is more readily available than the Händelgesellschaft edition, is completely butchered.

Handel not only failed to recognize the significance of his success with his English works, but remained adamant when this was brought to his attention by an old friend who had once written for him a successful libretto, *Rinaldo,* and who was so helpful and understanding at the beginning of his career in England. Aaron Hill's letter is as perceptive as it is moving. He fully recognized the portent of Handel's latest activities, sensing the possibility of the establishment of English opera if Handel would only assume leadership. He earnestly invited the composer of "inimitable genius" to be

resolute enough, to deliver us from our *Italian bondage;* and demonstrate, that *English* is soft enough for Opera, when compos'd by Poets . . . I am of opinion, that male and female voices may be found in this kingdom, capable of every thing, that is requisite; and, I am sure, a species of dramatic Opera might be invented, that by reconciling reason and dignity, with musick and fine machinery, would charm the *ear,* and hold fast the *heart,* together.[11]

Here was a blueprint, most of whose features Handel had already apprehended, and he had also found the native voices, male and female, that could do justice to song in "soft English." Handel's answer, if there was any, is not known, but he evidently disregarded Hill's appeal. Since his powerful reaction to the unauthorized performances also erased the men in the Little Theatre, any hope for English opera was gone. Piracy or no piracy, what the Arne-Carey-Lampe trio was trying to do was not a subterfuge; when they said they were offering English opera they meant it. The qualifying "after the Italian Manner" did not refer to castratos, coloratura pieces, and all the other components of the Italian opera seria, but to a genre distinguished from masque, semi-opera, and ballad opera. It is true, of course, that there was no English composer within sight who could have realized this dream, but Handel could have made it possible for some to arise by showing the way. It is sad to think that this tragedy of lost opportunity was to be repeated later under even more auspicious circumstances.

As we have seen, subsequent events seemed to confirm Handel's deep-seated optimism in regard to Italian opera. Having succeeded in gaining access to the Theatre Royal in Covent Garden and having organized a company, he produced *Ariodante* and *Alcina,* two great and successful operas. Yet even so he had to round out the repertory with the reworked *Acis, Esther, Deborah,* and *Athalia,* which, with the organ concertos played between the acts, were popular and virtually bailed him out. This return to oratorio in 1735 was not due to a recognition of the feasibility

[11] The complete letter in Deutsch, p. 299.

and viability of the oratorio but solely to the circumstances. Opera was in bad straits and something had to be done to retrieve his fortunes. Either he had no Italian singers, or those he had could not measure up to the competition's galaxy of stars; the only solution was the employment of English singers (and the ever-faithful Strada) in English works. Also, it is not inconceivable that with his sober business sense he realized the savings unstaged works would effect in this difficult situation. There were no artistic or esthetic reasons for the change. It is most interesting to observe that while Handel instantly reacted to piracy, he paid no attention to rival oratorios. When his erstwhile friend Greene produced a *Jephthah,* and Defesch a *Judith,* they remained ignored, but the minute the challenge came from opera, from the Italians, he was full of fight—and creative fervor.

In January 1736, Handel suddenly decided upon a new English work. By February 19 it was not only finished but performed in Covent Garden to considerable applause—and the money started to flow into Handel's rather depleted coffers. With *Alexander's Feast* we are back in the situation we found in Italy in Handel's youth, where the dividing line between serenata, cantata, and oratorio was a very tenuous one. *Alexander's Feast* might be termed a large cantata, but since we are in England its proper name is an ode. That it is called an "Ode to St. Cecilia" is a little more far-fetched. The dramatis personae—Alexander, Timotheus, Thais, and the chorus of Greek warriors—have little to do with the Christian saint, who at the end of the ode is virtually dragged into the story. But the ode offered good poetry, the arranger, Newburgh Hamilton, obsequiously respectful of Dryden, did not hurt the original, only arranging it for recitatives, arias, and choruses, and Handel found many opportunities for the genre pictures he always loved.

Since the foundation of the London St. Cecilia Society in 1683, the feast of the patron saint of music, November 22, had been celebrated annually in music. Although there is only a passing reference in her legend to her praising God in music, Cecilia somehow acquired fame as a musician, and the painters early appropriated her as a favorite subject, creating magnificently anachronistic scenes in which the second-century martyr plays on beautiful Renaissance and Baroque organs. In literature, too, she found admirers in Chaucer and others. It was Dryden's second *Ode to St. Cecilia* that was the subject of Handel's great new work. Dryden, the classicist, made a big detour to reach St. Cecilia, going back all the way to Plutarch, perhaps because this was his second Cecilian ode and he wanted to do something different, and his preference in any case was for antiquity. He chose the famous feast of Alexander, held many centuries before St. Cecilia in celebration of the conquest of Persepolis. To enliven things, Dryden introduced Timotheus, known to have been a singer of unusual powers of persuasion. The allegory of the power of music, which is the subject of Cecilian odes, is thus present, though somewhat incidentally, and calling for more classical learning than the simple traditional eulogy of musical instruments. Dryden, the playwright and polemicist, the satirist and critic, the cool, precise, brilliant, and seemingly unemotional observer, aging and left behind, turned to lyricism. He himself was convinced—and said so—that an ode of similar merit had never been written and never would be. The ode is indeed a fine piece of poetry and most suitable for musical setting; its climax is reached by well-organized stages which Handel followed not only in the quality of his music, but in the instrumentation. Given a well-constructed piece and beautiful words, Handel was bound to create a masterpiece, and an extraordinary masterpiece *Alexander's Feast* is.

There were some precedents he could follow. Dryden's ode had been set to music by Jeremiah Clarke in 1697 and by Thomas Clayton in 1711—Clarke's a minor work, Clayton's less than that. Hamilton, who thought that Handel alone was capable of doing justice to Dryden's poem, forgot another St. Cecilia ode which, though not composed on Dryden's text, hovers over Handel's: Purcell's of 1692. As usual, Handel does not borrow directly from his great predecessor, but the imprint of the English master's particular delicate art is everywhere. Shelley's words on Raphael's St. Cecilia: "She is calmed by the profundity of her passion," is perhaps the most fitting description for Purcell's ode.

There is something truly "classical" about *Alexander's Feast*, a happy and serene score, with its simplicity, diatonic directness, pellucid choral writing, and refined orchestration. Handel now proceeds with the newly-won rapport between the arias and the choral pieces that we have seen established in *Athalia*. Right at the beginning there is a remarkably fine alternation between the chorus and the solo voices. "Bacchus ever fair and young," a bass aria with chorus, reminds us that of all the gods Bacchus was the only one who demanded not worship but conviviality, a god who was willing to sit down at the same table with his devotees. For a moment a darker tone appears as the soprano sings of the sad fate of Darius, immediately commented upon by the chorus, a magnificent dirge, a choral arioso that ends in no thunderous Hallelujah but stalks away, pianissimo. "The many rend the skies with loud applause" is one of Handel's fine agitated pieces, but its brisk and animated quality hides an extraordinarily *raffiné* construction, in which a basso ostinato goes its own rigid way while the chorus proceeds with constantly variable phrase lengths. Now the trumpets and drums appear as the chorus of warriors clamors: "Break his bonds of sleep asunder." This also is an ostinato construction, a choral chaconne, but simple and direct, and is followed by a great bass aria, "Revenge, Timotheus cries," one of the blustering rage arias Handel likes to give his villains in the operas, but the busy orchestra gives it a comic undercurrent. That Handel seems indeed to be secretly smiling in his Homeric way at the whole affair lends *Alexander's Feast* a particular charm. The bass continues with an *ombra* scene: "The Grecian ghosts, that in battle were slain." The bassoons and the organ's *tasto solo* running with the strings create a mystery-laden atmosphere. The King then takes a torch and led by Thais makes ready to destroy the temple to a gently flowing pastoral accompaniment; Handel again has tongue in cheek. The final chorus, quite Purcellian in gait, ends the scene, and properly with it the ode. But where does that leave St. Cecilia?

By a real tour de force Dryden now rings in the saint. Commentators have found this hard to accept, though some have advanced the not implausible if a bit tenuous solution of regarding this as the triumph of St. Cecilia over Timotheus, Christianity over paganism. Is it not possible, though, that Dryden, the old and incorrigible satirist, perpetrated in this abrupt transition from antiquity to Christianity a sly little parody, which was well understood by Handel? By hinting at the universally known symbol of Cecilia, the organ (but see Handel's mocking ritornels that surround this brief recitative), he paves the way for a fine chorus in which "At last divine Cecilia came." Then Dryden builds a rather strange situation: a competition between Timotheus and the saint, which results in a draw. In a recitative the tenor suggests "Let old Timotheus yield the prize" but the bass counters with "Or both divide the crown," for "He rais'd a Mortal to the skies," while "She drew an Angel down." Now the superb final chorus takes up this proposition enthusiastically, the Timotheus theme dancing lightly toward the skies while the angel steps downward in solid quarter notes; only in the last measures, marked Adagio, is the conflict finally resolved by the simple expedient of letting the angel have the last word. Once we realize the innocent satire we notice some other things. Dance rhythm prevails in *Alexander's Feast* (as it does in *Acis and Galatea*). The majority of the solo numbers and half of the choral numbers are in triple time, and some of those in duple time are marches. The role of the tenor is reminiscent of that of the Evangelist in the Passion, and this too seems to have been more than a coincidence, more than a mere traditional technical device, especially when the narrator's role is shifted to the soprano.

When the scene moves from antiquity to Christendom, Handel is willing to display the full measure of his contrapuntal art; "At last divine Cecilia came" is a grand fugue. The final chorus is even more remarkable, a combination of solo ensemble and chorus, as it were, a solo ensemble in choral form. The mastery and inventiveness of this number make it one of Handel's supreme compositions.

At this point *Alexander's Feast* really ends—or should end. Hamilton was of a different opinion; he graced Dryden's verses with a few of his own wretched lines, which Handel set to music, but subsequently wisely cancelled. Though the music is not bad, these additions, printed in the appendix of the new Halle edition, are rightfully omitted as spoiling the effect of a wondrous final chorus. Mozart, in his re-orchestrated version, also ignored the additional numbers; every musician would feel that Dryden's poem and the magnificent ending as set by Handel do not suffer continuation.

The German exegetes had a great deal of difficulty with Dryden's *Ode,* the opinions ranging from the naive to the preposterous. Chrysander, the good old Romantic, denounced Dryden for writing on commission: this practice, he said, was debasing for a true artist and incapable of resulting in a masterpiece.[12] Surely he must have heard of the Esterházys and Rasumovskys and how they debased some true artists! Most of the others resent the small role assigned to the saint, whose "Christian" and "churchly" role is ignored. But Dryden and Handel found the ambiguity that envelops the work attractive, and the composer, with his fine instinct, seized upon the poet's *"salto mortale* from antiquity to Christendom" (Kretzschmar), turning it into one of his finest choral scenes.

This lovely work, whose popularity for a long time was second only to *Messiah's* and whose performance, properly adorned with an organ concerto or two, could not fail to enchant an audience no matter what its preferences and prejudices, is today seldom heard in America. Goethe and Herder admired it, but our choral societies cannot exercise their Christian lungs sufficiently on its Grecian beauty. Handel seems to have been equally insensitive to these beauties once the creative urge was satisfied. Abandoning a clearly promising trend, he doggedly returned to opera, to three consecutive failures, and the enterprise came crashing down in ruins.

[12] Chrysander did not even bother with the original manuscript—this was not a "sacred" work—but worked from the printed edition. The new Halle edition (Bärenreiter), still ignoring the fact that "The praises of Bacchus" was originally written for bass, gives it to the tenor, though in the following "Bacchus ever fair" the bass takes over.

XII

T HE ARTISTIC GRAVE COULD NOT HAVE YAWNED MORE ominously for Handel than in the early fall of 1737, when, afflicted in mind and body, he repaired to Aachen. But commiseration with his plight yields to admiration for the way he faced it. Music-loving physicians are fond of reconstructing case histories of their favorite composers, an occasionally illuminating pastime somewhat similar to inquiries into the performance practice of old music, and, one imagines, with as inconclusive results. At any rate, Dr. Wilhelm Reinhard, a Düsseldorf physician, in *Die medizinische Welt* (1935) questioned the "stroke" Handel is supposed to have suffered in 1737 and arrived at the diagnosis of "rheumatic muscle and nerve condition of the right arm." Considering the rapidity of Handel's recovery of the full use of his paralyzed arm, the modern diagnosis may appear correct, but it does not explain the mental disturbance verging on derangement hinted at by all contemporary witnesses.

Whatever the illness was, it could not cancel the iron will and energy of this man. Dr. Reinhard thinks that Handel must have undergone what the Germans vividly call a *Pferdekur* (horse cure), taking the cure in double or triple doses, which would be entirely in keeping with his impatient and determined character. The balmy climate of Aachen and the warm medicinal baths must have been helpful, and even more so the congenial atmosphere of the Rhineland city, which, with its many churches and monasteries and easygoing and rather "Latinized" Catholic population, must have recalled the Italy of his youth. Soon he regained the use of his arm and fingers, and naturally he immediately looked around for a place to exercise them by playing his favorite instrument, the organ, not a difficult task in Aachen. He found a fine instrument in the Abbey Church at Aachen-Burtscheid. The sudden complete recovery of their famous guest and his mastery of the instrument so awed the good nuns that they ascribed his cure to a miracle wrought by St. Cecilia, thus starting a legend that *Alexander's Feast* and the *St. Cecilia Ode* were Handel's thanksgiving offerings to the saint for her succor. Unfortunately, as with most such legends, history neglects to cooperate and corroborate—*Alexander's Feast* was composed the year before. As to the smaller *Ode,* it was composed, as were many others before and after, back home in London for the November feast of the patron saint of music, observed in Protestant England more fervently and regularly than in the Catholic Rhineland.

Even more important than his physical recovery was the return of Handel's mental faculties. As we shall see, his creative power welled up with undiminished force. The equation between the inward state of an artist of Handel's magnitude and its outward expression is, of course, difficult to establish. There were not a few who believed that the composer of *Arminio, Giustino,* and *Berenice,* all failures, had shot his bolt; they noticed that the "Paraletick Stroke" had induced depression, apathy, and "the most violent deviations from reason." These facts were known not only in England but in most centres of music on the Continent. The Crown Prince of Prussia, the future Frederick the Great, who was a cousin of Anne, Princess of Orange and Handel's pupil and ardent friend, did not share the former English princess's enthusiasm for Handel. Writing to her husband in October 1737, he expressed his conviction that "Handel's great days are over, his inspiration is exhausted, and his taste behind the fashion."

Returned to London in November 1737, Handel found a city empty of opera—and of competition; the Opera of the Nobility was bankrupt, Porpora and the great singers had gone back to Italy. Recent estimates show that Handel was not plunged into bankruptcy as has been supposed, but the situation was bad enough. He was in debt, with virtually nothing but his royal annuities to keep him afloat. That his finances were in a bad state is proved by the absence of dealings with the Bank of England during 1737–38. But Heidegger was still in business, once more a lessee of the Haymarket Theatre, where he opened the season with a pasticcio, *Arsace,* just about when Handel returned from Aachen. The two old campaigners came to an understanding, and soon we see Handel hard at work composing an opera, *Faramondo*. That Heidegger was still willing to experiment with Handelian opera is truly remarkable in view of his past experiences. *Faramondo* was hardly begun when on November 20 Queen Caroline died and all places of entertainment were closed for a period of mourning. Handel dropped the opera, and by December 12 finished the great *Funeral Anthem* for the Queen's obsequies, which took place in Westminster Abbey on the seventeenth. All newspapers praised the "fine Anthem of Mr. Handel's," and the performance, which is reported to have employed some 150 to 180 singers and instrumentalists, must have been impressive. In the words of the Bishop of Colchester, it was "reckoned to be as good a piece as he ever made," a feeling shared by many a modern critic. If there were any misgivings about the aftermath of Handel's illness, the *Funeral Anthem* (see p. 226 f.) should have dispelled them, for it showed Handel's creative faculties not only unimpaired but rising to the summit. Nor was the tempo of his productivity slowed: *Faramondo* was finished on December 24, and two days later Handel began work on *Serse*.

January 3, 1738, saw the première of *Faramondo* at the Haymarket Theatre. The cast contained the latest find in castratos, Caffarelli, Porpora's prize pupil. The great singer, a difficult, vain, and irascible man, lasted only for one season in London, but for a time he created a sensation. Montagnana and Merighi were back at the Haymarket, but the faithful Strada was gone, although replaced by a good soprano, Elisabeth Duparc, called Signora Francesina, and there were a few other new singers. The company was recruited by Heidegger prior to Handel's joining him. The original libretto of this opera, written by Zeno for Pollarolo, was undoubtedly good, but it was so whittled down and twisted around by Handel's unknown adapter that it resists any reasonable analysis; the confused goings-on and the complicated intrigues prevented Handel from shaping the fine music he composed into a coherent whole. *Faramondo*, which eked out a few performances, is usually dismissed as a deserved failure, but we cannot so simply disregard this music, which, beginning with the exceptionally fine overture, is very attractive, if not always outstanding. The texture is light and elegant, both vocal and instrumental writing spirited, and as Leichtentritt neatly puts it, "every leap fits, every accent suits." Surely, the sophisticated, varied, and sprightly rhythm that infuses this score with remarkable liveliness does not reflect the working of a mind inflicted with illness. There is much engaging love music in

Faramondo, though little characterization; on the other hand we notice
the tendency towards architecturally built scenes in which the chorus is included. However, all the musical refinements could not save *Faramondo,*
because it completely lacked theatrical values.

The pasticcio *Alessandro Severo,* which followed on February 25,
also disappeared after six performances. Even if we record as many as six
or eight performances of these works, they were poorly attended, and
Handel was in real financial straits. Finally he had to yield to the entreaties of his friends, consenting to a benefit, which was given on the
twenty-eighth of March, offering a mélange of anthems, songs, duets, and
an organ concerto. The theatre was so filled that tiers of "Benches upon
the Stage" had to be fitted to accommodate the overflow. The success was
complete, yielding £1,000 and effectively relieving Handel's plight, at
least for the moment.

If the reader wonders why such a crowd would assemble for a nondescript concert, while on opera nights the theatre would be half empty
or worse, the explanation lies in Handel's personal popularity, which was
never really threatened. The London newspapers, reporting the first performance of *Faramondo,* which was also Handel's first public appearance
after his illness, say that "he was honour'd with extraordinary and repeated Signs of Approbation." Indeed, Handel was famous and well liked
even when his fortunes were at a low ebb, and when he was used as a tool
for political ends. Perhaps the best proof of the respect in which he was
held is the attitude of his creditors, almost all of whom waited patiently,
confident that in one way or another Handel would be on top again and
would honor his commitments. On many occasions his music was played
to attract a public for a charitable cause. Thus at the annual benefit service for the "Sons of the Clergy" at St. Paul's, the *Utrecht Te Deum* and
some of the anthems were always a drawing card.

We might mention here the erection in 1738 of Handel's marble
statue in a public park—an unusual honor, then as now, for a living composer. The public gardens in Vauxhall on the south bank of the Thames
had been for years a favorite resort of the great city when in 1732 Jonathan Tyers, who had acquired a lease, developed it into a fashionable
place of entertainment. He built a covered orchestra shell, open at the
front to the Gardens, and in addition there was an entirely covered
rotunda also suitable for concerts. In 1737 an organ was built and a
permanent organist engaged; organ concertos were a popular item on the
programs. The place had of course "loose morals" and "open immoralities"
(Flower), but the food was good and the music was good and much of

that music was by Handel. The "loose morals" did not seem to have deterred either the nobility or the artistic gentry from frequenting the place; Hogarth, among them, helped with the decorations and designed the handsome silver season ticket of which Handel was an honorary recipient. Tyers, about whose musical or other propensities we know little, was a great admirer of Handel (he purchased fifty tickets for the March benefit), and he commissioned the sculptor Roubillac (spelled Roubiliac in England) to carve a marble statue of the composer "in Consideration of the real Merit of that inimitable Master." The statue was "placed in a grand Nich, erected on Purpose in the great Grove" of the Gardens in April 1738. Louis François Roubillac (1695–1762) was a French sculptor who settled in England in the early thirties. A protégé of Walpole, he soon became the most fashionable portrait sculptor in England. His sepulchral monuments (including Handel's) are to be found in Westminster Abbey, and his statues of kings and notables populate many a public square. Roubillac was a skilful craftsman but an artist of modest taste. His statue of Handel is unimaginative, though contemporaries considered it a good likeness. It remained in the Gardens until 1818, after which it was removed to the premises of Messrs. Novello, where it keeps good company to that firm's unimaginative editions of Handel's scores.

On April 15, *Serse*, finished barely a month before, was presented at the Haymarket Theatre with the full cast headed by Caffarelli. It was even less successful than *Faramondo*, and Handel had to be satisfied with five performances. This opera puzzled its contemporaries no less than its modern critics, whose opinions range from Sir Newman Flower's indignant "a musical farce . . . an absurdity that has no raison d'être," to "rein komische Oper," or a genuine opera buffa. Burney, puzzled by this highly sophisticated and actually modern score, considered it the work "of a mind disturbed, if not diseased." Obviously, *Serse* was a comic opera, but historians are flogging sundry dead horses when they find the mixture of the serious and the comical objectionable, as they have done from Burney to Leichtentritt. *Serse* is not an opera buffa, nor was it "a desperate attempt to keep up with the taste of the day," as Dent judged it to be. It is the spirit of the old Venetian opera-comedy that returns here, as indeed the libretto was an old Venetian book by Minato, once set by Cavalli, and in Stampiglia's version by Bononcini. *Serse*'s comedy is more subtle than that of the opera buffa and rests on the incongruity of showing great and solemn historical personalities in their unsolemn and unhistorical moments, notably in the throes of love intrigue, where they do not show to advantage. The comicality is in this incongruity and is ex-

ploited by almost purely musical means; the hilarious situations and
contretemps of the buffa are largely missing, the only bit of time-honored
situation comedy being the delivery of a love letter by a slow-witted servant to the wrong person. Handel was aware of the latest operatic developments in Italy; during his most recent visit there Leonardo Leo,
Leonardo Vinci, Pergolesi, and others were already well known and the
early buffa was rapidly gaining in popularity. Our notion that the opera
buffa began with Pergolesi's *La Serva padrona* is an old historical error:
far from opening a new era, this engaging work only crowned a movement that was at least a generation old. But while Handel's style became
lighter (we have noticed this when he tried to cope with Bononcini's light
music) and the texture more elegant, and while he was willing to banter,
whatever he took over from more recent Italian opera did not essentially
change his life-long adherence to the older Venetian-Neapolitan type of
opera which he carried to its apogee.

The dramatis personae in *Serse* are two brothers opposed to a pair of
sisters, the usual subplot to complete the intrigue being supplied by a
princess enamored of Xerxes, and, for the first time in Handel's operas,
the old, old comic servant, the buffo character. The whole plot can be
summarized in one sentence: the King of the Persians is interested in one
of the sisters, whose lover is of course none other than Xerxes's brother,
and since the other sister has designs on the same man, they must find
ways to overcome the king's rather commanding position in the affair.

Now this comic opera begins not with an amusing situation that can
be exploited but with magnificent love lyricism: the famous "Ombra mai
fù," better known as "*The* Largo," appears in the very first scene. Nor is
there anything comic about the ravishingly sensuous music of muted
strings and recorders that follows, which so affects the middle-aged
amorist, Xerxes, that he wants to know who the person is who sings "O
voi che penate." Romilda continues her song as her lover, Arsamene, begins to worry about the king's interest in the sweet singer. He and the
king sing a duet which, as to situation, is anything but *sehr komisch*, as
some would have it. As a matter of fact, most of Arsamene's arias are very
moving. The king makes no headway with Romilda, yet he is more and
more taken with her, and sings more and more in the grand pathetic
manner of the seria—which is what makes things comical. In the meantime the Princess Amastre's "Sapra delle miei offere" is again comical because it is a light travesty of the traditional rage aria. The two sisters spar,
very attractively passing from the lovelorn to the waspish.

In the second act, Elviro, the servant, is charged with the delivery of a love letter. Disguised as a flower vender, he punctuates his song with the street vender's calls, no doubt authentic cries which Handel is known to have noted down. The letter is cunningly used as the imbroglio deepens, but Romilda is steadfast, causing an outbreak of royal fury in the Neapolitan comic style of Scarlatti. Now it is Amastre's turn to pine. Her aria "Anima infida" is a jewel of sophisticated operatic writing. And so the action goes—or what passes for action—but its quality is immaterial because there are live persons on the stage; they are interesting, and they sing interesting music. In the end, of course, everything is straightened out: the king, an irritable monarch, works up to another rage aria, but takes back his pursuing princess while the others are properly sorted out. The characterizations are excellent. The two sisters show quite different personalities, and all the others in this delightful if unusual opera are well handled. Xerxes's role, designed for Caffarelli, is of course less positively drawn, but in this particular situation his character is quite credible. *Serse* is rich in the most sophisticatedly charming needle-point music which was far over the heads of Handel's audiences, as it is over those of today.

On May 23, 1738, Heidegger invited subscriptions to his forthcoming season of Italian opera, but by July he had to abandon the project for lack of interest. After the season closed on June 6, therefore, Handelian opera was not to be heard until the fall of 1740. The rest of 1738 was seemingly an idle period, and Handel was not heard from, not even being mentioned in the periodical notices in the newspapers. But he was not idle: on July 25 he began the composition of a new oratorio, *Saul.*

[2]

CHARLES JENNENS WAS A wealthy man who converted his ample leisure into activities in harmony with his literary ambitions. Somewhat pompous and, like rich amateurs in general, feeling superior to most other literati, he was nevertheless a cultivated man, a fervid Shakespearean, and not unacquainted with the classics. Jennens lived in such splendor that the nickname "Suliman the Magnificent" was bestowed on the Squire of Gopsall in Leicestershire. He maintained a round table and, as in the Burlington and Chandos residences, Handel could there meet very able litterateurs. Among these, Richard Bentley, nephew of the great Cambridge classical scholar of the same name, must have been an intellectually invigorating person. A lesser edition of that storehouse of knowledge that was his uncle, he also united classical erudition with Christian theology and archaeology, a combination that had an impact on Jennens's mental processes and hence also on Handel. The "Gopsall Circle" and its influence on Handel has not yet been sufficiently explored.

The Handelian literature, taking its cue from Dr. Johnson, tends to deprecate Jennens, but this is manifestly unjust. He was intelligent; he had a good eye for dramatic possibilities and for continuity, and he not only knew what lends itself to musical treatment and choral commentary but correctly estimated Handel's own particular capabilities. Although he neatly paraphrased the Bible, the delineation of characters was his own. Jennens's libretto made a genuinely dramatic piece out of the biblical story of Saul, with characters and motivations. Though not much of a poet, he was quite knowledgeable as a dramatist, and he must have been interested in music and possessed of some knowledge of it. Apparently Jennens fancied Handel's music and had followed his career for some time, because we find his name (as we do Newburgh Hamilton's) in Handel's first subscription list, for the opera *Rodelinda* in 1725, and he had a number of Handel's scores copied for his own use. The two men somehow became acquainted, undoubtedly on Jennens's initiative. We know of a letter Jennens addressed to Handel in 1735, with an offer of a libretto, which for the moment was politely evaded. Whether the composer remembered Jennens's offer or was again approached cannot be ascertained; we do not even know whether the libretto offered in 1735 was *Saul*. But at the later date Handel gladly accepted Jennens's text, starting to set it at the end of July.

The work did not progress with his accustomed speed and ease; something was disturbing Handel deeply, and one gets the impression that for the first time real doubts about his future course were undermining his security and optimism. After a few weeks he laid aside *Saul* and on September 9 turned to the composition of a new opera, *Imeneo*. But, and this shows his inner turmoil, the opera too was laid aside. A few days later *Saul* was taken out of the drawer and Handel continued to work on it. A visit from Jennens about this time must have contributed to the settling of his mind, and a measure of emotional security must have returned, because when *Saul* was finished by the end of September, Handel immediately embarked upon the composition of *Israel in Egypt*, which was completed within a month. If he did suffer a mental derangement in the previous year, there was assuredly no trace of it left; the man who composed such colossal masterpieces in a few weeks was in command of creative faculties as fresh and luxuriant as ever.

The story of David and Saul having always been popular with poets and musicians, oratorios on the subject were composed by a number of masters, among them Carissimi. Only three of these, however, need concern us here. Keiser's *Der siegende David* (1728) is not a significant work, but it may have been known to Handel; it does employ a carillon, an instrument that makes its first appearance in a Handelian score in *Saul*, a rather unusual coincidence otherwise. Porpora's *Davide e Bersabea* (1734) we have already mentioned (p. 248); it went unnoticed by Handel. The third of these precursors, *David's Lamentations over Saul and Jonathan*, by John Christopher Smith, Jr., came practically from Handel's household. This oratorio was also composed in 1738, though earlier in the year than Handel's *Saul*, and was not performed until February 1740. There may be something more than coincidence in the timing of the two settings, although nothing is actually known about their relationship, and Smith, though a good musician, was certainly not in Handel's class. At any rate, Handel owes nothing to these earlier settings, though Jennens studied them for his purposes.

The story of Saul in the Book of Samuel is complicated and diffuse. That Jennens succeeded in working it into a good dramatic libretto is attested by the very high level of the music—Handel always responded to true dramatic stimuli. *Saul* is pure tragedy, without a trace of religious philosophy; its entire conception is visual and theatrical; it is a music drama. Considering the spectacular aspects of this score, the festivities, the ghost scene, the funeral cortege, the two attempted murders, and so forth, one might say that there is a good deal of "grand opera" in it. The original division of the work was into "acts," not "parts," and the score contained stage directions even though it was called "An Oratorio or Sacred Drama." Only staging would bring out the true grandeur of this tremendous work, for *Saul* is full of action, far more so than any opera of the period, or, in fact, than any for some time to come; compared to it most of Gluck is statuesque.[1] Saul is Greek tragedy; Jennens and Handel only removed mask and cothurnus to give us the men behind them. This is no longer the mythus of the Bible but the mystery of life, as in the Attic tragedy, where not the sinner is punished for his sins but man for being man. Librettist and composer realized that the tragic is always the futile struggle of human will with *Ananke;* this *Ananke,* however, no longer resides on the snow-covered peaks of Zeus's domain but in men's own souls. We carry our destiny in ourselves, and we fall when we rise against it, when

---

[1] Percy M. Young, in his *The Oratorios of Handel,* rejects, as recently as 1950, the staging of *Saul* and the other oratorios as being "aesthetically inadvisable." But his old-fashioned bias is immediately evident from the sentence that precedes this judgment: "It is fascinating to bribe sensuousness into acceptance of Handel the oratorio writer by staging, as operas, his oratorios."

we want to be something other than what we are.

Handel must have found the pairing of the figures of Jennens's drama familiar from opera. Michal, Saul's gentle younger daughter, loves David; the older daughter, Merab, a haughty princess, resents being offered as a prize to the slayer of Goliath; while Jonathan, the king's son, a noble youth, offers his friendship to David. At first everything seems to be resolved satisfactorily: Merab finds someone socially more acceptable than the shepherd's son, and David and Michal are happily married. This was not an unskilled dramatic move; the coming tragedy is hinted at, then delayed, temporarily easing the situation. The king's jealousy grows—his general wins too many battles—and he resolves to destroy David. Now the conflicts mature between father and son and between the king and David. Saul bids Jonathan kill David, which the youth refuses out of loyalty to his friend, thereby coming into conflict with his filial duty. Saul, who had previously attempted to slay David, now turns on his son, but the javelin again misses. He is clearly bereft of his senses, though later he composes himself and realizes that he is preparing his own ruin. He therefore goes to Endor to consult the Witch, who calls upon the Ghost of Samuel the prophet, whom Saul implores for help. What he hears is the announcement of *Moira*, his inevitable doom, which duly follows. Jonathan is also killed, as is the messenger who brought the fallen king's crown to David, and then the dead king and his son Jonathan are carried away to the strains of the famous Dead March.[2] The ending is a little pat: *Le roi est mort, vive le roi!* Merab's change of heart, as she finally approves of David, if not as husband at least as brother-in-law, is perhaps an unnecessary touch of family solidarity, but on the whole the libretto was put together capably, if occasionally with rather platitudinous words.

The oratorio starts *in medias res,* all the principals are immediately involved and are vividly before us. The first scene, entitled "Epinicion, or Song of Triumph for the victory over Goliath and the Philistines," is one of the great ceremonial pieces, ending with a magnificent Hallelujah Chorus. As a piece of musical architecture, the Epinicion, a string of five numbers forming a self-contained *scena,* is a departure from older practices, showing that Handel was fully aware of the advantages of the oratorio over the opera seria. This is the victory ode of the ancients informing us of the situation as the drama opens. No time is wasted, the

---

[2] That the Dead March is not in minor but in C major has caused as much uneasiness as fancy explanations. Aside from the fact that the march is clearly a *Tod und Verklärung* piece, only one of the Romantic worriers noticed that C major is the principal key in *Saul.*

pieces are well-proportioned, the fine opening chorus, "How excellent Thy
name, O Lord," returns and then is replaced and crowned by the great
Hallelujah Chorus. In the opening phase of the work the expressive
recitatives and the great choral pieces over-shadow the arias, demonstrating both the essential stylistic feature of the new genre, the English
oratorio, and Handel's emancipation from the canon of the seria, but
when Saul appears with his great rage songs the personal drama begins at
top dramatic pitch.

In the second scene the exchange of views between Merab and
Jonathan is perhaps a little lengthy, but the following scene is a wonderful dance piece that begins with the charming chorus of the maidens,
"Welcome mighty King," rising in intensity when the male voices join the
chorus. The carillon theme was taken from Francesco Antonio Urio, but
Urio would scarcely believe what possibilities his theme (in itself altered)
discloses in Handel's elaboration. The core of the drama is reached when
the king's envy is aroused by "this upstart boy," David, and he begins to
rage. David's soothing song only draws a javelin that misses its mark. In
the meantime everyone sings music perfectly in accordance with his character, Jonathan's difficult position being presented by a fine recitative, "O
filial piety," followed by an aria that is less impressive. The exchange of
friendly endearment between David and Jonathan is somewhat routine
Handel, but the minute the overwhelming figure of Saul reappears the
dramatic tension is back in full force, and the music of the secondary
figures is informed by the same quality. The act ends with a fine fugue, a
choral prayer for David: "Preserve him for the glory of Thy name." The
people enter the drama by expressing their uneasiness.

The second act opens with a scene built on the same admirable dramatic principle as the first-act opening. The chorus begins with "Envy,
eldest born of hell," as mighty a piece as Handel ever composed. It
evolves over an ostinato bass which in the middle of its relentless repetitions is interrupted by the dark warning, "Hide thee in the black night."
This chorus no longer comments, it takes a hand in the unfolding drama.
We are again witnessing the birth of tragedy from the spirit of lyricism,
for this is Atridean lyricism, the profound and fearful dilemma of human
nature, full of contradiction and subject to the irrational strokes of fate.
Now Handel calms Saul's rage, and when the father answers Jonathan,
who beseeches him "Sin not, O King, against the youth," he is composed
and kingly. The recitative before Jonathan's fine aria is somewhat perfunctory, but then so are the words: "he has done important service to
you and to the nation." Such flat words never roused Handel's poetic im-

agination. The love music of Michal and David is a nice interlude in which Handel's recently renewed experiences with pastoral music are shown to advantage. The people fully approve "virtue's charms," in an affecting choral piece.

The sinfonia heard at this point is a purely theatrical device, equivalent to the lowering of the curtain in staged performances, to link events that take place after the lapse of a certain time. Like the fine overture, the sinfonia is an elaborate organ concerto.

David's return from another victorious campaign, only increasing the king's jealousy, is followed by a duet between David and Michal, not amorous this time but fraught with fear and foreboding, even though David protests that "At persecution I can laugh." Now Handel carefully and sympathetically develops the tender girl's character, and she finds an unexpected reservoir of strength to defend her husband. "No, let the guilty tremble," she sings with almost heroic accents. After another sinfonia, the king, brooding in a recitative heavy with tension, attempts to kill Jonathan, whereupon the chorus sings "O fatal consequence of rage," a stunning piece expressing indignation over this "violation of every law" and horror at "this furious monster." These are the king's outraged subjects, not disinterested bystanders. The theme of this great choral piece also hails from Urio's Te Deum but is developed beyond anything Urio could have foreseen.

The whole third act is tightly composed, tense and pressing toward a climax. The tremendous opening recitative shows Saul's inner collapse— "Wretch that I am," he sings, "Of my own ruin author." Perhaps the only comparable scene in all operatic literature is Philip's soliloquy in Verdi's *Don Carlo*. Handel, the great connoisseur of men, stands in awe before Saul. In the traditional biblical figure he discovers a tragic human being. The scene at Endor is Aeschylean: fate does not stalk in, it envelops everything as the orchestra prepares the appearance of the Ghost. The unconquerable impulse of a man proceeding to his ruin is depicted, the *Ate* of Greek tragedy, which strikes the sinner and sweeps him away with his sins. But Saul's sin is of an altogether human quality, not a direct defiance of God but pride in his power and bitter jealousy of its challengers. The scene is superbly calculated to prepare the final tragedy: Handel avoids everything formal and symmetrical, the king stands alone, undeluded and fully aware of the portent of his evil deeds, yet not contrite. He is not going to be subdued, for "If Heaven denies aid, seek it from hell!" The ensuing confrontation with the Ghost, musical theatre of the first water, has worried sentimental critics and historians, not least among them Chrysander, who once more forgot the duties of editor and scholar, lapsing into those of the moralist.

A sinfonia prepares the change of scene. David is encamped waiting for the news of the battle between the Israelites and the Philistines. An Amalekite messenger comes carrying Saul's crown, with the tidings of Saul's death by his hand; his reward is to be put to death. David's aria "Impious wretch" is a remarkable piece, for as is sometimes Handel's way, his music changes and even negates the meaning of the words. After the first part, angry in tone, when David repeats "Since thy own mouth hath testified, by thee the Lord's anointed died," it no longer sounds like a justification of the death sentence, but like a realization of the futility of the act.

The final scene, like the very first in the oratorio, is put together from several numbers, really a compound finale which the authors called "Elegy on the death of Saul and Jonathan." At first Handel wanted to use his labor-saving device of borrowing wholesale, this time from the *Funeral Anthem*, but his heart was in this somber tragedy; changing his mind he wrote superlative original music. After the Dead March the chorus sings "Mourn, Israel, mourn thy beauty lost," a heartrending dirge. From the final notes of the magnificent instrumental introduction Handel creates the mood of the choral lament "Thy choicest youth on Gilboa slain," the almost unbearable pathos of youth destroyed. David's aria, "Brave Jonathan his bow ne'er drew," is not on a par with the following "In sweetest harmony," but when he sings with the chorus in the manner of a precentor "O fatal day," we once more hear mourning music of breathtaking beauty. The Greek tragedy could end here, on the profoundly pathetic observation "how low the mighty lie!" But—perhaps a remnant of the operatic dénouement—now the living must receive their due. The people are summoned by Abiather: "Ye sons of Judah, weep no more," and the people respond with "Gird on thy sword," urging the new king to "Pursue thy wonted fame." Abiather is a sort of perfunctory public crier, but the chorus soon makes us forget him, for in this rousing piece one can physically sense the tumultuous, surging crowd. The theme of the fugue, "Retrieve the Hebrew name," which constitutes the middle part of this great chorus, also comes (again altered) from Urio's Te Deum (*In Te Domini speravi*).

Both Jennens and Handel realized the greatness of the theme of the wild darkness of the driven mind, and they concentrated on Saul's towering figure. Though intermittently deranged by jealousy, the king is a tragic figure, for while he has moral flaws of character, he is not without heroism when he faces his fate. In his clear moments, Saul analyzes himself with a sensuous misery, a witness to his own sorrow. He is interested in nothing but his own dark consciousness and the sensations exploding within it. But if the fire of Saul's passion is gross and ugly, Handel shows that even the gross and ugly can be wholly burned away in the full and courageous acceptance of the consequences.

Jonathan and David are clearly secondary figures. It seems that Jennens was not altogether in sympathy with David and that Handel accepted and shared this view, because while David's traditional role as singer to the harp is well served by the music he is given, his character is less heroically drawn than is usual in works, poetic, pictorial, or musical, where he is the principal figure. Jonathan is touching, but he weakens and gradually fades out. Michal is lovingly sketched, a young woman deep, warm, and sweet, while Merab, though priggish, is really a passionate woman. While the script shows her in this mood she comes to life in her music, but when she drops her haughty opposition to David, Handel drops her; he is no longer interested in her, as the music plainly shows. The Witch and Samuel's Ghost are powerful dramatic characters, but Saul's real foil is the chorus—his people. The role of the chorus is altogether on the pattern of the classical tragedy, for the king's actions involve his people and a tragic conflict is inevitable.

Anything like a conventional "sacred oratorio" performance of *Saul* would certainly call up the wrong associations—Jehovah is in the picture as a mere accessory. Supernatural forces agitate human destinies, but these fates are nevertheless decided in the terrible struggle of human souls. Nor is any moralizing in order, as Handel himself made clear by eventually cutting out the role of the High Priest, the only figure through whom Jennens indulged in a bit of moralizing. This is stark drama in which Handel realized to the highest degree what was always his aim: to extract from his hero the finest and the greatest that is in him in the moment of his supreme trial. And this drama demands the resources of an opera house, resources that would delight those Handelians who like their Baroque music massive, with phalanxes of singers and players. *Saul* calls for the largest ensemble in all of Handel's works, and Handel himself made it massive. It is the only one of his oratorios that employs trombones in addition to a full Baroque orchestra, solo organ, and carillon; also, he borrowed from the Tower a pair of outsize military kettledrums which sounded an octave lower than the usual orchestral instruments.

The use of the organ in *Saul*, as in some of the other oratorios, calls for special study on the part of modern organists, for Handel uses it in many instances as an orchestral instrument and not simply to fill in the continuo. Indiscriminate use destroys a considerable amount of the orchestral color envisaged. Organists should be particularly alert to Handel's instructions when he explicitly excludes the organ, or when he demands *tasto solo* or *organo pieno*. On the other hand, the splendid overture, more extensive than any of Handel's opera sinfonias, is really a four-"movement" suite *ossia* organ concerto intended for his own use, as are a number of the other instrumental pieces where the organist can excel, especially if he knows how to improvise tastefully.

Saul is not without its weak spots. Fortunately they are few and can easily be eliminated, for it cannot often enough be repeated that such inordinately long Baroque works must be pruned. In general one might say that there are too many arias in *Saul* and even when they provide great music, they tend to retard the pace of the drama. A number of them should be cut—always with an eye on tonal concordances—and the result would be a tight and relentlessly developing drama.[3]

A refreshing change from the operas is the remarkable fact that all male parts in *Saul* were designed for natural male voices and were so sung at the first performance. Saul was sung by the bass Waltz, Jonathan by the tenor Beard, David by the countertenor Russell, the Ghost of Samuel by the bass Hussey. La Francesina took the part of Michal, Mrs. Arne that of Merab. This cast was not comparable to the great Italian ensembles to which Handel was accustomed, but it was a competent crew. The less than modest acclaim *Saul* received was not due to their modest talent; the London public could not as yet grasp the significance of this work. Two years later in Dublin *Saul* proved to be a great success.

On February 17, 1739, *Alexander's Feast* was revived, followed on March 3 by *Il Trionfo del Tempo e della Verità*, the cantata Handel wrote in Italy. This is not among the best of his Italian compositions; the didactic tone of its text is one that never fired Handel's imagination. Although somewhat expanded for this revival, it was laid aside after one performance, to be once more taken up and reworked at the end of his career. March 20 at the Haymarket was an unusual evening, a benefit for charity, for which purpose Handel had "generously given the Use of the Opera-House, and directed the performance of *Alexander's Feast*," also playing a new concerto. Thus we see Handel in the midst of the consider-

---

[3] Brahms, a great admirer of Handel, and in particular of *Saul*, conducted the oratorio in 1873, during his first season as musical director of the Gesellschaft der Musikfreunde. Interesting hints can be gleaned from the cuts he made. See the Brahms *Briefwechsel*, III, p. 53.

able difficulties of maintaining a sagging theatrical enterprise, working day and night on new compositions, yet characteristically taking out time to help a charitable purpose. On this occasion, a number of well-to-do musicians, led by Michael Festing, Maurice Greene, Pepusch, and others, organized a Fund (later Society) for the Support of Decayed Musicians. Handel was among those asked to join the charitable society, the first of its kind in the world. Everyone was enthusiastic, even Heidegger joined, donating £20 to defray the expenses of the performance, and the benefit brought in handsome returns. Handel remained a benefactor of the Society for the rest of his life.

[3]

Israel in Egypt, which saw the light in the King's Theatre on April 4, with "several concertos on the organ," is almost as remarkable for its defects as it is for its excellences. The construction is loose; it can hardly be maintained that the parts are carefully related to the whole, since the work was not composed on a dramatic poem. It has been suggested that Jennens may have helped with the selection of the verses from the Bible, which is possible, but we know that Handel was thoroughly familiar with the Bible, and that on a previous occasion he had refused such assistance proffered by a bishop. We must also suppose that Jennens would have disapproved of such an undramatic juxtaposition of excerpts from Exodus and the Psalms; he admired Handel but he admired even more his own talents as a dramatic poet. The manner of composition was also peculiar in that Handel first set the second part (Israel in Egypt is the only oratorio in two "acts").

The work is completely different from Saul; in fact it differs from the dramatic oratorio pattern to such an extent that Streatfeild's suggestion that it was originally intended as a large anthem should be given consideration. Perhaps Israel in Egypt was indeed planned as an anthem or a set of anthems like the Coronation Anthems, but somehow it got out of hand and assumed the proportions of a large oratorio. The original title was The Song of Moses, and the present first act was to be preceded by the Funeral Anthem, which Handel was apparently determined to use in one way or another. One can hardly blame him for not wanting such a superb work buried with the late queen forever. But the plan had once more to be abandoned, though not the idea of taking a short cut: Israel is the most heavily padded of all Handel's great works. Almost half of the oratorio's numbers depend on borrowings, in part or even in whole. The anthem character is also plain from the exterior of the oratorio: there are only four arias as against almost ten times as many choruses, and practically no recitatives. There must have been some purpose in this "ceremonial" construction, but it is impossible to ascertain its nature; the war with Spain was in the air but not yet a reality.[4] Nor can we find a trace of any commission. Though long, *Israel in Egypt* remains a torso; the first part was never written, and the work opens abruptly with a perfunctory recitative. Yet with all its shortcomings, there is an impressiveness about *Israel in Egypt* that deeply satisfies.

After a brief recitative, the oratorio opens with a large, anthem-like double chorus, "And the children of Israel sigh'd," and thereafter one superb choral piece follows another. "He spake the word" owes its core to a sinfonia from the now-famous *Serenata* of Stradella, and "He gave them hailstones for rain" also descended from that fine Neapolitan composer, though in both instances the borrowing resulted in something so Handelian that only scholars armed with documents can point out the foreign goods. The alto aria, "Their land brought forth frogs," is descriptive but in a story-telling sense, as indeed the whole oratorio is a vast, loosely connected epic poem. The various plagues are described in this manner; hailstones can be heard dropping on the orchestra; flies and lice (the latter ennobled in Germany to the status of gnats) buzz and flutter. Stradella would have been amazed at this extraordinary entomological accompaniment. No plagiarism was ever more imaginatively treated. It was to amaze Haydn, too, but that genial elderly retired *Kapellmeister* picked up the idea like a youthful experimenter—he understood Handel.

"He sent a thick darkness," in its free declamation, construction, and ambiguous harmonic scheme, is startlingly different from the severely contrapuntal lines of most of the other choruses. This choral recitation is a magnificent musical description of the uncertainties of the night which, indeed, "might be felt" physically. We seldom know in what key we are until the piece ends on a solid E major, but near the middle we surely hear E-flat minor! "He smote all the first born" was derived (as was "They loathed to drink of the river") from a set of Handel's own keyboard fugues, once more transformed with unparalleled skill, and of course with newly devised orchestral accompaniment. "But as for his people," letters patent owned by Stradella, affords, with its pastoral tone, a little respite among

[4] Walter Serauky's interpretation certainly oversimplifies the problem. "We must assume," he says in his biography, "that Handel composed this oratorio responding to a profound inner religious motive." Neither Handel nor any other 18th-century composer did any such thing; they were professionals who worked for specific occasions.

the great anthems. The following fugue largely continues this tone. This time Handel borrowed Stradella's beautiful tune "Io pur seguiro" in its entirety, without changes beyond removing one dot to accommodate the rhythm of the English text. "Egypt was glad" is an undisguised adaptation, almost without change, of an organ *canzona* from Johann Caspar Kerll's *Modulatio Organica*.[5]

Now Handel reaches into his own choral reservoir: his *Dixit Dominus* of the Roman days furnished the material for "He rebuked the Red Sea." *Dixit Dominus* was the masterpiece of his youth; now the mature and experienced musician recasts it, and the Italian piece sounds altogether English. The Chandos Anthem, *The Lord is my light*, is converted into "But the waters overwhelmed their enemies," again perfectly at home in its new habitat. The first part (the second of the work as originally planned) ends with another loan from Stradella, assuming the shape of "And believed the Lord."

The second part rises to new heights of splendor. Now Handel does his own work and does it in the grandest of the grand manner; everything is on a large scale, neither composer nor listener has time for meditation. Indeed, he seldom wrote a more dazzling choral piece than "I will sing unto the Lord," a great anthem for double chorus. Another original piece is "And I will exalt him," a fine double fugue. Erba's Magnificat and Urio's Te Deum furnished the material for several of the following numbers, but always with original touches added by Handel. We should really be thankful that these two minor composers existed for assuredly their music became ennobled and immortalized. "The people shall hear" is once more Handel at his most exultant and triumphant, a tremendous double chorus full of strokes of genius in the interpretation of the words. This piece is more dramatic than epic, with telling pauses, exclamations, sudden turns, and complicated polyphony alternating with block chords. Nor does the music sag after this heaven-storming, as Handel, his dramatic sense alert, follows the paean with a gentle piece, "Thou shalt bring them in," only to explode anew with "The Lord shall reign," an anthem for double chorus, and still another one, "Sing ye the Lord."

The solo pieces are pale compared to this splendor, although the alto aria, "Thou didst blow with the wind," is engaging, with its undulating accompaniment depicting wind and water. Since they are impersonal, Handel fell back on his vast experience and bedecked them with coloraturas. The same might be said about the duets, though they are well

[5] This organ piece, though printed in 1686, was probably taken from Handel's childhood notebook. See p. 13.

worked out, if somewhat archaic in Steffani's style. "The Lord is my strength," a canonic duet, hails from Erba's Magnificat (though he would scarcely recognize it), while "Thou in thy mercy" switches to Urio, this time verbatim, but the orchestral accompaniment is new. The third duet, "The Lord is a man of war," is interesting because this time Handel leans on both of these mysterious Italians, the patchwork recalling the old *chanson fricassée* of the 16th century.

Israel in Egypt remains unique among Handel's oratorios as, in its way, *Messiah* is unique. It has no dramatic plot, no individual characters, and since Handel freighted himself with borrowings from the past century, a certain archaic touch repeatedly makes itself felt. Julian Herbage calls this curious work "Handel's most superbly magnificent failure," a judgment that comes closest to the truth. For, whatever the objections, the choruses are great music, and they offer a wide variety of mood and technique, ranging from grim intensity to tender humility, from simple narrative to grandiose jubilation. Every device in the choral arsenal is used, choral recitative and arioso, fugue and double fugue, through-composed dramatic setting, and so on. And we should bear in mind that some of these choral pieces are exceptional not only in Handel's copious output, but in the entire choral literature. Another noteworthy feature of *Israel in Egypt* is the role assigned to the orchestra, which remains independent and colorful even in the polyphonic choral numbers. As to the "embarrassing" borrowings, a course in composition could be based on the study of Handel's reworking of the loot.

All of this goes to show that something must be done in the way of proper presentation of *Israel in Egypt* to salvage its greatness and diminish its flaws. By eliminating most of the solos, recitatives, and duets, as well as the archaic pieces such as the Kerll *canzona,* we would gain a sequence of exceptionally fine choral pieces. This would amount to a concert, but then *Israel in Egypt* is in fact a choral concert; we can turn it into a "benefit"—for our enrichment. Though the choruses are disconnected, at times they do form certain groups, unified by repetition or even a suite-like pattern. These groups should be retained intact whenever possible but separated from one another by concertos as Handel separated the acts by playing such pieces. An avalanche of great choral music can easily cause fatigue, and this may well have been the chief reason for the original failure of *Israel in Egypt.* Instrumental interludes would ease this congestion very effectively. And of course a proper beginning must be provided for in the form of an overture, of which there are many fine ones buried with unknown operas.

Israel in Egypt was a failure, and it is sad to watch Handel tampering with the score within a week. Since the public's reserve was presumably due to the preponderance of choruses, the remedy was obviously dictated: the second of the total of three performances was "shorten'd and intermix'd with Songs," and Italian songs at that!

[4]

WHEREVER WE LOOK we see only failures and near failures, but if the experience brought Handel disillusionment, it certainly did not give him pause. In September and October he composed the *Ode for St. Cecilia's Day* and his chief orchestral works, the Concerti Grossi, Opus 6. These, as well as sundry new organ concertos, were to be played between the acts of the English works. The 1739 season at the Haymarket Theatre, though precarious, was peaceful. Handel had learned to live and let live (or was he soothed by the character of the competition?), since a *modus vivendi* had evidently been arrived at with Covent Garden, where an opera company under Pescetti was functioning. Giovanni Battista Pescetti (c. 1704–1766), a pupil of Lotti, was originally appointed to replace Porpora. With the demise of the Opera of the Nobility he was left on his own, staying for a few years in London before returning to his native Venice, where his presence is attested in 1747. A composer of modest talent, he presented no threat to Handel. That some sort of amicable arrangement was made between the two establishments is clear from their respective calendars, and even more from the fact that they shared several of the singers.

During October or early November Handel decided to return to his own management, leasing the Theatre Royal in Lincoln's Inn Fields from Rich. He gathered an English company, and the season opened on November 22 with *Alexander's Feast* and the *Ode for St. Cecilia's Day*. The advertisements refer to Mr. Dryden's "New Ode," or even to "Mr. Dryden's Last New Ode," but actually this was the earlier, and lesser, of Dryden's two Cecilian odes. Unlike *Alexander's Feast,* this is the traditional Cecilian ode in which there is no plot, no epic story-telling, but a simple eulogy of the saint and of music, expressed through the praise of the individual musical instruments. While it is undeniable that there is some conventional music in Handel's *Ode* and that the composer depends rather heavily on Gottlieb Muffat's *Componimenti Musicali per il Cembalo,* this short and relatively minor work is an attractive piece, very Purcellian, and beautifully worked.[6] The manner in which the borrowings from Muffat were absorbed and developed affords a liberal education in the art of imaginative craftsmanship.

The arias are beguiling. The one for soprano with solo cello, "What passion cannot Music raise and quell?," is a ravishing saraband; the tenor aria, "The trumpet's loud clangour," is proud, with a graceful nod to Purcell. Surely no one should call it a "Kampfszene," nor is the unassuming march a "Siegesmarsch"; what we witness is a delightful game to bring into relief "The soft complaining flute" for soprano, with its delectable accompaniment of flute and lute. The aria is a delicate piece, even if a little conventional. The tenor aria, "Sharp violins proclaim their jealous pangs," is not so sharp as it is coquettish, rather belying "fury and frantic indignation," but the tune is a spanking good one and wittily developed. As usual, at the mention of the organ Handel is emotionally involved; the soprano sings "The sacred organ's praise" in a most engagingly tender air. When Handel accompanied this aria on the organ, the public was treated to some extraordinary improvisations; we, unfortunately, must be satisfied with what is printed in the score. The soprano continues with "Orpheus could lead the savage race," an aria with the inscription *Alla Hornpipe*. This old English dance, which Handel knew from Purcell's theatre music and from the various country-dance anthologies published in the early 18th century, gave him an opportunity to deploy a sharply accented and syncopated orchestral accompaniment. This almost symphonic development of a motif in the orchestra is quite characteristic of the *Ode,* reflecting the proximity of the Concerti Grossi, Opus 6.

The choral numbers are all of the finest. Especially attractive is the interplay of chorus and orchestra in the opening choral number, "From Harmony, from heavenly Harmony." When the chorus declaims, the orchestra, elaborating a prickly motif, scurries around the voices; then, when the choral texture becomes more linear, the two groups engage in animated play, running up and down "through all the compass of the notes." There follows a section, "The diapason closing full in Man," where over long pedals the original motif in the orchestra, now chastened, becomes elegiac—a truly poetic musical realization of the imagery of the words, light, fragrant, and as English in feeling as Purcell, who himself would have smiled at it with pleasure (as did Chopin, who worshipped

[6] Handel did not waste any time. Muffat's work came from the printer's shop in the first part of the very same year! *Componimenti Musicali per il Cembalo* is available in a modern edition; see *Denkmäler der Tonkunst in Österreich,* III, 3.

the piece).[7]

The final chorus, alternating with the unaccompanied soprano, is stunning, as is the sudden entrance of the trumpet at the words "The trumpet shall be heard on high." Now, in the final fugue, "The dead shall live," Handel rises to grandeur. This is a rich, expansive, and festive piece, yet it is amiable rather than Olympian, as befits Dryden's poem and the happy occasion. When performed as a *componimento da camera*, by a modest-sized ensemble and with singers who prefer poetic expression to bawling, the *Ode for St. Cecilia's Day* is a most charming piece, easy on the ear.

The year 1739 closed with a revival of *Acis and Galatea*, and with new concertos, probably from Opus 6. Handel had some time on his hands: London experienced the worst cold in its known history, and the theatres were practically closed for two months. He used part of this unexpected leisure for the composition of *L'Allegro, il Penseroso, ed il Moderato*.[8] This fine holiday piece is not the work of a troubled or tired man; it is perhaps Handel's most accomplished pastoral composition, for which Milton supplied the incentive with his wondrous poetic imagery. *L'Allegro* certainly contradicts the popular image of the Puritan. This is the work of a pure poet, full of sensitivity, sympathy, admiration for the exuberance of nature, and tender feelings. It is not yet the work of the Titan whose awesome creative force will break through the reserve of the crippled, lonely prisoner of darkness. In *L'Allegro* Milton is a young poet with a radiant view of life and as yet without the heavy ballast of political-moral philosophy. Nor is *L'Allegro* affected by the formal, didactic, satirical, and philosophical poetry of the Augustan Age; there is no sign of the spirit of Locke, which banished imagination and the marvelous, nor does it reflect the elegant classical art of the English Rococo of Pope. *L'Allegro* was the work of a Spenserian poet of exquisite perfection of verbal finish and musical lilt. And this poet, who came from a musical family, knew and understood music, his companion—as was the Bible—from infancy.[9]

Milton was a friend and collaborator of Henry Lawes, the best-

---

[7] It defies the imagination how a serious scholar could see in this lilting English pastoral direct connections with Leibniz and his philosophical order of the universe. Even more amazing is that "From Harmony" is seen as a manifestation of the maternal strain in Handel's ancestry, of the Evangelical pastors, "lovers of church music, whose spirit guided our Handel from opera to the oratorio." This nonsense was not written by a Romantic patriot a century ago but by Walter Serauky in 1956.

[8] We shall follow Milton's original spelling rather than the corrected "Pensieroso."

[9] See the excellent study of the musical accomplishments of the elder Milton, *John Milton the Elder and his Music*, by Ernest Brennecke, New York, 1938.

known result of this collaboration being the musical setting of *Comus* in 1634. The original *Comus* intrigued many composers and librettists, several of whom made attempts at refurbishing it. Paolo Rolli, who, though house librettist to the various Haymarket Theatre companies, saw the essential exoticism of Italian opera in England, watched the English theatre for usable materials. In 1737 he reworked Milton's *Comus* for an opera, *Sabrina*, but it was a failure. Arne's *Comus* (1738) relied on still another version concocted by John Dalton, who "dramatized" Milton's original book with the aid of additional characters. It has been suggested that Handel was drawn to Milton because of Arne's new setting of the masque, which is quite possible. There are unmistakable signs that he studied Arne's music, and perhaps he asked Jennens for a Miltonian libretto; but it is more likely that both the idea and the selection of a poem originated with Jennens.

Jennens's arrangement of the libretto is altogether praiseworthy; he showed not only skill but very good understanding of the requirements of music. In the original poem (of which about one-third was used) *L'Allegro* is a self-contained entity constituting Part One, while *Il Penseroso* similarly forms its own section as Part Two. Jennens extracted the lines most suitable for musical setting and intermixed them. From the musical point of view this was a remarkably shrewd idea, preventing monotony by encouraging a variety of moods. The construction is also able. First there is a brief exchange in two recitatives and two arias between the Cheerful Man and the Pensive Man, which is in the nature of an introduction, announcing the forthcoming contest. Thereafter the two moods alternate, each having two or more numbers before yielding to the other. While Jennens very commendably sought contrast in the libretto, his attempt to resolve the Miltonian dichotomy by a sort of reconciliation in the third part, of his own devising and called *Il Moderato,* was unfortunate. Aside from the impossibility of matching Milton's poetry, the removal of the bucolic quality negated the *raison d'être* of the poem and inhibited Handel's imagination. *Il Moderato* also abandoned Jennens's excellent device whereby contrasting moods prevented sameness: all of the third part is given over to the Moderate Man.

Milton's exuberant heaping of image upon image, the lightning swiftness of apprehension that snatches a dozen meanings and compacts them into one, were qualities that found a foil in Handel. In Handel's rendering of the words there is a depth beneath the surface, a meaning not so much grasped as felt. The description of nature that abounds in *L'Allegro* is not an end in itself; both Milton and Handel bring nature into harmony with man's moods. They show him in his sunny moments, as he enjoys life in the countryside or in the teeming city. Opposed is the other mood, the contemplative, ruled by the goddess Melancholy, conjuring up the power of the past, the rewards and pleasures of the theatre, poetry, and music. The work has the ripeness and passion, the truth and experience, and the transfiguring imagination that together make what is lasting in art.

A delightful aspect of *L'Allegro* is that the arias extend to the chorus invitations that are taken up gracefully and most naturally, the chorus often sharing thematic material with the preceding solo. "Come and trip it as you go" sings the tenor, and the chorus responds with a gentle dance song, but "Laughter, holding both his sides" evokes a polyphonic merriment that makes the listener indeed hold his sides, for nothing like this "laughing chorus" has ever been set to music. "Come, but keep thy wonted state," with its ground bass and stately air, is entirely Purcellian. "Far from all resort of mirth" has most attractive *slow* coloraturas, but in the "bird songs" an extraordinary voice and skill is needed to cope with them. Singing skill of the highest order is indeed required everywhere: the ineffable song "Hide me from Day's garish eye" is consistently in the highest range of the soprano, and elsewhere the singers must vie with the lark and the nightingale.

The bucolic pieces, usually with obbligato instruments, are delightful. Whenever Milton speaks of "sweet birds," of "hounds and horns," of the "hedgerow elms or hillocks green," he evokes from the composer charming musical accents, lovely rhythms, and delectable sounds. (Incidentally, Urio's Te Deum is still remembered by the flute in "Sweet bird.") In "Or let the merry bells ring round" Handel uses the carillon he had had constructed for *Saul;* the descending scales, typical of English church-bell ringing, he knew from Purcell's "Bell Anthem," *Rejoice in the Lord Alway.* In the fine air "Oft on a plat of rising ground," the deep pizzicatos in the basses also echo distant church bells. Only once does the Cheerful Man lapse into a pensive mood, in "And ever against eating cares." Here we see how purely poetic is Handel's imagination and how he avoids any literal symbolism. The words "in notes with many a winding bout" are set to a melody that does wind gracefully, but so convincingly musical is this pictorialism, and so unobtrusive, that its naturalness is nowhere threatened. Almost any other Baroque composer would have seized the opportunity to set "soft Lydian airs" in the Lydian mode, but while Handel's music is "soft," he avoids the obvious symbolism, thereby depriving the exegetes of a splendid document. Such "documents" can be found, though, with a little diligence. It is rather amusing that Handel's only known Shakespearean "commentary," "sweetest Shakespeare, Fancy's child," is a march bearing the instruction *Pomposo:* it almost seems that Handel is being a little sarcastic. Later the aria, not a particularly outstanding one, turns into routine virtuoso coloraturas. Here was a chance not to be missed by later commentators, for the coloraturas were immediately declared deeply symbolic and named—the good Lord forgive the namer—"Shakespeare-Koloraturen."

The choral numbers are mostly intimate and beautifully coordinated with the arias, at times serving as the middle part for da capo combinations. At the end of the first part of *L'Allegro,* "Thus past the day, to bed they creep" is admirably expressive—and suggestive—of the mood of being "lull'd asleep." The chorus hums and buzzes in "The busy hum of men," and the trumpets and drums fall in with bright fanfares to illustrate "knights and barons." The ineffable calm and peace of "May at last my hoary age," with its gentle organ accompaniment, prepare the way for the final choruses, the first of which, a fine fugue, "These pleasures, Melancholy, give," resurrects a portion of the early Italian trio, *Quel fior che all'alba ride* (1708).

It was a mistake, similar to that in *Alexander's Feast,* to follow this ending with anything, least of all with poetry of Jennens's own making. The music composed for *Il Moderato* is still of very high quality, but the moods have wilted; it is difficult to follow apotheosis with homily. Handel ends *Il Moderato* with a grand choral piece, but he now feels that a lesson is called for, and resorts to a chorale *cantus firmus* to bring it home. *Erhalt uns Herr bei deinem Wort* is a great tune, and it is elaborated with great skill, but it is neither Miltonian nor English; both the spirit and the remarkable workmanship of this piece are out of character in this Purcellian work.

With *L'Allegro* Handel entered into a more intimate relationship with Purcell, but it was not only Purcell who bound him to the English scene; the music of his young colleague, Arne, attracted him—and was to attract him on future occasions. Arne's is not strong music; it is tender and guileless, there are few dramatic accents and even fewer tensions, but there is a felicity and domestic security present that is as attractive as it is thoroughly middle-class English. Arne is altogether un-Handelian, completely lacking in heroic grandeur, but it was exactly this quality that attracted Handel. While the impact of this fine composer on Handel was not comparable to that of Purcell, it was nevertheless perceptible and real.

L'Allegro is again one of those works that suffered constant alteration and perhaps the largest number of transpositions, ranging all the way from soprano to bass. Yet, though he changed and transposed, Handel never really hurt this score, and some of his later additions (which were considered in our discussion) became valuable permanent parts of the work. *L'Allegro* needs supporters—there is a noticeable coolness towards it in the Handelian literature. Even Julian Herbage considers it "a somewhat unsatisfactory entertainment," while other critics deplore the lack of dramatic interest and characterization, a criticism that would equally apply to *Messiah*. It seems to us, though, that this adverse judgment is due mainly to the mistake of considering *L'Allegro* an oratorio, which it is not. It is not even a "Klein-Oratorium," nor is it either a dramatic or a "sacred" piece, but an extended English ode-pastoral.

The lack of form and organization that some writers see in it is contradicted by the features of construction related above, but we suspect there are other factors at work here that cause misunderstanding. *L'Allegro* has a large number of accompanied recitatives, every one of them carefully composed and most of them superbly expressive. The recitative is usually a stumbling block for persons not close to opera. In a "sacred" work, such as a Bach Passion, they accept it without question because the text sanctifies everything, but in operas they would just as soon omit them, and indeed many recordings of operas do so. Recitatives usually begin with traditional formulas and the superficial observer does not notice when a piece assumes a physiognomy of its own. The recitatives in *L'Allegro* often approach the arioso, and their melodic line is vaulted. Another puzzling phenomenon is the presence of not a few unaccompanied or sparsely accompanied solo passages (often without bass or continuo) which seem "incomplete" to those accustomed to full and continuous harmony. Those, however, who can concentrate on the expressive qualities of the human voice will not find anything strange in such passages. No, *L'Allegro ed il Penseroso* is a masterpiece; the first part is surely Handel at his imaginative best, while Part Two, perhaps less consistently fresh in invention, is very close to it. In many ways this is the most adventurous and exploratory of Handel's works, looking far into the future. *L'Allegro*, to use Milton's words, "is most musical," and if its popularity is limited, that is because it "shuns the noise of folly."

The performance on February 27, 1740, for which the management still had to assure the public that the theatre was "secur'd against the Cold," presented sopranos Signora Francesina and "the Boy," the latter probably a son of the organist John Robinson and Ann Turner Robinson, who for some time was one of Handel's sopranos. The alto part was taken by the countertenor Russell, the tenor was Beard, and the bass Reinhold. It seems that *L'Allegro,* while not exactly a success, pleased more than the two large oratorios that preceded it, yet Handel found it necessary to revise the score repeatedly, mainly because of the different requirements of the ever-changing casts.

In March Handel revived *Saul* and *Esther,* and in April *Israel in Egypt* had one performance. Something, however, was amiss, because in September Handel suddenly resumed work on *Imeneo,* two years after it had been abandoned in favor of *Saul.* Immediately after this score was finished early in October, he embarked on still another opera, *Deidamia.* Thus his second—and as it turned out, last—season at Lincoln's Inn Fields was to be once more an opera venture. By acquiring Andreoni, a soprano castrato, and using his English singers and La Francesina, Handel scraped together an opera company. For the opening early in November, *Parnasso in Festa* was revived; then on St. Cecilia's Day *Imeneo* was presented and was a total failure that survived for only one repetition. The year 1741 opened bleak and cheerless. The cold wave no longer deterred the patrons of the opera house, yet they still failed to come in numbers. *Deidamia* opened on January 10, but by the 10th of February it too reached its end—there were only three performances. Walsh, always carefully timing his publishing affairs, was on hand with his invitation to subscription, but the response was so meagre that it had to be abandoned.

[5]

HANDEL'S LAST TWO operas are less known than *Agrippina*. That first of his full-fledged Italian operas, written thirty years earlier, is at least always mentioned with pride by all writers as having conquered the Venetians; the last two are merely recorded as utter failures. This is only one of the examples of the astonishing insufficiency of our knowledge of Handel and his works, because both of these operas are crammed full of delectable music. *Imeneo* may very well defy resuscitation because of its inane libretto, but *Deidamia* is a genuine masterpiece that will certainly come into its own when such works are prepared and performed by persons whose horizon is not limited to the operatic routine of the late 19th century. In both of these operas the music is worked with the finest brush, the melodies, many of them in dance forms and rhythms, are light, capricious, often bordering on the *style galant.* The short two- or four-measure tunes of the opera buffa make their entry into Handel's vocabulary; these tunes are "popular" in the best sense of the word. Once the tune is launched, there is, however, no telling what metric tricks Handel will play on its symmetry. Between these fresh tunes there appears the great pathos of the seria with its long-breathed, arching melodies, the grave accompanied recitatives and virtuoso coloraturas, but in most instances this tone is used for subtle contrast that serves comical ends. The texture of the score is transparent, the orchestral writing is of chamber-music delicacy, with particular attention paid to the bass line. Handel avoids the typical rumbling-ambling bass line of the Baroque; everything is light and airy, the composer repeatedly specifies cellos without basses, and at times there is no bass at all; more precisely, the violins are in charge of it. Both operas continue on the tack Handel took with *Serse*, but they depend even less on the da capo aria than does that fine score. That these last operas were not just dashed off and that Handel fussed a good deal over them is indicated by the alternate versions of arias; and the deliberate attempt at "modernization" is further attested by the ensembles and the use of the chorus.

Imeneo vacillates between opera buffa and comic pastoral; it is quite different from Porpora's setting of the same libretto for Venice in 1726. To be sure, what Handel composed was not the same book; Stampiglia's original text was put through the usual intellectual shredding process by an anonymous librettist until it became unrecognizable. Though a resounding failure as a theatrical piece, *Imeneo* contains delightful music; the harmonic scheme is bold, the tunes charming, and the writing always fastidiously elegant. There is a fine trio and an extended and well-constructed finale with chorus. The arias show the virtuoso but light style of the newer Neapolitan opera, something its contemporaries must have noticed because they called *Imeneo* an "operetta." Unfortunately, dramatic continuity and the theatre are so badly served by the lengthy simile arias ("I am like a vessel driven by storms"), and other irrelevant insertions, that nothing beyond a string of fine concert pieces can be salvaged from *Imeneo*.

As we have seen on other occasions, Handel was not a vindictive person. Paolo Rolli, who had deserted him for the Opera of the Nobility, was now taken back into Handel's good graces, and the wily and indestructible Italian rewarded him with a good libretto for *Deidamia*. Rolli, an inquisitive character who carried on an extensive correspondence, was evidently familiar with the latest operatic developments in Italy, at the same time keeping a weather eye on the popular English theatre, especially the ballad opera. While the libretto of *Deidamia* is not an opera buffa, it is decidedly comic in intent, if in a more subtle way than the contemporary buffa, perhaps as a result of Handel's discussions with the librettist, for, as we shall see, Handel had positive views on this subject. We know that he was not interested in opera buffa, but also that he had a good sense of humor, and that from *Faramondo* onward he was groping for a type of comic opera for which there was no precedent. Nevertheless, *Deidamia* does approach the buffa a little more closely than *Serse*, Handel's one declared comic opera, for the comedy in the former work is not altogether dependent on purely musical means. There are several scenes that are authentic comic opera in the theatrical sense.

On this occasion Rolli did not find it necessary to observe the traditions of the seria and proceeded to create good theatre. The story, taking its subject from the Trojan War, is well spun. The Greek kings on their way to Troy visit Lycomedes, whom they suspect of hiding Achilles. The oracle having told them that without Achilles they cannot succeed, the allied kings, Fenice (Phoenix), Nestor, and Odysseus, decide to ferret out the great hero, who is disguised as Pyrrha, one of the palace ladies. The leader of the group is Odysseus, an accomplished diplomat; we shall follow the Latin form used by Rolli and call him Ulysses, though here he is disguised as Antilochus.

The opera opens with a grave and splendid overture; but Handel's mocking intent is immediately made clear by the following aria of Deidamia, Lycomedes's daughter, delicately accompanied, which shows an ambiguity that is far removed from the spirit of the seria. She not only suspects the identity of Pyrrha but lets the listener understand, if he follows both text and music closely, that she knows Achilles more intimately than her innocent protestations would indicate. That Achilles, for a girl, is quite an enthusiastic huntsman worries Deidamia lest his disguise be detected. Her misgivings are expressed in a lilting minuet aria. Even Achilles's declaration of love (with a proviso for the paramount rights of the warrior) is in this delightful dance idiom. Nerea, the princess's confidante, attractively characterized as a sort of soubrette, is let in on the secret and promises assistance in charmingly tuneful, coquettish music. The resourceful Ulysses has a pretty good idea where to look for the great general and sees the means at hand; accordingly, concealing both his real identity and the fact that Penelope is waiting for him at home, knitting, he resorts to the old stratagem of extracting information by making love to Deidamia. At the same time, he instructs Fenice to open a second front with Nerea. The act ends with a "nightingale song," which, though one of those simile arias that can bedevil the action, is very charming and appropriate for the spot.

In the second act, Ulysses decides on more ardent wooing. Deidamia, anxious not to alienate him, does not protest, for while Ulysses is busy with her Achilles is safe. This scene is really a *conversation galante* and the music is no less *galante,* minuet-like, and full of refined little melodic turns. Achilles, listening from behind some bushes, is furious at this apparent acquiescence of Deidamia, and so is the music of his aria. Deidamia's following arias are all beautifully turned, even rising to the chromatic pathos of old. Nerea comes along, informing her mistress that Fenice has been making similar advances to her, and suggesting that both of them continue to play the game. Presently a stag hunt is organized by Ulysses, the ladies to play the part of Diana. What Ulysses wants to see is how the maiden Pyrrha handles the spear. Upon seeing her performance he no longer has any doubts. The scene where Lycomedes and his guests are getting ready for the hunt, solo and chorus nicely alternating, is dotted with short, simple, popular melodies. Dent correctly and very amusingly calls this chorus "beefy" in the English manner. There are indeed English characteristics, not "beefy" but Purcellian, in many another spot of this opera.

Now Ulysses attempts the dangerous trick of trying to make love to Pyrrha, hoping he can coax an admission from the embarrassed Achilles, but the move fails. Moreover, Deidamia overhears the scene, and now Ulysses finds himself under crossfire. At this point the opera frankly turns toward the buffa, as in desperation Ulysses tries to convince each of his sole devotion to her. He is ably abetted by Handel, who in the same aria provides different accents for the different appeals. After Ulysses leaves, Achilles gets a tongue-lashing from Deidamia, a superb *aria di carattere,* but her *perfido* and *barbaro* do not sound convincing; Handel is mocking, for the music is delightfully light. The intended travesty on the pathos of the seria is only enhanced by the fine middle portion of the da capo aria, where Deidamia gravely announces that the only solution to her predicament is death. The fermatas and the general pauses emphasize her dilemma in *hochpathetisch* style. Fenice, who also tries the courting game with Pyrrha-Achilles, concludes in no uncertain terms that "No, che ninfa non è," which is genuinely funny where its exact counterpart in *Siegfried* —"Das ist kein Mann!"—is merely ridiculous.

Rolli outdoes himself in the third act; the trap laid for Achilles is pure comic opera and excellent theatre. The crafty Ulysses invites the ladies of the palace to select presents from a treasure chest, but among the finery are hidden some weapons and a helmet. When Pyrrha sees these accoutrements of the warrior "she" forgets about ribbons, laces, and trinkets and reaches for the sword. At this moment a trumpeter, stationed outside by Ulysses, sounds an alarm. "The enemy is upon us," cries Ulysses, and before realizing that he is giving himself away, Achilles discards his disguise and rushes out to get at the invaders.

This excellent comic scene is followed by a serious exhortation, as Ulysses reminds the boyish Achilles that he owes his services to the Hellene cause. The unfrocked lady enthusiastically declares that he would like nothing better than to fight Hector, brandishing the sword and singing an aria that could come out of one of Verdi's operas: "Ai Greci questa spada sovra i nemici estinti." He no longer sings minuets but a heroic song, the orchestra seconding with fanfares. Rolli's skill is still in evidence in the next scene. After the stage empties, Ulysses is left alone with Deidamia, whom he tries to comfort. With mingled anger and sorrow she protests that since he has robbed her of her lover, what good are his words to her? She hopes that he will perish with his ship at sea. Ulysses understands her feelings and answers in a fine extended aria, distinguished by elaborate motivic work.

After everyone has assumed his rightful name and status, Handel turns to love music. Deidamia sings a tender aria; Nerea's is a more extroverted song. In the finale all are on the stage. First we hear a remarkable duet, sung by the principal pair, a busily hopping gigue—Handel has his tongue in his cheek, for everything in this brilliant piece smacks of "fooling." The pleasant final chorus draws the sound moral that opportunities of the moment should be enjoyed on the spot.

Deidamia would delight audiences even without any historical conditioning, but this extraordinary masterpiece must be properly prepared for a revival. There is a modern performing edition of the opera, published by Rudolf Steglich, which is a good beginning. With Dent he was one of the few to recognize *Deidamia* as a viable masterpiece; even Leichtentritt, usually a warm admirer of just about everything Handel wrote, is lukewarm towards this work. Walter Serauky, perhaps the most uncritical—and certainly the most prolix—worshipper of Handel, naturally has boundless admiration for *Deidamia*, which he expresses in no less than seventy pages, only to come to the conclusion that this opera is still another triumph of German versatility. To return to Steglich and his laudable efforts to make this score available to theatres, the musicologist in him unfortunately gets the better of the man of the theatre: his stage directions are naive where they should be sophisticated, his concept is Romantic and German, where it should be modern and Italian. One glance at the personnel of the first performance will show that for modern audiences the distribution of the roles is forbiddingly lopsided. Deidamia was sung by soprano Francesina, Nerea by soprano Monza, Achilles by soprano Edwards, Ulysses by castrato soprano Andreoni, Fenice by countertenor (or alto) Savage—five high voices to one lone male voice, the bass of Reinhold who sang Lycomedes. (Nestor does not sing.) While this is bad enough, Achilles, a female soprano, is disguised as a girl! It was not unusual in those days to write a male part for a soprano or alto as distinguished from a castrato, but in the case of Achilles this causes a theatrically impossible situation, contradicting Rolli's often almost da Pontean lines of believable comedy. All this will have to be considered by an enlightened editor, and he must also bear in mind that in most cases the original simple arias are preferable to the second, virtuoso, versions.

[6]

The season wore on. Handel, seemingly undisturbed, went back to the English works. On January 31, 1741, *L'Allegro*, "with several new Additions and Concertos," did a little better; Handel added eleven new numbers and shifted the parts, "the Boy" being replaced by the new Italian soprano, Monza. February 3 was given over to a benefit for Handel's old friend, John Christopher Smith, Sr. Then with the final *Deidamia* on the tenth the curtain was rung down on the opera composer, never to rise again. The season was rounded out by a command performance of *L'Allegro*, revivals of *Acis and Galatea* and *Saul*, and on the last evening a presentation of *L'Allegro ed il Penseroso*, without *Il Moderato*.

And now quiet settled down both on the theatre and on the house in Brook Street; Handel seemed at last to have acknowledged defeat and given up opera. What was his state of mind? He must have been baffled; neither oratorio nor opera was successful, only the pastorals found favor with the public. We see him compose, early in July, two fine Italian duets, *Quel fior ch'all'alba ride*—not to be confused with the early Italian piece by the same title—and *Nò di voi non vuò fidarmi*, for which there is no particular reason that we have been able to discover. Rumors once more began to circulate that Handel was ready to strike his colors, his career ended, and return to Germany. But personally he was still widely popular, and an open letter to the *London Daily Post* indicates the existence of an equally widespread sentiment deploring the decline of the composer who for a generation had been a prominent figure in London's artistic life. The anonymous author of the letter laments the neglect into which Handel has fallen, appealing to the reputation of Englishmen as "encouragers" of the arts, and exhorting them to "take [Handel] back into Favour." [10]

It is at this point that biographers paint a pathetic picture of a man whom life has defeated, who is bereft of his fighting courage, but who now finds lasting serenity by turning away from the theatre to Holy Scripture, henceforth dedicating his gifts to the service of religion. "The powers of his art," said Sir John Hawkins, "never appeared to so great advantage as when he made use of passages selected from Holy Writ." The danger of such a simplified and generalized interpretation is that it inhibits further investigation; it seems to explain the course of events without actually doing so. *Messiah,* which at this point is always the chief exhibit, does not reflect a change in Handel's artistic habit and thought.

Handel cannot be considered a compromise phenomenon. Only his time was that, and only his time can be censured. A lesser man would have perished in attempting to acclimatize English taste to the opera theatre, as indeed all the others did perish. Among the victims we must sadly count one of the greatest musical talents of the 17th century, which was rich in them: Purcell. He is of course far from forgotten, and enough of his music lives to assure him exceptional rank not only in Britain but everywhere else. His great dramatic powers, however, were not permitted to develop to full maturity, and he departed young from a scene where his particular talents were hobbled.

The impression that in Handel's case we are dealing with a categorical "conversion" is misleading; it is the result of half-serious historiography. As a matter of fact, such a conversion is inconceivable; in the case of a truly great creative personality, we shall always be made aware of the continuation of his earlier art, only perhaps enhanced. An undramatic composer will never become dramatic, and a miniaturist will not give us great symphonies. It could not be otherwise, because temperament is inborn; there is no such thing as a changing temperament, and this manifestly applies to Handel, but we cannot dismiss the circumstances that affect temperament. Unlike the artist in more recent times, whose every move seems to be influenced by his surroundings, the art of the Baroque masters was remarkably stable, yet this stability, so prominent on the Continent, did not extend to the free artist in England who managed his own affairs. The world had a greater influence on such an artist than on the *Kantor* in the service of a church or school or the *Kapellmeister* in the service of a princely court. There is here, then, a dichotomy that has led many a writer to false conclusions.

It is agreed that at this juncture of his career Handel reached a posi-

[10] April 4, 1741. Full text in Deutsch, p. 515.

tion that was to hold good for the future; but earlier biographers—and not a few later ones—consider his reorientation a "conversion to a sacred calling," implying that oratorio is noble and sacred while opera is something not quite clean and Christian. Time and again these critics bewail the "waste" of Handel's creative years on this frivolous and alien form of music. The same regret is expressed by some literary critics for the twenty years "wasted" by Milton during the interlude when he put aside his "singing robes" to engage in prose polemics. Burke was also seen "squandering his time on speeches and pamphlets." But could either of these men be imagined without their complementary activities? And who could say whether *Paradise Lost* and *Samson Agonistes* would have been created without the interlude of prose, or whether the great oratorios could have been composed without the operas preceding them?

More recent historians, fully aware of the fallacy of the religious conversion theory, advance the contrary view that Handel turned to the oratorio out of sheer necessity, fleeing into a safe world for lack of force to put up with the rough realities of opera in England. Stated thus categorically, what truth there is in such a statement becomes veiled. Handel did not lose the game because of lack of force. How can we speak of "lack of force" in the face of the resurgence that followed his repeated "bankruptcies"? Handel continued to compose operas in the face of defeat, remaining intrepid, competitive, and willing to take risks, until he became convinced that he had found a new and suitable outlet for his dramatic talents. Seen from this perspective, we must also question the theory of Müller-Blattau, set forth in an otherwise good article in *Die Musik in Geschichte und Gegenwart*, that *Alexander's Feast* is the turning point, the proof of Handel's decision. But this is to confuse a masterpiece such as Handel was likely to produce at any time and under any circumstances with a "decision" to which he had not come even after his disastrous collapse and his return from Aachen. There was no such decision made at the time of the composition of *Alexander's Feast*, for Handel did not yet see the situation clearly; the final crisis was the result of cumulative factors. In a speech at Halle University, Dent said that it was only in the middle forties that the period of experimentation ended for Handel. This is an equally untenable view, for the experimentation itself ended with *Athalia—Saul*, composed in 1738, is one of the greatest of the oratorios. The decision must have been made before *Samson* was composed, that is, in 1740–41. It may be helpful at this stage to review the process by which Handel was brought to a point of evident crisis that forced a decision.

Until about 1728, despite apparent variety, Handelian opera was confined within the relatively narrow limits of the composer's variant of the Venetian-Neapolitan opera. Meant to appeal in the main to aristocratic audiences, this opera inhabited a realm of experience not common to the vast majority of Englishmen. "The opera," says Hawkins, "was an entertainment calculated for the better sort of people in this country." Could it, if continued on this plane, have reached out to include the chief patrons of the English theatre, the educated middle classes? Italian opera did not have this capacity in 18th-century England. After Handel's return from his second Italian journey we notice a gradual change in the operas; they become lighter, and several of them won considerable popular success, being indeed very fine works. Still, he was decidedly constricted, and in the final operas one senses a conscious attempt to break through the routine of the opera seria. Some of these changes, as well as the employment of the chorus, were the result of his experiences with the first oratorios. It is interesting that this intelligent man, whose art grew out of opera, who lived his entire life within its sphere, never expressed his thoughts on the matter. But *Serse* shows that he began to ponder its nature as the English works proved to him that the great vessel of his imagination was too large for the restricted waters of the opera seria, and he must have recognized that even the new, lighter, and more popular style he essayed in the last operas would not lead anywhere; the public simply rejected Italian opera.

There were some other inhibitions that increasingly turned Handel's attention towards English works. Because the regulations affecting opera during Lent began to be enforced in earnest, from 1737 onwards Handel organized what amounted to oratorio "seasons," which of course also included odes and pastorals. It was during that same year, when he was in dire straits and his health at a low ebb, that the Lenten season at Covent Garden demonstrated that while the operas played to scant audiences, *Alexander's Feast, Deborah,* and *Esther* filled the house. We noticed that this astute observer and good businessman chose at that time to ignore these important omens and continued to risk his fortune and health in fanatic defense of Italian opera. But the great success of the English works at Oxford must again have been in his mind when the final curtain went down on *Deidamia*.

He now saw that there was absolutely no future for Italian opera, and that not even the temporary successes of the past decades could be repeated—the fate of *Serse* and *Deidamia* must have been a bitter disappointment. Yet it was the businessman in Handel who sized up the situation ahead of the composer. Beginning with 1739, Handel abandoned the subscriptions, the only known safe system of providing working capital and basic income for a repertory theatre.[11] Henceforth anyone who could afford a single admission fee was able to attend the theatre, and it was thus that Handel made the first move towards attracting the cultivated English middle classes instead of the aristocratic patrons of the Italian opera. So the impresario; but the composer was not yet convinced that he should altogether forsake opera for oratorio; after all, both *Saul* and *Israel in Egypt* were failures. At this point there was a crisis, perhaps the only real crisis in his life; here, then, would be the human explanation for Handel's "conversion" to oratorio. But beyond this we must find the purely artistic reasons; and it seems to us that the solution of his dilemma owes a good deal to that "magnificent failure," *Israel in Egypt*.

Clearly, the greatest attraction to Handel in the English works was the chorus; we have seen that under the influence of oratorio, ode, and pastoral, he tried to use the chorus even in the operas. Had it not been for the lack of a permanent chorus in the contemporary opera house (though not of course in Vienna and Paris), he undoubtedly would have extended its role in the opera. As it was, most of the time he had to be satisfied with a "chorus" made up of a solo ensemble. In *Israel* Handel overreached himself, presenting a plethora of great choruses without "songs." The public did not like it at all, and Handel realized that he must return to the reasonable balance of the two elements achieved in *Saul*. The moment he understood that this oratorio was still music drama—theatre—even though the visual element was suppressed by a hypocritical society, the course of his remaining creative years was irrevocably set, and the resilient old warrior immediately threw off his indecision. That this is more than a guess is borne out by the events that took place about this time.

Lord Middlesex, who had already tried his hand at managing theatre, the New Theatre in the Haymarket, now founded a replica of the Opera of the Nobility, moving across to *the* opera house, the old Haymarket Theatre. Heidegger, whose masquerades and ridottos were still remembered, must have been in some way connected with the affair but avoided publicity so as not to embarrass the distinguished "undertaker." The peregrinating Rolli was immediately on hand, and Middlesex acquired a first-class composer, Baldassare Galuppi, for musical director. A good Italian cast with two castratos, one of them the Andreoni of Handel's last troupe, was assembled, the season opening on October 31, 1741,

[11] It was in England that "subscription" opera and concert series originated, an example later emulated wherever music became an organized business, wrapped in social amenities.

with a pasticcio, *Alessandro in Persia,* put together by Galuppi from the works of half a dozen composers, including himself. The pasticcio was very successful—twenty-one performances during the season—and it seemed that this new corporation of aristocrats would restore Italian opera to its erstwhile glory. A year or two before, Handel would have considered the mere formation of such a company *casus belli,* exploding into frantic activity, recruiting a troupe and composing operas, ready to vanquish, before they could gain a foothold, the foolhardy who dared to challenge him. Instead, he attended the opening night at the Haymarket Theatre as a spectator—and "laughed." The laughter was not directed at Galuppi's pasticcio—Handel was guilty of many of those himself—but at the realization that he no longer had to struggle with such things. The whole situation now seemed to him so ridiculous that, as he wrote to Jennens, it made him "very merry all along the journey" to Dublin. His mind was made up; he no longer saw competition in Italian opera because he had altogether different plans.

So when Handel left for Dublin early in November 1741 (to paraphrase Penseroso somewhat), "old experience attained to something like prophetic strain." At fifty-six he was to start the artistic voyage to reach final equilibrium, turning altogether to the oratorio. That he realized he had at last made landfall cannot be doubted; the great works that follow prove this conclusively. Now he becomes the composer of giant events and giant feelings; the world widens before him as space and time widen before De Quincey's opium eater. To the much-tried composer the oratorio now becomes, as neither Italian cantata nor German Passion could, a personal genre.

XIII

WHILE THE ACCUMULATED REASONS FOR A RADICAL
artistic reorientation related in the preceding chapter should have sufficed
to bring about the change, the *deus ex machina* was still needed to give it
a concrete beginning and direction; throughout Handel's life this was so,
and the momentous step he was about to take was no exception. The calm
we have seen in the Brook Street house where Handel whiled away the
time composing Italian chamber duets was suddenly shattered by furious
activity. At the end of the summer of 1741, Handel began *Messiah*. Part I
was completed in six days, another nine days were needed for Part II, and
six more for Part III; after three days for "filling out" the score, i.e. completing the orchestration, the great work was achieved. The new incentive
was so powerful that upon affixing the date to the last page of *Messiah*,
September 14, Handel immediately began *Samson*, and this other gigantic
work was fully sketched by the end of October.

Messiah is a unique work in Handel's *oeuvre*, the only biblical
oratorio calling on the New Testament.[1] *Messiah* is not typical of the
Handelian oratorio because, while it is a justly admired and appealing
masterpiece, it is undramatic. We notice that immediately upon finishing
Messiah, Handel returned to the dramatic oratorio. There must have been
an unusual incentive for him to compose so special a work, and this incen-

[1] *Theodora*, the other "Christian" oratorio, was not, of course, derived from Scripture but from a 17th-century historical novel. It goes without saying that *La Resurrezione* (p. 84), apart from being a youthful work, cannot be counted among the
English oratorios.

tive clearly came from Dublin, whither Handel was invited by the Lord Lieutenant of Ireland, the Duke of Devonshire, on behalf of three of the Dublin charity organizations. When this invitation was extended is not known, but there is a report that the Duke was in London in February 1741. Handel was well known in Dublin, where his works were often played, especially for charity benefits. *Messiah* must have been especially planned for such a charitable benefit, a fact that would explain its specific nature, the consequence of a request based on his reputation as a composer of church music.

When Handel arrived in Ireland he was described in Faulkner's *Dublin Journal* of November 21 as "a Gentleman universally known by his excellent Compositions in all kinds of Musick, and particularly for his *Te Deum, Jubilate, Anthems,* and other compositions in Church Musick." The notice emphasized that works of this nature "for some Years past have principally consisted the Entertainments in the Round Church, which have so greatly contributed to support the Charity of Mercer's-Hospital." Only one piece of available documentary evidence, however, specifically backs up our conclusion. Reporting on the final rehearsal of "Mr. Handel's new Grand Sacred Oratorio, called, The MESSIAH," the *Dublin Journal* expressly stated that the oratorio was "composed for this Noble and Grand Charity." Though the *Journal's* writer echoed a belief shared by most Dubliners, we cannot positively ascertain whether he spoke from first-hand knowledge, because the communications on the subject known to have taken place between Dublin and London in the fall of 1741 have not survived; but the chronicles furnish strong circumstantial support.

Upon arrival in the Irish capital, Handel immediately mapped out his plans, as was his custom, by scheduling everything he considered attractive to the public. A subscription series of six concerts was announced in December, and another set in February 1742, but in neither of these very successful series was *Messiah* included, though the finished score was in Handel's travelling bags. It was not until April 13, almost five months after his arrival, that *Messiah* was introduced on the occasion of a great and very special charity gathering "For the relief of the Prisoners in the several Gaols, and for the Support of Mercer's Hospital in Stephen Street, and of the Charitable Infirmary on the Inn's Quay." That this was regarded as an extraordinary event is clear from the long preparations supervised by a committee, and from the interest shown by the highest civic and religious authorities. Handel had the assistance of the choirs of both Christ Church and St. Patrick's Cathedrals, the latter also an Anglican church, whose dean at the time was Jonathan Swift, known for his dislike of music. The request of the Governors of Mercer's Hospital, however, was for such a noble purpose that even the irascible Dean had to give his permission for his choristers to participate.

A number of other signs point to an exclusive arrangement for charitable purposes. For all of Handel's concerts in Dublin, the tickets were obtainable at his house in Abbey Street, but the sale of tickets for *Messiah* was expressly taken out of his hands; they had to be procured at the music hall itself or at Neale's music store. Now William Neale was not only the head of the consortium that built the New Music Hall for the Charitable Music Society, but also Secretary of the Dublin Charities' Commission. Evidently the Society was in complete charge of the production; in fact, they even procured the singers from the cathedral choirs. That this was so is once more documented by the fact that with the repeat performance of *Messiah* Handel's privilege of selling tickets at his house —and hence for his own ends—was restored, indicating that the original purpose having been achieved, Handel now "owned" his *Messiah*.

Mainwaring, speaking of the role *Messiah* played in the deliverance of the prisoners, wrote: "There was a peculiar propriety in this design from the subject of the Oratorio itself; and there was a peculiar grace in it from the situation of Handel's affairs." *Messiah* remained a work that "fed the hungry, clothed the naked, fostered the orphan" (Burney). Its final popularity was due to its association with the Foundling Hospital; it was the yearly charity performances given in the chapel there from 1750 on under Handel's leadership that started the oratorio on its unexampled career.

It is highly significant that Handel never again returned to the Christian-contemplative oratorio; there must have been a reason for that. As we shall see, though the reception of the Dublin production was one of the greatest artistic triumphs of his life, when Handel returned to London he at first refrained from presenting the oratorio to the London public. It was only at the end of a very successful run of *Samson* that he virtually slipped *Messiah* into his repertory, carefully avoiding even mentioning the title. In all announcements save one, the word *Messiah* was avoided until 1749; the title was always "A new sacred Oratorio." *Israel in Egypt,* which had no libretto paraphrasing the Bible but offered selected lines from Exodus in a musical setting, deeply shocked many Englishmen. So here it was, the unbelievable, Holy Scripture in the flesh, uttered—nay, sung—by the most lascivious and immoral of persons, theatre folk, and accompanied by a detestable band of fiddlers in the Play-House, that damnable institution where no true Christian could enter without being

A Schlop
B Vnfer Frawen Kirch
C J Morits Kirch
D S Vlrichs Kirch
E S Georgen Kirch
F Geben Alter
G Gottes Haus
H Rats Keller
I Badstube
K Cantoley
L Der Dom

M Rats Thurn
N Schlos
O Wasser Kunst
P Cuy Hauf
Q Spital Johann
R Vlrichs Thor
S Gebr Thor
T Galck Thor
V Morits Thor
W Mosker Brücke
X Neue Mühl

Hall in Sachsen
Gegen Abend.

New York Public Library

PLATE I

Halle in the 17th century. Engraving from *Topographia Saxoniae inferioris*
(1653), by the heirs of Matthaeus Merian. The Liebfraukirche is slightly
to the right of the center; the Cathedral is the bulky building with the
small cross on its roof, partway to the left

PLATE II

Queen Anne, with the Duke
of Gloucester. Painting
after Sir Godfrey Kneller
(c. 1694)

King George I. Painting by
Sir Godfrey Kneller

PLATE III

King George II. Painting by
Thomas Hudson

Queen Caroline. Painting by
Charles Jervas

PLATE IV

George Frideric Handel. Engraving after a portrait by Thomas Hudson

PLATE V

Handel's house on Brook Street. Water-color signed "L.M."

Mr. Gerald Coke

The first London announcement of *Messiah*, in the *Daily Advertiser*, March 19, 1743. Note the absence of the oratorio's title; its use was not risked until 1749

British Museum

By SUBSCRIPTION.
The Ninth Night.
AT the Theatre Royal in Covent-Garden, on Wednesday next, will be perform'd
A NEW SACRED ORATORIO.
With a CONCERTO on the ORGAN.
And a Solo on the Violin by Mr. DUBOURG.
Tickets will be deliver'd to Subscribers on Tuesday next, at Mr. Handel's House in Brooke-Street.
Pit and Boxes to be put together, and no Persons to be admitted without Tickets, which will be deliver'd that Day, at the Office in Covent-Garden Theatre; at Half a Guinea each. First Gallery 5s. Upper Gallery 3s. 6d.
The Galleries will be open'd at Four, Pit and Boxes at Five.
To begin at Six o'Clock.

PLATE VI

Johann Mattheson

Alessandro Scarlatti

PLATE VII

The Bettman Archive

Thomas Arne

John Gay

Music Division, The New York Public Library

John Christopher Smith, junior

The Bettman Archive

PLATE VIII — *Handel's Competitors*

Giovanni Bononcini

Nicola Porpora

John Christopher Pepusch

PLATE IX — *Handel's Singers*

Susanna Maria Cibber (*left*)

Francesca Cuzzoni (*above*)

Faustina Bordoni (*bottom left*)

John Beard. After a portrait by Thomas Hudson

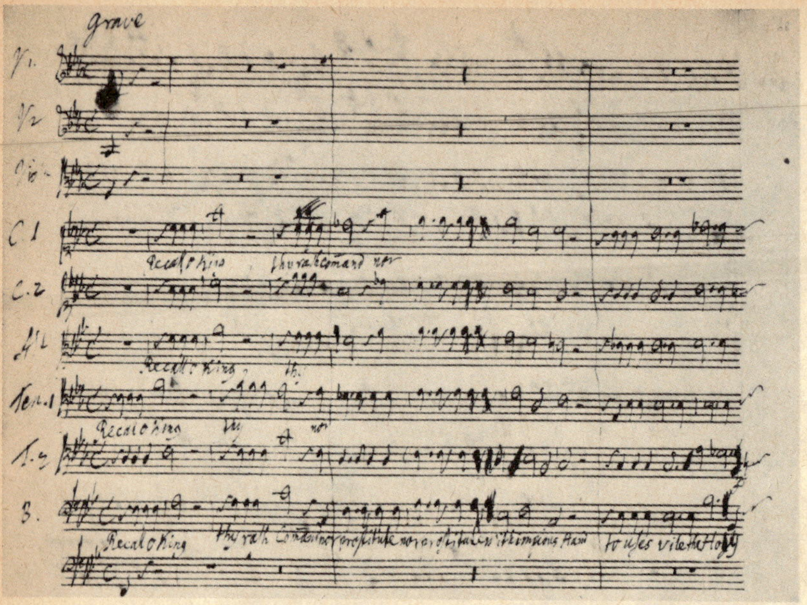

Page from the autograph manuscript of the oratorio *Belshazzar*

PLATE X

British Museum

Page from the autograph manuscript of the opera *Tolomeo*

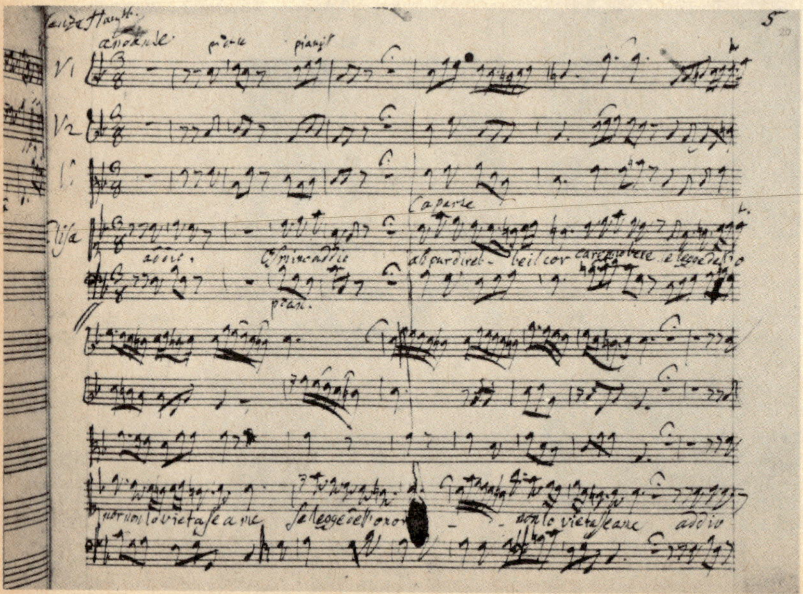

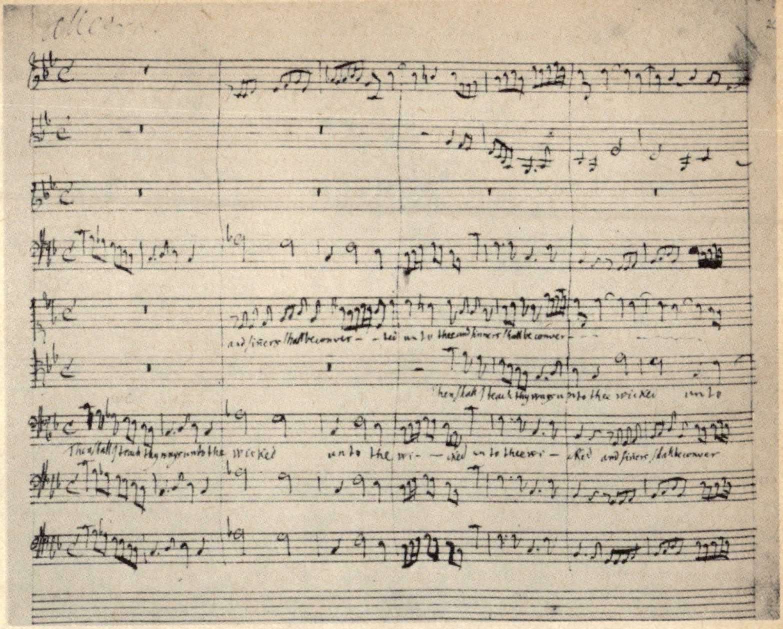

Page from the autograph manuscript of the anthem *Have mercy upon me, O God*

British Museum PLATE XI

Page from the autograph manuscript of the third *Grand Concerto,* Opus 6

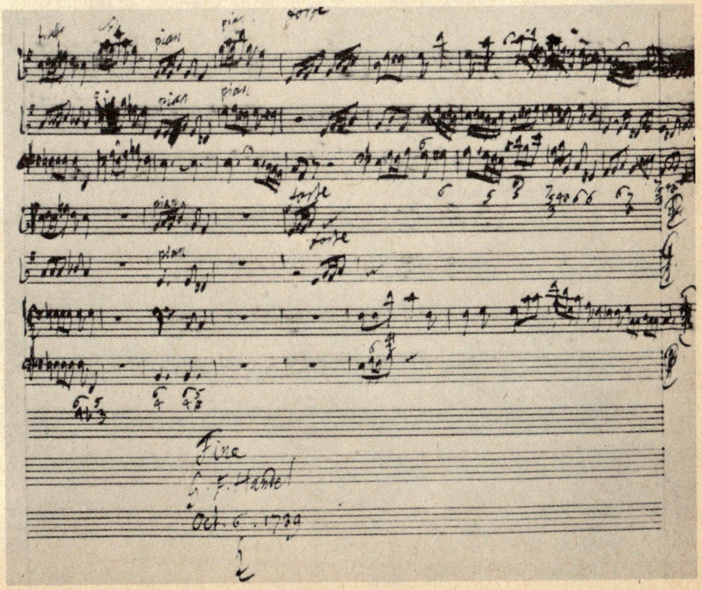

PLATE XII

SIX
CONCERTOS
For the
Harpsichord or Organ
COMPOS'D BY
Mr. HANDEL.

∴ These Six Concertos were Publish'd by Mr. Walsh from my own Copy Corrected by my Self, and to Him only I have given my Right therein. George Frideric Handel.

London. Printed for I. Walsh in Catharine Street in the Strand.

Of whom may be had
The Instrumental Parts to the above Six Concertos.

Just Publish'd for the Organ or Harpsicord.

Rameaus Concertos	Hasse's Concertos	Alberti's Lessons
Robengrave's 6 Double Fugues,	Handel's Fugues	Pelcetti's Lessons
with Scarlatti's Celebrated Lessons,	Rolengrave's 18 Voluntaries	Handel's Lessons
Stanley's Concertos	Zipoli's Voluntaries	Loeillet's Lessons
Avisous Concertos	Palquinis Voluntaries	Handel's 60 Overtures
Burgh's Concertos	Baltasris Voluntaries	Handel's 80 Songs

Title page of the first set of organ concertos, Opus 4. Note Handel's warning, which was one way to discourage or disavow pirated editions

ACIS and GALATEA:

AN ENGLISH

PASTORAL OPERA.

In THREE ACTS.

As it is Perform'd at the

NEW THEATRE in the HAY-MARKET,

Set to MUSICK

By Mr. HANDEL.

LONDON:

Printed for J. WATTS at the Printing-Office in
Wild-Court near Lincoln's-Inn Fields.

MDCCXXXII.

[Price Six Pence.]

Title page of *Acis and Galatea*. Note the designation "English pastoral opera," though to this day the work is often listed as a secular oratorio

PLATE XIII

Title page of Walsh's edition of the opera *Rinaldo*. As a rule, only "songs" were printed, with a simple accompaniment, to prevent performing material from falling into the hands of unauthorized persons

British Museum

S A M S O N.

AN

O R A T O R I O.

As it is Perform'd at the

THEATRE-ROYAL *in* Covent-Garden.

Alter'd and adapted to the Stage from the SAMSON AGONISTES of *John Milton*.

Set to Musick by GEORGE FREDERICK HANDEL.

L O N D O N:

Printed for J. and R. TONSON in the *Strand*.

MDCC XLIII.

Title page of the libretto of *Samson*. Although it explicitly states that the word book was "adapted to the Stage" from Milton's *Samson Agonistes*, the work is always treated as a "sacred biblical oratorio"

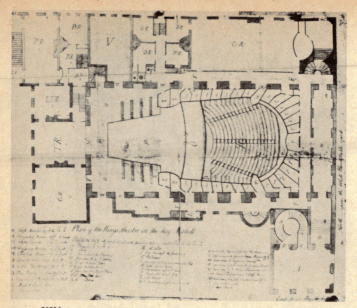

PLATE XIV

The King's Theatre in the Haymarket. After a drawing by William Capon (between 1777 and 1789)
British Museum

Interior of the Theatre in Covent Garden, as it was in Handel's time. From an engraving showing John Beard addressing the audience during the price riots, March 3, 1763.
Raymond Mander and Joe Mitchenson Theatre Collection

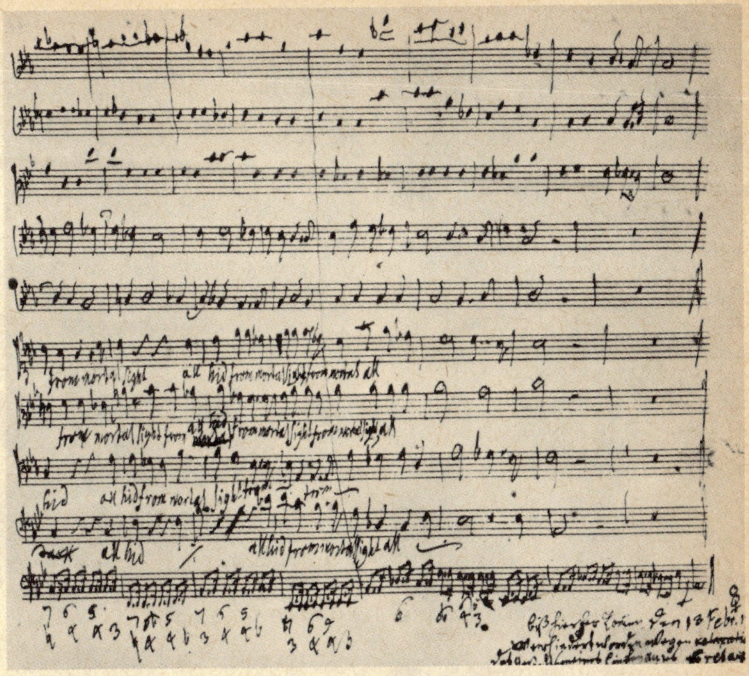

PLATE XV

The page from *Jephtha* where Handel temporarily stopped composing. At the bottom of the page he wrote: biss hierher kom̄en den 13 Febr. 1751 verhindert worden wegen ~~relaxation~~ des gesichts meines linken auges so relaxt. (got so far as this on Wednesday, February 13, 1751, unable to continue because of [the?] weakening of the sight of my left eye.) By this time, Handel's command of his native language was insecure; first he used the English word "relaxation," then, crossing it out, turned it into a verb, "so relaxt"

British Museum

PLATE XVI

Charles Burney. After a painting by
Sir Joshua Reynolds (*left*)

Sir John Hawkins (*right*)

Friedrich Chrysander. Detail from a painting
by Leopold Graf von Kalckreuth
(*bottom left*)

soiled. This indignation contributed to the dismal failure of *Israel in Egypt*. Considering the situation in London, it was hardly possible that Handel would have contemplated, out of sheer religious ecstasy, a work that quotes not only from the Old Testament, hitherto his only source for oratorio in England, but from the Gospels—episodes from the life of Christ presented in the theatre! The subsequent history of *Messiah* amply proves that Handel knew what he was doing; he could write such a work for Dublin, where everyone understood its purpose, but not for London. Another remarkable fact should be mentioned here: no score of *Messiah* appeared in Handel's lifetime. *Samson,* composed only a few days after *Messiah,* was almost immediately published by Walsh, but he made no effort to produce any edition of *Messiah,* which did not appear until 1763. That there was uncertainty about the advisability of publishing the oratorio, or even the customary selection of "songs," was demonstrated by William C. Smith (*Concerning Handel*), who proved that the engraved plates were ready in 1749! It stands to reason that once this great work was in existence, Handel was not disposed to let it languish, and he was not unmindful of its original purpose, to aid charity, which was eventually what made *Messiah* acceptable to London.

Now let us examine the musical elements that clearly support the contention that *Messiah* was composed for a specific occasion, and thus was conditioned by available musical forces.

Contrary to the impression firmly established for almost two centuries, the original orchestra Handel used in *Messiah* was not massive but slight and delicate. This unusually modest orchestra also indicates that *Messiah* was planned for the small Dublin State Band under Matthew Dubourg, an ensemble that Swift called "a club of fiddlers." The ubiquitous oboes and bassoons of the Baroque orchestra were missing; only the two trumpets and kettledrums were added in some of the choruses (one trumpet also appears in one of the arias because the text calls for it). The string body itself was so small that Handel did not find it possible to subdivide it in the concerto grosso manner, as had been his custom; the "senza ripieno" signs first appear in the London performances. Subsequent productions of *Messiah* saw the orchestra considerably enlarged, the Foundling Hospital parts using a fair concerto-grosso string orchestra of about twenty, four oboes, four bassoons, two each of trumpets, horns, and timpani. We also have at least one set of oboe parts in Handel's handwriting that he wrote in 1749 to "Their sound is gone out."

Handel composed the alto arias in *Messiah* for Mrs. Cibber. As Larsen demonstrated, an aria like "He was despised" could not have been composed with an Italian singer in mind but for one particularly adept at good, affective English declamation. This is corroborated by Burney, who also states that the alto arias "had been originally composed for Mrs. Cibber." Burney says that "Handel was very fond of Mrs. Cibber, whose voice and manners had softened his severity for her want of musical knowledge." Susanna Cibber was a great tragedienne who played opposite Garrick, and though her singing voice was minuscule, her power of communication made even Handel forget about her "mere thread of a voice." Their friendship dated from about 1738, and it rested on mutual fondness.

Mrs. Cibber's private life is harshly judged by most historians, though it is difficult to see on what they based their strictures. Even Sir Newman Flower, highly suspicious of her—after all, she was an actress—grudgingly admits that Handel's relationship with her "matured into a great and clean friendship." A more solid moral affidavit than this is unimaginable. But Susanna was unhappily married to a besotted scoundrel, Theophilus Cibber, the playwright's son, who pursued her with a lawsuit. Terrified of her vicious husband, she fled to a hideaway, known only to Handel, the actor Quinn (a mutual friend), and one or two other intimates, who visited her frequently. Evidently a public appearance in London was out of the question in 1741. Her friends sought more security for the panic-stricken actress, and Handel must have been party to the plan for Mrs. Cibber to seek refuge in Ireland, out of reach of her husband. Though the first notice of her presence in Dublin is from December 12, 1741, she must have been there earlier, for she was ready to sing in Handel's concerts from the very beginning.[2]

Against these facts in support of the opinion that *Messiah* was composed in response to a particular commission, all that the contrary view can offer are stories of rapture during the composition of *Messiah*, stories that remain unsubstantiated. Handel is supposed to have sequestered himself in his study for weeks, "barely touching food," and his servant and the few visitors that were admitted found him alternately weeping or praying, or just staring into eternity, a physical-emotional condition that surely would not permit the incredible achievement of composing this colossal score in twenty-four days. "I did think I did see all Heaven before me and the great God Himself," he was supposed to have declared. *Mes-*

[2] The stories that Mrs. Cibber and Handel travelled together to Dublin are obviously apocryphal. Because of adverse winds, Handel was detained for several days in Chester, where the future historian, Charles Burney, then fifteen, was at school. Burney, who "watched him narrowly as long as he remained in Chester," would surely have discovered such a celebrated companion.

siah is a great work clearly conceived with love and creative rapture, its inspired quality being consistently high; nor should anyone doubt Handel's sincere Christian devotion. But the mental conditions described in these stories are wholly uncharacteristic of both the man and the composer. It is remarkable that in this trance-like state, that marvelous apparatus, Handel's memory, worked so superbly, for *Messiah* is studded with the most imaginative adaptations of Italian love lyrics. To be sure, these were his own compositions, but while there are no foreign borrowings in *Messiah,* the parody technique is conspicuously present, and that requires far more musical concentration than prayer. We find it rather touching when one of our German colleagues, commenting on the famous statement that Handel "did see the great God Himself," says that this "is hardly susceptible of proof." This is a sound step toward a saner approach to *Messiah* and its role in Handel's life and work.

Dublin, the Irish capital, the birthplace of Swift and Sheridan and the city where Congreve was brought up, could look back upon a long musical past when Handel's memorable visit took place. One of her native sons, the monk Tuotilo, who became famous around 900 in the Irish settlement of St. Gall, Switzerland, is still remembered with admiration for his Christmas trope, *Hodie cantandus est nobis puer.* The two cathedrals of the city, though partially rebuilt, are of great antiquity, and their musical history is an honorable one; in Handel's time they had small but well-appointed choirs. Being Irish, the choristers were good not only at singing: a late 17th-century decree forbade them or anyone else the wearing of swords near the cathedrals. Many fine musicians resided or visited in Dublin; besides Handel, Arne and Geminiani were fond of the city in the 18th century. The reader will remember the stormy career of Sigismund Kusser in Hamburg (see p. 30 f.). After leaving the German maritime city he settled in its Irish counterpart, becoming in 1710 the leading musical light in Dublin. At his death he was succeeded by Matthew Dubourg. A Londoner by birth, Dubourg (1703–1767), a pupil and lifelong friend of Geminiani, was a very good violinist and all-round musician who began his career as a child prodigy at Britton's concerts in the loft above the "small-coal man's" bins; Handel liked and trusted him. As Kusser's successor in 1728 he became vice-regal conductor. Opera started immediately following its introduction in London, and Dublin not only performed Scarlatti's *Pyrrhus and Demetrius* in 1711 but imported the famous Nicolini to sing in it. The phenomenal success of the *Beggar's Opera* caused a spate of Irish ballad operas, and the London Royal Academy of Music also soon found a replica in Dublin. In 1731 a concert hall was built on Crow Street, and a second very fine hall in Fishamble Street opened its doors in 1741 a few weeks before Handel's arrival. Though small by modern standards, seating about six hundred, the New Music Hall was excellent; Handel praised it highly. Its normal capacity could be extended when the ladies came without hoops and the gentlemen without swords. This they were requested to do for the performance of *Messiah;* as a result "an Hundred Persons more" could be accommodated "with full ease." The request for the ladies to appear without hoops became as firm a custom at important concerts (as long as hoops were worn) as the rising of the audience at the singing of the Hallelujah Chorus.

Dublin had several musical societies, for the Irish were and are a music-loving people, but these societies were unusual in that they were organized for charitable purposes. This was owing to the wretched social conditions in Ireland, compared to which London's poor and the inmates of her prisons and hospitals were well off. A public-spirited citizenry, shocked by the conditions in the prisons and hospitals, wanted to alleviate the misery of these unfortunates, raising funds for this humanitarian purpose through public concerts. The New Music Hall in Fishamble Street was built at the behest of the Charitable Music Society under the guidance of William Neale, a music publisher, and was known for a while as Neale's Hall. Since Neale, as we have noted, was also the secretary of Dublin's Charities Commission, he not only had a commanding position in the great events that were to follow but in all probability was party to the invitation that resulted in the creation and production of *Messiah*. Many a hopeless prisoner wasting away in jail for paltry debts was freed by payments to his creditor from the proceeds of the concerts.

On November 18 "the celebrated Dr. Handell" arrived in Dublin; the newspapers soon learned he neither possessed the doctor's degree nor wished to have one. The trip was delayed for several days by unfavorable winds. He must have travelled with an inordinate amount of baggage, for the scores and parts of the eight major works performed, and of the concertos and other numbers, must have filled a large trunk. But apparently he took with him a small organ too, for in one of his letters to Jennens he refers to "my organ." This is quite probable because the New Music Hall did not as yet have an organ.[3] It was the first time that Handel had to rely on untried local forces for the bulk of his performers. We know that he was responsible for the presence in Dublin of Susanna

[3] Grattan Flood, in his *Fishamble Street Music Hall*, reports that as a departing gesture Handel presented an organ to the Hall; it was used when the new season of the Charitable and Musical Society opened on October 8, 1742.

Cibber, and two other singers and the organist were also his appointees. One of these was an Italian soprano, Christina Maria Avoglio, who appeared from nowhere in London in 1740 and just as suddenly disappeared without a trace four years later. She was a good soprano, and Handel took her to Dublin. While waiting in Chester, Handel made the acquaintance of an organist by the name of Maclaine and his wife, a soprano, both of whom he engaged for Dublin. Apparently they were good enough musicians for his purposes, but absolutely nothing further is known about the couple.

On December 14 the subscription sale of tickets began at Handel's home in Abbey Street, though his first public concert was preceded by a charity event at the Round Church (St. Andrew's), where the *Utrecht Te Deum and Jubilate* and one of the Coronation Anthems were performed and Handel played the organ, for which he was officially thanked. The first concert took place on December 23, the program consisting of all three parts of *L'Allegro*, "two concertos for several instruments, and a concerto on the Organ." The reception was enthusiastic: "The Performance was superior to any Thing of the Kind in this Kingdom before," said the *Dublin Journal*. Handel reported to Jennens in a long letter (Deutsch, 530) that the subscription was such a complete success that for all six nights "I needed not sell one single Ticket at the Door." He praised the performers and found that "the Musick sounds delightfully in this charming Room, which puts me in such Spirits (and my Health being so good) that I exert myself on my Organ with more than usual Success." For the rest, this is a careful letter. Handel assures Jennens that "the Words of the *Moderato* are vastly admired," and requests his correspondent to convey his "most devoted Respects" to a bevy of aristocratic patrons and friends. The praise bestowed on the poetry of *Il Moderato* did not prevent Handel from omitting it in subsequent performances in favor of the *Ode for St. Cecilia's Day*.

The fare for the ensuing concerts consisted (in addition to a repetition of *L'Allegro*) of *Acis and Galatea*, the *Ode for St. Cecilia's Day*, and *Esther*, each program being repeated together with the various concertos. When only half of them had taken place, the success of the subscription concerts was so manifest that by February 6, 1742, a second series of six concerts was advertised in the *Dublin Journal*, "on the same Footing as the last." In this series Handel performed *Alexander's Feast*, *L'Allegro*, *Esther*, and *Hymen*. The latter, "a new Serenata," was in reality a concert performance of *Imeneo* (see p. 322); Handel still had a lingering fondness for this unlucky opera.

The first announcement of *Messiah* appeared in the *Dublin Journal* on March 27. The public rehearsal, held on April 9, was reported in the newspapers as a most successful "elegant Entertainment" and "was allowed by the greatest Judges to be the finest Composition of Musick that ever was heard." Finally, on April 13, 1742, the "New Grand Sacred Oratorio, called The MESSIAH," received its official première. Signora Avoglio and Mrs. Maclaine took the soprano parts, the altos were Mrs. Cibber, William Lambe, and Joseph Ward, the tenors James Baileys and John Church, and the basses John Hill and John Mason. All the men came from the local church choirs. It will be seen that although *Messiah* has no dramatic figures (only the four customary vocal designations), Handel employed nine solo singers. This was of some importance, because in contemporary practice the soloists sang with the chorus, and they must have constituted a substantial part of the small ensemble, which was reinforced by several other singers from the two cathedrals.

The Charities Commission, which carried on the negotiations for obtaining the singers with the deans of the cathedrals, had no difficulty with Christ Church, but Dean Swift of St. Patrick's, already close to a mental collapse, caused them a good deal of anguish. At first he gave the Committee permission to draw six singers from his choir, subsequently denying that he ever gave such permission. The document, printed in Swift's *Correspondence*, is more than an irascible man's animadversions.

> And whereas it hath been reported, that I gave a licence to certain vicars [choral] to assist at a club of fiddlers in Fishamble Street, I do hereby declare that I remember no such licence to have been ever signed or sealed by me; and that if ever such pretended licence should be produced, I do hereby annul and vacate the said licence; intreating my said Sub-Dean and Chapter to punish such vicars as shall ever appear there, as songsters, fiddlers, pipers, trumpeters, drummers, drum-majors, or in any sonal quality, according to the flagitious aggravations of their respective disobedience, rebellion, perfidy, and ingratitude.

Eventually permission was granted by the intercession of friends.

The orchestra was good—Burney called it "very respectable"—and since it not only had an excellent drill master in Dubourg but by the time of the performance of *Messiah* had been functioning through the two sets of subscription concerts and rehearsals under Handel's exacting leadership, it was in fine shape for the great event. Handel directed from the harpsichord, and Maclaine played the organ. The Dublin papers again spoke of "the most finished piece of Musick" and of "exquisite Delight" but praised even more warmly Handel's generosity in donating all proceeds to charity (the performers also donated their services). Four hundred pounds was distributed to the three "great and pious Charities," and 142 prisoners released when their creditors were satisfied.

[2]

THE "libretto" of *Messiah* is rather extraordinary, for virtually every word is scriptural, selected from a great variety of passages from both Books. Jennens did his work with considerable skill; the selections from Prophets, Gospels, Pauline Epistles, and the Revelations of John were ably blended into a text eminently suitable for musical setting. Some doubts later arose about Jennens's ability to make such a good compilation, and a legend grew up according to which his secretary, Pooley, an impecunious clergyman, was mainly responsible for its excellence. Debunking is of course great fun, but it works only with the aid of solid evidence. The trouble with the Pooley story is not only that there is absolutely no evidence to support it, but Pooley himself is so insubstantial a phenomenon that no trace of him can be found. Yet the story gained credence and is still repeated, for the Squire of Gopsall invited ill will both during his lifetime and afterwards.

Jennens was always ready with comforting words, and if what he said was not in the Bible, it always sounded as though it should have been. He was one of those ready to assert high principles and to justify his desertion of one after another of them, but, when his own literary exertions were not involved, he was a genuine admirer of Handel. In a letter to one of his friends in 1745, he claims that he "made Handel correct some of the grossest faults in the composition," averring in another passage that though Handel's setting resulted in a "fine entertainment," it is "not nearly so good as he might and ought to have done." Evidently the pompous and vain Jennens kept on pestering the composer ever since the first setting of *Messiah,* for—and with uncharacteristic patience and forbearance— Handel wrote him in July 1744: "Be pleased to point out those passages which you think need altering."

The selection of the words has also been attributed to Handel alone, a theory contradicted by Handel's distinct acknowledgment of Jennens's authorship and his references to "your *Messiah*" or "your oratorio." Whatever is said, while Handel undoubtedly had more than one session at Gopsall and took a hand in the shaping of the libretto, Jennens was the compiler.[4]

---

[4] Kretzschmar flatly stated that "Handel himself put together the biblical text," adding that it was only his modesty that made him acknowledge full honors to Jen-

The libretto was more than a compilation, for it had a subtle plan behind it: the sequence of Promise, Incarnation, Passion, and Resurrection provides an epic unity that dispenses with a dramatic plot. Thus *Messiah* does have a religious basis, but as Winton Dean crisply states: " 'Sacred' refers to the subject, not to the style of music or Handel's purpose in writing it." And we must bear in mind that Jennens, as well as the Dublin papers, always refers to *Messiah* as a "fine" or "grand" or "elegant Entertainment," a designation that posterity found very embarrassing. Indeed, the oratorio does not present the life and Passion of Jesus but the lyric-epic contemplation of the *idea* of Christian redemption. It was to be altogether non-dramatic and non-descriptive. There is scarcely any narration or action in it, and most of the recitatives are undramatic, not a few even perfunctory. Comparisons with the North German Passion are inadmissible, if for no other reason than the combination of Advent, Christmas, and Easter, which makes a *de tempore* use possible only if the great work is taken apart—which is exactly what our churches do, thereby destroying the whole plan. Nevertheless, the *turba* and "scourging" choruses do come, of course, from the German Passion, while many of the arias and all the accompanied recitatives are pure opera.

The fact is that while Bach's Passions, notably the *St. John,* are highly dramatic, with Jesus represented in person, *Messiah* is undramatic, without even a dramatis personae. In *Messiah* not only were the individual parts simply designated by vocal register, but various numbers were divided between the same vocal type. Handel used from five to nine soloists; only once, in 1749, was *Messiah* performed with four soloists. Yet the theatre is not altogether absent in *Messiah;* Handel's freshness and flexibility, his incomparable capacity for seeing and retaining significant nuance, could not be so severely disciplined as to pass up every opportunity for dramatic expression. Inevitably the elements of dramatic music, of Italian opera, were present, as they were in Bach. Certain formulas, intervals, repetitions, and sequences are so basic to the species that even the altogether different English speech rhythm cannot eliminate them. The accompanied recitative, in particular, is purely dramatic-theatrical, it cannot become "churchly"; to call these recitatives in the oratorios *geistig-religiös* is nonsense.

---

nens. But surely the same man who gruffly told the Bishop of London that he did not need his help in selecting passages from the Bible for Queen Caroline's funeral anthem would not have hesitated to disavow Jennens's claims. But Kretzschmar was not the first one to disregard all evidence. In 1822 Zelter simplified everything by declaring that *Messiah* was put together "aus Lutherschen Bibelworten" and was astounded that it should be sung in English.

What distinguishes *Messiah* above all from the North German Passion, and from most of Handel's own oratorios, is the choruses. No, *Messiah* is neither cantata, nor *geistliches Konzert,* nor Passion, nor North German *Betrachtungsoratorium,* but an English anthem-oratorio, full of stately ceremonial music, and in this sense related to *Israel in Egypt.* Next to the great Exodus epic it has the largest number of choruses in relation to solo numbers. This was recognized as early as 1763 by Dr. John Brown, who remarked that though *Messiah* "is called an *Oratorio,* yet it is not dramatic but properly a Collection of *Hymns* or *Anthems* drawn from the sacred Scriptures." As a matter of fact, for some time, especially in Germany, the arias were felt to be so inferior to the choruses that some amusingly radical changes were advocated. In 1820 it was seriously suggested in the *Allgemeine musikalische Zeitung,* a most respectable musical journal, that because of this discrepancy in quality the leading composers of the time should get together and recompose the arias! And this at a time when Graun's gaudy imitation Italian arias in *Der Tod Jesu* were held up as the models of profoundly religious art.

There can be no question, indeed, that the unparalleled popularity of *Messiah* is due mainly to its anthem-like choruses. It is not the subtle idea of Redemption that captivates the listeners but the rousing choruses that are first cousins to the sumptuous ceremonial anthems. The Deity that finally emerges from this great work is the triumphant God of the Old Testament whom Handel so often praised in his oratorios, not Christ the Redeemer, whom he so magnificently evokes in one of the arias—and this in spite of the fact that *Messiah* is essentially a paean of Redemption. And when the Hallelujah Chorus is thundered, its wondrous strains exuding power and pomp, the audience gets to its feet to greet a mighty ruler in whose presence we do not kneel but stand at attention.

This exceptional work, a type to which Handel never returned, was nevertheless almost solely responsible for posterity's adulation; Handel was enthroned as the Christian church composer par excellence. Of the other oratorios only those of the anthem type, such as *Israel in Egypt* and *Judas Maccabaeus,* led a modest existence next to *Messiah,* and the dramatist was completely unknown. For this reason, though *Messiah* is familiar to all of us, we should take a closer look at the music. This is the more necessary because no other oratorio—in fact no other choral work—is so burdened with the most fantastic symbolic interpretations.

Beginning with the overture we are faced with extraordinary metaphysical speculations on the part of the commentators. Even the usually sober and judicious Streatfeild succumbs here, speaking of the world steeped in sin and despair awaiting the Redeemer. But of course any solemn Grave in the minor key could be so interpreted. The sinfonia that opens *Messiah* is a French overture, like countless others Handel composed, except that it is one of his best and well suited for an introduction to this work. The important point is a purely musical one, namely that after the E minor of the overture, the friendly E major of the following recitative is indeed "comforting." The minute Handel begins setting the text, the sort of exegesis that became popular at the beginning of this century under the name of "hermeneutics" can be used with abandon, for old and trusted formulas are to be met with everywhere. We do not dispute the validity of such interpretations; after all, the whole of the Baroque *Affektenlehre* was predicated on it, and all composers of the age attempted to portray words, even ideas, by using musical figures that have a pictorial quality expressible in the very graphic image of the score. But both the term hermeneutics and the notion were borrowed from scriptural exegesis; the procedure is highly subjective and is liable to far-fetched exaggeration. Our main objection is directed against arbitrarily selective use of it; the commentators often pick what suits them and just as often pass in silence the contradictory examples. Thus when the tenor, in his first and exceptionally fine accompanied recitative, sings "and cry unto her," the voice vaults upwards on the word "cry," just as it does on *Aus tiefer Not,* or in practically all settings of *Et ascendit in caelum.* But it is just as incontestable that in "Speak ye comfortably to Jerusalem," the octave leap on "comfortably" is unanimously ignored by the exegetes; it cannot be exploited symbolically because one does not leap in comfort. Granted that word painting was second nature to all Baroque composers, and Handel was especially felicitous in its use, one must guard against too literal interpretation; Handel never indulged in tone painting that could not be justified on purely musical grounds.

The following cavatina, "Every valley," where on the word "exalted" the melody breaks into lush coloraturas, is one of Handel's enchanting nature pictures, and the chorus "And the glory of the Lord" follows the poetic plan naturally. The dance-like character of this magnificent piece adds greatly to the feeling of rejoicing. The combination of contrasting themes is masterly, but what overwhelms is the typical Handelian concentration on chordal outbursts, as with the words "and the glory of the Lord." Curiously, the dance character was found a little objectionable by Streatfeild—shades of Purcell! In the bass recitative "Thus saith the Lord," Handel again indulges in tone painting on *"shake* the heav'ns." This is a robust recitative, and indeed the bass part—as in Handel's operas—is robust throughout.

"But who may abide" exists in versions for bass, alto, and soprano, but the bass version is preferable, not only because Handel carefully saved the high soprano voice until the arrival of the Child Jesus but because in the following prestissimo the equable, slightly pastoral piece turns into a regulation "rage" aria, which by time-honored tradition is the province of the bass. "And He shall purify" is a choral fugue, quiet in the polyphonic sections, but as usual proclamatory in the anthem-like homophonic-syllabic measures. Though exquisite in workmanship, this is not, on the whole, an inspired piece, and some slight discrepancy arises as the tone painting originally devised for the second part of the Italian cantata *Quel fior che all'alba ride* is applied to the English text without further ado. The aria and chorus "O thou that tellest" is again in the pastoral vein, the gently florid dance tune expressing intimate peace and rejoicing. This is a strophic song which gains in intensity in every strophe. Highly refined is the gradual acceptance by the voice of the little expressive motif that first appears in the orchestra during the held notes and rests in the vocal part.

"The people that walked in darkness" is a remarkable example of tone painting by unison of bass and strings. Its hesitating meandering does indeed suggest the tentative groping of those who walk in the darkness. This compelling piece was completely misunderstood by Mozart, who composed very fine—and totally un-Handelian—additional contrapuntal parts to it, presumably to relieve what to him appeared as monotony. J. M. Coopersmith, in the preface to his pathbreaking critical edition of the vocal score of *Messiah* (New York, 1947), follows Leichtentritt's advice in recommending full continuo harmonization of the entire piece; both of them are woefully wrong. The harmonization would remove the very groping Handel intended to represent by the use of stark unison. There are many examples in Handel's operas to show that the unison was deliberate. Furthermore, Handel's intentions are clear, for full harmonization appears whenever the text mentions "light."

It was a stroke of genius to follow this dark piece with the happy madrigal "For unto us a Child is born." To some the provenance of this delectable piece beclouds its irresistible charm. As in several other numbers in *Messiah*, Handel utilized portions of his earlier Italian chamber duets, in this case the lightly amorous "No, I will not trust you, blind Love." These duet-descended choruses are a miracle of craftsmanship and musical sensitivity; with their delicate, unforced, and free linearity, in which all four parts seldom appear simultaneously, they retain a good deal of the intimacy of chamber music, without suggesting the original species. So extraordinary are they that they constitute a special category, the "duet-chorus," altogether different from the great choral fugues and massive anthem choruses. Handel was so enamored of this affecting piece that he repeated the exposition twice, ending with a fine coda. But "For unto us a Child is born" is far more than a skilful parody-transcription. True, Handel did not pay too much attention to the changed accents; the "Nò" in the original (*Nò, di voi non vuò fidarmi*) does not fit the "For" at all, but what does it matter? When Handel suddenly makes the delicate madrigal erupt in tremendous ejaculations—"Wonderful, Counselor"—he gives the composition a significance the original never had. At the great cries the discreet accompaniment ceases as the violins swing upward in bright, jubilant thirds. Beethoven always marvelled at the elemental effect of this passage, and Mozart exclaimed, "When he chooses he strikes like thunder." The performance of this piece demands particular attention on the part of the conductor. The "andante-allegro" prescribed by the composer is usually misunderstood—we are dealing with 18th-century notions of tempo. But no historical erudition is needed when dealing with this ever fresh and modern music; a madrigal must never be sung at breakneck speed. Nor should it be performed with the full chorus, which should fall in with "Wonderful." [5]

After this radiant piece the mood turns to the pastoral; since the 19th century this part of *Messiah* has been most notoriously exploited in a lachrymose way. But how can we blame the country organist, choirmaster, or music teacher for sentimentalizing such a delicately poetic piece as the *Pastoral Symphony*, predicated on pure string sound, when Chrysander, the great Handelian scholar, himself suggests the addition of woodwinds, organ, and harp!

We are perfectly willing to agree that the ethereal violin accompaniment in the following recitatives ("And lo, the angel of the Lord"; "And suddenly there was with the angel") represents the soft beating of the angels' wings, but the remarkable aspect of these pieces is that they are neither rhetorical nor dramatic but simple scriptural narratives which are most attractive and appropriate in context. Eventually the dramatic instinct rebelled against such a "lost opportunity," and in the London ver-

---

[5] Steglich thought that he had discovered a basic motif in *Messiah* upon which the whole work rests. It is the interval of the fourth, which he calls *Gewissheits-quarte*, the "Fourth of Certitude," presumably referring to Redemption or Salvation. If so, it is astounding that the Italian duet, scolding Love as "too treacherous, too charming a deity," should also be based on this motif.

sion Handel introduced a more expressive arioso. Even though this is a fine piece, the first version is preferable.

Now the trumpets enter—but not the way we usually hear them. Handel demands that they should sound *da lontano*, "from a distance," i.e. off stage, then gradually move nearer. Nor is "Glory to God" supposed to burst upon us—the dynamics of the trumpets makes this clear. The change after five measures to basses and tenors ("and peace on earth") is the more arresting because the previous measures avoid the bass register. The emotional-dynamic scheme of this piece is extraordinarily *raffiné*, for as Handel passes from homophony to polyphony ("good will toward men"), then to antiphonal exchange, and finally to a full-voiced and full-throated ensemble, the effect is overwhelming. The fine orchestral postlude gradually fades into the "distance" whence it came. "Rejoice greatly" is a true da capo aria, embellished with coloraturas, the accompaniment worked out with particular care. "He shall feed his flock" offers the quintessence of southern Italian suavity, and it is this very quality that makes it so tenderly expressive of Christ the Good Shepherd. The pervasive charm of this song resists any verbalization. The chorus "His yoke is easy" once more returns to *Quel fior*, yet in the choral version it somehow acquires a Purcellian flavor with its lilting, dotted coloraturas. As in "For unto us a Child is born," the fugal treatment is light and transparent, the four parts seldom appear simultaneously. Handel carefully indicated the dynamic contrasts so as to make this transparency unequivocal, but at the end the anthem character takes the upper hand, and the splendid homophonic setting, in wide open chords (the treble is carried to high B-flat), is the epitome of sonorous choral euphony.

So ends the Advent-Nativity part of the oratorio; unflagging in inspiration and rich in the most wondrous invention and craftsmanship.

The second part is the Passion-Resurrection "cantata," but, as we have said, it is not modelled after the North German Passion; the drama is eschewed for contemplation. Nevertheless, "Behold the Lamb of God," which opens this section with majestic solemnity, does have a good deal of the tone of the old Passion music. It is noticeably archaic in style, only to turn to a smiling sorrow as the soprano holds the pitch on "the sin of the world" while the three lower parts sing a sort of gently rhythmicized lullaby. When this wonderful chorus is sung too loudly—as it usually is—all its tender mourning is lost. "He was despised" is one of Handel's great arias, a lament in which the sadness becomes physically expressed through an individual, even though unnamed, making the magnificent piece dramatic and operatic in spirit and tone, as is further attested by the expressive rests and the little dialogues between orchestra and voice. Here the melody does not flow; it gets under way with difficulty, in little gasps—"rejected," "despised"—then in the middle portion of the aria, in the sharply accented C minor chords of the orchestra, the real drama is upon us.

The Passion music is then carried to its conclusion in a group of choruses. Handel's imagination continues unabated on the highest plane. Now he reaches back for the accompaniment of the middle section of the preceding aria, but turns it into the darker F minor, pounding along relentlessly with dotted sixteenths. But above this grim orchestral tableau the chorus is not agitated; it comments, in hushed astonishment, that "Surely, He hath borne our griefs." Handel took "surely" to be a tri-syllabic word, but the inflection expresses the idea so perfectly, and is so English in tone, that we have no reason to bewail the metric slip. Indeed, the two-syllable *Wahrlich* in the German translation does not fit into the situation at all. It is in this sense that we must consider Handel's supposed lack of understanding of the English language; he does occasionally mis-handle the tonic accent and meter but not the spirit of the language.

"And with his stripes" is a fugue in the old style. Though masterly in execution, this chorus does not seem to be so spontaneous as the others, a fact that gave an opportunity to the writers of *scholia*. A whole literature arose in Germany about the piece's spiritual and religious meaning. Such meaning, if it exists in an abstract fugue, "is hardly susceptible of proof," to quote our colleague's wise words about Handel's heavenly vision; but the warning was disregarded, and the fugue was taken to represent the cross. So we have a *Kreuzfuge,* even though nothing is said about it in the text. Actually, this is an ancient peregrinating fugue theme, used by many composers all the way up to Mozart, and it had seen service before in Handel's keyboard music.

In the next chorus, "All we like sheep," Handel is again back in the world, communicating with his listeners directly, pictorially, and without need of any metaphysical assistance. His alert imagination seizes upon every image: the concise ejaculations on "All we like sheep" are followed by meandering figurations that indeed "go astray," and on "we have turned" roulades appear. How these symbols are then converted into the most appealing musical constellations demands a chapter by itself, which we propose to undertake farther on in this book. The figures on "turned" course from voice to voice in admirably rolling counterpoint, their attraction so strong that the orchestra cannot withstand it. Significantly, the end is in F minor, tying this marvelous piece, over the preceding fugue, to

"Surely."

With the sharply dotted rhythm of "All they that see Him," Handel reverts to the two earlier instances of accompanied recitative, but the orchestra is now angrier as Handel writes a near-realistic piece of action. The immediately following chorus, "He trusted in God," presents a fugue subject so capriciously asymmetrical that in lesser hands it would surely have come to grief in the course of the exposition. Handel glories in it, plays with his material with sovereign ease, modulates rapidly, and throws in countersubjects. This time the commentators are within their rights in speaking of a "mocking fugue," or as Schering plausibly says, "a *turba* of soldiers." "Thy rebuke," an accompanied recitative originally for tenor but presently almost always sung by a soprano, is again the work of the dramatist. The piece is heavily affective and the harmonic scheme disturbed by constant modulation. The tiny arietta, "Behold and see," restores peace, but the ending is very sad. After a brief recitative, "He was cut off out of the land of the living," which is curiously perfunctory considering its text, the A major aria, "But thou didst not leave his soul in Hell," sets the tenth verse from Psalm XVI, which seems rather arbitrarily applied to the Messiah. It is a good piece, but one is aware that Handel wants to get at the great chorus that follows.

With "Lift up your heads," the jubilant theme of "Glory to God" returns, but Handel varies the simple homophonic anthem proclamation with the whole arsenal of his redoubtable choral counterpoint. Polyphony gradually gains, only to yield to the massive antiphonal homophony ("The Lord of hosts") of the coronation anthem style. This is one of the great choruses. The second chorus, "Let all the angels," is often omitted, but Larsen plausibly defends it and its importance in the scheme of the oratorio. The air "Thou art gone up" is known in four versions, but the original, for bass, is the preferred one. Though on the whole the aria itself is not outstanding—Handel begins to miss the opportunity for direct dramatic representation of individual characters—its rollicking accompaniment is very spirited. The composer obviously struggled with the vocal part of this piece. "The Lord gave the word" revives the expansive anthem type of chorus. From here onward one feels that occasionally the conspicuously Old Testament anthem style is somewhat incongruous with the Gospel. Christ emerges more and more as a hero, perhaps as King of Kings, but not as the Lamb of God. The musical level remains high, however, even though this particular piece, a good anthem, is not on a par with the great ones. "How beautiful are the feet" is known in five versions, but today the aria with its lovely gliding siciliana rhythm is usually given to a soprano. In it Handel is at his suave—and Italianate—best. The short madrigalesque chorus "Their sound is gone out" replaces the da capo in the aria.

"Why do the nations" is a fine old thunder piece of the rage-revenge aria type of which there are many notable examples among Handel's bass roles in the operas. There is something grimly determined in the ritornel, which grumbles angrily, three times exploding in a spiteful shout, each time at a higher pitch, to end, after a dozen measures, in a helpless trill. The bass solo starts with a widely arching trumpet-like call, but is afterwards lost in bewildering coloraturas. It is a great mistake to tack on a da capo to this piece; the chorus is the third section of the aria, which never had a repeat. By now Handel was wary of the da capo aria, and whenever he could he avoided the repeat. Yet this chorus, "Let us break their bonds asunder," is often omitted in favor of a da capo, which not only upsets Handel's formal plan, but robs us of a fine piece. Forgetting the anthem for the moment, Handel here again conjures up the madrigal; the delightfully frivolous "fugue" theme is opposed by an entirely different one composed of a broken triad and a running figure in sixteenths. Most attractive is the deception Handel plays on our musical expectations. Instead of the expected combination, the two themes never appear together, but throughout the composition one gets the impression that eventually they will. By almost general agreement this is considered one of the *turba* choruses. According to the text it should be, but unless the music is sung loudly (Handel gives no dynamic indication), in which case it loses its musical character, it surely belongs to the transparently light choruses. In the tenor aria "Thou shalt break them," the orchestra does justice to the words; the vigorous theme almost physically suggests "breaking and dashing," but the vocal part, after a good start, turns into a rather routine affair.

And now we come to the most famous of the *Messiah* pieces, indeed the most famous choral piece in the English-speaking world. While our German friends often call the Halleujah Chorus a *Glanzstück*—which it most assuredly is—they also see in it "the expression of spiritual-religious introspection"—which it most assuredly is not. No more magnificently extrovert music has ever been composed. Interestingly enough, a musical dilettante—but a great philosopher—Wilhelm Dilthey, could have shown the way to the musicological exegetes. He found the exact definition for this exhilarating work by calling it "a coronation march." [6] The triumph of God, says Dilthey, here assumes a *secular* character. The Berlin philos-

---

[6] *Von Deutscher Dichtung und Musik.*

opher was indeed right, for the Hallelujah Chorus is a pure coronation anthem, built with an unerring sense for gradual intensification to an irresistible climax. This point is reached when the treble declaims in solidly repeated tones "King of Kings and Lord of Lords," holding on to the same pitch while the other parts excitedly approve with their "forever, Hallelujah." Six times this is repeated with ever-rising pitch as well as tension, when at last, the treble having moved upwards the distance of a seventh, all parts join in proclaiming the Lord of Lords. The effect is overwhelming. Beethoven, who admired Handel above all other composers, used the bass motif on "and He shall reign forever" for the fugue theme of the "Dona nobis pacem" in his *Missa Solemnis.*

The remarkable gradation of intensity we just spoke of is unfortunately almost invariably disregarded in the ferocious fortissimo bellowing of our choral societies, who give their lungs a sturdy Christian workout in this piece. Handel indicated precisely the dynamics he desired at the beginning of the great chorus by demanding that the orchestra play *senza ripieni,* which of course cannot mean forte, but in our performances the bedlam starts with the opening notes. Though it is an extraordinarily fine and rousing composition, the Hallelujah Chorus should not be considered the summit of Handel's choral art. It is one of the finest of the anthem choruses, but among the dramatic choruses there are many that are superior works of art; Handel himself declared the final chorus in the second act of *Theodora* far superior.

One would expect that anything that followed such splendor and power would suffer. Handel did experience difficulties in the third part of *Messiah,* working hard, correcting, amending, replacing, and in some instances improving upon the earlier versions. The situation in this third part is somewhat like what we see in a number of his operas and oratorios, where he shows a certain lack of interest in what follows after the dénouement. And, of course, a dénouement of a sort was undeniably reached with the tremendous chorus that ends the second part. This slackening of interest is not, however, in evidence in the aria that immediately follows the Hallelujah Chorus, "I know that my Redeemer liveth." This is the more surprising because textually its quiet faith is in contrast with the finality, the convinced certitude expressed in that rousing chorus. This ineffably beautiful aria is sheer transfigured enchantment, at the same time having the pastoral quality of a chaste awakening of nature in the early morning sun. It affords another example of Handel's complete assimilation of the spirit, the sound, and the meaning of the English Bible. We say "the spirit" because the declamation itself is faulty, but only

the grammarians could be troubled by that. It is perhaps of some significance that "I know that my Redeemer liveth" was never altered in the
many subsequent versions of the score.

The following chorus, "Since by man came death," carries us—like
the preceding aria—into the Christian orbit par excellence. The stunning
opening phrase for the first time in this work offers a quality of sacred
music one finds, for instance, in Antonio Lotti's church music. To search
for antecedents in Schütz is as futile as to invoke Purcell; this is the latter-
day "Palestrina style" of Venice (see above, p. 70 ff.). After these two
pieces, Handel's inspiration does not reach the consistently exalted level
of the first part. The aria "The trumpet shall sound" not only resembles
the trumpet aria so popular in 17th-century opera but has a good deal of
its spirit—as well as its routine. One would be tempted to call this aria
naive, but the epithet does not fit Handel. It is much safer to assume that
this piece is well within the English tradition of anthem arias or welcome
songs which afford pause between the great choruses. The general plan of
Messiah forbade the grand *scena* that Handel would normally have built
in such a situation in an opera. But if the piece is not grand it certainly is
long; from Mozart onward everyone tried to cut it, with varying results.
To speak of "considerable symbolic significance" in discussing this harmless aria is nothing but fantasy.

The only duet in *Messiah*, "O death, where is thy sting," also descended from an earlier, amorous Italian duet. Handel reworked it considerably, but in its present form it is still altogether of the Italian
chamber duet style, suggesting a different musical climate. Not so the
chorus "But thanks be to God," in which we once more witness the masterly extension of a duet into a full chorus. Though the polyphonic work is
very attractive, this piece is often omitted. Amusingly enough, the dance
rhythms of "If God be for us" have made some Handelian authorities unhappy. Did they never look at the superb gavotte or minuet arias in
Bach's cantatas that sing of the most hallowed themes? This is a good
"English" piece, Purcellian Handel. Mozart recognized it for what it is, a
minuet, but was severely taken to task by the later analysts, for the aria is
supposed to represent the descent of the Holy Ghost from heaven. The
poor little Viennese musician, untutored in hermeneutics, could not be
expected to divine such things.

The final choruses, "Worthy is the Lamb," "Blessing and Honour,"
and "Amen," which form a sort of compound finale, return to the grand
anthem style. The first two are rather simple, but the final "Amen" fugue
is a dazzling piece. It is the amplest choral number in *Messiah*, built on

exceptionally large and characteristic themes, which Handel develops
with all contrapuntal stops pulled out. His sketches in the Fitzwilliam
Museum show that the many canonic imitations and strettos received considerable preliminary scrutiny, which reminds us that the chances of a
fugue being grandly constructed may perhaps be a matter of contrapuntal
skill and imagination not requiring assistance from metaphysical sources.
Handel meant this stupendous chorus to be the crowning glory of the
oratorio; it will remain forever the envy of all choral composers.

That *Messiah* was an exceptional work even in Handel's own estimation is attested by its immunity from his notorious habit of shifting music
from one oratorio to another, a practice from which none of the others
was exempt. That is one of the reasons it is called "the most homogeneous
of all Handel's larger works." But this is hardly true even if we willingly
admit that few of Handel's works show such a consistently high and rich
inventive power. Even "ideologically" there is a distinct dichotomy in
Messiah, as Handel alternates between the concept of the Lord of Awe,
Power, and Retribution, and that of the other, the Galilean. The magnificent anthem choruses show that by this time there was no turning back;
the ceremonial style was in his bones, and unless he could employ the
chorus for specific dramatic purposes or to illustrate a pastoral scene, the
result would usually be an anthem, and one feels the presence of "Jehovah with thunder arm'd." Nor could the contemplative intention be kept
intact, though Handel wrought wonders in the arias, which proved that
he could be as lyrical at fifty-five as he had been twenty years earlier. If
anything, there is more tenderness and magnificently controlled eager
melodic compulsion in some of the *Messiah* arias than in their predecessors. But the dramatist, the lover of imagery, could not always be repressed; single words that suggest action could unleash his imagination.
An interesting example is afforded by the second version of the recitative
"And they were sore afraid," in which *sore* received a sharp emphasis,
whereas in the first version it is unaccented, a simple narrative.

Much of *Messiah* was repeatedly altered, even recomposed. As a
matter of fact, not even in Dublin was the oratorio performed according
to the original manuscript; several important numbers were altered or altogether replaced before the première. However, this was largely due to
local conditions, as some of the London reworkings had to take into account the singers' capabilities—and desires. Nevertheless, Handel was
clearly not altogether satisfied with some portions of the work and, responding to his marvelous sense of form and propriety, improved many a
detail, even whole numbers. These many changes led to the belief that a

"definitive" version of the score is an unattainable goal. Modern scholarship, free from the hobbling "tradition" that surrounds this work, holds a different opinion. The earlier editions were like gaudy plaster copies of a noble marble statue. Arnold Schering's was the first modern edition (1930) based on a thorough knowledge of, and nice feeling for, the style and on patient collation of the historical facts. In the meantime, J. M. Coopersmith, Jens Peter Larsen, Alfred Mann, and Watkins Shaw, with their enlightening studies, have proved that the many versions and variants of individual numbers often represent changes that Handel considered permanent. On the basis of these findings, Alfred Mann, Watkins Shaw, and John Tobin published excellent scores.

Critical appreciation of *Messiah* in the modern literature presents a bewildering variety. We shall not list the hymns of praise Handelian authors composed in their own right; the great work deserves all the admiration it has won, even though we can no longer accept the tradition that made *Messiah* a quasi-liturgical work. But it will be of interest to mention some of the quaint misreadings of style and time. Leichtentritt, expressing the consensus of his generation of German scholars, thought that whereas the other oratorios build on Italian foundations, *Messiah*'s construction rests on its composer's German heritage: the German Passion and church cantata. This view was seconded by a number of British authors. More recent writers, while still insisting on a basically German-Lutheran quality in *Messiah,* attempt to fortify their position by minimizing the Italian element in the making of the score. Bücken (*Die Musik der Nationen*) calls the Handel of the pastoral portions of *Messiah,* so full of Calabrian and Sicilian rhythms, tunes, and echoes, "the greatest musical representative of the German pictorial Baroque." Serauky goes farther—he claims the entire work. "*Messiah* belongs among those rare oratorios of Handel in which the Italian sweetness of the melodies retreats behind the homely tone of German musical feeling." Indeed there are three homely German sicilianas in the first part alone! Finally, one more example of the inadmissible and misleading application of hermeneutics that plays havoc with an esthetic appreciation of this splendid music. We have mentioned Rudolf Steglich's fantasy about the "Fourth of Certitude," the *Gewissheitsquarte.* He also insists that D major is the "Messiah key," citing as proof the act-ending choruses, all of which are in D. But that would make Bach's B minor Mass, most of which is in D, or almost any other major Baroque work *calling on trumpets,* a kindred work; for all the composers did was to accommodate those instruments, which were tuned in D. They counted on the festive brilliance of the trumpets.

[3]

THE DUBLIN DAYS drew towards their end. The great success of *Messiah* was followed by a nonsubscription presentation of *Saul* and by a second *Messiah;* on June 3 Handel conducted his last performance "with Honnour, profit, and pleasure." Lingering for a while in the hospitable city, he attended Garrick's performance of *Hamlet* and paid his respects to Dean Swift. One imagines that he wanted to thank the Dean for lending St. Patrick's choristers for his concerts, but if so, his gesture of courtesy was in vain: the man Handel tried to talk to was no longer sane. On August 13 he embarked on the journey to London, fully resolved to return to that "generous and polite Nation" within a year. This hope was never realized.

The man who returned to London after ten months' absence was an altogether changed creative artist. In a letter to Jennens written shortly after his return, Handel reflected on the rumors that had him taking up opera anew. "The report that the Direction of the Opera next winter is committed to my Care, is groundless. . . . Whether I shall do some thing in the Oratorio way (as several of my friends desire) I can not determine as yet." But it was not long before Handel "determined" that "the Oratorio way" should be his for the rest of his life. The decision was not a direct consequence of the great success obtained in Dublin by *Messiah,* though his self-assurance and determination were certainly greatly helped by the months of glory enjoyed in Ireland and the corresponding rest from malicious intrigue.

The history of *Messiah* following its warm reception in Dublin is rather peculiar. As we have related above, London heard it three times in 1743 and twice in 1745 and then it rested until 1749. Though after the yearly Foundling Hospital performances it gradually gained in esteem, even at the end of the century, after the monster commemoration performances, at a time when both the work and its composer had been beatified, there were still voices denouncing *Messiah* as blasphemous. In the second third of the 19th century, a distant successor of Dr. Gibson in the see of London would not permit *Messiah* in Westminster Abbey, though by that time the oratorio had become a religious landmark in the English-speaking world, seemingly as immune from criticism as the articles of faith. Handel was aware of the unique nature of *Messiah* and never intended to duplicate it. "One might have expected *Messiah* to have been the starting point for a new tradition," says Larsen, "but this did not happen," and Myers perceptively observes that "*Messiah* embodied all Handel's methods and typifies none." We must ask, then, what is the meaning of "the Oratorio way"?

XIV

I F "SACRED" MUSIC IN GENERAL OCCUPIES AN IMMENSE CHAPter in the history of music, one of its forms, the oratorio, fills a sizable subchapter by itself. In the English-speaking world the oratorio form is dominated by Handel, though not by Handel the composer of a score of oratorios but by Handel the composer of *Messiah*, or, more precisely, of what *Messiah* has become. (In Central Europe the "Bach style" is the frame into which all choral works are fitted.) So, in the English-speaking world, performances of any oratorio of the 17th, 18th, and 19th centuries have been so closely bound to the *Messiah* ideal that stylistic differences largely disappear; Bach's *St. Matthew Passion*, Mendelssohn's *Elijah*, Haydn's *Creation*, and Elgar's *Dream of Gerontius* all are presented in pseudo-Baroque style, unctuous and heavy, serving up grandiloquent sentimental-religious tableaux. When hearing *The Seasons* performed in this manner we are reminded of certain German and English translations of Dante, which gave this most Catholic of poets a distinctly "reformed" countenance.

Serious composers were aware of the dismal decline of the oratorio in the second half of the 18th century. Most of what was produced by the official purveyors of "sacred" music and by other composers who still felt called upon to continue the tradition was but a play with old forms. Indeed, the oratorio became a *l'art pour l'art* enthusiasm for old sounds and techniques and artistic mannerisms; the content was lost and only melancholy reminiscences played a tired game. Even Mendelssohn's fine

Elijah, whose choruses breathe a certain Handelian splendor, is badly marred by the archaic recitatives—the oratorio had become a pseudo-religious genre, as it never was with Handel. Its spirit could no longer inspire a discerning composer, for it was artificially surrounded by severe restrictions, artistically at odds with the times, which were imposed by popular taste upon both composer and audience. This explains why for such a long time most major composers gave a wide berth to the genre.

The irony of this state of affairs is that not only the biblical Handel of *Messiah* and *Israel in Egypt* but the Handel of the classical *Hercules* is clad in ecclesiastical robes, and so, for that matter, is the gentle, genre-painting Haydn. Since these works refuse to reveal their greatness under such restrictions, they are not understood and are seldom performed. The oratorio has become no longer a musico-dramatic genre but a problem in the psychology and sociology of art. We are prone to see in the biblical figures dramatized by Handel spiritual athletes, but even if we realize that they are men and women who struggle, suffer, love, and kill, we are inhibited by finding them in a matrix long since appropriated for preconceived religious purposes. Yet somehow we feel that perhaps these figures might be ourselves at an earlier time, or that these strange, stiff creatures are our long-forgotten and still scarcely remembered brothers. It is this vague feeling of kinship upon which the understanding—and revival—of Handel should be based, for the men and women in the oratorios can be brought back to life if we can see them as human beings, if we can remove the fixed bliss from their faces and the unctuousness from their voices. It is monumental nonsense to have the biblical protagonists stand in concert halls in stained-glass attitudes, in white tie and tails or in modish evening dresses, backed by a chorus gowned in church vestments, and all affecting that diluted Tudor English which is conventionally decreed to have been spoken in all periods from 1066 to Dr. Johnson.

The oratorio is looked upon as a form dealing with abstract, though codified and hallowed, ideas, and with ideal experiences far removed from actual life; the public does not see, or expect to see, in them immediate, tremendous forces close to life. The Victorians who first made Handel widely available to the public by publishing his scores in large popular editions sought and found only one mood in the oratorios, the "religious," and found it in every utterance, or, failing to find it, resorted to shameless falsification. Musicians, editors, clergymen, and historians all shared in this activity. They made the Handelian world a very tight and narrow one, every little liberty of action and thought becoming suspect, and if their suspicion was confirmed by the text, or by the musical treatment of it, or if the text admitted any interpretation that ran counter to their own bigoted and prudish beliefs, they did not hesitate to modify it. It is only detail and torso that this conception gives us, for it silences the drama itself. There is no such thing as purely religious drama, any more than there is purely esthetic drama. Tampering with the original texts of Handel's oratorios falsified the dramatic perspective and made symbolic what was not so intended. Handel wanted to represent relationships between men, background and circumstances being accessory and fortuitous.

Perhaps the most important consideration is that these oratorios are altogether independent of the church and do not require its assistance in any form. The Handelian oratorio is not church music, not even religious music. Newburgh Hamilton, in the preface to *Samson,* described the oratorio as a music drama in which "the Solemnity of Church-Musick is agreeably united with the most pleasing Airs of the Stage." Jens Peter Larsen, though he leans toward the "sacred music" concept, states unequivocally (*Handel's Messiah,* p. 94) that the Handelian oratorio "is not church music; it is, like opera of the time, music for entertainment." To the Victorians, and, through their legacy, to our modern public, the human figures in the stories are only puppets who are being driven by the word of God either to find the true way or to perish because they worship foreign gods. With this religious connotation everything that the composer's imagination conceived as visible and audible disappears; for the direct sensuous perception is turned into an indirect intellectual one. The individual work of art becomes schematicized, a category with a priori values, separated from its creator's imagined world; the historical drama is turned into religious oblation. This religious-moral-didactic concept of the Age of Propriety is still so strong that it invades even scholarly musical literature. Kretzschmar voiced the consensus when he stated that Handel's intention in his oratorios was to represent the promulgation of Christianity. This was the view of a society that desired to be instructed, whose interests were predominantly ethical, and that expected art to be, if not subordinate, at all events directed to some earnest purpose.

Years later Leichtentritt still echoes the traditional view that "Handel drew from his memory and confident Protestant faith the powerful religious feeling which made possible the oratorios." Since he counts *Semele* and *Hercules* among the oratorios, this is a curious surrender to a dated and untenable popular belief. Friedrich Blume, in his fine monograph *Die Evangelische Kirchenmusik* (1931), was among the first to take an unequivocal stand, declaring that Handel's oratorios have nothing to do with sacred music, a judgment supported by all the evidence, if such evidence is used with scholarly detachment. In *Handel, a Symposium*, Basil Lam puts this idea very neatly: "The oratorios are historical dramas and have acquired an adventitious sanctity for which they were not designed." With Winton Dean's monumental work on the Handelian oratorio, the whole question should be considered settled, but it is not, and even some very able scholars are still misled by the biblical exterior. Jens Peter Larsen, author of the distinguished essay, *Handel's Messiah*, speaking of *Saul* says that "there is a clear tendency for character drawing to become the central dramatic feature at the cost of the main idea of heroic-biblical drama." The first part of this statement correctly presents the essence of Handel's whole concept of the music drama, the second part negates it. Later Larsen excuses Handel's wandering from what is seen as the true type: "This does not imply that the principle of oratorio had been wholly abandoned." But what is this principle but an arbitrary post-Handelian construction? The eminent Danish musicologist is not alone in holding this view, the thesis leading him to conclusions that are difficult to accept. He considers the oratorios after *Messiah* "somewhat stereotyped," and consequently sees *Israel in Egypt, Messiah,* and *Saul* "more typical of Handel's characteristics and power" than the great works that followed.

Handel himself felt the limitations of the genre better than anyone else. He was unwilling to confine his creative power to religious exposition; he wished to bestow it on love and loyalty, happiness and sorrow, crime and punishment. Except in some numbers in *Messiah,* there is nowhere a truly religious, let alone a Christian, message in these oratorios, nowhere a Christian thesis advanced or defended. The biblical texts and the frequent mentioning of the Lord do not change the preoccupation with human matters and sentiments. Handel was not a theological poet like Milton, in whose works the role of the Deity is so overpowering that it crushes mere men. In spite of their biblical setting, Handel's dramas come from life, they are dramas in the actual theatrical sense. In this music there is no preaching, but the free play of the imagination; the humanizing forces are not decorative by-products of Holy Writ nor are they the staffage of a cultivated and elevated "moral entertainment." And there is in the Handelian oratorio a vital strain coming from classical antiquity. Handel's public for some time refused to follow him; contemporary English religious opinion, in fact, saw near-blasphemy in his oratorios. It did not approve of the employment of the Word of God for dramatic purposes, fearing that the Old Testament would lose in religious and ethical meaning when translated from sacred to secular use.

It is impossible to appreciate these figures, who bear Hebrew names but act like men from the Attic drama, from a religious-moral view, as has been done for generations. Handel the dramatist was concerned with men, how they stand up under the impact of fateful conflicts. If it were at all imaginable that a composer should express nothing subjective, that he should give us merely a musical accompaniment to biblical themes, which alone supply the work's strength and purpose, then the composer would become an inhuman automation. The art of the Handelian oratorio is an eminently theatrical one, and once the public becomes accustomed to the idea, when it learns to appreciate Handel's true intentions, these works, universally held to be the antithesis of the lyric stage, will exert their full dramatic force. Following the Handel opera renaissance in Germany in the 1920s, scenic productions of his oratorios became popular there. The cultic theatre those performances represented completely missed the spirit and nature of these works. So long as the oratorios are hedged with a "sacred" character, they cannot be directly experienced as music drama nor compared with other music, because appreciation of their merits is unconsciously biased by their presentation as quasi church music.

There can be no question that originally the oratorio was considered a sort of opera. We have seen that Handel's *Resurrezione* was staged in Rome, that the very first of his English oratorios, *Esther*, called a masque, was written to be staged and acted. The aristocratic patrons of opera, used to the virtuoso singing of the Italian opera troupes, found the oratorio dull and uninteresting. They did not object to the "theatrical quality" of the new musical form; on the contrary, they objected because they did not find enough of it, for without scenery and acting they could not imagine drama. It was another matter with the Puritan-descended guardians of English morals, whether High or Low Church; Bishop Gibson's edict against *Esther* gave a proper weapon to the zealots. It is noteworthy, though, that even thereafter a "story," that is, a dramatic plot, was expected in the oratorio, and some of Handel's finest works in this genre were not successful because they had no clear-cut heroes and villains. The oratorio libretto had to be dramatic, otherwise it was a failure, which might contain single numbers that Handel could shift to dramatically more advantageous positions in other oratorios. Handel demanded, especially after *Messiah*, that his librettists provide him with a theatrically effective text, and if they did not, he himself took a hand in the shaping of the libretto. Victor Schoelcher, Handel's first able modern biographer

(*The Life of Handel*, London, 1857), saw clearly that these oratorios are music dramas, and deplored that even in his time staged performances were prohibited. (A century has since passed, but there is still validity in his description of a listener at a concert performance of a dramatic oratorio—like a blind man at the opera.) But even a century before the French Schoelcher, Englishmen were aware of the oratorio's theatrical quality. In 1763 the author of *An Examination of the Oratorios which have been performed this Season at Covent Garden Theatre* states that "an Oratorio if acted becomes immediately an Opera." Being a good Englishman, however, he rejoices that an oratorio is "unincumbered with the absurdity of a dramatic exhibition."

Like Shakespeare and other great dramatists, Handel took any known story and plot in which a usable idea was present, then proceeded to work it out for the theatre. His dramatic and humanistic ideal was strongly influenced by his English environment, which in a way imposed certain limitations upon him. At times the result of this influence appears as a manner which must be accepted and to which the listener must get accustomed. Handel's is an attitude that acquires significance when the premises are understood. Since dramas based on historical events count on the historical sympathies of the public, this often limits the composers' choice of subject to the country in which those events took place. The same limitation applies to English biblical dramas because of the particular place the Old Testament occupies in English Protestantism. The English concept of the Old Testament is, to the non-Briton, a rather perplexing mixture of the cult of great men, ethical and moral precepts, historically defined categorical order, socio-economic and juridical philosophy, all somehow linked with Christianity. There was, of course, the magnificent King James translation that made the Bible virtually English; there was, too, a sense of identification with the Old Testament that made it almost national history, as antiquity is to the Italians. Handel paid a high price for his fidelity to this national ideal, for aside from *Messiah* few of his other oratorios became popular in the world at large, and some of the finest are known only to musicologists.

The biblical theme was a tradition obligatory to all Protestant composers. The Germans used it for prayer, contrition, and thanksgiving; familiar texts were invoked constantly but without any particular relevance to the problems of the present. Unlike the British, they preferred to celebrate the New Testament, they preferred Jesus to Jehovah, because in Germany Lutheran orthodoxy had to supply a substitute for a national instinct that was slow in forming and that afforded no substance for a national art as it did in England. The great gestures of kings, war lords, high priests, and powerful matriarchs, so prominent in the Handelian oratorio, are absent in the German cantata and oratorio. In the German works the fundamental approach is not one of identification with the dramatis personae but one of a strong congregational consciousness.

The historical subject limits the artist because the known data and the known characters reduce his freedom. If he remains absolutely faithful to the original, artistic quality may suffer; if he takes too much liberty with his material, historical truth may suffer. But the prestige of historical material is great, especially if it is scriptural, and it possesses a good deal of attraction. The figures did exist; they are accepted even before the artist develops them; when Saul or Solomon or Joshua appeared, Handel's audience recognized them as lifelong acquaintances. Moreover, these biblical figures lived in animated times, took part in tremendous events, wielded great power, and their lives and actions influenced whole nations. In them the conditions of life and its passions are projected larger than lifesize. What is the life and death of an ordinary man compared to theirs? But the historical or scriptural subject has its serious pitfalls, chief among them the problem of characterizing larger-than-life public figures —kings, high priests, generals—as individuals. They must act the roles history has assigned to them, and the artist will want to shape their character in conformity with their historical role, but historical acts often have a coldness that even the power of a great artist cannot change into living warmth. Their faults and their virtues are equally oversized and somewhat monotonous, and are, moreover, of a generalized type difficult to make convincing in dramatization. In the historical drama patriotism may call forth undue rhetoric, which kills the drama, while in the biblical drama the moral-religious attitude can be benumbing, especially since it is a priori. The threads of a historical drama come together from every direction and are spun before the birth of the hero, continuing throughout the piece: elaborate kinships, old grievances, ambitions, plans for revenge or conquest. The artist does not see in them a synthesis, yet the greatness, the power, the pathos of tremendous conflicts in the historical drama compensate for its many weaknesses.

Ever since its inception, the musical drama, whether opera or oratorio, has been more interested in historical-mythological subjects than has the spoken drama (though at times the theatre was historically oriented, especially in France and England). The esthetic significance of mythology rests on the fact that concrete stories project in concrete symbols the problems of man's life. These stories are not so rigid as to preclude a great variety of sentiments and feelings, though the mythological subject, or history become mythology, unquestionably takes away from the dramatist some of his independence in dealing with his subjects. On the other hand, the myth is living naturalism, unfaded history, ever fresh and ever present; it offered Handel a ready-made, naive, and truly epic-dramatic synthesis that is timelessly poetic. Historical or scriptural mythology can be assumed to be unquestioningly accepted by the listener. This gives an immediate advantage to the composer, who can then do more or less what he likes, and the listener may be led unresisting, and often unaware that a composer like Handel does not intend to sacrifice his characters as individuals in their own right to the impersonal forces and tendencies they exemplify. There can be found in even the most monumental personage an irrational residue which the great artist can seize upon and can convert into memorable characterization. Librettist and composer can invent and fill in as much as they please, and few of the characters of such a remote era can be glaringly misrepresented, few facts offensively distorted. This is propitious for the dramatist, and Handel does like to concentrate on invented detail, concealing or merely alluding to the main biblical theme. The oratorios are, indeed, full of "sensible perplexity." The historical writer and composer must resuscitate life anew, from pieces that have fallen, forever mingled with the unknowable secrets of the past, into the great pit from which they can never again be drawn out untangled. They must be seen with the aid and illumination of intuition, with the power of the force of imagination. Still, the reconstructed picture can be true and deep.

The scribes of the Old Testament wrote as chroniclers, without the force of actual experience, whereas the creative artist can play with his pliable material; he can shape, motivate, and combine freely, having only to remember that the illusion must be perfect and artistically authentic. The biblical dramatist can select models for the individuals and peoples of the past from the raw materials of his own present, like the painter or novelist when he turns to historical subjects. In them such a procedure is almost self-evident; in a musician, composing on texts culled from the Bible, it is less easy to perceive. The musical language that Handel uses in his great biblical oratorios is replete with the echoes of great events and great men, but its spirit is individual, and it has an artistic unity wholly personal. It echoes not the language of the age it depicts but of the age of its composer; everything becomes the dramatic present.

The Old Testament frame is often insufficient, forcing Handel into compromises. At times his protagonists, as he depicts them, have no authentic place in this biblical world, and the ideas the librettists put into their mouths are not convincing enough to permeate their character. Some of the librettists' creations are more, some less than what their roles demand. But when Handel was secure in his bearings he could fuse his figures with any background. The old woman Nitocris in *Belshazzar* grows out of her surroundings with absolute naturalness. The situation into which she was born demands exactly the type of creature she is. Her tragedy touches the essential features of her being: friendship, maternal love, politics. But though the Old Testament offers attractive and musi-cally advantageous subjects, with ever-changing scenes, to Handel it had an attraction and meaning that went far beyond the lively story, the ex-otic milieu, and the colorful landscape. He turned to it for two reasons. The first, as we have seen, was the special position it held in Protestant England. It furnished him with models, lessons, symbols, majestic statutes that he could apply to the nation. But, secondly, it provided him with heroic characters in action, which he could elaborate in his own fashion. The statutes are before us in utmost clarity; the men appear in their most passionate moments. The treatment of the individual characters was en-tirely personal, the work of the born dramatist who espies life, but the characterization of nations and institutions was English and could have come from no other source.

Handel's great strength rests on his ability to fuse psychological penetration with representation and then to present the combination in wondrous pictures and expressive colors. His grand tableaux sparkle with fiery life, history made human and contemporary; their message is con-veyed with all the complications and contradictions of life, yet clearly and unmistakably. It was not so much the quality of the libretto that mattered as its emotional possibilities. The rhyme could be atrocious, the story flat, but if it presented dramatic situations and characters that could be fas-tened upon, a poetaster would do almost as well as Milton. Everywhere Handel shows a strong sympathy—even kinship—with those of his char-acters who, once they have thrown the dice, be they kings, prophets, heathen, or scoundrels, go towards their aim by means fair or foul and cannot be deflected from it.

Incidentally, Handel obviously did not find anything objectionable about the heathen; in fact, he seems to have liked them and shared enthu-siastically in their pantheism and nature worship. Thus the Baalites in *Athalia* are far from detestable; their music is most pleasant and the choral sound delectably tender. It is interesting to observe how often Handel simply overrules the librettist, refusing to follow him, by either removing or changing disparaging or contemptuous words, or setting them with a totally different sense. In *Theodora* the Romans, despicable in Morell's words, are not at all unsympathetically treated in Handel's music; they act like Romans, in the light in which Romans see the world. Streatfeild noticed this tendency in Handel, praising "the voluptuous beauty of heathendom" in *Athalia*, while Edward Fitzgerald thought that "Handel was a good old pagan at heart." A pagan he was not, but a humanist always.

Categorical distinction among genres always seems arbitrary whenever a significant new type appears. The English oratorio as created by Handel refuses to be tabulated by any method of classification deserving to be called precise. Should it be considered to belong to the oratorio genre that preceded it, or is it something entirely new? In Handel's time they made at least this distinction in England: a work was called an "oratorio or sacred drama" if it had a biblical theme and otherwise was variously known as a "musical drama," "pastoral," or "ode." Following the Victorians, we place even the classical pastorals and English operas such as *Acis and Galatea* and *Semele* among the oratorios and, what is worse, perform them as if they were oratorios. Leichtentritt deals with all choral works other than anthems and Te Deums under the heading "oratorio," while *Handel, a Symposium,* divides these works into secular and sacred categories. Thus, while the collection of essays just named is altogether modern and critical, it does maintain a classification that is basically misleading. Larsen makes the following subdivisions within two main categories: heroic-, anthem-, and narrative-oratorio within the genus "Biblical Oratorios," and concert- or cantata-, and mythological-oratorio within the class of "Non-Biblical Oratorios." However, as we have seen in Chapter III, while in Italy the distinction between sacred and secular cantatas, serenata and oratorio, was tenuous if it existed at all, the English oratorio represents a new category in the sense of Brunetière's conception of the rise, predominance, and decline of genres. "Handelian oratorio" is, therefore, a term justified by the uniqueness of the species, but within this generic term we must not include works that do not belong there. The arbitrary religious interpretations play havoc with Handel's intentions not only where they palpably fly in the face of the composer's expressed wishes, but even where these intentions are not clear. Winton Dean was the first historian clearly to see these contradictions; his classification of Handel's oratorios into dramatic and non-dramatic classes brings sense and order into this chaotic situation; it should give Handelian criticism its bearings.

While some of its musical ingredients go back to, say, Carissimi, in concept and tone the Handelian oratorio is altogether different from either the Italian or the German type. Religion, politics, technical necessities, influences coming from sister forms, all played an important part in its formation even though it was carried by strong individual creative force. Handel united three different and seemingly irreconcilable strains in the English oratorio: Old Testament story, Shakespearean characterization, and classical form. Of his ability to create human character in music we have seen many examples in the operas. In the oratorio, the biblical milieu notwithstanding, what he wanted was simply to seize those moments when fate elicits the supreme possibilities of life. In order to arrive at these moments, his protagonists must first traverse a long road. It was this road only that presented any problem to the composer, but if his librettist made it even moderately passable, the result was a masterpiece; his music picks up what it has to say as naturally as a mother picks up her child. Handel's musical language at times hovers between the extremes of the lyric and the epic-dramatic, thus creating the particular and individual forms that made the Handelian oratorio a most personal and inimitable vehicle. The other two strains, Old Testament and Greek drama, are much more difficult to assess even though their role is paramount and pervasive.

[2]

NOWHERE DID Handel acknowledge any particular indebtedness to classical antiquity, yet the conclusion is inescapable that his oratorio, with its choral action and commentary, owes a great deal to the Greek theatre. Handel's studies in the humanistic school of Halle gave him a good foundation, but it was only in Italy that he discovered that this classic spirit does not exist in books alone, to be admired from afar as a magnificent example of the culture of an age now dead. He realized that the classical legacy is not restrictive but is an artistic force. Coming face to face with the spirit of antiquity stirred him as deeply as Mozart was stirred when he first met the spirit of living polyphony in Bach. Mozart, too, knew polyphony as it was taught in school, but here it was a living force, an ideal of beauty. Handel made the classical ideal of beauty his own, first expressing it in formal opera. Opera, the mother of all modern music, has stood from its inception to this very day under the influence of the classical spirit, at first overwhelmingly, after the 18th century in ever diminishing but still perceptible degree. Then in England Handel discovered a very particular English conception of Hellenism: the combination of the Puritan Bible with pagan poetry as exemplified in Milton.

We have come a long way from the time when literature, music, and the arts were indivisible. Certainly, in the culture of classical Greece, literature was *primus inter pares,* but today it is mainly her art that still exerts a tremendous influence. For centuries upon centuries thousands and thousands of men who did not understand a word of Greek and were never interested in any other aspect of Greek civilization, endeavored to imitate or utilize Greek art.

The English spirit annexed that of the classical era with alacrity. The Augustan Age, like its Renaissance forebear, still looked upon an idealized vision of classical antiquity, a life where beauty and freedom met in a perfect union never again attained. To the English men of letters, especially the poets, Greece was the gateway to Paradise, and this in spite of the fact that the Greek language itself was always something of a luxury in English culture. It was, Dr. Johnson said, like lace—"every man gets as much of it as he can." In the heyday of English classicism it was rather the Latin poets who were the common possession of all educated people; the heroic age of verse translation, Pope notwithstanding, was a Latin age. This was a matter of natural affinity: Latin is woven into the very texture of literary, and in particular rhetorical, English. For the same reason it is in rhetorical passages, that is, in the speeches of tragedy and sometimes of epic poetry, that the line connecting Greek with English letters is most direct and unbroken, though the spirit of Greece was conveyed through Latin translations. The Puritans' deep-seated aversion to the many classical elements in Latin Catholicism, to the statuary and pictures, to the veneration of the great pagan, Aristotle, as a quasi saint, should not mislead us; it could not efface the memory of Greek poetry, the spirit of Pindar, which remained living. This heritage must have been responsible for the fact that it was the English who first gave the modern world a deep and wide-ranging poetry.

It is no accident that the drama, the most immediate representation of reality, has such an ancient and distinguished history in England. The theatre lost its religious connotations sooner in England than anywhere else and was no longer the dilettante undertaking of guilds and clerks as in the time of the mystery plays; professional actors appeared and the theatre grew as opera did in Italy. These actors were either servants or protégés of court and aristocracy, those quarters from which the wind of the Renaissance was blowing. As we look around we can see that these English poets and playwrights knew and practiced everything in vogue in

Europe. Spenser imitates Petrarch, Ronsard, Virgil, as well as Tasso, who was his contemporary. *The Fairy Queen*, that magnificent, decorative, Ariosto-like epic, one would be tempted to call un-English were it not for the luxuriant flood of English verse. But where decoration is for the Italian convention or substitution, for the Englishman it is the continuation of reality. It was the English poets who gave the world the engaging and modern charm that appears in Spenser, the construction of a fairy world from pictures, similes, rhymes, old and unusual words, alliteration, and assonance. Thus the Englishman, who always wanted reality, made real what is beyond reality.

Chapman translated Homer and Hesiod; Marlowe delved into Musaeus, the last great poet of declining Greek lyricism, the incomparable storyteller of love and death, of "the waves of the sea and of love," sweet, warm eroticism; *Hero and Leander* became the period's favorite piece of literature. Milton—like Racine—was convinced that he constructed his works on classical principles and so were the Augustans who followed him and who once more translated Homer. But all these men also knew the Bible, and of course several of Handel's librettists knew it ex officio, staying pretty close to the original wording even when dramatizing Scripture. Though clergymen, they also knew the classics and dramaturgy. Even that graceless pedant, the Reverend Thomas Morell, D.D., was the author of a lexicon of Greek prosody and wrote such classical plays as *Prometheus Bound.* In the universities, where at the opening of the 18th century instruction and religious controversy were preferred to original and critical scholarship, there were nevertheless men of great learning, and gradually the English school of Hellenic studies became an inspiration to the great Continental scholars.[1]

The classical dramatic tradition reached England in the 16th century through the translations of Seneca, and that influence remained strong. Soon, however, the English dramatists evinced a predilection for native subjects taken from English history. This national-historical drama reached its summit—and its virtual end—in Shakespeare. Neither the religious drama nor the classical drama as represented by the academic plays proved to be congenial and fruitful in the 17th century; it was in the masque, the pastoral, and the comedy that this period produced its best. Then in the latter part of the century, under the influence of the French

---

[1] This lively interest in the classics remained unbroken, and one encounters its manifestations in the most surprising places. Gladstone, to mention an example, was a Homeric scholar, the possessor of a library in which translations of Homer in the languages of five continents formed a truly magnificent collection.

classical theatre, English drama returned to rhyme in the "heroick play." The best of the playwrights, such as Otway, though indebted to the Elizabethans, leaned heavily on the French. By the time of Pope, English tragedy was completely hamstrung by the French model, and as late as the 1750s, Hume the philosopher advised his kin, Hume the playwright, "to read Shakespeare, but to get Racine by heart." The old plays, as Evelyn, referring to *Hamlet,* pointed out half a century earlier, had "begun to disgust the refined age." Yet, the luminosity and the lucidity of the great Augustan literary men notwithstanding, French classical drama was essentially alien to the English mind, which, through all changes and vicissitudes, was moored to Elizabethan taste. Even under the Restoration there had never been any real Gallicizing of the English theatre. But Shakespearean productions during the 18th century attempted to profit, if in a naive way, by the precept and example of the French. Aaron Hill, Cibber, and others were trying to make use of French drama for the English stage, but theirs was a crude imitation. The two nations were able to learn from each other, no doubt, but even in the use which each makes of its acquisitions they reveal the impassable gulf between them. Soon definite attempts were made at reconciling the classical spirit with the tastes and preferences of the nation. These tastes and preferences were naturally influenced by the conditions and restrictions of the period as well as by the social composition of the theatrical audiences—and the odds against the reconciliation were high on all counts.

"As the social changes in the 18th century gave a new influence to the middle classes and then to the democracy, the aristocratic class, which represented the culture at the opening stage, is gradually pushed aside; its methods become antiquated, and its conventions cease to represent the ideals of the most vigorous part of the population." [2] The domestic tragedy of Lillo and Moore and the rising novel show this convincingly, moving from the heroic-classical to the everyday. Significantly, the date of *Pamela,* of the new morality, is practically the date of *Messiah.* In 1740, when Handel made his great "decision," there was no English tragedy, no English opera, no masque, only good comedy turning towards burlesque. Distaste for and moral revulsion from the theatre were by no means restricted to militant Puritans; a large segment of the population shared these attitudes before and after the Commonwealth. There was a great deal in the theatre of the age that seemed to Handel (as it does to us) indecorous and coarse, but he was equally repelled by the sentimental comedy that was the expression of the playwrights' repentance. We have

[2] Sir Leslie Stephen, *English Literature and Society in the 18th Century.*

no record of his attending any of these plays, but many of them were performed in the theatres with which he was associated, and it is highly improbable that he was not aware of them. At any rate, we do know that he read the newspapers and pamphlets, which were full of theatre criticism and controversy, and he had many acquaintances in the literary world.

The moment was crucial for him; opera was a total failure, yet he could not compose a "modern" drama because he was altogether wedded to mythology, and contemporary life had no mythology, it could not fuse the timelessly poetic with the excitingly actual. To him the bourgeois drama was too close and hence trivial, its heroes were painted with exclusively local colors; their pathos therefore lacked drama and the natural poetic resonance of ancient tradition. The great parallel of the old drama, that of ethics and esthetics, was missing. *Style galant* and Rococo tried to reconcile classical antiquity with "progress," but could not muster enough strength for either tragedy or epic poetry. It excised the essence of Calderón and Racine, substituting bombast and elegantly effective emptiness, while Dryden and Fénelon diluted epic poetry. Under these circumstances, the Handelian music drama, the oratorio, was not, like the bourgeois drama, the satisfaction of an organic necessity but the isolated creation of a man of genius responsive to the cultural currents of his adopted country. It has been misunderstood because its resonances were mistuned, but once the components of those complicated chords are recognized and brought into concord, we can understand and follow the astonishing and unique development of the English oratorio.

One of these components was, as we have said, classical Greek drama. Greek drama was in intimate connection with the national religion, and like Aeschylus, Handel was imbued with the lofty moral and political convictions of his society. For, like the Greeks, he was seeking the great necessities, the inexorable logic of events, the fatefulness, the eternal validity of conflicts not restricted by time and place. But between the world of ancient Greece and Handel's was a great gulf. In order to bridge it, to endow his drama with the feeling of immediacy and national consciousness, Handel had to transfer the spirit of the Panhellenic nationalism of Greek drama to English nationalism. The English Bible was the providential means at hand. Without taking into consideration the national significance of the English Old Testament it would not be possible to account for the Handelian oratorio. Nevertheless, that not only its specifically English middle-class attitude but also its magnificent artistic quality and integrity were turned into an "adventitious sanctity" was a perversion of Handel's intentions, a grievous calamity that will be very difficult to undo unless we return his oratorio to its rightful place, the theatre. And that theatre was the theatre of the Greeks.

Sophocles dealt with religious myths, national, political, and ethical ideas, but everything, including the ever-recurring idea of destiny, was treated from the dramatic angle, as an instrument of human characterization. Aristotle had already defined "mythus" as an element in tragedy, where it stands very nearly for what we call the "plot." All these human beings of the Sophoclean drama are alive, because what dominates them is emotion. Similarly, the subject of Handel's drama is man, with the words and gestures of particular states of mind; religious abstraction is thereby excluded, as well as the complicated intrigues and counter-intrigues of the Venetian-Neapolitan opera. The Bible, serving as mythus, gave him a deep and colorful background from which man in the foreground rises with tremendous power. But Handel also liked epic enlargements, idyllic scenes, ever-affecting pastoral and love scenes; the lyricism often brings him closer to Aeschylus than to Sophocles. These episodes at times suspend the action, as in opera, and dilute that concentration which is so typical of the Sophoclean tragedy, but then such lyricism is precisely what distinguishes the music drama from the spoken variety. It is an essential element, and its mixture with the epic and the dramatic is what makes for the unique genre that is Handelian music drama. The lyric, the dramatic, and the choral now coalesce in a way unknown in opera or in any other species of drama since antiquity.

As can be seen, Handel used the natural ingredients of the theatre of classical antiquity, but he could not write Greek drama with Greek themes, or rather, whenever he did, the reward was stony incomprehension. He was thwarted by what had become the basis of Christian philosophy: the moral difference between antiquity and the Christian world, the "Heathen or Christian?" asked by the young Nietzsche. It is obvious that so long as orthodox Christianity supplied the universal background of belief, tragedy in the classical sense was impossible. Moreover, classical mythology no longer fell naturally on the ears of the English public, it could not be used as a matter of course, as can be seen from the unpopularity of the opera librettos, and even of the classical "oratorios" such as *Hercules*. But the Old Testament was a living mythology to this public. We have seen that the *tragédie bourgeoise* was absolutely foreign to Handel, but so too was the "universally human," for that was a fiction invented by bourgeois humanism. He was a draughtsman of character; and what the Romantics so fondly call *reinmenschlich* in man, freedom from all special traits, an unbroken, unlimited being, was therefore also foreign to him. Handel could not be tempted by an unspecific man, his man had to have feelings, loves and hates, jealousies and ambitions, virtues and sins, all of these contributing to his fate. Indeed, we may confidently apply to Handel what Matthew Arnold said about Sophocles: "He does not produce the sentiment of repose, of acquiescence, by inculcating it, by avoiding agitating circumstances; he produces it by exhibiting to us the most agitated manner under conditions of the severest form."

Handel's problem was to attain the monumentality of the Greek drama without jeopardizing human values, to safeguard the great symbolic content within the ever-changing richness of life. Here the music drama is at a considerable advantage over the spoken theatre, for it can greatly modify the effect of severely stylized language and sharply formulated thought by means of musical lyricism which allows within the drama pictures that are not exclusively determined by the words. Even the eruption of a great passion can find perfect expression in a lyric aria. The aim—and the greatest problem—was to give through this stylization a comprehensive yet sensuous symbolism—that is, theatricality. In Handel's case this theatricality was inborn. Though proceeding from the French classical drama, he largely escaped—because of his music—the rhetorical reflections of Corneille and Racine. Unbiased study will disclose that the truly dramatic moments in the great oratorios are theatrical-operatic, and these moments, we cannot repeat often enough, call for the theatre in order to exert their full impact. Even when there is no stage, the oratorio is a music drama, a form of opera.

[3]

THE ENGLISH ORATORIO grew out of the circumstances of Handel's life, and could not have so grown anywhere but in England. The unique combination of Greek drama and the Old Testament developed from personal experience, from a social order, and from a historical consciousness that were not indebted, as were some of the musical elements, to Italian oratorio or German cantata. The old mystery and miracle play was more didactic than religious, and the didactic quality is likewise present in the *sacra rappresentazione* and the early oratorio in Italy. Such an art cannot, except in the hands of a few rare creative artists, rise above local, educational, and ethical effect. Thus, even though all these elements, especially the Italian oratorio, are usually listed among the ancestors of the Handelian oratorio, we may safely disregard them. The idea that Handel's concept is indebted to Greek drama is so clear that one wonders why it was not examined long ago. Rolland perceived it more than half a century ago, but little attention was paid to his hints until Winton Dean took up the question. "It was as though the spirit of Handel had been led unconsciously towards the Hellenic ideal," says Rolland; yet one wonders whether the process was so passive.

The crucial point for Handel was Racine's reintroduction of the classic chorus which, significantly, took place in the French dramatist's last, biblical dramas. This the literary historians consider no more than a "scholastic experiment appropriate to a conventual atmosphere," [3] but then why does this reactivated chorus rapidly gain the Italian spoken theatre, opera, and then the English oratorio? In the ancient drama the chorus gradually changed from a lyrical to a dramatic role, only to disappear altogether in the new comedy. When it returned, many centuries later, it was a conscious revival and imitation that went far beyond scholastic experiment. The literary historians neglected to examine the proper place of opera in the development of Baroque drama, for in spite of the essential misunderstanding by the Florentine antiquarians, opera did, in effect, cause a *rapprochement* with the drama of the ancients. Giovanni Vincenzo Gravina (1664–1718), Apostolo Zeno (1668–1750), Scipione Maffei (1675–1755), and Pietro Metastasio (1698–1782) were the principal representatives of this new classicism that was closely allied with music, as indeed the music drama was the most congenial medium for it. They exerted themselves for the improvement of dramatic art in Italy and all of them did so by deliberately falling back on the "ancients."

This second Camerata, as it were, was no less learned, but far more musical than the original Florentine group.[4] Zeno, the first great reformer of opera, attenuated the crudities of the Venetian opera libretto by accepting and introducing into opera elements of the French classical drama. His successor, both in literary tendencies and in the office of Imperial Court Poet in Vienna, Metastasio, created the new art of *poesia per musica*. He may have been reviled by the Gluckists, and dismissed by most modern estheticians of opera, who seldom took the trouble to read these books as literature or to consider them from the point of view of Metastasio's time, but a great poet he was. (His detractors, it may be

---

[3] See, about Racine and his *Esther* and *Athalie*, p. 285 f.

[4] Gravina was one of the founders of the Roman Academy of Arcadians, and Handel should have met him there before Gravina left for the Academy of Quirina, a secessionist organization. There is no record of his having met Maffei (for whose learning Burney is full of admiration), although the latter visited London. The works of Zeno were well known to Handel, also those of Metastasio, at least up to the late thirties.

Classical Tradition in Opera 375

said, might have been misled by the fact that he outlived his style and his time by forty years.) Many of Metastasio's librettos are remarkable literary works in their own right, despite the conventionality of the plots. He was the true late Baroque classicist of the theatre, who in his time spoke from the very soul of musicians and public. His versification is sheer perfection and his love lyrics are tender and suave, but his particular strength—as often in Racine and Handel—was in the characterization of women. Metastasio adhered to Aristotle's dramaturgical principles, and his dramatic figures speak the language of the Greek Olympus even in his biblical oratorios. At that, he was not really a tragic poet; the secret of his immense success and reputation rests on a certain sympathetic lightness of touch, which made for a musical verse. He was a poet of love, even if that love was the *amour raffiné* that in his time was no less fashionable in life than on the stage. Voltaire still considered Metastasio's best writings worthy of Corneille and Racine.

But, as we have said, the historians failed to realize the significance of these developments; the opera libretto appeared to them as something outside the realm of literature proper, though the example of Philippe Quinault, Lully's librettist, should have warned them. Quinault's librettos were regarded by French literary critics as forming an integral part of the French classical theatre—hence the title *tragédie lyrique* rather than opera. Metastasio never apologized for being a "mere" librettist, nor was he so regarded; the title his contemporaries gave him, *Il Sofocle italiano*, was thoroughly deserved, for his drama was *the* Italian drama of the High Baroque. Parenthetically we may add that it was not only in Italy and France that the classical tradition was acknowledged to have been propagated by opera, but even on occasion in England. Dryden, in the preface to *Albion and Albanius* (1685), speculates about the relationship between Italian opera and Greek drama. In his *Dissertation on the Rise, Union, and Power, &c., of Poetry and Music* (1763), John Brown saw an unbroken tradition from the drama of antiquity to Baroque opera.

In France, as in Italy, the classical theatre was naturalized. In the mid-16th century Sophocles and Euripides were translated into French verse by Ronsard, and soon we observe a short-lived vogue of biblical tragedies under Calvinist influence but also cast in the Greek mould. The chorus was employed and the Alexandrine soon ruled the language. Subsequently Spanish and Italian influences criss-cross this French theatre, and by the time the great tragedists, Corneille and Racine, arrive on the scene, the chorus had disappeared, a loss that was paralleled in opera.

The reasons for this were largely economic, for ever since public, "commercial" opera began in Venice, the managements had had to cut corners to make the inordinately costly opera production profitable. They settled on a few principals, reduced the orchestra, and dispensed with the chorus. Metastasio, who understood the artistic and dramaturgical advantages of the chorus, made tentative efforts for its restoration, but it was only in the second half of the 18th century that it gradually returned to Italian opera.

Not so in French opera. Racine, summoned from retirement by Madame de Maintenon, reinstated the chorus, and it became the starting point of a new flowering in French opera and subsequently in the Italian theatre and opera. Padre Martini still praised the superiority of the French in operatic choruses. Handel faithfully followed the Italian custom of solo opera; it is only in his later operas, already under the influence of the oratorio, that the chorus appears. But in the English music dramas, the oratorios, he made the chorus paramount, and for the same reason that the French made it so: the chorus was an integral part of the Greek drama. "One must admit," said Voltaire, a sworn enemy of opera, "that the opera-tragedy recalls in many ways the tragedy of classical Greece," and Du Roullet, the librettist of Gluck's *Iphigénie,* still was convinced that "by following Racine with scrupulous attention" the true music drama along classical lines could be achieved. This French tragedy, especially Racine's plays, was considered in the 18th century the embodiment of *le naturel, la raison,* and *le bon sens,* qualities that were seen as flowing from Greek drama.

Thus the men of the Enlightenment. They were right, except that these qualities, very French qualities, were attributed to the wrong source. Racine's drama did descend from the Greeks, but it was the expression of a particular national culture, that of Louis XIV's France. The parallel with Handel is startling. With him, we see once more a dramatic conception based on that of the Greeks, but by choosing to make the Old Testament his theatre, Handel represents English national culture. He departed considerably from the classical exterior, at the same time giving his music dramas a Grecian strength the English spoken theatre of his day did not possess. The literary men of the Augustan era may have acquired Racine's elegance, but not his power; Handel displays this elegance in the application of the métier, the art of composition, and his power not only equals Racine's but exceeds it. The elegance that is so attractive in the love songs and pastorals is superseded by stark dramatic directness and economy when in the accompanied recitatives, the ariosos, and the choruses he goes to the core of a situation.

The more or less strict schematicism of the French classical drama was nevertheless the source of great beauties. If its rigidity, solemnity, rhetorical effusion seem to exclude real action, Racine (like Handel), in compensation, at the decisive moments comes much nearer to final values than the free drama, for his rhetorical pathos could drive even abstractions to the most profound dramatic explosions. This French classical drama, which exerted so great an influence on the Handelian oratorio, was addressed to an aristocratic minority, whereas Handel sought to address the much wider middle classes, and with them the nation as a whole. The reconciliation of this fundamental difference is very difficult, and we can approach it only with the critique of the historical point of view. We must realize that the whole development leading up to the oratorio was a series of efforts to find the right relation between Handel's sensations and his creative power—which is really the case with every great artist. Neither the record of sensations nor the constructive expedient can, however, be considered apart; the misunderstandings that arose around Handel have been due to precisely this mistaken separation.

[4]

It is said that before writing his *Iphigenie*, Goethe spent days drawing Greek statues to immerse himself in the spirit of Hellenism. Greek drama was in his day considered to be most effective when its figures came closest to the statuesque. Stravinsky still condenses the action in his *Oedipus Rex* into a few deliberate, marmoreal scenes. The pictorial —that is, the active participation of the milieu—was believed to weaken the plasticity of the drama. What did Greek drama mean to Handel; how did he prepare himself for the task of dealing with it; how was he to utilize what undoubtedly attracted him to the classical drama, its ability to form great symbols, its stylization of great destinies?

After an artistic lifetime spent in the world of Italian opera, he realized that, aside from the English public's hostility to this foreign importation, the conventions of Venetian-Neapolitan opera, though descended from classical sources, did not permit the monumental-heroic scale. Yet the transition from opera to oratorio was not so startling as the proponents of the "conversion theory" see it, for while the exteriors of these works are different, their method of composition is fundamentally the same. In the oratorio, however, Handel was largely freed from the rules governing the opera, from the stereotyped handling of the subsidiary actions and episodes, and the sudden unmotivated turns created by the *deus ex machina*. As a result, his scenes could broaden into epic sketches, then, suddenly halted, condense into sharply dramatic pictures.

What was altogether new was the role of the chorus in the drama; in its concinnity and its grandeur it is no longer the *turba* of the German Passion but is akin to the choral ode of the Greeks, for these choruses usually stand in some precisely planned relation to the principal figures. A chorus such as the "Jealousy" chorus in *Hercules* or "O fatal consequence" in *Saul*, in its inexorable and all-embracing power, is truly Sophoclean; it summarizes and comments on the tragedy with sombre and at times fearful intensity. "Grandeur" must be interpreted in this Hellenic sense, which was what Handel had in mind when he requested in one of his letters to Jennens a change in the libretto: the conclusion seemed to him "not grand enough." At times the chorus, like the *parodos*, the first choral passage in classical tragedy, enters right after the *prologos*, or moves from place to place (*peripateia*), or addresses the public in the manner of the *parabasis* of Aristophanes. There are also instances resembling the *kommos*, the Greek lament in which the principal alternates with the chorus. Of particular relevance is the position of the arias, which, unlike the pattern in the operas, are at times introduced between two choric songs—the *epeisodion* of the classic drama. Only the *exodos* is treated differently. In the classical drama this is the part following the last song of the chorus, but, because of the nature of the music drama, Handel likes to end with the chorus itself.

With this role of the chorus the Handelian oratorio leaves the romanticized classicism of the opera to enter the orbit of the true classical drama. And this Handel owed to Racine, who stated in the prefaces of his two late dramas that he used the chorus in the tradition of the ancient Greek theatre. It was in *Esther*, which Rolland called "one of the greatest tragedies in the old style written since the Grecian period," that Handel first made contact with the living spirit of classical tragedy, and this encounter, though not immediately, became eventually decisive for the future development of his creative imagination.

[5]

THE SIGNIFICANCE OF Racine and the classical theatre for the Handelian oratorio is clear; but that of the Old Testament we have not yet examined with sufficient critical insight; it has an importance over and above the historical conditions that steered Handel toward it. More precisely, over and above the historical factors giving rise to the English oratorio there must be something in the content of the scriptural subject, in its message, in its values, that transcends the original conditions as transmitted from Racine to Handel. There may be some point in returning to the genesis of the Handelian oratorio, for in history each thing depends on something else.

The genesis was by no means so sudden as it may have appeared in the discussion of *Esther* and *Athalia*. In those two oratorios Handel was setting to music stories from the Old Testament taken from Racine's plays by the same titles. In a Catholic country like France the Old Testament as a whole had something of an exotic air. Only the Huguenots were devoted to the Psalms. Their translation into verse and their musical settings represent a unique feature of the Reformation in Latin countries. In England, on the contrary, the Old Testament was not only the pervading source of religious thought, but was liable to political-social interpretations, for the relation to the Deity in the Old Testament is a national one. But are form and content in these oratorios compatible? Can they be intellectually reconciled? The formative principle, we are told again and again, is an essentially Christian world view. But within the stylized drama Handel turns almost exclusively to the dramatis personae giving us their essence and their character as completely as permitted by the illusion of life. This illusion of life is not, however, imparted by Scripture, by revelation; it comes from the inner life of the drama. The use of scriptural language may have the effect of intensifying the pathos of the drama, but that is only through an assumed attitude. Similarly, seeing a universal story in a scriptural setting inclines us to attribute to the work a spirituality it in no wise possesses. But though a biblical drama may have a religious connotation, the drama itself must be expressed through the souls of the acting human characters; the uniqueness of the conflict, its sole relevance to a given occasion in a given drama, excludes any other approach. The material of the drama is social, involving relationships between men, and the first requirement here is a stage—there is no true drama without a stage. Every drama that does not grow from the spirit of the theatre, or at least from a theatrically conceived and inspired milieu, is prey to the rhetorical or the didactic. Drama requires a certain sensuous culture, the expressive motions of the human body, the beauty of the human voice, even pomp and ornament. Nor is the theatre in itself enough, for it does not exist without a public, and that public usually represents a certain dominant class of society whose economic, political, and other beliefs and circumstances, the tempo and rhythm of whose way of life, give birth to the manifestations, even the forms, of its culture. As we have remarked above, Handel's operas—like Racine's dramas—were written for an aristocratic public, but the oratorios were addressed to the English people, and that people was, said John Richard Green, "the people of a book, and that book was the Bible."

Christianity absorbed both Judaic and Hellenic elements and throughout history they alternated in prominence. The strong impact of the Judaic was felt mainly in the principles of revealed law, while the rich Hellenic elements furnished a source for esthetics. The Greek world was the cradle of beauty to all ages, and it retained this role within Christianity. The Renaissance heard Moses's voice in Plato and sought David's words from the sybil's mouth. Perhaps the most brilliant synthesis was the work of Michelangelo, who not only succeeded in coupling the figures of the Old Testament with those of ancient mythology but in a miraculous way could unite the primitive force of the former with the freshness and charm of the Greeks.

In England, Milton also linked the Muses of Mount Sinai with those of Mount Helicon, and in general English Protestants were well disposed towards this union. But Protestantism evinced a certain hostility towards the ideal of beauty, which it tended to equate with popery. The English Protestants shared with their continental brethren a desire to "cleanse" Christianity of the beauties of "paganism," but their approach to the problem was quite different and uniquely their own. Hellenism exerted a powerful attraction on them. Its spirit of human self-sufficiency found a congenial expression in the polity and philosophy of the Englishman, upon whom, apparently, the sea had much the same effect that the "city" had upon the Greek, encouraging independence and self-centered isolation from the rest of the world. But this was curiously felt and communicated in a Hebraic spirit, satisfying the interests of a civilization that had become particularly aware of history.

The English not only equated their history with that of the Hebrews, but there were numerous attempts to show kinship between classical antiquity and the Hebrew world, the fusion of which they felt produced not so much Christianity in general as English Protestantism in particular. They were wary of linking classical antiquity with the New Testament, according primacy to the Old Testament not only over the New but even over ancient Hellas. Latin civilization was synonymous with Catholicism, a view of life with which the English did not sympathize. Only once did Handel transgress the limitations imposed by this concept, in *Messiah;* he never again returned to the New Testament.

The Old Testament and Greek drama are considered mutually exclusive, two extremes—but are they? Both grew from mythological-religious sources, and the passions visited on their human figures were symbolized by deity. The liberty of the dramatis personae in both to make choices and decisions is more or less restricted by fate or divine commands. There is, indeed, a certain kinship between the two sources; for instance, in the profound difference that separates them, even in their external manifestations, from Christian spirituality. Greek drama was living mythology, the Old Testament living history, both originating from the imagination of the people.[5] Even the arrangement of the Greek theatre was different from the stage produced by the Roman-Christian West. The ancient Greeks sliced from lush green hillsides the magnificently curving tremendous stone benches of their theatres; the lapping waves of the sea marked the pace for the slow measured unfolding of their tragedies. The Romans cut up the great boulders and sent the blocks to the cities to be built into amphitheatres, the tragedy eventually turning into the circus. True, in the Handelian drama the protagonists do not wear masks and they no longer announce through a voice pipe, in solemn, stentorian tones, the decisions fate has made for kings and heroes. But there is a new voice pipe, more powerful than any the Greeks may have had: the polyphonic chorus. For what we hear is no longer speech, but music, beautifully articulated, powerful, massive, and gentle. Yet many of the echoes do come from the Ionian Sea.

As has been said before, in the new English music drama called oratorio, Handel's problem was to attain the monumentality of the Greek drama without losing human values. This meant that a distance had to be found from which a great event could be seen as containing a whole complex of life. The representation of the Gospels, which he tried in his youth, could only be done in lofty general terms, excluding the personal and psychological elements, the essence of the Handelian drama. Christ appears—to the dramatist—in an unapproachable seclusion. For a long time Handel had thought he found the necessary distance in formal opera, but though emotion and character are often powerfully represented there even through the conventional forms, what was needed was to amplify this ardent dramatic lyricism to epic proportions. This is what he proceeded to do by marrying Greek drama with Old Testament history, adding to the biblical story the schooled humanist's art, the simplicity and directness of the true classical spirit.

Thus he came to create true drama of a Sophoclean tone with biblical

[5] Friedrich Schleiermacher's theological school declared the Old Testament a collection of folkloristic tales.

themes. *Belshazzar* exudes the spirit of Greek drama, and, though taken from the Book of Daniel, it received important additions from Herodotus and Xenophon. Or, to mention another example, *Jephtha* also strongly suggests the Attic drama, and its choruses are unimaginable without their Greek antecedents. What made the blend successful was not only the fantastic frame of the tremendous biblical stories, but all the materials of life from which this fantasy was built, and all the life that it represents: of the composer, of his nation, of his time. The reign of Saul or Solomon does not date these oratorios and does not limit them to an ascertainable historical period; these works present human characters under certain conditions. But the conditions, the manner, that is, the concepts, ideas, and reactions of the protagonists and of the people—the chorus—have their roots in ascertainable English social usage. It is in this setting, physical and spiritual, that Handel the oratorio composer must be apprehended; for the center of gravity of his oratorio is for the most part immovably fixed in England and its people, and most of its great strength, as well as certain weaknesses, springs from that remarkable fact.

The Old Testament offered natural themes for Handel, but these were not religious themes. His biblical learning was considerable, but to the *composer,* the Old Testament, which fascinated him endlessly, was not revelation but a complex of concrete, sensuous appearances and events that he made his own. These settings are not expressions of biblical faith but dramatizations, the projections of character. With all his earnest devotion Handel was a dramatist with a strong Dionysian streak; to him the biblical figures were not historical-mythological models but men, present, valid, and usable by a dramatist at all times and under all conditions. This Old Testament is ancient and modern at the same time; modern, because in Handel's setting everything historical, everything that comes from the past, is cast anew in the present by his dramatic force. In the hands of most composers, the biblical story becomes subject matter—in Handel's it is life; others do not really know what is dramatically living in it, for few of them feel altogether free to regard the scriptural text with the critical eyes of the dramatist. To Handel it made for creativity, it aroused and enhanced his perception of life. He saw in the heroes of the Old Testament not what they were thousands of years ago but what they became thousands of years later; they are visions and creatures of his own. He is a later brother of the great figures of ancient Israel, an English brother, who recognizes the kinship. His Old Testament characters speak like inhabitants of the biblical country, and yet they constantly betray their 18th-century English citizenship. It makes sense, for to the English Protestant the Old Testament was inextricably associated with the ideals, the national and political aims of his country. These ideals became reality for Handel, and he represented them on a heroic scale.

It makes sense, yet it is this very matter that is at the bottom of the process that has led to the misrepresentation enveloping Handel's person and life work. We have quoted the German writer who said that Bach and Handel were "Christ's singers." Another says, "Bach and Handel became the singers of Christendom, this is their final and decisive importance; in an indissoluble embrace they unite the Old with the New Testament." Still another person of standing, a German divine, praises Bach and Handel for their artistic achievements "which rest on divine inspiration and which is the continuation of Luther's work"! From this point on the arguments cease to be orderly and are lost in hazy reasoning in which theology, musicology, and German and English local patriotism are thrown together in a tangle of speculations difficult to analyze or even to follow. The writers could not help seeing the preponderance of Old Testament texts in Handel's works, as they could not miss the preponderance of the New in Bach's; but this is explained by the simple expedient of declaring Handel to be "the musician of promised salvation," and as such naturally attracted to the Old Testament. In this way they come to the conclusion that Handel's aim was identical with Bach's; "at the summit both meet in solemn worship of God and the praise of Christ as the Redeemer of the world." There is a curious contradiction here, a sweeping ignorance and denial of historical and even theological facts that surely calls for explanation.

[6]

NOTHING is more difficult to determine than the real force of conviction with which a creed is actually and individually held. Christianity in Handel's England was preached more earnestly than it was practiced, and professed more stoutly than it was believed, but a decent—if formal—respect for the observances of the Church had for a long time been imposed by social sanction. The 18th-century Church in England was well-mannered and decorous but highly political and certainly deficient in its spirituality. Religion was widely taken for granted; to be a member of the Church was just another act of man in society. Yet, though the Church of England may at that period have become somnolent as a Christian institution, and though the philosophers were busy, in England as in France, undermining the foundations of religion, the masses firmly held to faith in the hereafter.

Their emphasis, however, was on the earthly present. The Englishman was convinced that there should be an ultimate value in the things of the world. He found no support for this view in the New Testament, whereas in the Old the prophetic genius of the Jews was profoundly "thissided." The prophets did not preach a theoretical but an eminently practical monotheism that was attractive to the English. Handel's Englishmen admired and fully accepted the Jewish Old Testament concept of collective action, whose symbol was a king leading his people by virtue of a covenant executed under the auspices of a Deity who would not tolerate oppression and injustice. This concept was the blueprint for constitutionalism. The institution of the monarchy, the concentration of military as well as civil power in the King (as is clear from Pentateuchal legislation), shows a startling resemblance to British institutions. The legal system, the revolutionary concept of social justice described in Deuteronomy with its judicial sessions held in public, the witnesses, their examination, all was eminently congenial to the British mind. They could read in the Old Testament about commerce, territorial expansion, competitive nationalism, and political autonomy, subjects with which their own existence was closely bound up. All these things were relevant to the social and political problems of their day.

As we examine the English Protestants' relationship to the Bible we discover that theirs was a very particular view among Christian denominations in the Handelian era, and what is most striking is the exceptional role the Old Testament played in their conception of Christianity. Their acceptance of the principles of the Sermon on the Mount was not an unconditional but a selective one to suit political and economic aims and conditions. At the same time, their ever-present historical sense made them turn to the Old Testament rather than the New. The English love their institutions not with mystical fervor or mere local patriotism, as do some other peoples, but with an intelligent and steadfast loyalty to principles. Their attitude tends to the hortatory and rhetorical; their national solutions must have a moral foundation.[6] This rhetoric of the English is

---

[6] One may of course argue that while morality is not identical with religion, it is directly involved in the religious attitude, and, conversely, the genuinely moral attitude, the recognition of moral obligations, directly involves religion. When a man believes in God his belief inevitably affects his conduct, and to affirm duty is implicitly to affirm God. But religious relationship to God comes with prayer, and "it may be held," said Coleridge, "that the most deep and original moral interpretation is not likely to be that which most shows a moral purpose." Moreover, Hutcheson's motto, "the greatest happiness for the greatest number," announces a practical result of moral steadfastness independent of religion. Thus divine ethics is converted into

not mental gymnastics and the pathos of words, as with the Latins, nor sentimental-metaphysical as with the Germans; it originated from a moral necessity, it is the voice of conscience, the spokesman for national morality. The concreteness of its language furthers the concreteness of its thought.

It was in the Old Testament that the English found the roots of this national mystique. The historical Israel of the Bible offered to England a most congenial parallel. Judaism presented an intense national consciousness of a people divinely set apart, a destiny that English Protestantism applied to itself, the English nation becoming the new Israel, chosen by God as His instrument. This identification with the ancient Hebrews dates from the Reformation, when the Bible, until then a hidden book, not accessible to persons unable to read Hebrew, Greek, or Latin, was made generally available in the vernacular. It was strengthened by England's experience of what became a Holy War, in which it saw itself as a righteous people opposing the power of the idolatrous, foreign-god-worshipping Spaniards. The fate of the Armada, with its almost miraculous outcome—*Flavit et dissipati sunt*—had the force of a biblical confrontation of good and evil. The idea was inherited and accentuated by the Parliamentarian party during the Civil War, who thought of themselves as the Chosen of the Chosen, strongly and deliberately identifying with the Old Testament, even to the use of Hebrew names in preference to those of the saints, a practice previously rare. The idea survived the Parliamentarians' political defeat to become, after the Restoration, the most prominent of English attitudes. By Handel's time this Puritan-descended concept had been translated from a religious idea into a broad social assumption, a prime example of the interaction of religion and politics.

The Jews of the Old Testament were a disciplined people who lived by the Law. That the Jews not only created a remarkable system of law but stanchly upheld it, firmly believing in a government of law rather than of men, appealed to the English mind. For the Jews there was no term that more adequately expressed the essence of their religion than "Law." The Maccabees died for the sake of the "Law"—that is, for the ancestral faith. If we examine the writings of prominent English churchmen of the Handelian era we shall find a similar attitude. Bishop Gibson, leader of the Church-Whig alliance, had a great antagonist in Bishop Thomas Sherlock

human law bound to material things instead of the hereafter. But this characteristic English compromise in ethics and religion has only brought the English into subjection to the theory of material necessity and the practical sway of Mammon.

of Salisbury, the leader of the Tory clergy. But to both the Bible was *Scripta Lex,* and both dealt with religious questions like lawyers. The religion of the Law shared by Hebrews and Britons had its noble ingredients, but it also had a fondness for negatives, for a mercenary spirit, and its attempt at redemption through human effort contradicted Christian doctrine. The English greatly admired also the passionate belief of the Jews in the righteousness of the mission of their people. However, while this idea of a Kingdom of Heaven on earth was a religious-theocratic idea to the Jews, to the Englishman in Handel's time it was an eminently practical, secular proposition. He most certainly wanted the Kingdom of Heaven—but right then and there. In many affairs the rest of Europe would have considered purely spiritual, King and Government took precedence over Canterbury. Handel's contemporaries noted with satisfaction that the Old Testament's perspective was not that of eternal life, but of a present existence for which the Jews organized their society with skill and solicitude. They were proudly confident that a righteous, strong, and prosperous Englishman was fully capable of achieving the good life by his own strength. To the English mind Ezekiel's view that man is capable of exercising sufficient will power to enable him to live in accordance with the purpose of Yahweh was welcome.

The Englishman fought his own battles, after which, in ringing anthems, he asked God's concurrence. This is the spirit of his wonderful ceremonial music. The Christ of the New Testament was difficult to place in this picture; He had qualities that contradicted the English anthropocentric-humanistic concept at every step. Yahweh, however, could be made into a constitutional God who was all-powerful and exacted obedience yet whose speech from the throne could be prepared, like that of the monarch, by the government. We should recall Milton's *Pro defensio populo Anglicano,* which insists that power does not descend from God but is vested in the sovereign by the people. This the Englishman believes with unshakable faith, though with similar tenacity his kings claim their office "by the grace of God." Here, too, they found a parallel, for Yahweh was regarded as the Lord of his People. (That He became a universal God was owing to the genius of Moses.) It should be remembered that as early as Milton's *Paradise Lost* the Kingdom of Heaven is the model of a well-organized earthly state. One can find hymns there, but also commands and war chariots. The Lord's heavenly armies enact the same deeds as Israel's soldiers down on earth. It is only a different, larger Earth. The Briton will not accept a faith that does not spell out its tenets; he accepts religion as something that gives human life the reassurance of being part of a higher order of things but insists that this order should have particular relevance to earthly life, should offer a frame for, but not be the overpowering aim of, his existence. For all this he found abundant precedent in the Old Testament but little in the New. The Gospel is essentially a message of spiritual redemption, not of social order and reform. And it offers a drastic revaluation of earthly goods.

To the English Protestant, God appeared as He did to the Jews, as the powerful ruler of a kingdom on earth. The Jewish concept was a national organization under the effective kingship of Yahweh. To the prophets the kingship of Yahweh was an actual reality. And when the monarchy came to an end and the Hebrew state was broken, there arose the expectation of the coming of a future king, who henceforth was an ideal king because he was not present to enforce his laws. The *political* idea of the Messiah, the restorer of the Jewish state, remained alive as part of rabbinical theology, and it is well known that during the Middle Ages more than one false Messiah appeared, arousing ardent hopes. But the Jews did not believe in a suffering and atoning Messiah; the first disciples of Jesus could only gradually extricate themselves from the elements of Jewish *political* doctrine to arrive at their understanding of the Saviour.

The English, too, chose to see in God a Lord Protector and were devoted to maintaining this role with great ceremonial elaboration. But while the Nonconformist was earnestly interested in the observance of the severe moral principles laid down in Scripture and mistrusted the Established Church, he united with the Anglican in expecting God to observe His part in the contract and not to meddle with the political-economic order of the modern state. While the Yahweh of the Old Testament was a deity with concrete power, in the religious view as embodied in the 18th-century Church in England, heavily touched by political philosophy and by the ideas of the rising Enlightenment, the God of the New Testament was acknowledged without being allowed to interfere with constitutional life, though all the decorum due a reigning monarch was observed. To the straightforward and practical Englishman the simple, dramatic, and visually apprehensible stories in the Old Testament seemed more real and congenial than subtle abstractions, complicated theological and philosophical articles of faith. (The contrast with the Lutherans, who favored the musical representation of the Gospels, is significant.) The Old Testament story could always be interpreted in ethical and moral terms, and there was a lesson to be learned from the fate of those who defied the authority of the Lord, for they were punished not unlike the guilty defendant in a British law court.

The Christian Church has traditionally lent support to the assumption that the powers that be are ordained by God, a view that gave rise to the glamorous ideal of the Holy Roman Empire. After the Reformation the idea received fresh impetus and found a new realization in England. Here the Church, being a national institution headed by the King, had a particular role. The Kings of England had always been accustomed to surround themselves with clerical advisers, whose duties were as much secular as ecclesiastical; and whenever the coming of a new dynasty made strong support for the throne more than ever desirable, that support was sought as much from the lords spiritual as from the temporal counsel of the Crown. By Handel's time, the episcopate was regarded as a political body whose duty it was to offer advice on matters of state, and the obvious method of advancement in the ranks of the Church was by party appointment. The bishops sat in the House of Lords throughout the session, their solid Whig block counted upon to deliver the votes, and they did indeed frequently help to decide purely party matters in favor of the government, while at election time they were expected to influence the constituency in their diocese. All this left little time for spiritual matters; the bishops spent the winter in London, attending Parliament and showing up at court. William Warburton (1698–1779), Bishop of Gloucester, Pope's friend, a Shakespearean and one of the most doctrinaire critics of the age, in his *Alliance between Church and State* (1736) clearly demonstrated that in this alliance the state was not concerned at all with religious doctrines or defense of the truth but with the practical advantages secured to itself by the addition of religious sanctions to its own authority.

The Englishman was engaged in commerce, industry, and finance; he was building an empire, organizing the world. Like the old Roman, he must lead and enlighten the barbarian, defend civilization. (Kipling, still more recently, wrote verses that could have been written by an ancient Roman.) As he civilizes, he also converts, the cause of empire becomes the cause of Christianity; in this cause he needs not other-worldliness but hard-headed practicality. He was comforted by the Old Testament, which showed an appreciation for private property and wealth, the cornerstone of modern Protestant ethics.[7] Renunciation no more appealed to him than poverty, which he felt to be practically synonymous with sin. He saw that in the Old Testament those who lived a righteous life and obeyed the

[7] The sanctity of private property is one of the Commandments, the Tenth, which English Protestants significantly retained in its Hebrew form, the neighbor's real estate, livestock, *and* wife being on the same list of prohibited covetousness. Lutherans and Catholics separated goods from the neighbor's wife by dividing the Commandment into the Ninth and Tenth.

laws could invariably count on Jehovah's support. Doing well in business was almost a corollary of religious observance; success and status were the good to be pursued, and he felt no doubt of God's support so long as he observed the letter of the law. Actually, all the camouflage notwithstanding, this was the victory of the modern secular state dedicated to material well-being and civic progress and to its protection. As Crane Brinton succinctly observes: "Protestantism did help to make the non-Christian world-view of the Enlightenment." [8]

The Old Testament supported the Englishmen's view, and they liked the Old Testament for its exaltation of righteousness, the constant emphasis on morals, the primacy of law, its Puritanism, its unequivocal endorsement of private property and "free enterprise." And they loved the elaborate ritual, administered by a priesthood of high estate, the role of the King, and above all the staunch defense of the nation's ideals, laws, and institutions by great commoners who rose to heroic leadership. No one in their entire history has realized for the English these ideals, these thrilling ceremonies, these dramatic figures, with more conviction, more majesty and grandeur, and more exhilarating immediacy than Handel in his anthems and oratorios.

The enthusiastic celebration of the *genius loci* should not suggest, however, that at every minute we must remember "1066 and all that." Handel had centuries of the Christian tradition and the Christian paradox behind him but did not see his artistic duty in the light of any theology. He did not directly revert to this Christian tradition in his English works, but neither did he discard it, though the devotees of the religious conversion theory never notice the true manifestations of the tradition, notably at the end of Handel's career. The last oratorios, while not religious in the Victorian sense of exhortation, are informed by religion as a landscape is informed by light. Handel had absolutely no use for sanctimoniousness, though never disputing true piety. He felt strongly for the suffering of others, and compassion, the sacredness of sorrow, is a Christian trait absent from the Old Testament. He laid himself open to life in all its manifestations, and when in old age and sickness he continued to wrestle with his art, consolation, the philosophy of Christian revelation, appears unobtrusively and in an altogether personal form. This is the Christian belief in

[8] This picture was not altogether unfamiliar to Handel, for he had witnessed the vociferous quarrels of Lutherans and Pietists in his youth in Germany. Equally familiar was the thoroughly materialistic attitude of faithful churchgoers in Hamburg, who transacted business right in the pews. In the end, materialism is characteristic of all well-organized mercantile societies, where wealth, and political influence to protect and promote it, is in a curious way combined with religion.

Christian experience rather than in a book. In these last works an iron door had shut on the interests for which posterity will esteem him. The quiet ecstasy, the note of stillness and spiritual security, indeed of prayer, wholly escaped the sober middle-class mind then as now; *Theodora* and *Jephtha* were total failures. But what does sobriety know of true piety— and of true poetry? Perhaps in the end there is a special impressiveness in the way Handel's life and work leaves so much to our awed conjecture.

[7]

JOHN LOCKMAN, in his introductory essay to the libretto of *Rosalinda* written for John Christopher Smith, Jr., in 1740, deplores that "notwithstanding the wonderful Sublimity of Mr. *Handel's* Compositions, yet the Place in which Oratorios are commonly performed among us, and some other Circumstances, must necessarily lessen the Solemnity of this Entertainment, to which possibly, the Choice of the Subject of these Dramas may likewise sometimes contribute." Here is the principal prob-lem posed by the new English oratorio, a problem of tradition: the ora-torio had to abandon the stage practically at the moment of its inception. Yet it was not welcome in the church either. The English example is not unique; the same suspicion surrounded the oratorio in other Protestant countries in the 18th century. In Hamburg, oratorios were performed as "musical concerts" because churches often prohibited their presentation within sacred precincts. If in London Handel produced oratorios in thea-tres and inns, the Hamburgers did so in armories, harbor installations, and even the local prison! It is somewhat amusing to observe that eventually the complacent English had to emulate those idolatrous Italians by per-forming oratorios during Lent as a substitute for opera.

In Rome—or Vienna, or Dresden—this was considered the decorous thing to do, and everyone was clear about the subterfuge, but in England the practice, which started in earnest after Handel's death, was sur-rounded with a large aura of hypocrisy. The 19th-century Puritans still wanted to exterminate everything in the oratorios that would even faintly recall the stage; Chrysander himself was horrified at the idea of imputing dramatic-theatrical qualities to the oratorios, though towards the end of his life he began to see the light. It was only after the First World War that staged oratorio performances, begun in Germany, could be mounted in England with impunity. But it took several more decades before Win-ton Dean could arrive at the logical conclusion that "*Semele* and *Hercules* are the greatest full-length musical dramas in the English language."

These two works were composed on classical subjects and were called oratorios without the "sacred" prefix, but the "biblical" and hence "sacred" oratorios are every bit as theatrically conceived music dramas as the "secular" oratorios.

A scene such as the one in the first act of *Solomon* may give the impression of a very religious affair; the High Priest, famed Zadok, is certainly pious and fervent, and even the King has some nice things to say about his religion. Just the same, what is uppermost in Solomon's mind at that moment is to retire with his young and tempting Queen to a bucolic spot, which he presently does to the delight of the chorus, which wishes him a pleasant time in one of the most charming choral ballads ever created. How Handel's imagination flares up at the prospect of love and the contemplation of nature! The horrified Victorians took appropriate steps to remove King Solomon's unequivocal statement that his "love admits no delay." Most expressions of this sort were suppressed, for these good people wondered uneasily whether the composer of *Messiah* was not something of a sensualist. The "Nightingale" scene in *Solomon* is one of those instances to which Lockman refers as a questionable choice of subject, and it is quite possible that without the "sacred" label, the judicious excisions and alterations, and the purported religious edification, the biblical oratorios would have shared the fate of *Hercules* or *Theodora,* both of which are about as well known as the opera *Ariodante.* The theatre makes conscious the processes of life, compelling us to look them in the face and understand their necessity, but Puritans of all eras dread sex and link its sinfulness with the theatre. Handel's oratorios had enough love scenes to worry them considerably. The tepid "sacred" performances given today do not even suggest the oratorios' great richness in mood and expression.

It is significant that the two non-dramatic works, *Messiah,* and *Israel in Egypt,* became the most popular of Handel's oratorios, indicating the continued, if latent, bias, the fear of the theatre and its unsuitability for sacred music. (Amusingly enough, *Parsifal,* a full-blooded romantic opera, with a scorchingly sensuous second act, does, on Good Friday, transform the opera house into a church.) Handel was convinced that dramatic music demands the stage, and since he was first and foremost a dramatist, his mind was so preoccupied with opera that it took him some time to realize that he could not only create dramatic music in the oratorio but could go much farther afield than the conventions of opera permitted. While the bishop's ban on staged performances forced some compromises, the drama and the stage were not separated in the oratorio: the detailed stage directions testify to this even though most of them were removed from the published scores. One constantly feels something in the oratorios that should be realized but for two centuries could not be realized: Handel's true dramatic intentions. In Elizabethan drama and in the Greek drama, intention and realization went together; in the Handelian English music drama, though the intentions are clear, the realization was —and is—prevented by what we have called the "religious issue." Thus, even though Handel's numerous stage directions make his artistic intent clear, it was neutralized if not destroyed by the injection of another extraneous and irrelevant issue, the essential moral degeneracy of the theatre versus the revelatory nobility of Holy Writ. The rising bourgeois civilization insisted on a moralizing, religious, political, and didactic interpretation for fear that otherwise the sacred subjects would be lowered to the level of theatrical entertainment. For two centuries the humanity was sucked from the core of the Handelian oratorio.

The religious exercise is still carried out at performances of Handel's oratorios, but the artistic problems are honored in the breach. The Romantic era, and our own musical practice which is still largely based on it, could not solve these problems because it could not see the musico-dramatic values. Important things are neglected and nonessentials accented, so that the intended effect is usually distorted. The many fine nuances in the solo numbers are ruined by breast-beating, while the choruses turn into brutal melodrama. The irony of it is that in just those works where Handel attained that dramatic continuity which he was unable to create under the handicap of the formal conventions of the opera seria, we destroy this continuity in our performances of the oratorios by pauses that isolate the numbers. By the time of *Saul,* Handel used the da capo aria with circumspection, though he still resorted to it as a vehicle for lyric effusion; now the accompanied recitative and the extended arioso come into their own. Both of these are highly dramatic means of expression, demanding the vigor and experience of the opera singer, not the church musician. The Handelian oratorio may appear undramatic in the concert hall, but with few exceptions it is essentially theatre music and therefore eminently dramatic. What in the spoken drama seems unduly to stress the epic and lyric qualities, and consequently loosen dramatic form, is in the music drama a fundamental necessity. It makes possible the conversion of the intellectual element into mood and feeling, both intimate and monumental. And that mood and feeling are not uniformly devotional; the enemy of the poetic and the dramatic is custom.

"The plays of Shakespeare and the English Bible are, and ever will be, the twin monuments, not merely of their own period, but of the perfection of English, the complete expression of the literary capacities of the language, at the time when it had lost none of its pristine vigor." It was this language, and Shakespearean characterization, that appear in Handel's oratorios with pristine vigor. They are not quaint period pieces, but the musical embodiment of Saintsbury's "twin monuments" of English art.

XV

AFTER AN ABSENCE OF NINE MONTHS IN IRELAND HANdel came home to London and quietly took up residence in his Brook Street house. There is something curious about this quietness. In former years his comings and goings were publicized—the "famous Mr. Handel" was newsworthy—but this time one might have thought that London had completely forgotten him. Handel retired into solitude and for months nothing was heard of him. Once more we see him in the seemingly incongruous occupation of writing Italian duets: incongruous, because Handel seldom composed without some definite purpose in mind, and there was no apparent reason for the musician now firmly resolved to follow the English "oratorio way" to write Italian vocal chamber music. One recalls, however, the Italian duets composed during the deceptive rest that preceded *Messiah,* and, as at that time, the present inactivity does not appear to be lacking at least some signs of conscious purpose.

The pleasant and heartwarming intermezzo in Dublin did not efface the memories of the hard years that had preceded the Irish journey; Handel knew very well that a return to the musical marketplace of London meant a renewed struggle. At that time London gave the impression, said Dr. Johnson, "of a people not only without delicacy but without government, a herd of barbarians, or a colony of Hottentots." Though these words are palpably an exaggeration, we are tempted to apply them to Handel's enemies, high and low, who, as we shall presently see, continued to attack him with unremitting ferocity. Even Horace Walpole was ready to turn the fusillade of his destructive wit upon Handel. The serenity and confidence acquired in friendly Ireland did not, however, dull the entre- preneur's tactical sense; Handel bided his time and made his plans while shunning publicity. Then one day he picked up the score of *Samson*. Though the oratorio had been practically finished the year before, he subjected it to a thoroughgoing revision, in the process making many changes dictated by the as yet uncertain composition of his troupe. Thus again, though far more extensively than in *Messiah,* the composer meddled with the original score even before its première, and again the changes were not always to the advantage of the work.

If Homer and Virgil represent the greatness of the pagan world, Dante and Milton must be assigned their position in the Christian. One stands for Catholicism with Aristotelian forms, the other for Protestantism with Platonic theories. But Milton was also one of the makers, for good or ill—or both—of modern England. He gave a permanent turn to Eng- lish literary thought, he completed and sealed the triumph of Protes- tantism. To his mortification, the ardent Puritan lived to see the return of the old system of church government, restored on a much firmer basis than he had ever known it to enjoy. With the monarchy returned, the great poet stood in a hostile world, blind, poor, alone, and proscribed, but even this did not break his spirit, and now he began writing *Paradise Lost.* Besides being a Puritan, however, Milton was also a classicist; there are judges of Latin literature who on the strength of his Latin poetry do not hesitate to give him a high place in the long line of Latin poets. His Puritanism is now modified by lyric passion, from his classic reminiscences arises an involuntary worship of beauty. The order and harmony he brought to his poetic forms are more than the harmony of a cold mind; they are rather the resolution of the tension between the ascetic and the man of vivid imagination. Religion and reason meet in *Paradise Lost,* Platonic and Augustinian ideas in the middle of the Baroque, the Puritan Bible mated with pagan poetry. Macaulay sees the hero of this great poem as neither Adam, nor even God, but Satan, the fallen angel, for to the Puritan everything revolves around the problem of evil. Adam and Eve shrivel in this tremendous perspective and the work becomes a heavenly drama, the drama of the eternal tension of the world that col- lides in the microcosm of man.

But Milton could also write Greek drama, in a severe Sophoclean tone, though again with a biblical theme, for he was a Protestant. *Samson Agonistes* was his last work. Although *Samson Agonistes* is a Greek trag-

edy to the point of preserving the unities, Milton, as a Puritan, did not of
course intend it for the theatre; Handel's librettist had to make a semblance of a play out of it. While the subject comes from the Book of
Judges, it is less a biblical than a Miltonian drama. The blind Milton appears to have seen in Samson a symbolic parallel. In treating the motif of
feminine treachery, the poet altered the biblical story to make Dalila
Samson's wife. We must recall Milton's distressing first marriage, which
haunted him increasingly in his old age. He also invented Harapha, the
Philistine giant, and a happy dramatic invention it was. The changes
made by Handel's librettist, Newburgh Hamilton, closely followed Milton's ideas, some of which were uncongenial to Handel. The gallant musician, fond of women, could not sympathize with Milton's misogyny, nor
could he hate the Philistines with Milton's fervor. The musician chose not
to wrestle intellectually, theologically, and artistically with the poet, but
contented himself with Milton's general outline of the drama and especially with his rich language, trying to sustain the rather over-spacious
and leisurely form in which the librettist unfolds the story.

Considering all this, one wonders why Handel went to Milton for a
work that was to follow *Messiah*. Apparently it was Hamilton who was
responsible for the choice of the Miltonian subject. His first venture, *L'Allegro ed il Penseroso*, was successful, but that was the poetry of Milton's
youth, most inviting to Handel, whereas *Samson* was the old poet's moral
philosophy, altogether unshared by Handel. Though the poet and the
composer had some traits in common and possessed similar and unparalleled artistic recuperative powers, what primarily attracted Handel to
Milton was his poetic language. Milton's visual imagination was so powerful that it was at times a disadvantage to his poetry, from which the sense
of mystery fled when it was most needed. T. S. Eliot, in his *Note on the
Verse of John Milton*, maintains that Milton's poetry appeals to the ear
alone, and that his involved syntax is deliberately introduced for the sake
of pleasing sound. No one could better appreciate whatever truth may be
in this opinion than a composer with Handel's ear for pleasing sound.

Samson Agonistes is a Greek tragedy only in ideal form and intensity
of expression. As Hamilton's preface shows, this was clearly recognized in
Handel's time: "That Poem indeed never was divided by him into Acts
and Scenes, nor design'd for the Stage, but given only as the Plan of a
Tragedy with Chorus's, after the manner of the Antients." Hamilton did
not do a bad job. His addition of a second chorus, that of the Philistines,
as a foil to Milton's chorus of the Israelites, was an excellent dramatic
idea, and since the confidant or companion, so necessary in musico-

dramatic works, was missing in Milton's closet drama, Hamilton resource-fully borrowed Micah from another part of Judges. The rest he executed with skill and piety. The recitatives and choruses are all Milton's, taken, if not from *Samson Agonistes,* then from other poems, and the patchwork quilt of sentences from here and there was as neatly stitched as Jennens's similar operation in *Messiah.*

So far so good, but even though Hamilton greatly reduced the origi-nal work, he did not altogether succeed in eliminating its basic *longueurs,* nor the occasional didactic tone, always a trap for Handel's imagination. The drama gets under way with difficulty and builds rather gradually be-fore erupting with tremendous intensity in the third act. Dr. Johnson had a very low opinion of *Samson Agonistes,* a drama in which "the inter-mediate parts have neither cause nor consequence," he said; Percy Young avers that "any *mise en scène* is superfluous," and that Handel's *Samson* is as "unstageable" as Milton's original drama. At first glance, both seem to be right; Samson is blind and in chains, immobilized almost to the very end of the work. Yet it is obvious that both Hamilton and Handel looked at the subject with the theatre in mind, and in recent times staged per-formances of *Samson* have proved to be not only feasible but a means of blanketing the work's minor faults with its major force.

While on a colossal scale, *Samson* is readily intelligible in its musical-dramatic form. What it offers is not so much a full-sized drama as an incident—a highly dramatic incident, it is true, but one considered in iso-lation. With suitable pruning and editing the oratorio displays its com-poser's characteristic qualities: his power to impart vitality to his dramatic figures, his capacity for warm, rich, and expressive music. Though there is scarcely a plot outside the hero's fate, the dramatic interest steadily rises, and the close of the work is chilling in its tragedy, shot with flashes of fearful beauty. The tragedy of Samson has a terrible grandeur. Over-thrown and in bondage, he still kept the vision and the dream, and con-quered amidst the collapse of hope. That agony is his triumph. At his first appearance, he calls out from the shadow of eternal twilight. As the drama unfolds, he reaches a passionate inward peace, understanding and reaching out towards his fate. Still, it is undeniable that the choice of Mil-ton's drama was not a felicitous one; Handel the dramatist was not inter-ested in castigating sin; he did not want to set to music moral issues; he was interested in character.

Manoah, Samson's father, is a typical figure of the paternal fidelity that Handel always venerated. Micah, the friend and companion, did not interest Handel very much; for the better part of the work Handel gave him a role of passivity, though a very melodious passivity, for some of his songs are fine indeed. Harapha, the Philistine giant, is fully realized. He is gross and loud-mouthed, but not really wicked; that every one saw a bit of Polyphemus in him is not insignificant. Dalila shows to what pains Handel went to remove Milton's ideological wires, strand by strand. Everything in his life and character indicates that many aspects of Milton's poem were distasteful to him, who was not plagued with the problems of sin nor particularly attracted by chastity. He approached this situation as he did every other, as a dramatist, and the first thing he did was to transform Milton's despicable harlot into a persuasive woman of beguiling femininity.

The result caused discomfort to the guardians of morals, both in England and Germany. The discrepancy between Milton's conception and Handel's music was glaring and called for corrective commentaries. Even the usually clear-headed Streatfeild tried to invest Handel with Miltonian moral views: "The disgust with which he regarded sensuality that he saw rampant around him is, I think, to be read in *Samson*." But he goes even further: "turning with loathing from the sordid and sensual amours of Samson and Dalila, he lifts his voice in a triumphant paean in praise of chastity." Percy Young also is convinced that Handel, a man of moral strength, abhorred the sensuality of the pair, though he admits that the music illustrates Dalila's "blatant charms." Young's subsequent remarks, approving Handel's celibacy—indeed, he finds that in *Samson* Handel expressed his pride in bachelorhood—makes one wonder how the English nation managed not only to survive but to multiply. Perhaps Hans Joachim Moser's conclusion is the most curious. To him the scene where the "hypocrite, Dalila," appears is "undesirably operatic," though he must have been aware of Schering's logical finding that Dalila is indeed an operatic type for which there are many precedents in Handel's operas. But then curious things can happen when Milton and Handel are presented as an integral part of a *Geschichte der deutschen Musik.* It is most interesting to compare the views of these scholars, learned in historical detail and obedient to the moral precepts of their society but insensible to poetry and the theatre, with those of musical laymen who, stumbling left and right in technical matters, nevertheless grasp the dramatic-poetic meaning. Wilhelm Dilthey, the great German philosopher, can be utterly naive in matters musicological, but he cannot be fooled by preconceived attitudes. To him Handel's Dalila was not a harlot but the type of seductress who could be moved to tears, could touchingly plead, and could be gentle—if she cared to.

Since *Samson* was repeatedly reworked, with many changes, subtractions, and additions, our description will be somewhat arbitrary, both incomplete and generous, for at times one must choose between as many as three arias. Since no "definitive" edition of the score exists, and both the Händelgesellschaft and the Novello scores are tentative and heavily manhandled, we have attempted to hew to a reasonable compromise version.

After a fine overture, pleasantly adorned with horn parts, we witness a scene that is a reflection of the Epinicion in *Saul:* the Philistines are rendering homage to their god, Dagon. While it does not reach its prototype's freshness, this is a good opening scene; the chorus is brisk and the trumpets lively. The Philistine Woman's aria "Ye men of Gaza," interpolated between two choruses, is charmingly lilting. It offers *Samson's* first example of the unaccompanied beginning of an aria or arioso, a device later frequently used, even to the point of setting the motto to be sung by the naked voice, the orchestra taking up the ritornel afterwards. This procedure, heretofore seen occasionally, is quite characteristic of this work and is particularly effective when the betrayed and despairing hero sings, all alone, forsaken even by the orchestra. Handel bogs down a little as a Philistine (tenor) sings a long aria, followed by still another by the Philistine Woman. The music, especially hers, is pleasant, but the drama fails to get underway. It is still static in Samson's first recitative, but "Torments, alas!" is made of sterner stuff; the many pauses in the melody give this arioso a truly grieving quality. Samson, a blinded, helpless prisoner, broods bitterly over his fate, accusing himself for yielding to a woman and forfeiting his God-given strength. Micah, the confidant, sings his first aria. It is once more good music, and the accompaniment is finely worked, but it does not contribute to the drama.

Following a dialogue in recitative, Handel begins in earnest: Samson's arioso-aria "Total eclipse" is one of those pieces that baffle one's understanding. It is as simple as anything could be, yet its pathos is profoundly moving. The simplicity of sensation passes beyond the understanding into the simplicity of imagination. The following chorus, "Oh first created beam," a superb piece beginning homophonically but ending in a short fugue, so impressed Haydn that he quoted the line "Let there be light" practically verbatim in *The Creation.* The effect is, indeed, magnificent, especially since the outburst on "and light was over all" is preceded by a measure sung unaccompanied, piano. The fugal part becomes luminous when the treble sings the theme in augmentation, sounding like a chorale cantus firmus—in fact it does quote the first six notes of *Aus tiefer Not.* The loquacious Micah continues, regretting that Samson had not sought a woman from his own race. Manoah, the father, appears, appalled when he beholds the wreck of one who once was a great and forceful man. But before he can sing his first air, an Israelitish Man sings a little philosophical disquisition, "God of our fathers, what is man?" which, though a good piece, once more arrests the unfolding of the drama.

In the old man's song "The glorious deeds," the dramatist is completely in his element. The first part of this aria is a fairly routine operatic bass number with plenty of coloraturas, but the largo ending is very moving. What distinguishes the piece is the manner and form; it is through-composed, and every idea expressed or hinted at in the text is searchingly rendered in music. Manoah, reminding his son of his glorious former prowess, makes a deeper impression on Samson than his friend Micah; we feel the first signs of something stirring in the giant's despairing lethargy. Suddenly aroused, Samson, in an impassioned aria, lashes out against Jehovah's indifference: "Why does the God of Israel sleep?" It is the old style rage aria traditionally reserved for the bass but here given to the tenor; Handel thus created not only one of the first principal tenor roles in dramatic music, but the first aria for a *tenore di forza*. He knew very well what he was doing; the ritornel is exceptionally elaborate and the challenge is hurled unaccompanied. That the tone was found blasphemous is clear from Handel's subsequent alteration of the text to the less direct "Let not the God of Israel sleep." In the chorus "Then shall they know that He whose name Jehovah is alone," the crisp fugal work yields to a tremendous anthem-like homophonic exclamation: "Jehovah is alone." The accompanied recitative "My genial spirits droop" vividly conveys Samson's distress after the flareup. Micah now resumes his oration in an aria. Just as Milton said, in reference to his political tracts, that he "used only his left hand," so Handel does in this aria, which is more interesting in construction than in content. But "Then round about the starry throne" is a typical act-ending chorus with Handel in full command; "The music seems to glow with a white heat of rapture," says Streatfeild. It is a large anthem chorus, once more proceeding from bright homophony to a gradual polyphony and back to the chordal.

As the second act opens, Samson and Manoah are still conversing, the father singing a long, earnest aria, "Just are the ways of God," with a very attractive concerted accompaniment, but now, surprisingly, it is Micah who suddenly catches fire, singing one of Handel's great arias, "Return, oh God of hosts!" The song is as warm as it is bold, its harmonic scheme and adventurous modulations are fascinating. This is really a *scena*, for the following chorus, "To dust his glory they would tread," is

the third part of the aria, and Micah continues as a sort of precentor, sep-
arating the choral sections by his lovely melody. This is an unusually
beautiful piece. Now the drama takes a sharp turn as Samson's "wife" appears, "bedeck'd and gay, sailing like a stately ship." Handel sets the
words he was given by the libretto, but his music gives them a different
meaning. This Dalila certainly does not move with anything like the stateliness of a ship, let alone a "frigate," as the awkward German translation
has it. Those who like to quote analogies may see in Dalila and her retinue of virgins a prefiguration of Kundry and her flower girls, but Handel
stays away from any attempt at super-erotic sorcery, as well as from Milton's professed loathing of sex. The music is lightly erotic but only because it emphasizes femininity and might seem oddly decorative but for
its intent: the underlying give and take indicates that both Samson and
Dalila remember better and more pleasurable days.

Dalila approaches Samson "with doubtful feet and wav'ring resolution," which is amply justified for she is greeted with "Out! thou hyaena!"
Nevertheless, she begins a song, "With plaintive notes and am'rous moan
thus coos the turtle left alone." It is a delectable piece, the orchestra
depicting the cooing of the turtle dove; everything is light and graceful,
even the bass fiddles move in ballet slippers. The aria is perhaps a trifle
long and eventually one becomes aware that, as with Hoffmann's doll,
something is missing in Dalila. She continues with the assertion that her
jealousy prompted her to act as she did: "to keep you there both day and
night, love's prisoner, wholly mine." As the two converse there is little
spirit of vengeance, but neither is there any remorse; instead of breaking
into violent denunciations, Samson sings a fine siciliana ("Your charms
ruin led the way") which of course is generally omitted in performance as
not being in accord with Samson's high moral principles. Whether encouraged by this or out of sheer feigned piety, Dalila in her recitative
promises to nurse Samson with "redoubled love . . . to extremest age."
What ensues, with the virgins joining Dalila's song, is pure stage music
that loses a great deal of its charm in a mere concert performance. The
three numbers add up to a *scena* that begins with a slow minuet aria in
which Dalila invites Samson to "hear the voice of love" and ends with a
reminder that no moment should be lost because life is short. Handel
sketches here with his finest pencil, the workmanship being no less admirable than the mood, which is completely dominated by femininity.
Nothing is heard during this *scena* but high soprano voices, even the continuo is careful not to rumble. At this point perhaps we should quote
Schering, who in his valuable book on the oratorio perceptively character-

izes this remarkable scene. He notes the resemblance to Kundry and the flower girls, but observes that Handel's procedure is the exact opposite of Wagner's, for the erotic is symbolized by the voices singing alone, without the aid of suggestive harmonies, "thus moving the listener by their natural melting sweetness and their captivating echo play of brief sentences." The reiterated "Hear me, hear the voice of love" is indeed utterly attractive and feminine without being provocatively sensual.

But Samson overcomes the attraction of his memories and in the duet "Traitor to love" the true situation reasserts itself and they begin to slash at each other. The duet is tense and sharp, not the Steffani type but a genuine dramatic ensemble. After Samson's "I'll hear no more," Dalila, at the end of her resources, admits defeat and leaves. The following philosophical observations on the shortcomings of the female sex are not convincing. Handel's heart was not responsive to this; at this juncture in the drama, however, the moral conclusions were inevitable. In fact, the imprecations threaten to get out of hand, spreading contagiously not only to Micah, always ready with some commentary, but also to the chorus. Handel could silence Samson's newly won insight into the qualities of a true spouse by giving him a secco recitative of only five measures, but the following chorus undertakes to present Milton's summary condemnation of womanhood: "To man God's universal law gave pow'r to keep the wife in awe." Surprisingly, this un-Handelian idea is set to music in masterly fashion, but after the solemn beginning, when the details of this "universal law" are discussed in a spanking fugue, the meaning of the words is completely ignored. The wickedness of "female usurpation" is a wholly incongruous jolly piece that Handel himself omitted in later versions. It is a pity that this excellent choral piece is dramatically useless; it rolls with effortless grace and the part-writing is of the finest.

Harapha comes to see the fettered hero, taunting him about his reputed strength and refusing Samson's angry challenge to "combat with a blind man . . . a slave half-slain." Harapha's aria, "Honour and arms," has the aspect of the conventional operatic rage aria, but at the same time there is a decidedly basso buffo quality—echoes, as we mentioned, of Polyphemus. Samson answers in a very fine aria, "My strength is from the living God," marked *Larghetto e pomposo,* but the piece lacks real conviction. The theatrical qualities increase in the duet "Go baffled coward," in which the two giants sing in turn, until at the end Handel combines the music of both in a truly dramatic confrontation.

The stage becomes even livelier in the act-ending *scena* of three choruses, every one of them of the highest quality. "Hear, Jacob's God" is sung by the Israelites in a spacious six-part setting; the pleading "save us," with its accents displaced by syncopation, is quietly piercing. This piece, which was borrowed from Carissimi's *Jephte*, does not, however, merge smoothly with the others; for some reason Handel failed to perform his usual transplant surgery. Now the Philistines answer with their four-part "To song and dance we give the day." It is a magnificent piece built on an ostinato bass, but handled with freedom, and the counterpoint is genially loose. This has been interpreted as representing a piece of *Völkerpsychologie*, illustrating the lower culture of the Philistines as opposed to the Jews', but then this lower culture managed to produce a much more sophisticated orchestral accompaniment in this piece than the Jews showed in the preceding and contrapuntally much tighter chorus, and the Philistines have French horns, too, which are apparently unknown to the less primitive Jews. In the third chorus ("Fix'd in his everlasting seat") Philistines and Jews sing together. In a way this is a summation; each group invokes its own god but with the same music, though within the setting Handel distinguished the parties. This is a real ensemble finale, with the whole cast assisting the chorus; it is also rather Purcellian with its sprightly minuet quality.

With this we are well prepared for the tremendous third act. Harapha is dispatched to bring Samson to perform at Dagon's feast by demonstrating his strength. The invitation is rejected with scorn, and though this time Harapha has blood in his eye, he still sings in a not too well disguised buffo style. The chorus of Israelites implores Jehovah to "arise with thunder arm'd"; Samson is now fully aroused from his agony of despair. The dramatic pace is shrewdly planned, for instead of breaking out into open and active belligerency, Samson sings a very beautiful aria, "Thus when the sun forms wat'ry bed," which with its gentle pastoral quality, full of Handel's pictorial touches, depicts his quiet but firm resolution. The spark for action comes from Micah's animated accompanied recitative and from his aria "The Holy One of Israel." Micah ceases to be an observer-commentator and turns into a sort of leader. His music changes, too; the popular simplicity of the tune appeals to the people, and seconding him, the chorus eagerly takes it up. Samson leaves on his final mission as Manoah reappears to reiterate his plan to ransom his son. But a Philistine is heard expressing his pleasure that "Great Dagon has subdued our foe," which, like "Ye men of Gaza," is a splendid Purcellian dance air the substance of which moves to the chorus on the same text in an appealingly open and light texture. The "oriental-primitive" Philistines once more treat us to a piece of exceptional quality, with fine points of imitation and a jubilant orchestra reinforced with horns. The heathen are innocent of danger; the approaching dénouement is superbly calculated on Handel's correct assumption that the audience knew what was in store for the self-confident Philistines.

Manoah sings "How willing my paternal love," a warm and noble air, after which the supreme dramatist throws in his reserves. Manoah returns to his unfinished recitative but is again interrupted by the wild music of a sinfonia which announces the catastrophe that has taken place offstage. The mood is filled with tension as the noise abates and everyone waits for the next move; the concept is altogether theatrical even though the original stage directions are omitted in the printed scores. Events chase one another rapidly as Handel, with equal rapidity, alternates recitative with chorus; his orchestra is now violent. The Philistines are desperate: "Hear us our God," they cry, and by a stroke of genius Handel supports their chorus with materials taken from the wild sinfonia. The Philistines— "chorus at a distance" is Handel's suppressed stage direction—are collapsing: "Heav'n, we sink, we die!" A messenger arrives announcing Samson's death, and we are again reminded of *Saul* as Handel ends *Samson* with an elegy which, though shorter, is as magnificent as the one in the earlier oratorio. It begins with Micah's "Ye sons of Israel now lament," which is taken up by the chorus "Weep Israel," both sharing the key of F minor. A dead march follows very like the one in *Saul,* and again in the major key. In fact, this *is* the Dead March from *Saul,* somewhat reorchestrated and transposed, and with an obbligato organ part added; Handel discarded his first version. The culminating point in the elegy is the final chorus, "Glorious hero," which, though only a half-hundred measures long, is a little compound finale in itself and one of the most moving choral scenes ever composed. The dirge, in a rondolike form and abounding in delicate Purcellian touches, consists of skilfully coordinated sections, each of only a few measures, but with a continuity as remarkable as their variety; here Manoah is the *choragus,* there an Israelitish Woman, while the Virgins alternate with the full chorus. They mourn Samson, but the tone is gentle, for all Israel is elated over Samson's redemption. The mystery of beauty that pervades this scene is due to the reconciliation of hero worship with piety, which in the final measures, "rest eternal, sweet repose," creates an indescribable atmosphere of peace and fulfillment.

These are not, however, the final measures of the oratorio. The elegy constitutes the true lyric end of *Samson,* as Don Giovanni's descent to hell is the true dramatic end of that opera. Mozart added a magnificent, if irrelevant, postscript to illustrate the maxim that crime does not pay, while Handel had to satisfy the public's desire for a sort of happy ending with the trumpets in full cry. As in *Don Giovanni,* the result was at once oddly unsatisfying and oddly memorable. Manoah calls the Israelites from mourning, "Come, come! no time for lamentation now . . . Samson like Samson fell, in life and death heroic," adding (this was lated excised) "Why should we weep or wail, dispraise, or blame, where all is well and fair?" Indeed, everything can be settled by the mandatory thanksgiving anthem; but first Handel gives the Israelitish Woman a brilliant trumpet aria, "Let the bright Seraphim," which became a Handelian landmark. Fine as the piece is, it is essentially an *aria di bravura* or *d'agilità* as in the old Venetian operas, where arias with concerted trumpet were very popular. The final chorus, "Let their celestial concerts all unite," is a great anthem. The soprano begins with an unaccompanied sentence in the manner of a psalm tone, in agreeable contrast to the effectively mobile full chorus.

Though a great work, *Samson* is not quite in a class with *Saul.* Every act contains magnificent music and whole scenes that are top Handel, and in the third act the composer is at the summit of his powers, but between these absorbing scenes his inspiration did not fully respond to the lengthy soliloquies. This is due mainly to the moral philosophy of Milton, in which Handel was not at home. Hamilton saw the danger but could not altogether eliminate it; its effect is particularly hobbling in Micah, who is a sort of narrator charged with the delivery of lessons and observations. In the choruses Handel could escape the pitfalls by use of the technique, so characteristic of him, of concentrating on single words and ignoring the others. *Samson* does approach *Saul* in rich scoring, but the orchestra is treated differently. The number and variety of instruments is almost as great as in *Saul* (even the trombones, used in *Saul,* may belong here too, though this is somewhat conjectural), but all these instruments are seldom used together; apparently horns and trumpets were played by the same persons.

Though there are many fine choruses, *Samson* is not really a choral drama; the arias and recitatives are prominent, and Handel shows a newly found preference for the use of the chorus to continue situations and feelings expressed in a preceding solo by elaborating on the same musical substance. This is a powerful agent of cohesion, and an essentially modern operatic device. (This relationship must be carefully weighed when cuts are made for performance.) The symmetry of the da capo aria is now largely abandoned. The arias in *Samson* tend to the two-part cavatina or, if there is a ternary plan, the place of the da capo is taken by a chorus. Also, many numbers that are listed as arias are more nearly elaborate ariosos. The accompanied recitative has grown into a supreme dramatic vehicle, but together with its rising importance, we see a rather surprising reappearance of the basso continuo aria, long since abandoned. However, Handel employs it for dramatic purposes, to accentuate what follows. Though Handel was not, compared with Bach, particularly devoted to basso ostinato constructions, they do appear felicitously here and there; *Samson* has several of them, always treated in a spirit of freedom rather than by literal repetition. A remarkable new element is the exploitation of the "Symphony of horror and confusion" in the following chorus; this accompaniment is in a genuinely symphonic vein.

After *Messiah*, Handel once more fell back on foreign borrowings; *Samson* is rather liberally indebted to Carissimi, Astorga, Legrenzi, Giovanni Porta, Telemann, Gottlieb Muffat, and Keiser. Some of these loans were not repaid with the usual generous interest; Handel did not bother to adjust them to his own style, which makes them somewhat conspicuous. But the others show his astonishing capacity for assimilation, for making everything he touched his lawful possession. The score was repeatedly reworked, and since it was a popular oratorio, often revived, Handel kept up the alterations to the very end of his life, in later revivals making changes in the text also. To restore the score will require a great deal of study, ingenuity, and tact, but with suitable excisions and selections *Samson* will prove to be one of the great oratorios. It would seem though that a really satisfactory performance, especially when staged, should omit the portions after the dirge, which is the natural close of this tragic work. Finally, we must note that the title role was given to a tenor. This was not only because the faithful Beard was available; as Handel became altogether wedded to works in English, his dramaturgical ideas changed, leading him away from the practice of the Italians, who favored the virtuoso singing of the castrati and were not disturbed by the incongruity of the male soprano or alto. A castrato will still appear here and there, but henceforth the tenor will rule in the oratorio, promoted from an accessory role to the eminence heretofore occupied by the castrato.

The first performance of *Samson* took place in Covent Garden February 18, 1743, the singers consisting of Signora Avoglio, Mrs. Clive, Mrs. Cibber, Miss Edwards, Beard, Savage, Reinhold, and Lowe—a large company that permitted alternate casting in the première. Incidentally, it is quite significant that Dalila's part was given to an accomplished actress, Susanna Cibber. The success was genuine. *Samson* became the most im-

mediately successful of all oratorios; it ran to full houses for eight performances in one season—a record. Dubourg, temporarily in London,
joined Handel's company, playing, from the fourth performance onward,
"A Solo on the Violin," while Handel played one of his organ concertos in
the other intermission. This success was lasting; *Samson* remained popular
throughout the rest of Handel's life. It was not only that the public liked
to hear native singers in English, but the Miltonian concepts and words
suited English middle-class feelings. The public did not look very deeply
into Handel's rendition of these concepts and words, and it is easy to see
why subsequently *Samson* became a "sacred oratorio."

Samson was the mainstay of the six subscription concerts announced
on February 12. Apparently the Dublin experience had convinced Handel
that he must return to the subscription system if a guarantee of financial
returns was to be achieved. The response was so encouraging that the
series was extended to eight concerts, and on March 12 a second set of six
evenings was announced. On the eighth night, *L'Allegro ed il Penseroso*
and the *St. Cecilia Ode* were given with the usual concertos; on the
ninth night "A New Sacred Oratorio" was advertised without a name.
Handel was cautious; this time he did not challenge, rather he tried to
smuggle in *Messiah* on the coattails of the successful *Samson*. But *Messiah*, presented on March 23, was unsuccessful. Religious scruples, of
which Handel was well aware, played a large part in this, but the musical
reasons were not negligible. As with *Israel*, the public missed the "story,"
the lack of arias, and was surfeited with "too many choruses." The delicacy of such things as the "duet choruses" (see p. 346) was unappreciated
by most contemporaries. After three performances *Messiah* was quietly
given up for this season, as well as for the next.

[2]

WITH THE CLOSE OF the season Handel returned to creative
work. There are indications in the spring of illness; Mainwaring and
others mention "some return of his paralitick disorder." If so, it must have
been soon shaken off; *Semele* was composed in June, *Joseph* in
August-September. The Battle of Dettingen, in which George II led his
victorious army—or was led by his horse—took place on June 27. The
glory of the sovereign had to be properly celebrated; accordingly, in the
last two weeks in July, Handel composed a great Te Deum (see above, p.
228). Sung at the Chapel Royal on November 27, the *Dettingen Te Deum*
impressed everyone by its martial splendor. Thus passed 1743. The next

Lenten season of oratorio, announced on January 9, 1744, was initially planned for twelve performances. *Semele* opened the series on February 10, and with it the London public was once more treated to an unexpected and radical change in style, subject matter, and conception, for which their only preparation was the announcement's careful wording: "After the Manner of an Oratorio." The public expected Handel to act the musical poet laureate who in his works returns thanks for his purse, but neither *Messiah* nor *Semele* showed this gratitude in suitable form.

Was Handel's "conversion" so complete that henceforth he was to dismiss every memory of opera? We have noticed that *Samson* is not really a choral drama; its many arias and recitatives are of vital importance. One has the impression that Handel was consciously attempting more than a *rapprochement* between opera and oratorio, even a virtual reform of the music drama. After *Samson* he found the formula, for *Semele* is a new type of music drama: English opera, in which the dramatic element shifts from the contemplative chorus to high personal tragedy. Mainwaring saw this as early as 1760: "Semele is an English opera, but called an oratorio, and performed as such." Dr. Delany, though a great music-lover and of course thoroughly indoctrinated by his wife in Handelian lore, did not attend *Semele* because the "profane story" was too operatic for a clergyman. The many highly dramatic accompanied recitatives, which are often descriptive, the ensembles, among them an unusually fine quartet and a number of duets, the almost exclusive use of the da capo aria (even in the choruses), and the unmistakable presence of Venetian and French operatic traits—all these take *Semele* bodily from the genus oratorio. We cannot therefore agree with Julian Herbage (in *Handel, a Symposium*) that *Semele* is "totally unlike his Italian operas, and shows unique understanding of both the English masque and the Purcell-Dryden semi-opera." *Semele* certainly shows Handel's thorough understanding of the English lyric stage, and he made the most of it by combining with great skill two traditions: English masque and semi-opera with Italian opera. But the dramatic action, the recitatives and arias, are pure opera, Italian-descended opera, the stylistic ingredients always clearly in evidence. Herbage himself says that "the dramatic continuity of the last act is remarkable, and is effected through the exclusive use of accompanied recitatives and the omission of the chorus." Indeed, the more *Semele* advances, the more the operatic comes to the fore, and masque and semi-opera—let alone oratorio—are left behind. Recent German attempts at compromise terminology—*oratorische Choroper*—are also mistaken; Hermann Abert correctly identified the operatic nature of *Semele* decades ago. Percy Young, in his book on the Handelian oratorio, is quite explicit on this point: "*Semele*, not being an oratorio at all but an English opera without action, falls outside our terms of reference." This master-piece of airiness, ingenuity, and exquisite finish was a long step backward—and upward. It was as if Handel looking backward repented his repentance.

All good Handelians of the old school were uncomfortable with *Semele*. Chrysander's preface consists of one short paragraph on the middle of the page.

The libretto has the curious title *The Story of Semele. As it is Perform'd at the Theatre Royal in Covent Garden. Alter'd from the Semele of Mr. William Congreve, set to Musick by Mr. George Frederick Handel. MDCCXLIV.* The title, *History of Semele*, was chosen because its secular tone excluded the designation "oratorio," while its oratorio-like nature did not permit the use of the term "opera." Nevertheless, Congreve undoubtedly wrote *Semele* (1707) as an opera libretto and it failed to find a composer solely because its lack of dramatic force made it unsuitable for the stage. By making certain changes, Handel was able to treat it as an oratorio, and we call it that in the sense in which we used the term for *Hercules*.

Brief as this preface is, it is full of contradictions as well as faulty information. The work continued to languish even after the English editors dampened its amorous ardor by deleting or changing lines. Thus *Semele*, with music that is irresistible and as fresh as when it was composed, has long suffered from the silly prejudices of an "insensible" (to use a good 18th-century term) bourgeois civilization, though its more recent neglect was due less to prudery than to inertia and musical illiteracy. The Oiseau-Lyre recording of 1958 and various recent performances, some staged, seem to indicate a growing awareness of the exceptional qualities of this wondrous tragedy of love.

The libretto of *Semele* was not the work of an amateur, but of a great English comic dramatist and impeccable stylist, William Congreve. Written early in the century, it was published in 1710 as "An Opera," and indeed it was originally planned for John Eccles, who set it in 1707. More precisely, the performance of Eccles's opera was announced in 1707, but there is no indication that it was actually produced. Chrysander was unaware of Eccles' setting, but surely a hundred years later it is inexcusable for a Handelian scholar to ignore the score, preserved in the British Museum. Serauky, obviously working, as usual, from antiquated secondary sources, in this case copying Chrysander, flatly states that Handel was the first to attempt the composition of Congreve's book. But Handel did not set the original libretto; it was arranged for him by someone, perhaps, as Winton Dean guesses, Newburgh Hamilton. The arrangement is quite serviceable and the graceful ease of Congreve's dialogue is preserved. The additions are skilful, and the arranger was evidently under instructions to find more opportunities for the musician than Congreve provided. He also eliminated some lines that must have been thought offensive, but even what was left after these excisions shocked the English and puzzled the Germans. Handel found the piece very congenial; he liked the Greek myth (Congreve combined Euripides with Ovid) and composed it as a human drama, without any deference to the supernatural status of some of the figures. He found ample opportunity for the creation of characters, and the uninhibited passion of the protagonists fired him to write love music of pervasive beauty and ardor.

Semele was composed in a spirit of content; the pure fancy of its melody shows this. The creative rapture is clearly in evidence in the total lack of borrowings. Handel so skilfully intermingles narrative with moments of lyric intensity that the story becomes a sustained song; but the love lyric is in the carnal mode, the passions are deep, intimate, and undisguised. *Semele* is an opera of love, a radiant work celebrating, with a kind of ecstasy of the senses, the glory of a woman's form and presence. Handel approached it with masculine feelings, with a purely human— even heathen—energy. There is no sentimentality in his concept; in the tragedy of love what matters is love,

> *Love that is first and last of all things made,*
> *The light that has the living world for shade.*

Contrary to certain interpretations, there is absolutely nothing symbolic in Handel's treatment of the story. *Semele,* daughter of King Cadmus of Thebes, loves Jove, who courts her in the guise of a mortal. She is also loved by Athamas, prince of Boeotia, who in turn is loved, though secretly, by Ino, Semele's sister. We are dealing here with a timeless love quadrangle (to which we may add Juno, with her jealous attachment to her husband), the very stuff of the lyric stage. The lyric cries and protests against the bondage of earthly life hold communion with yearning in a profoundly human sense altogether free of the supernatural. Indeed, perhaps we should reverse Anatole France's line: *Les dieux sont cruels quand un homme les agite.*

Semele is a beautifully developed character, a very real if unusual woman who takes shape and becomes vital in her first sentences, stays alive throughout the work, and is still living after it is finished. She seems to be half-numbed by her great passion, a complete egoist wholly devoted to the rapture of the moment, a voluptuous, yielding coil of flesh, who nonetheless is possessive and demanding. Juno is a fine portrait of a jealous woman who will not rest until she destroys her rival by any means at her disposal. And, as we know from mythology, she had a good deal of experience in such matters. At that, she does not lack nobility, and hers is the most forceful personality in the entire cast, a superb characterization. Jove is not really the "mighty thunderer"; all he wants is to make love, and in his eagerness to attain his desire he makes mistakes unbecoming to a god. But beneath that exterior there is revealed a nature capable of deep feeling and a personality who in the end is shaken rather than frivolous. Somnus, the God of Sleep, is engagingly drawn, with a goodly touch of the Italian buffa, but Iris remains quite impersonal. Nor do Athamas and Ino attract Handel's full attention; both of them are rather pale accessories, though Ino is not without passion. Cadmus, the old King, being a grieving father, Handel warms to him; his uncomprehending sorrow is touching. The chorus has a reduced role in *Semele,* but it forms an integral part of the drama, and its music is throughout of exceptional quality.

Semele begins with a broad and strong overture, though its third part is a delicately pensive gavotte whose rhythm and tone are carried over into several of the songs. The opening chorus, "Lucky omens," immediately creates an operatic situation; this is not an anthem but a wedding ceremonial. The rhythm is still dancelike and remains so in the choral fugue that ends the scene. No one knew better than Handel that in essence the fugue is a dance piece. But this finely wrought choral piece, like most of the others in *Semele,* merely furnishes the background; it does not, as in *Saul* or *Samson,* enter the drama proper. The latter is immediately evident, though as yet without tragic overtones. King Cadmus urges his daughter to "invent no new delay"; it is time to "obey, hear, and obey." Athamas, a bit pompously, repeats the King's demand. This at once indicates that these two are dealing with a rebellious woman who will not marry against her choice. The real world does not exist in the face of all-embracing love, and just as Juliet is absolutely indifferent to the fact that Romeo killed Tybalt, her kinsman, Semele cares neither for her father nor for her suitor, addressing herself to her lover, Jove. Handel immediately shows us what manner of woman she is: the wide interval of the ninth on "Oh Jove" cuts into the innocuous scene with instantaneous fervor. This is opera music of the first water, the voice part later punctuated with eloquent, "composed" pauses. In her next aria, "The morning lark to mine accord his note," Handel slips a little into the old routine of Baroque opera, for this is a "bird" or "lark" song like the many delightful ones he composed as simile arias.

Presently the dramatic situation becomes tense, for neither Athamas nor Semele understands Ino's state of mind, and they are surprised at her outburst, "I can no longer hide my passion." The old king is also distressed by the behavior of his two daughters. Here something extraordinary happens. Handel unites the four principals in a quartet, a genuine dramatic ensemble. This piece, quite unusual in Handel's day (though, as we shall see, *Solomon* has an equally remarkable trio), does not resemble anything in any masque or oratorio; it is of a type that was to become the glory of opera. Every one of the figures retains his individuality, and Handel makes them enter the ensemble one by one at the right psychological moment. Now the chorus falls in, adding an effective postscript to the fears and indecisions expressed in the quartet. The choral setting is Handel at his sturdiest. Cadmus and Athamas are dismayed as the flame on the altar dies, but Semele sings—"aside," say the stage directions— "Thee Jove, and thee alone, thy Semele adores." Everyone is now angry, and the chorus explodes with wrath: "Cease your vows," it thunders, " 'tis impious to proceed" with the nuptial ceremony, and the cast is virtually expelled except for Ino and Athamas.

Ino pleads, "Turn, hopeless lover, turn thy eyes." The aria is carefully constructed, but Ino still appears a somewhat pale woman. Athamas, unable to grasp the situation, tries to comfort her in a brotherly way, which does not make the music glow. Ino, realizing that her oblique allusions are wasted, bursts out into a rather fiery recitative, "Insensible! Ingrate!" whereupon Athamas finally recognizes the true portent of her complaints. The following duet aptly illustrates their predicament; Athamas is shocked at the discovery of unrequited love, and Ino is dismayed at having lost her head. Since both are now emotionally aroused, their music picks up in intensity.

Now comes a typical example of Baroque operatic *deus ex machina*: Jove, in the shape of an eagle, abducts Semele. While Cadmus in a touching accompanied recitative is crushed by this turn, the chorus does not see any calamity; instead it congratulates Cadmus in a fine dance tune, because a member of his house has risen to the rank of divine mistress. The horns added to the orchestra lend it the joyous sound Handel always likes to give to the heathen. After this, Semele's voice is heard from above to the tune of a delectable gavotte: "Endless pleasure, endless love Semele enjoys above." The aria was originally not intended for her (it is written in the third person), but Semele surely sings in character, leaving the impression that she can hardly contain herself recounting the delights of love. The music is so ravishing, its lucid directness, its sensuous-poetic power so pervasive, that the act-ending chorus can do no better than appropriate it, further enhancing its charm with fine madrigalesque imitations.

After a remarkable—and capricious—sinfonia, the second act opens with Juno questioning the Olympian messenger, Iris, who tells Jove's wife about the "sweet reatreat" of her rival, and the pleasures she is enjoying, the music resembling Galatea's in its neat *galant* simplicity. Juno is incensed, and this magnificent woman elicits strong music from Handel. In a particularly expressive accompanied recitative, "Awake, Saturnia," marked *allegro concitato,* she vents her rage, warning the whole universe of the consequences of her wrath. This recitative, abounding in affective text illustrations, is one of the most dramatically expansive of all Handel's recitatives. After Iris's description of the formidable monsters that guard the lovers' retreat, Juno, far from being intimidated, sings an impassioned aria, "Hence, hence, Iris hence away." This da capo aria, magnificent in its *élan,* uses the middle section to give Juno a brief respite at the mention of Somnus, the God of Sleep, but after that her frenzy returns.

The scene changes to Semele's palace. "She is just awakening and rises," say the stage directions, which Handel carries out admirably. Semele begins her song unaccompanied, as if still half asleep. "Oh sleep, why dost thou leave me?" is a continuo aria, rather rare at this stage of dramatic music, but Handel resorts to it so that he can altogether concentrate on the singing voice. Semele does not want to awaken because that would rob her of her dreamy bliss, yet while she appears to be a woman completely absorbed and satiated by sensual pleasure, we realize that all is not well; the tragedy is already hinted at, for she senses that her rapture cannot last. When Jove appears he is greeted with a short recitative: "Let me not another moment bear the pangs of absence." Jove answers in a fine aria, "Lay your doubts and fears aside," but the tone is *galant* and not quite convincing; there is something evasive in his protestations that "though this human form I wear, think not I man's falsehoods bear," adding that "Love and I are one." Significantly, the aria is a dance piece, a minuet-saraband, with a smoothly gliding melody and elegant accompaniment.

The *galant* song is followed by a rather sober little recitative in which the god reminds Semele that she, being a mortal, needs a little rest once in a while. Semele, now alert, immediately answers Jove's "Love and I are one" by contending that "not you alone, but Love and I are one." The construction of her aria is extraordinary, for the lilting dance rhythm is in contrast with the coloraturas, which have a strange urgency about them, nor is the tonality of D minor a happy one. The concluding chorus once more pays handsome tribute to the masque; its text is new, "How engaging, how endearing is a lover's pain," but the musical substance is from Semele's aria. In the light and graceful choral version there is even more of the undertone of passion and disquiet than the same music had when Semele sang it.

Now Semele begins to tempt the fate that will ultimately destroy her. She complains that "I am a mortal, still a woman." This disturbs Jove; "Aiming at immortality [is a] dangerous ambition." In an aside he concludes that he must "amuse her, lest she too much explain." Jove repeatedly sings "apart," which in an "oratorio" performance is altogether lost. The ensuing chorus, *Alla hornpipe* ("Now Love that everlasting boy invites"), is love music, delightful in rhythm and in sound, the garlands of imitations in the orchestra caressing the voices. Jove decides that Semele needs a playmate; he will fetch Ino from Boeotia, so that the two sisters can romp together like happy nymphs in Arcadia. The aria he sings, "Where'er you walk," is indeed Arcadian (a poem borrowed by the arranger from Pope), but aside from its bewitching melody, it is an incomparable masterpiece in the way the vocal and instrumental parts are woven together. An astonishing feature of this miracle of melody is that though poetic and pastoral, it is not descriptive—the leaves are lacquered. The dreamy piece—*Largo e pianissimo per tutti,* demands Handel—is a paean of love that became famous all over the world. Some of the other songs, equally admirable, deserve to be equally well known.

The same exquisitely worked texture holds our attention in Ino's song "But hark! the heavenly sphere turns round," in which she relates her adventurous journey through forests populated with dreadful beasts. The following duet still echoes the fairy tale atmosphere; it is not a dramatic ensemble but one of those chiselled chamber duets with delicate imitation and magnificently sustained melodic writing. The concluding fugue is again an astonishing composition—a pastoral fugue!—which stands nearly alone in the choral literature. Now the chorus disappears until the end, because the dénouement concerns the dramatis personae alone.

The introduction to the third act evokes the world of the God of Sleep; the shadowy arabesques played by the bassoons and basses are wonderfully suggestive. This is a theatre piece that directly prepares the raising of the curtain. The spell is broken by Juno's stern "Somnus awake." The sleepy god stirs, singing a slow, trance-like song, "Leave me loathsome light," which fairly simulates sleep. Handel's uncanny skill in depicting the half-awake drowsiness of Somnus in a beautiful song fascinates with its combination of the real with the unreal. Juno, a good psychologist and well acquainted with the personal foibles of the corps of gods, offers the lethargic Somnus a nice little nymph, Pasithea, for his delectation. The response is remarkable. Somnus is transformed; jumping with joy he breaks into a genuine buffo aria—but one with an erotic undertone. Juno and Somnus sing a duet, not a chamber duet but a superbly operatic scene. Juno is all calm determination as she precisely repeats her demand and sets the price upon it, but Somnus only utters Pasithea's name and is ready to carry out Juno's wishes. So the conspiracy to punish Semele by magic gets under way.

The scene changes back to Semele, and we realize that Jove's endeavors to keep her occupied have come to naught. "My racking thoughts by no kind slumber freed" is once more a beautifully ornate largo aria, filled with restlessness and foreboding. The operatic element is not only all-pervasive by this time, but obviously rests on traditional Italian principles entirely missing in the English semi-opera. As Juno, disguised as Ino, enters Semele's presence, the old Venetian "bedroom scene" is before us, complete with mirror. Juno's approach is very smooth and deceiving; she is both shrewd and contemptuous. (The asides of both women are meaningless unless the work is acted on the stage.) Upon her fulsome praise, Semele picks up the mirror and sings a suavely ravishing coloratura aria. Anticipating immortality, she becomes giddy, declaring that "no object sure before was half as pleasing" as what she beholds in the mirror. The aria is a little long and requires superlative singing and acting skill to bring it off. Juno, aware that the right moment has come, tells Semele in a crisply dramatic accompanied recitative the best—and oldest—method to bring an ardent male to terms. (Incidentally, one wonders whether "adieu" was deliberately used in this affair between gods.)

Semele, grateful for the advice, which she believes to come from her sister, sings a gently waving siciliana, and now the crisis approaches. Jove enters, with rather unseemly haste: "Come to my arms, my lovely fair." The fine aria is built above a pseudo-ostinato bass, and Handel withholds the violins until the piece is well under way. But Semele does not respond and Jove is stunned: "Oh, Semele, why art thou insensible?" Semele is now all woman, sure in instinct, and even surer in timing. "I ever granting" is a fine piece, but no longer expansive—every note counts, and the repetitions ("I always am wanting") are indeed insistent. Jove loses all his senses but one and is ready to promise anything, which he presently does in a powerful accompanied recitative. The reaction to Semele's demand for immortality is instantaneous: Jove forgets all else in consternation. "Ah! take heed what you press" is a rushing, impatient, and sternly warning aria; Handel dispenses with any ritornel but keeps the orchestra in an uproar. Semele does not yield: 'No, no, I'll take no less!" She also launches into a fast coloratura aria, skipping the customary recitative. There is something defiant and determined in this whirlwind piece in which the voice stops racing only when the word "oath" is sung on a long-held note. Yet one must regretfully agree with Winton Dean that here, for a moment, Handel's dramatic sense failed him. At this crucial spot, where one would expect an accompanied recitative, he permits Semele to reca-pitulate a long aria verbatim, after which she leaves abruptly. *Semele* is studded with da capo arias, another sign of the return to opera, but they are either so placed that they ideally suit their purpose, or are skilfully manipulated to avoid literal repetition. Fantastic coloratura can be a very effective dramatic agent, and Handel was thoroughly adept at using it, but in such symmetrical application it is a double-edged weapon.

Jove, left alone, upholds the drama. Now we see a god in an alto-gether human predicament, and the frivolous Olympian becomes a griev-ing mortal; profoundly moved, he turns flesh and blood in the shadow of onrushing death. "Ah! whither is she gone" we may perhaps call an ac-companied recitative da capo; it is an example of the remarkable new species we have encountered in *Samson,* which straddles recitative, arioso, and aria. Juno reappears to savor her victory, but even though her music is very good, this scene can be safely omitted. Elaborate stage directions preface Semele's death scene, for it is a struggle to memorialize beauty in the face of death, to render the stillness of surrender to the fear of death. It is a brief piece, again in the free dramatic arioso-aria style, but, a pendant to Dido's lament, it is one of the memorable moments in all opera. "Ah, me," sings Semele, "too late I now repent . . . I feel my life consuming," and then the last pitiful unaccompanied words: "I can no more." Now the chorus, absent throughout this act, returns with the *epodos,* which is one of Handel's tremendous choral frescoes. Having wit-nessed the tragedy, they show their emotions by their halting singing of a choral arioso, "Oh horror and astonishment," which is followed by a flow-ing polyphonic texture ending again in arioso. The gradual vanish-ing into pianissimo is carefully indicated by the composer.

Once more we feel that a work has been finished, that the "Story of Semele" really ends here, that the anguish and the tragic dénouement should not be dissipated. We are little interested in what happens to Athamas, who finally gets a spouse. Moreover, it is not without embarrassment that he accepts the consolation prize, Ino. A surprise awaits us. The customary Hallelujah Chorus, with the trumpets and timpani added, does appear, but it announces that the offspring of the idyll has been saved from the catastrophe. He is none other than Bacchus, and the chorus, knowing what he will mean to posterity, jubilates in a fine "prelude and fugue." Indeed, this splendid fugue is "free from care, free from sorrow," but all this good music is dramatically expendable; it weakens the somber drama with an enforced happy ending.

Semele was performed on February 10, 1744, at Covent Garden with an experienced cast headed by La Francesina, Avoglio, Esther Young (Mrs. Arne's sister), Beard, and Reinhold. A complete failure, it was withdrawn after three performances. Handel tried it again in December, but after one more performance *Semele* was retired, never to be revived in Handel's lifetime. We notice with regret that at the December revival Handel disfigured this enchanting English opera by the addition of several Italian songs. It is amazing that he should have resorted to this old and long-discredited subterfuge. Perhaps it made some sense when he tried to stiffen the sagging popularity of *Israel in Egypt* in this manner—it has scarcely any "songs"—but in this case there was an embarrassment of riches. *Semele* was composed with care, dedication, and a high sense of artistic integrity, an integrity still in evidence when Handel subsequently reworked the opera. If we throw out the Italian insertions and consider the changes made between the few performances, we shall see that Handel substantially improved the score. Since the autograph and performing material are available, a critical edition, using some of the fine unpublished material and indicating recommended omissions, would not only give us a most viable work, but would elevate *Semele* to its rightful place: that of the first great full-length English opera.

There was, however, a certain reason for the desperate expedient of spicing the work with Italian songs: Handel was facing an opera war reminiscent of the old campaigns. *Semele* is an opera, and it was so recognized by the opposition. The opera party and Lord Middlesex were not fooled, bitterly resenting that Handel should produce opera without incurring the expenses of scenery and costly Italian singers. In spite of the failure of *Messiah* and *Semele,* Handel's subscription concerts were on the whole successful, and he siphoned away from Middlesex's opera house a good portion of the public. In one of her letters Mrs. Delany says "the houses have not been crowded, but pretty full every night," and Handel once more became a regular depositor at the Bank of England. Even Horace Walpole remarked that "Handel has set up an Oratorio against the Operas and succeeds."

The opposition was really ruthless. Verbal insults being no longer sufficient to stop Handel, they resorted to the crassest measures: hired ruffians made attendance at Handel's productions hazardous as people were set upon, beaten, and robbed. The scandalous situation was eased only upon the King's attendance at the theatre, when known troublemakers and members of the underworld were arrested; after the royal visit the disturbances resumed. In fact, the disorderly acts were so constant that their occasional absence was an event worth mentioning. Mrs. Delany, writing about a performance of *Semele,* remarks "there was no disturbance at the play-house." The war was not restricted to the low level of physical brawls; it was just as vigorously prosecuted in aristocratic salons. Burney mentions a Lady Brown as "a persevering enemy of Handel" who helped Middlesex's cause. This must be the same person to whom Mainwaring refers as "a certain fashionable lady who exerted all her influence to spirit up a new opposition against him." The wife of Sir Robert Brown, merchant and diplomat, Lady Margaret organized lavish concerts for the aristocracy, favoring, according to Burney, musicians "of the new Italian style."

It was not only the opera party, however, that was up in arms. When seeking the Lord Chamberlain's permission for the production, Handel had described *Semele* as a work "after the manner of an oratorio." This was supposed to placate that august official as well as the clergy, but in this instance he also had to reckon with the hurt moral sense of the great and virtuous public. They saw through the deception. Why, even Tristan's love potion is foreshadowed as the jealous Juno bribes the God of Sleep to excite Jove's already quite virile desires by an aphrodisiac dream. And they saw illicit love, a perfectly decent marriage project ruined by lechery. It is true whoever arranged the libretto for Handel took pains to eliminate Congreve's less felicitous and more "suggestive" language. To quote an example, in the original text Congreve has Jove propose rather impatiently

> *Say what you require*
> *I'll grant it—now let us retire.*

The final phrase was omitted. But all such lines could not be eliminated without seriously hurting the play, and such passages as

On her bosom Jove reclining
Useless now his thunder lies

created considerable uneasiness. The Victorians were even more scandalized by Jove's extra-marital adventures and by Semele's uninhibited passion, and the moral censors used their blue pencils with a vengeance. At the turn of the century *Semele* was still found to be unworthy of the composer of *Messiah*. Ebenezer Prout, who edited a vocal score for Novello, forever disgraced himself by his high-handed and altogether irresponsible mutilation of *Semele*. It is incredible that a modern musician should find a word such as "desire" morally objectionable. As to the removal of "bed," one wonders whether the Victorians even used that piece of furniture for resting. What Prout did to the music is even worse. Chrysander himself, as we have said, is curiously equivocal; he was not interested in this radiant score. But his dilemma was of his own making: by calling *Semele* an oratorio, he came into conflict with his idea of religious music.

[3]

THE NEXT new oratorio, *Joseph and his Brethren,* presented on March 2, 1744, at Covent Garden, affords one of the saddest examples of how a poor libretto can completely hobble the creative powers of a genius. *Joseph* is a frightful concoction of the worst sanctimonious trash ever wished on a composer. The story is lacking not only in continuity and coherence but even in the most elementary meaning. If plot and construction are wretched and senseless, the "poetry" is even more so. Handel was not moved by Asenath, the heroine, and when such a thing happens a work is doomed. He himself got tired of it; for the final chorus, he simply inserted the *Dettingen Te Deum.* It was not because of clerical limitations that the author, the Reverend James Miller, failed in his task, for the good pastor was a confirmed friend of the theatre and a playwright to boot. He was simply unfit to wield a pen. Even though *Joseph and his Brethren* contains a few very fine numbers, notably some great choral pieces, we must regard it as a complete failure. But though far from popular success, the work was sufficiently well received to encourage Handel to offer several subsequent revivals, the last taking place two years before his death, when he was already blind. But it never eked out more than two or three successive performances.

The subscription series ended on March 21 with *Saul.* Rumors once more predicted Handel's impending artistic demise, but instead it was Middlesex's opera company that expired in June. The noble lord's intrigues against Handel had proved of no avail, and for a while Middlesex even found it necessary to leave London for Paris, where of course he "lived a dissolute life"—at least Flower so reports. But Handel, far from being eclipsed, immediately exploited the situation. On June 9 the old warrior informed Jennens that he had leased the Haymarket Theatre vacated by Middlesex, engaging a company consisting of Francesina, Miss Robinson, Beard, Reinhold, "Mr. Gates with his Boye's and several of the best Chorus singers from the Choirs," and expressed the hope that Susanna Cibber would join the ensemble. Eager to proceed, he asked Jennens for the first act "of the new Oratorio [*Belshazzar*] with which you intend to favor me." After this we lose track of Handel for about a month—perhaps he went to Tunbridge Wells—but by July 19, the man who was supposed to fade from the scene was so impatient that he began the composition of *Hercules* even as the first act of *Belshazzar* arrived from Gopsall. By the time *Hercules* was finished, towards the end of August, the second act of *Belshazzar* was at hand, and without waiting for the rest, Handel immediately began setting the new oratorio. Two tremendous masterpieces composed in two months! On October 20 a subscription series for twenty-four evenings was announced, which duly began in November with *Deborah*. Then, on January 5, 1745, *Hercules*, "A new Musical Drama," was first performed at the fifth subscription concert.

XVI

HOW HANDEL HAPPENED ON THE REVEREND THOMAS
Broughton and who was responsible for the subject of *Hercules* is not
known. But Broughton managed to prepare a libretto that supplied all the
stimulus needed by Handel's responsive imagination for the creation of the
crowning glory of Baroque music drama, the near-perfect confluence of
observation, expression, passion, and music. The Reverend Dr. Broughton was another clergyman dabbling in letters, but while a creative nonentity, like the Reverend James Miller, he was a man of learning
and of much more experience than the author of *Joseph and his Brethren*. His preoccupation with the classics and with English letters gave
him a good idea of the nature of the theatre and of the expressiveness of
well-chosen words. As we read his book, derived from a combination of
Sophocles's *Women of Trachis* and Ovid's *Metamorphoses* (IX), it becomes clear why this divine could accomplish what his hapless colleague
could not. *Hercules* is a drama, not a potpourri; it has construction and
continuity, the first essential conditions for a dramatic composer; it has
motivation, providing plausible figures that a dramatic composer can endow with life; and, finally, though its author was not a poet, he had a
good memory combined with a partiality for the great English poets, and
his text is liberally strewn with fine echoes. This favored another important element in the Handelian canon, for the imagery of words was a
powerful stimulant to the composer.

Broughton showed good theatrical sense in arranging the old legend.

He tightened the conflict by peeling off almost everything extraneous to the drama of jealousy, which made for sharpness of image, for unblurred edges. In Sophocles's play, Hercules does commit adultery with the captive princess, Iole; by making both innocent, the tragic passion of Dejanira is enhanced. But perhaps most important was the change that made possible a confrontation of husband and wife; in the original play Dejanira's husband never reaches Trachis. In this rearrangement of a rather complicated play, Broughton was aided by Ovid, but his own additions are numerous and on the whole sound and useful.

Hercules does not open with the usual banquet, thanksgiving, or ritual scene. Mindful of the type of drama he has decided upon, Broughton proceeds with a good design: the introduction of the characters before their conflict is developed. Dejanira, desolated by the long absence of her spouse, Hercules, fears that he will never return to Trachis from the wars. Her misgivings about his fate are reinforced by the Herald, Lichas, and her son, Hyllus. The priests, too, predict his death as the chorus sings with sepulchral power. Young Hyllus is resolved to end the uncertainty by searching for his father in foreign parts, but even as he is about to depart, the Herald announces that the victorious hero is returning with rich booty, which includes the beautiful princess Iole of Oechalia and her retinue of virgins. The tone changes, the populace rejoices, and everyone appears ready to settle down to the pleasures of a peaceful domestic life.

The stage is now set for the drama to burgeon as the two women are enmeshed in a conflict. Iole is completely possessed by her grief for her father, slain by Hercules, and her distress at being a prisoner. She has no thought for anything else, but Dejanira, a passionate woman, senses in her a rival. Though Iole protests her innocence, Dejanira is more and more convinced that Hercules is unfaithful. The chorus warns of the terrors of jealousy, but even as the somber theme of this most insidious of passions is developed, Hyllus proclaims his love for Iole, inducing a new moral in the chorus as it expresses its faith in love as the greatest gift of life. Iole rejects Hyllus. Dejanira denounces the conjugal treachery of Hercules, who, surprised, for the moment takes the accusation lightly, but Dejanira misinterprets his reaction as a confession of guilt. The centaur Nessus once gave her a magic garment supposed to rekindle love in its wearer; Lichas is charged with delivering it to Hercules as a token of Dejanira's forgiveness. But Nessus, mortally wounded by Hercules, had plotted revenge: the garment does not arouse love, it poisons the wearer. Hercules puts it on and dies, cursing Dejanira, as the furies rise to haunt her. Iole is filled with compassion for her enemies in their hour of tragedy.

In the mandatory Baroque epilogue Hercules ascends to Olympus, Jupiter commands the young pair to wed, and the work ends with a choral piece extolling everything and everybody.

Hercules is a music drama, like *Semele*, virtually an opera; there are in it no national, religious, or political motifs, as in many of the oratorios. Handel is completely absorbed by the theme; his intention to crystallize its essence, to capture the meaning at once elusive and comprehensive, dictated a more complex and concentrated idiom than that followed in *Saul*, the other great drama of jealousy. This desire to grasp and exploit the essence produced in Dejanira a character that dwarfs all the others. Julian Herbage, a little too severe with Broughton, recognizes the exceptional stature of Dejanira, but exaggerates when he calls the other figures "merely puppets that adopt the conventional postures of the 18th century tragic stage." Winton Dean epitomizes Dejanira when he calls her a "female Othello"—nothing less would do justice to her character. She is a figure in the round, this ardent woman whom Handel presents vis-à-vis the other characters the way a spire is placed next to a human figure to show its height. Few of Handel's heroines are as determined as she, and yet she does not sin against femininity. The swift stir of her jealousy, growing into primeval recrimination and then into spiritual blackness, reaches a pitch of frenzy in her aria; the listener feels as if he were struggling for breath while a flood of music sweeps over his head.

As Iole first appears she wonders about sin and love, still knowing neither. The simple directness of her utterance is very moving. Gradually, as she is drawn into the conflict, her personality develops. Hercules, who appears only twice, is really only an accessory, the object of Dejanira's jealousy; not the mighty demigod of the myth but a likable warrior with deep sanity, vitality, and a muscular eloquence that at times is almost amusing. This, too, has led to misunderstanding: "Hercules himself is merely sketched as a bluff, vigorous character," says Herbage. But Broughton and Handel realized that the psychological impact of insane jealousy would be the more telling if the subject provoking such passion is not a towering hero but a simple type who would not even think of adultery.

Handel did not penetrate into the character of Hyllus, though he gave him fine music, and Lichas's role is definitely over-extended; several of his numbers are expendable, for Lichas owes his eminence to Handel's regard for Mrs. Cibber. When her participation in the new oratorio venture became assured Handel understandably wanted to make room for her in the cast. The only adaptable role was that of Lichas, originally a minor part for a tenor, which Handel proceeded to convert and expand far be-

yond its dramaturgical needs. This gallant generosity did not help the
drama, but as remarked above, continuity can be achieved by the simple
expedient of omitting a number of Lichas's songs—the suggestion comes
from Handel himself. When subsequently Mrs. Cibber was no longer
available, he cut the part of Lichas altogether. As in *Semele,* the chorus is
employed not so much as a direct agent in the drama but as clarifying and
summarizing lyric body in the spirit of the classical *choros.*

Hercules opens with a scene oppressive with forebodings. Lichas, in
a fine accompanied recitative, bewails Dejanira's dejection over the absence of her husband. His following aria transgresses the boundaries of
the Baroque style; its *galant* tone was noted by several Handelian critics,
who liken it to Gluck and Jommelli. The little unison passages interspersed in the aria are particularly effective in creating a mood of tense
grief. Dejanira's first aria, "The world, when day's career is run," is also a
"modern" piece, the chromatic passages followed by a simple cadence
have the effect of causing an oscillation between light and shade. Hyllus's
"I feel the God" is in the spacious heroic style that one would assign to the
mature Gluck were it not for the typically Handelian largeness of gesture.
Upon hearing the oracle, Dejanira no longer doubts the death of Hercules, consoling herself with the thought of being reunited with him in the
hereafter. "There in myrtle shades" is a fine aria in which grief is blended
with renunciation in a pastoral tone. Hyllus now sings a song, "Where
congealed the northern streams," in which the mood is depicted with all
of Handel's ability to illustrate a text; the voice literally "congeals" when
the passage is repeated for the third time. The chorus approves of Hyllus's
resolution to seek out his father; "O filial piety" is a tremendous choral
fugue framed by two homophonic pieces in slow dance rhythm. In the
first of these one can clearly recognize the origin of the first chorus in
Gluck's *Orfeo.*

The heavy atmosphere is lightened with the announcement of Hercules's safe homecoming. Now Dejanira exults: "Be gone my fears." Lichas,
too, in his lilting aria "The smiling hours," dismisses gloom, nicely preparing the entry of the chorus with "Let none despair, relief may come." This
is a remarkably free and inventive double fugue with sharply contrasting
themes. The transparent construction, with many passages for pairs of
voices, reminds one of the "duet" choruses in *Messiah.* Iole enters. In her
magnificent aria "Daughter of Gods, bright liberty," she is altogether preoccupied with her unhappy status as a prisoner. The long ritornel is startling: it is through-composed as though the requirements of the text were
already present. A march is heard and Hercules appears. He addresses

Iole in a friendly tone, but this awakens in her the dreadful picture of his slaying of her father, and we are treated to one of the great laments in the dramatic literature: "My father." The slow arioso is introduced by a ritornel of dark, rich color. Instead of the expected continuation of the motto, a sudden diminished seventh chord turns the aria, for a moment, into an accompanied recitative before it continues upon its course.

Hercules, satisfied with the situation—his requirements are modest —wants to forget about the carnage and enjoy love. "The god of battle quits the field," he sings in what would be a simple strophic song were it not for the exquisite accompaniment. Once more we are astounded by Handel's new, modern idiom, by the refinements he can put into a fifteen(!) - measure ritornel, and the manner in which he exploits this material in the course of the air. The chorus seconds Hercules. The Thessalian shepherds who come to celebrate the victory and acclaim the hero have brought along their bagpipes and shawms, and by turning from B-flat to D Handel adds the trumpets to the rejoicing. "Crown with festal pomp the day" is a typical act-ending chorus, but the mixture of the heroic and the pastoral makes it extraordinarily attractive.

The spirit of rejoicing at the end of the first act disappears when, at the opening of the second, Iole appears, still dominated by the awful realization of her loss of freedom, and questions her fate: "Why was I born a princess?" The aria "How blest the maid" is again one of those remarkable pieces that point far into the future. The two women now come face to face. Dejanira is at first restrained, more sorrowful than angry: "When beauty sorrow's liv'ry wears, our passions take the fair one's part," but soon she begins to accuse. Iole, innocent and inexperienced, replies "What ills the jealous prove." Lichas, hearing the accusation that "Hercules is false," comes to his master's defense in an elaborate da capo aria.

Now the chorus takes up the theme of jealousy in a piece of an intensity extraordinary even with Handel. "Jealousy, infernal pest" recreates the tone of Greek tragedy as it had not been heard for two millennia. At the same time it is a wholly modern and prophetic musical composition far beyond the confines of the Baroque. The form is da capo, the means symphonic, for the orchestra does not accompany—it is charged with a genuinely symphonic texture of its own. The convolutions are so calculated that significant thematic elements intrude into the pauses of the vocal parts, and when later both unite on the exclamation "Jealousy," the effect is crushing.

After this tremendous scene all concerned—including Handel—have difficulty in collecting themselves. Hyllus and Iole meet alone as Handel proceeds to elaborate the subplot, as he so often did in his operas. Hyllus confesses his love for Iole, but his tone is somewhat formal and distant. Here the librettist, strong in dealing with the great abstract themes but obviously uncomfortable in depicting young love, did not help his composer. The recitative is a rather sober dialogue. The gentle and chaste Iole speaks words of mature wisdom that do not suit her. Her following aria, "Banish love from thy breast," a charming piece, is also a little miscalculated in tone; Iole's brilliant coloraturas do not accord with the sentiments expressed. But now Handel takes to the smitten young prince and gives him a warmly romantic siciliana, "From celestial seats descending," that once more evokes magnificent endorsement from the chorus. "Wanton god of amorous fires" is an exquisitely tooled late Venetian madrigal supported by a symphonic accompaniment whose motif capriciously intrudes here and there into the vocal parts, while elsewhere it is ingeniously combined with the vocal theme.

The conflict quickens as Dejanira confronts Hercules, who does not quite realize the seriousness of her charge and replies with a blustering aria in which he recites his accomplishments with such gusto and naive self-satisfaction that we are on the borderline of the buffa. Unimpressed, Dejanira counsels him to lay aside his weapons for a spinning wheel. This aria also has in it elements of the opera buffa, but here they are used ironically. Dramaturgically, this is a master stroke, for Dejanira is yet at the stage of annoyance rather than wrath; she is acid and sarcastic. The unsophisticated—and innocent—Hercules, not knowing how to deal with the situation, simply leaves, pleading urgent business, but this hasty departure, which Dejanira takes for a form of admission of guilt, stings her to action. With a sure dramatic instinct, Handel first makes her pensive in a fine slow aria, "Cease ruler of the day to rise." In the following recitative she decides to employ magic to recapture her husband's love, charging Lichas with the task of carrying Nessus's magic garment to Hercules. Lichas accepts the embassy with a little dance tune, compact, charming, and dispensing with the ritornel. Sure of her success—or out of guile— Dejanira shows magnanimity towards Iole, whom she no longer considers a rival, sending her an olive branch. The two women sing a carefully worked pastoral in the chamber-duet style. But Steffani can no longer claim to be the godfather; the piece has decidedly Purcellian echoes. The chorus is pleased by this turn of events, expressing its sentiments in a delectable gavotte, "Love and Hymen."

As in *Samson,* the sinfonia preceding the third act describes the catastrophic events taking place offstage. This is a program prelude, bold in form and substance. Handel now gives Lichas a very moving piece, "O scene of unexampled woe." The chorus weeps: "Tyrants now no more shall dread." This is truly Sophoclean in its all-embracing grandeur as it summarizes and comments on the whole tragedy with sombre intensity. Hercules's animated accompanied recitative and aria, marked *concitato,* is not simply a rage aria for bass; the orchestra never relents, even where Hercules intermittently abandons his tumbling coloraturas. The dramatic tension is now considerable, presently becoming fearful. Hyllus sings a particularly attractive aria with a superb symphonic accompaniment ("Let not fame the tidings spread"), but at this point the long da capo aria hurts the action. With Dejanira's final song, an extensive through-composed *scena* with constant change of mood and tempo, the drama reaches its climax. The astounding variety of the music faithfully follows the constantly changing thoughts and feelings of Dejanira, now half-demented with revulsion and fear. No shattering sound, no shuffling crowds here, but one of the most expressive and intimate character studies to be found in the operatic literature. Dejanira is one of those extraordinary visions who visit the imagination of a great creative artist, a tragic though heroic figure, who as she drains her cup of suffering reveals in an image the inner meaning of a total situation.

Iole arrives, singing a song, "My breast with tender pity swells," which has an unmistakable resemblance to "I know that my Redeemer liveth." Yet this ineffable piece is an altogether different and complete creation. Now Handel's attempts to conjure up a happy ending become quite evident. Lichas, Hyllus, and Iole all sing lengthy numbers, and the chorus, assisted by two horns, closes the work with a jolly bucolic piece. Broughton, intimidated by the period's unwillingness to accept a tragic ending, demurred at driving Dejanira to suicide, as the original story demanded. This not only dampened the effect of the appearance of the furies, but compelled Handel to compose a conclusion that obviously held little interest for him. Unlike the epilogues in some of the other works, however, this music is not easily expendable. *Hercules* contains no weak or routine music; every number is worked out with meticulous care, with well-turned and always interesting accompaniments and construction. We feel astonishment not only at the consistent beauty of the music but also at its copiousness.

The pace of this oratorio is slow; largos predominate, as do tonalities in the minor mode. The harmonic language is bold, often heavily chromatic, and the accompanied recitative, which is used profusely, reaches an intensity, as well as dimensions, heretofore unknown to the Baroque. *Her-*

cules is highly dramatic, modern, new, and romantic. Handel borrowed very little, and the little he did was incomparably enriched. Ritornels are elaborate, but often are treated like delicate chamber music. The orchestra is not large, though trumpets and horns appear in some numbers; the string orchestra, without even the oboes, is the mainstay, and there is scarcely one measure in which it is not manipulated with imaginative craftsmanship. The moving up of the bass into a higher position, so characteristic of the crystalline orchestra of Haydn and Mozart, is already noticeable in this score. This Handel did either by omitting the double basses, thus leaving the cellos in charge of the lowest part, or by dispensing with the entire apparatus of the basso continuo. Curiously, among all these novelties we again encounter the archaic basso continuo aria, but its use was deliberate. Whenever Handel felt that the mere continuo had served its purpose, he called in the orchestra, usually in the closing ritornel. There are subtle reverberations from *Semele,* especially in the love music. Dejanira's song, as she recovers from her melancholy at the news of Hercules's approach to Trachis, is not without a slight amorous-erotic tinge. This is the kind of music Handel usually composed when promising pleasures to the gods visiting earth; apparently mortal women had an attraction for the Olympians (as for the denizens of Valhalla) that goddesses could not match. *Hercules* has one shortcoming: the romantic bravura of some of the larger arias (there is a trace of this in *Semele,* too) seems to be a little out of place. These arias are decidedly close to the *style galant,* and indeed *Hercules* contains so much that we associate with the music of the new generation emerging towards the middle of the century that Handel must be counted a powerful influence in the operatic reform ascribed to Gluck. In fact, Gluck knew, admired, and utilized *Hercules.*

The "new Musical Drama" *Hercules* was presented on January 5, 1745, with Handel's faithful and experienced cast: Reinhold (Hercules), Miss Robinson (Dejanira), Beard (Hyllus), Francesina (Iole), and Mrs. Cibber (Lichas). It failed. It had to fail because there was something in *Hercules* that the vast majority of Handel's listeners could not understand, something Handel himself, though he understood, could never again attain. The note of distress, mixed with a vital expressive impulse, is too much even for our generation. Thus the greatest of Baroque music dramas still awaits the recognition it deserves. Handel had to acknowledge defeat, cancelling the rest of the subscription concerts after a few days. With characteristic honesty he offered to "pay back the Subscription Money" for the unused part of the series. The announcement, which appeared January 17 in the *Daily Advertiser,* is a moving document, a proud confession, but also a quiet indictment of the public. In a few sentences Handel told all the world what he believed in, what he endeavored to do, and, a curious but significant matter that has not been properly appreciated, he declared his faith in the suitability of the English language for his music.

As I perceived, that joining good Sense and significant Words to Musick, was the best Method of recommending *this* to an English Audience; I have directed my Studies that way, and endeavour'd to shew, that the English Language, which is so expressive of the sublimest Sentiments is the best adapted of any to the full and solemn Kind of Musick.

Handel's faith in "a Nation, whose Characteristick is Good Nature" was not disappointed; the response was instantaneous. In the very next issue of the paper several subscribers suggested that "with Justice to the Character of the Nation, and the Merit of the Man," the subscribers should decline to withdraw the remainder of the fees. Indeed, the public's response to this dignified manifesto was such that within a week Handel could announce in the *Daily Advertiser* that, moved by the generosity of the subscribers, he ought not content himself with "bare expressions" of his gratitude, but would proceed with the fulfilling of the originally announced obligations, at least to the extent it might prove feasible; "let the *Risque* which I may run be what it will." So a seventh subscription concert was announced for the 16th of February, featuring *Hercules,* but resumption of the concerts had to be postponed until March 1, when a safer course was followed. The popular *Samson* was substituted for the unappreciated *Hercules,* followed by *Saul* and *Joseph.* The "new Oratorio, call'd BELSHAZZAR" was offered at the twelfth concert, March 27.

[2]

WE HAVE touched upon the correspondence between Handel and Jennens concerning *Belshazzar* and have seen that in his impatience at his librettist's tardiness Handel turned to the composition of *Hercules.* In the meantime, portions of *Belshazzar* began to arrive, and they caused him uneasiness as the proportions grew larger and larger. Jennens used twice as many words as the composer needed and even so felt that he had not yet said everything he wanted to say: one more scene, one more verse still seemed called for here and there. Handel was aghast at its length, and though he set the enormously long first act, he demurred about the rest, cautiously at first, as in general he showed surprising forbearance towards Jennens. In his letter of July 19, 1744, he accepted Jennens's "reasons" for the length of the first act, but added "and it is like-wise my Opinion to have the following Acts short." Upon receiving the third act, however, he became worried and began to complain, though tactfully and with the help of a little flattery, praising the "sublimity" of Jennens's work. "I retrench'd already a great deal of the Musick, that I might preserve the Poetry as much as I could," wrote the composer, now making concrete suggestions for cuts. In the end he set the text the way he saw it, omitting about two hundred lines. Yet the book offered drama-tic continuity and characterization and Handel was clearly aroused by it. If any proof is needed of his literary dramatic sense, a comparison of the libretto with the score will supply it. Handel cut words, lines, and whole airs whenever the pace of the drama seemed to him too slow. The cuts can be ascertained with accuracy; as in the past, Jennens's admiration for Handel was not unconditional when his own literary effort was involved. While grudgingly accepting the cuts, he insisted that the printed libretto contain all his words, including the portions not set by Handel.

Belshazzar is a biblical drama inasmuch as the core of the story is taken from the Book of Daniel, but the chief protagonist comes not from the Bible but from Herodotus, from whom, together with Xenophon, Jennens drew with considerable skill and acumen. Even the historians' account was used with the poetic license of the dramatist in order to create character, motivation, and a continuous action. Jennens may have been verbose, but by and large he provided Handel with a good dramatic libretto. He knew his classics and the Bible, as well as the august themes treated by these sources, and he also knew, like da Ponte half a century later, how his composer would react to a dramatic proposition. So the enormously long first act, with its dramatically unpromising social-philosophical observations, turned out to be a magnificent preamble to a tragic tale of fate within the spirit of the Attic drama.

At first sight the idea of a music drama whose background is historical-philosophical seems strange, if not altogether unfeasible. Carnal love is not involved in this drama, and consequently there is none of Han-del's exquisite love music, but there is again one of those towering matri-archs Handel was so fond of creating in music. And the antithesis of Jews, Persians, and Babylonians gave him an opportunity to employ the chorus for the most remarkably consistent musical characterization of different nations and cultures. After *Semele* and *Hercules* the style once more changes; it becomes thrusting, and brings back the grandiose imprecatory element of the Old Testament, the pronouncements of punishment and revenge.

The story is very simple. Nitocris, the Queen Mother, a spiritual disciple of the captive Jewish prophet, Daniel, contemplates with dismay the approaching collapse of Babylon. Cyrus and the Persian army are besieging the city, and aided by information obtained from Gobrias, who has abandoned Babylon to join the hosts of righteousness, the Persian king plans to enter the city by diverting the protective flow of the Euphrates. While this plan is hatched—indeed, while it is being carried out—Belshazzar is occupied in the drunken revelling of the Babylonian feast of Sesach. During the orgies of the feast "a hand appears writing on the wall over against him." The king faints with fright, and upon recovery he commands the wise men to be summoned to explain the meaning of the message on the wall. They being unable to solve the riddle, Daniel is sent for, and he tells the King that he and his empire are doomed. The Persians break into the city and slay Belshazzar, but Cyrus is magnanimous towards the conquered, professes his faith in Jehovah, and promises the Jews freedom and the rebuilding of their temple in Jerusalem.

No libretto is more than a potential living drama until it is realized in music. Out of this story Handel made an almost savagely powerful, robust, and severely sumptuous score. *Belshazzar* is a stirring and spirited work, a masterpiece of eloquence and sympathy as well as incisive skill. The book is well constructed, and there is just enough psychological observation to deepen the interest without overburdening the plot. The narrative, in the smooth corpulence of its phrasing, shows a readiness, at times really extraordinary, to accommodate itself to musical treatment.

Nitocris is a tremendous figure, like Dejanira, though quite a different woman. A patriot and mother, she is not carried away by senseless passion; rather she is possessed by an intelligence clarified by suffering. Her despairing sagacity, her Cassandra-like clearsightedness, warn her that her son's acts are ruining the realm, and she tries, though without confidence, to change his course. At the same time her love for her son adds a moving note that sounds from true human depths, from a heart wrung with pity and stricken with loss. The antinomy that confronts Nitocris exercised a spell upon Handel; the conflict remained as strenuous to him as to Nitocris. Handel did not bother to make Belshazzar really interesting, he is only the traditional biblical lawbreaker, for his role is nothing but to be destroyed. He is not a tragic hero but someone who seeks his own downfall without reason. Yet, as with Harapha and some others, Handel did not make an out-and-out villain of Belshazzar; he is a drunkard, an irresponsible satrap. Cyrus is an unusual warrior, beneficent, remote, and serene, who takes his emotions with a priestly solemnity. His utterances are at once delicate and determined. That the role was originally composed for a soprano, rather suprisingly at this stage of Handel's career, offers a stumbling block for modern theatrical performance, as does to a lesser degree the alto of Daniel. But Handel helps here, for when he was forced to reshuffle the parts for lack of a suitable prima donna, he gave it to the bass Reinhold!

The Prophet Daniel has an attitude so rigid that his personality makes little impression. He luxuriates a little in his elevated sentiments; nevertheless, he has a solid core, though one is brought to it slowly; Handel entrusted some very great music to him. Gobrias is an honest old man, torn by the same problems faced by Nitocris. Though a moving figure—Handel always endows his old men with warmth—he does not have the Queen's stamina and flees from the tyrant. Now under Cyrus's protection, he has to work up his anger anew. *Belshazzar* has not one but three choral groups—Jews, Babylonians, and Persians. Every one of them receives music of its own: the Jewish choruses are richly contrapuntal and elaborate, the Persian brilliant, and the Babylonian roisterous in an attractive way.

The fine overture, with its startling, sudden interruptions, is no doubt programmatic in intent, for which reason Handel omits the customary minuet or gavotte at the end. Handel holds on to the somber E minor as he embarks on the difficult dramatic assignment of the opening scene. Nitocris, wise in the ways of men and their political creations, contemplates the laws of the rise and fall of empires. Thus the drama commences with a philosophical meditation on the "fluctuating state of human empire," which one would think could hardly amount to more than a preparatory statement. But Nitocris is deeply concerned, and Handel translates her philosophy into vibrant dramatic music. Nitocris asks Daniel whether there is any remedy for the situation. Daniel answers, perhaps a little professionally, that the only remedy is to submit to God. His following aria, "Lament thus not, oh Queen," is, however, a fine piece. The second scene is merely another grand choral number in the concert hall, but in the theatre, where the Babylonians hurl their taunts at the besieging Persians from the battlements, it is stirring music drama. Handel gives a superb musical rendition of the text; the smugly confident Babylonians sing flowing garlands of tone that sound like laughter. The choral writing is as airy as in any of the "duet" choruses, yet there is a certain massiveness in this wonderful piece. Gobrias's air, "Oppress'd with never ceasing grief," is a little complete drama in itself as the plaintive beginning gradually recedes before rising anger, ending in stark vindictiveness.

Now Cyrus appears. First he accepts Gobrias's motif, counselling "haste, your just revenge to speed," but in the following accompanied recitative he shows his ultimate magnanimity; he wants neither ransom nor prisoners. The latter half of this recitative is again pure theatre as Cyrus elicits combat intelligence from Gobrias. "Behold the monstrous human beast" is again one of those utterly simple yet powerful deceptive pieces where unadorned unison is more eloquent than the most expressive harmonies. In Gobrias's song the wastrel is more graphically before us than in Belshazzar's own acts. After listening to the old man's description of Belshazzar, Cyrus sings a noble prayer, the scene ending with another fine chorus. "All empires upon God depend" begins with a homophonic introduction, but at "Begin with prayer" Handel proceeds to an extraordinary choral fugue built on a gigantic theme and elaborated with all manner of combinations. Now Daniel, who is given an entire scene in three parts, rises to eminence. First he sings a fine largo, followed by a recitative and by a most impressively constructed passacaglia. The unison strings introduce the ostinato, whose elaboration remains largely independent of the rhetorical voice part, though here and there the latter takes up bits of it. There is solemn drama when Daniel declares that "from the rising sun to the setting sun, the nations may confess, I am the Lord"; the inexorable ground bass is interrupted, the voice, accompanied by simple chords, dominates. The chorus of the Jews is jubilant. Preceded by a long ritornel, it begins hymnically, ending with a triumphant Hallelujah-Amen.

Handel surmounted every difficulty threatened by the philosophical musings of the opening scenes; the tone is one of grandeur, and the musical substance inspired. Now he has a chance to vary the grandeur with some of the vulgar tones of earthly existence. Belshazzar appears, surrounded by his people, inviting all to take part in the saturnalia of Sesach: "Let festal joy triumphant reign." The gestures remain large, however: the ritornel is thirty-six measures long, almost a sinfonia. That Belshazzar begins alone serves to enhance the boisterous quality of the dance—Sesach is the Babylonian god of debauchery. Nitocris, in "The leafy honours of the field," really a simile aria but in this case quite appropriate, tries to forestall the orgy. The piece is of course descriptive, but also highly poetic. Nitocris fails, and as Belshazzar orders the sacred vessels from the temple to be used as wine cups, the Jews, horrified at his sacrilegious intentions, warningly urge him to reconsider. "Recall o King thy rash command," in the dark key of F minor, is built with a shrewdly effective dramatic sense. The six-part chorus presents men and women antiphonally; they sing unaccompanied until on the word "Jehovah" the orchestra joins them with heavy C minor chords. Throughout this remarkable piece harmony, dynamics, and pauses are used for dramatic ends.

Nitocris is stirred by the Jews' plaint and warns Belshazzar anew, but he is tired of "frivolous dispute" and wants to proceed with the feast. Mother and son now confront each other in a magnificent duet. Each of the participants contends at length, but Handel gradually diminishes the distance between entries, the phrases become shorter and tighter, and presently the two parts are interwoven. The chorus of Jews re-enters, this time more solemn than excited and thereby more dramatically taut. The pattern is familiar: from homophony to polyphony, but in the mighty fugue that ends the act, Handel knows how to be pictorial within the framework of intricate counterpoint.

The second act opens with a large chorus of Persians. They have carried out Cyrus's stratagem of diverting the Euphrates. Though quite different from the tremendous closing chorus that precedes it, "See from his post Euphrates flies" is equally as accomplished. In the large tripartite construction the counterpoint is deliberately small-jointed, and as the independence of the parts decreases so the impact of the homophonic ejaculations increases. We are in the presence of a duet-chorus: Handel derived this fine piece from his chamber duet *Fronda leggiera e mobile* (1743), and the transformation is once more a stunning piece of craftsmanship and imagination. This time the airy theme exactly fits the situation: the coloraturas on "mobile" could nicely serve for "[Euphrates] flies" without the changing of one note-value; the notion of borrowing this piece must have been spontaneous. The tone is a beguiling scherzando, and the ever-changing combination of voices keeps the piece indeed *leggiero e mobile*. The Babylonians, represented by a three-part chorus of women's voices, deplore the river's "faithlessness" in simple chordal style. The Persians' chorus of men answers in the same style. The concluding double fugue has a lucid structure in which the strongly contrasting themes are elaborated with a freedom that must have chagrined theorists and pedagogues then as it does now.

Cyrus orders the advance through the dry riverbed. His long da capo aria "Amaz'd to find the foe so near" is a little misplaced at this juncture, and though it contains fine music, it could be cut out. A short martial sinfonia calls the Persians to arms, while the Babylonians, not yet aware of their danger, indulge in their orgiastic feast. The boisterous tone returns in "Ye tutelar Gods of our Empire"; the ponderously jolly theme is catchy, the phrases drunkenly asymmetric, the melodic convolutions capricious but always in a good popular vein, all of which adds up to a powerful piece. The same tone lingers in Belshazzar's aria "Let the deep bowl thy praise confess."

As he defies the God of Judah, there begins the most extraordinary scene in all the oratorios. It is largely lost unless the work is staged, for as in Verdi's *Macbeth,* the King's retinue does not see the apparition until after the King recovers from his faint. The excited chorus wonders "why our mirth so sudden ends"; then they discover the writing on the wall. The panic and consternation are masterfully rendered. The King, a little more composed, sends for the Chaldean sages to interpret the meaning of the message. At this point Handel borrows from Telemann's *Musique de Table* (1733) a posthorn signal. Entitled "Allegro Postillons," the sinfonia, a program piece, describes the mission of fetching the seers, but it also admirably serves to enhance the suspense.[1] The wise men are baffled, and now fear descends on the courtiers as a wailing, piercing cry, "nor God nor man affords relief," passes from voice to voice. Upon Nitocris's recommendation Daniel is consulted. Daniel's aria and recitative again exhibits the admirable new device of forming larger units by connecting two or more pieces through the symphonic elaboration of themes common to them. In the aria, reproachful and haughty, the postillion motif lurks in the background, a reminder that the wise men could not interpret the meaning of the writing. The customary order of recitative and aria is reversed for dramatic emphasis; the interpretation of the fatal message demands the freedom of the recitative. Now it is the authentic prophet who speaks, predicting Babylon's doom.

Nitocris's despair does not take the form of an accompanied recitative, as one would expect in such a scene of shattering conflict. Handel has her sing "Regard o son my flowing tears" in a siciliana whose normally smooth flowing lines are studded with the large intervals of sixths and sevenths. The mother's song has a crushing effect on Belshazzar, who is silent. Meanwhile the Persians are advancing on Babylon, with Gobrias acting as their guide. Cyrus's aria "O God of truth" shows his determination to advance. It also shows that he tends to be somewhat sententious, though his counsel of moderation and the avoidance of "needless slaughter" is of course a most commendable quality in a conquering general. The

---

[1] For those who want to study the mysteries of the creative process, a comparison of Telemann's original with Handel's version offers an enlightening lesson. Max Seiffert gives a good analysis of this piece in *Bulletin de la Société Union Musicologique,* IV (1924).

Persians acclaim their "glorious prince" in a fine large anthem, which
again represents the aggregate of three distinct pieces, ending in a splendid fugue. One does not mind the almost didactic tone of the text, for
Handel's imagination is at white heat, the richness and variety of choral
detail are captivating, and the great double fugue rises to majestic height.

The third act, though well planned by Jennens, could easily have de-
generated into watery sentimentalism—it is perilously undramatic.
Handel brought it off magnificently, once more demonstrating that in a
music drama it is the musician who gives the text its meaning. That Handel was conscious of the pitfalls is demonstrated by the existence of two
or even three versions of almost all the important pieces in this act, and
our choice is made difficult because all of them are excellent. The act begins with another fine piece by Nitocris. "Alternate hopes and fears distract my mind," sings the Queen, but the grieving mother, who sees her
son's unavoidable fate, recognizes the moral justification of the impending
tragedy. There are two versions of this appealing piece, but surely the
second, which uses the thematic material of the E minor recitative that
opens *Belshazzar*, should be preferred. Nitocris, in a brief secco, asks
Daniel whether there is any hope for her son. The prophet's continuo aria,
"Can the black Aethiop change his skin?" is obviously a simile aria, a little
smug, and not up to the level of Daniel's best music.

The Persians are nearing, and the Jews predict the fall of Baal, but
not yet jubilantly; "Bel boweth down" is a dark, menacing piece. Belshazzar, fortified with wine, decides to make a stand, but is immediately
cut down. Gobrias, in a moving larghetto lament ("To power immortal")
tries to forget the past and hope for a better future, which is promised by
Cyrus: "Destructive war, thy limit know; here tyrant Death, thy terrors
end." The aria again tests Handel's powers, for the oriental potentate acts
like an English general touched by the Enlightenment. But Handel gave
the piece a tone that completely neutralizes the platitudinous sentences;
what we hear is a paean of victory with an accompaniment unusually rich
for a solo air, as oboes, trumpets, and timpani are added to the orchestra.
The ritornel is an almost jaunty tune, the kind one cannot dismiss from
one's mind for days. It is the composer who speaks here, not the reform
monarch. The great dramatic duet that follows, and in which Nitocris
bows at the victor's feet while Cyrus offers himself as a son to replace the
slain one, is marked by the nobility of its melody, the stateliness of the
accompaniment, which has stretches in ostinato, and the manner in which
the antiphony of the voices is arranged. Daniel's short recitative, which
follows, is a little unctuous; but the minute the soprano intones the engag-

ing dance tune, "Tell it out among the heathen," he is forgotten. This is a happy transplant. The fifth Chandos Anthem, *I will magnify Thee,* reworked with care for the occasion, is most appropriate for the grand ending Handel envisaged. While the score does not so specify, the soprano and alto solos in the last portion of the great anthem are clearly meant to be sung by Nitocris and Cyrus. Serving as a compound finale, the wondrous piece steadily rises to a flooding Amen.

Belshazzar bears evidence of a craftsmanship that alone would make it a monument. It is well constructed and has distinction of style. Here, in contrast to the classical dramas *Semele* and *Hercules,* the da capo aria is used sparingly; Handel relies on the dramatic flexibility of the arioso combined with passages in accompanied recitative. The latter, also used in choral numbers, reaches great intensity in this oratorio. The ritornels are long, elaborate, and often descriptive-programmatic; thematic elements from them are used as symphonic subject-matter binding together several numbers. In general, the scenes in *Belshazzar* tend to be large interlocking structures, a prefiguration of the "reform" opera of the next half-century. Borrowings are few, the one significant instance being the fifth Chandos Anthem at the end of the work. This was a happy idea, not accidental but deliberate and well planned. Handel discussed the employment of the anthem with Jennens, a fact that sheds considerable light both on his dramaturgical concepts and on the question of borrowings. (See below, p. 559 ff.) The "military music" comes from the English semi-opera, and several other numbers show a decidedly English quality. Interestingly enough, it is in Belshazzar's songs and the choruses of his banqueting people that this is most noticeable. Their popular tone —and popular tunes—have the quality of English folksong.

But there is far more in this work than skilful execution. Setting aside questions of craftsmanship, there is a splendor, an intensity, a vibrant feeling in *Belshazzar* that make it one of the greatest of Handel's dramatic works, one of the most convincing demonstrations of poetic-dramatic genius. So ardent was the creative fervor that Handel, impatient with Jennens's slow delivery of the libretto, precomposed many important numbers, which subsequently had to be changed to suit the occasion and the available personnel. There is an embarrassment of riches to choose from, because the several versions are often equally fine and attractive. Neither the Chrysander nor the Macfarren edition of *Belshazzar* is satisfactory in this regard, though Chrysander at times does print one alternate version. The new Halle edition should print all of them, with considered recommendations as to the final choice. Provided with this material an intelligent conductor would know how to proceed.

The first performance of *Belshazzar,* on March 27, 1745, featured Handel's reliable cast: Beard (Belshazzar), La Francesina (Nitocris), Miss Robinson (Cyrus), and Reinhold (Gobrias). Susanna Cibber was to take the part of Daniel, but there seems to be considerable doubt that she actually sang in the initial performance; her absence would account for some of the hasty revisions and transpositions that Handel made before the première. There were two repeat performances, but the oratorio was unsuccessful. The subscription season dragged on, and Handel once more risked *Messiah,* though still not naming it by its title. But the concerts refused to catch fire and after the sixteenth of the projected twenty-four performances the enterprise was called off altogether. Thus ended the season on April 23. It also ended Handel's connections with the Haymarket Theatre, the scene of so many of his triumphs and tribulations.

Handel's friends, especially such devoted ladies as the Countess of Salisbury, paint in their correspondence a sad picture of his plight, but the popular story of his renewed "bankruptcy" is once more false. Handel's financial situation was precarious—there is the melancholy note of his offering the two organs at the Haymarket Theatre at a bargain price —but he met his obligations. The records show that all his singers were paid. Speaking of the singers, we must also bear in mind that perhaps Handel's troupe also had something to do with the unsuccessful season. His faithful cast was not exactly youthful, while the younger members, Beard and Mrs. Cibber were young, but then they had undistinguished voices. Far worse was the matter of Handel's health. Evidently he suffered another physical collapse; not only did the "palsy" return but also the mental fatigue that had plagued him when he was forced to seek the cure at Aachen. The Earl of Shaftesbury found that at the end of October (1745) Handel looked "somewhat better," but, significantly, in expressing hope for full recovery, the Earl remarks that "he has been a good deal disordered in his head."

XVII

WE DO NOT KNOW WHAT EVENTS FOLLOWED THE
closing of the unfinished series of subscription concerts, except that Handel was ill, physically and mentally, and that he must have gone somewhere to recuperate. At sixty he was no longer able to carry the enormous burden of the double life of composer and impresario with the robust defiance of earlier years, and it seems that the collapse and near tragedy in 1738 had permanently diminished his fantastic stamina. Yet it was only the year before the present defeat that Handel had reached the highest peak in his artistic career when in a dozen weeks or so he composed *Hercules* and *Belshazzar*, an accomplishment still unexampled in the history of music. So it could not have been sterility that now silenced him, but natural exhaustion; everything had gone into the making of these colossal masterpieces. Whatever the nature of his ailment, a brief rest still sufficed to restore him to action, and his combative spirit drove him back to London. Sometime late in August 1745 he returned, perhaps from Tunbridge Wells or Cheltenham; and while he was still showing signs of strain, the few who met him reported that the composer was on the way to recovery, and the "disorder in his head" had subsided. He must have had some plans, because he leased the Covent Garden Theatre for the coming Lenten season.

But the Handel who returned to the Brook Street house was nevertheless a changed man; his heartiness and optimism were gone, he shunned the outside world, and his creative instinct was almost completely dormant. The only ascertainable composition from this barren year is an Italian chamber duet, *Ahi nelle sorti umane,* his last in the genre. Curious, how during times of internal conflict and indecision he always turns to the fountainhead—Italian melody. When we read the reports of sympathetic friends about Handel's appearance and demeanor during the last subscription performances—the women among them especially were good observers—we realize that something beyond fatigue was reflected by the melancholy, wan appearance of this man of usually commanding presence. Handel was fully aware of what he had accomplished in *Hercules* and *Belshazzar;* we have many testimonials that the critic in him was quite distinct from the impresario. The almost complete lack of understanding for these masterworks must have hurt him deeply, and he must have been puzzled about his future course. Would oratorio end in fiasco as had opera? The months went by and nothing was heard from Brook Street, and it seemed that the aging composer would have to subsist on the annuities received from the court. Not altogether surprisingly, it was a political event that roused him from his creative slumber, and once more he struck into the current at exactly the right moment.

Prince Charles Edward, the Young Pretender, landed in Scotland to claim the throne of England for the Stuarts. Sir John Cope, the English commanding general in Scotland, had been defeated; Edinburgh opened its gates to the Stuart prince, and soon his army rolled south from the border. His triumphant advance to Derby frightened Hanoverian London to the very recesses of its soul. There was a run on the Bank of England, and in the absence of a substantial regular army, all sorts of volunteer corps were formed; even the lawyers of the Middle Temple exchanged wigs for helmets. The threat to London caused a temporary disappearance of many a timid heart from the capital, and to the King Hanover seemed a very inviting place.

Stirring slowly, Handel at first contributed a few patriotic songs, but caught up in the martial fervor, he soon decided upon a more massive demonstration. The old flair for responding to the atmospheric pressure asserted itself and now came an entr'acte in his creative life, which Dean aptly calls the period of the "victory oratorios." They were also personal victories, hard won because a good deal of this did not suit his dramatic genius. The first two of the new works, the *Occasional Oratorio* and *Judas Maccabaeus,* have since called forth extremes in judgment that vividly illustrate the still shaky and often simply emotional attitude taken by devout Handelians. The *Occasional Oratorio* was, to be sure, as Young calls it, "plain propaganda" for Protestantism and the reigning dynasty. But to both of these Handel was genuinely devoted. Moreover, if seen in the light of its own day, the *Occasional Oratorio* was magnificent propaganda. For us this work has lost not only its effectiveness but its very *raison d'être*, but to the besieged English in London it was a dignified and splendid appeal to national unity *in tempore belli*. Granted, it was thrown together in a couple of weeks, for Handel had to hurry; the rebels had been repulsed, but the decisive battle was yet to come. A pasticcio it was, and most of the borrowings are familiar, but it contained some pretty solid fare, and the wild glory, the vast cascade of sound of the fine choruses (from *Israel in Egypt* and other works and equipped with new texts) gave Londoners the uplifting sense of crowded and important events. Those who peremptorily dismiss it as a "hodgepodge" violate the historian's Xenophonic oath. The German scholar Arnold Schering saw in the *Occasional Oratorio* a demonstration that "Handel participated in the fate of his adopted country with all his heart."

While the *Occasional Oratorio* retired into the dust that lies heavy upon forgotten splendor and stands today with the forlornness of a burnt-out firework, *Judas Maccabaeus*, filled with the same dead-alive grandiosity, was and is acclaimed as a supreme masterpiece. The most famous of the oratorios next to *Messiah*, and the work that finally turned Handel into a national institution, henceforth unassailable, is a child of many of the previous oratorios, and the parent of not a few composed in many lands after Handel's death. Yet *Judas Maccabaeus* was also an occasional oratorio. It has many borrowings, its construction is tenuous, and it contains a fair amount of insignificant or unillumined music. But it also has many eloquent numbers showing Handel at full stature. To call it, with Young, "a decline into claptrap," or with Herbage to consider it a shamelessly cynical exploitation of the low artistic instincts of the "groundlings," is to be far off the mark. Equally mistaken are those who read into this simple and somewhat haphazard collection of airs and choruses profound moral and religious parables, and consider it a monument of German fortitude. Indeed, there are even voices—recent ones—declaring *Judas Maccabaeus* to be fully the equal of *Messiah*.

Once more we should take a glance at history. The public that lived through the Spanish and Austrian wars and the Stuart rebellion was eager to hear Britain praised. They were not so naive as the Elizabethans, who wanted to see duels and murders and love-making; they were the successors of the Puritans and wanted to see the empire as divinely ordained.

The powers attributed to music as a patriotic evocation and tonic antedate recorded history, and they are still called upon. The *pièce d'occasion*
is a dangerous form, however, and the sea of musical history is strewn
with craft that came to grief because they were overladen with homage.
In one of his books Malraux says: "It is not emotion that destroys a work
of art, but the desire to demonstrate something." No such disaster, however, threatened Handel in *Judas Maccabaeus*, which bore its cargo triumphantly to port. The harsher critics see only that there is neither dramatic continuity nor design and that much of this music lacks inwardness;
they ignore the vigor of the rest. In such a work neither great complexity
of design nor great subtlety of tone is to be expected; *Judas Maccabaeus*
is stirring rather than moving, but the choruses often display a rugged
and elemental beauty. And they also display the brilliance of a genius
who even when he nodded would never wholly abandon his prerogatives.
We may safely declare that nothing Handel wrote illustrates so well his
tremendous effectiveness as a composer for occasions as does *Judas Maccabaeus*.

The *Occasional Oratorio* was composed sometime in January 1746,
that is, before the decisive victory. A morale booster, its ceremonial,
anthem-like rhetoric was bolstered by a text patched together from Milton's psalm translations. There is a certain plan in this oratorio, though
there is no structure. The first part depicts the "misery of the world" and
the "threatening vengeance," warning the nation that "scattered like
sheep, ye perish on your own way." But Jehovah will sustain the English.
The second part extols liberty and expresses renewed trust in God, whose
"mercies shall endure." The bass solo, "To God our strength," and the following chorus, a great anthem, exude confidence and a sense of power.
Leichtentritt and others here detect echoes of *Ein' feste Burg*, which is
possible, but to call this small excerpt from the tail end of the first sentence of the chorale a "cantus firmus" and the piece itself the "old German
form of *Choralbearbeitung*" is patently a fantasy. The concluding Hallelujah Chorus is solid and impressive. In the third act the "warlike ensigns
wave on high," "trumpets pierce the vaulted hall," and the Duke of Cumberland is promised that "millions unborn shall bless the hand that drew
the sword in virtue's cause."

The oratorio ends, quite appropriately, with a festive chorus—but it
is none other than the Coronation Anthem *Zadok the Priest*.

For the purpose for which this pasticcio was put together it was no
doubt admirable, but today, with its many borrowings firmly associated
with their original habitat (it is somewhat disconcerting to hear the

famous hailstones rain down anew, this time presumably on the Scots),
the *Occasional Oratorio* is little more than a historical document. Interestingly enough, it is the first act that contains most of the original music,
and good music at that; apparently Handel's creative power returned
overnight once he summoned it. The national-dynastic homage is most
prominent in the second act, ending in the Hallelujah Chorus mentioned
above, a grand and elaborately contrapuntal piece. Acts Two and Three
are made up of numbers taken from *Athalia, Israel,* and others—half of
the third act is from the latter oratorio; what new music is in these acts is
negligible.

The unfilled subscription concerts of 1745 still worried Handel, as
can be seen from the *General Advertiser* of January 31, 1746. "We hear,
that Mr. *Handel* proposes to exhibit some Musical Entertainments on
Wednesdays or Fridays the ensuing Lent, with Intent to make good to
the Subscribers (that favoured him last Season) the Number of Performances he was not then able to complete . . . " The notice also was the
first news in many months about Handel, and the first intimation that his
creative activity had been rekindled. The *Occasional Oratorio* was announced for February 14 in Covent Garden. The previous year's subscribers received free tickets, and the oratorio, well received, had two repeat
performances in the same month. These three performances constituted
the entire Lenten season of oratorio for 1746—a modest resumption of the
activities of both the creative artist and the entrepreneur, but a definite
resumption it was.

The Battle of Culloden was fought on April 16, 1746, and early in
July Handel began composing *Judas Maccabaeus;* the score was finished
in a month. With it a new librettist appeared in Handel's life, a man
whom we would just as soon forget for his initial contributions to the
composer's *oeuvre* but not for his later books, upon which Handel composed the sublime works of his declining years. One would have expected
that Handel, who showed appreciation of Jennens's not negligible skills
and who, despite the failure of *Messiah* and *Belshazzar,* knew in his own
mind that Jennens had provided him with excellent librettos, would have
stayed with such a tried collaborator. It is not clear what affected their
relationship, but though they seem to have remained on polite terms,[1]

---

[1] In 1749, when Jennens rebuilt his Gopsall residence in a princely manner, he
asked Handel to design the organ to be erected there. Handel's letter is polite but
contains nothing beyond strictly business matters relating to the instrument. Yet he
remembered Jennens years later, bequeathing him two fine pictures by Balthasar
Denner.

there was an undeniable cooling in their friendship.

Then again we know that *Judas Maccabaeus* was in a sense a commission, and its librettist, the Reverend Thomas Morell, D.D. (1703-1784), was not Handel's choice. In his memoirs [2] Morell states that it was the Prince of Wales who recommended him to Handel. This was said years after Handel's death, and though there are some incongruities in Morell's recollections, there is no reason to doubt his veracity—why would Handel have approached this ecclesiastical poetaster of his own volition? Flower found an excellent phrase when he called Morell "a bad copy of Jennens." In fact, judging from his initial efforts as a librettist, he was another Reverend Dr. Miller. A good-natured man, he got along with Handel; that they were on friendly terms is evidenced by the bequest of £200 in Handel's will. Contemporaries describe Morell as a sociable fellow with many artistic friends, a good raconteur, fairly learned, and a lover of music. But Morell was sententious to an alarming degree, and his initial influence on Handel was artistically unwholesome, for with his texts the great dramatic oratorios temporarily ceased. The Doctor succumbed too easily to the undoubted charms of illogicality, and his verse lacked the poet's perception of beauty, yet, as we shall see, there could be a dramatic idea behind his feeble structures. The worthy divine also had delusions of grandeur and, like Jennens before him, berated Handel for not doing justice to his deathless words. But while Handel was remarkably patient with Jennens, he was little disposed to take criticism from this pedestrian dramatist and said so plainly. There is a well-known anecdote that one day Handel burst in upon Morell with the cry "Damn your iambics!" On the other hand, unlike the pompous Jennens, Morell was an easygoing man who did not hold a grudge, as can be seen from his pleasant recital of this very anecdote, to which he admiringly adds that upon his changing the meter Handel composed the piece on the spot.

In his memoirs, Morell also says that "the plan of *Judas Maccabaeus* was designed as a compliment to the Duke of Cumberland upon returning victorious from Scotland." Thus the immediate fate of Handel was determined jointly by the Prince of Wales, an amateur librettist-clergyman, and the semi-grotesque figure of "Billy the Butcher," the Duke of Cumberland, Frederick's brother.

Judas Maccabaeus, which ranges from the static to the turbulent, is a work not easy to come to terms with. It has no real plot, characterization is rudimentary, there being only two protagonists distinguished by a name, and the chorus, though it is the principal carrier of expression, has

[2] In *Hodgkin Manuscripts,* published by the Historical Manuscripts Commission.

no antagonist as in the earlier oratorios. The subject was taken from the First Book of Maccabees, but Morell, the classical scholar, also used historical sources. The action is very simple. The work opens with the Israelites mourning their departed leader, Mattathias, father of Simon and Judas. The Israelites under the divinely designated leadership of Judas battle victoriously, but soon have to muster the army against another foe, Antiochus. Judas again triumphs, and the third act extols his valor. This is hardly a plot, and the libretto offers no construction, only a sequence of pieces.

The absence of dramatic construction is betrayed by the scarcity of accompanied recitatives. With its many allegros, this is a comparatively "fast" oratorio; Handel wanted to get at the hortatory choruses and did not waste much time polishing the arias. Perhaps the most surprising lapse of critical vigilance on Handel's part is the perfunctory nature of most of the recitatives and many of the arias. On the other hand, this oratorio has an unusually large number of duets, some of which are excellent. That the score is musically more substantial today than it was originally is due to the additions Handel made a year or two before his death. Several of these fine pieces were not written for *Judas Maccabaeus* but for other oratorios revived in the late 1750s, but they found a permanent resting place in the more popular *Judas*. This work also contains numbers shifted from other oratorios that, having acquired squatter's rights, refuse to be returned to their original surroundings. "Oh liberty" is better off here than in the *Occasional Oratorio*, which can scarcely hope for an afterlife, but "See the conquering hero comes" is from *Joshua*, a good if not great oratorio that sooner or later will claim its property. Indeed, when the oratorios are restored to their proper shape and rightful position, a good deal of stock-taking, bookkeeping, and reorganization will be necessary.

Judas Maccabaeus begins on a note of high originality that, unfortunately, is not maintained for long. The fine overture with an unusual, and undoubtedly programmatic, fugue is followed by a magnificent choral scene of mourning. "Mourn, ye afflicted Children" is a great choral ode built upon a funeral march in the orchestra. Equally magnificent is the duet with chorus, "For Sion lament"; not only the people weep but the bassoons, which are used in an astonishingly modern operatic manner. The form is attractively original: a siciliana with what we might call a choral arioso over a rhythmic ostinato. Though the melodic material is borrowed from Bononcini, Handel made the piece altogether his own. But now he relaxes his grip: "Father whose almighty power" is a routine fugue, "I feel the deity within" an unoriginal *ombra* piece, and Simon's

"Arm ye brave" an ordinary aria. By turning from personal to patriotic passion Handel reaped popularity, but at a price. He has no difficulty with the choruses but cannot find warmth for the solos—even Judas, the hero, does not materialize as a character. One notices this especially in the recitatives, which limp. As we have said, "O liberty" was taken from the *Occasional Oratorio;* now Handel adds two more "liberty" pieces. All of these are in a peaceful, pastoral, lightly lilting and gliding dance form as if to epitomize the felicities of freedom. These movements, especially "Come ever smiling Liberty," became very popular and were often sung as concert numbers. The final chorus in the first act, "Hear us O Lord," is a motet-anthem, an impressive contrapuntal piece—Handel is again in his element.

The inspiration still holds at the beginning of the second act: "Fall'n is the Foe" is top-drawer Handel. The chorus is robust, with sharply accented pictorial intervals stubbornly announcing an accomplished fact with a degree of amazement that is expressed by a masterful dramatic stroke as Handel interrupts the vigorous choral texture, the chorus stammering, piano, "fall'n, fall'n." It is a gripping moment. The duet "Sion now her head shall raise," admirably connected to the following chorus, offers a brace of exceptionally beautiful pieces. This was a much later addition to the score; some even claim that "Sion" was Handel's last composition. The scale-like runs on "raise" are used with infinite ingenuity, and the part-writing is masterful. This is one of the rather unusual cases typical of this oratorio whereby duets are connected with choruses, a procedure Handel usually employs with solo arias. The rest of the second act contains a good deal of minor Handel, but there are some exceptions. "How vain [i.e. "useless" or "inefficient"] is man" is a somewhat incongruously jolly air, but pretty. Dean was the first to point out that Handel —as well as all his German commentators—must have misinterpreted the meaning of "vain." This is surprising in view of the occurrence of the same word and idea in one of Simon's recitatives, "Not vain is all this storm and grief." Another example of incongruity is Simon's aria "The Lord worketh wonders," which is written on the pattern of a bass rage aria but is very friendly, full of harmless roulades.

Kretzschmar called attention to the fact that the pattern of mourning-despair followed by rallying-victory is repeated in this oratorio. The messenger having announced "new scenes of bloody war," the Jews must now start their lament anew, but they do it just as beautifully as in the first act. "Ah wretched Israel" starts with the mourning plaint of the soprano (Israelitish Woman) in a continuo aria, the strings join her, then the chorus; the freely flowing treble melody is in admirable contrast to the ground bass. Presently the mood changes, though hardly because of Simon's pale song, "The Lord worketh wonders." "Sound an alarm" is the only music where Judas makes his individuality felt. This too is a continuo aria, but when the chorus falls in and the trumpets limber up, Handel lifts us out of our seats. When we look at the score we can hardly understand why this piece should be so effective; the words alone—"We hear the pleasing dreadful call"—would induce a smile, and the choral parts are little more than simple chords without a genuine treble line. It is by the way everything is timed, with a most impressive general pause inserted, that Handel achieves his objective and annuls our objections. The air, "Wise men, flatt'ring may deceive you," is an old acquaintance from the Italian days. Though originally it appeared in *Agrippina,* it is best known as the ineffable air "Ah when the dove laments her love" in *Acis and Galatea.* This too is a late addition; Handel reworked it in 1757 or '58 for *The Triumph of Time.* The ingenuity of the composer, at the end of his long creative life and blind, gave it again an altogether new and fresh charm. In this final reincarnation the graceful song received a delectable accompaniment with recorders, oboes, bassoons, and horns. "Oh never bow down" is a good duet with a nice pastoral interlude. It leads into a chorus using the same material, the group ending in a somewhat old-fashioned choral fugue, "We worship God." Even though the curious fugue is worked with diligence, this piece has little distinction.

The opening aria in the third act, "Father in heaven," is Handel at his peak. Its warm, beautiful melody completely envelops the listener. Then Handel nods a little until "See the conquering hero comes," one of his most celebrated pieces. Although it does not belong in *Judas Maccabaeus,* having been shifted, as we have noted, from *Joshua,* a couple of hundred years of association with *Judas Maccabaeus* have given the loan a permanence that obliges us to deal with it here. And a remarkable piece it is, one of those incredibly simple things whose effect is elemental. But the presentation is anything but simple. First the chorus of youths sing, then the chorus of virgins, all high voices, each group accompanied by characteristic orchestration. Then the full chorus and orchestra join in an ever-swelling volume of sound. The following march, just as simple and just as attractive, is thematically related. Of the rest, "Sing unto God" is a good anthem, Judas's recitative "Sweet flow the strains" is considerably above the average, and his trumpet aria "with honour let the desert be crowned" is also one of the better pieces. "Oh lovely peace" is again a fine duet, but the final number, "Rejoice oh Judah," is little more than a standard

Hallelujah Chorus.

The oratorio season of 1747 opened in Covent Garden on March 6 with the *Occasional Oratorio,* which was twice repeated during the month. This was followed by a revival of *Joseph and his Brethren,* then on April 1 *Judas Maccabaeus* was first presented, the main cast consisting of Signora Gambarini, Signora Galli, Beard, and Reinhold. It was instantly successful and has remained extremely popular to this day, and not only in England. It was one of the major Handelian oratorios to attract attention in Germany, where Johann Adam Hiller, founder of the Gewandhaus Concerts (1781) in Leipzig and subsequently cantor at St. Thomas's, became the first of its many "arrangers." It became a favorite work for patriotic-military celebrations after the Napoleonic wars, but the jubilant, ceremonial nature of its choruses caught the fancy even of the Latins, not really attuned to this kind of British-Protestant pitch. French and Italian editions of the score were published in the 19th century. The success of *Judas Maccabaeus* in England was unquestionably due partly to the historical circumstances, but its popularity elsewhere shows that the generally simple and undemanding nature of the work and the fine quality of many of its numbers surely had much to do with its remarkable career. Realizing both the temper of the times and the futility of addressing only one social class, Handel abandoned the subscription system, now addressing himself to the large and artistically less experienced middle classes, who responded enthusiastically to the brave patriotic trumpeting. But the King and the aristocracy were equally carried away. Never again did Handel return to subscription series; his final triumph was owing to the support of the wider public, and he recognized a good thing when he saw it. *Judas Maccabaeus* became a reliable money-maker, achieving more than fifty performances during Handel's lifetime.

The triumph of *Judas Maccabaeus* has also been attributed to another cause. "A Jew on the stage as a hero rather than a reviled figure was a thing practically unknown in London, and Handel at once found himself possessed of a new public." This opinion of Flower well summarizes the widespread belief that this oratorio's success was chiefly due to the patronage of the Jews of London who came to acclaim their national hero. One wonders whether Samson, David, Daniel, and all the other celebrated figures in the previous oratorios were biblical Yorkshiremen. Why would the Jews suddenly become interested in oratorio and just as suddenly lose this interest with the following two oratorios, both of which were composed on the pattern established by *Judas Maccabaeus,* and both of which had Jewish heroes, one a Maccabee? A "new public" he undoubtedly had, because anyone who could afford the fee was admitted, and that new public must have included some of London's Jews, but there could hardly have been the concourse of the Jewish population that nearly all biographies claim. Those of the Jews who went were animated by the same feelings that prompted their fellow Englishmen to attend: patriotism. Sir Newman himself quotes Dr. Morell as saying that the "plan of the oratorio was to honor the victorious Duke of Cumberland," and he certainly knew that Morell dedicated the libretto to the Duke. More than that, this printed preface plainly states that Judas is a portrait of the Duke, "a Truly Wise, Valiant, and Virtuous Commander."

In view of all this it is equally futile to insist that *Judas Maccabaeus* is a "sacred oratorio." In this connection the selection of this particular scriptural text is of significance because Maccabees is not concerned with religion but with the national cause. We must remember that with few exceptions the Apocrypha were declared canonical by the Council of Trent, but Protestants never accepted them as such. Both Luther and Coverdale separated them from the other books of the Old Testament, and in general, while highly respected, they were considered merely human writings. The First Book of Maccabees is pure history; the Second, which goes over the same ground, though less soberly, is full of denunciations of the nation's enemies and tends to homiletic reflections.

Opinions and judgments concerning *Judas Maccabaeus* show an astonishing variety, as we have already remarked. Much of it should be dismissed out of hand were it not that otherwise eminent scholars have engaged in ridiculous speculations. The judges who considered *Judas Maccabaeus* next to *Messiah* the greatest of the oratorios evoke only a sympathetic smile. Let us cite an example from an older generation. Once the victory of both the Duke of Cumberland and Handel became history, the unevenness of this music began to be noticed. An anonymous critic in the *Morning Herald* (February 19, 1852) wrote, to the consternation of loyal Handelians, including the outraged Schoelcher, that "the airs of *Judas Maccabaeus* are occasionally feeble and insipid, but two or three of them are exactly the reverse." This, of course, is an exaggeration, but it has foundation; in the case of some of our German colleagues, however, we are facing veritable "pious orgies." There is no need to go into detail; suffice it to say that even so distinguished a scholar as Hermann Abert saw in the figure of Judas a "German knight." The prize goes to the incredible Serauky who swallows every hint he has ever read. He not only fully endorses Judas as a typical German warrior, but insists that the English could not possibly understand the true nature of this paragon of German virtues.

During the course of the large number of revivals—*Judas Maccabaeus* was repeated every season but one during Handel's remaining years—the score was heavily retouched, and, as has been noted, Handel crammed it with popular numbers from other oratorios. The many versions make this work a nightmare for editors, as is reflected in the large number of editions, both English and foreign, few of which agree in content and sequence.

[2]

WHATEVER CHANCE brought Handel to Morell, the great success of *Judas Maccabaeus* induced him to continue not only the partnership but also the successful recipe. *Alexander Balus,* composed during June 1747, was a deliberate sequel to *Judas,* the material once more roughly taken from Maccabees. Unfortunately, sequels are often unsuccessful, and one that is an improvement on its predecessor is quite rare. The story is confused enough in Maccabees, and Morell was unable to create a musico-dramatic situation until the better part of the oratorio was spent. Alexander, victorious King of Syria, compels Ptolemy, ruler of Egypt, to accept his suzerainty. The Egyptian schemes to cast off this dependence, and in his villainy does not spare his own daughter, Cleopatra, whom he has married to Alexander and has now abducted. Alexander takes the field against Ptolemy but is killed. Jonathan the Maccabee continues the punitive expedition and wins; Ptolemy is killed, and the Jews are liberated. The theologian-librettist now added to the heroic goings-on a love story, welcome of course to Handel, but having such a miserable plot and such atrocious poetry that the composer's task was made virtually hopeless. The liberal splicing into Morell's verse of bits of Shakespeare and Milton only gives the impression of a pedestrian d'Annunzio juggling a torrent of swollen words. Morell also demonstrates that he did some conscientious homework on the *oeuvres complètes* of his composer: snippets taken from a number of Handel's earlier texts are also mixed into the stew, though they were altered in the librettist's own fashion.

The setting of this literary gem caused heavy weather for the composer; he toiled with difficulty, borrowing left and right. *Alexander Balus* has few choruses, is destitute of fine counterpoint, and reverts to the long-abandoned formal opera scheme, with the da capo aria returned to its prominence. The work as a whole suffers through being strung on a very slender thread of continuity, and in the first two acts is it apt to run into shallows of expression. The hero of the drama, Alexander Balus, never emerges. Morell's fatuous moralizing left Handel cold; but the German Handelians took it to heart, constructing upon it a strained mysticism purporting to represent a struggle between spiritual and destructive powers, "the divine order of the world" being the victor. Far from being steeped in nebulous spiritual struggle, *Alexander Balus* is pure opera, insignificant and wayward in the first two acts, magnificent in the third. In the first two acts the main props of the Handelian music drama, accompanied recitative and actively participating chorus, are either missing or greatly reduced, while the routine of the da capo aria returns. But in the third act Handel takes a firm hold and is once more in top form. The figure responsible for the return of full creative force and imagination was Cleopatra, so in the end, the Maccabean heroism and the heavy moralizing notwithstanding, *Alexander Balus* is the tragedy of a woman.

"Age cannot wither her, nor custom stale her infinite variety," says Shakespeare's Enobarbus of Cleopatra. Handel remembered the seductress from his *Giulio Cesare* (see above, p. 181), and the lush, sensuous oriental tone returns as the exquisite orchestra of strings, oboes, bassoons, trumpets, and drums is augmented by mandolin, harp, and flutes. The same charm of mysticism mingled with sensuality also returns, but Handel adds to her "infinite variety" the affectionate intimacy of a woman in love. In her rich radiance the male heroes turn pale. Once Handel rediscovered her, the divine *Weltcrdnung*—if there ever was such a thing in his mind—is thrown to the winds as both she and Handel come to life.

We get a glimpse of her attraction in the first act. Her song "Hark, hark! he strikes the golden lyre" is a charming piece drenched in color. There is little else in this act that deserves attention, though it must be admitted that even the dull numbers show a most remarkable elegance of workmanship that recalls the texture of the last operas. In the second act there is not much more of interesting music, but "O calumny" is in a class with the other two great "jealousy" choruses from *Saul* and *Hercules*. Its tremendous ostinato theme rumbles inexorably, the whole creating an atmosphere charged with fear and a sense of overwhelming desolation.

In the third act everything changes as Handel's sensitivity, stretched on the rack of experience yet determined to be true to the reality of its intense moments, makes itself felt. It opens with Cleopatra's "Here amid the steady woods," a song that has all the bucolic Handel's delicate, exact, and fragile beauty of expression. The noisy festival atmosphere disappears; these are ideas that may be played with, there is no need of urgency, and the composer's skill and grace find their proper scope. But the gentle and poetic musing is suddenly shattered as Cleopatra is set upon and seized by Ptolemy's henchmen; a very dramatic scene of real theatre. Alexander's air "Fury with red-sparkling eyes" is a fine rage aria, presto, with a sharply contrasting larghetto middle section that makes the da capo quite proper. Then Aspasia, Cleopatra's companion, meditates on the "strange reverse of human fate," but Jonathan must give the situation an "ideological" turn—Alexander's heathen gods are not powerful enough to deal with this problem. In "To God, who made the radiant sun" he beseeches Jehovah; the grand piece, even if perhaps a little stiff melodically and its hymnic quality a little *voulu,* did not miss its intended effect.

The following chorus, "Sun, moon, stars," is also a very fine piece, but it is Cleopatra who really dominates everything. She constantly increases in stature, and by the time she confronts her father, the clash is between two marked personalities. Ptolemy rages in "O sword"; he is no Polyphemus but an authentic villain whom Handel fully realized in music. His daughter's reply, "Shall Cleopatra ever smile again?" has simplicity, masterful serenity, and a thrilling stillness. Fate presently strikes with brutal terror: a messenger brings word of Alexander's death. "O take me from this hateful light," sings Cleopatra; we feel all the tenderness and wistfulness that underlie the pain and sorrow of a woman trembling like the windblown river reed. Handel is now really fired, developing Cleopatra's character "from bride to widow" (Schering) with sympathy and penetration. Scarcely realizing the full meaning of her bereavement, now she learns that Ptolemy, her cruel tormentor but nevertheless her father, is also dead. Her lament, "Convey me to some peaceful shore," is a song of broken-hearted ecstasy; rapture and sorrow alike seem to have lost their meaning in the unutterable grief. Jonathan praises God and the chorus sings a fine Hallelujah and an Amen fugue, but both of these are subdued, for the end is still altogether under the spell of Cleopatra's tragedy.

So the tragic moment passes without being followed by the forcible means so often employed in some of the other oratorios to end in exultation. Indeed, Cleopatra's charm radiates all around her and is reflected by the initially somewhat insubstantial Aspasia, her confidante. In the second part of Aspasia's fine aria "So grace the sweet attractive smile," the light, fluent manner of Bononcini, but even more the neo-Neapolitans' narrow-gauge but very attractive melody, with capricious inner repetitions, take us back to the delightful texture of *Faramondo* and *Serse.* Ptolemy aside, the men are much less interesting. Handel was undecided about Alexander; the lover is quite pleasant, but the military hero is not alive. The martial trumpeting in his aria "Mighty love now calls to arm" does not quite take care of this lack of characterization. Jonathan is too saintly for human nature's daily food; it is difficult to feel any friendliness towards him.

The orchestration is throughout interesting, modern, and piquant; especially in Cleopatra's music, where delectable combinations of the plucked instruments with pizzicato strings and woodwinds once more remind us that Handel treated the heathen with fondness. Whenever he deals with "Asiates" (as the heathen of the Middle East were called), counterpoint is banished and color takes over, the tunes become lively, even catchy, and the orchestra scintillates.

And yet this "sacred oratorio" was stillborn. Some librettos fail to affect because they turn too much light on at once, others because they turn on too little. *Alexander Balus* is one of the latter; the first two acts cannot be salvaged. A performance of the third act, preceded by excerpts from the first two, as part of a concert would be very worthwhile, or perhaps a good one-acter could be made of it for the stage. Anything that would preserve the remarkable third act would be welcome, but revival of the entire score would be a very doubtful enterprise, though it has been done. Composed in June 1747, *Alexander Balus* was performed on March 13, 1748, that is, after *Joshua*, with Casarini (Cleopatra), Sibilla (Aspasia), Galli (Alexander), Lowe (Jonathan), and Reinhold (Ptolemy). There were two repeats, but the work's reception was cool and remained so whenever Handel attempted a revival.

[3]

Joshua, composed July-August 1747, is a continuation of the *Judas Maccabaeus* scheme, the last of Morell's victory oratorios. This libretto, too, is very bad. It has the same poor construction and lack of dramatic content, with a makeshift love story added to the clamorous acclaim for the Israelite-English arms. Handel obviously disliked it, and this time he made it short, did not exert himself unduly, and borrowed a great deal. There is a tenuousness in this work, as if the deeper mysteries of the spirit at war with itself demanded a firmer imaginative grasp. The story is taken from the Book of Joshua; historically unreliable, it is nothing but a recital of wars of extermination offering little scope for a dramatic plot. The combination of this with Morell's lack of dramatic sense resulted in another anemic text aggravated by a gauche love story. *Joshua* does at times, however, rise to great imaginative intensity, though not without frequent lapses, for the work reveals a deficiency in that easy ample power which yields lasting creations. We do not find in it the great individual hero who as a central organ nourishes the drama; the characters are squeezed to fit the situations. There are certain aspects of character that a dramatist, even a Shakespeare or a Handel, is greatly hampered in depicting. Joshua is an oracle rather than a leader, and oracularly ambiguous. At times when he is supposed to represent the divine beatitude of wisdom he appears more like an egregious prig. The emotions he expresses have no proper foundation, and the strategic humility he occasionally shows makes him a forerunner of the modern Socialist lords. And his image lacks precision. Handel made no attempt to impose symmetry on the naturally formless personality depicted by the libretto. Caleb, being a patriarch, had the good fortune to be made into a dignified basso, while Achsah and Othniel are youthful lovers rather innocent of any deeper passion.

Handel went to work on the libretto with the same lack of real enthusiasm he displayed in the first act of *Alexander Balus*. The recitatives are uninspired routine, like those in *Judas Maccabaeus*, but this *laissez aller* is extended, as it is not in that work, to many of the choruses, and Handel depends a good deal on borrowings. But where there is a semblance of drama he musters all his power, and an undimmed power it was.

The libretto presents the story of the conquest of Canaan under Joshua with Caleb as chief of staff. Caleb's daughter, Achsah, is betrothed to a young warrior named Othniel, but he has yet to prove that he is worthy of the prize. In this oratorio the ratio of solo to chorus is restored to almost normal proportions, and *Joshua* opens with a fine polyphonic piece ("Ye sons of Israel") with elaborately refined motivic work. The solo numbers that follow are unimpressive, but the chorus "To long posterity we here record" once more rises above the average. The ensuing episode with the angelic messenger, "Awful, pleasing being, say," is a little awkward, while "The Lord commands," in which Joshua is designated to lead the Jews in battle, has a share of Anglican anthem solidity; therefore the love episode between Achsah and Othniel comes as a welcome relief in this act, which contains plenty of warlike noise but few inspired pages. As usual the love music is pastoral and charming with its "birds" and "limpid streams." Even in the victory oratorios, whenever Handel turns to such intimate scenes, a delicate chamber-music style relieves the somewhat perfunctory bellicose setting.

The second act picks up noticeably, and we hear some sounds of a supreme and characteristic beauty. Now Joshua commands the storming of Jericho. Muffat's *Componimenti* furnished the material for the march, but after that Handel takes charge, unmistakably and with a vengeance. "Glory to God" is one of his most powerful choruses—no wonder the walls of Jericho tumble. The middle section, "The nations tremble," gave him opportunity for some grand descriptive music that deeply impressed Haydn when he heard *Joshua* in London in 1791. The following arias of Caleb and Achsah are not particularly moving, but the Passover feast is celebrated by a fine ostinato chorus, "Almighty ruler of the skies," in Handel's best form. As in *Judas Maccabaeus,* at this point there is a military reverse, the Jewish arms are defeated at Ai; we have to start all over again. But Handel rises to the occasion, the mourning chorus is a striking triumph over the agreeable pieties that reign in this oratorio; a fine piece in which acute emotional sensibility is matched by a poetical freshness of sympathy. The Jews take heart: "We with redoubled rage return." It is a pity that the *choragus* who introduces these fine choruses should be such a self-important person as Joshua, who dwells on heavenly rhetoric and contents himself with a mere summary of the stirring actions he has set in motion.

Now the clanging of weapons and the hortatory tone are given a rest as Handel jettisons the heavy historical ballast he is compelled to drag along, to indulge in the gentle lyricism of young lovers. But Caleb soon warns that this is not the time for amorous dallying, and Othniel obediently turns to a higher moral sphere. His song encompasses all known and accepted virtues, but Handel's music attenuates the homily. Though "Heroes, when with glory burning" is based on a conventional melody, it is a fine piece. The military music returns (this time it is taken from *Riccardo I*), but the finale is a matchless masterpiece. This is the famous scene where Joshua bids the sun and moon to stand still so that the battle will not have to be fought in darkness. The effect is marvelous, almost graphically representative, like the slow opening of a fan disclosing the landscape pattern upon it; the expression is concentrated, the picture almost impressionistic. Handel employs the whole store of his pictorial technique, but this is not "eye music"; the technique is used with incomparable felicity and the impression is completely aural. As so often with this composer, a single word suggestive of imagery unlocks his imagination. The exact balance between musical effect and exquisite scenic harmony, between conception and execution, is struck with perfect accuracy of touch and security of hand.

The third act opens with an anthem, "Hail mighty Joshua," which though well set is not impressive, as in general in this act Handel again relapses into routine. But Caleb's great song "Shall I in Mamre's fertile plain" and its connected chorus are an incisive caesura which brightens the drabness with a clear note of poetry. Now it is found that still another victory is needed, and since Othniel's status as a warrior must be raised so that he can claim Achsah's hand, he is charged with the conquest of Debri, the city of the giants. Othniel is ready: "Place danger around me." The piece is nice enough though it seems more concerned with the bride than with the fearful giants. This gives the chorus an opportunity to pray for the young warrior, which it does most impressively in "Father of mercy." Particularly attractive is the fine antiphonal prayer with the choral sopranos acting as precentors. Achsah's song "O had I Jubal's lyre" is again a charmingly gliding piece—in general, elegance and poetic orchestration are not wanting in any of the victory oratorios after *Judas Maccabaeus*. This aria quotes materials from Handel's earliest youth, but it is fresh and new even after half a century of repeated reworkings.

Othniel succeeds, of course, in conquering the giants, hence "See the conquering hero comes," which was expressly composed for this spot, but which we were compelled to discuss when dealing with *Judas Maccabaeus* where it has been preserved for two hundred years. The final chorus offers the customary praise of Jehovah and its tonality of D is mandatory because of the trumpets. It is a short piece and what looks like a double fugue (at "the great Jehovah") is not developed in earnest. It seems as if Handel got tired of the oratorio before the listener would have been likely to and merely coasted to the end on momentum. But *Joshua*, first performed in Covent Garden on March 9, 1748, with Galli, Casarini, Lowe, and Reinhold, was a great success, and remained so for some years. Although not one of the great oratorios, it deserves to be better known, for alongside the many routine pieces there are some that represent Handel at his best. The alto-soprano combination makes the pair of lovers a little abstract for modern audiences, but that could be remedied, and with some of the deadwood removed, the great pieces would easily carry *Joshua*.

[4]

As we look back upon this phase of Handel's career we realize that considerable stress seems to have been placed on what should be a minor thread in his life work. He should not be represented here solely as the great-souled mouthpiece of freedom and patriotism but as an artist awakening from a brief creative slumber to reassert himself. His librettist misled him with books quite exceptionally unserviceable for dramatic purposes. Though at first they held a quality of delusive promise, soon we see the tendency to lose the reality of the experience in the embellishments of it. At this stage there is often more windy rhetoric than tempered steel in the writing, and the surface emotions of joy and elation that abound in Morell's texts forced Handel to bow to a somewhat tortured respectability. Nor was the cumbrous movement of Morell's lyrics suited to musical setting. Many of them make little pretense of being verse apart from being cut up into lines. Their graceless grace called forth in Handel a neat simplicity in the solo pieces, too neat to be expressive. There is a good deal in them that reminds us of the more formal aspects of opera. The airs may contain poetic ornament but they are not very often poetry. The "helmeted phrases" of Milton, which elicited such a bounty of great music, are missing in Morell's vocabulary, and if he slips gleanings from Milton and Shakespeare into the body of his books, they merely sound an alien and puzzling note. Indeed, he saddled Handel with words that surely must have sounded ridiculous even then, although in many cases the composer somehow managed to overcome this handicap.[8]

On the other hand, the characterization of the great historical figures is, if not unconvincing, conspicuously bald in spite of the moral-religious significance read into them by some critics. These figures act and speak with high-sounding sentiments and almost exasperating complacence quite detached from the environment, which is often no more than an unconvincing backdrop to the story. The rush of events exceeded the activity of critical control, and borrowings are frequent. In most instances Handel retold the old musical stories gracefully but he did not reconceive them. We must not forget, though, that all these were *pièces de circonstance,* and since they were overcharged with the emotional atmosphere of the times, they have a typical quality which gives them an empirical significance and interest. That is, indeed, the only note of unity in these works, without which they would stumble. There were some acute observers who realized this at the time. The Reverend William Harris remarks in a letter that "had not the Duke carried his point triumphantly, the [Occasional] Oratorio could not have been brought out." (Deutsch, p. 630.) Indeed, when we look at the ensemble of these four oratorios, we recall a statement made by Edmund Waller which, though coined in

---

[8] One can imagine the trouble the German translators had with Morell's verbiage. "Fromme Andacht" certainly does not come close to "pious orgies," but then we ourselves could not come close to such freaks.

quick-witted self-defense, expresses a lesson applicable to this case. When asked by Charles II why the eulogy he wrote on Cromwell was superior to the poem addressed to the King on his return, Waller answered, "Sir, we poets never succeed so well in writing truth as in fiction."

We must remember that crumbs are still bread, that a great composer by the sheer force and grace of his imagination and style can invest with a degree of vitality what would otherwise be casual gleanings. In spite of its untidiness, *Judas Maccabaeus* is a durable and often very impressive work, and in the others too there are some stretches rich in imagination and ideas as well as some numbers that can be ranged next to the greatest in *Hercules* and *Belshazzar*.

Whether one feels that Handel was the victim of a generous error in giving so much of his time to this kind of music, or fully admires *Judas Maccabaeus*, there is no gainsaying that the victory oratorios, particularly the last-mentioned, radically and decisively altered his life and position. His enemies were silenced, their weapons dulled; Handel was no longer an intruding foreigner but a popular poet laureate—the oratorio performances were turning into memorable events. Embarked upon the seventh decade of his life, he was now assured of an unassailable stature, supported not only by the entire royal family, including his erstwhile enemy Frederick, Prince of Wales, and by aristocratic patrons of Middlesex's opera, but also by all strata of the "general public." [4]

The times had indeed changed. In his preface to the word book of *Samson* (1743), Newburgh Hamilton, bewailing that "so many mean Artifices have been lately us'd to blast all his [Handel's] Endeavours," consoled himself by the consideration that "all true Lovers and real Judges of Musick" know that "we have so great a Genius among us." Nevertheless, it took the musical settings of the themes of a great national crisis to swell the ranks of these "true Lovers" with a multitude of fickle ones, who only a short time before were either indifferent or hostile. Perhaps the most interesting example of this newly won loyalty and admiration is furnished

---

[4] Concerning the share of the middle classes in this final triumph of Handel, we must call attention to the observations of that excellent and critical interpreter of documentary evidence, William C. Smith, who claims that this question is by no means as yet fully elucidated. Handel's admission fees had always been and still were at this date scaled far more to the purse of the aristocratic patron than to that of the man in the street—half a guinea or more was a large sum of money for an ordinary citizen. The fees charged by Handel for his oratorio performances were actually higher than those obtaining at the King's Theatre with its expensive Italian singers and costly décors and machines. Smith throws in a new idea worth investigating, namely that this policy may have been "a very important factor in Handel's struggle." (*Concerning Handel.*)

by Lord Middlesex and his opera party, whose anti-Handelian moves and defamations had surpassed anything he had had to endure from his wily Italian competitors.

After its debacle (see above, p. 420), the Middlesex company was reconstituted for the 1745–46 season. The resident maestro, Giovanni Battista Lampugnani (1706–1781), who took over from Galuppi in 1743, was retained, but he had to share his office with visiting celebrities. The company had a good roster of singers, and it seemed as though Italian opera had made a comeback. "The opera flourished more than in any latter years," remarked Horace Walpole. The visiting maestro for the 1745–46 season was Gluck, but he does not seem to have cared for the position; after a few months in London he was back on the Continent. In former years Handel would have considered Gluck an antagonist and would have moved heaven and earth to crush him as he did all the other "Italians" (Gluck was consistently billed as Signor Gluck), but by now he cared little for what the opera party was about, and the two musicians got along without any undue contretemps. This was no doubt largely due to Gluck's great admiration for the senior composer, an admiration he retained all his life. The derogatory statements about Gluck attributed to Handel have not been correctly assayed. There is an anecdote connected with Gluck's visit to London that made the rounds of biographies as well as of those anthologies that are devoted to the delights of seeing great men make fools of themselves. Handel is supposed to have remarked to Mrs. Cibber that "Gluck knows no more counterpoint than my cook." While the accuracy of this story cannot be ascertained, it is entirely plausible, but we must also take into consideration the work that invited this sarcastic remark. Gluck's first offering, *La Caduta de' giganti*, was a pasticcio made up of youthful works of the composer, then in his thirty-first year. Moreover, the "cook" referred to was Waltz, a well-trained musician of the old school.

This minor work of Gluck's deserves a closer look not because of its intrinsic merits, but because of its purpose, which parallels Handel's. During the rebellion the theatres knew hard times and most of them were closed when the Scots threatened the south. The idea of exploiting the situation, especially when the tide began to recede after Derby, seemed as attractive to the opera partisans as it was to the oratorians. Gluck was persuaded to adapt his music into a hastily arranged allegorical homage to the valiant Prince who led the English hosts. Being unfamiliar with the form such a piece would take in England, he naturally resorted to its Italian equivalent, the serenata, but the Duke of Cumberland was as clearly visible underneath the Italian garb as he was under the Jewish. Presented on January 7, 1746, *La Caduta* was very successful and played to full houses. The Italian opera's foray into English politics was not without an ironic touch. Gluck, as well as the entire personnel of the Italian opera, was of course a Catholic; it must have been a little embarassing for them to assist at the "anti-papal" rallies. But life, especially operatic life, must go on, and perhaps they scarcely realized the issues at stake. Another small but historically significant detail did not escape the keen eyes of Deutsch. Though an old-fashioned Italian pasticcio serenata, *La Caduta* "was called in the bill 'a Musical Drama,' as had been Handel's *Hercules* a year before at the same house." The new dramatic species created by Handel had begun to make its mark.

Responding to the new climate, the opera party not only called off the war, but switched to what seemed a friendly co-existence; this really concealed piracy, an unashamed exploitation of Handel's rising fame. On November 14, 1747, *Lucio Vero* was performed at the Haymarket Theatre. The advertisement simply stated that "This Drama Consists of Airs, borrow'd entirely from Mr. Handel's favourite Operas." Another pasticcio, *Roxana,* an arrangement of *Alessandro,* again announced as "Compos'd by Mr. Handel," was produced in February 1748. After that the Haymarket Company gave up all pretense, simply snatching an original opera, *Ottone,* thus virtually setting up Handel as a competitor to himself. The irony of the situation was that while the advertisements paid lavish compliments to Handel, in the absence of copyright laws with teeth, he neither had control over his music, nor did he receive any compensation. This should have been even more galling to the old warrior than the previous enmity, but he was not perturbed; by this time he was used to being in the public domain. It became customary at theatrical benefit performances to sing a Handel air or two as a bonus; even *Hamlet* received such embellishment.

Handel found a bonus of his own, however, in the Haymarket performances: badly needed singers to relieve his aging leading ladies. While formerly the Opera of the Nobility not only prohibited their singers from appearing with their competitor but even had an efficient program of proselytizing, now the King's Theatre singers were permitted to sing at Handel's Lenten seasons while remaining in the employ of the opera house. Giulia Frasi, who became Handel's leading soprano until the end of his life, he spotted at a performance of *Lucio Vero,* her first engagement in London. Aside from her fine voice (though Burney called it "cold and unimpassioned"), Frasi's English diction was impeccable. The two became fast friends. Contralto Caterina Galli was also a Haymarket discovery. Under Handel's watchful and expert tutoring, Galli, endowed with a fine natural voice, developed into a great singer who remained with Handel till the end. Her performance in *Judas Maccabaeus* was a triumph, and she became a great favorite with the public, though in later years she grew fat, indolent, and intractable; only Handel could manage her. Elisabetta Gambarini, an even younger singer than Galli, did not stay long with Handel; she must have been an accomplished musician, judging from the harpsichord pieces and songs she published and the organ recitals she gave. Casarini, a soprano with the Middlesex troupe, and Sibilla, a German free-lance singer, neither of whom is known beyond her last name, completed the female contingent of his Lenten casts. Of the men, aging Reinhold was steady, and Lowe took over the tenor parts when Beard was not available or was out of favor.

Handel now lived a calm and secure life. He held to a regular schedule: two oratorios composed during the summer, preparation and performances during the season. He no longer cared either for publicity or for society; old friends were retained, the ones who had been too prudent during the trying days were quietly ignored, and a very few new ones were accepted. The friends of the early decades in England, such as Dr. Arbuthnot and Queen Caroline, were long since gone, but there were some staunch ones of more recent date. Among these the Harris family was particularly faithful. James Harris (1709–1780), the oldest of three brothers and a cousin of the Earl of Shaftesbury, was a man of considerable distinction. Member of Parliament, classical scholar, esthetician, philologist (his collected works were published in 1801), he had a deep admiration and affection for Handel. Harris was also an enthusiastic and excellent amateur musician. Morell recalls a performance of *Jephtha* under his direction in Salisbury which he declared to have been the finest he had ever heard. The second brother, Thomas, was a jurist; the third, the Reverend William Harris, was chaplain to the Bishop of Salisbury. The family's ancestral seat was in Salisbury, where James took a very active part in the local music festivals. The descendants of James Harris, the Lords Malmesbury, collected the family letters and papers, which contain a good deal of Handelian lore.[5] But some of the happiest hours Handel passed with his lady friends, Mrs. Delany, Mrs. Cibber, and La Frasi, whose house was always a welcome refuge. When he was in their company he was altogether different from the reserved quasi recluse he

---

[5] William C. Smith thinks it likely that part of Handel's convalescence in the fall of 1745 may have been spent in Salisbury.

had become to the rest of the world; he was relaxed, friendly, and full of wit. The ladies pampered the now corpulent and slightly bent but still impressive man to his heart's content.

Handel's creative vitality may have been somewhat circumscribed by Morell and the events that called forth the victory oratorios, but it was not lessened; *Alexander Balus* and *Joshua* were composed in ten weeks, which had been the tempo of the creation of *Hercules* and *Belshazzar*. By the time the 1748 season ended with *Judas Maccabaeus* on April 7, he must have been tired of victory music; a glance at Joshua's "Haste, Israel, haste" will show that it is barren of real conviction. It was time for a change, and Handel did not waste any time: on May 5 he began *Solomon*, which was finished by June 13, and July-August was spent in the composition of *Susanna*.

XVIII

Solomon, AN INCESSANTLY VIVID PANORAMA, IS ONE OF THE
richest of the oratorios; Handel seems to be intent on seeing how much
sail he can crowd on without wrecking his ship. This oratorio is not a
story of blighted love or damaging passion; there is no conflict because
there are no antagonists among the principal figures, and there is no jealousy because the King and his ardent wife are young lovers who have
eyes for each other only. Handel composed a work that is part pageant,
part idyll, part allegory. The action is still skeletal, as in the victory oratorios, the librettist working with tableaux and individual acts rather than
with a unified three-act drama, a choice that precluded dramatic characterization of the sort Handel created in *Saul* or *Belshazzar*. At times the
figures seem more like abstractions than fully vitalized personalities, yet
the mood is so pervasive that a certain personality of more than momentary validity does come through. On the other hand, the theatrical-visual
conception of course suited Handel admirably, and while there is no comprehensive construction, the individual acts are well formed. *Solomon* is
one of the "sacred" oratorios and in a sense it *is* concerned with religion,
though with a religion neither Hebrew nor Christian. What it conveys is
the apprehension and the love of life's mystery and beauty, the conviction
of meaning in all things; in a word, a pantheistic view of the world. This
being the case, one wonders why King Solomon was selected as the subject of this work.

Solomon is commemorated in centuries of folklore, all versions agreeing in praising his wisdom, wealth, and glory, although in fact he was not very different from other oriental potentates. He did realize the plan of David, his father, by completing the Temple, and he built as well a number of other splendid edifices. Among these was a palace for the Daughter of Pharaoh who, alone of the reputed hundreds of occupants of his harem, was retained by the librettist as his Queen. There are other aspects of the history of Solomon, however, that had a great deal to do with the purpose of the oratorio named after him.

The Messianic teaching of Judaism cannot be understood apart from the role that Solomon played as an empire builder. Nor can Solomon's prayer in the Temple be understood correctly unless it is interpreted from the standpoint of a political act intended to strengthen and further his imperial design. The King's reign marks the zenith of Israel's power, perhaps because Solomon realized, as did the English, the dangers of subjecting the royal power to the spiritual authority of the priests. He was a diplomat who, like the English, preferred to treat and bargain rather than go to war but nevertheless organized his country's military affairs very competently. Even from the biblical tale it is obvious that the Queen of Sheba did not visit Solomon just to ask him questions, as the story goes; she was alarmed by Solomon's commercial policy and by his fleet. In the best tradition of statecraft she came to offer an entente. All modern scholars agree that the Queen of Sheba never entertained any amatory designs upon the person of Solomon, but the creative imagination of folk art supplants the sobriety of the chroniclers.

The librettist of *Solomon* made his own interpretation of the biblical tale. In the old and well-tried manner of "official history," he omitted all adverse nuances, making of the King of the Israelites not only a paragon of monogamy but an irreproachable figure that could not have displeased the King of the English, who knew well that he and his subjects were beholding their own portrait. Thus, in a sense, if not one of the victory oratorios, *Solomon* is at least an epilogue to them. It is still full of magnificent pageantry, but it is better integrated than its immediate predecessors; it still glorifies king and country, but now the king does not lead in battle but rules over a peaceful and prosperous land; it still praises Jehovah, but these choruses have the potent and magical quality of creating an atmosphere in which by purely epic-rhetorical means universal human emotions are at once idealized and intensified. Musical rhetoric, we must remember, cannot be judged by the canons of other arts; it can be unalloyed beauty.

English authors were not slow in recognizing in *Solomon* a glorification of George II and the eulogy of a nation secure in its power and living the plentiful life of a golden age. Even the Queen of Sheba, who should be an exotic figure, resembles a British sovereign on a political state visit, and Pharaoh's daughter is just an amorous girl emerging from the English countryside. This is not new, of course: *The Taming of the Shrew* is played in Padua, but Katherina is certainly Kate, an English girl. What is really epitomized in *Solomon* is not arms and the man but the nation, its stability and its prosperity. Young puts this succinctly: "*Solomon* exalts reason, wisdom, wealth, and cultural ostentation." Yet while *Solomon* is a variety of the victory piece, or at least a eulogistic homage, it is "of permanent rather than occasional significance" (Dean).

The German authors have been baffled by this oratorio. With few exceptions they are not sufficiently familiar with the temper of the times and with the history of the English musical theatre from the Stuart masque to Purcell's semi-opera, to which *Solomon* stands in considerable debt. As usual they tried to read profound moral and metaphysical lessons into what is essentially a brilliant theatre piece. Not so Ernst H. Meyer, who has a thorough knowledge of English history, musical and cultural. He saw in *Solomon* and the other late oratorios Handel's increasing identification with the English people and English life, which became a prime source of his inspiration.[1] His, as well as other excellent modern essays were available to the quasi-official German biographer of Handel who was entrusted with the completion of Chrysander's work, yet Serauky blithely goes on record as saying that "one thing must repeatedly be emphasized: Handel never became an Englishman in his adopted country."

Chrysander, Leichtentritt, and Schering consider Morell to be the unnamed author of the libretto, but Dean disputes this. Perhaps the shrewdest part of his careful examination of the text is the botanical analysis, which proves that whoever wrote the book was a nature lover, something Morell assuredly was not. Even if we grant that the librettist's references to nature are based on scriptural allusions to Solomon's interest in nature, the anonymous author's partiality to nature pictures (which may have been the very thing that attracted Handel to him) goes far beyond antiquarian zeal. Since nature's moods and aspects were always within the call of Handel's memory, he now freely indulges in his favorite pastoral scenes, reaching a culmination in the intoxicating freshness of the "Nightingale Chorus." All the choruses are those of the Israelites; the counterpoint, always reserved for them, is therefore extensive, rich, and elaborate. The orchestra is used on the same large scale as the mighty

[1] *Händel in seiner Zeit*, in *Wege zu Händel*, Halle, 1953.

eight-part choruses; the iridescent delicacy of *Alexander Balus* is seldom present; brilliance, solidity, and expansiveness largely overrule color.

The plot can be told in a couple of sentences. In the first act the recently built Temple is consecrated, the King, the priests, and his people offer songs of thanksgiving, after which the King retires with his young Queen. Act Two presents the famous story of Solomon's judgment over the infant claimed by two women, while Act Three is devoted to the entertainment of the Queen of Sheba on a state visit. The story was put together from I Kings and II Chronicles, but some historical writings were also consulted.

As can be seen, the first and third acts offer no drama whatever, but the judgment scene in the second act is flesh-and-blood drama which, though episodic, is actually the rallying point for everything happening before and after. There are several disparate elements in this work, each of which is dropped after its exposition: conjugal bliss, kingly wisdom and justice, and the eulogy of a great and well-administered realm. Aware of this, the librettist's solution is not without merit—he bases each act upon one of these elements. At that, it is quite possible that, given its immediate purpose, there was no intention of making this oratorio a through-composed drama. By the some token, Handel was somewhat hampered by the restricted degree of characterization such unconnected acts offered. The Levite is virtually a piece of décor, but even Zadok, the high priest, is too distant; the cuts that will have to be made in performances should come largely at their expense. But even the principal figures leave something to be desired, though their music is consistently admirable. Since Handel had the gift of evoking personality at will, one wonders why Solomon, his Queen, and Nicaule, Queen of Sheba, were not drawn with a sharper stylus. Perhaps a eulogy demands more universal than particular traits; indeed Handel seldom lets us forget the symbol of the office or position held by these figures. He compensates with the choruses—linear eloquence has its own charm—and with a poetically powerful thread that goes through the entire work: the evocation of nature. He could almost always respond with a fresh immediacy to the enchantment of nature, or conceive out of the depth of his own creative mind a glittering musical landscape.

Solomon keeps a measured, unhurried stride throughout the narrative, but he can forget that he is a mighty ruler and dwell on the beauties of his domain, and can turn with ardor to his young wife. Hers is the eloquence of simple and untutored passion; she is prettily rapturous and pleasantly sensuous. It is in the characterization of the two harlots that

Handel fully exerted his powers of representation. Again, one is inclined to believe that he felt free to do so because they are an accessory to the eulogy and thus true portraits can be drawn. The distribution of the singing roles is most peculiar in *Solomon:* the title role is given to a female mezzo soprano, all four of the other women are sopranos, Zadok is a tenor, and the insignificant Levite a bass. Such a preponderance of high voices we have not encountered since some of the operas. Herbage makes the plausible guess that "Handel seemed temporarily to lose faith in the tenor voice for his leading role." It is quite possible that in his eagerness to rid himself of the helmeted heroes he retired the *Heldentenor.* And if he had tired of the tenor heroics, is not there a sly intention in making Zadok, the high priest, a dignified and official professional, a tenor? Winton Dean speculates that Handel may have assigned Solomon's role to a female voice to emphasize the symbolic, "unnaturalistic" portrait of the King, adding that "it is possible however that this concentration on the female voice was intended to balance the weight of the double choruses." But whatever the original reasons, they no longer have any validity for us; a baritone can easily sing Solomon's part in his own range. The resultant masculine quality immeasurably enhances the oratorio's effectiveness for modern audiences.

Solomon contains some of Handel's grandest choruses; as in *Israel in Egypt,* they are the chief glories of the work. Handel sets them in five and eight parts, the latter predominating, sumptuous and rich. After a fine overture the oratorio opens with one of those scenes of rejoicing that Handel almost always manages to make impressive or at least interesting; "Your harps and cymbals sound" is no exception. The piece is one of the rare instances where Handel falls back on the cantor's art of his youth: it has a sort of cantus-firmus construction with a royal scope. This is not a chorale elaboration; there is nothing "strict" about the manipulation of the tune, but the rocklike solemnity this style so well suggests is most appropriate for the occasion. The following chorus, "With pious heart and holy tongue," separated from the first by an air of the Levite, is even more splendid. Over the steadily pulsating string accompaniment in eighth notes, the simple choral declamation in halves creates the feeling of a great hymn. The second part then becomes polyphonic, close imitation alternating with antiphonal passages. There is something insistent in this piece; "till distant nations catch the song" is stubbornly repeated, always ending in a resounding homophonic passage on "and glow with holy flame."

Solomon appears, singing an exceptionally fine accompanied recitative-arioso, with a type of accompaniment that shows a new finesse in Handel's orchestral art. By dividing the violas, Handel obtains a five-part string choir, to which he adds two obbligato bassoons. The descending figurations of the bassoons render this a startlingly modern operatic scene. In contradistinction, Zadok's air "Sacred raptures cheer my breast" is a somewhat old-fashioned and extended piece that would match the insubstantial loquacity of this worthy were it not for the admirably flowing melody over a marchlike accompaniment, which suggests a subtle tongue-in-cheek intention. The concerted element is very skilfully meshed with the vocal part. Handel was obviously bored with the high priest, giving him only one other good song. The next chorus is again a marvel. "Throughout the land Jehovah's praise" is a fugue, then again it is not, because there is nothing of that sort in any rule book. Beginning in four parts, it widens into eight, the motet-like polyphony yielding to majestic chords which on "full power" indeed exhale impressive power. The tone changes altogether in Solomon's air "What though I trace each herb," the first of the nature pieces. The tune is glorious and the garlands of the gently intertwining violins convey the peace of the countryside. The da capo is perhaps a trifle formal, but we are listening to a genre piece, not to an *aria di carattere*. To those who see in *Solomon* a religious work, this pantheism is a bit disturbing, but not nearly as much so as the scene that follows.

The Queen begins her air, "Bless'd the day when first my eyes saw the wisest of the wise," which is fine and proper, but she follows this with "Bless'd the day when I was led to ascend the nuptial bed," which was found embarrassing by the Victorians in a "sacred oratorio." The charmingly uninhibited Queen now goes to the superlative: "But completely bless'd the day, on my bosom as he lay," which prompted the uneasy Romantic editors of the score to exercise strict censorship. Sex, even when sanctioned by holy matrimony, does not belong in an oratorio, even though the freshness of this music and the delightful accompaniment create a tone of frank innocence. Now the amorous couple sing a bewitching duet, "Welcome as the dawn of day," one of those melodies that stay forever with us.[2] Zadok enters to offer moral advice about faith and truth dragged in by the librettist quite irrelevantly. The royal pair pays little attention to it, and the King's "Haste to the cedar grove" is answered by

---

[2] This wondrous piece caused an amusing contretemps for some of the exegetes. B minor is supposed to be the *Schmerzenstonart*, the key of grief and pain, yet Handel here contradicts all authorities—and Bach himself—by using B minor for warm, happy, and ravishing love music.

the Queen: "With thee th' unsheltered moor I'd tread." The music continues to be utterly charming, and its youthful grace is enhanced by a borrowing from an Italian cantata from Handel's own youth. This cluster of
love songs is capped by a chorus, "May no rash intruder disturb their soft
hours," better known as the "Nightingale Chorus." Its chaste lines are
filled with tenderness, the perfect union of sentiment, design, and pictorial detail making this, perhaps the finest nature scene ever rendered in
music, into an old Dutch landscape painting come to life.

This group of pieces forms a pastoral-amorous interlude, a picture
rather than a story. Its purpose seems to have been to extol conjugal love
after established religion had been extolled in the previous numbers. That
Handel poured into them some of his loveliest music does not change the
episodic nature of the entire scene, which of course should not discomfort
us. To some of the biographers and critics it was nevertheless discomfort-
ing, though the musicians among them could not have remained insensible to such gems.

Now, to quote Keats, "we take but three steps from feather to iron."
The second act opens with a tremendous chorus. It is not a choral aria,
like the Nightingale Chorus, but a mighty rondo-fugue in which the introduction returns as a refrain. "From the censer curling rise grateful incense" is in Handel's amplest anthem style, exhibiting his choral versatility
at the other extreme. The piece is ceremonial-documentary, it aims not to
move but to overwhelm, yet there is a ponderously playful element in the
fugue theme, which Handel apparently toyed with for his own pleasure.
Solomon's aria returns to the more intimate tone of his nature scenes,
though "When the sun over yonder hills pours tides" does not reach the
exquisite poetry of "What though I trace." Sung by a woman, as originally
written, this is no more than a well-designed number, but a male voice
gives it nobility of utterance. The Levite offers a bass aria that is altogether impersonal to the extent that some of it sounds like a two-part
invention, but presently everything changes. To demonstrate the wisdom
and discernment of the King, a case history is presented. This is not at all
badly fitted into the general scheme, and though also episodic like the
love scenes, inasmuch as it has no bearing on what follows in the oratorio,
everyone, with the exception of Sir Thomas Beecham, has seen in it the
dramatic core of the oratorio.

The two harlots appear before the King to seek justice. Handel here
departs from the tradition that places ensembles at the culmination of
dramatic plots and begins the scene with a trio, the dramatic pace controlled with admirable insight into human nature. The First Harlot, who

is the true mother, begins in F-sharp minor with a magnificently pathetic and romantic song. What seems to be an aria changes into a duet when the Second Harlot, to prevent her rival's plea from affecting the King, interjects that "false is all her melting tale." When the King sees that this is going to be an altercation, he too joins the ensemble with a solemn warning that "Justice holds the lifted scale." The dramatic-musical situation is one of great poignancy as the three present their individual thoughts simultaneously. The first woman, forlorn and distressed, yet with the nobility of a loving mother, sings haltingly, while the second's fluent Neapolitan patter betrays her falseness. The King's reiterated invocation of Justice and her lifted scale—really an ostinato—provides the anchor for the shifting intensity of the emotions. As the others drop out, the true mother is left alone to end the beautifully constructed piece as she began it, claiming "my cause is just." The characterization is sharp, brittle, and precise, drawn with an unsparing hand. The true mother is a heartbreaking figure, but just as the false mother is mercilessly exposed for what she is, the King appears a trifle pompous. In the preceding recitative the librettist paints royal integrity a bit too thickly. The King, consenting to hear the litigants, says: "Admit them straight; for when we mount the throne, our hours are all the people's, not our own." This fits the description neither of the absolutist in Jerusalem nor of the constitutionalist in London, and Handel, quite knowledgeable in such matters, seems to be having a little private fun at the expense of this self-negating king.

Solomon now pronounces his celebrated verdict which the Second Harlot hastily accepts. The accompaniment, which grins like a gargoyle, well illustrates the emptiness of her soul, and the frivolous convolutions of the bass effectively contradict her concurrence, "Thy sentence, great King, is prudent and wise." The true mother, stricken with fear for her offspring, offers to give up the child rather than see it killed. The words are trying—"Can I see my infant gored?"—but Handel simply breaks through the librettist's snare and gives us a deeply felt and pondered piece, a remarkable dramatic juxtaposition of grief and beauty, shading from unanalytical emotion to a sense of illumination. The composer's solicitude for a proper dramatic presentation of this song is plain from the detailed instructions he gives for the performers in the score; here he interrupts the largo aria with "adagio," there he follows it with "risoluto." The two women never utter a sound that is not characteristic of their diametrically opposed personalities.

Solomon, in an accompanied recitative that begins in B-flat and ends in G-sharp, solemnly pronounces sentence. Turning to the second woman, telling her that she "must be a stranger to a mother's name," he orders her out of sight. (With a good English sense for jurisprudence, the librettist has the King admonish her to refrain from any "further claim.") Then Solomon restores the infant to its rightful mother, who sings a duet with the King ("Thrice blessed be the King"). The deceptively easy-flowing piece has very attractive canonic passages.

The following chorus, "from the east unto the west," is a splendid eight-voiced composition with elaborate concerted parts for the orchestra. Distinctly popular in tone and syllabic in construction, this chorus, the quintessence of ceremonial choral art, would surely warm the heart of any king "so worthy of a throne." It also warms Zadok's, who "from morn to eve could enraptur'd sing the various virtues of our happy king." Fortunately, he selects an unsacerdotal mood for his effusions, a simile aria that refers to the stately palm tree. At this point, instead of the expected act-ending paean, we are treated to a far more delectable pastoral than the priest's. The true mother, who has somehow remained on the scene, sings a song that resembles the Pastoral Symphony in *Messiah.* But now the chorus takes over with an appropriately resounding piece, "Swell, swell the full chorus of Solomon's praise," which does justice to the text.

With the third act a new scheme is presented. Except for Solomon and the priest, the protagonists of the first two acts are omitted as a new figure, Nicaule, Queen of Sheba appears. If there ever was a "basic religious idea" in this oratorio, its last vestiges are now abandoned, for the third act is an entertainment within an entertainment, an almost self-contained masque whose motif we might call *épater la reine.* A bustling sinfonia introduces Sheba, whose entrance aria no critic seems to like. While it is perhaps not particularly distinguished, the air has a fluently vocal melody and a nice concerted accompaniment. "Ev'ry sight these eyes behold" is a gavotte sung by a Purcellian English princess. Now the masque commences. Solomon's plan is to show the Queen the four temperaments as sung by his singers led by the King as the precentor. What follows is unmistakably English theatre music; Handel enriched the traditional genre with unflaggingly magnificent music. The first piece of the masque is a miniature Cecilian ode: "Music, spread thy voice around." The delightful madrigal is in five parts, dotted with antiphonal passages. It is indebted to one of Steffani's motets, but the exploitation of the germinal idea is altogether Handelian. The King then commands the martial mood. "Shake the dome and pierce the sky," a double chorus, is in Handel's full-dress manner, with all decorations and sashes worn. The thrilling piece does not really end; Handel wants to sharpen the contrast with the next number, which is introduced by a tiny recitative so as not to dull the exhilarating effect of the preceding dynamic chorus. "Draw the tear from hopeless love," one of Handel's greatest choruses, speaks of love but also of "death and wild despair," a veritable *Tod und Verzweiflung*, creating a mysterious hush of awe and fear. As the tenors' anguished cry wanders through all the parts we suddenly have the feeling of listening to Passion music. The fourth temperament is represented by "Thus rolling surges rise," a charming madrigal, a Baroque *La Mer* with its airy and elegant counterpoint. This is the happy ending of the masque and of the command performance.

With the end comes, unfortunately, an end in Handel's interest in what remains to be done—we are witnessing his typical post-dénouement indifference. But he still has a few tricks up his sleeve. Sheba gives her thanks for the entertainment, and the Levite pronounces both host and guest covered with eternal glory; a poor piece that is expendable. Zadok also returns, this time with a good air. "Golden columns" has a brilliant, almost jaunty, concerted accompaniment that really makes the piece. The following chorus, "Praise the Lord with harp and tongue," is not on the same level with the great choruses but it is a massive and effective anthem, its resilience compensating for its thinness in ideas. Dean's recommendation that this Hallelujah type of chorus should be shifted to the end is well taken. Schering thought that at "God alone is just" Handel borrowed from the Sanctus of Luther's *Deutsche Messe.* Whether or not this is so—the resemblance is tenuous—it is immaterial; the piece is in the old "Jehovah with thunder arm'd" style that is particularly English no matter whence its ingredients.

Of the rest only one number deserves particular attention: Sheba's superb farewell song, "Will the sun forget to streak." Here Handel once more rises to the summit as the intensity of the writing is sublimated in the ordered beauty of the form. This scene where the Queen of Sheba takes leave after having been shown the wonders, beauties, and riches of the land, having admired the piety of Zadok and the people, and above all the wisdom and statesmanship of Solomon, is an exact prefiguration of a visit of the present reigning British sovereign to one of her dominions. It is official, decorous, nothing untoward is permitted to intrude, and everything is on a high and noble tone. Yet it *is* real and heartwarming. It is this quality that makes *Solomon* so English, for in no other country do the people feel the same way about the monarchy. The following duet between the King and Sheba has none of this magic, and the final chorus is notable more for carrying power than for musical substance.

[2]

THE DIVERSITY OF mood and content in *Solomon* and *Susanna*, composed as a pair, is as remarkable as the consistent creative and technical capacity they reveal. *Susanna*, which no longer runs in Hebrew-Hellenic grooves, is so difficult to fit into any survey of Handel's oratorios that it is often allowed to drop out of the picture altogether. With this work, Handel commits himself to a tone that rings oddly against the works immediately preceding it, those that insured his final triumph. *Susanna* seems to show the after-effects of transplantation into a richer soil, with some consequent rankness of growth. Paradoxical as it may seem, this rankness is manifested in the choruses. *Susanna* seems so remote in subject matter, sentiment, and manner from nearly everything else Handel composed (except for some of the late operas) that even his most sympathetic critics have been baffled by it and a diligent search was instituted to find the antecedents. But it is useless to seek such antecedents in the old Italian oratorio; *Susanna* has no ancestors, it is a Handelian creation, albeit a very particular one, more a chamber opera than an oratorio. It is in effect an opera, with the largest number of da capo arias in any of the oratorios, and it has nothing whatever to do with the biblical locale. The tunes are delightfully light, in the English folksong vein which is not at all veiled by the equally pronounced elegance of the setting. The music owes a great deal to the rhythm and cadence of the language and to the kind of tunes Handel heard around him; several authors rightfully point to Arne's influence. Though *Susanna* has delightful touches of unobtrusive humor, and scenes drawn with a light and whimsical hand, neither can we simply call it a comic opera. Many critics have been puzzled: is *Susanna* an oratorio, an opera, or perhaps a mystery play? What could have prompted Handel to set to music such a tale? The strait-laced were shocked by some of the scenes, and even to many others the oratorio's subject matter was of doubtful character. They should have remembered what Maitland said: "Sin in some shape or other is the great staple of history and the sole subject of law."

The tale of Susanna and the Elders is one of the "additions" to the Book of Daniel. The legend, placed in the early days of the Captivity, relates the familiar story of Susanna, the beautiful, pious, and chaste wife of Joachim, who was surprised bathing in her garden by two old men, who were judges. "Inflam'd by lust" they made immoral advances, and when indignantly rejected, they spitefully had Susanna condemned by falsely charging adultery. She was about to be executed when Daniel, then a young man, by skilful cross-examination of the accusers proved the falsity of the charges. This is clearly a folk tale adapted to a specific milieu, and it must be much older than the scriptural version, which is placed by modern scholars long after the Captivity. The legend enjoyed considerable popularity—as a good tale would—and was subjected to many interpretations. During the Renaissance both painters and musicians favored it as a theme; *Susanne un jour* was among the most popular of chanson texts and tunes. Kenneth Levy, in his fine study in *Annales Musicologiques I*, mentions thirty-eight vocal settings between 1548 and 1642. It is perhaps of some importance to note that *Susanne un jour* originated as a "spiritual chanson"; Levy describes it as a poem intended for devotional use among Protestants. In the Catholic lands it became a decidedly secular piece, but the Huguenots' conception was readily echoed by English Protestants, though the rich, disarming humanity of Handel's approach to the story offers a subtle but definite shift of emphasis.

The "oratorio," a combination of abandon and economy of means, and demonstrating the alert radiance of a new simplicity, has scenes that recall the vivacity of miniatures in an illuminated manuscript. Regrettably, the anonymous author of the libretto, probably the same person who supplied the book for *Solomon,* once more did Handel a disservice. His exposition presents divagations that have no connection with the core of the drama, and the gigantic choruses in these scenes do not suit the intimacy of the work. Indeed, this tone is ill mated to the manifestations of the spiritual as well as of the amorous scenes. It gives an excuse for saying that the librettist's belief in Jehovah and in the supremacy of Heaven is merely decorative. Handel summoned his mighty thunder in the choruses and all his sensuous suavity in the love scenes. Each of these two extremes is magnificent, the *élan* of some of the choruses is sweeping, but the shadow of these great choral friezes lingers around and blankets some of the delectable rural badinage. The trouble was of course that since *Susanna* was virtually an opera, it was difficult for Handel to find adequate scope for his popular trump card, the chorus. Not until we get to the court scene is the role of the chorus fully motivated. The dramaturgical mistake of forcing the grand ceremonial style upon an intimate drama is only compounded by the majesty and power of a number of these choruses; the very first of them could stand in the greatest of Handel's choral dramas and still rise above its surroundings. The presence of these interpolated choruses was bound to create confusion in the minds of those who are constantly on the lookout for moral-religious issues. To them—as to the librettist—an oratorio was unthinkable without a chorus of Israelites mourning, girding for battle, praising Jehovah, expressing victory or indignation. The Hellenic mould did not suit *Susanna* either.

But the core of *Susanna* is intact. Where there is real dramatic conflict and action, the growth, the fragility, the sprightly movement as well as the exquisite nature pictures of the great master are all there. The dramatist's fidelity to character and the poetical humanity with which he invests his figures give such scenes a rare integrity of emotion. We feel increasingly the precariousness of innocence until inevitably the crisis comes. In these scenes there is neither roughness nor loose ends. Handel is preoccupied with creating a musical language that really has the stress and shape of what he feels. The comic touch is subtly present in the unmistakable travesty of such well-known types as the rage and trumpet arias. Regarded in this spirit, and with a realization of the extraneous nature of the "religious" choruses, *Susanna* becomes no less remarkable though considerably less edifying. However, when the play turns from internal conflict to objective commentaries, the drama can easily collapse, for the anchor is not strong enough to hold the design together.

Susanna's role is winning for the individuality of her characterization and the climactic effect of her vindication, but even more because her inner vision, penetratingly clear, is translated into musical poetry. Her innocence and pining for her absent husband show her a gentle, accepting, and impressionable creature, but when wronged her steadfastness makes her charm come out even more freshly without sticking a single romantic-sentimental plum in her hat. Her role confirms our belief that the anonymous librettist could not have been a divine like Morell, or if so, he was an unusual one, because Susanna is gloriously aware of the facts of life. This "oratorio" is full of what the moralists called carnal love, portrayed without inhibition, though very properly within the frame of wedded bliss. Thus Handel was well served by the book, and from this point of view *Susanna* is an unclouded masterpiece. Susanna's Attendant (the old operatic confidante) also turns in a haunting scene, but husband Joachim is clearly an accessory; a loving husband, yes, but not a very interesting person. He is one who, despite qualities that are not unattractive, is nevertheless destitute of any real strength of character. The two Elders are superbly characterized. The first one, the tenor, may be a lecher, but he also has a genuine horror about a passion unseemly to a man of his age. The librettist gave him a large selection of expressive metaphors—"raging fire," "purple torrents," "burning smart," and so on, all of which were welcome to Handel's pictorial imagination. But, as on other occasions, what he made of the character differs from the librettist's intentions: this one shows an emotional instability restrained by a form of urbanity. The Second Elder, the bass, has no such inhibitions; he is after his quarry, impatient, with an air of splenetic repression about him. For once the patriarch, Susanna's father, is not a warmly dignified old man. Handel gave Chelsias some very good music to sing, but his person remains floridly ceremonious in speech and gesture and in the end a bore. Eventually Handel threw him out of the cast, and his absence is not even noticed. Daniel, the future prophet, may be an excellent lawyer, but he is the type whom only some transient passion can illuminate. He has wit of the legal variety and, if *Susanna* were rightly presented on the stage, would have theatrical liveliness, but his personal character is hinted at, not established. Handel did not bother to give it imaginative expression.

After an excellent overture, Handel immediately gives our heartstrings a mighty pull: "How long, o Lord, shall Israel groan?" is a great choral passacaglia in Handel's weightiest manner. Alas, this glorious lament on the plight of Israel is in no way connected with the subject of the drama, and Handel, unable to make a connection with the following scenes, simply drops the tone, abruptly turning to the delights of marriage. The music in this group of songs, consisting of a bouquet of da capo arias and one duet, flows most invitingly and the pieces are daintily composed, but they have charm rather than a deeply clarifying passion. They have a decided folksong quality, eschewing counterpoint even in the duet. The outstanding number is Susanna's "Would custom bid the melting fair," a dulcet, simple song. Love has a poignant sweetness and the young life pushes aside the old. Chelsias supplies two seriously worked contrapuntal pieces in which voice and strings are carefully integrated. "Who fears the Lord may dare all foes" reminds us of the closely imitated instrumental pieces of the North German composers. Though the air is too long, and the old man's pious meanderings do not contribute anything to the drama, this is good music. Chelsias's other song, "Peace, crown'd with roses," a short, dark-colored piece, is also attractive. A reversion towards old ways of thinking and feeling, these songs are not the less impressive for that. Unfortunately, from every other point of view they are expendable. Susanna's "Without the swain's assiduous care" also abandons the folk tone; the almost *galant* piece has an engagingly elaborate accompaniment. Joachim's simile aria, "The parent bird in search of food," offers a nice blend of folksong-like simplicity with *galant* elegance; the key of F-sharp minor does give it, though, a slight tension.

Susanna, left alone, is invaded by doubts and forebodings of coming evil. She asks in an accompanied recitative, "What is this weight that in my bosom lies?" The answer almost gives away what is to come as the librettist makes her divine premature death, threatened innocence, and "falling without a crime," but Handel rises to the occasion. "Bending to the throne of glory" is a moving little ballad, sighing in gently tearful suspensions. The chorus's "Virtue shall never long be oppressed" retains this mood. This is a fine madrigal with elaborate concerted accompaniment whose thematic subject gradually infiltrates the vocal parts. Though somewhat extraneous to the play, it is a rewarding composition.

The First Elder appears, singing a dramatic accompanied recitative, "Tyrannic love." The rapid change of tonalities depicts his worry about the "purple torrents" that rage in his bosom. As contrast to the agitated recitative, his "Ye verdant hills, ye balmy vales, bear witness to my pain" is a simple strophic song that recalls the ballad opera. The Second Elder joins his colleague, and the two engage in a recitative, conversing like two judges discussing the day's legal events. The First Elder politely inquires whether it was a difficult case that makes the other seem so miserable, but soon they discover that both of them are under Susanna's "magick spell." The Second Elder now launches into an impetuous air, "The oak that for a thousand years withstood the tempest," another simile aria, but this time patently a buffo piece, a sly travesty on the rage aria and very characteristic of the man. Handel interrupts the running coloratura of the vocal part with some ungainly skips made very funny by the bassoons playing *colla parte*. The First Elder is more smitten than ever, the Second, observant and spoiling for action, spots Susanna on her way to the garden. The two decide on an ambush: "await our time, then rush upon the fair, force her to bliss, and cure our wild despair." The First Elder now sings to himself as if to bolster his courage, "When the trumpet sounds to arms." Handel avoided the obvious; instead of writing the customary aria with an obbligato trumpet, he only conjures up the instrument. The mock bravery is very entertaining as Handel sharpens the travesty by surrounding the trumpet-like vocal line with capricious runs and rhythms in the violins. At the end of the first act Handel again returns to the grand style of the opening. "Righteous Heaven" and the immense fugue "Tremble guilt" threaten to obliterate everything that took place before. These two choruses belong among the greatest of Handel's many great ones, but it is difficult to account for them in their surroundings. Incidentally, here Handel once more remembered Erba and his Magnificat, but he changed the small coins into large banknotes.

The second act opens with Joachim who, away from home, reminisces; *partir, c'est toujours mourir un peu.* "On fair Euphrates' verdant side" is a pleasant pastoral air with attractive accompaniment, but Joachim still does not emerge as a positive personality. The next scenes constitute a dramatically tight, well-constructed whole. Susanna, her "spirits faint beneath the burning heat," wishes for the cool shade of the tall trees and the refreshment of the "swiftly trickling fountain." Her song "Crystal streams in murmur flowing" is one of Handel's most entrancing pastorals. The strings murmur delectably as they are alluringly intertwined with the voice, imitation and complementary rhythms and phrases preventing any check in the gently undulating motion. This highly sophisticated pastoral is followed by a simple strophic song. Susanna, longing for her husband, asks her Attendant to sing her the song Joachim wooed her with. This sort of thing is an old operatic recipe that never fails if the music is good; "Ask if yon damask rose" is a prizewinner. This English song is another little ballad, ineffable in its moving simplicity. Susanna's companion understands her mistress's frame of mind and sings her another song, this time about her own long departed lover: "Beneath the cypress' gloomy shade." The unadorned siciliana of sixteen measures sings of love that seems so far away as never to have been, yet she dreams of her sorrow, which will never altogether pass.

Presently Susanna sends her away to fetch the ointments while she bathes in the pool. The two Elders see their opportunity and advance, to Susanna's consternation. The First Elder, even though seeing her in the nude, tries his luck with gentlemanly courtesy; "Blooming as the face of spring" is a suave air, and his first request is modest—he wants only a smile. Not so the excitable Second Elder, who insists that his passion is strong as the torrent, which Handel renders in a blustery "torrential" buffo aria. But in the middle portion there is an undertone of real menace as he bursts out "then yield to entreaty, you proud fair," his voice leaping up the interval of a twelfth. Susanna, who first thought that this was a crude joke, is now enraged and denounces the "deceitful wolves." In the ensuing trio, one of the best and brightest specimens of Handel's wit and skill in characterization, each protagonist is provided with his own music and special accompaniment. Susanna is accompanied by delicate imitation, the First Elder's song calls for solemn chords (he is still *comme il faut*), but the Second Elder sings in unison with the strings in the buffo patter manner. Then Handel combines all three with a skill not to be found that side of Mozart. Seeing that they are defeated, the old men raise an alarm, calling for witnesses to come and see the adultress whose lover, they announce, had just escaped. They want her tried on the spot.

Susanna summons courage to deal with the situation: "If guiltless blood be your intent" dispenses with ritornel and motto, starting directly as the song is directly addressed to the heart. The flower-like melody, rising and falling, is tender, and though Handel unfolds it effortlessly, a certain tension is maintained by an insistent rhythmic pattern in the accompaniment. Remarkable dramatic use is made of the da capo principle as in the middle section Susanna falters, only to regain her resolve in the reprise. Now the chorus enters with perfect naturalness; its comment, "Let justice reign," is relevant to the action. The piece is distinguished by smooth counterpoint freely exchanged between the voices and the instruments. Needless to say, all these scenes are so theatrically conceived that in the concert hall their effect is considerably diminished.

Joachim, pondering the message he received, cannot believe that his wife should be unfaithful; he must hasten home to stand by her. "On the rapid whirlwind's wing" is another fine nature piece. All Handel needed was the word "whirlwind"—the violins whistle with abandon not only in the elaborate ritornel but throughout the song. It is a stunning virtuoso piece. The act-ending chorus begins with a simple but effective homophonic declamation that completely ignores the stilted—almost legal—tone of the text. The following fugue, though skilfully worked out, fails to impress except for its craftsmanship. We notice, as we have in some of the other choruses, that this counterpoint has something curious and old-fashioned about it. It is perfectly singable, and the choral setting is idiomatic and euphonious, yet this fugue theme is instrumental, like an organ fugue's, as its elaboration is also organ-like. This was of course a Baroque phenomenon, the universally adaptable musical substance, but Handel seldom used it to such an extent in a choral fugue.

The scene in the third act is the courtroom after the verdict has been pronounced. The chorus, its role again proper and plausible, announces that "The cause is decided." There is something decisive and final in the ritornel; the violins stubbornly repeat a running figure while the oboes play an almost chorale-like solemn tune. The tone is conversational, depicting the crowd in the courtroom discussing the verdict, but every once in a while all of them dramatically unite in a shout: "Susanna is guilty, Susanna must bleed." Handel was constantly incommoded by the exceptionally silly and stuffy lyrics, but almost always found a way to overcome them. Susanna's largo air "Faith displays her rosy wing" is a good example of this. Handel starts the magnificent F minor recitative-arioso with a grave ritornel but does not wait until it is finished; Susanna's sad but proud song, protesting that "innocence shall never fear," begins in the third measure, rising out of the dark background independently. This anguished yet composed woman is a sister to Theodora, Handel's only martyred heroine. The song moves even one of the Elders, the first one, who tends to be sentimental: "Round thy urn my tears shall flow" expresses a certain sympathy for the doomed Susanna. But the music, to quote a famous statement of Gluck, "does not lie." Handel made the air into a psychological study, modern, sophisticated, and pantomimic. The plaintive and pleasantly melancholy air has the appearance of a trim and tidy song, but no sentence is ended as its beginning would lead one to expect. Handel uses deceptive cadences, internal repeats that upset the symmetry, sudden tiny coloraturas, and other unexpected turns to prevent a clear-cut musical statement. The rascally Elder is a hypocrite who covers his true feelings with pretended sympathy. Susanna knows it: " 'Tis thus the crocodile his grief displays." She charges those "who see me over the verge of life" to tell her husband about her innocence, but the Second Elder is getting impatient: "The sentence now is past, the wretched convey to instant death."

At this moment Daniel appears, exhorting the people not to believe such a "varnished tale," whereupon the Second Elder angrily calls him a "presumptuous boy." Daniel accepts the challenge. " 'Tis not age's sullen face that is the sign of wisdom," the song demonstrating more an eminently judicial temper than strong personal conviction, though it is not altogether without a certain wrath. A third Judge is sufficiently impressed by Daniel's invoking the sanctity of the legal concept that a verdict cannot be reached without sufficient inquiry and proof, and orders the case reopened. This entire scene has been declared an unconvincing operatic *deus ex machina,* but such court thrillers are usually theatrically unexceptionable, and this one is supremely well managed.

The procedure is quite according to English jurisprudence. First Daniel, a sort of *amicus curiae,* requests the setting aside of the verdict and the freeing of the accused; presently, as a retrial is ordered, he assumes the role of defense counsel. At this point the librettist remembers that divine sanction or aid must be worked into the proceedings to keep the chorus occupied. Handel obliges with a very fine "prelude and fugue": "Impartial Heav'n, whose hand shall never cease." Now the defense counsel undertakes the cross-examination of the accusers. "Thou artful wretch," he addresses the First Elder, "what tree stretch's her boughs to screen the guilty pair?" "A verdant lentisk," answers the sentimental one. Then, to the Second Elder, "And say, thou partner in the impious deed, beneath what tree you chaste Susanna saw embrace her lover and transgress the law?" Since the choleric one names a different tree "far to the west," the falsity of the accusation is proved and the table is turned. Daniel's song "Chastity, thou cherub bright" following the acquittal is puzzling. It is a winsome piece, good melody, sensitive accompaniment with an intermittent ground bass which at the same time is elaborated thematically—yet it is not quite successful. Handel in his usual way picked out the words that appealed to him: "gentle as the dawn of light," "swift as musick's dying strain," which turned the piece into a shapely pastoral-like song. What is puzzling is its neutrality, why Handel composed a simile aria instead of presenting the future prophet's feelings at having rescued Susanna.

Joachim now arrives at the scene. The text of his love song, "Gold within the furnace try'd," is poor, nor is this a character piece, but inviting music it is. The piquant alternation of the same thematic material in symmetric and asymmetric patterns is captivating. Now Chelsias also appears as a character witness, but after the dénouement, again, Handel lets his imagination yield to the expertise of the craftsman mopping up. Everything is skilful and agreeable, but the spark is gone. Chelsias's brief air is perfunctory, the chorus's "Bless'd be the day that gave Susanna birth," with the trumpets making their first appearance, is also a routine number, but Susanna's charms are not yet exhausted. She now sums up everything in her "Guilt trembling spoke my doom." The song is passionate, but we also see the sparkling of the amorous tear. This piece could easily be shifted into the latter part of the century; it is *galant,* homophonic, and the accompaniment has a symphonic-operatic quality. The slackness returns with the following duet and the final chorus, both of which are less than minor Handel.

Performance of the two oratorios took place in inverse order of their composition. *Susanna* was presented on February 10, 1749, with Frasi in the title role, Galli as Joachim, Lowe and Reinhold as the First and Second Elder (Reinhold also singing Chelsias's role), and "the Boy" as Daniel. There were four performances and, though we hear of full houses, *Susanna* disappeared for ten years; Handel revived it for one performance shortly before his death. *Susanna* was not heard for another hundred years, and less than sparingly after that. One of the reasons for this neglect is undoubtedly the unfortunate circumstance that sex is unavoidably and palpably present in this oratorio, which never bore the "sacred" epithet despite its Bible-descended text. Even Chrysander, who was strait-laced and inclined to make as much of a celibate of Handel the artist as he was in life, counsels against prudery, warning in his preface that

Handel never excised anything of importance from the part of the two Elders. But his colleagues went to work on the wicked libretto with hard blue pencils. The revival in Cologne in 1859 may have been occasioned by the appearance of the first of the Händelgesellschaft volumes, for, most curiously, Chrysander selected this work to inaugurate both his great undertaking and the first centennial anniversary of Handel's death. Chrysander's score is on the whole one of the better edited ones, but the Novello score, the one in general use in the English-speaking world, though published several years after Chrysander's, is an outrageous travesty that should have been withdrawn and banished long ago. In his preface to the score Chrysander acknowledges that *Susanna* is very long and in need of abridgment; he mentions the cuts Handel himself made and justly observes that Chelsias could be altogether dispensed with.

Handel, well aware of the limitations and idiosyncrasies of the public, now accepted them stoically. He continued to compose with devotion and integrity, but he knew that his livelihood depended on the proven successes and was no longer downcast when a new work failed to catch on; his revivals filled the house. Yet even here we notice that he often smuggled in among the favorites one or another of his orphans. The première of *Susanna* was followed by revivals of *Hercules* and *Samson,* then on March 17 *Solomon* reached the public for the first time, followed by *Messiah,* now announced by its rightful title but sung only once. In the cast of *Solomon* Galli sang the title role, Frasi appeared in the triple part of the two queens and the First Harlot, the Second Harlot was Sibilla, Zadok fell to Lowe, and the Levite to Reinhold. We have no information about the work's reception, and though the performances seem to have been well attended there were only two repetitions, and, as with *Susanna,* Handel did not revive *Solomon* for ten years. This assuredly is surprising. The subject matter of *Susanna* may have displeased many, the exquisite miniature work and subtle humor may have been lost on a public expecting lusty Hallelujahs, but the splendor of *Solomon,* and the dynastic as well as moral message it conveyed, should have appealed to audiences well-conditioned by the victory oratorios.[3] But musicians did not fail to

[3] We cannot blame Handel's contemporaries, however, when two hundred years later one of Britain's leading musicians, Sir Thomas Beecham, completely misjudged this glorious score. His recording of *Solomon,* the first to reach countless listeners unacquainted with Handel's works outside of *Messiah, Israel in Egypt,* and *Judas Maccabaeus,* is a capital crime by any artistic code. The smugly superior baronet, always ready to deal cavalierly with defenseless composers, outdid himself by excising the entire judgment scene, thereby demolishing the core of the drama. Other numbers were shifted helter-skelter out of context, the entire score reorchestrated in

recognize the greatness of this oratorio. Haydn heard several excerpts from *Solomon* in Oxford when the honorary degree of Doctor of Music was conferred upon him in 1791. Greatly impressed, he took the text of Sheba's recitative, "Thy harmony is divine, great King," setting it as a three-part canon, which he offered in homage to the university.

[3]

POLITICAL EVENTS once again demanded musical acknowledgment; Handel was invited to contribute the music to the celebration of the Peace of Aix-la-Chapelle. The preparations for the festivities began soon after the armistice in May 1748, their gargantuan scale in odd contrast to the negligible gains Britain achieved by the treaty. Italian specialists in pyrotechnics were engaged, and the general scenic design was in the hands of Jean Nicolas Servan, a celebrated French architect, scene designer, and decorator, who for some reason went under the name of the "Chevalier Servandoni" (which fooled Flower into calling him a "hotheaded Italian"). Under his direction a large wooden edifice was built in Green Park. The firework display, held on April 26, 1749, was a questionable success and ended in near-tragedy. Many of the rockets failed to go off, while those that did managed to set the building itself afire, causing a bad panic in the large crowd, with many injured in the stampede. But the *Royal Fireworks Music,* as the suite came to be called, pleased, though Handel had had his difficulties with this score. The King wanted "martial instruments" only, but the Duke of Montague, in charge of the festivities as Master General of Ordnance (a couple of hundred cannon also participated in the noise-making) believed that "Handel will never be persuaded" to leave out the strings. Apparently Handel did give in to the monarch's wishes, for the string parts were added later. The original score called for 9 trumpets, 9 horns, 24 oboes, 12 bassoons and one contrabassoon, 3 pairs of kettledrums, and one or more side drums. The suite is pleasant if inconsequential outdoor music, but the overture, when played by a good wind band, is a brilliant piece. Handel's friend and admirer, Tyers, the owner of Vauxhall Gardens, arranged a public rehearsal of the music on April 21. Converging on the Gardens, the crowd of some 12,000 created such "stoppage" on London Bridge that carriages were held up

---

the most conventional 19th-century *Kapellmeistermusik* style, with juicy harmonies, senseless doublings, and ridiculous thematic imitations added. The recitatives are elephantine, the retards asthmatic, the cadences brutal, and such cheap effects as cymbal clashes complete this incredible travesty.

for three hours.

Handel was now indeed popular. On May 9 the grateful General Committee of the Foundling Hospital elected him a Governor of the institution. On May 27 there was a great benefit performance in the Hospital's chapel, at which the *Fireworks Music* (with strings added), the new *Foundling Hospital Anthem* (see above, p. 226), the *Dettingen Te Deum* (now designated as the *Peace Anthem*), and selections from *Solomon* were performed to a full house, with the Prince and Princess of Wales in attendance. This was the first of many charity performances in the Hospital to which Handel, devoted to the cause, always contributed his services. The resultant income substantially added to the Hospital's operating capital. Handel was now the admired master, with a large stock of works that had become famous and well liked. The recognition he now enjoyed had already begun when he was still in deep distress. Pope, in the fourth book of *The Dunciad,* came to his rescue in 1742, and Horace Walpole eventually also endorsed him. Neither Pope nor Walpole knew anything about music, or had any taste for it, but, like other men of letters, they distrusted and even despised Italian opera as an intruder upon the English scene. They sensed that the oratorio was something English that they could and should support. There was, too, a growing public for musical performances. Mercantile England was bringing into being large numbers of people who were strange to the uses of their own wealth and leisure and who were eager to know how to live. Handel could have run oratorio seasons with his established successes alone, but he kept on composing new works that carried him into hitherto unexplored regions. This was a bold undertaking, for this astute connoisseur of the game must have known that the public could not follow him into the domain of the spirit that he chose to enter. Though he was no longer the adventurous speculator with buoyant optimism as his main weapon, his imagination was yet abundantly alive, and, like the aged Verdi, he was ready to embark upon his last masterpieces. *Theodora* was composed during July 1749.

After a brief creative interlude, the composition of incidental music to Tobias Smollett's *Alceste,* Handel made his usual preparations for the oratorio season when London was struck by an earthquake. In the confusion and fear few had a mind to attend the theatre; rather they sought the provinces to escape the tremors which seem to have centered upon London. A month later, after confidence had returned, the city was again shaken, and a veritable exodus followed. The earthquake affected Handel no more than had Prince Charles and his Scots; while others panicked, he quietly went ahead with rehearsals for his spring oratorio season, which opened just before the second series of tremors, on March 2, with *Saul*. After a repeat performance *Judas Maccabaeus* followed, and on March 16 *Theodora*, "with a new Concerto on the Organ," was presented for the first time.

XIX

IT MAY BE THAT GENIUS IS NEVER ENTIRELY AWARE OF ITSELF, and Handel in particular gives evidence even in old age of still exploring his powers and still coming upon surprising discoveries. The more one studies the last two oratorios, *Theodora* and *Jephtha,* the more one is aware of a substratum of thought that is elusive. No musically perceptive person can fail to realize that there is here an atmosphere not easy to account for from what is generally known about Handel. There is a spiritual serenity, a tranquillity in facing a host of contradictions and assailing questions, and a preoccupation with the profundities of this life—and of that to come. Poise that is almost detachment, betraying only the merest hint of moralizing and therefore exercising the subtlest of attractions, is typical of the last two oratorios. But it should not be inferred that the tone is always sombre and melancholy; the music often moves with lightness and delightful ease. This music, and it includes some of Handel's loveliest and most affecting, is quite different from the idiom with which his name is generally associated; yet even those who have no experience in the new, autumnal style will not be slow to recognize its subtle charm. His style has been deepened by experience without losing any of its frank impulsiveness. The emotional stream ripples, but never eddies against either the Scylla of sanctimoniousness or the Charybdis of pomposity, and the tenderness all through these works (in an age with "sensibility" the fashion) never descends to the sentimental. There has been a change, however, in many of those aspects of Handel's musical and mental processes characteristic since his "conversion" to the oratorio—or is *this* the conversion? *Theodora* has a Christian subject, the only English oratorio aside from *Messiah* of which this is so. But then *Jephtha,* which is not a Christian oratorio, exhales the same spirit. This tension, and this conception of tranquillity not as an end in itself but as a condition of future events, creates its own particular world. For, indeed, while in *Theodora* and *Jephtha* we discern no formal message hidden below the configurations, and the details of the works are not intended to provide symbols and lessons, they do yield more than a story; they leave us with a sense of human nobility.

Our postulate up to this point has been that within the generally accepted tradition of the "sacred oratorio" the Handelian music drama is unconcerned with Christian philosophy. We have seen that Handel created dramatic poems about individual men and nations, *Messiah* being the only exception, and it was this exception that became the rule that decided for posterity the reputation of Handel. *Messiah* was called a "sacred oratorio," but *Theodora* never carried the qualifying adjective— Handel always called it "an oratorio" or "a music drama." This was partly owing to the convention that reserved the "sacred" designation for works that had either biblical texts or biblical connotations. We have noted that, with some exceptions, *Messiah* is still in the Old Testament oratorio style; it still contains Old Testament texts, and many of its choruses are pure ceremonial anthems. In *Theodora* Handel for the first time deals with Christian dramatis personae, the story concerning itself with the vicissitudes of Christian persecution and the spiritual travails of the Christian martyrs. And a characteristically Christian idea appears here also for the first time: the insistence on death as a gate to life. Leichtentritt declared *Theodora* to be "the peak of the Italian saint- and martyr-oratorio," which it very well may be, if we grant it a place in the Italian genre on the basis of its subject matter. That subject matter is commonplace enough; the theme is human will and human fate; but Handel has treated it with what one is tempted to describe as final clarity, evoking a vision of the inner world, which he affirms and expounds with illuminating grace. We must ask, then, what is the place of *Theodora* in Handel's *oeuvre* and what if any are the connections between the two "Christian" oratorios?

Surely they cannot be directly compared; at most we can range the two works side by side as great music. There is no resemblance in the treatment of the religious motif. The appearance, though impersonal and undramatic, of Christ in *Messiah* brings a new spirit and a new problem

into the Handelian oratorio. In this work, the composer of dramatic
passions shies away from the dramatic treatment, but he does not on the
other hand ascend the pulpit. *Theodora* is in a different category: it is an
intimate work. Even the choruses are intimate, and there is none of the
Old Testament grandeur to which we are accustomed in the other oratorios, including *Messiah*, neither rousing Hallelujahs nor majestic double
fugues. Of sophisticated religious dogma there is no trace in *Theodora*,
but—and *Jephtha* shares in this—of immediate experience of God as revealed in all life there is much convincing and moving evidence. The fusion of action and suffering dominates Handel's imagination in the last
two oratorios; the conflict is more and more an inner one. The love story
in *Theodora*, presented with great delicacy, nevertheless quickens the
pace of the drama, emphasizing the appeal of its spiritual qualities by the
lovers' intense endeavor to transcend—though without denying—the
flesh. And there is the shadow of death falling on everything, but it is not
oppressive, for the mood is lyric, the application of the most delicate art to
the conception of tragedy.

Morell took the story from a historical novel, *The Martyrdom of
Theodora and Didymus* by Robert Boyle (1627–1691), which appeared in
1667. The original novel is both unctuous and gory. Boyle's heroine,
Theodora,[1] with her beauty, her secret terrors, and her unvarying virtue,
confronted Morell with a difficult task, yet he managed to turn the very
weakness of the material into a kind of strength by stripping the story of
Boyle's worst features and composing a preface to form Act One. While
Morell's style is atrocious, the action is fairly continuous and constant; the
story is complete and intelligible. Even so, he worked out that story with
a kind of resigned relentlessness. Here is life, the Doctor seems to say, and
character—the composer must face it to the end. But the librettist also
provided something that was welcome to Handel, the clash of two worlds,
two faiths, and two different sorts of humanity. Thus the libretto was
quite serviceable, though it seldom conveys a sense of spiritual reality.
Handel penetrated beneath the shabby poetry with the aid of the miracle
we so often observe in the great music dramatists: the music changes and
transfigures the meaning of the words, and the story thereby acquires the
quality of a true myth which at its best is grave and compelling.

Theodora opens with a scene honoring Jove and the emperor. Valens,

[1] Theodora, a Christian martyr during Diocletian's rule, died in 304. She should
not be confused with Theodora, the more famous and notorious wife of Justinian (6th
century), a courtesan become empress. The confusion, which is frequent, comes from
the fact that the latter's body lies in Corfu Cathedral as St. Theodora. Piquant, if
Procopius told the truth about Justinian's consort.

the Roman prefect, threatens with death all who refuse to offer sacrifice. Didimus, a young Roman officer secretly converted to Christianity, pleads conscientious objection, though professing complete loyalty to the emperor. This is not acceptable to Valens, who decrees death for all recalcitrants. Didimus seeks the help of Septimius, his friend and immediate superior, who is sympathetic but avers that soldiers must obey. In the next scene we meet Theodora among the assembled Christians; she is a young noblewoman accompanied by Irene, her confidante. They too defy the decree and Valens, a Roman who cannot understand why common sense does not make the Christians avoid such a deadly conflict, has Theodora arrested, condemning her to serve in Venus's temple—with all that this implies. Didimus pledges his life to save his beloved and the Christians invoke heavenly blessing upon the couple. In Act Two the Romans are preparing for the pleasures awaiting them in the temple of Venus. Septimius, on Valens's behalf, once more tries to convince Theodora that sacrificing to Jove is preferable to becoming a temple prostitute, but Theodora places her trust in divine help. Didimus confesses to Septimius that he is a Christian and wholly devoted to Theodora. The two soldiers are old comrades, and the senior officer permits the younger to visit Theodora in prison, where he proposes to change clothes with Theodora so that she can escape. Though willing to die, she finally accepts his offer. In Act Three, Theodora returns to the praying Christians to great rejoicing, but soon it becomes known that Didimus has been condemned to death for his part in the escape and a similar fate awaits Theodora if she is apprehended. In a final court scene, Valens sees no reason to avert the martyrdom both defendants seek.

[2]

THE SAINTS OF Christian history are a line of great eccentrics, the inspired fools of the world. But sympathetic readers of Christian mysticism also know that the great lovers in history were not the Antonys and Cleopatras but the saints. Having conquered all human desires, they burn with an intense flame of love. Handel's heroine is haunted, regretful, and desolate, but beneath all this the pulse of an inner serenity and assurance beats, an ever-present consciousness that death is but the gate to life. She is not a sensuous woman, yet in her music she is ardent, albeit with the ardor of a St. Theresa. Only imagination extended to its fullest could compass the spiritual mystery of this woman, and the mystery was translated with the poet's directness into a language lacking all trace of pulpit gravity. Morell conceived Irene as the usual auxiliary in the drama, but Handel makes her rise to impressive heights—she commands half an act. Irene is very different from her mistress but equally authentic and no less poignant; Handel gave her affectionate and lingering care. Didimus is both in search of his soul and in flight from it; his arias are here a confession, there a claim. One detects a slight insecurity in Handel's approach to this character, and there is a touch of floridity in the latter's expression, both undoubtedly because the role was written for an alto castrato, very unusual in an oratorio, especially so late in Handel's career. But in the end Handel shows Didimus as a man who enters noiselessly through a door that normally creaks. Morell saw Valens as a harsh, even cruel monster; Handel's Valens is rather a man hard and unbending but upright, a Roman through and through, a masculine figure of ruthless efficiency convinced that the Roman way is the right way, that duty comes first and deviations from it cannot be condoned. Eagerness for martyrdom makes no sense to his orderly military mind. Septimius should belong to the same class of Roman military officers, but his is a far less unequivocal personality than Valens's. He has sympathy for the Christians and his friendship towards Didimus is genuine, but such help as he may give must be surreptitious. Perhaps the beautiful music Handel gave him is justified if we consider him a man touched by compassion.

[3]

THE ORATORIO opens with Valens's order to Septimius, "Go my faithful soldier, let the fragrant incense rise to Jove." The aria has a military, imperative tone, but when Handel reaches "fragrant incense" we realize why the flowing runs in sixteenth-notes were added to the fanfarelike ritornel. The following chorus, "And draw a blessing down on his imperial crown," retains the fanfares from the previous aria but not the runs connected with "rising incense." With the trumpets added, the martial character is enhanced. Didimus's cautious plea to his commander not to force everyone to sacrifice to Jove is answered by "Racks, gibbets, sword and fire shall speak my vengeful ire." The situation and the text should have brought about the traditional rage aria, but Handel forgoes the roulades, giving Valens simple though sternly angular sentences, in the manner of a man used to command, and imbuing the aria with a certain tone of finality. The chorus of Romans, "For ever thus stands fix'd the doom," supports the prefect. Here again we are dealing with a marked freedom from the expected and the conventional. The chorus sings a siciliana, suave and melodious, the light choral style alternating with attractive bits of imitation. Both the situation and the cruel and bloodthirsty words of the libretto would seem to call for violence of musical expression, but Handel's pagans are always natural people whom he sees in their own light. The Romans now take the role of the Baalites in the earlier oratorios, and, indeed, the French horns appear to give added charm to the pastoral quality that so strongly contrasts with the words. It is interesting to see how this is done. On the words "their [the Christians'] groans and cries are sweeter than the trumpet's sound," Handel fastens himself to "sweeter," repeating it five times in a gentle echo play between soprano and alto.

Didimus sings his first air, "The raptured soul defies the sword," its theme borrowed from Clari's chamber duet *Quanto tramonta il sole*. Handel sets the words—and interprets them—with considerable rhythmic interest, but, while the piece offers warm and appealing music, it is a little abstract, most of the time sounding like an elegant trio sonata. Only in the middle part does Handel resort to dramatic vocal writing. Also, the da capo makes this a very long piece. Septimius shows sympathy for Christian sentiments but insists on "Roman discipline." His aria "Descend kind pity, heavenly guest" is again musically most attractive. The long ritornel betrays Handel's pleasure in composing this music; repeatedly we feel that the decisive cadence is at hand and that the aria will begin, but Handel, loath to give up the flowing ritornel, turns away from the cadence and continues to spin the lovely music. As the voice enters—this time pure bel canto—we see the same pleasure in extending a nice sentence, now from eight to ten measures, with a curiously dilated cadence. Handel, as so often in his elaborate music, catches sight of the particular object, the factual detail, and seizes upon it. He plays with the cadence, dilating it even more at the repetition. The ritornel at the end of the first portion of the da capo, with its pleasure in internal repetition and little capricious ornaments, is very close to Pergolesi's light style.

Theodora, accompanied by Irene, makes her first entrance, and Handel immediately presents her in full stature with characteristically penetrating music. Though this is a sort of da capo piece with a very short repeat, fundamentally it is a free dramatic *aria di carattere*. The ritornel begins with a thrice reiterated theme full of dark possibilities which are immediately stifled by a resigned cadence. As the listener is waiting for a clue to where this leads and as the ritornel momentarily rests on the dominant, the voice enters, alone, with a statement that immediately fixes the mood: "Fond flatt'ring world, adieu!" Henceforth the orchestra may try, as it repeatedly does, to sound the dark motif, but Theodora always falls in with the soothing cadence. The antithesis is fascinating, creating a tone of firm if gentle resolution. Irene's air "Bane of virtue," in the warm key of E major, reminds one of Semele's most beautiful songs, though without the erotic undertone. The richly dotted rhythm ceases in the middle portion, where Irene suddenly changes to a quiet arioso in C-sharp minor. As we look at the text we are once again surprised to see Handel composing fine intimate music that suits Irene's feelings but not the painful platitudes Morell puts in her mouth. There follows (with a nod to Clari) some exquisite choral polyphony of the madrigalian variety, "Come mighty Father, mighty Lord." While the texture is fluent, without real stops, the whole is dominated by one quietly lovely theme that seems to suggest "Grace and truth flow from Thy word," the word "flow" eliciting runs through the compass of all voices and instruments.

When a messenger arrives counseling flight—the Romans are threatening—Irene expresses trust in the protection of God. Her air, "As with rosy steps the morn advancing, driving the shades of night," is a magnificent sunrise piece, the ritornel rising and rising to a crescendo indicated by Handel. The voice enters, but while the nature picture remains intact, there is a firmness in Irene's melody, for this is a simile aria, and as the sun rises so do "our hopes of endless light." The energetic bass motif lives an independent life not unlike the pedal motifs in some of Bach's chorale preludes. The Christians' chorus, "All pow'r in heaven above, or earth beneath belongs to Thee alone," while not one of the grand choruses, is well declaimed and suits the situation.

Septimius comes upon the Christian assembly and sternly warns against defiance of authority. "Dread the fruits of Christian folly" begins well, in the sharp tone we associate with the Roman military, but Handel intersperses the good musical material with somewhat perfunctory coloraturas. When Theodora challenges him, Septimius orders the guards to carry out Valens's sentence to take her to the temple of Venus. Morell's words for the short recitative are coarse, but they are soon forgotten and only their brutal meaning remains. Theodora's da capo aria "Angels ever bright and fair" is very brief, almost nothing happens in it, but we get the first moving glimpse of the procedure so characteristic of these last oratorios: the passing from dramatic representation to the contemplation of the idea.

Didimus arrives too late to intervene. Though a soldier, he too is imbued with a religious devotion and serenity like Theodora's, but at the same time he loves her and wants to protect her. Handel expresses the

Roman's conflict by abruptly inserting recitatives in his aria. The motto-ritornel itself comes after the first dignified sentence of the aria. The violins are wild and excited, punctuating the voice part, but Didimus never wavers in his devotion, which, in the middle part of the song, reaches deeply romantic pathos. The da capo should be ignored in this fine piece; it would nullify the startling entry of the ritornel. The act-ending chorus of Christians, "Go, generous, pious youth," is neither an anthem nor a fugue but a simple and gentle choral aria reflecting the confident faith of the protagonists. Handel's first audiences, accustomed to a rousing ending with trumpets and drums, must have felt disappointed when the moving song faded away, piano, its hesitant rhythm emphasizing the feeling of farewell.

Morell forgets about his doctorate in divinity and becomes a playwright of sorts in the second act, which is short but varied, its excellent dramatic continuity inspiring Handel to compose an exceptionally fine act in which his artistic concentration never relaxes. Every one of the arias is as limpid as a still pool, yet each has a delicate necessity so that every piece falls into place and helps to build a satisfying whole.

Morell, as we said, provided variety, and the scene in the Temple of Venus introduces a subdued sensual glow with a strong feeling of the dance, which does not, however, reach the extrovert hedonism of the music of Handel's Oriental pagans—the Romans are Westerners. Their first song, "Queen of summer," is a delectable bit of English theatre music, a fragrant choral minuet. Yet something is amiss in this appealing piece; the tone and rhythm are wholly English, but they do not fit the natural gait of the words. This is surprising because in this instance Handel could not have objected to Morell's text. Valens sings a song of praise, whether to Jove or Diocletian is not entirely clear. He starts in his sturdy Roman manner, but the lively accompaniment and the occasional coloratura seem to indicate that he is not unmindful of the forthcoming feast of Venus and perhaps has had a beaker or two in advance. Morell again has the right dramatic idea when in a secco recitative Valens enjoins Septimius to try to bring the "stubborn maid" to reason. The second song to the goddess of love, "Venus laughing," is quite different from the Purcellian minuet-chorus that preceded it. This, too, is neither boisterous nor openly erotic, but the continuous reiteration of one motif—in itself gentle—creates a sort of euphoria that anticipates more animated pleasures. Streatfeild interpeted the monotony of the repeated tune as "a picture of purely soulless religion," but Handel was not at all concerned with Roman religion. Used to the hearty and unbridled feasts of Sesach and Dagon,

Streatfeild did not realize that Handel here deliberately avoided the orgiastic, representing instead the disciplined stage of religious observance that comes before.

The symphonic element used for dramatic purposes, which we have increasingly noted in the later oratorios, now comes to the fore. The scene shifts to Theodora's prison. The flutes, withheld up to this moment, shrill on single tones as they relieve the strings; the terrors and uncertainties of the night are conveyed with verisimilitude. "With darkness deep as is my woe" is a night piece indeed, but the night is not all terror; the wondrous arabesques in the accompaniment add a mysterious pastoral charm that only enhances the forlornness of the song. On the words "your thickest veil around me throw," the strings break into a soft undulating pattern studded with warm, highly pathetic suspensions which stop at the phrase "or come, thou death" but return at "embosom'd in the grave." These are the wistful and evanescent tints of the haunted. The tonal order is unusually bold: the first sinfonia is in G minor, the aria in F-sharp minor, and the return of the sinfonia in E minor; Handel enlarges the sinfonia, and the flutes become more insistent. The key of E minor is retained for Theodora's next song, "Oh that I on wings could rise," the middle portion turning toward B minor. The second song begins with a surprisingly robust ritornel and with one of those incipits that usually end in melodies stretching beyond the horizon. But when Theodora begins to sing, everything turns into sadness, though no longer the sad searching for an answer of the first aria, for there is a certain confidence and resolution in this fine piece. The first part again shows pastoral-descriptive writing ("the silver dove is swiftly sailing"), but in the middle section a motif is reiterated thrice in the voice and thrice in the accompaniment in a way that virtually halts the piece with its resolution "that I might rest, for ever blest, with harmony and love."

Didimus confides to Septimius his love for Theodora and his secret espousal of Christianity. Handel now delves more deeply into Septimius's character, but the piece is also descriptive in that felicitous way where the melodic, the graphic, and the gestural are all clearly word-begotten yet entirely musical. Septimius's aria is dramatically important, for he is the key to the ensuing action. Handel introduces the scene with a long ritornel which immediately expresses the mental conflict by opposing a *galant* theme to a military fanfare that reminds us that Septimius is a Roman soldier. This large aria is composed upon one sentence of text: "Though the honours that Flora and Venus receive from the Romans this Christian refuses to give, yet nor Venus nor Flora delight in the woe that disfigures their fairest resemblance below." The music must take care of the unspoken ideas, which it does handsomely. Notably interesting is Handel's way of accentuating what might be called the "Roman loyalty motif" by reinforcing it at its fifth appearance with an insistently rushing upbeat. Though the music flows with admirable ease and melodic felicity, we clearly feel the indecision in Septimius's mind, the conflict of duty and compassion. When Didimus, in a secco, pleads "Oh save her then, or give me pow'r to save," Septimius gives him permission to visit Theodora in prison. Didimus's following aria, "Deeds of kindness," is no longer *galant;* it goes beyond that, practically into the Mozartean world. Irene's prayer, "Defend her, heaven," opens with a magnificent ritornel, which is then symphonically developed. The symphonic-thematic urge is so strong that Handel altogether omits the customary echo play in which the orchestra repeats the motto and the cadential phrase endings of the voice. The accompaniment goes its own way, furnishing harmonic support to the voice, but its own contribution is highly dramatic. Irene maintains a steady, solemn vocal line, but the orchestra is agitated and full of tension. Handel's creative power is at such a pitch that through number after number he maintains this rich flow of music.

In "Sweet rose and lily" Handel returns to the Baroque aria, the orchestra lovingly repeating the chiselled motto phrase as Didimus, deeply moved, watches the sleeping Theodora in prison. The tenderness of this piece recalls the music of *Acis and Galatea,* but at the same time the "new" Handel is strongly revealed. The same man who only a few scenes back bewitched us with his Venus music now writes a love song that is altogether innocent of the flesh. Theodora refuses to escape at the expense of Didimus, preferring death from his "hand and sword." "The pilgrim's home" could have become maudlin, but Handel avoids all pathos as Theodora chooses death in a simple strophic song, a siciliana that makes the scene not only believable but moving. But finally yielding to Didimus's entreaties, Theodora joins him in a farewell duet. This is ablaze with the heat that purges yet is infinitely tender and pure; the lovers hope to meet again on earth, "but sure shall meet in heaven." Handel turns to polyphony, the obbligato bassoons making the structure a five-part one. There is a vigorous and comprehensive linear design which takes little account even of grace in the figures but compels them to its own dusky harmonies and angular curves.

There is yet a summit beyond this peak; indeed, the act-ending chorus is perhaps the absolute summit of Handel's choral art; it was so considered by the composer himself. "He saw the lovely youth" is a recounting of the parable of the youth whom the Lord raised to life in Nain. The chorus is epigrammatic without being false, packed without being obscure. This is the mysterious moment of the union of the internal and the external, the soul and the form, the content and the expression. For this is the aging composer's profession of faith, a faith not limited to the narrow terms of stated articles; it is like the harmony of the spheres which no human ear can hear but which the human mind feels with elation. The piece, in the sombre key of F minor, begins with a funeral dirge in the orchestra, upon which is built a severe vocal setting in continuous imitation. But when Christ commands "Rise, youth!" the texture becomes entirely homophonic, even descriptive, interpreting the motion of the young man. Now something like a double fugue begins, the themes again interpreting the words, leading to a final utterance of considerable and eloquent power.

Irene, this most musically attractive of all confidantes, opens the third act with another magnificent song, "Lord to Thee each night and day strong in hope we sing and pray." The aria is full of extraordinary melodic "irregularities." In the middle part, where the text speaks of convulsive earthquake and rolling thunder, the tone changes as Handel indulges in his favorite nature pictures. But inwardness never leaves Irene's song; the orchestra alone is pictorial, though neither vehemently nor literally descriptive. Clearly, Handel refused to be distracted from Irene's prayer. Yet Morell's cataclysmic words must have brought back memories of the many animated and dramatic nature pictures of the past, otherwise he would not have hurled the chilling Neapolitan sixth into the closing cadence; it is far too strong a dramatic effect to be mated with the words "still to Thee we sing and pray." In the aria "When sunk in anguish and despair" the intriguing metric asymmetry returns, combined with a capricious rhythmic scheme. The orchestra has a quietly lively accompaniment, but the voice is serenely unperturbed. The Christians respond to the story of Theodora's escape with a fine chorus, "Blest be the hand and blest the power that in this dark and dang'rous hour sav'd thee." The construction of this piece is once more extraordinary. Starting without a ritornel, and vaguely in the manner of a fugue, it immediately lapses into homophony, twice repeated; though the themes are typical fugue subjects they are not so developed, and Handel savors the full sound of the homophonic chorus. Thus the poet triumphs over the conventional. Now Theodora like a precentor gives the chorus a theme, "Lord, favour still the kind intent." The procedure is still the same, for the chorus freely alternates between polyphony and homophony, but when the ripieno sopranos take up

Theodora's motif in earnest, as a quasi cantus firmus, the setting assumes the quality of a chorale paraphrase. A remarkable piece, this, and most suitable for the spot.

A messenger announces that the rescue plot has been discovered, and now Didimus is threatened with death. Theodora resolves to return to prison to save Didimus, answering Irene's anxious questions firmly. The duet they sing is one of the few fast pieces in the oratorio; in a situation such as this there is no time for extended discussion. The piece is not only swift in tempo, it is what the French call *serré;* not a chamber duet but altogether dramatic. Neither voice is permitted to develop a melody, there is a constant give and take, but the last word is Theodora's: "I must obey."

Irene's subsequent aria in C minor, "New scenes of joy," shows this courageous woman admirable in adversity. Unfortunately, she has to face not only a tragic situation but also Morell's singularly inept words—the text makes little sense at this juncture in the drama. In the face of impending tragedy Irene sings of "new scenes of joy." Perhaps Morell had in mind Christian rejoicing in martyrdom, but he certainly made a mess of it. This did not prevent Handel, his creative impetus still unbroken, from writing exceptional music by ignoring the words; the purely musical-emotional momentum is so strong that the literary factor must take second place. But the audience cannot altogether ignore the words, and unless a new text is fitted to it, the great aria will remain obscure. Irene's melody is simple, though the motto theme is one of Handel's typical wide-ranging pathetic themes; it is again left to the orchestra to develop it. Handel worked with manifest care; the polyphony is both subtle and pervasive, the da capo written out so that the composer could indicate his own little melodic variants. There is no ritornel, only the one-measure motto is stated.

The ensuing "court scene" is introduced by a recitative that in Chrysander's edition is obviously severely cut. In five brief sentences Valens expresses astonishment at the Christian ethics of disobedience and condemns Didimus to "repentance or death." Didimus justifies his stand, Theodora offers herself to expiate Didimus's crime, while Septimius, a little fatuously, comes to the conclusion that there is "virtuous courage" even in the female sex. The long da capo aria Septimius presently sings is an exceedingly well-made minuet-like song, but it is *galant,* righteous, and distant; Handel's Septimius is not a character of full integrity. He holds that "from virtue springs each generous deed," and goes on to urge, "Let justice for the hero plead, and pity save the fair." The only show of emo-

tion is in the last part of this sentence. Morell undoubtedly meant all this
to be taken at face value, but Handel did not care for Septimius; he
wanted either a true Roman or an avowed Christian. Valens fulfills Handel's requirements in his air (*furioso*), "Cease, ye slaves, your fruitless
pray'r." The opening sentence is like a trumpet call and is echoed by the
strings. This is a compact piece and could have done without the traces of
"rage" coloratura of old that Handel understandably carried at the back
of his mind.

In a recitative, Didimus and Theodora offer their lives for each other,
which prompts the Christians to comment with all the majesty of the ancient Greek *choros*. The sombre piece carries us back to the spirit of "He
saw the lovely youth," the great chorus at the end of the second act, for
Handel again searches his own soul. Under the guise of the conventional
act-ending number he presents a meditation upon the mysteries of love
and death. The theme of "How strange their ends, and yet how glorious"
is another borrowing from Clari, but it magnificently suits the sense of our
mortal instability that informs this chorus; what Handel made of the borrowed theme is sheer miracle. In a way, this piece, in which emotion is
not so much recollected in tranquillity as evoked by it, is the climax of the
act, although it does nothing to precipitate the dénouement. Indeed, arriving at this point in the oratorio, one has vague apprehensions about
Handel's frequent habit of losing interest in post-dénouement matters.
This tremendous chorus expresses everything; what can come afterwards?
The immediate dramatic needs the composer fulfills quite properly. The
pair pleads before Valens in secco recitative; they renew their contention
that each of them alone has incurred the penalty of death. Whether
Morell the classical scholar wrote out of knowledge of the Roman mind or
just naively hit upon the authentic tone, Valens's reaction to this is characteristically Roman. "Are ye then judges of yourselves? Not so our laws are
trifled with: if both plead guilty, 'tis but equity that both should suffer."
Then he dismisses them with an aria, "Ye ministers of justice, lead them
hence." The brief aria is most appropriate, and its brisk, angular melody
expresses the prefect's annoyance and impatience, as well as the finality of
his decision. For some unknown reason Chrysander relegated the piece to
the appendix of the score, though it surely is superior to the perfunctory
recitative that replaced it.

But now, with the drama really ended, came the critical moment for
Handel. He still had two numbers to compose: the protagonists' farewell
and the mandatory final chorus. First he wrote an aria for Didimus, then
a farewell duet for the two martyrs. Though the musical material was

superb, the long da capo aria at this point in the drama followed by a duet must have seemed too formal. Then his dramatic sense found a marvelous solution: he combined the two pieces by grafting the duet upon the aria as a substitute for the da capo, a procedure that gives the illusion of Theodora's song gradually joining Didimus's. The move required a number of changes which were executed with his wonted skill, the result being a remarkable scene. "Streams of pleasure ever flowing" evoked a simple flowing music. A good deal of the sweet simplicity of southern Italian church music, with its parallel thirds and sighing suspensions, appears here, and most appropriately because all suffering is past, the two lovers are in sight of the Elysian fields.

The final chorus, "O love divine," is a sublime berceuse, half smiling, half in tears. There is in it an element of abandon amounting to a true surrender in Handel's yielding to inspiration. Both Schering and Dean liken the chorus to the great lullaby that ends the *St. Matthew Passion,* and perhaps for once the two great composers of the Baroque who had nothing in common did find a common ground: the singular expression of the identity of poetical and religious feeling.

[4]

MORELL IS OUR WITNESS that Handel valued *Theodora* more than any other of his oratorios. This was not merely the librettist's self-compliment; Handel himself made remarks to others that, if not so explicit, corroborate Morell's statement. The technical quality of the work also indicates that *Theodora* held an exceptional place in the composer's affection for his progeny. The construction is tight and controlled to the smallest detail; tempo (mostly slow) and tonality (and concordances thereof) are carefully assigned to the individual numbers, and so are melodic intensity and dramatic pace. Handel borrowed a good deal. A new source appears in *Theodora:* the chamber duets of Giovanni Carlo Maria Clari (see above, p. 58), but whatever is borrowed is rarely more than an incipit; the finished product is completely beyond the reach of the original composer. One look at Clari's duets (which Chrysander commendably published in the supplement to the Händelgesellschaft edition) will show this. Only in the overture did Handel use an entire movement, from Muffat's *Componimenti.* Bononcini (*Griselda*) also reappears, and of course our composer lent himself some material from his own works.

Finally, we must account for the presence of a castrato in the cast of an English oratorio, an event that had happened only once before. The role of Didimus was composed for Gaetano Guadagni (c. 1725–1792), a young man who later became one of the great international favorites, creating the role of Orfeo in the first version of Gluck's opera. Handel admired the voice of this fine singer, who took the trouble to study with Burney and with Handel himself in order to acquire a first-hand knowledge of the English style. Burney praised his ability to sing in English, adding that during his first years in England "he was more noticed in singing in English than in Italian." Handel subsequently gave many of the roles originally composed for Mrs. Cibber and other altos to Guadagni in revivals. Still, it is difficult to explain why Handel should have employed an Italian castrato at this late stage of his career unless one is willing to grant a nostalgic and half-conscious remembrance of the triumphs of yesteryear.[2] In the end, however, all such details lose their significance in the face of the freshness of original genius and the confident mastery over the whole region of his knowledge. *Theodora* was a remarkable departure for a man of Handel's age, and an eloquent proof of undiminished openness and plasticity of mind.

[5]

Theodora was first performed in Covent Garden on March 16, 1750, the cast consisting of Reinhold (Valens), Lowe (Septimius), Guadagni (Didimus), Frasi (Theodora), and Galli (Irene). It was a total failure. Some hold that the earthquake that to a degree had emptied London of those who could well afford to attend the theatre was responsible for the near-vacant houses; but the anecdotes connected with the three performances tend to dispute this. Morell relates that Handel said "the Jews will not come to it because it is a Christian story, and the Ladies will not come because it [is] a virtuous one." Whether true or not, the story is *ben trovato*. Young puts it more seriously: "[*Theodora's*] uncomfortable insistence on the ultimate devolution of Christian values in an unchristian

---

[2] This assumption is given support not only by the part that Handel composed for Guadagni in *Theodora* but also by some of his subsequent acts. The Tenbury manuscript of *Messiah* contains a version of "Thou art gone up on high" that Handel composed for the revival of *Messiah* in May, 1750, in which Guadagni sang. It is bedecked with runs and ornaments. The castrato was so indelibly associated with formal opera seria, and the style of writing for his kind of voice so stereotyped, that it was difficult for Handel to dismiss from his mind the habit of many decades. He admired great singing, and once he set his mind on using Guadagni, some of the idiosyncrasies of style also had to come back. We have seen that he could not altogether free himself from the similarly stereotyped effects of the rage aria, vestiges of which remain in many a fine bass number in the English oratorios, not least in *Messiah*.

world" was embarrassing to a public that wanted great paeans from the Old Testament, love stories, and vigorous trumpeting in the choruses. Everything seems to have militated for *Theodora*'s failure. The tragic end, the introversion, both were unaccustomed; nor could the public understand the character of such a figure as Theodora, who does not "wear the robes of formalized virginity" (Dean). Handel's unwillingness, while according Christians their due, to deprive the pagan Romans of theirs was found objectionable, and there have even been recent voices in England expressing dismay at Handel's failure to provide a triumphant ending. But though *Theodora* was the least successful of all the oratorios, Handel treasured it, even trying to revive his favorite in 1759, but death intervened. This shameful fate seems to cling to the great work; it is still unknown and a reliable score remains to be produced. Chrysander's is too arbitrarily put together, and the omission or abbreviation of many of the recitatives not only hurts dramatic continuity but often destroys it. Macfarren, who followed Chrysander's edition, outdid the German scholar: being a Victorian prig, he eliminated all references to the punishment contemplated for Theodora, an omission that, of course, gravely affected the dramatic motivation. If Chrysander used the correct text, Handel surely set to music a different one for Macfarren.

A sad postscript must be added to this already sad story. Handel butchered the score of this oratorio right after the first performance, and again in 1755, on the occasion of the sole revival during his lifetime. Fortunately, the original can be reconstructed without undue difficulty.

[6]

WE MUST RETURN TO late December 1749, when within a few days Handel composed incidental music to Tobias Smollett's *Alceste*. Smollett, a novelist but eager for theatrical laurels, is said to have offered *Alceste* to John Rich, who in turn induced Handel to compose the music in lieu of repayment of a debt. Rich went about his plans with a lavish hand. The Chevalier Servandoni, who built the pavilion for the Royal Fireworks, painted the scenery, and a large cast was employed to take care of both the speaking and the singing roles. But *Alceste* was never performed. The reasons for its abandonment are unknown, though the earthquake could have been one of them. More likely, the obstacles were neither physical nor esthetic. Sensing an impending financial failure, Rich, a shrewd businessman, probably decided to cut his losses before they reached appalling proportions. *Alceste* was neither opera nor play; it reverted to the pattern of the masque, that is, to a theatre tradition no longer in vogue. Smollett's libretto is lost, and from the remaining song lyrics we can form but a vague idea of what *Alceste* may have been, though it was undoubtedly a masque or semi-opera. This being the case, the play was the thing; the protagonists spoke, and the music was of secondary importance. We do possess the complete score, in its present shape no more than a torso, though it must have been a better work than what was ultimately fashioned from it. In the 18th century lost opportunities were seldom final, and the scenery as well as every musical ingredient of the unperformed *Alceste* was salvaged for other purposes, the bulk of the music going into *The Choice of Hercules,* while some of the other pieces were used as additions to newly revived oratorios. *Alceste* was a play in four acts, but since the music was incidental, if played continuously it would not suffice for more than one act. Handel did not attempt to enlarge it to a full-evening affair but cast about for a one-act libretto; apparently the resulting work was to be used as a complement to such shorter works as *Alexander's Feast.* In fact, *The Choice of Hercules* was announced as an additional third act to *Alexander's Feast.*

The new libretto to which *Alceste*'s music was adapted within one week at the end of June provides one of those biographical riddles to which there are a number of possible solutions. Each Handel biographer has had a favorite author, ranging from Spenser to Morell. The confusion, made richer by the misreading and misspelling of names, was greatly lessened by Dean, who established with near certainty that the play was based on an original poem whose author was Robert Lowth (1710–1787), clergyman, biblical scholar, and poet. That still leaves us with the problem of finding who made a libretto from the poem. Given Handel's relationship with Morell during these years of his life, it seems likely that it was the latter who shouldered this task, and perhaps even selected the subject. It does not really matter. The piece is a routine allegory in which Hercules must choose between the blandishments of Pleasure and of Virtue, with Virtue, if not more persuasive than the other goddess, nevertheless the winner. But the piece has some fine music, notably one of Handel's great ensemble pieces.

While the Smollett play was entirely within the tradition of the English theatre *with* music, *The Choice of Hercules,* a lyric work *in* music, is much more difficult to place. It is neither a full-fledged oratorio nor an English opera, nor can it be called a cantata, though Bach composed a cantata by the same title. Perhaps we should consider it a sort of English serenata.[3] At any rate, Handel's own designation, "a musical interlude," does not make much sense. At subsequent revivals *The Choice of Hercules* was placed between the two parts of *Alexander's Feast,* which made it an interlude in fact, albeit a totally irrelevant one. But this was an arbitrary arrangement that does not justify the designation.

The Choice of Hercules did not provide material stimulating to Handel. The book had no dramatic interest, no opportunity for characterization, nor even what usually saved the day in a pastoral or allegorical play without action—poetic language. Morell's words were not a trellis for imagery. Handel did not give the piece much attention, though he decked it with isolated beauties. Though a wizard at transplanting music, in this instance his lack of care in the adaptation is often evident, especially when illustrative-descriptive music is applied without change to an altogether different situation. He did not even bother to write out a new score. There were instructions to the copyist on how to handle the pieces taken from *Alceste,* only the new music and the numbers that underwent considerable reworking being scored by Handel. But the latter, as usual, are lessons in the composer's skill.

The first part of *The Choice of Hercules* is given over to Pleasure. The music, pastoral in tone, is delightfully orchestrated, the participating flutes, bassoons, and horns giving it an outdoor tinge. Pleasure's songs are graceful, sparkling, and warm, with a soupçon of eroticism. The aging Handel writes with remarkable simplicity, yet everything is musically telling. Virtue's songs, equally well made, are nevertheless perceptibly different; the warmth that makes Pleasure's music so engaging is absent. Pleasure first tries her charms—and they are considerable. "Turn the youth to joy and love" is a beguiling gavotte aria equalling the best in *L'Allegro.* The chorus takes up the inviting song in "Why, ah why this fond delay?" with Pleasure in the role of precentor. Finally Hercules must say something, and his "Yet can I hear that dulcet lay" is a very fine song even if the transfer from *Alceste* does not quite suit the mood. But its lightly sensuous languor does convey sentiments that do not offer encouragement to Virtue. Pleasure immediately takes advantage of this hesitation in an

---

[3] Bach's *Hercules auf dem Scheidewege* (Schmieder 213) was called a *dramma per musica.* It was, like a number of his secular cantatas, a little Baroque serenata-opera, though to designate it as such is not looked upon with favor. There are some aspects of Bach and his music that are as much in need of reinterpretation by the removal of pious mystifications as is the case with Handel. Bach's *Choice of Hercules* shared the fate of Handel's, though in reverse: a good deal of its music was bodily transferred to the *Christmas Oratorio.*

entrancing air, "Enjoy the sweet Elysian grove." Why she does this by proxy, through An Attendant on Pleasure (tenor), is an incomprehensible riddle, for this is perhaps the finest song in the entire score.

Now we come to the new music, the trio, the following two pieces, and part of the finale. Here is drama, if innocent Arcadian drama, and trim and tidy dramatic continuity. The trio, one of the masterpieces in ensemble writing, is dramatic-elegiac with a transparent tone. Pleasure remains winsome and alluring, Virtue retains her cool elegance, and as they alternate in their wooing, Hercules, vacillating, constantly interjects, "Where shall I go?" Handel's characterization—for in a way such it is—is masterly; the youth is the victim, not the master, of his fate. The dramatic continuity is ably maintained even though we know in advance that Virtue must be victorious; Handel is not satisfied to do the obvious, however nicely. Virtue now enjoins Hercules to be faithful to his "celestial birth" and "rise from earth immortal." The chorus seconds her impetuously: "Arise, arise, mount the steps ascent and claim thy native skies." The robust choral piece "breathes fire celestial," and Hercules responds: "Lead, Goddess, lead the way, thy awful power supremely wise." The large da capo aria is shapely and even a little heroic—Handel never permits compliance with destiny to be entirely unheroic—but one distinctly feels a difference in nuance hinting at a still unresolved conflict. Pleasure so clearly dominates the entire "oratorio" that one is not convinced that this was a free choice. The last chorus, "Virtue will place thee in that blest abode," is the one number in *The Choice of Hercules* with the proportions and weight of the great oratorio choruses. Its almost overwhelming power and cold violence is a brilliant stroke of the imagination, but at the expense of the work as a whole. It is completely extraneous to the framework, and misplaced at the end of such a slight, bucolic composition. Perhaps the strangest thing about it is its grimness. For some inexplicable reason Handel changed the piece from the original major to minor, thereby intensifying the dark atmosphere, then crowned it with a giant double fugue. Surely the ponderously menacing theme in the ritornel, which remains in the orchestra as a quasi ostinato, growling relentlessly, does not in the least suggest the heavenly bliss promised by Virtue. Perhaps Handel was annoyed by the mandatory surrender to Virtue—he clearly favored Pleasure—and in his anger loosed some of Jehovah's thunders of old. Magnificent as the great anthem is, it is not a suitable close. In general we might say that even though the music of *Alceste* and *The Choice of Hercules* is largely identical, the former was probably a better and more homogeneous work. Perhaps a skilful librettist could recreate the play—the legend is well known—and thus make possible the use of Handel's original setting.

The Choice of Hercules was first performed on March 1, 1751, as "an Additional New Act" to *Alexander's Feast*. We do not know the cast, but we can assume it to have consisted of Handel's steady company: Frasi, Galli, Lowe, and perhaps Guadagni. Whether it was successful of itself or was carried to success with the always popular *Alexander's Feast* is difficult to determine, but Handel had four full houses and made four worthwhile trips to the Bank of England.

[7]

AT THE BEGINNING OF 1750 the Earl of Shaftesbury in a letter to his cousin, James Harris, remarks that he never saw Handel "so cool and well. He is quite easy in his behaviour." He also reports that Handel, always an enthusiastic lover and connoisseur of painting, purchased "several pictures, particularly a large Rembrandt." This explains the withdrawal of a good deal of money from Handel's account in the Bank of England, which evidently went into the acquisition of the canvases. Handel's well-being was enhanced by his pleasure in seeing the Foundling Hospital prosper. In May he inaugurated the new, if as yet incomplete, organ he had presented to the Hospital and conducted a performance of *Messiah* in the institution's chapel. The house was oversold and a large number of persons, though ticket holders, had to be turned away. A second performance was therefore given a fortnight later (there is no instance in Handel's career when he did not honor tickets sold), and another full house doubled the Hospital's take. The successful yearly performance of *Messiah* became a tradition, with Handel playing and conducting as long as his health permitted. But what the Earl of Shaftesbury saw was only external; the aging musician's private thoughts must have been different. The year before he had lost one of his oldest comrades in arms, alongside whom he had fought many a battle: Heidegger, completely forgotten, died at the age of eighty-five. One year later Aaron Hill, Handel's first English librettist, followed. And now a living ghost came to remind him of the passing of time. Cuzzoni, the great prima donna of his early London years, the onetime toast of the musical world, reappeared on the London scene in May 1750, a faded woman, her voice gone, eking out a miserable existence. In an advertisement she requested the public to attend a benefit concert she was undertaking. After one more pathetic appeal to the public, "which shall be the last I will ever trouble them with" (May 1751), she left England.[4]

It was time to take stock of affairs. On June 1, 1750, "considering the Uncertainty of human Life," Handel made his will. It is a straightforward document without any rhetoric. He remembered his servant, his amanuensis, and several of his cousins, the bulk of the estate going to his niece, Johanna Friderike. According to newspaper reports, late in the summer Handel made a visit, his last, to Germany. Since he no longer had professional interests, such as recruiting singers, on the Continent, the trip must have been solely for the purpose of visiting the few relatives he still had. Nothing is known, however, about this journey beyond a notice that Handel was "terribly hurt" in an accident when his coach overturned while en route in Holland; but that it took place is confirmed by a reference Handel made to it in a letter to Telemann. The composer, now sixty-five and a heavily corpulent man, still had physical reserves to throw off the effects of the accident. Returned in the fall, he soon felt the creative urge stir in him; on January 21, 1751, Handel began the composition of *Jephtha.*

[4] Flower has Cuzzoni sing in *Messiah,* evidently confounding the benefit concert with the Foundling Hospital events. His story was duly repeated with proper embellishments by all popular biographers. Handel was charitable by nature and instinct, and he undoubtedly contributed to Cuzzoni's benefit, but he drew the line where artistic capability was concerned. Cuzzoni, a shadow of the great diva, could no longer sing such an exacting part. The poor woman soon disappeared, ending her life in Italy as a buttonmaker.

XX

THE YEARS HAVE THEIR OWN CAPRICE; RICH HARVESTS ARE
sometimes followed by meagre ones. The year 1751 was seemingly meagre;
yet it was in this year that Handel created what in many respects is
the most poignant of all his works. *Jephtha,* the last of the oratorios, is
an artist's vision of the life of the mind. Though not the most dramatic of
the biblical works, it is the most poetic, differing in character from all the
other great ones. The mood recalls Euripides's tragedy where Theseus and
Hercules have their last talk: a tender and sometimes terrible privacy full
of dark perplexities. The composer, after more than half a century spent in
incessant creative work, has now arrived at his last stage. The change is
momentous, wholly original, and shows a deeply searching mind, a stout
soul, and a clear composure. His mind is as enchanted in its suggestibility
as ever, his reaction to stimuli as swift and definite, but we now witness
the unusual: a mystical experience coming to a non-mystic.

There are neither prophets nor saints nor villains in *Jephtha,* only authentic human beings whose voices echo clearly, like a fountain in a still
courtyard. Thus this "sacred oratorio" is once more a human drama, the
Old Testament religious background notwithstanding. Even more than
Theodora, Jephtha is personal and depends little on Morell's vanities. The
elaborate background of thought on which the human drama is sustained
is unfailingly impressive, never shallow or insincere, nowhere obtruded
beyond the requirements of the characters and the scene. In fact, the
characterization is so convincing that the background creates itself; the

dramatic form is needed only because through it verities can best escape false accents. Thus Handel performed a tour de force, expressing undramatic feelings in a dramatic form. There is a certain conflict now between his cheerfully external technique and the introspective style of old age, yet the conflict was not at all to his disadvantage. Indeed, the aged composer, his eyesight failing, shows qualities we should not expect from the extrovert musician of earlier years. This great soul, much tried, seeks to find the final equilibrium, and the epic-dramatic composer becomes a pure lyricist, like Aeschylus, but one whose lyricism has a distinctly religious hue.

Jephtha has a story, characters, incidents, and development. Handel deals with all these with his wonted skill, but gradually we become aware (as we were earlier in *Theodora* but now increasingly so) that almost everywhere the libretto seems the lesser part. As we become familiar with the score we begin to divine the hidden ideas that are not in the script yet fill the great choruses. It is almost as if he uses the libretto as a pretext. This is the lyricism of a man who strikes against his own fate; it is not Jephtha who struggles here but Handel. To struggle with exterior elements is not so oppressive as to struggle with oneself. What drives Handel now is a peculiar "holy egotism" that uses men and human relationships for the ennobling of his own ideas. Solitariness—not solitude, for that he had always known—the ultimate loneliness of a sensitive man, drew those laments of one left in the world alone and in increasing darkness. But even in darkness, with total blindness threatening, he won equanimity, and the muse amid silence sings loud. The loneliness betrays itself in utterances whose cadence is almost stifled, and results in music hard to parallel anywhere.

It was in *Jephtha* that Handel took leave of his artistic career and created a symbol of his entire art. He did so with his old power and mental alertness and with that newly won serenity which he carried into his remaining years after the inner struggles were past. In our emotional admiration we cannot believe that a great dramatic composer could leave the arena without a farewell. It cannot be categorically denied that Handel, who hid himself so consistently both in his private life and in his works, stumbled on *Jephtha* as he did on some other of his oratorios, and what we perceive as intention is perhaps mere appearance created by accident. But there are some things about *Jephtha* that are so unusual as to constitute an exceptional case. In this work his imagination ranges even farther afield than in *Theodora*, and there is a peculiar distance from which he views earthly things, as if he were no longer altogether of this world. I cannot believe that he does not identify himself with Jephtha to a considerable extent, perhaps subconsciously, trusting the incognito that the biblical dignity confers on his hero.

"Sing, goddess, the anger of Peleus' son Achilles." These are the first words of the *Iliad*—world literature opens with a song of emotion, of passion. The ancient poet of patriarchal life already saw the eternal danger and curse in human passion, the anger of men who must live in a constant life-and-death struggle with themselves and with their environment. The great Attic dramatists represented this struggle by strokes of fate, and the principal problem of a tragedy of fate came to be to what extent the situation itself ruled the drama. When we say that a man's fate is in his character we are referring to the way he meets a fate coming from an external source. But it is necessary that fate should be something other than the person it would destroy. Only in the final moments of confrontation is there a mystic union between the two. The Greeks with their marvelous artistic sense symbolized by deity a passion that descends on a man from without. This was stylized mythology which at the same time became sensuously concrete. To Handel the hero and his fate do belong together, and once they have met they cannot be separated, but he was more fascinated by the moment that preceded their meeting. It is at those moments in *Jephtha* that his lyricism reaches its richest depths, the depth of a questioning mind regarding itself, wondering whether the divine is the upper side of the human or whether the human is the under side of the divine. This is the drama of doubt, perhaps Handel's most personal drama. Here, in the great choruses, it is more than anything else the pregnancy of poetic statement, the eloquence of thought, the expressiveness of the imagery that underlie Handel's effects.

But to what extent is man the generator of his acts? The relationship between the doer of an act and the act itself is the central problem of such a drama; every stylization, every arrangement depends on where these two are separated and where they are one, how one determines the other. Handel saw the tragic in *Jephtha* not so much in the situation created by fate as in the inner experience of suffering. To him there was no large gulf between suffering and action; suffering was action turned inward, the words of the libretto notwithstanding. The greater the compulsion of the external action in *Jephtha* the more deeply inward does the centre of the tragic struggle move. Handel wanted to dissolve in music the sharply formulated words that he found unequal to cope with the moments where a man reveals himself. Where Morell merely gives the rhetorical reflexes of impending catastrophe, Handel burrows downward, into the depths where the moral dilemmas dwell. Morell could see only an exterior problem created by fate and the suffering it brought with it; Handel saw an inner purification. This inevitably led him, however, away from the purely dramatic to the lyric, to the sombre choric lyricism of the Greeks; he no longer needed realistic bas-reliefs around the statues of the heroes. Thus he reached the perfection of antique form, of the great Greek dramatists, at the same time embracing the supreme individual experience of a Christian. The Greek drama in Hebrew vestments is only a theme and background; it merely goes to show how independent of actualities is true poetry. The characters no longer expose themselves through action but through meditation. Jephtha is no longer facing fate, he has become the symbol of a deep and universal human relationship. His feelings are revelations of transcendent purity, for they have ceased to be merely individual manifestations.

Theodora and *Jephtha* show how different the musical setting can be from the libretto that called it into existence. This ability of Handel's to refine a mediocre libretto through his music, to endow it with a core and with psychological penetration, is most admirably carried out in *Jephtha*. And perhaps the difference is strongest where the external happenings are seemingly faithfully followed. Handel's failing eyes see far into the distance with prophetic clarity, yet he no longer sees the reality around him. He revels in the world he created—the music shows it if the words do not—and at the same time he sees his own tragic situation: there is little time left in life. At sixty-six he was past the ordinary 18th-century life span, his life work was finished—and much of it even forgotten. The choruses in *Jephtha* seem to tell us that they are visions that, though long in gestation, have little to do with those which preceded *Theodora*. Handel does not descend to Hell as did Dante before starting his ascent to Paradise; the great Olympian composer descends from Olympus to discover from mortals what is Olympian. The religion that is expressed in *Jephtha* is not the religion of an epoch but that of a soul, and the hereafter toward which the choruses lead is not the fantasy of an imagination detached from life. This religion is life itself, enhanced, condensed, deepened and fulfilled, still strongly reflecting life's trials but also its warmth, its sounds, its pictures. This was something so personal and so profoundly human that Handel repeatedly removed Morell's references to the Almighty; his religious sentiments must be expressed through human suffering. The human spirit appears in *Jephtha* as a profound solvent; not that of the Enlightenment, but indeed that of Christianity. This is the triumph of the new synthesis which recaptures the almost forgotten spiritual discipline of centuries.

Jephtha is striking in its mingled strength and delicacy. There are few slack passages, the writing is throughout firm and controlled. If it is not the tight drama that it sets out to be, the composition's exceptional qualities do not in any case rest on dramatic-theatrical consistency. The construction, except for the core of the piece, is perhaps a little loose, especially in the first act, though the masterful concentration, power, and boldness of expression combined with admirable technical efficiency make us forget this. Yet towards the end of the work, as the dénouement approaches, there are scenes that are nearly fatal to the oratorio.

[2]

THE SUBJECT OF *Jephtha* was familiar, and the several musical settings of the biblical story were not unknown to Handel and Morell. But with one exception, the prototypes—if we may call them that—should not detain us. The only exception, Carissimi's *Jephte,* was certainly well known to Handel because he earlier borrowed from it for *Samson.* We Carissimi, but the attraction lay more in the new means of expression offered by the Italian composer than in the genre he so significantly advanced. Even when Handel quoted from Carissimi he seldom tampered with the essence of the music, using it rather as an insertion suitable for a certain occasion. Significantly, his *Jephtha* shows no borrowing from have seen (p. 81 ff.) that Handel was impressed by and indebted to *Jephte.* Morell, who studied not only Judges, where Jephtha's story is told, but the several librettos fashioned therefrom, proved to be quite independent of all of them. As a matter of fact, while he retained the essence of the biblical story, all his characters except Jephtha himself are his own invention. In the Bible, Jephtha (or Jephthah) was expelled from Gilead because he was the illegitimate son of a harlot. His half-brothers, born in wedlock, resented his questionable status and drove him away from their common home. Jephtha grew up in a friendly region, where he made a name for himself as a God-fearing man and a born leader. During his absence from Gilead the country was invaded by the Ammonites and held in subjection for eighteen years. Sorely tried and without hope, the elders of Gilead, among them Jephtha's brothers, appealed to their erstwhile victim to "come and be our captain." Jephtha acceded and while girding for battle made a vow that if he were victorious, "whatever cometh forth of the door of my home to meet me when I return . . . I will offer it for a burnt offering." There followed "a very great slaughter" of the Ammonites; and on Jephtha's return, the first person emerging from the house to greet him was his daughter, unnamed in the Bible. Though deeply shaken, Jephtha felt obliged to keep his sworn word, so he "did with her according to his vow." So far the Bible. The tragic ending of Jephtha's story is not only parallel but palpably identical with that of Agamemnon's in which his daughter, Iphigenia, was similarly selected by fate as an innocent victim. There are other variants of the legend, all of which, whether from Greek or Hebrew antiquity, obviously go back to a much older common source; folklore migrates and is very tenacious. Morell, who was also a classical scholar, undoubtedly knew the plays of Aeschylus and Euripides; the name he gave to Jephtha's daughter, Iphis, appears to be derived from Iphigenia. Perhaps he even knew Racine's great tragedy, for he conscientiously explored the relevant literature and utilized the librettos made from the biblical story. Among the latter was an oratorio composed by Handel's erstwhile friend and subsequent bête noire Maurice Greene.

Morell went about his task with fair skill, even mustering here and there a language that is vivid and colorful and which, of course, was of considerable help to Handel. Though admittedly even poor versifiers can exhibit sudden flashes of poetry, Morell's were not due to such rare inspiration. He resorted to the old literary trick of plucking suitable lines and words from the best available poets, including Milton and Pope. In Morell's time this was an accepted procedure in letters as well as in music, and Morell did not disguise his sources. The characters he invented are Zebul, a soldier and half-brother of Jephtha, who is instrumental in obtaining the command of the Jewish army for Jephtha; Storgè, Jephtha's wife; and Hamor, suitor of Iphis. The roles as well as the continuity are well developed, all the threads converging neatly enough in the great choral scene where the priests, loath to carry out the sacrifice, plead: "Hear our prayer in this distress."

Now suddenly Morell proceeds to scatter the lines apart again. The great wall of tragedy frightened him, and he was looking for a flower in that crannied wall. To elaborate the stories of the Bible is always tempting and always dangerous. While the original story presented the librettist with a fundamentally simple and logical dramatic situation (as of course did Euripides), Morell sentimentalized it, but sentimentality was anathema to Handel. The cleansing effect of tragedy rests on a peculiar mood which shakes and tears before it elevates; this Morell was unable to face. The motives underlying the radical change he gave the drama are obscure. Morell was in a double dilemma, which he did try to solve in a Christian spirit—and he failed dismally. With Euripides everything is in

the struggle of passions, and the knot can be untied only by divine intervention. But Christian faith rejected human sacrifice, it could only tolerate it symbolically. Thus Morell wanted to avoid dealing with death with
the customary ease—or brutality—of the Old Testament. In addition
there was the reluctance of the age to see a tragic ending, all of which
drove Morell to a compromise for which he invoked an *angelus ex
machina.* There was of course the obvious scriptural precedent in the
story of Abraham and Isaac. The Angel comes and, accepting the sacrifice
symbolically, promises eternal bliss to everyone. The recitative must be
quoted in its entirety to show its incongruity.

Rise, Jephtha. And ye reverend priests, withhold the slaught'rous hand. No vow
can disannul the law of God; nor such was its intent, when rightly scann'd; yet
still shall be fulfilled. Thy daughter, Jephtha, thou must dedicate to God, in
pure and virgin state for ever, as not an object meet for sacrifice, else had she
fall'n a holocaust to God. The Holy Spirit, that dictated thy vow, bade thus
explain it, and approves thy faith.

This comes close to negating the drama, as well as introducing an extraneous New Testament note. The Angel and the Holy Spirit are new
elements not even remotely connected with the original plot. Worst of all,
it now appears that the stirring drama, Jephtha's agonized suffering, was
all sham: the sacrifice was never intended to be carried out; Jephtha just
failed to scan the script "rightly." The changes could have wrecked the
whole work, but Handel once more was able to bypass Morell. As in
Theodora, he largely disregarded the new meaning and sentiments arbitrarily imposed upon the story. The beauty of the music does not depend
on the text or even on the theme. Reality evaporates into a sort of fluid
dream in which images are formed. The tragic, perplexity-ridden Jephtha
does not simply turn into a happy paterfamilias whose only daughter became a nun; his suffering is transfigured into joy, while the neat and
tender fadeout of Iphis makes an impression of moving comeliness that
remains in the listener's mind. This could not be kept up, however, beyond a point. The great chorus "Theme sublime of endless praise" gives
plausibility to this unexpected dénouement; anything that follows is
clearly an excrescence. Indeed, it appears that this chorus was originally
intended to close the oratorio; it should in modern performances be
adopted as the finale. Only a quintet, added in 1753, should be salvaged
from what follows; it could easily be inserted before the finale.

Jephtha, more than most other characters created by Handel, grows
steadily from beginning to end. There is something simple but eloquently

powerful in him, disdaining every flower of rhetoric; he wants to affect
with one quality only, but with that tremendously. Like Colleoni he sits
on a magnificent horse, but no matter how splendid his mount it does not
detract attention from its rider. It is Jephtha who sustains the large fabric
of this tale upon his shoulders. Iphis, that young woman led by fate into
identifying herself with a cause of which she has little understanding, is
an admirable figure, and the episodes in which her personal fate is involved are spirited and moving. Though related to Theodora, she is of this
world. She does rise to transcendence, but her road is a longer one than
Theodora's; she has to renounce life, which Theodora does not even cherish. Handel breathed a rare spirit into Storgè, one of the great, forceful,
and passionately unresigned matriarchs of Nitocris's breed. She remains
moving and memorable in spite of Morell's attempt in the finale to make a
sentimental provincial matron out of her. Zebul and Hamor are accessories, but Hamor especially is used to advantage in propelling the
drama.

[3]

The solo numbers in *Jephtha* are all music in a modern language, but the choruses, as in the Greek drama, retain their Doric
language, which gives them a particular solemn elevation. They are not
exercises in rhetoric, in grandiloquence; *pectus est quod disertum facit.*
All the emotional overtones and undertones that ordinarily hover upon
the very borders of consciousness are given powerful and moving expression; we see the visionary's native skies.

The musical world was somewhat shaken when it was discovered
that most of these choruses were based on borrowed material, that, indeed, *Jephtha* is heavily indebted to a Bohemian composer, as well as to a
number of Handel's instrumental and vocal works, among them *Agrippina, Ariodante, Lotario,* and *Acis and Galatea.* The new investor who
lent musical funds to Handel was a German-Bohemian by the name of
Habermann (1706–1783), called Franz Wenzel or František Václav,
according to which part of the hyphenated heritage is considered dominant. He was one of the large fraternity of German musicians who under
the long Habsburg rule found a congenial home in that musical country,
Bohemia. Well-regarded in his time and occupying good positions both at
home and abroad, Habermann as a composer shows little more than the
natural musicality and excellent craftsmanship of his clan. He would have
shared the obscurity of the many solid fellow choirmasters active in his

time, all competent and devoted to their calling, had he not supplied ideas to Handel. Upon discovery of his exalted role, he was promptly invested with the title "the Bohemian Handel," which is a curious case of immortality acquired by inverted history.[1] *Philomela pia seu Missae 6 a 4 vocibus* . . . was printed in 1747. How and when the score got into Handel's hands is unknown. Dent believes that Mattheson was the intermediary, but this is not documented. The matter is unimportant; Handel always kept a weather eye on new publications, subscribing to many, and it is quite possible that he asked his correspondents to supply him with copies. The charge that his failing health and waning inspiration compelled him to resort to more borrowings than in many other dramatic works is falsely true. Such music did stimulate him, and perhaps at this stage of his life he preferred to choose a star to navigate by, but he was never enveloped in its light, his identity was never in danger, and he was never confined by the materials used. We shall discuss the whole complicated question of the borrowings in Chapter XXII; suffice it to say at present that whether the borrowings can be justified is not the point at issue. What concerns us is that Handel has justified his material. The thematic material borrowed from Habermann acted as a musical fertilizer, providing the stimulus for a variety of ideas, but the final shaping of these ideas seldom depended on the original mould.

The overture to *Jephtha*, an excellent piece, was borrowed from *Alceste*. Handel composed a new minuet for the third part, leading directly to a recitative that presents Zebul without any preliminaries in the midst of an agitated situation. Habermann appears in the first aria, Zebul's "Pour forth no more unheeded pray'rs," and in the following chorus, "No more to Ammon's god and king, fierce Moloch shall our cymbals ring." The aria is routine, and those who detect fatigue in Handel's procedure could point to the sinfonia, which was taken over from Habermann's Mass without significant alteration, thus affecting the entire accompaniment to an undistinguished vocal part. But perhaps Handel was simply not interested in Zebul, for in the chorus he bestirs himself, and although the material still comes from Habermann, its development is out of all proportion to the original idea. This chorus did descend from the Kyrie of Habermann's First Mass, but while the background is by no means left in obscurity, the foreground is taken by heartier and lustier

---

[1] This sort of history is further complicated by some recent lexicographical gaffes. The new *Riemann Musik Lexikon* (1959) dutifully cites Handel's indebtedness to Habermann's six Masses, adding a list of works in which Handel made use of them. The list begins with *Agrippina* (1709)!

sounds: Handel is writing "pagan music." The fugue "Chemosh no more will we adore," with its stubborn insistence on the same tone, conjures up the old zestful Handel.

Jephtha enters, greeted by Zebul. "Virtue my soul shall embrace, goodness shall make me great" is one of those arias that some critics find "a little too conventionally pleasing." Perhaps the *galant* tone is to blame; the aria is in the modern style of the neo-Neapolitans. But this piece, and most of the others, despite an occasional glibness in the drawing, are perfect of their kind, achieving frequent and sensitive if evasive beauty. Handel did not care for Morell's platitudinous words and simply proceeded to compose an eloquent stream of music rather than a concentrated movement. His dramatic instinct warned him that Jephtha was not as yet a compelling figure, and since no conflict threatened, there was no need for a higher emotional temperature. The melody is exquisite, the setting delectable. Handel's musical sensitivity evokes admiration in the very first measures, as the angular intervals of the ritornel are smoothed into a gliding melody the minute the voice enters. Storgè, at her first appearance, is the loving wife bemoaning "a painful separation" from her husband, who is about to take the field. Her brief secco recitative shows the particular care Handel took with the secco in this work. The adjacent aria, "In gentle murmurs will I mourn, as mourns the mate-forsaken dove," with its light melancholy recalls the many fine "dove" songs of the past, but this engaging piece has a symphonic insistence in the accompaniment coupled with harmonic boldness that is characteristic of Handel's late style. Very attractive are the frequent unaccompanied entries of voice and solo flute, which are then balanced by long-held notes either in the bass or in the voice.

Hamor, espying Iphis, welcomes "the sight of thee, my love," changing from the recitative to a perfectly proportioned aria, "Dull delay, in piercing anguish bids thy faithful lover languish while he pants for bliss in vain." Once more Handel was confronted by a text supposedly the expression of ardor, but more nearly expressing self-pity and even the posturing a man assumes before a mirror. Ignoring the words—and pretty nearly Hamor himself—Handel wrote a warm love song of natural and impetuous bent. Iphis's reaction to this is a little cautious; her aria, as she reminds Hamor of his military duties, sounds like temporizing: "Take the heart you fondly gave, lodg'd in your breast with mine . . . Thus with double ardour brave, sure conquest will be thine." Nor is the music particularly impressive, though pretty enough with its capricious rhythms. The two lovers now unite in a duet, "These labours past, how happy we," which offers much more attractive music. Handel here leaves behind everything he used to cherish in this genre, forgetting Steffani and Baroque opera, for what we hear could just as well have come from an opera by John Christian Bach or the young Mozart.

Jephtha, ready for battle, now utters his vow. At this point we should expect him to sing his words with an apocalyptic ring, like Jove making his vow in *Semele;* strangely, all that Handel could or would muster is a pallid echo of the old Venetian *giuramento* recitative. Even more surprisingly, he never later changed this short recitative, although he must have felt its inadequacy. But then the indifference is suddenly shaken off, and the clean edge of thought, the heated thrust of feeling of a solitary spirit teeming with uncomfortable questions, burst upon us. "O God, behold our sore distress" is the first of this oratorio's great choruses in which Handel infuses into his music the strange emotional tension of a dream, the first of the personal confessions that make *Jephtha* unique among the oratorios. The largeness of the design and the solemn opening recall the anthem choruses of old, but this is not a paean praising the king or Jehovah, the scene is lit by a darkened sun. The material comes from Habermann's Fifth Mass, in which the *Qui tollis* begins with a double fugue, now serving the same function in Handel's chorus. But he instantly whittles away any excess musical verbiage, the substance becomes compact and expressive, it no longer owes allegiance to anyone but Handel.

The charged emotional climate churned up by this great chorus is not permitted to soften, though Storgè's following scene offers sombre and powerful music without the fearfully contorted chromaticism of the choral piece. "Some dire event hangs o'er our heads," she warns in the introductory recitative, but the aria already deals with "scenes of horror." This is violent music, but what is envisaged is the carnage of war; the impending family tragedy is not yet suspected. Handel borrows a little figure from the fourth movement of his A minor Concerto Grosso (Opus 6, No. 4), a wild and romantic piece, which he uses with telling effect in the accompaniment. The composer's superscription calls for *con spirito;* this is not a lament but a protest, and he resorts to magnificent pictorial illustrations, racing unisons, to bring out with visual clarity the dark forebodings.

Presently Handel relents as Iphis tries to dispel her mother's "black illusions of the night." Her air, "The smiling dawn of happy days," reveals at its best Handel's capacity for combining feeling and formal elegance, and the sun suddenly shines in the grimly sheltered place. The air is a dance piece, a bourrée, and somehow one feels that in its misty loveliness there is a poignancy of recollections of days and ways informed with the piety of Handel's remote childhood. In the act-ending chorus, one of the greatest "tone paintings" ever achieved in song, the earth is no longer pained by man; he is scarcely noticed through the whirling dust cloud kicked up by this tremendous musical poem, full of action and massive in detail and imagination. Here is a picture in which there are no subdued tones; it is as if Handel himself were powerless to curb the surging feeling that he is still bound to this world, he will not listen to the voice which bids him loose his ties. This is a renewal of faith in life, a reawakening to the strength of nature, which stands constant in the march of doom; the nature worshipper of earlier days is back at his altar, as compelling as ever. Then, with the line "They now contract their boist'rous pride and lash with idle rage the laughing strand," the supposedly weary old composer indeed lashes out with a vigor that few young men could summon. Chorus and orchestra, the latter reinforced with horns, forget all discipline and, flushed with elation, burst into rejoicing, the roaring, shaking peals of joyous laughter filling page after page with dancing black notes. This revel, incidentally, is a fugue! The idea also came from one of Habermann's Masses, but Handel struck it with his majestic stride, after which the "Bohemian Handel" had to relinquish all claims to his title.

Hamor opens the second act by announcing victory over the Ammonites. Since the victory was achieved with the active help of angels, the following chorus, "Cherub and Seraphim, unbodied forms," is not martial. Light figurations in the instruments accompany a harmonically simple and transparent choral setting. The fugue that follows this prelude is another matter. While nothing like the tremendous first chorus in Act One, the imagery of "they ride on whirlwinds" was sufficient to kindle in Handel's imagination a lusty descriptive piece. There follows Hamor's assurance to Iphis that even during the stress of battle he thought of her. While his air is pleasant enough, Hamor does not commit himself, and the music tells little of his character. Iphis, preparing to meet her returning father, asks her companions to adorn her like a bride and "tune the soft melodious lute, pleasant harp and warbling flute." The air has the quiet and gentle sincerity of its predecessor in the first act but a considerable gain in substance. Iphis is still a young girl, undisturbed by doubts or fears. Zebul's aria "Freedom now once more possessing" is an entirely superfluous piece borrowed in toto from *Agrippina,* though as we look at the score we are amazed at the stamina of that first opera.

Now Handel must cope with Morell's pious entr'acte, the mandatory obeisance to Jehovah, before he can continue with the drama. Jephtha praises the valor of Zebul and Hamor, "but the glory is the Lord's." There follows an aria, "His mighty arm with sudden blow dispers'd and quell'd the haughty foe." Handel took care of the situation by returning to the old opera aria with a military accompaniment. This is a good piece and appropriate for the occasion, but its inordinate length makes cuts necessary. One observes with amusement the presence of *galant* elements in what is essentially an old-fashioned opera seria aria complete with coloratura of a decidedly dated vintage. At that, the *galant* element came from Habermann's First Mass; the vocal part is Handel's. According to the oratorio code all this must be crowned with a grand chorus, and for the first time in *Jephtha* Handel gives us an honest ceremonial anthem with all stops pulled out. "In glory high, in might serene" is a splendid chorus of the old Hallelujah cut, except that the stately choral part is supported by an orchestral accompaniment more mobile and imaginative than in the old days.

The charming little sinfonia that opens the third scene of Act Two is clearly a theatrical device to portray Iphis while giving her time to approach her returning father. The pastoral quality of the siciliana sets the tone for her "Welcome as the cheerful light," a gavotte. Handel is careful to safeguard the innocence of the victim of the drama, who is still unconscious of the fate awaiting her. Every number Iphis has sung has been a graceful dance piece, and the intense perception of loveliness gives sublimity to the sweetness and radiance of mere beauty. The virgins take up the gavotte as if to prolong the calm before the storm.

When Jephtha realizes who is the first one to greet him, joy at once turns to raging grief. He cries in despair: "Begone, my child, thou hast undone thy father!" Iphis flees. The recitative is short and wild, Jephtha is in despair, but in the aria "Open thy marble jaws, O tomb, and hide me" he takes hold of himself. This magnificent dramatic piece is controlled, essentially singable and rounded, yet it conveys almost suffocatingly the father's grief. Handel achieves this by an angular melodic line, unexpected pauses, and rhythmic and prosodic irregularities. (Chrysander, as he so often does, hurts the powerful unison ritornel by harmonizing it.) In the consternation that follows, Zebul asks his brother why he is so cruel to the daughter who came to greet him. Jephtha answers sadly by telling of his vow, ending with "alas! it was my daughter, and she dies." "First perish, thou, and perish all the world," cries Storgè tearing into her husband with outraged and unforgiving fury. The scene is overwhelming, as is this woman who, seeing life's fruit turn to ashes, challenges the whole world.

The construction of her scene is remarkable. It starts as an accompanied recitative marked *concitato,* but every time Storgè remembers her daughter she softens (Handel marks it *adagio*), only to burst out anew (*concitato*). The orchestra seethes as the accompagnato imperceptibly turns into an aria, Storgè frenziedly demanding "let other creatures die." Suddenly she stops (*dolce*), thinking of her only child, "so fair, so chaste, so good," the words sung in little desperately touching gasps. But the frenzy returns; Handel is unsparing in such moments.

The drama now proceeds relentlessly as Hamor offers himself for the sacrifice. He did not show much temperament in the preceding scenes, but this air, like all the others here, is full of tragic force and a naturalness that, of all qualities, is the most poignant in a tragedy. This poignancy is carried to unsurpassed heights in the quartet in which the four chief characters of the drama unite. The ensemble, rare in serious works of the mid-century, is timed with uncanny sensitiveness; it is like a cadenza that sums up the action but is inseparable from it. This is a piece in which there is not, as they say of athletes, an ounce of spare flesh, even though the subject is rich. The quartet is not only gripping in concept but is composed with singular grace and delicacy, the diction masterfully clear and true. The short ritornel, with its falling augmented fourths and grave repetitions, brings back memories of the old ostinato of grief. Handel's, as usual, is not a true ostinato, but it creates the same feeling of fatality. "O spare your daughter," begins Zebul, "spare my child," begs Storgè, while Hamor, overcome, can at first only sigh, "my love." They continue, their vocal line becoming more and more animated, while Jephtha stubbornly insists, "Recorded stands my vow in Heav'n above." "Recall thy impious vow," the others demand, but Jephtha angrily counters, "I'll hear no more: her doom is fix'd as fate." He has the last word. The music responds sensitively to the changing pulse of mood and movement, while preserving an underlying gravity of rhythm in the accompaniment, which is independent of the vocal ensemble.

Iphis returns, ready to die. Morell, with remarkable clumsiness, makes her orate: "This vital breath with content I shall resign." Though Handel's music is not tailored to the words, he composed an aria that is once more simple but true and good; the dance rhythms remain, but only as a reminder. Handel labored hard on this little song, he knew that a young girl could not instantly turn into a tragedienne. His efforts produced a brief tragical epigram, *aperçu* rather than tragedy. Such simplicity of expression can seldom be found allied with such depth of feeling. The song has a devastating effect on Jephtha. It has been said that *un Inglese italiano è un diavolo incarnato.* An Italianate Englishman now sums up a century and a half of Italian opera, creating an accompanied recitative—the essence of Italian dramatic music—the like of which we shall find only in Florestan's anguished recitative at the beginning of the second act of *Fidelio.*[2] If there ever was a "through-composed" piece, this is it. It was in *Orlando* that Handel first tried to depict a man bereft of his senses; then came the powerful scene in which Saul desperately struggles to retain his sanity; but now he creates a figure sunk in bottomless misery. "Deeper and deeper still, thy goodness, child, pierceth a father's bleeding heart." By setting broken phrases, Handel achieves at the end an effect of psychological disintegration, at the same time throwing sharp intermittent gleams of light on the man Jephtha was. "Tears are for lighter grief"; we suffer, we do not weep, as when Lear is betrayed to the storm, and we live through every detail of his dreadful agony.

The composition of this scene was an exhausting experience, yet it left Handel with the strength to dive into the unfathomable blackness of life, to compose his greatest choral piece, one that is unparalleled in the entire choral literature. "How dark, O Lord, are Thy decrees," a colossus of a score in four sections, carries us into a place of darkness and exile and shadows, a place of deadly disquiet. What Handel achieves in this passionate self-confession cannot be summed up verbally, but, paradoxically, it is with this chorus that we can perhaps explain Handel himself. An entrepreneur and *maçon d'art* (as Rodin called himself), who provided entertainment for the aristocracy and later for the wider circles of the English middle classes, who always had an eye for his audience, who in this very oratorio still composed arias that aimed to please, he now completely abandoned his public. He can see solace nowhere and comes to the shattering realization that "No solid peace we mortals know on earth below." Formal faith, morality, and prayer no longer suffice. The great oaths and curses of the Old Testament, its verdicts and lessons he was accustomed to carry out magnificently in his music, but here the problem is more vast, for now he wonders whether man is the heir or orphan of creation. And the question must be answered by ploughing the endless unharvestable seas of a man's soul; his own soul, because this great threnody mourns Handel himself. His enormous vitality had by now ebbed; while he was younger and robust, fate could not defeat him, but now he was old and alone, and the faithful companion, the body, was fail-

[2] The comparison has occurred to others, too, and we think it justified. But to call Handel's recitative a *Vorahnung* of Beethoven's is neither criticism nor history but spiritualism.

ing him. It was during the composition of "How dark, O Lord, are Thy decrees" that he was forced to lay aside the score because of the onslaught of blindness. One eye's vision was gone altogether; intermittent clearing of the other eye permitted him to resume work, but it took months to finish, and he knew that this was the end, that his remaining days would be spent in darkness. Yet now the once ardent fighter and artistic speculator, stricken, discovered in himself a humility able to range itself against all the trials of life. He now felt himself to be freed from bondage to a cruel fate, in the recognition that life is governed and ordained. This was a religious confession, arrived at after a terrible struggle. The struggle is depicted in this awesome chorus, and as we listen to it we discover that we are intruders upon passionate privacies.

Theologians have doubted whether divine transcendence can really be conceived by the human mind on the plane of esthetic genius. God can be addressed but not expressed. But can we accept the thesis that spiritual man as artist always reflects and never creates? This proud and noble man, who has been declared to be with Bach the "singer of Christ," "the musician in ordinary to the Protestant religion," did write music that outwardly meets standards set by posterity on the basis of *Messiah,* but essentially he was always an entertainer, a glorious man of the theatre. With very few exceptions, he never wrote music that could be called devotional. It was music filled with a shrewd and kindly humanity, dramatic force, and incomparable musical inventiveness. If after *Theodora* and *Jephtha* we look back at the masques and pastorals and the great biblical dramas, we see that their religious exterior is but a garment draped by a sculptor on his marble effigy. But with these two works it was really a question of his personal faith, to represent Christianity, but without reference to its customary symbols. He remembered the sentimental-sensuous conception of Brockes, whose Passion he once set to music, in which "the believing soul" sings, and he remembered such songs as *Ein Lämmlein geht und trägt die Schuld.* But Pietism and facile Evangelism, as we have seen, had never appealed to him, and after a few youthful essays he had abandoned them. Neither, now, did the secular pomp and circumstance of the English Church, for which he used to compose grand and stately anthems and Te Deums. Nor could he return to the visions and ecstasies of the medieval German mystics, or to the spiritual love songs of the Latins. He wanted to submit to a higher order, but he could do so only apart from traditional religion, reaching an understanding and salvation by himself, as a person, as a feeling, thinking human being.

The struggle was titanic but he found the answer. In the first chorus of this tetralogy, with its implacable iambic rhythm steadily pounding in the orchestra while the voices grope questioningly in darkness, we feel that Handel is so steeped in despair, so entangled in doubts, that he will not be able to reach any affirmation. But at the end he cannot tear himself away from the one sentence that shows him the light. Morell ended the fourth and final section of the chorus with "What God ordains is right." Handel set the words but then changed them to "Whatever is, is right." The quotation from Pope is in his handwriting. Now the text read: "Yet on this maxim still obey, whatever is, is right." At first we feel that this idea is put as a quasi question. Handel separates the last line: "Whatever is," sung by the soprano, stands apart, then the full chorus nails down the answer with a clipped "is right." At this point Handel quotes from Theodora's farewell to the world; the eloquent sentence fits miraculously into this situation, both musically and spiritually. Then in the final measures certainty supplants the remaining doubts: the chorus is united, solemnly proclaiming "Whatever is, is right."

The third act opens with Jephtha ready to carry out the sacrifice. He has regained his composure and now laments in more coherent tones: "a father off'ring up his only child in vow'd return for victory and peace." But he is still agitated, the sombre arioso-recitative has lost little of the poignancy of the earlier pieces. Jephtha's next air is somewhat puzzling. It is an exceedingly beautiful song about which opinions may nevertheless differ, though most critics acclaim it enthusiastically. Jephtha seems to have undergone a sudden spiritual change. Calling on the angels, "Waft her, angels, through the skies," he sings in *galant* style an aria that contrives to entrap these pages in a tender charm. Jephtha finds solace in the thought that after her death Iphis will be carried "far above yon azure plain" to eternal bliss. But the fine song anticipates; the *angelus ex machina* is given away, and the sudden-risen piety has the appearance of a mask. The aria is a well-constructed piece, though it might be considered just a little too well rounded off. Some may find that this is sorrow drawn to an exquisite point of pain, while to others, and we are among them, the elegant coloraturas are a little too fluent and incongruous in the mouth of this deeply stirred man. The piece, with its almost cloying richness of texture, fills us with pity and perhaps wrings a few tears, but the great perspective of the tragic, the peculiar mixture of shock and elation, is missing. Equally masterly in composition but far more felicitous in expression is Iphis's farewell song, "Farewell ye limpid streams." The flush of life that so irresistibly coursed in her previous songs is recalled by the suavely gliding siciliana, but this melody is enfolded in silence. Her open innocence is still here; nevertheless one is aware of disturbing potentialities beneath it—this song is also a poem of the lure of death. The solemnly pacing basses of the second, E major, section and the polyphonic accompaniment lend the melody an almost hymnic quality, as if Handel, who never wrote one, now celebrates her apotheosis in a chorale paraphrase or prelude.

The priests, distraught by the role assigned to them, beseech Jephtha to abandon his vow. With this aching chorus Handel returns to the shadows. The pronounced chromaticism interprets the priests' troubled uncertainty and their abhorrence of taking the child's life. There is no ritornel, the stifling atmosphere of the earlier "personal" choruses is back. And so is something else that we seldom encounter in Handel: echoes of the old chromatic motet of the German cantors, the kind they composed when they beheld with awe the Venetians' new, modern, and expressive art. The mighty double fugue is far beyond the reach of these cantors (always, of course, excepting Bach), but this music does reflect their world as in a glass that is colored but not distorted.

To prepare for the happy ending, Handel called upon the last movement of his early Violin Sonata in D to furnish the sinfonia, a sort of *Engelskonzert*. It is a pretty piece and wears well after all those years. The Angel appears and, after proclaiming the message of deliverance, sings, "Happy, Iphis, shalt thou live." This is a very good song, rhythmically piquant and with a spirited accompaniment, but it is also a long one.[3] Much shorter and much more admirable is Jephtha's "Forever blessed be thy holy name." Though only a few measures long, it movingly translates the mind of a man who has found comfort and peace.[4] Handel now proceeds to a chorus that has all the earmarks of a dignified yet warm and unostentatious finale. "Theme sublime of endless praise" is an attractive and engaging piece, closer to the anthem than to the other dark choruses. It does start with the great choral gesture, but what follows is a warm and peaceful choral song, the many suspensions preventing hardening of the texture. The vocal writing is superbly euphonious, the orchestra simply tagging along. There are neither trumpets nor drums; Handel wanted the choral sound to dominate—there was no need for brilliance. Impressive

---

[3] The Angel's aria found great favor with the latter-day or neo-Victorians. Suggestions have been made for the performance of this song—and from respectable quarters—that even Hollywood would envy. A recent German book dealing with choral works proposes to have the Angel sing *da lontano*, with organ accompaniment, and with an "ethereal voice."

[4] I am amazed that no one has yet tried to make a metaphysical case of this melody; its resemblance to the Passion chorale, *O Haupt voll Blut*, is unmistakable.

are the passages where long-held notes over a pedal point proclaim "[thy mercies still] *endure.*"

Unfortunately, what Morell did at this juncture really plays havoc with atmosphere and dramatic meaning. Perhaps he remembered the public's apathy toward the tragic ending of *Theodora*; at any rate, he was determined to make everyone happy, on stage and in the audience. As Dean remarks, "the finale is characteristic of that mixture of Puritanism and sentimentality that permeated so much religious thought in the England of 1750." First comes a happy family reunion. "Let me congratulate this happy turn, my honour'd brother," begins Zebul, after which he sings an aria. Storgè's recitative, "O let me fold thee in a mother's arms," is similarly followed by an aria; and Hamor also has his turn. Finally, the reprieved heroine joins the family circle in the role of a good bourgeois marriage counselor. "My faithful Hamor," she advises, "may that Providence which gently claims, or forces our submission, direct thee to some happier choice." And of course she too sings an air. What we have here is the old operatic recipe: every protagonist must get an exit aria no matter what the dramatic situation may be. This must have been trying to Handel, who had long since given up the practice; it is surprising that three of the four airs are quite acceptable pieces. But Storgè's is poor; its tripping little coloraturas are more suitable for a soubrette than for this woman of iron. They make her vivaciously wrongheaded.

And now it was time for trumpeting and Hallelujahs. Handel not only obliged but composed two rousing anthems that could grace any of the oratorios except this one, for here they are anticlimactic and superfluous. The quintet, which was added in 1753, is really a duet with the other voices later joining in a ripieno fashion. This is an excellent piece that should and could be salvaged. As suggested above, by omitting the final numbers and ending the work with the fine chorus "Theme sublime of endless praise," *Jephtha* would gain a coherence that too much insistence on a happy ending denies it.

[4]

HANDEL BEGAN *Jephtha* January 21, 1751. On February 13, well advanced in the score, he had to stop. "Got so far as this," he writes in the middle of the great chorus in the second act, "unable to continue because of weakening of the sight of my left eye." [5] Ten days later the composer

---

[5] The annotation is in German with a curious English twist: "biss hierher komen den 13 Febr. 1751 verhindert worden wegen des gesichts meines linken auges so relaxt." See the illustration on Plate xv.

felt "a little better" and resumed work, but the relief was short-lived; on the 27th he had to break off again. In the face of this calamity he remained steady and disciplined. The oratorio season took place as usual, and he even played the organ. The deposits in the Bank of England show that *Belshazzar, Alexander's Feast, Esther,* and *Judas Maccabaeus* were as popular as ever. The season came to an abrupt end with the death of the Prince of Wales on March 20, and all entertainments were cancelled. His vision now was gravely impaired, and Handel tried to rest. After a short "cure" at Cheltenham he returned to London, receiving treatment from an eye surgeon, and on June 18 resumed work on *Jephtha,* but he was no longer equal to his usual phenomenal tempo; fall was approaching before the score was finished. The autograph itself shows the struggle; it is full of corrections and second thoughts. The Lenten season of 1752 started on February 14, with *Joshua* followed by *Hercules;* then on February 26 *Jephtha* had its première, the cast consisting of Beard (Jephtha), Galli (Storgè), Frasi (Iphis), Brent (Hamor), and Wass (Zebul). Brent, a counter tenor, was a new Handelian singer of transitory importance, but Wass, the bass, became a frequent replacement for Reinhold. Chrysander was aware of the significance of *Jephtha* and took unusual care with the editing of the score, even issuing a facsimile of the autograph. Unfortunately, at that stage the technique of such reproductions was still unequal to the nuances; the many important alterations that Handel made in pencil do not show. Yet while much of Chrysander's work is admirable, and his detailed comments are valuable, his arbitrary ways did not desert him. He failed to heed Handel's corrections in Morell's text even though these corrections touch upon the essence of the composer's frame of mind.

We do not know how *Jephtha* was received. Mary Delany thought it "a very fine [oratorio], but very different from any of his others." Whether her perceptive observation was shared by the public, or whether they found the happy ending sufficient to cancel the searching, sharp, and stirring power of the rest, we are unable to ascertain. The oratorio was revived the next year, and again in 1756 and 1758; a total of seven performances indicates it won at least a modicum of acceptance.

XXI

O N AUGUST 17, 1752, THE *General Advertiser* REPORTED
that "George-Frederick Handel, Esq; the celebrated Composer of Musick
was seized a few Days ago with a Paralytick Disorder in his Head, which
has deprived him of Sight." On November 3 [1] he was "couch'd by William
Bromfield, Esq," the Princess of Wales's surgeon. There was a certain improvement in January 1753, but only for a few days; by the end of that
month Handel had a relapse and almost total blindness ensued. The
newspaper notices were manifestly incorrect in their diagnosis of paraly-
sis; the stroke Handel suffered when he was compelled to go to Aix-la-
Chapelle was probably recalled. This time he was in full command of his
mind, and though suffering from other physical ailments brought about
by age and obesity, his eyes were the victim of no cerebral disorder but
of cataracts, which inept surgery worsened.

"Aetatis 66," Handel wrote on the last page of *Jephtha*. The annotation, unusual for him, brings back Penseroso's lines:

> *May at last my weary age*
> *Find out the peaceful hermitage.*

This was the end, the last original work, and all the other concerns of life
seem to retire into the background. The outside world disappeared not
only from his sight; he no longer went anywhere except to his concerts

[1] The English calendar changed on September 3, 1752; henceforth our dates follow the "New Style."

and to the services at St. George's Church. Posterity has in general accepted as fact that, with the extinction of his sight, Handel's spirit collapsed under the strain, that the crippled composer's remaining years bore only fruits of frost. "That fortitude which had supported him under afflictions of another kind now deserted him," says Hawkins, while others speak of "broken spirit" and "great despondency." It seems to us that such a view is unreliable in fact and controvertible in interpretation. Blind and ill, Handel was still Handel; idleness and mere drift were impossible for him, work was his anodyne, and he filled his sightless days with incessant labor. No, the flame was not extinct. A man who has lived in continuous creative activity, who has lived strongly and resolutely through much adversity, could not, by being dealt one more blow, become a disburdened Atlas. There is no question that at times one is aware of a creative fatigue, but Schering already warned that such manifestations in certain numbers of *Jephtha* are misleading, that there is no sign of the failure of powerful imagination. As we take a closer look at Handel's remaining years we shall see at every point a more virile and positive figure than the helpless recluse who has hitherto represented the blind musician in the general imagination. He retired into his sightless world without rancor, without a feeling of defeat. With his mistress, Solitude, who understood him and accorded with his feelings, he was in uninterrupted and happy contact with a host of familiar spirits. He will still have some beautiful days, for even in November there are such days, recalling a more vivid season; and he will find a strong supporter—Wisdom. Handel's spirit was alive until the end; then, in his last days, he turned from life ready to face whatever new enterprise death might turn out to be.

To make some kind of adjustment to his blindness was Handel's first challenge, and he met it. Though without the lifelong habit of making music in darkness that made John Stanley an accomplished performer not in the least restricted or inhibited, he still managed to continue playing and directing.[2] He still conducted some performances in the year of his death, and up to 1758 rehearsals were held in his home the day before the performance. Only eight days before his death he attended a performance of *Messiah*. Though unable to read, he had not lost his former interests. We see him subscribing at the end of 1753 to the works of the late Aaron

[2] John Stanley (1713–1786), blind from childhood, nevertheless received a thorough musical training. Gainsborough's portrait shows a pensive, sensitive person who, according to Burney, was an excellent and exacting musician. Stanley, with John Christopher Smith, the younger, became Handel's chief exponent, conducting various performances of his works during his last years and after his death.

Hill, a four-volume collection of the writings of his old friend and sometime librettist. The many alterations and additions to the oratorios revived
during these seven years reveal a firm grip, a comprehension both of form
and substance. How fully the physically invalid composer was in possession of his mental powers, though dictating his music as the blind Milton
did his poetry, is perhaps most eloquently illustrated by the alterations in
"Wise men flatt'ring may deceive you," done for the revival of *Judas
Maccabaeus* in 1758; its freshness and delicate orchestration rival the best
of his work in that genre. The year before he had added to *Esther* a magnificent duet and chorus, "Sion now her head shall raise." In both cases he
had to rely also on his phenomenal memory, which apparently remained
intact, because in both instances he developed borrowed material in his
inimitably inventive manner. Finally, 1757 saw another major, full-
evening "new" work, *The Triumph of Time and Truth.*

[2]

THE ORATORIO SEASON OF 1753 began on March 9 with *Alexander's Feast* and *The Choice of Hercules.* No concerto was announced,
though the performances themselves may have been conducted by Handel. *Jephtha, Judas Maccabaeus, Samson,* and *Messiah* followed, all of them
except *Messiah* repeated. (The annual charity performances of the latter
oratorio obviated the need for repeating it in public performances.) The
following year's Lenten season saw revivals of *Alexander Balus, Deborah,
Saul, Joshua, Judas Maccabaeus,* and *Samson,* the season again concluding with *Messiah.* On May 15, 1754, Handel conducted *Messiah* for the
last time in the Foundling Hospital; soon afterwards John Christopher
Smith, the younger, was appointed organist and conductor for these benefits, but Handel always attended them. The 1755 and 1756 seasons also
presented the old favorites, though Handel insisted on one performance
of *Theodora* in 1755. As we scan this list we observe how the public held
fast to its original judgment. *Israel in Egypt* still puzzled them, or as Mrs.
Delany remarked in 1756, it "did not take, it is too solemn for common
ears." And of course *Theodora,* as we have seen, was simply not accepted.
But Handel's account at the Bank of England grew steadily.

By this time the aged composer had become nationally famous, his
works were performed everywhere in the provinces, and his name was the
chief attraction on the programs of the many charity events. The times
had changed indeed. From 1753 onward at the King's Theatre in the

Haymarket, which used to be the headquarters of his enemies when not tenanted by Handel, his works were performed under Stanley's direction. Deutsch tells us that there were instances when Handel's name appeared simultaneously in the advertisements of three of London's theatres. Oxford too had changed since the days of the irascible Dr. Hearne. Now the university had a professor of music, William Hayes, an ardent Handelian, under whom a number of performances took place yearly "attended with very crouded Audiences." These performances were considered to "equal in Grandeur and Elegance any of the kind that have been exhibited in this Kingdom." Some of Handel's experienced singers were in great demand for such occasions, travelling over the country. Among the conductors, besides the indefatigable Dr. Hayes, Stanley, and Christopher Smith, we find such notable composers as Dr. Boyce. There is even on record a performance of two of Handel's songs at a concert in New York in 1756. Handel's fame was such that as early as 1753 Walsh offered twenty-two of his oratorios in a sort of *Gesamtausgabe,* bound in twelve volumes.

On August 6, 1756, Handel executed the first codicil to his will, taking care of the shares made vacant by the death of several persons, increasing the benefits to others, and assigning new bequests to Morell and Newburgh Hamilton. John Christopher Smith, the elder, Handel's copyist, amanuensis, and friend since the Halle school days, with whom he for some unknown reason fell out for a while, was reinstated and his legacy generously increased. No provisions were made for the younger Smith, a pupil and loyal aide to the old composer. Handel presumably expected the younger man to inherit his father's effects, as indeed he did.[3] The few ties Handel still had to Germany were not overlooked. In September 1754 he wrote, or rather dictated, a letter (still in French) to Telemann. The friendly note inquired about the other old composer's health and announced the consignment of a shipment of "exotic plants" to his colleague, who was a devoted horticulturalist.

Esther opened the 1757 season on February 25; on March 11 *The Triumph of Time and Truth,* "altered from the Italian, with several new Additions," introduced the first new full-evening entertainment offered by Handel since *Jephtha.* The new "oratorio" was the third version of *Il Trionfo del Tempo e della Verità* of about 1707, the second being the 1737 Covent Garden production of *Il Trionfo del Tempo e del Disinganno.*

[3] These effects included all of Handel's original scores, which the younger Smith eventually surrendered to King George III, an ardent Handelian, who settled a pension on him.

Morell now made an English version, adding a new figure, Deceit. Since the mandatory gestures of the biblical oratorio were absent, Morell felt free to indulge in what for him was high poetry. Handel, too, felt free to put together on a sufficiently simple plan a series of happy ideas separately elaborated, picking up the thoughts as he found them in his capacious memory. *The Triumph of Time and Truth* is an allegory that does not lead anywhere in particular. It may at times be loosely knit and wandering, but it never loses its charm and poetry. Without mystery, it is full of clear and definite detail, such as could be shaped only by a brain altogether unencumbered by "great despondency." The unchanging rhythm of quietude and contentment that informs it evokes an atmosphere of peace and kindliness. Fifty years of music passes before Handel's mind's eye. He reminisces, putting into the score all the things that were close to his heart, the bucolic nature pieces, the great choruses, arias, here melting, there meditative. *The Triumph of Time and Truth* for a moment brought together the two worlds of Handel, the years brimming with activity and the ones restricted to memories. The revisions, new accompaniments, new orchestration, and the few new pieces are all done with thoughtful care, the music, except where Handel deliberately departs from Morell, always ably adapted to the new words. This is perhaps not a work for the repertory, too many of its numbers being well known in other contexts, but it should be heard, for it is an admirable summary of Handel's entire musical career. Going back all the way to the serenata composed in Rome, following with excerpts from the Chandos Anthems, some of the operas, and up to the Foundling Hospital Anthem, he touched upon every phase. Yet *The Triumph of Time and Truth* is not a potpourri, the pasticcio of old; Handel was holding a review. If he could no longer see his beloved pictures hanging on the walls, he could still hear the ones he himself created in sound. Memories have a way of being vagrant, but also fragrant, and to describe this work as esthetic pantheism is to use a cold formula. The public liked these memories; there were three repeat performances and a revival during the next season.

A second codicil was added to the will on March 22. His faithful attendant, Peter le Blond, having died, Handel now remembers the servant's nephew. In general, we see that whenever a beneficiary is removed by death, rather than cancel the bequest Handel would extend it to the next of kin. A third codicil was drawn up on August 4. It contained the following new items: John Rich was given the "Great Organ that stands at the Theatre Royal in Covent Garden"; Jennens received two pictures by Denner; and Bernard Granville, Mary Delany's brother, two Rembrandts; while the Foundling Hospital became the possessor of "a fair copy of the Score and all Parts" of *Messiah*.[4]

After the close of the 1758 season, in the summer, Handel went to Tunbridge Wells, allegedly to be treated by John Taylor, Sr., an eye specialist also known as "the Chevalier." This "ophtalmieter" was a quack, though eventually boasting the title of court oculist to George III. If the operation really took place (Taylor's memoirs are filled with unreliable and inaccurate stories), this suave adventurer can claim to have contributed substantially to the misery of the two greatest musicians of the age. It was Taylor who in 1750 operated on the blind Bach—equally unsuccessfully.

During his last season the seventy-four-year-old and seriously ailing Handel still oversaw the performances, even playing and conducting intermittently. When John Christopher Smith conducted, the blind man was led into the theatre, and occasionally to the organ or harpsichord. This last season was as strenuous as many in his heyday: *Solomon, Samson, Judas Maccabaeus*, as well as again one of the orphans, *Susanna*, were given in several performances, all of them with "additions and alterations." But Handel knew that the end was near, and he was ready for it. The season closed on April 6, 1759, and on the 11th Handel dictated the fourth and final codicil to his will. His old friend Dubourg was remembered, also Thomas Harris, and a gift of a thousand pounds was earmarked for the Society for the Support of Decayed Musicians.

In addition to the personal items there was a curious paragraph in this last codicil.

I hope to have the permission of the Dean and Chapter of Westminster to be buried in Westminster Abbey in a private manner at the discretion of my Executor, Mr. Amyand and I desire that my said Executor may have leave to erect a monument for me there and that any sum not Exceeding Six Hundred Pounds be expended for that purpose at the discretion of my said Executor.

It was altogether unheard of for anyone to suggest that he be buried in the national pantheon; the suggestion usually came from a "grateful nation." At first glance, Handel's wish appears either naive or preposterous,

---

[4] In the gradual appreciation of Rembrandt, England played an honorable part. From the first quarter of the 18th century there was a lively interest in the painter among English collectors, the unwanted corollary to this interest being the production of forged Rembrandts as early as 1750. That the authenticity of one of Handel's Rembrandts was questioned even then is shown by Handel's wording of the bequest. "I give to Granville Esquire of Holles Street the Landskip, a view of the Rhine, done by Rembrand, & another Landskip said to be done by the same hand." The second Rembrandt was an earlier present from Bernard Granville. Both pictures are now lost.

but if we follow his career in England we shall realize that it was neither; it was entirely in keeping with his character. It is impossible not to see in this act of Handel's a profession of faith that is also a clear refutation of the national claims advanced by a number of German scholars. The qualities of heart and mind that enabled Handel to identify himself with England, and the courage and force with which he triumphed over all obstacles to end his life as an English institution, devotedly acclaimed by his compatriots, naturally called for some sort of acknowledgment. We are convinced as we read about the infirm old man's continued activities, running his oratorio seasons, dictating the changes and new numbers to Christopher Smith, that if he had to go through all the struggles and defeats of his career again he would do so, because this was his world. He never capitulated and after each resurgence his forum became larger until it encompassed the nation. His character did not deteriorate, he never became pretentious or snobbish; he accepted himself and his genius with simplicity and with immense gusto and enjoyed fame and power to the full, but he also took every opportunity to be kind. He belonged in England, and since by the end of his life he was considered a great Briton, not only *de jure*, by virtue of his naturalization almost forty years before, but by acclamation, which no legal document, only a people's heart, can offer, he simply wanted to be laid to rest where such persons in England are laid to rest. His was not a preposterous demand but a request that seemed perfectly natural to him. His wrestling with reality now gave way to quiet certitude; he stated his wish in plain terms, including the request for private interment. This wish, unusual as it was, was neither questioned nor even considered out of the ordinary; his place among the nation's great seemed as natural to his fellow subjects as it did to him. When he died the newspapers were unanimous in extolling the greatness of "the most excellent Musician Any Age ever produced." Earlier in this book we called Handel's purposeful wanderings a great quest, and it was a quest in which he had very early decided that the will must play a large part. It was one of his abiding characteristics to dismiss the past; his mind was always on the present and the future. He forgot himself in the cause and was able to identify the cause with himself. Westminster Abbey was the logical end of the quest, the one thing conceivable among all that was inconceivable.

[3]

SHORTLY BEFORE his death, Handel was visited by Selina Hastings, Countess of Huntingdon, the celebrated religious leader of a sect of

Calvinistic Methodists, the founder and generous supporter of many chapels, and an energetic collaborator of Wesley and Whitefield. In her recollections [5] she says that she visited Handel, whom she seems to have known, at his request. "He is now old, and at the close of his long career; yet he is not dismayed at the prospect before him," adding that the Reverend Martin Madan "has been with him often, and he seems much attached to him." There is no proof to support this version of Madan's role in Handel's life. During his last days Handel saw few persons outside his valet John Duburk, the two Smiths, Dr. Warren his physician, and James Smyth, a London perfumer who seems to have been an intimate during his last years. Madan, a cousin of William Cowper and a favorite of "the Queen of the Methodists," was not the type of person to whom Handel would be attracted. Originally a barrister of pronouncedly debonair habits until converted by John Wesley, he became a minister and a fervent worker for the Countess of Huntingdon. A man of extreme views, he later became the centre of a storm when, on "scriptural authority," he advocated polygamy.

During the April 6 performance of *Messiah*, Handel suffered a fainting spell. As we have seen, he executed a final codicil to his will on the 11th; he knew that his final hour was at hand, and it came in the morning of April 14, 1759. We have an account of his last moments by Smyth, who, though not present in the death chamber, was close by. His report is in a letter to Bernard Granville, printed in the *Autobiography and Correspondence of Mary Granville, Mrs. Delany* (London, 1861).

According to your request to me when you left London, that I would let you know when our good friend departed this life, *on Saturday last at 8 o'clock in morn died the great and good Mr. Handel.* He was sensible to the last moment; made a codicil to his will on Tuesday, ordered to be buried privately in Westminster Abbey, and a monument not to exceed £600 for him. I had the pleasure to reconcile him to his old friends; he saw them and forgave them, and let all their legacies stand! [6] In the codicil he left many legacies to his friends, and among the rest he left me £500, and has left to you the two pictures *you formerly gave him.* [7] He took leave of all his friends on Friday morning, and desired to see nobody but the Doctor and Apothecary and myself. At 7 o'clock in the evening he took leave of me, and told me we "should meet again"; as soon as I was gone he told his servant *"not* to let me come to him any more, for that he had *now done with the world."* He died as he lived—a good

---

[5] *The Life of the Countess of Huntingdon,* London, 1844.

[6] This undoubtedly refers to John Christopher Smith, the elder; we are not aware of any other reconciliation.

[7] This is a mistake, only one of the pictures was a gift.

Christian, with a true sense of his duty to God and man, and in perfect charity with all the world.

The funeral took place on April 20. According to the *London Evening Post* "The Bishop, Prebendaries, and the whole Choirs [singers of the Chapel Royal, St. Paul's, and the Abbey itself] attended, to pay the last Honours due to his Memory; and it is computed there were not fewer than 3000 Persons present on this Occasion." The English people disregarded Handel's wish for a private service. Dr. Croft's Funeral Anthem was sung to a large gathering, an English composer's tribute to the man who wanted to be buried in Westminster Abbey because "having, with universal Applause, spent upwards of fifty Years in England," he too had become an English composer.

XXII

THOSE TO WHOM THE ROMANCE OF HISTORY MAKES A strong appeal will always be attracted by the story of the musician, reared in the humble atmosphere of the cantor's guild, who succeeded by sheer force of character and talent in making himself the musical ruler of England. Romance, however, is the wrong word to apply to a life that contains so much that cannot by any stretch of language be called romantic. The story of Handel may perhaps be best described as a stern drama in which the masterful will of a man of genius is in conflict with a variety of forces, which he succeeded in dominating but to which he also in part succumbed. Handel belongs among those who, irked by stability and settled jobs, follow the beckoning of adventure with unconquerable optimism. His ingenuity and confidence would never recognize obstacles. He was intolerant of delay, indifferent to formalities, had a genius for organization and great powers of persuasion, and his driving force was incalculable. Always possessed of a central calm, he found the fortitude, even in the midst of time-consuming and vexatious affairs of theatrical production, to muster the exacting labor necessary for large new works. Bluff, sagacious, immensely persevering, but consistently human alike in his virtues and his failings, he was a real man dealing with a real world. Questions of whence and where did not interest him; he was not a philosopher nor a religious contemplative. It is when he allows his mind to be anchored in earth and humanity that he is most distinctly a poet. To cast his story in a religious-romantic mould is to do his greatness disservice. He had the

English spirit: he liked the beautiful but he liked the useful too; nothing was farther from him than *l'art pour l'art*. He could have said with Dryden, "my chief endeavours are to delight the age in which I live."

Handel always royally assumed the privileges of a great man. Patient at one moment, irascible at the next, resolutely courageous in the face of threats, he was an optimist with a fearless propensity for taking chances, always summoning the energy to extricate himself when his hopes proved elusive. Indeed, his was a philosophy of risk and leadership. It may perhaps be said that Handel's life was from beginning to end a magnificent gamble, and his works were merely the most serious gamble of all. He took a long series of dangerous corners and took them in his own way. As a composer-entrepreneur he ignored many of the accepted rules of the game, yet most of the men and women who worked with him, after some initial bewilderment, fell under his spell and into his difficult, exacting step. He never bothered to explain himself, and the varied episodes of his career, bracing though they are as studies of valor in action, are teasing in the final questions they pose. The numerous Handelian anecdotes are no substitute for more illuminating self-confessions when a tricky biographical landscape is surveyed. Besides, the proportion of truth to legend in these anecdotes is far smaller than is generally the case. Here is a man who in a peculiar sense made the musical theatre his home, but divest him of the footlights, follow him home in a London street—how does he look then? Formidable in power and even more so when left out of it, he won resounding triumphs and courted egregious disaster. He is as difficult to appraise as the nation whose spirit he so superbly embodied. Is there a final sense to be made of him? No man could have chatted and played more genially in Mary Delany's or Susanna Cibber's music room, but no man was more rigorous in barring his threshold to others. He was a solitary man, hard to know and hard to portray, but what most eludes description is the singularity of his essential being.

Carefully reasoned scholarly essays are gradually displacing those legends which inevitably adhere to the name of a man so remarkable in character and achievement and so studiously secluded from the public eye. There are few historical characters who display so little of their secret thoughts, and few who make us more inclined to believe that the inner man differs markedly from the outer. We know what he looked like, what he liked to eat and drink, what he wore, and what jokes he made, and whenever he lost his temper we are told about it. Further, it would not be difficult to compile from his known utterances, few as they are, some sort of philosophy of life of which no one need be ashamed. The bones of his

life are thus easily resurrected, but the life they supported is a very different matter. Sincere and forceful as he was in his actions, Handel never
cast aside his reserve, and his works remain the chief key with which he
chose to unlock his heart. He lived until 1759, but a span of seventy-four
years is inadequate to suggest his output of energy; his recreation was a
change of work. But vitality alone does not constitute greatness, and
quantity, though evidence of vitality, is not quality. During those many
years he enjoyed few idle moments, and his competitors and adversaries
certainly enjoyed no quiet ones. Burney recalled that Handel worked so
incessantly that he had no time "to mix in society, or partake of public
amusements." But he took everything seriously; above all he took life seriously. No one knew better what a struggle life is, how the consequences
of the smallest weakness can snowball, and how constantly one must be
on guard in order to prevail. In the end, when all the material has been
sifted and ordered, when scholarship has drawn its inferences and framed
its inductions, the mind is left overwhelmingly aware of something transcendent. In Edward Arlington Robinson's words,

> *There are complexities and reservations*
> *Where there are poets, for they are alone,*
> *Wherever they are.*

[2]

We have vivid records of the impression Handel made on a
number of observers. He was a tall man, always well dressed though not
ostentatiously so. We know that in his younger years, before he became
corpulent, he was considered handsome, but to the irreverent eyes of contemporaries his later massiveness was obvious and ridiculous. Nevertheless, the gluttony attributed to him, as in Goupy's famous caricatures (see
above, p. 244), is questionable. Handel was a very large man who needed
considerable food; he insisted on a bountiful table and was something of
a gourmet. But had he been a real glutton he would have been a gouty
invalid, as were so many of his English contemporaries in comfortable circumstances, instead of living to the ripe age of seventy-four at a time
when average life-expectancy was considerably below that. The portraits
and busts [1] usually show him in repose, and what strikes one above all in

---

[1] See J. M. Coopersmith's *List of Portraits, Sculptures, etc., of Georg Friedrich
Händel*, in *Music & Letters*, 1932. Aside from the curious clinging to the German
spelling of Handel's name by an American in an English publication, this is an excellent summary of the subject. (As early as 1715 the composer signed himself George
Frideric Handel.) The fine chapter on Handel's portraits in W. C. Smith's *Concerning*

these likenesses is the fixed look of the eyes, eyes of a calm and fearless arrogance, with a look of determined remoteness. In ordinary unconvivial society, and when not under the stimulus of excitement, he was distinguished by his dignity and ceremonial manner. Or as Dr. Johnson would have said, he was "knowing and conversible." A cultivated man of the world, well read, he could hold his own in discussions, and he was a connoisseur of painting.[2] But when affronted he could burst out violently (Burney attests that Handel could swear fluently in five languages), for like many men of genius he was of an autocratic disposition, intensely jealous of his independence, and his self-confidence was like a rock.

He could be obstinate and unyielding, and as Hawkins says, he "had a fixed resolution never to admit a rival," but there was a largeness and loyalty about him that prevented him from indulging in pettiness. Most of the time he was good-natured, full of humor, kindliness, and charity, and no fact concerning the inwardness of his private life is better established than his delight in children. He was always attentive and generous to his family. When he learned that a relative by marriage, a widowed Frau Händel living in the old family home in Halle, was being charged rent, he instructed his brother-in-law, Michaelsen, to permit her to live there free. Never vindictive, he was also a realist. Owen Swiney, who absconded with the box-office receipts of *Teseo* in 1713, thereby causing an almost catastrophic financial difficulty, became, twenty years later, a useful business associate. The same is true of the exasperating singers who, after joining the competitors' camp, were readmitted to his company. Of his humor Burney said: "Had he been as great a master of the English language as Swift, his bon mots would have been as frequent, and somewhat of the same kind." Burney also quotes "an Irish gentleman, Dr. Quinn," whose veracity he respected, as a person who in Dublin "had the pleasure of seeing and conversing with Handel." Dr. Quinn relates that "Handel, with his other excellences, was possessed of a good stock of humour, no man ever told a story with more. But it was a requisite for the hearer to have a competent knowledge of at least four languages: English, French, Italian, and German; for in his narrative he made use of them all." In small and congenial gatherings he was amiability itself, not disdaining to accompany amateur singers and playing the harpsichord hours on end. Mary Delany (then still Mrs. Pendarves) described such an occasion in a letter to her sister, Ann Granville, in 1734. "Mr. Handel was in

---

Handel (1948) contains valuable additions to the reconstruction of Handel's physical appearance.

[2] "Among the few amusements he gave into, the going to view collections of pictures upon sale was the chief" (Hawkins).

the best humour in the world, and played lessons and accompanied Strada and all the ladies that sang from seven o'clock till eleven."

He was definitely partial to the ladies, who wholeheartedly reciprocated. Of George II's five daughters the three older princesses, Anne, Amelia, and Caroline, were his pupils and faithful auditors. Anne, the Princess Royal, his favorite pupil, was a musician of near-professional capabilities. She was a good singer and harpsichordist and well versed in composition. After her marriage to William of Orange she formed a little orchestra, which she directed from the harpsichord in frequent palace concerts. The admiration was mutual, and the Princess often used her influence to help Handel in difficult situations. We have seen Susanna Cibber's warm friendship for Handel, and Mary Delany idolized the composer throughout a long life. Mrs. Delany, previously Mrs. Pendarves, was born Mary Granville in 1700 and died, with faculties unimpaired, at the age of eighty-five. She first heard Handel play when she was ten.[3] Always surrounded by distinguished people, she corresponded with many, among them with Swift during his last sane years. Interested in science, letters, and art, and a great music-lover, she acquired a certain fame with an art form of her own devising: the representation of flowers in "paper mosaics," of which there is a large collection in the British Museum, praised by no lesser judges than Sir Joshua Reynolds and Horace Walpole. Her admiration for Handel was unbounded. She even "made a drama for an oratorio out of Milton's *Paradise Lost,* to give Mr. Handel to compose to." It was tactfully passed over by Handel.

Handel grasped without effort the social as well as the economic and esthetic aspects of his surroundings, an important ingredient of his success being that he was not only a composer but a man of the world, a Londoner who knew his town in success and failure. Everything essential to the pattern of contemporary life found some counterpart in his experience.

Since English men of letters enjoyed social privileges and all sorts of important appointments, they were more or less actively engaged in political intrigue, like the clergy, and this unfortunately left its mark not only on their dealings, which were often unscrupulous and even vicious, but also on the quality of their works. Most of Handel's friends were Whigs, but his principle was always to stay out of politics and not to join positively any of the sets into which the literati were divided. It was

---

[3] Incidentally, the Wyches and the Granvilles were related and one wonders whether Handel's early acquaintance with Mary and her family was not due to some recommendation from Hamburg.

nevertheless unavoidable that Handel, a public figure, a German like the unpopular King, should be drawn, if innocently, into political maneuvers.

It is characteristic that Handel's charitable activities and contributions increased with his affluence, though, as we have seen, he was ready to lend a hand even when his personal fortunes were at their lowest. His awareness of supreme capacity made him sometimes intolerant of criticism and impatient of opposition, and in the hurry of events he sometimes judged amiss, acted hastily, even unjustly. But throughout he was borne up by the consciousness of high purpose and unfailing resource. For all his inconsistency, he never changed his aim; he only modified his methods to suit a changing world.

Handel's was an era when the whims of the singers had to be obeyed. In Italy, and in the musical colonies established by Italians, if a singer did not like an aria it had to be changed, and the composer usually submitted every number to the appropriate members of the cast for their approval. Even such powerful personalities as Legrenzi or Scarlatti had difficulty in asserting themselves. Not so Handel; he knew better than anyone since Lully how to enforce the composer's rights and wishes. Hawkins puts this amusingly: "In his comparison of the merits of a composer and those of a singer, Handel estimated the latter at a very low rate." Mainwaring reports that "the perfect authority which Handel maintained over the singers and the band, or rather the total subjection in which he held them, was of more consequence than can well be imagined." During rehearsals he could be a tyrant, giving offenders a fearful tongue-lashing. He "subdued the humours" of the capricious singers "not by lenitives but by sharp corrosives," says Mainwaring. These "corrosives" could take the form of bodily threat. His first biographer tells the story of Handel seizing the recalcitrant Cuzzoni "by the waist, and if she made any more words, swore that he would fling her out of the window."

As an opera director, he was a singular phenomenon. The insatiable enjoyment of creation he united with the bravado and readiness for action of a *condottiere*. We have seen that Handel used members of the English diplomatic service for recruiting singers abroad, and he seems to have been on excellent terms with several of them—the banker Joseph Smith in Venice was a veritable postal agent. Incidentally, it is quite possible that the various envoys procured for him new musical publications. He experienced financial difficulties, but W. C. Smith has proved that there is no evidence that he was ever close to "bankruptcy," the favorite contretemps of romantic biographers. Hawkins estimated that the income Handel received from oratorio performances after the establishment of regular seasons was more than £2,000 a year, a very respectable sum, to which must be added the income from the published scores and his various annuities from the Crown, not to speak of the dividends from his investments. He was not really interested in money for its own sake, for his way of life did not change in his days of affluence, but he regarded it as a symbol of success and recognition. Handel's banking operations (in which he was interested and knowledgeable) were in the care of Gael Morris, "a broker of the first eminence," says Hawkins. Indeed, Handel was an English middle-class squire of sound business sense, living in comfortable circumstances. When he died he left an estate of some seventeen to eighteen thousand pounds. He maintained a simple household with a few servants, did not keep a coach and horses, and on the whole "he had at all times the prudence to regulate his expence by his income." But there was always money for those who needed it, and he spent large sums on paintings.

Towards his English colleagues he was courteous—though there were some exceptions. One notices that his name appears on many subscription lists for works, such as those of provincial organists, that could not have interested him. In turn—again with exceptions—his English colleagues treated him with respect and consideration. Several of them showed forbearance unusual in the highly competitive theatrical world. During the 1745 season, for example, Arne, who operated from the Drury Lane Theatre, announced the performances in the newspapers by stating: "This Day is fix'd on to avoid interfering with Mr. Handel." It was another matter with the Italians in London, who either were part of the cabal or were used by his enemies in the way Piccinni was later to be used against Gluck. They received no quarter from Handel and as a rule had to return to Italy with bloodied noses. Though he was a keen observer of the international scene, what he thought of the music of other composers we do not know. During the early years his admiration for Scarlatti, Pasquini, Corelli, Steffani, and of course Zachow was genuine and warm, but in his mature years he refrained from showing any preferences or even appreciation, though Hawkins mentions an expressed admiration for Rameau. He subscribed to publications from abroad, but only towards Telemann did he show an interest that went beyond courtesy. His regard for Telemann remained constant for more than half a century. In 1735 his old friend and boon companion, Mattheson, dedicated a volume of organ fugues to Handel "as a token of singular homage." Handel's answer, beginning stiffly with "Monsieur" and ending with "avec une consideration parfaite," is cold and formal. Though complimenting Mattheson, Handel makes it clear that he is too busy to pay too much attention to such things. "My continual application to this court and nobility keeps me from any other business." This was a curious tone towards an intimate friend of his youth; however, Mattheson was anything but a *chevalier sans reproche,* and Handel may have had his reasons. At any rate, the dedication was omitted from future editions of the collection of fugues.

As for Bach, although their names were linked by German writers as early as the 1730s—Scheibe in his *Critische Musikus* (1737) declared Bach and Handel the two greatest keyboard artists—the two never met. So far as we know, Handel knew little about his greatest contemporary and was familiar with none of his music. As we have pointed out, Bach knew some of Handel's music and appreciated it, copying a few scores and even borrowing from them.

[3]

THE PROBLEM OF Handel's relationship with women has puzzled his biographers for the last two hundred years, producing ingenious and conflicting theories, a few of them cogent, most of them dubious, if not inept. Psychoanalysts were quick to conclude that Handel, like Brahms, had an unnaturally strong attachment to his mother, which made him incapable of passion for other women. Many of the writers seem to regard celibacy as a higher and more spiritual state than marriage, which is a rather curious attitude coming from English Protestants. Flower called Handel "sexless and safe," while others attributed his bachelorhood to a "moral revulsion to carnal passion." But it is clear from his dramatic works that he did not see anything prurient in sex. He did not consider erotic conflict to be of a lower order than moral conflict, and he never permitted the passions of his dramatic figures to be derided on moral grounds. We have seen what he did with such a part as Dalila's, where the warm music contradicts the moralizing text. But on occasion he directly intervened on behalf of his heroine when the librettist was too harsh. Thus in *Semele* he changed the original "the curst adultress" to "cursed Semele"; a woman in love may be cursed but not besmirched.

The solution to this mystery must be sought, I believe, in the artist rather than the man. It is evident that Handel was attracted to women in all stages of his life. The Mlle. Sbülens mentioned in a letter of the nineteen-year-old Handel, La Bombace in Florence and Venice, the shadowy Iberian princess, Donna Laura, and a number of singers and other women clearly interested Handel more than socially or professionally, although his amorous encounters with them were as carefully screened from view as were his political and religious inclinations. But all of these were peripheral affairs. One might say that he simply did not have time for serious engagement with women. Solitude for him was not loneliness, it was his deepest inspiration. He was imbued with a mixture of creative frenzy, the rapacity of a conqueror, and the enterprising zeal of a businessman, all goading him to incessant activity. He saw no place for a woman in his scheme of things. What woman would have been willing to keep pace with this driving personality who made his work a religion and expected others to treat it as that, who organized every moment of his life and every detail of his household with a hearty but thorough dictatorship? How would any woman understand the single-minded pursuit of any idea that took possession of him? Gossip is always eager to discuss the loves of artists, but in truth a poet or composer is not always created for love. Complete devotion, complete sharing of sentiments, which is what love means, are more difficult for the creative artist than for anyone else. The more profound his devotion to his art, the less can his identity be sacrificed by being dissolved in another person. Some women feel this instinctively and are wary of the poet's love. The Muse is a symbol, and the Muse's love is everyone's and no one's.

There is a certain kinship, both in nature and in expression, between Eros and musical poetry. It is the urge, the creative urge that drives the composer to work, and the pleasure he experiences while so engaged is akin to erotic experience. The kinship is much closer than that between, let us say, music and the emotion of patriotism. This is clear even quantitatively: there are many more love songs than patriotic songs.

Considering the extremely wide range of the characters of Handel's heroines, and the infinite nuances in their femininity, it seems incontrovertible that he must have been a man not only of normal masculine constitution but one attracted by and sensitive to feminine charms, as is borne out by his marked predilection for the women among his friends. Furthermore, one notices that the women in his dramas, no matter what the libretto requires, respond far more readily to strong instincts than to principles or viewpoints. He was little interested in their social problems and conflicts, the more so in their femininity. The attitude is that of a man who knew women, and whenever he speaks of them his voice is sympathetic. At times he mourns their frailty but it is clear that he would not wish them otherwise. His female figures were not created according to the conventions of the time, for he loved beauty and would have found the world bare without feminine grace.

Love changes according to climates, but that the Puritan, straitlaced,

biblical England of Cromwell or the Victorians was not the English norm
is well demonstrated by the Elizabethans and by the Restoration. The
ardent poem of Romeo and Juliet, the pure oxygen of love that kills, was
written by the epitome of an Englishman. And that voluptuous votary of
love, Semele, was portrayed in music by an Englishman with a German
intonation who in staid Halle could never have heard such accents. Such a
woman could never have risen from the imagination of a misogynist. Nor
were Semele and Cleopatra the only ones in Handel's enchanting gallery
of women possessed by love. Solomon's young Queen is as irresistible as
her sinuous, beguiling music. We may have no positive proof of Handel's
love affairs, but how could a man unacquainted with love compose the
wondrous idyll known as the "Nightingale Chorus" (*Solomon*), the lilting,
seductive promise of an enchanting night?

There are other memorable women, the Nikes and Aphrodites of old
Greek coins, who, stepping out of their hieratic confines, begin to live.
Some are fresh and fragrant in their youth, gentle, timid, innocent, and
utterly charming, some are not unaware of life's pleasures, some are ravishing, uninhibited lovers. But Handel also knew those who are driven by
demonic strength and overwhelming tragic passion. How magnificent are
these regal women—Dejanira, fierce, possessive, or Nitocris, a tragic
queen, torn between duty and maternal love. It is noteworthy that in the
last oratorios, *Susanna, Theodora,* and perhaps even in *Jephtha* (Iphis),
women are the principal figures, as they were in a number of the operas.

These passionate women caused consternation among the doughty
Victorians who could not reconcile such attitudes with the composer of
Messiah. They "cleansed" even *Semele* of what to them seemed immoral
indulgence in the pleasures of the flesh, but their real concern was with
the presence of sex in the "sacred" oratorios. Though Solomon became a
paragon of monogamy in the oratorio, Handel made up for the loss of the
harem by the ardor of the reformed king's love for his queen. Embarrassment at such earthy attitudes and episodes in biblical oratorios could be
avoided only by changing the words of the original libretto. "Editing" of
this sort was done with such thoroughness that even innocent words that
only faintly referred to anything sexual were eliminated as suggesting the
wicked and unseemly. This attitude is still reflected in today's performances
of the oratorios, for the figures in the love scenes are manipulated puppets;
they are not considered for their own sake but are subordinated to the
"sacred" theme. When Shakespeare wrote *Romeo and Juliet,* what he
cared about was the love story, not the quarrels of the Montagues and
Capulets, which remained for him a secondary piece of plot making. So

with Handel. When he composed love scenes—and there are many in the oratorios—every other consideration vanished. But the Handelian music drama with a biblical subject has unfortunately been represented as being altogether composed in the spirit of religion, its sole purpose being moral edification and nothing so trivial and ephemeral as love. Neither art nor love, however, is trivial, and a love story is not a sop to distract the mind.

[4]

HANDEL'S LONG contact with the English imparted to him a good deal of the essence of English genius. London, he realized, was not England but the vortex into which all currents of English thought are gathered up, whirled around, and from which they emerge with a new unity and new power. But the Englishman is at heart a countryman, and Handel, too, became an intimate of Nature's household. He was one with nature by intuitive identification; he responded to the individuality of each landscape and felt in every mood its corresponding season and time of day. Making these moods real in the listener's mind is only a matter of association of ideas. The transition from nature to art bends back on itself. When the Elizabethans wanted to commend a flower they said it was as beautiful as a picture of it. The realists miss this profundity of abstraction and are lost in the concretization of details. The ancient Greeks praised Zeuxis, for he painted cherries with such accuracy that the birds came to peck at them. But this only proves that the birds are no connoisseurs of art. The artist superimposes on nature what he considers desirable; he makes a selection from nature of elements that suit his interests. This is what Handel did, this is what all poets do.

To range the arts according to whether they are representational, taking their subject from "nature," like painting, or whether they are subjectless, like music, is primitive. Art does not directly take from nature anything but physical matter—stone, or canvas, or sound. To confuse the physical with artistic matter is fatal, for artistic matter is not of natural but of human origin. A metaphor or simile drawn by music from nature or everyday life arrests the hearer by its vividness or strangeness, leaving the mind in sufficient doubt about its precise application to tease it into active thought. The ready use of nature's material for images is a sure sign of intimacy with it. It was Handel's capacity to identify himself with the impalpable presence of nature, the inspiration of a rare surrender, that makes his nature scenes alive with wonder. He was a pagan in the true and original sense of the word, closely in contact with the earth, looking at it with an all-encompassing loving eye. The observer of nature is caught up in the visionary who sees detail and incident as part of a mystic whole, though not less clearly defined. Handel's imagery is as delicately and regularly near to nature as his vision, and he continually discovers in her something new to see and ponder and express. What Dryden, in his *Essay on Dramatic Poesy*, said concerning Shakespeare applies equally to Handel: "All the images of nature were still present to him, and he drew them, not laboriously but luckily: when he describes anything, you more than see it, you feel it too." Yet while Handel describes a landscape or a bucolic scene with incomparable felicity, his music can assume an intensity of feeling of which the source is merely the ostensible theme.

Handel already had had a taste of genre scenes and nature painting in Hamburg; Keiser was a master of them. This was long before nature as a whole had any deep significance for other German musicians or even poets. The Lutherans, preoccupied with the hereafter, did not understand nature and regarded it with anxiety; or, as in the case of Bach, were unconcerned with it. They looked upon the phenomena of the outside world with a medieval distrust of the inscrutable powers that it harbored. (Their warm espousal of the poetry of nature is of a considerably later date.) The humanistically oriented concept of nature Handel acquired in England was otherwise new. True, Dryden's and Pope's Nature still largely reflected the urban mind noting with superiority the oddities of the rustic. Yet they liked "nature to advantage dressed," and there was no feeling of disharmony between pagan and Christian ideals. Nature was no longer a strange domain in which man gropes, distrusting it, or subjugating it in the spirit of the Enlightenment or the New Science. It was not mysticism nor yet romanticism. The real mystics, such as Angelus Silesius, closed their eyes to the most magnificent landscape; it was they who coined the terrible saying *mundus pulcherrimum nihil.* To Handel and his Englishmen the colors of the earthly do not fade in the presence of God. To them nature was a pervading mood, and in art more a style than a form, its essential trait being the intimate. Nevertheless, the seemingly narrow little world that is the idyllic can be as serious as the widest and, in the case of England, it can represent the spirit of a people. *Susanna's* flavor is unmistakably that of the English country, and *L'Allegro* breathes the spirit of rural England.

[5]

WE MENTIONED a few pages back Dr. Quinn's letter to Burney in which the Dublin doctor praised Handel as a raconteur who liberally mixed four languages. Though undoubtedly true, the remark certainly does not indicate that Handel's "English" consisted of just such a panache; any storyteller might well resort to this device. German authors, who seldom fail to pounce on any evidence to emphasize Handel's "uncertain knowledge of English," use this story to bolster their claim that Handel remained a true and pure German even after forty-seven years of residence in England. If they would take a look at much 18th-century German writing, they would find a similar mixture, though more objectionable because foreign words are often inflected according to German grammar. It stands to reason that a man who already knew four or five languages would be able to acquire better than passable English, yet it is still the joy of the popular (and not so popular) biographies and histories to relate the many stories about Handel's difficulties with the English language.[4]

Many of the anecdotes do not bear close examination. There is, for instance, the famous story related by Burney and frequently quoted that when Carestini remonstrated with Handel about an aria, Handel was supposed to have lit into the haughty and pampered castrato with: "you toc! don't I know petter as your seluf, vaat is pest for you to sing?" The only flaw—and it has already been noticed by Chrysander—is that Handel would not have addressed an Italian singer in English. Carestini could not speak English and Handel's Italian was excellent. Actually his faux pas and his exploits in pidgin English are largely fabrications and are due mainly to his German accent. Such sneers are bound to arise in the case of a foreigner; even Lully's impeccable French settings were derided. D'Alembert found that the French recitative was created by a "foreigner," going so far as to accuse Lully of "deformed prosody," an absurd charge.

Hawkins, speaking from personal knowledge, says that Handel "was well acquainted with the Latin and Italian languages; the latter he had rendered so familiar to him that few natives seemed to understand it better." The historian acknowledges that Handel "pronounced the English as the Germans do," but his estimate of Handel's proficiency in English differs markedly from that implied in anecdotes. "Of the English also he had such a degree of knowledge, as to be susceptible of the beauties of our best poets; so that in the multiplicity of his compositions to English words, he very seldom stood in need of assistance." True, Handel did use a pasticcio language when annotating his scores. When a work was finished he would write *ausgefüllt*, and the title would also contain *angefangen*, followed by words in English. He composed on German,

---

[4] This misinformed view was shared by the present writer in his younger years (*Music in Western Civilization*).

Latin, Italian, and French texts, corresponded in French, and spoke fluent Italian, but essentially there were only two languages that closely concern his music: Italian and English. In the end, English became for him the principal language. It is noteworthy that by 1730 he used his mother tongue with a certain hesitation, as can be seen from a letter in German to his brother-in-law.

But all this is of small importance. Handel undoubtedly had a strong German accent, mispronounced, even misunderstood, some words, though his crimes against correct setting of English are no more conspicuous than those committed by Bach or Beethoven against their own tongue. The often mentioned gauche prosody is, in fact, frequently due to the incongruity of the altered texts with the original music. What matters is that he understood the genius of the language, notably the rich imagery of English, and not only understood it but, as is clear from his own statements, liked it and considered it well suited for musical setting. (See above, p. 290.) No English composer, not even Purcell, could set an English text with a finer ear for its true accents and inflections than Handel in the "Nightingale Chorus." "I know that my Redeemer liveth" affords another example of Handel's complete assimilation of the spirit, the sound, and the meaning of English. We say "the spirit" because the declamation itself is not faultless; nevertheless, Larsen is right when he contradicts Dent's cavalier dismissal of Handel's "Englishness" by saying that the relationship between words and music in Handel's English oratorios is altogether different from that in his German and Italian works. "This aria tells us something important about Handel's indebtedness to the English spirit, and how natural it is that Handel's music has been recognized for centuries as a true expression of that spirit." The English language with its plethora of consonants is of course quite different from the Italian, in which the many vowels produce an effect of a clear stream flowing over stones. But when approached from its own premises it can be as successfully adapted for musical setting as the Italian. It did not take Handel long to discover this, and once he felt secure, he challenged his librettists. There are many known instances where he changed the original text not simply to obtain more singable word combinations but also to improve the verse, which he did at times with surprising skill. While many of these changes found their way into the Händelgesellschaft scores, Chrysander ignored just as many.

What a difficult task for an artist that his most intimate thoughts should not be expressed in the language through which his entire culture was formed! But Handel was a little like the Renaissance humanists to

whom Latin became a mother tongue; for him English became a source
of the spirit.

[6]

VIRGIL HAD for a long time the reputation of being one of the
great religious poets of the world. Mystery attached itself to him from the
earliest times, and the ambiguity with which he hailed the coming savior
of the empire allowed him the dignity of a Christian poet. Handel
presents a somewhat similar case. He too had his "Fourth Eclogue"—
Messiah—upon which his religious reputation was built. Hawkins, attempting a summary of Handel's achievements, comes to the conclusion
(II, 913) that "in the first and highest class of Handel's works no competent judge of their merits would hesitate to rank his first Te Deum, and
the Jubilate, his coronation and other anthems, the Dettingen Te Deum
as it is called, and the chorusses of his oratorios." It is obvious, therefore,
that by 1776 a firm conviction was already held that it is the compositions
"in which the praises of God are celebrated" that "the power of his
harmony is beyond conception." But, as we have seen, the anthems and
Te Deums were ceremonial pieces, not true religious music, while in the
oratorios Jehovah is for the most part a poetic convention. Statements of
piety are from the mouths of the dramatic characters or in a context
where the plot, rather than Handel's personal belief, is the determining
factor. His rare remarks on religion show a remarkably wide tolerance
without any denominational specification or even reference. Ardent
Handelians completely misread the composer's basic character when, like
Chrysander, they declared him to be a religious mystic. This claim has
been maintained to this day, supported by apologists eager to credit
Handel with abandoning the frivolous opera theatre for a labor of devotion to Christianity akin to Bach's activity in Leipzig. Thus a firm tradition was created unchecked by objective scholarly reflection.

Until this day the change has been ascribed to a "conversion," a turning from the frivolity of opera to the service of religion. Just where the
popular assumption of this change of heart started is difficult to ascertain,
but it is so profoundly entrenched that it is almost impossible to remove
the vestments that clothe the oratorios. Let us examine this "conversion."
In the first place, the change is anything but sudden and emphatic. The
oratorio *Athalia* was a great success, but Handel returned to opera, completely ignoring for a time the new genre he had created. In the second
place, it is clear from all his acts, from his stubborn fight against all odds,

that he would never have abandoned Italian opera had he not realized that in the face of innate English antipathy for the genre there was no hope for its continuation. The decision had nothing to do with religion nor was it so fundamental a change as the critics of Italian opera have supposed. As a matter of fact, if the ecclesiastical authorities had not frowned on staged performance of scriptural subjects, we should have witnessed a form, a particularly English form, of "biblical opera," a phenomenon not unknown in the history of music.

The conversionists conveniently forget the vicissitudes of the Handelian oratorio, which for some time caused Handel troubles scarcely less wearisome than those suffered by his operas. The oratorio was condemned by those who felt grave misgivings about the propriety of uttering Holy Writ in the "play-house." But it was banished from the church, too! Clergymen considered even *Messiah* a blasphemous "religious farce"; it was not admitted to a church until eighteen years after its composition, nor were any of the other oratorios until the end of the century. In 1784 a performance of *Messiah* in Westminster Abbey provoked clerical indignation, and even a publication of a book of sermons preached against the oratorio by the Reverend John Newton.[5] It is sad to contemplate that William Cowper had a hand in this, for the unstable poet, then living with the Reverend Newton, was by that time wholly absorbed in an extreme sort of Evangelism.

However, the religious climate did change as English Pietism flourished in the wake of Methodism. The Wesleys themselves were fond of music and appreciated its role in religion, and while the more Calvinistically inclined shared the Reverend Newton's opinions far into the 19th century, Handel's hour did come, as we see from the elaborate commemoration acts in his honor beginning in 1784. The "conversion" theory was canonized, and though there were many persons living who had known Handel and were conversant with his setbacks and difficulties, the commemoration festivities were the nation's endorsement of the oratorios as an expression of "the fundamental truth of religion." As early as that we get a glimpse also of the atrocious distortion of Handel's music in performance which became characteristic of the 19th century. In 1787 over eight hundred singers and instrumentalists took part in the performances (already fortified with choirs of trombones), their number rising to 2,500 in 1857, and to 3,000 two years later, filling the Crystal Palace with the righteous bellowing we unfortunately associate with performances of

[5] See Robert Manson Myers, *Fifty Sermons on Handel's Messiah*, in *The Harvard Theological Review*, October 1946.

Messiah, a contemplative and lyric masterpiece.

Shortly before the first commemorative service we encounter the first literary affirmation of the "conversion." In fact, the theory had become fairly current by the time Sir John Hawkins published his *General History of Music* in 1776.[6] The excellent pioneer historian states that by abandoning opera and embracing oratorio "Handel gave another direction to his studies, better suited, as he himself used to declare, to the circumstances of a man in advancing years, than of adapting music to such vain and trivial poetry as the musical drama is generally made to consist of." Needless to say, there is no record of such a statement by Handel, as there could be none, because it is so much out of character. What Handel did say, and what is entirely in character, was in 1746 when the young Gluck called on the admired master to show him the opera he had composed for London: "You have taken far too much trouble over your opera; here in England that is a waste of time. What the English like is something that hits them straight on the eardrum." That, indeed, a grateful if misguided posterity accepted as the Handelian trait par excellence.

The conversion theory was well summarized by William Edward Hartpole Lecky, historian and author of *A History of England during the Eighteenth Century* (1878–1890). Endeavoring to find in the immense welter of data and sources those elements "which relate to the permanent forces of the nation, or which indicate some of the more enduring features of national life," he saw these features in Handel's music "only when interpreting the highest religious emotions." Indeed, Handel was one of those "whose lips the Seraphim had touched and purified with the hallowed fire from the altar."

Neither the preacher nor the psychoanalyst will get much satisfaction out of "Mr. Handell." Metaphysics had no meaning for him. His considered beliefs as they are revealed in his acts and his works appear even more latitudinarian than those of his friends. Again and again he seems to wrestle with the difficulties of reconciling with the fullness of life as he understood it the moral claims of Christianity as presented by the preachers and theologians. His fundamental religious position involved unqualified acceptance of what he saw as the essential faith, but his works show that he had his own mind about the crystallization of that faith into

---

[6] As a matter of fact, by this time the conversion theory was made retroactive, applied to Handel's entire *oeuvre.* A good example of this is furnished by Robert Falkener, author of *Instructions for Playing the Harpsichord* (London 1774): "The immortal Handel, in whatever Pieces he composed for the Entertainment of the Public was extremely cautious not to admit any thing that might excite either mean or lewd Ideas."

dogma, and his attitude towards religion is very different from that of the two churches he served. He relied on inner freedom and seems to have had for the mere fulfillers of the law a fine contempt. Indeed, to Handel the positive values he was seeking were to be found in creative energy, of which he had a superhuman stock. He acted individually and solved every moral problem for himself.

Handel was a practical man of the theatre, an expert professional speculator in the business of musical entertainment, sacred or secular. Life-loving but hard-working, shrewd in bargaining but generous, he was a man altogether untinged by religious mysticism; if anything, like a good Englishman, he mistrusted it. In the minutiae of religion he took no apparent interest. His whole cast of thinking was practical, his interest ethical-moral. We know that he was born and reared a Lutheran, but after he left Germany he gave not the slightest indication what communion he favored. Although biographers do not mention the fact, Lutheran congregations had existed in London since the 17th century. In Handel's time, St. Mary's Evangelical-Lutheran Church, adjoining the Savoy Palace, was available to him, yet he is never known to have frequented it. The court, too, was at least nominally Lutheran. George I brought with him two German Lutheran court chaplains and maintained a parochial school within the palace grounds. Formally Handel did not belong to the Church of England either, and his faithful attendance at St. George's would seem to be the conventional observance of an English gentleman's religious duties. He did not care for anything that he did not see and understand, he was natural even when describing the supernatural. One recalls Courbet's gruff bon mot when someone asked him why he never painted the Madonna: "Monsieur, I never had the pleasure of meeting her." Handel's mode of artistic creation was to shape with warm feeling but with cool and calm disciplined professional knowledge. His single-minded and unspeculative acceptance of life's hazards, his preference for a straight and undeviating course through them, is the antithesis of the mystical. He was not an unworldly preacher but an artist who happened to be endowed with exquisite sensibility in certain directions, in whom passion and emotion were intensified while they were sublimated by the severe "poetic pains" of creative genius.

For a long time Handel was alone and the target of much cruel satire, at times gross and unpardonable. We are aware of his disappointment at the thwarting of cherished projects, but never of bitterness. By the end of his life opposition had changed into nationwide admiration and affection, but the rise in the emotional barometer was not due, as has often been assumed, to his embracing of a Christian mission. Equally far-fetched and contrary to the evidence is the opinion of some writers who, deceived by appearances, have gone on record affirming that nothing in Handel's career "warrants the assumption that he was actuated by any motive nobler than desire for monetary reward."

This uncertainty in the final estimate of Handel's position proceeds from a doubt about the line of tradition in which he should be set. The influence of any nation, as a creative force in art, can be exerted either directly, through an already formed art, or indirectly, by lending elements impregnated with its colors and moods to an artist of another nation to shape and adapt and to pass on with his own stamp to the world of art. It was so with Lully, with El Greco, with Baron Grimm, and it was pronouncedly so with Handel. What appears to be the spontaneous art of an individual may acquire an entirely different significance when seen from the angle of the situation that prompted it—in a word, the milieu. Long before modern psychologists, Robert Owen already believed that human conduct is wholly the result of the action of the cultural and psychological environment upon the individual. It is the milieu that places man in the scheme of things, but the milieu is the fabric of hundreds of threads woven together. The two inspirations that biographers, especially Handel's German biographers, like to discuss separately, religion and the adopted nation's institutions, were not opposed to each other. The Church in England was an integral part of that collective spirit whose pressure on individual musical genius constituted a large part of English musical history.

What gave the Englishman's civilization its power and glory was his proud consciousness of a steadily forward-pressing humanity, reliance on his own powers, confidence in himself. Not only did he believe, all protestations to the contrary notwithstanding, that man is the measure of all things, but there was an element in his belief akin to the concept of the ancient Greeks, to whom the gods were only a higher form of the human. In Christian dogma man, though created in God's image, possesses a nature so weakened by sin that he cannot by his own powers rise to participation in the divine life. By virtue of this conception the measure of all things is God, not man, and man is no longer the most powerful but the weakest of creatures. But such a dogma was in reality foreign to the English mind and character, and wherever we look in English history we find a conflict between Jupiter, Jehovah, and Christ. Handel, though originally a German Lutheran, found this English temper congenial. He had a confirmed faith in the ultimate integrity, one might almost say divinity, of the individual human being whom he extolled in his English music dramas. Indeed, the presence of any specifically Christian ideas in his works (always excepting *Messiah*) is difficult to prove even though it is generally taken for granted. When at the end of his career he changed Morell's lines in *Jephtha* from "What God ordains is right" to Pope's "Whatever is, is right," he revealed that his religion was less that of a denomination, or hardly even of a "way," than an attitude of mind and heart. Yet, though the stern purposefulness of his life did not depend on stated articles of faith, Handel lived in a happy security of the conviction that there is an order in the world decided from above.

There are two different orders of reality, one human, the other super-human, and the point of junction between them is Jesus Christ. When all is said and done, Jesus himself is the essential fact in Christianity. He is both the Revealer and the Revealed. We have seen that after the few compositions of his youth in Germany and Italy Handel no longer set to music the symbols of Christianity. In the Old Testament, Handel's most frequently used source for oratorios, God is revealed in the moral law, in human relationships and experiences. In *Theodora* the characters live and act in a Christian background, but even that background is historical rather than religious. That leaves us nothing but *Messiah*, altogether an exception in Handel's *oeuvre*, a commissioned work destined for charity purposes. But all this is intelligible, and even warrantable, if we conclude that Handel's religion was a form of Deism. Leichtentritt, who sensed the problem, calls Handel "freethinking." If the term seems more a careless adjective than a seriously meant designation, we may recall that in 18th-century Germany, as in England, it had no hostile or pejorative connotation. Pope's *Essay on Man*, from which Handel's quotation in *Jephtha* was taken, was generally interpreted as an apology for the "freethinkers." Though a Catholic, Pope was not immune to the "natural religion" that so attracted his contemporaries.

The new philosophy and the new science had done away with many old beliefs more energetically in England than anywhere else in the world. Deism was a characteristically English way of looking at things; as Crane Brinton has said, "A respectable Deism was the ordinary position of the English mind." A natural religion based on reason alone, without the aid of any supernatural revelation, Deism posited belief in a personal God, both Creator and Judge, but not accessible to man in the Judaic or Christian sense. Its English form characteristically embraced a rather wide range of latitudinarian Christianity. Though it did not last very long, the movement left indelible marks on modern legal, political, and moral philosophy. It had many adherents, especially among the upper middle classes, and including many of the literary men with whom Handel was acquainted. It was in this part of the century that the third Earl of Shaftesbury, Matthew Tindal, Thomas Woolston, John Toland, Bolingbroke, Thomas Chubb, and a number of other Deists exerted considerable influence, eliciting from Joseph Butler the great protest that was *The Analogy of Religion* (1736). Like most of the Deists, Handel did not find it contradictory to accept the established outward forms of faith, and the ceremonial-theatrical quality in the services of the Church of England suited his music. Upright, honest, charitable, and kind, Handel, who seldom missed Sunday service, was, in the highest sense, an English gentleman, following his own dictates, and running his affairs by strictly minding his own business. We can now see the real meaning of the statement he once made to Hawkins when the latter asked him what he particularly appreciated in England: "He would often speak of it as one of the great felicities of his life that he was settled in a country where no man suffers any molestation or inconvenience on account of his religious principles." All his life, and from his early youth, Handel's acts showed a firm belief in a man's privilege to make what he can and will of his interior existence.

Posterity owes Handel, the artist and the man, a reappraisal. For the moment he still lives on "in the serene twilight of doubtful immortality," and in that deceitful medium he looms vaguely as a sort of fabulous high priest of biblical religiosity. There is seldom much of the prophet or priest in the man of the theatre, and Handel would not have denied this—and in his England he did not have to deny it. When we come to regard him closely, he appears as one of the most human figures among musicians of his or any other age. Now the light of art begins to shine on his oratorios, illuminating in them not dogmatic religious messages but the warm scenes of our earthly life, which were obscured from us for two centuries.

[7]

WE MUST NOT swing from neglect to blind eulogy; there were blemishes, too, in Handel's character. He could be an opportunist, he could sometimes subordinate art to business interests, and he could do shoddy work. When creative fervor dropped, he was an ordinary mortal, and we should look at his lapses with sympathy, as we do with other great men whose accomplishments dwarf their shortcomings. But there is one aspect of these weaknesses that cannot be passed over lightly. Poetry and music above all other arts have the power to raise a man above himself, to make him feel the tide of infinity flowing around him. It is this exalted status that Handel betrayed with maddening regularity.

Handel shows a contrast unique among great composers. Setting a text, he would battle the librettist, examine every word, make suggestions, or himself change the text for better dramatic logic, concentrating on the task at hand with a fierce creative ardor. While working on an original new score he was conscientious as were few in his time; the artistic moment was paramount. His judgment of music, whether his own or someone else's, was shrewd and correct. Hawkins tells the story of Handel's asking his opinion of "See the conquering hero comes." The historian frankly admitted that he did not consider it of any particular merit, whereupon Handel genially remarked that eventually this piece would be "more popular with the people than many other fine things." He was critical in reading and copious in correcting what he wrote, unerringly finding a better solution when second thought disclosed flaws or suggested new possibilities in a piece or even in a few measures. Implicit in all his original scores is the craftsman's jealous fidelity to the shape and substance of the material with which he works. But once the task was finished, he showed an incredible indifference, and more often than not simply ruined his carefully planned and lovingly composed work with senseless juggling of portions, transpositions, cuts, emendations, and interpolations of all sorts. Almost every one of his major scores became, after a few revivals, a jungle in which the traveller can hardly find his way. It is incomprehensible how this sensitive man of impeccable taste would throw together odds and ends without any regard to compatibility. The same composer, whose logic of tonal relationship was one of the most highly developed in the entire range of musical history, would shift and transpose unceremoniously until nothing remained of the original scheme. At times these rearrangements made no sense at all or resulted in comical distortion. In the revised score of *Solomon* (1759), a particularly botched performance, Solomon's wife was cut out altogether; as a result the king's invitation to love-making al fresco is addressed not to her but to his official guest, the Queen of Sheba. Since Handel failed to adjust what follows in the original score, Sheba appears to be embarrassed by her host's indelicate proposition and, as if to change the subject, says "this music is divine, o King." These were her original lines in praise of the formal entertainment staged in her honor. A similarly ludicrous situation was created when Handel exchanged the role of Alexander Balus for that of Cleopatra's confidante, Aspasia. There are many instances where he did not even bother to touch the shifted or borrowed material, simply instructing the copyist what to do with it.

How can we explain the careless, even destructive, attitude of one who in his original creations proceeded with such magnificent artistic insight and integrity? Some of the arrangements or reworkings were done in self defense against piracy, which was rampant. There was a sort of copyright act instituted by Queen Anne, later superseded by a licensing act; Handel even received a personal copyright from the King in 1720, a fourteen-year "Privilege and License for the sole printing" of his music. But all these acts were so ill-defined that they were unenforceable. Expediency and self-interest were the watchwords of all society under the Hanoverians. Handel's only recourse when an unauthorized version of one of his works was announced was quickly to rearrange and produce it himself, assuring the public that his version was new, enlarged with additional numbers, and so on, and therefore preferable to the competitor's production. It is likely, therefore, that a number of Handel's reworkings were done under a sort of duress to keep the would-be pirates off balance; he was a fierce competitor.[7] We must also bear in mind that new singers often had to be accommodated at short notice, making hasty transpositions inevitable, and that the public's craving for always new productions had long since sanctioned the practice of pasticcio operas. This practice is much more ancient than its modern critics realize. The transferring of portions from one play to another was already frequent in the Roman theatre of antiquity and was given by Latin authors the realistic technical term "contamination." In sum, what Handel did was not markedly different from what was being done at the same time in Naples, or Venice, of Vienna; it was the standard practice of the age. We might add that refurbishing was freely indulged in by Bach, too, and we find the practice still liberally employed by Gluck in his most hallowed "reform" operas, the *Iphigenias*.[8]

But these are partial explanations, they do not answer the question of extreme carelessness and unconcern. The real explanation is that there were two Handels: the composer and the entrepreneur. The composer who wants to compete, who is in fact an impresario, loses the ground

[7] It was for the same reason that full scores were not printed, only "favourite songs" and "symphonies" in reduced score, so as to prevent performing material from getting into the hands of unauthorized persons.

[8] Nor are cases of willingness to permit ridiculous travesties of an original work unknown among other composers. In a letter to Zelter (May 25, 1823) Beethoven calmly tells the director of the Berlin Singakademie that "large portions" of his *Missa Solemnis* "could be performed a cappella," adding that in such a case "the whole work would have to be revised." He was careful, however, to indicate that this unenviable—in fact, impossible—task he expected Zelter to perform.

from under his feet, he loses the basis of his art to stand upon. He no longer acts as a creative artist but as an ordinary businessman, he no longer exercises the discipline that comes from within but arranges things to suit external circumstances. Hawkins gives the reasons for the impresario's attitude, which are still valid after almost two hundred years: "In all theatrical representations a part only of the audience are judges of the merit of what they see and hear, the rest are drawn together by motives in which neither taste nor judgment have any share."

While this interpretation may solve this baffling problem, it is still hard to accept the fact that so overwhelming a genius could subordinate his art to such a degree for whatever reason. Art is not business, and the difference, for example, between the original *Solomon* and the reworked one is that between day and night. It was unfortunate that Handel did not realize that artists who betray their standards for any reason betray themselves. Happily, these scores can be restored. By starting with the original manuscript and carefully scanning the later additions and variants, accepting only those that bear the stamp of creative fervor, removing the bowdlerized or shifted numbers, a knowledgeable editor can produce a critically correct edition. But such an editor must steel himself and remember Spenser's lines:

> That which is firme doth flit and fall away,
> And that is flitting, doth abide and stay.

Handel the impresario often discarded some of the finest numbers, replacing them with inferior pieces that have nevertheless acquired popular sanction through the years.

[8]

AFTER THIS JOLT to our memories, we must turn to the interbreeding of ideas which under the heading of "borrowing" created for 19th-century scholars an almost insurmountable "moral dilemma." The moral issue was raised early in the 19th century. Thomas Busby, in his *A General History of Music from the Earliest Times to the Present* (1819), defended Handel on the grounds that he improved the material borrowed. This was angrily disputed in the *Quarterly Musical Magazine and Review* (1822) by an author who signs himself F.W.H.: "This is the first time I have ever heard of a theft being deemed less culpable by the improvement which the robber has afterwards made in the article stolen." Righteous consciences were just as alarmed eighty years later. Franklin

Peterson, in an article entitled *Quotations in Music* (in *Monthly Musical Record*, 1900), considers Handel's borrowings "flagrant," and any justification based on his artistic use of them to be "a puerile begging of the question." But we can advance into the second half of our own century and still find the same attitude. "Many of Handel's compositions," writes Henry Raynor in the *Monthly Musical Record* (1956), "are no more than plagiarism, showing no particular assimilation of other people's work, certainly not demonstrating that he has found in it significance which escaped the attention of its original composer." We are dealing, of course, with a romantic concept still widely shared by laymen: the composer creates in an intoxicated daze, at "white heat," and if he uses material of earlier creation, he is a plagiarist, a swindler, and a thief. One wonders why the other romantic conception of the artist as an irresponsible individual who must not be measured by the standards of bourgeois ethics is not applied in this instance.

Let us say at the outset that to represent Handel's borrowings as a weakness is not merely to pervert the simple evidence of the facts but to introduce an entirely discordant element into the total picture of a great artist who was also a man of magnificent moral courage. Many Handelians are embarrassed by their hero's interest in ideas proceeding either from contemporaries or older composers, an interest he had acquired early, when Zachow made him build up a library of models by copying interesting works by a wide variety of composers, and which continued to engage his piercing and delicate scrutiny to the end of his life. This propensity was altogether different from the haphazard shifting of material from one work to another (although actually most of Handel's borrowings were from himself); it was a time-honored device of composition used by the greatest masters well into the second half of the 18th century; no opprobrium was attached to it. Only those who do not understand the process of musical composition, who cannot see and feel the subtlety of transfiguration that can be created by a changed melody, even a single note, rhythm, or accent, have made a moral issue of something that is a purely esthetic matter. Have they ever considered the miracle that Beethoven made of a little torn rag of a waltz by Diabelli?—Brussels lace made of a piece of gunny sack. Far from condemning Handel, we should return to unrepentant appreciation and quote Romain Rolland's beautiful phrase: "Handel evoked from the very depths of the [borrowed] musical phrases their secret soul of which the first creators had not even a presentiment." There is an anecdote quoting Handel who was supposed to have answered the question of why he used material composed by Bononcini thus: "Well, it's much too good for him, he did not know what to do with it." While the authenticity of this is very doubtful, the attitude is typical for the times—and for Handel.

Handel was an assiduous student of music, a good reader. The good reader understands the other man's world and instantly recognizes its essential features. Bach, too, was an indefatigable student, and he, too, borrowed a good deal, but his approach was entirely different. With his analytical mind he carefully sought out what he wanted; once satisfied that a certain type of music would benefit him, he unhesitatingly adopted it for his own purposes. Handel did not search for his materials, rather he relied on his extraordinary memory. He could recall the smallest musical detail, a measure or a motif, forty years later. His powers of association and assimilation were unusual, and when he saw something he liked, something that was akin to his own style or could be converted to it, he instantly accepted and used it, whether it was a theme or an entire movement. He had an uncanny feeling for what was right for the occasion. The list of composers from whom we know he borrowed ideas is long: Graun, Kerll, Muffat, Telemann, Keiser, Kuhnau, Habermann, Carissimi, Urio, Erba, Stradella, Porta, Lotti, Legrenzi, Astorga, Steffani, Bononcini, Clari—even Cavalli; and it undoubtedly will be longer, because all of his borrowings have not yet been discovered. Certain types of music served him as a reservoir of ideas. Thus the collection of his own keyboard pieces was a favorite preserve for obtaining choral fugue material. Another favorite source was Italian vocal duets, mainly his own, but also Steffani's and Clari's. His cantatas composed during the Italian journey formed a faithful retinue in attendance throughout his life.

These visits of Handel to the caves of memory deeply worried his posthumous admirers and were seized upon by his detractors. Some advanced the senseless theory that he could not have proceeded to compose without first borrowing ideas. But Flower, the stern guardian of morals, who was keenly disturbed by the possibility that larceny might taint the memory of a man regarded as the artistic emissary of God, refutes this canard energetically, though not very accurately. "That Handel, more gifted with originality than most of the composers the world has known, should prowl about looking for the indifferent work of lesser and unknown people is a foolish charge." He immediately endorsed Percy Robinson, who in *Handel and his Orbit* declared Urio and Erba nonexistent, their names referring to certain places in Italy where Handel had stayed rather than to any composers. Robinson further insisted that Stradella's serenata *Qual prodigio*, incorporated in *Israel in Egypt*, was a youthful composition of Handel himself. These unproved flights of fancy may have helped to assuage moral scruples, but there is no place named Muffat or Habermann. Nevertheless, Sir Newman happily announced that Handel "was not a plagiarist—except on himself." Other commentators have thought that Handel resorted to quotations only when unsure of himself, because of mental fatigue or because of the aftermath of an illness. To connect Handel's borrowings solely with his illnesses is to admit to an ignorance of musical history, to an unfamiliarity with the creative process in music—and to a superficial knowledge of Handel's works. In the first place, Handel's habit of borrowing was well known in his lifetime and was not a discovery of posterity. Scheibe (*Critische Musikus,* 1745) says that though Handel often developed "not his own thoughts but those of others," he was nevertheless a man of "great understanding and of refined and delicate taste." Hawkins, like other musicians and historians of his time, also knew about the borrowings and mentions—with admiration— that in *Alexander's Feast* Handel "introduced a trio which he had set formerly to the words 'Quel fior che al alba ride,' which he adapted so well that most men took it for an original composition." He also gives a fairly accurate list of the choruses based on Handel's harpsichord pieces.

The pasticcio was of course an accepted form of entertainment and few listeners cared who actually wrote a particular piece or bit of music so long as it fitted the situation.

Chrysander himself was acutely aware of the problem and of its implications to his contemporaries; good scholar that he was, he decided to attack it in the open. In 1888, when the first of the six supplemental volumes of the great Händelgesellschaft edition, containing the original scores of Erba, Urio, Stradella, Clari, Muffat, and Keiser appeared, it required considerable intellectual courage to take an objective stand in the face of the ethical misgivings of the Victorians. Sedley Taylor followed in 1906 with a most interesting publication, *The Indebtedness of Handel to Works by Other Composers,* the first close examination of this problem. Taylor immediately reached its core when in the preface he remarked that Handel "also treated in precisely the same manner older works of his own." The theme is vaster than would have been thought possible in the days of Chrysander and Taylor, for "invention" and "imagination" represent one concept in the Baroque era and another in our own. But we are beginning to realize that like Nicias, who did not find it beneath his dignity to adorn with his brush sculptures made by other artists, great composers did not disdain to adorn with their notes the music of their fellows. Far more than in the sister arts, in music the rewoven tapestry becomes an entirely new creation.

Nothing is more difficult than to estimate the precise degree of consciousness in a creative artist of the distant past. Handel was one of those who are not so entirely submerged in their gift that they cannot watch and to a considerable extent guide it, even when they are possessed by it. Does the composer know what he wants? And if so, does this consciousness hurt his art? We can assume that at times it is the composer who is in command, at others the mood that envelops him; here it is consciousness that dictates, there instinct. But with the great composers, consciousness is always present even though it may not be the absolute master. This consciousness often wears a mask, follows the fashions, or defies them. Musicographers are very much interested in this question, which is one of their chief sources of material. The more ambitious—and less informed—of them have an exact way of dealing with it. They equate the "originality" of the composer with the remainder they obtain by subtracting the sum total of "influences" from the sum total of a composer's *oeuvre*. Since such research extends into the smallest details, this remainder often is pitifully small, for influences go through a composer's heart, lungs, and brains; they can tie him into a knot, intimidate him, if they do not make him ridiculous like more than one ponderous post-Wagnerian or perfumed post-Impressionist. However, it was this very same "influence research" that opened our eyes to the greatness of the past, that made us realize that the old maxim, "there is nothing new under the sun," is equally valid in music. The world is the same and the human ear is the same as before, and it is the same human heart that in its desires creates aims and directions and supplies propulsive force.

A particular form of "influence," always looked for, and as we have said, with great suspicion, is the borrowing of musical material from another composer. Some of Handel's works would shrink appreciably if the above-mentioned subtracting operation were carried out on them. In fact, this has been done and—with the exception of *Messiah*—he was found sadly wanting. Needless to say, things are not that simple, for obviously the mathematical is not the best approach to art.

What, then, is this "influence" or "dependence" of one artist upon another? It can manifest itself in the acceptance of an artistic view or philosophy that stands in some relation to a concept of life, or it can consist of a leaning to, a preference for, forms and idioms practiced by another composer, or in the taking over of a type, or in the borrowing of materials, even of substantial parts of compositions. The post-Renaissance composers, the *practici* of the north and west of Europe, still kept a good deal of the respect accorded in the past to the command of the métier, but the new emphasis on melody was seeking a compromise with the tremendous prestige of counterpoint. The new manner of hearing music was a middle road between spontaneous "sentiment" and the construction-conscious objective professional manner of the old masters. But while the increased pace of the dissemination of compositions created an entirely new type of artistic life, the conviction that an artist's distinction depends more on his productivity and professional skill than on the originality of his material was retained and was strongly shared by Handel. It was an artistic philosophy also evidenced in his steady adherence to such traditional forms as the da capo aria or the concerto grosso. But literal borrowing must be dealt with separately because it was made into a moral issue and confused with "invention" and "originality."

It is death to his genius, argues Ernest Hemingway, for a writer to write when there is "no water in the well," to write except when he feels he must. But surely this was not so before the Romantic age. Invention was well regulated in the Age of Reason, and to wait for divine inspiration as in the Romantic era was entirely contrary to the concept of musical composition. The musicians wanted to have as much power over their imagination as they believed the literary men had over theirs. They did recognize a particular form of invention called *ex abrupto, inopinato, quasi ex entusiasmo musico* (Mattheson), yet "originality" was still not a criterion; the individual masters were only characteristic representatives of the diverse schools and tendencies—that is, of individual artistic castes. The latter developed, within the national trends and schools, the more narrow artistic types, such as the opera maestro, the violin maestro, the cantor. A certain formalism was retained from the older traditions far into the 18th century, notably in the universal validity of certain genres. Thus the international lyric stage, the Neapolitan opera style, produced excellent masters, but they differ from one another only in the degree of their talent; in everything else they represent a type. As late as 1750 a Hasse cannot be distinguished from his Italian colleagues.

A corollary to this absence of originality was the widespread custom of borrowing. Mattheson, in his *Der Vollkommene Capellmeister,* states that "borrowing is a permissible thing; but one must return the borrowed with interest, that is, one must arrange the borrowed material in such a fashion that it acquires a better esteem [*Ansehen*] than the setting from which it has been lifted." Composers borrowed motifs, melodies, and entire movements without ever raising the spectre of plagiarism. It was considered possible and quite proper for one master to take over subjects or entire mood sketches together with all their thematic material, because what mattered was not the originality of the invention but the appropriate *affect* in the proper place. Handel did not necessarily borrow Urio's or Carissimi's music because of the originality of their thematic invention; he incorporated their work into his own because it was appropriate for the representation of a certain type of music. It was ready, in existence; why invent anything new? This was understood by every musician of the age, and no distinction was made between an "original" and a borrowed or converted piece. The musicians used each other's pens because they knew that there is no such thing as absolute originality in music, and they realized that a new work is the agglomeration of many inspirations, shreds of melodies that come from without, from all manner of sources. A borrowed piece when elaborated or worked in a new context is as much the borrower's original as it was when first composed. Though it may have been but little changed, it sounds different in its new environment.

Just as the literature of the period did not consider the borrowing of forms and subjects plagiarism, or even remotely connected with moral ideas and values, the musician was free to use accepted and known materials for his own expressive means without being accused of theft, imitation, or weakness. Harold Ogden White [9] showed that except for one or two minor authors, no Elizabethan can be found saying a word against borrowing as such. It was borrowing without proper digesting or reworking that roused their wrath. Pope still shared their views: "It seems not so much the perfection of sense to say things that have never been said before, as to express those best that have been said oftenest." The task of the artist was to give to a timely and well-known type of mood a new and pleasing shape and to contribute to its inner enrichment. Authors' rights were practically unenforceable; a composition once printed or acquired in copy was to all intents and purposes in the public domain. At that, it is remarkable that Handel, who knew far more music than most of his colleagues, used so few foreign goods in the shape he found them. He was content to quarry, on occasion, from various sources the materials for his more concentrated art. In most cases he stayed within the limits allowed by convention and was guided simply by his instinctive perception of the potentialities of a particular piece of music.

The layman is convinced that the creative soul is a sort of storage battery which when touched by life will instantly react by discharging electricity in the form of an inspired work of art. Well, the artist may re-

[9] *Plagiarism and Imitation during the English Renaissance*, Cambridge, Massachusetts, 1935.

semble a battery, but it is one that is constantly being charged, storing up impressions to be used when suitable for certain purposes. Beethoven's sketchbooks show this abundantly, and so do Handel's in the Fitzwilliam Museum. The very minute when the borrower looks at the material he is about to use, a process is begun. No matter how much it resembles the original, in the hands of a real artist it becomes a different plant, different sap will flow in its veins, it will acquire a different coloring and will occupy an entirely different spot in the garden into which it was transplanted. Even Handel's numerous borrowings from his own works sound in their new context quite different, for a different mood and different experiences are attached to them. The literal borrowings in particular need close examination. At times a superficial reading will yield the impression that Handel simply copied, but upon closer inspection all sorts of changes are discovered which, though each may be small, in the aggregate result in a new composition. Also, the original is often greatly enlarged in size and volume, not infrequently to three times its original proportions. It must also be understood that a melody is not at all bound to its erstwhile environment and mood unless it is universally known for that reason, like *The Star-Spangled Banner*. Even so, well-known hymn tunes, such as *A mighty fortress is our God* or *Gott erhalte Franz den Kaiser,* can be and have been used in a number of works as a purely constructive element without eliciting any extramusical associations.

To Handel, borrowing was not a diverting game during a pause in his creative activity, but the expression in his own terms of kindred experiences. Often the boundary line between the borrowed and the original is hardly visible, for he was a composer who not only learned the old tricks and formulas from the great store of Western music but who felt and knew the much more mysterious inner forms, the secrets of musical shaping. Among the great of music he is one of the greatest pupils. The masters of the past wanted no more than to be such good pupils, yet many of them became far more original than the phoenixlike Romantics who were convinced that they were reborn in every new work.

Perhaps the most enlightening and revealing glimpse we get into the mysterious ways of musical genius is offered by Handel's adaptation of duets. One of his favorite sources for useful reminiscences was his own vocal duets, delightfully sensuous love music whose beautiful undulating melodies radiate Mediterranean charm. He used them in a number of works—not least, *horribile dictu,* in *Messiah.* In *Theodora,* however, Handel did not fall back upon his own duets but borrowed some from Giovanni Maria Clari (1667–1754), a Pisan composer. They are available for comparison, since Chrysander printed them in the supplement to his edition of Handel's collected works. Handel would take a small segment, often no more than an incipit that none of us would dignify with a second look, and make it the germinal element of a tremendous musical edifice of his own. One marvels at the small alterations that would make a borrowed element coming from a totally different environment exactly right for the occasion. On the other hand, there are many instances when the new text to which a hasty borrowing was adapted failed to raise a spark, and all we see is an incongruous transposition, though such instances occur mostly when he whipped together a pasticcio for a revival of an older work. But if a new text has meaning for him, the transplanted piece may acquire a glow it did not possess heretofore. When borrowing entire movements he leaned to homophonic pieces—his idea of counterpoint was a very individual one. The manner in which he employed his keyboard fugues, by changing a single note, shifting one beat, or dotting one note to make them into models of choral material fills one with never-ending admiration. There is indeed something miraculous about the palingenesis of these "transpositions." Take a little keyboard fugue that became, in *Israel in Egypt,* a towering choral monument. Handel did not change much; he skipped some measures and made some adjustments in the part-writing, yet one would swear that the fugue was originally composed for chorus—more, for this particular chorus.

In his old age Handel was more inclined to seek borrowed material. This has been considered a sign of failing inspiration and invention, an interpretation that does not fully explain the situation. In his last original work, *Jephtha,* which shows him at the height of his creative powers, serene, profoundly engaged, and in unfailing command of the most refined technical mastery, he borrowed more than in any other dramatic oratorio. As we have seen, this time he used a volume of Masses by Habermann. A glance at the Habermann Masses will disclose well-worked compositions from the Czernohorsky-Zelenka wing of Austro-Bohemian music. These are decent, traditional works in the international and altogether impersonal style and idiom of instrumentally accompanied late Baroque church music. What Handel saw in them is impossible to understand, what he did with them defies the imagination; the innocent contrapuntal formulas blossomed into magnificent personal expression. No, neither laziness nor opportunism nor lack of imagination, and least of all moral deficiency, was the cause for this spate of borrowing in his old age. A peculiar inertia had to be overcome, the lassitude of the old and ailing man; and since his fierce creative energy and eagerness were unimpaired, all he needed was a push, a heave to clear the shore and hoist his sails. Almost anything would have served this purpose, for the minute he saw an idea, the fantastic *ars combinatoria* of old stirred in him, suggesting ways and means to shape the commonplace formula into warm living music. In this he followed the greatest composers from Perotinus to Bach.

Here I should like to quote Hermann Kretzschmar's fine eulogy of well over half a century ago, when no one else paid much attention to the recastings. Speaking of *Laudate pueri* he says:

In these reworkings of the same basic ideas one gets a deep insight into Handel's development and the altogether marvelous gifts of this blessed artist. So rich a measure of creative capacity, healthy feeling, and taste as we encounter when comparing these versions is unsurpassed in the entire history of art.

Only insufficient knowledge of music and its history could have brought critics to their absurd conclusions regarding the nature of Handel's borrowings. It appears that they have never heard of *cantus firmus*, *soggetto cavato*, and parody Mass. Many of the magnificent works of Palestrina and Lasso and hosts of others are built on the principle of borrowing, often a whole motet or chanson. Forty-nine out of Lasso's fifty-three Masses are "parodies." Nor have they examined such works as, for instance, Bach's adaptations of sonatas from Reinken's *Hortus Musicus* and his many borrowings from Legrenzi, Albinoni, Corelli, Vivaldi, and others. Bach reworked, shifted, and borrowed as much as Handel; in fact, to such an extent that "the chronology of his works is beclouded, compelling us to exercise the greatest care in judging every work whose time of creation and origin is not accurately known." [10] He reworked instrumental numbers into vocal ones and vice versa, converted secular into sacred cantatas, and so on. There are cantatas in three known versions, but individual numbers may have more than that. Blume also raises the question that is in our mind: "It is difficult to understand the sense and purpose of these reworkings; in many instances it would have been much simpler to compose a new piece than completely to refurbish an old one."

The reasons that induced Bach to work over an old composition are, we think, the same that actuated Handel. Something in the composer's subconscious flashes a memory that suits the mood, the affective requirements of the moment; it generates a creative spark, and since the age placed little value on absolute newness, the composer reworked a good

[10] Friedrich Blume in *MGG*. See also Arnold Schering, *Über Bach's Parodieverfahren*, in *Bach Jahrbuch*, 1921.

and usable idea. Gluck, as he advanced in years, borrowed material largely from himself, regarding his earlier works as sketches from which he might take whatever he fancied suitable for incorporation into his later scores. In *Iphigénie en Tauride* (1779) Gluck drew complete numbers from six earlier operas: *La Clemenza di Tito* (1752), *Antigone* (1756), *L'Ile de Merlin* (1758), *Telemacco* (1765), *Le Feste D'Apollo* (1769), and *Paride ed Elena* (1770). He returned to even earlier operas for orchestral accompaniment material: *Demofoonte* (1742) and *Semiramide* (1748). But Gluck also helped himself wholesale from the works of Sammartini, his teacher, long after he ceased to be a disciple. Vivaldi, too, borrowed from Corelli and Albinoni—even from Handel—but particularly from himself. Raguenet, in his celebrated *Parallèle*, accuses the French of pilfering from one another or themselves to such an extent that all their works are similar. All this was in the same spirit in which the Elizabethan poets rifled ancient literature and contemporary Italian books, as Shakespeare made use of Plutarch or Holinshed, or Tennyson of Sir Thomas Malory, as Dryden borrowed from Mlle. de Scudéry, or Washington Irving from a German tale for his *Rip Van Winkle*. Handel simply followed an old, tried, and in his day still perfectly natural practice: why should posterity have left only him so naked a prey to the cold winds of contempt?

The embarrassed critics and detractors still cannot divest themselves of the moral issue; they cannot see the particular principle that encouraged the speculative intellect to work from the primary experience of another. They are no more convincing than was Lady Mary Wortley Montagu who admired the dazzling virtuosity of Pope's *Essay on Criticism* only to reject it later "because I had not then read any of the ancient critics and did not know that it was all stolen." The romantic critics always think of Keats:

> *A theme! a theme! great nature give me a theme;*
> *Let me begin my dream.*

But the 18th-century composer believed in Racine: "All invention consists of making something out of nothing."

XXIII

Handel's style—The operas—Problem of opera in England—Handel and
the Italian tradition—Changed style in last operas—Ensemble and chorus
—Recitative, aria, arioso, *scena*—His opera librettists—Absence of buffa
vein—English oratorio a personal creation—The oratorio librettists—
Survival of operatic elements in oratorio—Handel's difficulties with
post-dénouement matters—The happy ending—Handel's role in the
operatic reform ascribed to Gluck—Inhibitions faced by modern musicians
approaching Handelian style

HISTORY, WHICH IN SOME RESPECTS WAS SO HARSH TO
Handel, obligingly eases the biographer's task, for Handel's work is neatly
divided into chronological events: Germany, Italy, England. Even the almost half-century spent in England is divided into two areas which,
though they overlap at certain points, are nevertheless easily distinguish-
able: the period of the operas and the period of the oratorios. In this long
creative life, seemingly diffuse and full of the most heterogeneous things,
there stands nevertheless Handel's *oeuvre* as a great organic whole. His
artistic development was tremendous, yet some of the essence of his last
works is present in the first ones. The young Handel was a hedonist, the
old and ill composer of the last oratorios rose above all reality. The early
composer was an Italian *operista*, the mature master was an English dramatist. The *caro Sassone* used the technique of the Italians, their language, their librettos, with scarcely an indication of his German origins.
Yet among the works composed at this early stage in his career there are
some that were to be imbedded in the works of his maturity without a
jarring note. Every element of his greatness is present in some of these
early works, like the rich petals of a flower in the bud. The more the hundred volumes of the old Händelgesellschaft edition are studied, the more
one experiences a feeling of awe at the scope of this universal musician
whose place among the great has not been generously enough recognized.
As we look at his life work from the perspective of the sum total of all
genres, we discover that he was at ease in every style and every type,

vocal or instrumental, capable of meeting Italians, Frenchmen, and Englishmen on their own grounds—and rising above them. Only the German style, the cantor's art, remained uncultivated.

There is a tendency in musicography to discern a Darwinian pattern in the several genres of music, seeing certain ones as resembling living organisms that have emerged from a chain of forms as the result of natural selection, while others succumb to the wear and tear of artistic life. Baroque opera is considered such a lost species, the general view being that these operas, and therewith all of Handel's, are old-fashioned and impossible to recover. They are old-fashioned, yet perhaps they were more so yesterday than they are today. Among the most interesting facts brought to light by modern research is the disappointment Handel felt on failing as an opera composer. This was a blow to his artistic aims and to his pride, a blow that seems to have hardened his reserve and impelled him to turn to the oratorio with the same intensity that characterized his stubborn defense of opera. To narrow his horizon by dismissing the operas is the way to misunderstand him; it has from the first been the source of many misjudgments. Within the last few decades the theatre has begun to repair the neglect by critics and historians, proving that there is much life in these operas and that though they have a strangeness for us their musical language is of the finest.

But perhaps it may be said that the judgment of posterity is the correct one and not the biased evaluation of some historians. Perhaps this old Baroque dramatic art is doomed, perhaps the consensus that makes Handel into the composer of *Messiah* alone is an example of natural selection. When we inquire whether there has actually been any "selection" based on esthetic considerations, the answer must be a resounding "No!" These operas require a much more stringent study than anyone has yet devoted to them. It is easy enough to account for them historically, and in the process we may also find artistic justification for them, as valid today as in the 18th century. The critics who dismiss Handel's operatic "phase" fail to consider how important that phase was in the wholly natural development of the English oratorio, made out of arias and recitatives of the opera with the addition of the chorus from the church and the theatre. The question is whether the artistic style of a given era is determined by that era's social organization, and if so, how? Is there an element in these operas that is a valid element of the age's mood? Was there an English public that would spontaneously respond to opera? The English stage, ever since Elizabethan times, shows how closely and immediately the dramatists reflected in their plays things great and small that agitated their times. The Commonwealth also proved that the theatre presupposes a certain freedom of political, religious, and moral life. During a severe, rigid, ideologically controlled period, that theatre cannot exist, except perhaps in some didactic or propagandistic form, as in present-day Russia.

The first thing one notes when contemplating the scene where Handel worked is that his opera was a class art, entertainment for the aristocracy. Though opera became the national theatrical art of Italy, its origins were aristocratic, and what Handel brought with him from Italy was a sophisticated entertainment for cultivated ears. Second, there was the foreign element, to which strenuous objections were raised, while the castrato created a moral issue, and the Italian librettos were found trivial. Yet none of this was altogether new to England. Evelyn, in his *Diary*, noted as early as 1673 that he "saw an Italian opera in music, the first that hath been in England of this kind"; the "voice of eunuchs" was known to Pepys in 1660. As to the Italian element, we may quote Dryden, who defended himself against the accusation that he "latinizes too much" by saying: "What I bring from Italy I spend in England, here it remains and here it circulates; for if the coin is good, it will pass from one hand to another."

The coin was good in literature, architecture, and painting, but on the operatic stage it could not "pass from one hand to another" for the simple reason that there was no such stage in England. In Italy, opera was by 1700 *the* theatre, as an institution having supplanted the spoken theatre, whereas everywhere else it was an importation that intruded upon the old and established spoken theatre. In France, and later in Germany, opera managed to grow roots, but in England, the home of the modern theatre, the public and the literary world alike refused to accept new and strange conventions and would not yield to opera's particular illusion. (Though we should not overlook the few enthusiastic admirers of Italian opera. Burney, who in his great history spent two hundred and fifty pages on 18th-century opera in London alone, considered it the highest form of music, "the union of every excellence in every art.") The point they could not understand was that opera is to be valued not for the representation of life to which the highly developed theatre had accustomed them but for the music's penetration of a reality beyond facts. To the theatrical public, individual character can be expressed only in spirited dialogue, and there is little dialogue in Baroque opera because it is not naturalistic theatre. The long musical sentences, the artificial figures of speech, the constant repetition of single words, and the kind of pathetic diction that Shakespeare called "King Cambyses' vein" all seemed ridiculous to them.

English theatrical history is as complicated as the history of the English musical stage, and it is particularly tortuous and obscure when the two strands are knotted together. We discussed this to some extent above (p. 194 ff.); suffice it to say here that, in the first place, because 17th-century England had no tragedy comparable to the French classical tragedy, the ground was not prepared for an English Lully. The English Lully, Purcell, nevertheless did arrive, but even he could not change the national taste; to compose for the lyric stage is to submit oneself, as even the playwright does not, to the chances of fashion. The social-artistic traditions are strong and inescapable, and their gradual abandonment is a very slow process. *Dido and Aeneas* is a genuine opera, but it is Purcell's only one, and it was not intended for the public theatre. His incidental music to such plays as *The Fairy Queen* or *King Arthur* is not a whit below the level of that of his sole opera, but the music consists of individual pieces, unconnected "numbers." Within this unoperatic frame Purcell time and again created superb scenes that are convincingly operatic. Thus an English operatic *language* was an accomplished fact; the only thing missing after 1695 was an English musician of sufficient stature to continue Purcell's work, break through the opposition from the spoken theatre, and effect a synthesis of all preliminary trends. There were some musicians who saw the problem and moved in this direction, but their talent was modest and they were given no encouragement. With the arrival of the Italians (and as an opera composer Handel must be considered one of them) any further hope for English opera was extinguished for a long time to come.

In the second place, the court masque was banished by the Commonwealth, and after the interruption of the tradition it was difficult to return to the distinctly aristocratic theatre. Now the musical stage became a more or less realistic entertainment in the public theatres; there was a *rapprochement* with the regular theatre and with the tastes of the middle classes. At any rate, it would be misleading to place the literature of the English play *with* music, which is a mere facet of its wide culture, beside the Italian play *in* music, that is, opera, which represents the fullest development of the artistic aspirations of a whole people. Imported Italian opera took the place of the old aristocratic court art, and for a few decades London became one of the colonies, like Vienna or Dresden, where the specific form, language, and tone of an alien culture, the Italian, held sway. Handel, who became the supreme representative of Italian opera of the late Baroque, was the focal point in the triumphs and failures of opera in London during these decades, and though in the end he had to abandon opera altogether, we do not leave this Baroque opera with the feeling that Handel's great gifts were wasted.

That they were, is the conventional view, but it does not stand objective investigation; these forgotten operas illuminate his whole path. Those who are puzzled by the disappearance of opera should remember that institutions that do not spring from an acknowledged social need lose their vitality, though not necessarily their artistic value. In the end, while it is unquestionably regrettable that Handel spent so many years doggedly promoting and fighting for something that had little hope of succeeding in England, and granting that Baroque opera had certain limitations inherent in the genre which he could not overcome, many of these scores are authentic masterpieces. That this is beginning to be understood is shown by the gradual revival of Baroque opera in Germany, Italy, and England. This is only partly the result of curiosity awakened by historical research; the law of the pendulum is asserting itself. The so-called orchestra-opera and the more recent *Sprechgesang* have destroyed singing; now we want to restore it, and nowhere was pure singing more exalted than in Baroque opera. However far and however long Handel's stage works fell out of operatic fashion, their sheer musical value, apparent even to those who are unable to adjust themselves to Baroque musical dramaturgy, insured their survival.

[2]

NEVER WAS THE style more candidly the man than with Handel. He was born for the theatre, and the Italian impressions sealed his artistic features. It is far from the mark to begin an appreciation of Handel's style by saying that "his music—like Bach's—is rooted in the instrumental and vocal art of the Middle German cantors" (Müller-Blattau in *MGG*). This sort of thing could perhaps be excused half a century ago, when German historians simply copied Chrysander, since scarcely any one on the Continent was concerned with English music. Today, and in the outstanding modern musical encyclopedia, such crass misreading of stylistic history is unpardonable. Both German and English writers, in eager haste to reach the "sacred" works, looked upon everything that preceded the oratorios as "preparatory" steps hardly worth more than a mention. The whole Italian period, consequently, was traced with indulgent superficiality, often accompanied, on the English side, by homilies on the futility of opera. The milieu from which Handel's art took its first flight was the chamber can-

tata, as far removed from the Middle German cantor's art as Vinci or
Pergolesi is from Bach. The cantatas, and their particular variety known
as the chamber duet, accompanied Handel throughout his life, springing
up like a mountain streamlet and with the most charming spontaneity
among the great sombre music dramas. Handel even composed new ones
on Italian texts as late as the 1740s.

While always retaining his individuality, he remained faithful to the
older Venetian-Neapolitan ideal of the musical stage, though towards the
end of his operatic career he does show signs of being influenced by new
currents coming from Italy.[1] He did not markedly develop in his operas
as he did in the oratorio, he only wrote better ones. We do not see the
tremendous broadening of conception that we can follow in the oratorios.
The operas do develop in finesse, in the wondrous handling of the orchestra, and in many other facets of the craft that a maturing musical genius
would naturally show in whatever he does, but the convention was too
strong, the genre held Handel in its grip. The technical construction was
more severely regulated in the old opera than in the new oratorio. The
latter, especially its lyric and epic variety, could arrange its episodes in
widely varied order, while the opera composer dealt with whole sets of
dramaturgical dogmas, constructional clichés, schemes, and schedules. If
such rules are applied too rigidly, if a genre becomes too stereotyped, it is
detroyed; this is what eventually happened to the opera seria, and this is
what undoubtedly caused a number of Handel's operas to lack viability.
But in a surprisingly large number of great works Handel coped successfully with the constricting conventions, for he often departed from the
strict observance of the "rules," even from tradition. Behind the conventional librettos (as behind the well-known biblical stories) Handel reconstructed the men who appear there as legendary or historical vignettes.

Though the form of Handel's opera was that of the aristocratic "court
opera," for him the essence of the drama was not the plot; he was far
more interested in the human nature of his protagonists. With the exception of *Riccardo I*, he never composed the type of allegorical homage
opera that the Italians wrote for the princes in whose service they worked
abroad. Vienna especially welcomed these thinly disguised paeans to the
ruling dynasty. In Handel's case homage to King and country was reserved for the anthems and, less formally, for the oratorios. When writing
for the theatre, to compose and to seize a dramatic moment were the

[1] The designation "Venetian" or "Neapolitan" must be understood in a rather
elastic sense, for neither Scarlatti nor Steffani nor Handel fits unconditionally in the
scheme.

same to him. Even the oratorios are music dramas conceived for the theatre; to place them in the church is absurd. Handel can reveal in a character dramatic possibilities that never occurred to the librettist, its creator, and his ability to conjure up a mood is well illustrated by the little ritornels that precede arias. At times, notably in the earlier works, he had some difficulty with his heroes, who tend to lengthy soliloquy and somewhat overdrawn pathos. Or on other occasions his hero simply walks through the drama toward his own scenes, making the work episodic. But when he reaches the great moments, the weak portraits are forgotten, and dramatic intensity can reach a peak that threatened the framework of Baroque opera.

While Handel was fighting his operatic wars in London, the fashions changed, and there began a vast shifting of operatic taste: the era of Scarlatti was declining as the era of Metastasio began. At first Handel seems to have been oblivious of these changes, or more probably he ignored them, for he was always well informed about musical trends. Nevertheless, a certain stirring in the operas composed for the new Academy of Music is noticeable. Handel's Italian recruiting trips, almost two decades after his first sojourn there, must have familiarized him with the new trends in Italian opera. Surprisingly, he was very slow to reassess his aims in the light of altered circumstances, but in the last operas there is a definite change. The texture becomes much lighter, assuming a decidedly popular cast; the melodies are often real "tunes." This has been attributed to the more modest capabilities of the singers Handel was forced to engage, the greater ones having been abducted by the competing companies. While this may have been a contributing factor—Handel was a pragmatic professional—the main reason was the rising neo-Neapolitan style of the opera buffa. The opera buffa was bound to be victorious over the seria, for the realistic and lively mimic sense of the Italians had always overcome abstraction ever since the Middle Ages; they loved a good story.

Now ensembles appear more frequently in Handel's operas, as does a long-forgotten element, the chorus. This operatic chorus (like the ensembles) is sparingly used, but it is definitely choral in nature as opposed to the "chorus" of soloists that Handel placed at the end of his earlier operas. Was this new phase a retreat from or an advance towards a creative truth? Earlier in this volume we said that when leaving Venice Handel had certain ideas about opera that he felt could not be realized in Italy. The vicissitudes of operatic life in London forced him to spend a long time in taking his soundings, but near the end there were great strides towards what in another quarter of a century would become the reform opera. He considerably lessened the distance between secco recitative and aria by increased reliance on the accompanied recitative and the arioso as well as a blend of these, and he moved from the individual aria to the group of pieces that make up a *scena*. But here his Italian opera ends. He had got himself into a situation from which he could extricate himself only by a complete reorientation: the English oratorio. He did not really cease writing operas—*Semele* among others proves it—but now he composed English works for English audiences. The premises had changed, and though it was within his grasp to establish what Purcell and all the others had failed to do, to create English opera, unaccountably he, too, failed. This failure could not be ascribed solely to insular conservatism, for a man of the world was at work here, and many of the materials used came from the ambassadors of European music.

Every one has denounced Handel's librettists—and some of them were very poor—but he could not have written masterpieces without at least serviceable librettos. One readily admits that the words alone may often look loose and even silly, but complete the words with the music (from which they never should be parted), and everything becomes quite different. In dramatic vocal music we can seldom consider the text apart from the music without injustice and stultification. If necessary, Handel did interfere with his librettist, but as a rule he did not pay too much attention to the story. It was different with the set pieces. Neither the Greek nor the classic French drama considered the novelty of the story of any importance, nor did Shakespeare. What they were interested in, and what Handel did, was to bring the figures to life; he was a creator of men. This, after all, is what makes a dramatist a dramatist. There is a good deal of accident in the story-telling as well as in the dénouement, but to the true dramatist accident is only the symbol of the accidental nature of human things. The absolute necessity, free of everything accidental, which is the dream of esthetes, does not exist in earthly life and is esthetically impossible, too; it would render human life into a mathematical formula. If during the course of composition Handel had a change of heart, or disliked what the librettist gave him, or was out of sympathy with one of the figures, he never hesitated to let the librettist know. If he could not get what he wanted he simply ignored the text and composed his music by favoring certain words, thus giving the piece the quality he wanted despite the text.

This Baroque libretto was not, however, dramaturgically primitive. Its aims were entirely different from the naturalistic, psychological drama of modern times, its main role being to create situations suitable for the introduction of arias, of lyricism. This has led to the musicological term "concert opera," a pejorative misnomer. But if we interpret "concert opera" to mean that a concentration on the music is necessary, we come closer to the nature of Baroque opera. During the aria, action was virtually suspended and the attention of Handel's public was riveted to the convolutions of the music. The spurious acting we usually require at this point interferes with this concentration. Our public, accustomed to the realistic theatre, will simply have to learn how to listen to this music, for it is the process that matters in this type of opera, not the action. At times Handel's stage is narrow, but it can be intensely lit; his plot makes contact with life at few points, but the contact is ringingly made.

[3]

IT IS REMARKABLE THAT the irrepressible happy world of Shakespeare and other English playwrights, the world of amorous comedy, banter, and playful humor, is rarely present in Handel's operas. His abstention from comedy is the more surprising because the English theatre consistently refused to divorce the serious from the comic. Furthermore Handel was well acquainted with Italian opera and oratorio, both of which contained buffo elements. In denying himself this mixture he denied himself an easy way of characterization, because comedy is the merciless critique of human foibles. Contrast of the serious with the comic is in itself a form of characterization. But though Handel had a healthy sense of humor and actually wrote delightful comedy, on the whole he seldom composed *parti buffe*. He may have been influenced in his early youth by some dramaturgical ideas that frowned upon comedy as part of a serious work. Barthold Feind, the Hamburg dramatist, was not the simpleton poetaster some historians made him out to be. His prefaces to his plays and librettos, as well as his treatise, *Gedanken von der Opera* (1708), show a considerable knowledge of the literature of dramaturgy and of the nature of opera. It is quite possible that it was from him that Handel first took the idea of excluding comic scenes from his dramatic works, for Feind had very positive views on the subject, even though low comedy was extremely popular in Hamburg. The other early impression may have come from Giovanni Crescimbeni, whom Handel met at the Arcadian Academy in Rome (see above, p. 54). In his highly respected *La Bellezza della volgar poesia* (1700), Crescimbeni expressed the Arcadians' conviction that the comic element has no place in a "classical" drama. A true dramatist does not make exalted persons mix with "base" people, such as buffoons. It is noteworthy that the original librettos for some of Handel's operas contained *parti buffe,* but almost invariably they were removed by Haym, Rolli, and the others in the reworking of the source material. Given the number of librettists involved, the consistent changes can be attributed only to Handel's insistence. Yet the Arcadians' principles were not observed by the successful opera composers, and Handel himself readily subscribed to such anti-classical devices as the mandatory happy ending, which Crescimbeni expressly prohibited, but which was the stock in trade of every composer and was demanded and relished by the public. Or was it perhaps the Restoration comedy, too coarse for Handel's taste, that discouraged him, or the earthiness of the buffa? To him passion was not to be mocked at. In almost every art there is a playful element, but Handel did not often like to play with his art. This playfulness is more natural to the Latin, whose spirit floats with liberty over artistic creation and does not easily surrender, like the German or Englishman, to sombre tragedy.

Every comedy is more or less realistic; or perhaps more precisely, no real comedy can be imagined without naturalistic elements. It calls for a different attitude, a different viewing, and a different lighting than does tragedy. One of its essential traits is the skepticism with which it views every form of heroism, behind which it wants to shine its light, seek the pose and the make-believe and the emptiness. It does not know, or refuses to acknowledge, anything in life that is perfectly secure, whose values, greatness, and beauty are above all criticism. And comedy, great comedy, always shows both sides of the coin simultaneously. Handel knew the buffa, but he did not compose comedy pure and simple, for he created characters of iron consistency, and in comic scenes a character drawn with consequence loses this very quality. On occasion he did use the buffo element very tellingly, but he was first and foremost a tragic and lyric artist.

This leaves us with the mixture, tragicomedy. Tragicomedy is a very complicated intellectual procedure, the realization that the event taking place before us admits to points of view that are mutually exclusive. This can only be the result of a subsequent intellectual act whereas spontaneous effect, the really theatrical, demands either of the two poles, the tragic or the comic. The older theatre did not know this combination; the most it admitted was the juxtaposition of tragic and comic characters, or the alternation of tragic and comic situations, in which case the two styles were separated. Nor can comedy be expressed sensuously—the situation is its chief means—and Handel's entire imagination was sensuous. He lacked the irony that was so strong in Mozart and enabled the Viennese master to compose superb comedy while it prevented him from debasing his characters to a point of being simply comical. The witticisms, the pungent comments for which Handel was known, have no echo in his music; but of delicate and sophisticated humor there are many more examples than *Serse,* always cited as Handel's only excursion into the comic vein. These range from single scenes, such as the duet of Dalinda and Lurcanio in *Ariodante,* to whole operas, such as *Deidamia.* This whimsical humor, which has little to do with the opera buffa, was lost on Handel's contemporaries. Burney rejected even *Serse,* obviously more because of his knowledge of the classical theory of drama than because of a true appreciation of the work. He objected to "the mixture of tragicomedy and buffoonery, which the reformers, Zeno and Metastasio, had banished from the 'serious opera.' " But *Serse* is not a "serious opera," nor is there any buffoonery in it, only genial love intrigue that has its engaging contretemps. Humor usually requires that things be looked at from close proximity, but Handel's view was seldom directed nearby. This, and the fact that there is no comic feeling, only comic thought and situations, explains the dearth of the comic in Handel's dramas. Speaking of the delicately humorous elements in Handel's last operas, Dean makes an observation that goes to the root of the matter so far as audiences of today are concerned: "It is a quality not easy to detect in a convention whose curious aspects seem ridiculous to a modern audience."

[4]

OPERA COULD NOT SUIT the social-cultural traditions in England. The spoken theatre, well known and well liked by the middle classes, rejected the etiquette and the classical props and puppets. The castratos—reprehensible to the British mind—the preening and jealously quarreling singers, added a moral touch to the distaste. When in 1737 the Covent Garden company collapsed, as did the rival establishment of the Opera of the Nobility, there was no opera left in England, and no one seems to have missed it even though by that time Handel had presented to Londoners over thirty operas. Somehow this mistrust and moral indignation gained in intensity, and by the time we reach the 19th century Handel's biographers were ready to rewrite history: the conversion theory appears as an explanation of his motives for turning to the oratorio. They honored the consensus that posited a sharp break between opera and oratorio. Not only scholarship but even ordinary common sense was lacking when they failed to see that only the locale, the scene of action, had changed, not the theatre itself. The means are the same except for the very important new element, the chorus. Handel experienced everything dramatically, instantly so, therefore even his epic-contemplative works eventually take a dramatic turn. Neither accident, nor compulsion, nor conversion is responsible for the change to oratorio; it was the result of a clear appraisal of the practical situation. Handel wanted a musical genre in which he could deploy his powers and which at the same time would appeal to all strata of the English public.

Two of the period's outstanding trends appear in his solution: the secularization of church music and the victory of the Italian musical Baroque. Therefore this art, while English to the core, is also of universal validity. It is unconfined by sectarian boundaries, and in an unsettled time it offered the most elevated spirit of community within a universal and popular style. There is no question that, aside from other compelling reasons, the change to oratorio was the result of a deep artistic insight. Handel saw the great line it made possible, and he also saw how to escape the restrictions of the opera seria. Nor is there any question that in his fidelity to this insight there was an act of renunciation, which few of his admirers are prepared to see and admit. Yet it is manifest in every one of his moves, as he went from crisis to crisis, facing the failures and humiliations with courage and determination. But to the reverent eyes of those who see in Handel the composer of *Messiah* only, and who have done little more than nibble at his operas, this determined and heroic fight was incomprehensible and ridiculous. They could not see here the struggle of a musician who was intimately concerned with the drama of human life and the texture of human emotions, for which opera, ever since Monteverdi, has always been the most congenial vehicle of expression.

Musically, Handel's progress from the "shallows" of opera to the "deeps" of oratorio follows such a delicate plan of gradation that the break between the two appears less as a plunge into deeper waters than a modification of form appropriate to a more intensely felt personal approach. He was still composing theatre music, even adding stage directions to those supplied by the librettists. It was Princess Anne, Handel's great friend and pupil, and a more perceptive Handelian than many a musician or historian of famous memory, who immediately saw the theatrical qualities in *Esther* and wished to have it staged and acted like an opera. While until recent times the aprioristic attitude towards the oratorio frowned upon any hint of the "theatre," some discerning and dissenting voices were heard even in Chrysander's time, though only in regard to the so-called secular oratorios. August Reimann in his *G. F. Händel* (1882) flatly declared *Semele* and *Hercules* valid only if staged.

Though oratorio was closely related to opera, there were some profound differences in the social and literary aspects of the new genre. The English music drama called oratorio reflected bourgeois thought and ethics, whereas opera was aristocratic. The bourgeoisie could see no reality in Italian opera, but the great conflicts of State *versus* rebellion, the defense of Jewish faith and institutions from the pagans had a social significance for them that accorded with their own aspirations. The Old Testament figures appeared to them as dramatic individuals of far greater dignity than the figures of classical legend and history, and the Old Testament also gave Handel a poetically fabulous distance: *major e longinquo reverentia.* The minute he returned to his favorite classical subjects, in *Semele* or *Hercules,* this *reverentia* disappeared and the English public rejected them as operas, which in fact they were. The behavior of Handel's characters had to conform to the expectations of his audience. That is to say, he was able, at the same time as he refrained from pointing a moral in his work, to rely on the uniform moral sense of his audience. For this reason the effect was far more powerful and moving than an express and positive appeal such as that in the sentimental family novel.[2] The other essential change was due to the complete reorientation of the phonetic structure upon which the melody was based, since Italian phonetics had to be replaced by English.

[5]

CATEGORICAL DIVISION OF genres always becomes arbitrary as soon as a new and significant composer appears on the scene. To deal with Handel's *Resurrezione* and the two German Passions as stages in the development of the English oratorio is inadmissible. Even the term "oratorio" is actually a misnomer when applied to Handel's English works, for they have little in common with either the Italian or the German prototypes. The oratorio flourished on the Continent during the Handelian era. Almost every composer of opera also wrote oratorios, and though today forgotten, there are many remarkable masterpieces among them. But these, including the works of such Germans as Fux or Hasse, were Ital-

---

[2] Handel was familiar with the family novel because Mrs. Delany was a great admirer of Richardson. A trace of this acquaintance does show through occasionally, as for instance in *Solomon.*

ian oratorios—that is, subterfuge operas. Even such an outstanding work as Leo's *Abel's Death* is pure Italian music drama, altogether different from Handel's English music drama. The fact is that there was nothing like the English oratorio before Handel. Hawkins proves that oratorio of any sort was practically unknown in his country.[3] He was aware of "the Concerto Spirituale, so frequent in the Romish countries, and which by the name of Oratorio is nearly of as great antiquity as opera itself," but he did not minimize its newness in England. "As to the risk that an entertainment so little known in this country as the Oratorio would be disrelished, of that too [Handel] was able to form some judgment." On the other hand, Handel's oratorios were unknown on the Continent, even though he was famous as a composer of operas, a number of which were performed in Germany and Italy. It is surprising that German scholars (and many of the English) avoided asking themselves the question that stared them in their face, namely whether Handel's oratorio was not an entirely personal form of English dramatic music. On the contrary, the tendency is to see in the Handelian oratorio a direct descendant of the German cantata and Passion, with some of its blood coming from Italy. Critics saw in the oratorio not passages from history, freely and imaginatively treated as dramas of persons, but symbols of religious and philosophical issues, and scholars made strenuous efforts to prove the presence of such issues in the most unlikely places.

This eternal search for *Weltanschauung* is misplaced in the study of a composer whose natural bent was towards representation of human passions, and not towards abstract theological problems. It is in the storms and ravages of the soul, its triumphs and tragedies, that his creative pleasure finds its most convincing tones, but he is also capable of the most intimate and refined accents, as well as warm—even searing—erotic transports. It is unfortunate that views on the oratorio are generally as blurred by excited religious acclamations as those on opera are distorted by sentimental prejudices.To most people Handel comes to life only when he raises his voice, that tremendous voice which could match Jehovah's, yet he can be like the giant who plays with a little child. Only the very great and strong can be so gentle and amiable. To Iphis he advances on tiptoes, but Belshazzar he strikes with a club. Nowhere in his dealings with his librettists does he allude to any doctrinal or philosophical questions; it is always the dramatic craftsman's imagination that speaks from his letters.

---

[3] While Italian oratorio was unknown in England, Carissimi's music was not entirely unfamiliar. Pepys describes an evening spent "in singing the best piece of musique counted of all lands in the world, made by Signor Charissimi, the famous master in Rome" (July 22, 1664).

"Your most excellent Oratorio has given me great Delight," he writes to
Jennens, acknowledging receipt of the libretto of *Belshazzar*. "It is indeed
a Noble Piece, very grand and uncommon; it has furnished me with Expressions, and has given me Opportunity to some very particular Ideas,
besides so many great Choruses."

This little paragraph accurately describes Handel's attitude as a dramatic composer; his way *ad lucem* was not, as the apologists maintain,
per crucem, but *per theatrem.* The world has heard a great deal of Handel as the pillar of Christianity but little of him as an artist who, like a
glass maker, shapes his material with blower and furnace into works of
exquisite limpidity. His sense of beauty is a quality our misguided tradition is often tempted to overlook in the supposition that he cared only for
grandeur. It did not produce the sort of beauty that those accustomed to
the great German Protestant sacred music are most ready to look for and
most likely to enjoy. It will be more readily appreciated when his dramatic
works, both opera and oratorio, are staged and acted with all their delicacy of characterization, avoiding the impression of repressed passions
and diverted instincts. The first requirement is a new edition of Handel's
works. It is hoped that with the new critical edition now in progress the
old religious and nationalistic bias will be forgotten in the interest of true
art and scholarship, so that this great music will once more sound in all its
glory.

[6]

LIKE HIS OPERA LIBRETTISTS, the men who furnished texts for
Handel's oratorios were no poets to speak of. Still, they could put together
a usable dramatic vehicle that suited Handel's genius. Unlike the Italians,
however, the pusillanimous English men of letters such as Humphreys,
when arranging a powerful drama for an oratorio libretto, would remove
its heart and make the rest into something comfortably bourgeois. Fortunately, if they kept a reasonable continuity and did not cut out all the
conflicts, Handel was able to make a work of art out of the poor dramatic
poetry. He was a good judge of librettos; his sense for the proper textual
vehicle for his music is shown by his correspondence with Jennens on the
inordinate length of *Belshazzar* and the unilateral cuts he made in it. But
when he was given a really wretched libretto, such as *Joseph and His
Brethren,* he was helpless to overcome its deficiencies and was reduced to
grasping at the little fragments of meaningful drama. At such moments,
even in his least successful works, his music immediately lights up, but

elsewhere the drama is inorganic. He aims at a unity that is absent in the libretto and that can be difficult to extract from the sometimes rather in-human figures of the Old Testament. As in any inorganic art, every virtue is at odds with some other virtue. The unifying monumentality of his lan-guage at times weakens the life of some of his figures, making them a lit-tle generalized, but he almost always compensates with his lyric intensity in the spiritual reflection of tragedy, with the conjuring up of the moods in which tragedy is conceived.

Good unity and continuity are usually destroyed in performance, as is not infrequently sense, too, by what might be called the "oratorio pause" between the individual numbers. The soprano finishes her aria, retiring with dignified reserve to her place on the conductor's right, and, when she is seated, the maestro beckons to the tenor who, with equal gravity and decorum, advances and gets set, the harpsichord sounds its warn-ing chord, and the recitative begins. But these two are dramatic adver-saries locked in a flaming contest; the recitative should follow immedi-ately upon the last cadence of the aria, for this is drama, theatre, and not a pseudo-divine service. We are presented with tableaux seemingly un-connected. This, in addition to the lack of staging, gives the false impres-sion that the dramatis personae are passive, symbolic figures. The operatic element survived in the oratorio and was if anything enhanced. At times one has the distinct feeling that Handel is more concerned with the dra-matic and communicative powers of his English singers than with the quality of their voices. Such a "star" as Mrs. Cibber was not even a singer by trade but an excellent actress.

To be sure, some of the disadvantages of Baroque opera were still present: male roles assigned to female singers and an occasional castrato part. But on the whole freedom from the restrictive practices of the opera seria is manifest everywhere. The da capo aria begins to be displaced as early as *Athalia,* and in some of the middle-period oratorios it is sparingly used, though Handel returns to it whenever a work, such as *Semele,* is closer to opera. Even here he permitted himself "liberties" and "irregulari-ties" such as he seldom used in opera arias. Ensembles, very rare beyond duets in the operas, are somewhat more frequent in the oratorios, and all of them are modern dramatic ensemble music of the first water. Even the duets are, as a rule, more dramatic in the oratorios than in the operas. They are often part of the action, whereas in the operas they are most of the time lyric-amorous episodes. It is remarkable that the instrumental pieces in the oratorios, the "symphonies," are far more telling dramatically than in the operas. Again, this was due to the absence of traditional rules governing the employment of instrumental pieces in the oratorio; Handel could indulge his imagination to a degree not possible in the operas. No modern composer surpasses him when it comes to such pieces as the description of the lair of the God of Sleep in *Semele* or the magnificent "sunrise" pieces and other nature pictures.

The older Handel becomes, the more he concentrates his efforts on the main characters in his dramas. There is a tendency to neglect the secondary figures and an unfortunate unconcern with post-dénouement matters. Time and again a magnificently taut and dramatically ever-growing third act will simply collapse after the hero's fate has been decided. Occasionally Handel does not even bother to mop up; he simply goes through the motions. Once he has done with the unfolding drama, his inspiration seems to flag, and he merely relies on his vast experience and facility—if he does not borrow a final chorus from some other work. This lack of interest in anything coming after the dénouement is however not a symptom of his old age. It is already present in the first, the Italian, *Acis and Galatea* of 1708, where, after Acis dies singing a wondrous little aria, the inspiration halts and the experienced technician takes over. Lessing said that "once the tragedy is over, our compassion ceases," but we think that Handel's curious unconcern was largely due to his aversion to the reigning tradition of the *fin felice,* the happy ending, which by its nature imposed restrictions upon the humanity of the story.

As we have remarked, it was in Handel's grasp to establish English opera, but he failed to do so. It is almost impossible to ascertain what prevented him from taking the few remaining steps, though the cruel rejection of *Semele* and *Hercules* may have convinced him that bona fide opera in any form was unacceptable to the English public. Still, there can be no question that the oratorio materially advanced the cause of modern opera. Schering (*Die Musik,* 1937) shows fine historical and stylistic insight when he—alone among musicologists—considers Gluck's endeavors to reform the music drama to have been judged onesidedly as the result of the literary influence of the Enlightenment. Calzabigi and others certainly had their share in this new dramaturgy, but the innate dramatic instincts of the musician are overlooked. Schering maintains that if one compares *Theodora* (1750) with Gluck's *Orfeo* (1762) one will not hesitate to ascribe to Handel's work everything—"and perhaps even more" —that has hitherto been attributed to the younger master. It is too bad that such perceptive thoughts by a great historian must be clothed in artificial patriotic garments. Schering goes out of his way to assure his compatriots that Handel's reforms were the result of "a pronounced German spirituality." No German spirituality is involved here, only the plasticity of ideas and the sound theatrical sense of a born dramatist who even in the stock phrases, nay even banalities, conveys warmth and expressivity. His powers of observation and his theatrical imagination were prominent from the very beginning; all he needed was to ask himself where and how beauty resides in the details. Long before Gluck, he was fully aware that certain theatrical elements serve to enhance the main features, that they place the essential in relief, and in his later oratorios he showed an increasing tendency to model in the round. When the handwriting appears on the wall in *Belshazzar,* the king's fright, the general consternation, the sense of doom, are dealt with in a purely theatrical conception that owes little to either old opera or German spirituality. Handel's dramatic instinct and imagination were closely allied with the practical care and savoir-faire of the expert performer. At the end of a work he did not inscribe the score with *Soli Deo gloria,* as Bach or Haydn would, but with the exact timing of the duration of the act.

The mixture of strains in Handel's music, the contrast between the sensitive grace of his intimate lyricism, the power of his dramatic scenes, and the epic grandeur of his anthems, may appear at first as something rhetorical and artificial. His style, because of its simplicity and "lack of problems," is still often unfavorably compared to Bach's. But once we penetrate a little deeper into it we realize that this music, like all great art, was the result of profoundly serious and exacting care, preparation, and organization. Simplicity and natural fluency can be very deceiving. Renan used to have a great reputation for the clarity and easy flow of his prose, which was held up as an example of a natural spontaneous faculty. Then a set of galley proofs was discovered mounted on wide sheets of paper, and the marginal corrections contained twice as many words as the original galleys. Yet the result was an admirably light and natural style that gives the appearance of simply flowing from the tap.

Then there is the incredible speed with which Handel worked, reflecting, surely, the facility and power of the born improviser. There is no mistaking the exaltation he felt using this power; he usually composed in some excitement, becoming burningly energetic as he raced with his subject. However, as with Mozart and Haydn, two exceptionally rapid workers, the time needed to commit a composition to paper does not tell the whole story. These musicians composed "in their heads," but they also made sketches and notes, Handel in this regard coming closer to Beethoven than to his 18th-century colleagues. Handel's sketches approximate the sketchbooks of Beethoven, a notoriously worrisome composer. They disclose that, while by nature a spontaneous, even explosive, composer, Handel not infrequently struggled with his material, though not so violently as Beethoven. We know that inspiration does not give the artist leave to neglect the impeccable exercise of his craft, but there was more at work here: the intellectual respectability of manipulative skill, a Baroque trait very strong in Handel, as well as a love of the opportunities offered by the moment for instantaneous exploitation, which then necessitated revision of the original ideas. In this last respect Handel fundamentally differed from Bach, his melodies in particular often growing under our eyes. They can be full of contrast, of capricious metric and rhythmic asymmetry, and they are yet of one piece. The recognition of the germ of a movement or aria, the growth of the germ in the warmth of the imagination, its attraction to itself of sidelights and reflections, its miraculous expansion quickened with emotion—all this makes Handel's style attractive and exciting. He could make interest beget interest, form reflect form, to create in the end virtually new types and genres.

[7]

Whenever we are faced with music as far removed from us as Handel's we must go back to the conventions, symbols, and principles of the age that produced that music. It is impossible to penetrate to the core of a world of art without knowing a good deal about the circumstances that produced and animated that art. Training in the understanding of such a musical style is still fairly rare today, even though Handel's musical language should be accessible to the most untutored mind. Distinguished performing musicians of the older generation who are still entirely under the spell of the esthetics of the Romantic era fail to apply their intellect, as distinguished from their instinct, to re-creation, but there are also musical inhibitions to be overcome, and these concern the younger musicians. A sense for tonal logic, for the architectural, dramatic—and expressive! —properties of a planned tonal order as opposed to piquant harmony is rarely present in musicians reared on post-Romantic and contemporary fare. Handel cannot be properly understood without such a feeling. Conductors are always ready to cut, shift, and rearrange portions of a Handel opera or oratorio, not realizing that they may inflict fatal blows not only to the structure of the work but to its dramatic and expressive qualities. But it is not alone feeling for long-range tonal connections and logic that is disappearing; the simple tonic-dominant relationship, the fundamental principle of "tension" that governed music for centuries, is about to depart and is undoubtedly meaningless to many young musicians. The same is true of the tension created by the leading tone, which for some time has freed itself from its traditional directional thrust. With understanding for all these elements absent or considerably weakened, it is difficult for a 20th-century listener to apprehend the infinite nuances based on tonal order and relationship. This is not to say that other musical means of creating cohesion, tension, and expression are not feasible or legitimate; but lack of tonal feeling places full enjoyment of the older style in jeopardy.

Before we categorize, we should agree that construction and organization are the result of an inalienable human instinct, but we should also bear in mind that formal arrangement does not necessarily denote inner construction, and while construction is an intellectual act, most of the time it is also a matter of "feeling" and expression. "Expression" is, however, an equivocal notion, especially when applied to music, where representation and expression are traditionally blended. Even when the composer expresses the most personal feelings, he is still following a purposeful intellectual process and not simply surrendering to the surge of spontaneous—that is, uncontrolled—creative excitement. We certainly experience great music before we understand it, before a rational accounting takes place, but the ability to experience can be trained and vastly extended.

This is especially true in the case of a composer like Handel, whose music is a treasure trove of elements strewn among the works of many masters in several nations. The most remarkable feature of this art, which he shares with such other universal masters as Lasso and Mozart, is that these combinations agree not only when the elements are compatible, but also when they are diametrically opposed. If we compare Handel's music to Alessandro Scarlatti's, which was one of Handel's chief sources, his art does not appear simply as bel canto carried to an even higher sphere. True, the cast of the melody is even nobler and can become breathtakingly beautiful, but Handel conveys this Italian art as if filtered through the entirety of the expressive taste of European music. That is, what Handel gives us is not the original Italian music but a variant in which southern sensuousness is paired with northern solidity, while the wondrous harmony of the forms, which with the Italians is a natural consequence of their composing process, is subjected to a governing authority. In Italy, where the two Saxons, Handel and Hasse, were acclaimed with enthusiasm, it was already noticed that Handel's music, while entirely within the Italian style and manner, had a stronger fibre than either Hasse's or Italian music in general. Indeed, even during his most hectic periods, when speed was essential to support his tottering operatic enterprise, Handel seldom fell into the suave but somewhat flat Italian manner of Hasse, the celebrated champion of Neapolitan opera.

It was the same with Handel's counterpoint, which was supposed to have issued from the German cantor's art. Handel, however, was not a cantor but a dramatist, for whom constant or indifferent use of polyphony, especially of "formal" or "strict" fugues, would diminish the dramatic quality; he therefore almost always blends homophony with polyphony even within the fugue, in a sort of improvisation that is altogether different from traditional German counterpoint. Perhaps the most interesting of these improvisatory creations are the quasi fugues which still cause discomfort to counterpoint teachers. A good example is "Thy right hand, o Lord," in *Israel in Egypt.* It begins like a fugue, the tenor commences, the soprano answers, but soon the fugue goes every which way, with many points of imitation, and what we hear is an essentially free-ranging homophonic piece full of witty turns. Handel did not have a fugue in mind at all; he improvised, but while the spirit is improvisatory, the piece is firmly and neatly anchored. In general one might say that Handel turned away instinctively but also deliberately from the stress and strain of a complicated design, even though this should have been his natural inheritance from the German cantor's art. What he retained from this inheritance was the sovereign command of counterpoint which he used in an entirely personal way. Handel shows a marked preference for designs into which happy thoughts that come in odd moments could be fitted.

XXIV

Handel's melody, harmony, rhythm, and metre—The improvisatory
element—Counterpoint—The fugue—Choral counterpoint—Other
stylistic features—The recitative—Difficult change from Italian to English
recitative—The aria—The da capo principle—The concerted aria—
Stylized aria types—Difference between oratorio and opera arias—The
ensemble—Illustrative symbolism—Hermeneutics and *Affektenlehre*—
Arguments for and against musical hermeneutics—Handel's use of
musical symbols—Handel and French music

HANDEL, LIKE BACH, USED COUNTLESS TRADITIONAL
contrapuntal subjects, formulas, themes, and motifs, but he also created
melodies of his own that tower above the everyday stock of the musical
craftsmen of his time. Bach, whose melodic gifts were extraordinary,
nevertheless was happiest with motifs that lent themselves to imitative-
ornamental procedure, to that marvelous interplay of contrapuntal parts
that is the essence of the linear conception. As soon as understanding for
this phenomenal art of musical design disappeared, Bach disappeared with
it and had to be rediscovered three generations after his death. The generations represented by his sons could not "feel" contrapuntally and found
such a texture lacking in expressiveness. The polyphonic composer exemplified by Bach knows no discrepancy between the means and his artistic will. He is so completely identified with his "instrument," he thinks and
invents so completely from the spirit of polyphony that his individual turns,
themes, and motifs lend themselves naturally to contrapuntal elaboration.
He is like the good chess player who always sees the whole board. When
such a composer turns to a "melody," a "tune," it is likely to be a reduction
and simplification of a many-voiced fabric into a dominant voice, the rest of
it being absorbed in the accompaniment. Quite different is a melody that
arises from a direct expression of feeling rather than from the manipulation of motifs.

A contrapuntal subject or symphonic theme is not an independent,
finished entity—it has only the capacity for development. It fulfills its

mission and reaches its full significance after elaboration and development; in a word, it is an element in an organism. A true melody is final,
unique, a closed entity which can be developed or changed only to a limited extent, and often not at all. Particular fugue themes and symphonic
subjects have been shared by many great composers, but melodies cannot be shared; at times they are borrowed, but they retain their individuality. Such melodies come to us in a flowing, streaming force
straight from the composer's soul. Yet Handel's great melodies, though
soaring and sensuous, can have a complicated structure; their constituent
members are often of unequal value and disregard symmetry, but they
follow their own inner blueprint to form a perfectly concentrated musical
organism. These melodies are ample in gesture and like to traverse various registers in swift succession (Examples 1, 2). Particularly characteristic of Handel are certain melodies whose opening strains start with such

Ex. 1 *Belshazzar*

Thou God most high and Thou___ a - lone. un - chang'd for - ev - er dost re - main

Ex. 2 *Agrippina* (solo cantata)

Co - me, o Di - o!   bra - mo la mor - te   a   chi vi - ta   eb - be da me?

an immense gesture that it scarcely matters what follows. Often when
such an idea occurs to Handel, he himself seems to "change the subject,"
embarking on a quasi-improvised continuation in a different vein from
the "head-motif" or motto (Example 3). Yet even such melodies are of one
piece, for this arch-improviser always kept his imagination in leash.

The heroic-pathetic Handel must always be balanced by the suave
lyricist. Melodies like those in Examples 4 and 5 are not less characteristic than his choral thunder. Nor should we forget the pastoral melodies,
whose charm, whether expressive of Mediterranean languor or the quiet

Ex. 3   *Theodora*

Ex. 4   **Solomon**

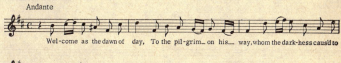

Wel-come as the dawn of day, To the pil-grim on his way, whom the dark-hess caus'd to

stray, Is my love-ly King to me

Ex. 5   *Rinaldo*

Ca - ra spo - sa, a-man-te ca - ra, do - ve se - i?

do - ve se - i? deh! ri - tor - na ai pian-ti me - il

of the English countryside, never fades (Examples 6, 7). Those who think of Handel only as *Jupiter tonans* should also look at the dainty grace of the tunes in his late operas, which obviously reflect the new Neapolitan style of the buffa. They give the impression of little intimacies recounted again and again with unwearied pleasure (Examples 8, 9). Against this we must cite Handel's Baroque penchant towards a certain melodic ecstasy that can result in a diffuse and flowery idiom, the melody luxuriantly

Ex. 6 *Ode to St. Cecilia*

Ex. 7 *L'Allegro ed il Penseroso*

overgrown with coloraturas. The choral melodies have an axis around
which the notes are grouped. Their inner construction is tight, full of tension, yet their quality is vocal no matter what their shape.

Both Bach and Handel show a preference for the large melodic design, but achieve this in different ways. Handel tends to freer stylization,
while Bach proceeds to more complicated and compound construction.

Ex. 8 *Imeneo*

Ex. 9 *Deidamia*

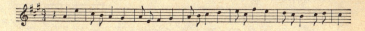

Handel preserves the vocal conception; Bach leans to a conversion even of vocal melody into the instrumental. In Bach's case this means that the music's relationship to the text may become vague and may even disappear, whereas in Handel the vocal basis is never missing and is subtly influential even in the most idiomatic instrumental compositions. His loyalty to the cause of the drama is often evident in unexpected turns as the sailing kite of melody is suddenly jerked from below by the composer's hand, the rhythmic flow exploded by a different accent. It is in this area that the Handelian melos differs fundamentally from the Bachian, for the "theatrical perspective" may demand a particular tone and pace. Often there is a certain urgency, a certain reckless quality in Handel's style, which Gerald Abraham calls his "broad slapdash style." This quality, which may be observed in Verdi and other Italian opera composers, can be very deceiving on paper; the stage is necessary for this kind of music to exert its intended effect. Opposed to this, though also rooted in drama, are the extreme condensation and plasticity of many of Handel's germinal utterances. Such compactness in turn has a latent propulsive—even explosive—quality that demands immediate continuation and exploitation (Example 10).

Ex. 10 Concerto Grosso, Opus 6, No. 1

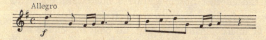

Then again, Handel, who was interested in folk music and is known to have noted down the street cries he heard in London, could compose melodies of the touching simplicity of an English folksong. The little ballad Susanna's companion sings is one of these. It looks—and is—charming, but its dramatic impact far exceeds its charm, for it was placed in context, in the "theatrical perspective," by the unerring instinct of the

dramatist (Example 11). While the great aria melodies are usually diatonic, in fugue themes Handel sometimes likes to follow the German Baroque practice, also dear to Bach, of building on chromatic, occasionally
even eccentric, subjects (Examples 12, 13).

Ex. 11 *Susanna*

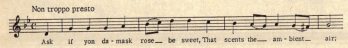

Ex. 12 *Belshazzar*

Ex. 13 *Israel in Egypt* (originally a keyboard fugue)

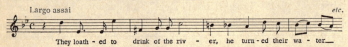

[2]

DENT, allowing his preferences to peep through the veil of
sound scholarship and discretion, found Handel's harmony "flat." Curiously, his colleague and another Busoni apostle, Leichtentritt, comes to
the exactly opposite conclusion, which we share. It seems that Handel's
not infrequent use of unaccompanied singing, his omission of the continuo as well as his fondness for unison passages, all of these serving dramatic ends, must have misled those whose harmonic taste was still anchored in the lush soil of late and post-Romanticism. This habit of renouncing the bass, and with it the entire apparatus of the basso continuo
(a procedure already employed in the Italian cantatas), has puzzled
those to whom "Baroque music" means a full-bodied texture supported by
a relentlessly rumbling continuo. Handel was ready to accompany his

singers with violins alone—or leave them altogether to their own resources. This is a matter of aural-theatrical imagination and not of flatness of harmonic sense. To indicate her loneliness Arianna, in *Giustino,* sings her aria "Per me dunque il ciel" without any accompaniment at all, which to ears unaccustomed to accepting even Gregorian chant without accompaniment is naked music. Chrysander often harmonized the unison passages, and editors and conductors like to add a little "body" to Handel's harmony, which they consider thin.

Handel's harmony is always sound, interesting, and often bold. His frequent use of tonalities such as B-flat, E-flat, and A-flat minor is exceptional before the Romantic era. His modulations, too, can be highly adventurous. A few examples will show that Handel's harmony is colorful even by 19th-century standards (Examples 14, 15, 16). In the final analysis one realizes that the flatness or boldness of Handel's harmony de-

Ex. 14 *Solomon*

Ex. 15 *Imeneo*

pended on the dramatic needs of the moment. At times the harmonies seem to have gone into hiding, while at others they glint in unexpected places, or fail where we expect them. In his instrumental music he is seldom adventurous; the harmony is always fresh and solid, but Handel relies mainly on his mobility, counterpoint, and fluent thematic continuity. In an accompanied recitative, however, he may advance far into the future. Furthermore, his harmony is also determined to a certain degree by the vocal concept that ruled his imagination. Mainwaring showed an early

Ex. 16   *Israel in Egypt*

and perceptive appreciation of the nature of Handel's harmonic scheme: "The harmony of Handel may be compared to the antique figure of Hercules, which seems to be nothing but muscle and sinew."

[3]

HANDEL HAD an exceptionally keen sense for rhythm and for metric refinement. His musical sentences may be compared to blank verse whose rhythm is complicated by enjambements. The frequent combinations and alternations, implicit or explicit, of different metres are enchanting, as are his combinations of dance types. Asymmetric constellations are frequent and always intriguing (Examples 17, 18, 19). His fondness for

Ex. 17   Concerto Grosso, Opus 6, No. 9

Ex. 18   Trio Sonata, Opus 2, No. 1

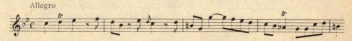

Ex. 19 *Susanna*

the hemiola, for time values whose relationship is 3:2, is noteworthy. This has been ascribed to English influences, but the hemiola, and the change from 6/4 to 3/2 (or vice versa) was a characteristic trait of Baroque music, resurrected later by Brahms in a typically archaic North German spirit. Even in his favorite dance form, the siciliana, Handel does not always observe the traditional rhythm; the spirit of the dance is there and so is the flowing, beguiling melody, but the rhythms are new and varied. Other interesting instances of subtle rhythmic-metric construction are shown in Examples 20 and 21.

Ex. 20 *Agrippina*

Ex. 21 *Il Moderato*

Perhaps the most engaging and most consistently intriguing quality in Handel's music is the combination of this preference for asymmetric design with the urge for improvisation. This great improviser at the keyboard was also a great improviser as a composer; in fact, this is an essential quality of his genius. The sudden capricious turns, unexpected internal repetitions, the brusque tangential departures, are all the result of the inspiration of the moment. It is fascinating to watch how Handel, having presented the antecedent, will delay the consequent, continuing to develop his thought by introducing new antecedents or questions, then answer them summarily, or in a series of consequents. These "irregularities" may seem to be separate portions, but are not really clauses, nor are they parenthetical; in spite of the improvisation there is a condition of dependence, a syntactical relationship arrived at by inductive musical logic (Example 22).

Ex. 22 *Theodora*

Opposed to this, though not unrelated to Handel's improvisatory-combinatory gifts, is his ever-growing penchant for thematic work that may assume genuinely symphonic proportions. This is notably present in the accompaniments to arias and choruses (Example 23). The often consistently thrusting and propulsive conduct of such thematically woven passages clearly testifies to the birth of the symphony from the spirit of opera. Finally, we should mention Handel's love of the ostinato basses of the Venetians. His use of the ostinato differs from that of the Germans and English, because it almost never offers a strict observance of the principle; it is only the effect that interests Handel.

Ex. 23   *Saul*

Gil - boan hills, on you

etc.

[4]

IF SOME HAVE questioned Handel's harmony, his counterpoint
has baffled many more. While his homophonic block-chord writing
(which overwhelmed Beethoven) is a typical characteristic of Handel's
choral style, his counterpoint is a sovereign art. A few pages back we
likened the true polyphonist to a chess player who always sees the entire
board; perhaps we should now add that the figures on this board are not
dumb bits of ivory but have their own sense, supporting one another con-
centrically. The born contrapuntist's chessmen always find themselves on
the right spot for action, second one another in imitations and similar procedures, sometimes without the composer's conscious awareness of the exact nature of the operation. Whether the theme was original was of no
particular importance—as we cannot often enough remind the reader—
but it had to fit into a musical organization and there occupy a central position. To a good composer a fugue subject immediately suggests many of
the possible combinations the minute he sees it. The experienced polyphonist knows at once whether a subject "will do," divining its possibilities;
he feels the latent counterpoint simply because he feels in terms of counterpoint. Only those reared on the music of the extreme individualism of
the Romantic era find in counterpoint something cold and cerebral. To
the average musician—let alone the layman—understanding for dense
counterpoint does not come easily; the texture is too rich and manifold.
One can go through Bach's more elaborate chorale preludes time and
again, know them and understand them, and then still hit upon some that
baffle. That Handel seems definitely "easier" is to be ascribed neither to
relative poverty of imagination nor to lack of technique. So far as contrapuntal technique is concerned, Handel knew everything his contemporaries knew. Yet wherever we look in the literature on the Baroque era,
even the authors most sympathetic to Handel often use such expressions

as "loose fugue," or "wayward part-writing," with implications of inferiority. The fact is that Handel's conception of polyphony was different from that of his contemporaries and was entirely personal. Loose as the counterpoint may be it is always thematic, only in the choral fugues are there exceptions to this for dramatic purposes. Perhaps the most characteristic difference between Handel's contrapuntal writing and that of the composers from whom he borrowed materials is that his *intentions* are seldom clear and he is always full of surprises, whereas even the inventive Gottlieb Muffat stays within the accepted fugal procedures of the Kuhnau tradition.

The relationship of the horizontal with the vertical in Handel's music was not clear to its critics because they were seeking parallels with Bach. They could find little the two composers had in common. First of all, the chorale, so prominent in Bach's music, is not at all characteristic of Handel's. He used it very sparingly and then usually only incipits of the traditional German hymns. The chorale as a genuine cantus firmus was alien to Handel's conception of polyphony and, as we have remarked on p. 208 ff., usually appears when Handel recalls the experiences of his youth or when he wants to be solemn in a somewhat archaic way. When he does so, he will use a species of cantus-firmus work, but even such textures generally serve dramatic purposes. Indeed, his writing is more the weaving of a free texture than actual cantus-firmus work over a given subject, as is often claimed.

What really upset the purists was Handel's fugal writing which, to say the least, is handsomely unorthodox. The fugue was for the Baroque composer what the sonata form was to the composers of the Classic era: the highest type of musical construction. But there were weighty differences in its practice. Bach, who wrote many great choral fugues, approached the genre in an instrumental spirit, whereas Handel's whole conception was vocal. While Handel composed some very fine fugues according to the book, the majority of his choral fugues are free, unpredictable, and gloriously unregulated. These agreeable levities cover the full range of Handel's highly imaginative fugal procedure; he was not bound by any rules of the *strenger Satz* of the German composers, because even the fugue served dramatic purposes.[1] The entrances can be orderly but

---

[1] Nevertheless, Handel was well acquainted with traditional German contrapuntal procedures; significantly, he used them only as examples—not in his compositions but in his didactic work. That Handel took the trouble to prepare such examples may come as a surprise because we know that he loathed teaching. Jakob Wilhelm Lustig, Mattheson's scholar, who visited Handel in London in 1734, reports that Handel emphatically declared to him that since Hamburg "no power on earth would move me

also quite capricious, the parts entering whenever they feel like joining in. Here the texture is imitative, canonic, there almost entirely homophonic; here the voices enter the traditional way, there after a couple of entries the remaining parts will drop portions of the theme to speed up the process, or entries will be delayed to create tension. At times the thematic substance is abandoned for the sake of a free flow, returning either imperceptibly or with a sudden jolt. The answer can be tonal or real—or neither.[2] The interruption of the polyphonic flow by homophonic passages, sometimes only a few measures long, only serves to emphasize the effect when the tumbling part-writing is resumed, sometimes reaching tremendous dramatic force, especially when a general pause is inserted. In some of his most magnificent fugues Handel does not pay much attention to the original theme; instead of developing it in the "correct" manner, he proceeds freely with snippets of thematic material, almost in a symphonic vein. If a motif strikes his fancy he will belabor it with gusto. What is decisive for him is the dramatic possibility, which overrules every other consideration. Also, if the vocal register is not advantageous, he is always ready to split up the theme or drop it and continue with free counterpoint. He will not permit his choral euphony to suffer from being forced into a weak register except when a deliberate symbolism is intended. We do find of course many fugues that open wide the door to the high art of "strict" fugal writing, if we may use that meaningless adjective so dear to theorists. "Oh God, who in Thy heavenly hand," an unusually beautiful chorus in *Joseph and his Brethren,* is a fugue *a tre soggetti* that even the most critical pedagogues would accept as a masterpiece. But as a rule the choral fugue with the regulation strettos, inversions, episodes, pedal

---

to accept pupils." But he made some exceptions, notably in the case of Anne, "the flower of all Princesses." He also taught the other princesses, and undoubtedly John Christopher Smith, Jr. Alfred Mann, in *Händel Jahrbuch,* 1964/65, pp. 35–57, thinks that a batch of manuscripts in the Fitzwilliam Museum served as exercises for his few disciples. One of the leaves carries the superscription "Madame," obviously referring to Princess Anne. Mann neatly proves that when all these pieces are put together one discerns a sort of graduated course in harmony and counterpoint. Moreover, the sonatas for recorder, also in this collection, must have formed part of the "course," for they seem to incorporate the principles presented in the exercises. Mann remarks that nowhere else is Handel's writing as tidy and legible as in these pieces—they were not meant for the copyist. In the exercises the old German tradition is preserved to a remarkable degree.

[2] Handel's "irregular" fugal entrances were the despair of pedantic counterpoint teachers then as now. But when such a spot was pointed out disapprovingly to Geminiani, his remark concerning the change of a semitone was: *Questo semitono vale un mondo.* We also learn from Mattheson that Handel's fugues "delighted the listener and kept both composer and player warm."

point, and so on is infrequent. Nor is there any set order in the exposi-
tions, since Handel is not at all averse to disregarding the proper relationship between *dux* and *comes*.

Handel was unmistakably attracted to the polyphonic practices of
the Italians, far freer than those of the Germans. The type of polyphony
Legrenzi, Bassani, Vitali, and others practiced towards the end of the 17th
century was light, fluent, unforced, vocal in origin and spirit even when
idiomatically instrumental. And of course the wonderfully balanced,
smooth, and flexible counterpoint of Corelli never faded from his memory. If we do not find in Handel's fugues the traditional elements at the
traditional places assigned to them, they are nonetheless present. He is
fond of the stretto but does not save it for the *pièce de résistance*, which
usually comes toward the end of the fugue; often he uses it right at the
beginning, even before the exposition is under way (Example 24).
Double fugues can take any shape or course, though he likes to develop

Ex. 24   *Berenice:* **Overture**

both subjects together from the very beginning. Perhaps the most interesting and unorthodox procedure followed by Handel is the insertion of a fugue into a different, larger structure, a practice that at times creates a most interesting and original quasi rondo form. The sections of the fugue will alternate with the recurring music of the number into which it is inserted and with which it has no thematic or any other connections. A choral fugue may be "accompanied"—that is, the instrumental portion is not *colla parte* but different from the vocal parts to the point where the instrumental bass is different from the vocal bass. It is clear, then, that we are dealing with a wholly individual conception of counterpoint that cannot be judged by textbook standards.

Writers on the fugue usually give Handel a wide berth. The *Harvard Dictionary of Music* does not even mention him in its article "Fugue," making a neat jump from Bach to Beethoven, while Percy Young avers that the writing of fugues was not one of Handel's strong points. Müller-Blattau, in his history of the fugue, glosses over Handel's fugues with a few general remarks, though among the older authors Chrysander and Seiffert valiantly tried to do justice to this unorthodox composer. There can be no question that this dearth of investigation is deliberate and not accidental. Bach's fugues have been studied and analyzed inside out, and since Handel is usually bracketed with Bach the various authors, especially in Germany, would have naturally sought out parallels, as they did when discussing cantata and oratorio. Moreover, no historian could have missed Mattheson's lavish praise of Handel's fugal writing. More amusing are the detailed analyses one reads in the biographies of Leichtentritt, Müller-Blattau, Serauky, and others, for they often cannot agree among themselves whether a fugue is double or triple, where the exposition ends, which are the episodes, and so on, or indeed whether a particular choral movement is a fugue at all. How little the nature of choral counterpoint was understood by the very persons who edited Handel's works for performance is illustrated in Prout's *Fugal Analysis* (1892), where the vocal fugues are printed without their texts, "for the sake of clearness." Nevertheless, Prout, who considered a good deal in Handel's fugues "irregular," bravely defended him against those who called his fugues "faulty and improperly treated." Surprisingly, Heinrich Bellermann, the staunch and archaic defender of the Palestrinian choral idiom, to whom Mozart was practically an avant-gardist, considered Handel "closer to the great masters of a cappella art than his famous contemporary Bach" (*Der Contrapunkt*, 1861). If the reader will return to the pages dealing with Handel's Italian studies, he will understand Bellermann's reasons, but the Italians' and Bellermann's views were shared by Englishmen too. Burney, in his volume on the commemoration concerts, remarks about "And with his stripes we are healed":

It is written upon a fine subject, with such clearness and regularity as was never surpassed by the greatest Choral composers of the Sixteenth Century. This fugue, which is purely vocal, and *à Capella,* as the instruments have no other business assigned them than that of doubling and enforcing the voice-parts, may fairly be compared with movements of the same kind in Palestrina, Tallis, and Bird.

No one in Handel's time, or before, used choral counterpoint as freely and ingeniously as he, and the vigor and terseness of the musical diction in his choral music is still unsurpassed. Handel's inner voice-parts are not "fillers"; usually they are worked out in the smallest detail, and often have considerable melodic value, but the severity of the cantor's art is absent. Perhaps the most typical aspect of this choral music is what is so well expressed by the German term *polyphonierende Homophonie,* which cannot be rendered in English with the same compact precision.

Handel's choral writing has an astonishing range, from light madrigal to giant fugue. A good example of a feathery madrigalian piece is found in *Semele* (Example 25). The polyphony is almost finicky in its tiptoeing. Accustomed as we are to the splendors of the anthem style, we do not notice the intimate Handel, the finesse of his chamber-music-like intimacy, the tensions he can create and resolve without massive dynamics. Particularly attractive is his way of proceeding from homophony to polyphony and then back again. This can take the form of a quasi prelude and fugue, with a clear break between the two, or can be marked by a subtly graduated ebb and flow. Handel may wheel a fugue into position with magnificent poise and dignity, the basses intoning the theme like so

Ex. 25   *Semele*

many high priests, but as the other parts enter, everything formal and expected gradually disappears. The variety and flexibility of his choral idiom is unexampled and unsurpassed. It is especially here that his freedom from the fetters of the opera seria is most noticeable. These choruses can assume every form of vocal or instrumental music; among them are choral recitatives, ariosos, and arias, as well as combinations of all three.

Here again we should single out Handel's ability to create stunning effects
with the simplest of means, for he knew that stillness can be awesome.
Example 26, from *Israel in Egypt,* shows that choral recitative can have

Ex. 26   *Israel in Egypt*

an almost graphic dramatic power. As a rule, the choral portions are accompanied by a *ripieno* orchestra, but seldom *colla parte;* the accompaniment can be of symphonic quality, with its own thematic material or utilizing elements from the vocal parts, or it can be imitative, and there are
usually little interludes that are purely dramatic. At times a homophonic
choral setting is accompanied by a linear texture or vice versa. The ritornels are often elaborate and significant. Perhaps the ultimate in dramatic
power is achieved in the "Jealousy" chorus in *Hercules,* where a predominantly homophonic choral setting is combined with a sharply accentuated
symphonic commentary in the orchestra. The entry of the chorus after a
menacing ritornel is shattering, and Handel does not permit the feeling of
apprehension to dissipate, for the rhythm of doom never departs from the
orchestra (Example 27).

In the end one realizes that aside from Bach there was no contemporary who could match Handel in contrapuntal skill, but as in all other aspects of their art, the two great composers cannot be compared because
their attitudes towards choral writing are diametrically opposed. Handel

made his style deliberately light, freeing it from the scholasticism of formal counterpoint. Weighty ideas he could present with a simplicity that made them accessible to all. Perhaps the greatest difference between the two masters, however, is that the highest concentration and expressivity

Ex. 27   *Hercules*

fer - nal   pest,   in - fer - nal   pest,

in Handel's choral music is not in polyphony but in homophony. With him choral homophony is usually the peak that follows upon the polyphony. That Handel is so different from his German colleagues rests on two causes: his Italian experiences and his residence in England. Ever since the Middle Ages English music had been distinguished from that of the Continent by its marked preference for well-blended vocal sound. Later, with Dunstable's gently rolling, soothing music, English composers influenced all of Europe, and it was for this reason that so euphonious a genre as the Italian madrigal found ready acceptance in England. Thus the German-born Handel, captivated while in Italy by the calm self-assured tone of Italian music, easily fell in step with the long-standing English tradition as exemplified by Purcell.

[5]

It will be remembered that the Beggar pointedly informed his audience that he avoided the "unnatural . . . for I have no Recitative." The distinguishing feature of the English "semi-opera" was the absence of recitatives and their replacement by spoken dialogue. The same procedure was followed by the German *Singspiel* all the way through the 19th century. Since recitatives were the carriers of the action and narration in Italian opera, Handel was faced with a dilemma when he turned to the English music drama. It was generally recognized—Burney deals with the question in some detail—that every nation found it difficult to come to terms with the Italian-born recitative, whose superiority was acknowledged even by Quantz and Mattheson. Many of the French partisans of

Italian opera also held this view. On the English scene, Pepys perceived this very early, commenting on it in 1667 when he heard an Italian singer perform excerpts from an opera: "The words I did not understand, so I know not how they are fitted, but I believe very well, and all in the Recitativo very fine. But I perceive there is a proper accent in every country's discourse, and that their setting of notes to words, therefore, cannot be natural to any body else but them." Addison, with his usual critical sharpness, expressed the prevailing ideas in a little essay (*Spectator*, April 3, 1711), reaching the conclusion that "an English composer should not follow the Italian Recitatives too servilely, but make use of many gentle Deviations from it in Compliance with his own Native Language." [3] These ideas were shared in other countries. That the Germans considered the music of recitative inseparable from the text is well demonstrated by their practice of dealing with it. When an Italian opera was performed in Germany (a number of Handel's operas were produced there, most often in Hamburg), the arias were equipped with a German text but otherwise not changed. The recitatives, however, were newly composed, the work devolving on such eminent masters as Keiser, Telemann, and Mattheson.

The difference between recitatives in the various national musical literatures rests not only on the genius of the language, but also on what species of speech served for the point of departure. In Italy composers set to music a manner of speaking that did not differ from everyday popular usage even when in a poetic vein, but the French *tragédie lyrique* patterned its recitative on the highly cultivated and somewhat frosty speech of the spoken drama as presented in the Comédie Française. Handel's Italian recitatives follow the normal practice, which, as various contemporary sources agree, was close to "natural speech." He had already learned something about recitative in Hamburg. Keiser, in the preface to his *Componimenti musicali* (1706), warns that a good recitative is as much a "headache" for the composer as an aria. Handel's secco recitatives in the oratorios satisfied the demands of the adherents of the doctrine of imitation by approximating natural speech, but he also gave his recitative distinctly musical values. The resultant English recitative thoroughly corresponded to the genius of the language, yet the controversy about the feasibility of recitative in any language but Italian continued. Burney himself, who endorsed Italian recitative, was inclined to favor spoken dia-

---

[3] Addison's remarks were known and appreciated by most Continental authors to the end of the century. Marpurg quotes him often, as does Rousseau, but even the Italians learned something from him.

logue in English works: "There is no recitative except the Italian which is fit for dramatic purposes." John Brown rejected recitative altogether.[4]

There is little to add to the discussion of Handel's Italian recitatives. When his operas are sung by Italian singers, the unbarred and free delivery, which is its essential feature, comes through naturally. Excited Italians, then as now, sing rapidly but with good diction. Not so in the oratorios, where the solemn, churchly delivery we usually hear is entirely out of style and character. If, in addition, the secco is accompanied by the organ instead of the harpsichord, the distortion is complete. There is no such thing as a "sacred recitative"; whether in oratorio or opera, the singer is given the pitch, after which he is left alone to deal with his lines freely, though observing a natural speech cadence. The barline is largely irrelevant, and the harpsichordist must never attempt to control the singer's pace.[5] Handel could be perfunctory, but he usually followed the requirements of the text, carefully planning his modulations and keeping the harmony moving to avoid the sort of turgidity our singers create artificially. In his earlier works he observed the rather sharp distinction between recitative and aria prevalent in the old opera, but later he eliminated this distinction more and more, making for a more fluent and continuous musical texture. The change was achieved partly by the use of transitional types, arioso-like recitatives (also favored by Bach), but the chief agent in eliminating the sharp contrast was the so-called accompanied recitative.

The accompanied recitative (also called *recitativo stromentato*) was already present in the Venetian opera of the 17th century. Scarlatti used it, though with a certain discretion, but with Vinci, Hasse, and notably Handel, it became the chief means to depict the transports of passion, crises, and violent dramatic moments. This type of composition, which Rousseau called *récitatif accompagné pathétique*, shows the dramatist at his peak; in this respect, Handel has been forgotten where most he should have been remembered. The vehemence of such recitatives as Jupiter's oath in *Semele* (Example 28) is matched by the tragic intensity of Saul's confrontation with the ghost of Samuel (Example 29). At times Handel inserts secco passages within the accompagnato with startling results. This kind of music, though impressive and telling when sung in con-

---

[4] *A Dissertation on the Rise, Union and Power, the Progressions, Separations, and Corruptions of Poetry and Music* (1763).

[5] The German cantata reformers, who introduced the theatrical element into the cantata (see above, p. 137 f.), did speak of a *Kirchen-Rezitativ*, which they recommended be more solemn and cantabile than the opera recitative. But they were dealing with a species of music new to Germans, and its operatic origin was under attack from religious quarters.

Ex. 28 *Semele*

By that tre-men-dous flood I swear, ye Sty-gian wa-ters, hear!

and Thou, O-lym-pus, shake, in wit-ness to the oath I take!

cert performances, would be far more effective on the stage, for it is thea-tre music par excellence.

Recitative and aria may represent a polarity, but they surely have a complementary function. Handel was well acquainted with the aria types even before he went to Italy. The da capo aria and the motto aria he knew from Keiser; he used them in his very first opera, *Almira,* as he did the continuo aria and the various dance pieces. The old Venetian aria was still flourishing, not yet displaced by the Neapolitan, when Handel was in Italy. He remained fond of it, adding various improvements, because the Venetian aria permitted a greater variety of structures than the Neapoli-tan. The mainstay was of course the da capo aria, which modern drama-turgy has belabored with surprising contempt (though we have never heard a dissenting voice when the device is used in Bach's cantatas and

Ex. 29   *Saul*

Passions). Of the innate artistic difficulty of this particular form composers were aware—witness the various operatic "reforms." Handel, like most of his confrères, did not find the principle inhibiting, and though in the oratorios the da capo aria was gradually displaced, he by no means abandoned it. Finding many ways of avoiding literal repetition, he never ceases to surprise us. His Italian colleagues could not match his skill in finding ever new ways to cope with the problem; they were wary of the countersubjects and themes Handel threw into the accompaniment, and would not engage in his bold modulatory scheme. Later, especially in the oratorios, he may begin the introductory recitative in a totally unrelated key, abruptly modulating in the aria, the rhythm shifting, so that the return of the original first section, even if unchanged, is welcome as a sort of resolution. While of course every aria requires individual attention for performance, we do possess a few in which Handel wrote out the da capo, adding embellishments and changes, or made an abbreviated reprise; they give us guidance that Handel's earlier editors largely ignored.

There were other means to make da capo arias attractively varied. Of particular interest is the so-called concerted aria, equipped with an accompaniment whose thematic substance is freely superimposed on the vocal melody instead of following it. This is an important characteristic of late Baroque dramatic music, both sacred and secular, and became one of the chief sources of the future symphonic idiom. It was as much liked by Handel and his contemporaries as it was naturally made for an imaginative composer. The concerted aria has various forms. It may actually assume the role of the concerto by treating a solo instrument in that manner, as in the brilliant trumpet arias that were so popular in Italy. Handel could write a concerted aria with a markedly virtuoso part for a solo instrument, as for instance, in Caesar's aria "Va tacito," in *Giulio Cesare*. Any modern horn player would blanch at seeing this part, yet the solo really enhances the vigor of the vocal part. Bach was particularly fond of this type, using oboe, violin, gamba, and the various *d'amore* and *da caccia* varieties of instruments. Such a concerted part may be based on the vocal melody itself and held to its style, in which case it usually takes the form of contrapuntal imitation and elaboration of portions of the vocal melody, thereby enhancing the latter's expressivity. Especially in the later oratorios Handel was partial to a type of concerted accompaniment that is not only altogether original but independent of the vocal part, only the harmonic scheme being common to both. A well-known instance can be found in *Messiah* (Example 30). This concerted accompaniment can be so independent that it is a veritable piece in its own right, self-sufficient even without the voice. This calls for a particularly refined

balance of musical content, otherwise the *raison d'être* of the aria is in
question. Undoubtedly many an aria with an obbligato concertante instrumental part was first sketched, or even composed, before the vocal
part had taken shape; hence our impression that the voice is trying to

Ex. 30   *Messiah*

make peace with the instruments. Bach, enamored of this species, occasionally permitted his imagination to run away with the accompaniment
to the detriment of the vocal part. The *Laudamus te* in the B minor
Mass is virtually a little violin concerto, worked out with minute care
and obvious relish, but the voice part is slighted and the piece could be
played by the instruments alone; so true is this that the uninitiated would
never miss the vocal part. Handel prized the concerted aria and showed

great versatility in its use, but the voice never loses its primacy. It must have been for this reason that he composed few arias with a solo concertante instrument sharing the honors with the singer; he preferred to use the orchestra as a unit.

Among the arias are many whose orchestral part exhibits a developed symphonic feeling quite extraordinary in the first half of the century (Example 31). Another notable feature of Handel's arias is the quality of the

Ex. 31 *Theodora*

later, in the body of the aria:

prelude-ritornels. Some are brief, but often they are quite elaborate, in themselves little da capo structures utilizing the thematic substance of the aria they preface. Sometimes they merely set the mood, but as a rule they have an important formal role, framing, as it were, the aria or chorus. Though every one is familiar with it, we cite the opening ritornel to the first recitative in *Messiah*. In four measures Handel admirably creates a mood sketch that determines the tone of the whole piece that follows (Example 32). Other remarkable instances have already been cited in Examples 3, 16, and 22.

Ex. 32   *Messiah*

To us the typified arias of the Baroque seem a little ridiculous: plaint, rage, jealousy, slumber, awakening, ghost, and battle arias were well standardized types which Handel, together with all other composers, accepted and used. They were stylized, as was the décor. Yet, though systematized, the variety the stylization permitted was great, and the character of such pieces was determined by tempo, time signature, tonality, rhythm, and so on—all musical criteria. A largo aria was quite different from a *tempo ordinario* (or *giusto*) aria, even if both dealt with jealousy. Those in dance rhythms were also well distinguished from one another, and one must beware of taking them for dance pieces pure and simple. They follow the rhythmic pattern of the dance form, but a minuet-aria can be profoundly tragic, while the gigue rhythm is used for arias that are anything but jolly. The siciliana in particular furnishes a good example. Handel usually sets it as a pastoral piece, but it can be highly dramatic or pathetic. Handel's aria technique developed steadily, though some of his most admirable melodies are present in his earliest operas and cantatas. A pure, transfigured lyricism appears in his old age, for the old poet may be more communicative than the young, he can no longer conceal his heart. The autumnal charm of declining years is more refined, more complicated, it reacts more subtly to stimuli.

The often noticeable difference between the oratorio arias and the opera arias is not to be attributed to the "sacred" character of the former.

This is an oversimplification, as is the "lowering of vocal standards," which even Hawkins seems to accept. It goes without saying that there had to be a certain difference between oratorio and opera arias; the former were in English and sung by English singers, no match for the castratos and Italian prima donnas. Yet while the English arias are far more varied in construction, they still remain Italian in their euphony and vocal requirements—we observe a corresponding case in *The Magic Flute*. The songs of Galatea or Semele, Jove or Solomon, and indeed, *all* the arias in *Messiah* still call for exquisite singing of full operatic calibre, which few of the specialized oratorio singers of today can furnish.

[6]

The Age of Reason rejected ensembles as being "irrational"; Rousseau still has some amusing nonsense to say about them. Furthermore, the old aristocratic opera, reflecting court etiquette, frowned upon the bad manners of several persons speaking when a noble figure delivered himself of a speech. But the Italians did not read philosophy or tracts on etiquette when they composed, and eventually they discovered that the dramatic possibilities of ensembles and finales enabled them to infuse some movement into the frozen majesty of the seria. They especially delighted in mocking the tradition of undisturbed soliloquies with the rapid ejaculations and asides in their ensembles. Handel's role in this development is far more significant than operatic history would grant him. It must be assumed that he arrived at the idea largely through his own dramatic logic; the dates support this contention.

The opera seria did not have true ensembles, nor did the early intermezzo and opera buffa; this development came after the middle of the 18th century. Leo and Vinci, both intent on ensembles, nevertheless had difficulty in arranging them because the construction of the librettos required the figures of the drama to fade away one by one. Furthermore, these composers (like Lully and Handel) could reach a dramatic crest with the single voice. Nothing could surpass in power and eloquence such a scene as the ending of the second act in Handel's *Orlando* (see p. 242). The presence of duets in the opera is understandable in view of the long-standing popularity of "twin singing," which had flourished ever since the *villanella* and the *madrigaletto*. The chamber duet was particularly favored in the 17th and 18th centuries and found its way quite naturally into the opera from its beginning. But these were, as a rule, dialogue duets, the singers sharing the same musical material; the dramatic kind, involving two distinct personalities, evolved gradually. Handel had his models in Scarlatti and Steffani; *Giulio Cesare* shows him a master of the operatic variety of the duet, far in advance of his contemporaries.[6] Though it may seem simple, the road from dramatic duet to trio or quartet is a very long one. This larger ensemble, the crowning glory of opera, for which there is no parallel in the theatre, was strenuously objected to on logical grounds. Baron Grimm, with typical French esprit, still inveighs against the "preposterous idea" of several persons speaking simultaneously. But the objections were made by men of letters who looked at the ensemble from the point of view of the spoken theatre; they could not understand that music is capable of presenting the simultaneous self-expression of several dramatic figures. In view of the rarity of ensembles beyond duets, it is astonishing to see how modern and prophetic Handel's few ensembles are. The trio in *Tamerlano* (1724), "Vogli stragi," reaches a long way beyond the limits of Baroque opera; it is a true dramatic ensemble that presents three recognizable characters simultaneously. There is a remarkable, if brief, quartet in *Partenope* (1730). Later, in the great oratorio ensemble, Handel created dramatic pictures that remained unexcelled until the advent of Mozart (Examples 33, 34.)

The act-ending ensembles are another matter. They are neither finales nor choruses, but "tuttis" by the assembled soloists. The introduction of the finale is generally ascribed to Nicola Logroscino in the late 1740s, but though a feeling for the spirit and function of the finale was unmistakably present even in the '30s, it is difficult to find any specific work

Ex. 33   *The Choice of Hercules*

[6] We know, of course, of his fine non-dramatic chamber duets. See above, p. 123 ff.

Ex. 34 *Susanna*

with a genuine finale before Piccinni's *La buona figliuola* of 1760. The character of the finale—that is, an elaborate compound piece made up of integrated recitatives, ariosos, and ensembles—is already present in *Tamerlano*, again showing Handel in the van despite his generally conservative adherence to the Venetian-Neapolitan operatic pattern.

[7]

IN CONSIDERING Handel's creative processes, we must now move into a less charted and more controversial region, into that province where a musical idea derives its contours from the words. Being a dramatic composer, Handel naturally depended a great deal on the words he set to music. His musical imagination was first kindled by a plot, personality, or idea, but he was highly susceptible to the pictorial and symbolical imagery of even single words. Music operates with symbols, which acquire a communicative meaning that transcends the purely acoustic phenomenon. The imagery is in the main dramatic in its intention, and a proper appreciation of this must precede any further inquiry.

The visual arts are fundamentally representational; music is fundamentally abstract. "The musician should always attempt to convey feelings rather than depict their actual causes; he should present the state of mind and body rather than that matter itself." This was the opinion of Johann Jakob Engel, expressed in his essay *Über die musikalische Malerey* (1780), and the statement reflects a conception that gained wide acceptance in what we call the Classic era.[7] The tendency to impose the representational on music is fraught with dangers, yet representation is not only possible but under certain conditions is an essential element in music. During the Baroque an illustrative symbolism derived from the text of vocal works was foremost in the minds of composers, and its association with the technical means of musical representation was intimate and pervasive. To us this is alien territory in which the expressive and the constructive elements are so intertwined that they virtually constitute an unknown language. Listening to music is a productive occupation, however; it calls for reasoning, conclusions—that is, participation—even though for the last century and a half we have been told that listening to music requires complete surrender of the mind to feeling. But music is a man-made art, its conventions are man-made and therefore accessible to

[7] The influential Engel was tutor of the Humboldt brothers, and it was from his book that Beethoven derived the motto placed at the head of the score of his *Pastoral Symphony*.

our intellect. Caroline Spurgeon, in her *Shakespeare's Imagery,* revealed that a poet's imagery is a part of his expression that can be studied, and profitably studied, by itself. This is true, *mutatis mutandis,* in the case of musical poets too. Even the untutored layman, in constantly searching for some "meaning" or emotion hidden behind a piece of music that bears the simple superscription "allegro assai," is recognizing implicitly that in a musical composition there is a premeditated will and intention at work.

The only trouble is that what we call "spontaneous expression" is difficult if not impossible to analyze, whereas the constructive-technical features do lend themselves to fairly unequivocal analysis. Dissatisfied with this uncertainty in dealing with the symbolic-metaphoric-descriptive aspects of music as opposed to the well-settled procedures followed in the theoretical aspects (harmony, counterpoint, and so on), musicologists decided to search for ways to deal with the problem in a systematic way. They knew that for centuries, and up to about 1770, vocal composers considered it their main task to express the sense of the words and to express the "affections" of the human soul. Indeed, the expression of the sense of the words, that is, text-interpretation in and by music, was one of the most important categories of Baroque musical thought. Since the means of attaining such expression in music were not always obvious and were mixed with what Hawkins calls "the common places," with the clichés of the reigning style, the musical interpretations themselves had to be interpreted conceptually and verbally. At the turn of our century hermeneutics was established as a branch of musicology affiliated with a sort of applied psychology. We have noted above (p. 344) that both the term and the methodology were borrowed from theology, but its transference to music was accompanied by a good deal of confusion concerning the boundaries of its new domain. In speaking of musical symbolism, a proponent may be referring to an advanced form of rationalism or to a simple interpretation of the theories of the *Affektenlehre,* the Baroque "doctrine of the affections." At any rate, hermeneutics usually denotes a synthesis of the conceptual with the autochthonously musical. The partisans of musical hermeneutics maintain that sound, like color, is inconceivable apart from objects, and that there can be no "pure" music devoid of associations. This symbolism takes the form of melodic, rhythmic, harmonic, and dynamic motion and configuration, but also uses the far more subtle means of form and organization.

Zarlino had already stated that "if any word expresses complaint, grief, affliction, sighs, tears, and other things of this sort, the harmony will be full of sadness." Morley, having thoroughly fortified himself by reading

Zarlino, goes a step farther when he quotes intervals and progressions appropriate for each affect. "You must have a care that when your matter signifieth 'ascending,' 'high,' 'heaven,' and such like you make your music ascend; and by the contrary where your ditty speaketh of 'descending,' 'lowness,' 'depth,' 'hell,' and other such you must make your music descend." These general suggestions the Baroque developed into an elaborate system of musical turns, figures, motifs, and chord progressions standing for a certain symbolic conceptuality that acquired a convention-sanctioned "meaning." Many of these symbols survive the particular time in which they flourished and are still understandable to us. Take for instance the falling chromatic bass of Bach that induced the feeling of pain and sorrow; it is still grasped instantly without the need of explaining the symbol. But many others are lost on the uninformed listener, for musical symbols are highly perishable. The decorative allegory and symbolic ornamentation of Baroque architecture show analogous traits in terms of particular esthetics of architecture. Today much of this is lost to us, yet the symbols live as architectural elements. So the musical symbolism, which similarly has lost most of its erstwhile meaning, lives on as elements of musical construction.

With the end of the Baroque the elaborate edifice built on the doctrine of affections collapsed and was soon forgotten. With it was forgotten its most notable exponent, Sebastian Bach. Handel survived because he was turned into a national-religious institution, but his musical imagery itself was also largely lost. Symbolism cannot attain its aims if the symbols used are private and therefore incomprehensible. The listener must either take such symbolism as expressed in descriptive music without reference to its intended meaning or occupy himself with a baffled search for an inaccessible meaning. Since with the great masters the link between symbol and the thing symbolized is often subtle, even disguised, it became an accepted scholarly pursuit to read all sorts of meanings into the simplest of melodic, rhythmic, and harmonic progressions, and exegetic ingenuity has been carried, notably in Germany, to fantastic extremes. There is always a danger of reading more into an old score than the composer could possibly have intended, and one may properly hestitate to accept a symbolic interpretation of a passage that has other functions that are quite clear and direct. A lavish application of hermeneutics encourages queer and unlikely analogies, and the whole thing can easily turn into a polite parlor game, such as one can find on almost every page of Serauky's *Händel.* Musical hermeneutics has, indeed, a dangerous attraction for the type of mind to which the appeal of mysticism is stronger than that of reason.

The fatal mania of the Bacon-Shakespeare school of interpretation of see-ing anagrams, acrostics, and cabalistic word jugglery in the most unlikely places has its counterpart in music.

Hermeneutics, while popular, also had and has its opponents. Many have refused to grant validity to what seemed to them no more than speculation. The simplest argument is, of course, that *Affektenlehre* is one thing, a great composer's poetry quite another. To turn the imagination of such musical poetry into a quasi psychic science, and its metaphors into statements of fact, has been viewed as being pretty close to an unscientific spiritualism. If one reads Ilmari Krohn's recent *Anton Bruckners Sym-phonien*, one must conclude that only a ouija board could have produced the results of these analyses, but the Bach, Handel, Beethoven, and Wag-ner literature, too, is rich in examples that come close to Krohn's spiritual-ism. Any explanation of content of the type hermeneutics indulges in seems to lift music from the sphere of esthetics and places it in the psy-chological orbit of everyday life; meaning is being forced upon things that have no logical meaning. An attendant danger is that one will take for a phenomenon of life what is an esthetic symbol. It can forcefully be argued that it is difficult to attribute esthetic value to phenomena that re-quire pragmatic interpretation; because the ear as a sense organ is in-different to symbolism, any such use of music involves all sorts of mediat-ing factors.

This opposition is not recent; long before Hanslick's celebrated trea-tise, voices were raised not only against the interpretation of symbolic and descriptive passages, but against the propriety of the composer's use of music for such purposes. Charles Avison (*An Essay on Musical Expression,* 1752) indignantly censured the composer who "for the Sake of some tri-fling Imitation, deserts the Beauties of Expression." He found it inexcusa-ble that so great a composer as Handel should "condescend to amuse the vulgar Part of his Audience by letting them *hear the Sun stand still* [in *Joshua*]." Sir John Hawkins, like Avison an admirer of Handel, was also embarrassed that this distinguished musician "has too much affected imi-tation," particularly regretting the attempt to "express the hopping of frogs and the buzzing of flies [*in Israel in Egypt*]."

It is true, of course, that "the charms and excellence of music are in-trinsic, absolute, and inherent" (Hawkins), but we cannot simply dismiss musical hermeneutics, for it is often in the light of such explanations that what we call in our everyday vocabulary the "beautiful" in art becomes clear. To give up hermeneutics altogether would mean to restrict all writ-ing about esthetics, and that surely would be an unreasonable sacrifice.

While overindulgence in fantastic conjectures is by no means rare even today, we have settled down to a sane and intelligent appraisal of the system of symbolic expression that constitutes an interesting and vital element in Baroque music and are able to recapture some knowledge of it.[8]

We may recognize the esthetic value of the Romantic view that music excludes anything purely intellectual, but we must immediately contradict it in some aspects. During the act of composition—that is, the actual "putting together" of the work—the prevailing feeling may be suspended in the working out of detail in order to make certain configurations more plastic. There are illusions in music not unlike optical illusions in function, and they force the composer to correct apparent distortions. The taper and the entasis of the Parthenon shafts are well known, but the architect's distant colleague, the composer, also deals with entasis, and none more skilfully than the Baroque composer. His fugal entrances, to mention one example, often require considerable adjustments. There can be no question that many a transition and development section, as well as clauses and cadences and a legion of formulas, can be such purely intellectual, feeling-free operations. One might go so far as to say that composition is in essence the constant alternation and mixture of the symbols of such objective and subjective processes, that in this musical symbolism and pictorialism there is a perpetual interplay of private and public meaning. The moment when apprehension passes through judgment into action cannot be exactly gauged; the coincidence between apprehension and art is so close as to be almost simultaneous. Exactly in what this mode of apprehension, which is neither truly conceptual nor merely emotional, consists remains obscure, but it is clear that emotion is not the only, the essential, unifying feature in this process; it is merely one link in the chain from cognition to conation.

The artist wants to make himself understood, and utilizes all possible ways to do so. Symbolic image and pure music come from the same creative mind. The difficulty for us is that the ratio and quality of these elements, which are of the utmost importance to both understanding and enjoyment, change, often radically, within a generation or two. Furthermore, the hermeneutical variability of musical constellations, such as intervals, rhythms, and harmonies, is very considerable, if not infinite.

[8] Those who look upon this system with a smile should not forget that their favorite 19th-century idols, led by Wagner and his leitmotifs, also used symbolism and text interpretation, and they too operated well within a recognizable system of clichés and conventions. Music always had them and, unless the machine takes over, will always have them. As to the serialists, their clichés and conventions dwarf anything seen before.

Some often-used symbols become practically immanent, but the rest depend on the particular situation and context in which they are used. Such musical metaphors and similes can be extraneous, inorganic, and altogether ornamental; on the other hand, a purely intellectual descriptive symbol, such as "falling" or "rising," or playful garlands of ornaments, can become entirely emotional in the proper context. The 18th century had far subtler means than the 19th to achieve translation of the optical or intellectual into the acoustical. This *is* a different musical language, for not even the polarity of major and minor, which the 19th century invariably interpreted as happy and sad, heroic and tragic, is unconditionally valid in Baroque music. But all this can become a direct and instantaneous experience once the symbols become assimilated.

It is clear, then, that to speak of music as the "katexochen art of feeling" is an untenable postulate. We are dealing, especially in Baroque music, with known intentions and acts; hermeneutics is therefore justified because these intentions are analyzable to a considerable degree. We realize that there is no musical concept that could have the unequivocal validity of a linguistic concept such as "cat." Even such expressions as "sorrow" or "jubilation," long and widely used in music, are lacking in any but convention-sanctioned precision of meaning. But the illusion of such conceptual meaning can successfully be created, and this was the main concern of all Baroque vocal composers. Daniel Webb, in his *Remarks on the Beauties of Poetry* (1762), expressed this cogently. He denies that music alone can express passions, "but let Poetry co-operate with Music, and specify the motive of each particular impression, we are no longer at a loss . . . general impressions become specific indications." The crucial requirement remains that all the musical elements employed to convey symbols should be capable of an autonomous expressive life even when freed of the conceptual. No matter how commanding the psychological situation, it should never threaten the supremacy of the esthetic. When Handel expresses the madness of Orlando by a constantly modulating, insecure tonality, he is almost graphically suggestive without ever straying from sound musical sense and logic; he merely uses analogies that can be symbolized. And since the symbols are idealized, their recognition is not absolutely necessary for the enjoyment of the music, though only by understanding them can we reach a truly penetrating insight. With Handel the auditive function of the symbol almost always remains purely musical, often achieving an intensity and a precision all the more arresting for its apparent casualness. Bach found in the final depths of the subjective something objective, an inner artistic conscience untouched by any exter-

nal purposefulness. This is true of *The Art of Fugue,* but it is also true to
a considerable extent of the first Kyrie in the B minor Mass and not a few
other vocal works. To Handel this was something totally alien; he depended on the words. Nevertheless, when Bach set to music a text more
elaborate than the few words of the Kyrie, he usually was entirely within
the symbolic world of the *Affektenlehre.*

The other extreme, as represented by Rameau, who once said "Give
me the *Gazette d'Hollande* and I'll set it to music," was equally foreign to
Handel. While the great passions of love, hatred, and jealousy were his
principal regions and he could be deeply stirred by them, the very imagery of words—even of single words—often sufficed to release his creative energies. In the midst of a dull piece he suddenly comes upon an
expressive or picturesque word and instantly his imagination catches fire.
Morell was aware of this and in order to keep the fire going often borrowed sentences or words from the great English poets, splicing them into
his own pedestrian text. They served their purpose well.

[8]

WITH A FEW exceptions Handel always deals with purely musical symbols, which he uses with such naturalness that the uninitiated
will seldom be aware of the "system" at work. His innate and incorrupti-
ble musicianship was not interested in facile onomatopoetic imitation, for
even the most glowingly descriptive and picturesque nature scenes are always smoothly within a musically unexceptionable texture. The stock figures of operatic "gesture music" are of course present everywhere, but
Handel often charges them with an individual cast. "Eye music," which
still survived in its oldest form, is seldom used by him, but like Bach he
was very fond of pictorial illustration of single words even at the expense
of the rest of the text, a procedure roundly denounced by the Romantics
as being a naive game. It was anything but that. Especially when used
with Handel's sparkling fluency, it is an effective agent of expressiveness.
The only caution one must proffer is that to the listener the symbolism is
not accessible beyond a certain point. Not even when the listener is familiar with the score can he instantly comprehend the reference, and in
the case of different symbols appearing simultaneously, no one but the
composer can be aware of them. But since with a composer like Handel
the symbolism is almost always audibly ordered music, if the symbols
have little or no meaning (though we can learn to spot them by meticulous study) the sheer grace of the music supplies such autonomous values

as to preclude any awkwardness caused by the loss of symbol-recognition. Indeed, often no intellectual analysis will tell us more, for it is impossible to flush out the heart of a composer's mystery.

Some authors intimate that the subtle "psychological" system of the doctrine of the affections and of musical imitation of life that Handel absorbed in Germany and Italy was wasted on his English audiences; but these doctrines were not only well known, understood, and spiritedly discussed in England, they lasted to the end of the century, long after the whole conception of imitation had been abandoned in Germany. Moreover, the topic was popular also with literary men, many of whom occupied themselves with the problems of expression in music. Robert Burton, in *The Anatomy of Melancholy* (1621), anticipates Athanasius Kircher by a full generation in discussing the power of music over our emotions. The doctrine of imitation, like the doctrine of affections, was taken over from the 17th century by most philosophers, critics, and artists; the old aims, *docere-delectare-movere*, were still paramount. They all believed, of course, in the other basic postulate, to express in music the meaning of the words, and from this point of view Handel's use of symbolism and imitation was well understood by Englishmen.

Esthetics as a discipline may date from Baumgarten (1750), but many "essays," "treatises," and "observations" earlier published in England nevertheless dealt with esthetics. Addison, Steele, Shaftesbury, and many others not only wrote about esthetics but busied themselves with its special application to music. At times writers even used examples from Handel's music to illustrate their views. James Harris (*A Discourse on Music, Painting, and Poetry,* 1744), when speaking of the power of music "to imitate Motions and Sounds," illustrates his contentions with a reference to "the walk of the Giant Polypheme in the Pastoral *Acis and Galatea.*" Harris, and a number of other writers who espoused the current theories of Aristotelian mimesis, were nevertheless cautious about its application to music, for it was clear to them that music was but "imperfectly" capable of literal imitation. "Musical imitation," says Harris, "tho' Natural, aspires not to raise the same Ideas, but only Ideas similar and analogous." Therefore, in the end, music is seen as gaining its power not from direct imitation but from the "raising of the Affections, to which ideas may correspond." This was a modern conception, far ahead of those current on the Continent. Mainwaring also warns that "a close attachment to some particular words in a sentence hath often misled [the composers] from the general meaning of it," a remark that could have been aimed at Handel, while Hawkins concludes that "these powers of imitation . . . constituted but a very small part of the excellence of music." But there were also unconditional adherents to the doctrine of imitation, among them that devoted Handelian, William Hayes, Professor of Music at Oxford, who considered the descriptive passages in *Israel in Egypt* the highest peaks in Handel's art.

An examination of Handel's music will show it teeming with musical symbolism. The simplest manifestations of the "doctrine" are easily discovered, and Examples 1, 35, and 36, illustrating motion or direction,

Ex. 35   *Saul*

Ex. 36   *Samson*

need no commentary. The more subtle forms require a closer scrutiny. Symbolism by rhythmic differentiation can be very effective, if not so apparent. In the anthem *Have mercy upon me o God,* the word "wicked" stands out with dramatic plasticity by virtue of the sudden change in the notes' rhythmic value (Example 37). Similar effects may be achieved by the use of coloratura, as in the next example where the word "wide" elicits

Ex. 37   Anthem, *Have mercy upon me, o God*

Then shall I teach— their— ways un-to the wick - ed

a garland that widens the vocal line (Example 38). Even more subtle is the musical illustration that the word "pass" ("till thy people pass over, O Lord") conjured up in Handel's mind. Divided tenors literally pass over divided altos in a piece of "eye music" that nevertheless makes perfect

Ex. 38   *L'Allegro*

Shal-low brooks   and riv-ers wide

musical sense (Example 39). Harmony is a powerful symbolic agent, as can be seen in Example 40, where on the word "strange" Handel places the chilling Neapolitan sixth. Finally, let us quote from the same oratorio a magnificent example of Handel's pictorial imagination. Representing

Ex. 39   *Israel in Egypt*

Ex. 40   *Theodora*

"the rosy steps" of the rising sun, the ritornel "drives away the shades of night" even before the voice enters with its explanatory words (Example 41).

Ex. 41   *Theodora*

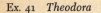
Larghetto

[9]

In his Handel biography, Romain Rolland speaks of a particular affinity Handel demonstrated toward not only French music but the French spirit in general. We know that Handel's command of the language was good and that most of his correspondence with non-British correspondents—even with his German relatives and friends—was in French by preference. But Rolland goes much farther than that: "If Handel had come to France, I am convinced that the reform of opera would have been brought about sixty years sooner, and with a wealth of music which Gluck never possessed." The idea, though conjectural (and surely Rolland's "sixty years" would have to be cut by half), is entirely plausible. Unfortunately, almost all we know about the palpably strong French influence in Handel's music rests on such nice conjectures. Müller-Blattau and Schering say that Handel was acquainted with Rameau's music, an opinion I wholeheartedly share with them, but they can offer no more documentary evidence than can the writer of these lines. Hawkins is even more tantalizing when he says "Mr. Handel was ever used to speak of Rameau in terms of great respect." This is not only one of the very few positive opinions Handel ever deigned to express about a fellow composer, but the sole statement by a qualified observer and first-hand witness we can hold to while expressing our beliefs.

Other authors point out Handel's consistent preference for the Lullian French overture as opposed to the Italian type. This is not surprising. The French overture was well known in Germany in Handel's youth, but even the Italians used it frequently. Draghi, Ziani, Badia, Bononcini all liked it, though Handel's exclusive preference for the French overture is indeed unusual.[9] Cuthbert Girdlestone (*Jean Philippe Rameau,* 1957), in stating that Handel heard French opera at the court in Hanover, where Cambert's son-in-law, Farinel, was music director, must have confused the performances of a French troupe of comedians with opera. The Hanoverian opera was brilliant under Steffani, but with Elector Ernst August's death in 1698 it was abandoned. By the time of Handel's two brief stays at the court there was no trace left of opera, the fine theatre being occupied by French comedians who *replaced* it. Cambert's "son-in-law" never laid eyes on Hanover; the Farinel mentioned by Girdlestone was his brother, Jean Baptiste (or Giovanni Battista) Farinelli, who seems to have reverted to the family's original Italian name.[10]

In Handel's time Hanover was known solely for its fine instrumental music. Telemann says that the French style was highly regarded and cultivated there and Handel may very well have come in contact with French music, for there were several French musicians in the little orchestra under his direction. But the French elements in Handel's music appear earlier than that—in fact, they are present from the beginning of his studies, for as we have seen the notebook he filled in Halle with model compositions contained works by Georg Muffat, a pronouncedly French-oriented musician. In Hamburg he was generously exposed to French influences. Although the Hamburg opera had performed Lully's lyric tragedies between 1685 and 1695, this was before Handel's time; the French influence did not really begin until Kusser was appointed director of the opera. Even then it was felt more in the divertissements and other instrumental music than in the operas themselves. Then with the advent of a

---

[9] The only Italian overture Handel composed is the one prefacing *Athalia.* But there is a good reason for that: the overture was a reworking of an earlier sonata.

[10] Farinelli must have picked up a pointer or two from Steffani, because he ended his career as King-Elector George's ambassador to Venice.

superior musician, Keiser, Italian, French, and German elements began to be reconciled in the opera; Keiser's example was not wasted on Handel; a French tone is evident in his first opera, *Almira.*

The French influence was not missing in London either, though the history of French music and musicians there is a very obscure one. The Restoration brought a wave of French music to England, but by the end of the century the tenacious native theatre subdued the French strain to such an extent that it is extremely difficult to follow its traces, even though some of them remain in Purcell's stage music. We know that Robert Cambert, having run afoul of the scheming Lully, found it prudent to go into exile in London, where he lived from 1672 to his death in 1677. Upon his arrival there he teamed up with Louis Grabu, a French musician resident in London since 1665 and very much in favor at the court, to the annoyance of John Banister and others whom he displaced. The two Frenchmen founded the first Royal Academy of Music on the Parisian pattern, but it soon failed. Eventually Grabu, a mediocre musician, faded away, though not before composing the undistinguished score to Dryden's *Albion and Albanius.* It appears, however, that repeated efforts were made to acclimatize French opera in London. Thomas Betterton, a highly esteemed actor and a great favorite of Charles II, was sent to Paris in 1683 to gather information on theatrical practices and to persuade a French opera troupe to come to London. It is not known whether he succeeded in engaging a French troupe, but Allardyce Nicoll, in his *History of Restoration Drama,* prints documents showing that Charles II attended "ye French opera" in 1685, and there are other references indicating that there was a French company playing in London and that their repertory included some of Lully's operas. It could scarcely be mere coincidence that Jacques Rousseau, Lully's chief scene painter, was also a resident in London about the same time. The French influence persisted, and it was strong enough when Mlle Sallé's troupe was active at Covent Garden to inspire Handel to compose his "dance operas." *Ariodante* and *Alcina* show familiarity not only with French opera but with Rameau himself. Even earlier, the "storm music" in *Riccardo I* was altogether French, and in general the arias in the French dance forms and rhythms are palpably due to French models, though of course this is equally true of not a few of Bach's compositions. Every once in a while Handel even designates his parts in the French manner; in *Teseo* we read *haute contre* and *taille.* I am convinced that Hawkins's statement about Handel's admiration for Rameau is based on fact, that Handel knew Rameau's music and profited from it—but how and when?

Hippolyte et Aricie (1733) and *Les Indes galantes* (1735) are the works that obviously must be considered; they are contemporary with Handel's "dance operas." But there is not the slightest proof that they were performed in London during Handel's lifetime, let alone in the '30s. The dates of publication are also discouraging, even assuming that the scores speedily found their way to London. Of the great theatrical works composed between 1733 and 1749, *Castor et Pollux* was published in 1733, *Dardanus* c. 1739, *Les Indes galantes* in 1740. Handel's "French" operas, *Ariodante* and *Alcina,* date from January and April 1735, therefore the only possible direct source could have been *Hippolyte et Aricie* and *Castor et Pollux.* (Rameau's harpsichord music was published earlier, 1724 and 1731, and circulated in London, but the affinities Handel shows with Rameau are with his theatre music.) Thus our evidence is rather circumstantial than direct, especially because one would expect that a composer admired by Handel would show up somewhere in a direct quotation.[11] There is only one case that may be a borrowing: the theme of "And the glory of the Lord," in *Messiah,* does sound like a passage in *Les Fêtes d'Hébé* (Example 42).

Ex. 42   Rameau, *Les Fêtes d'Hébé*

Que jus-qu'au cieux s'e - lè - vent nos ac - cords

Rameau himself offers no help; he was a man as reticent about his own person as was Handel. Even his wife was in the dark about her husband's first forty years of life; he never said a word about it throughout a happy marriage contracted with a nineteen-year-old girl when he was forty. Yet the two composers had many things musical in common. The use of the free, highly dramatic accompanied recitative, the blending of recitative with aria, the combination of solo with chorus, as well as the fine sense for the pastoral. To top our quandary, there are distinctly "Handelian" traits in Rameau; particularly, some of the dances in *Les Indes galantes* are astonishingly Handelian. While a good deal of this must be ascribed to the ubiquitous turns and phrases of the *Zeitstil*, there seems surely to have been a certain relationship between Handel and Rameau that is in need of elucidation. Neither Rolland, nor Masson, nor

[11] A good example is afforded by Muffat's *Componimenti* and Telemann's *Musique de table.* Both offer thoroughly Gallicized music, and both were copiously drawn upon by Handel beginning about 1741.

Girdlestone, all of whom knew this territory intimately, all of whom wrote perceptively and in great detail about Rameau and knew their Handel, gives us any guidance. But then the foreign radiations of the French opera of the Lully-Rameau lineage have not yet been examined in earnest. French music was pictorial, with a tendency toward the narrative; not necessarily program music, but characterized by a general tone and attitude. Also, there was a great tradition of theatrical orchestral music quite different from the Italian even though it had been established by a native of Florence. Handel somehow acquired an acquaintance with this style, though he rejected the dense orchestration of the French. What he liked most was the pathos of the slow portion of the French overture, its ponderous, heavily accented gait, interspersed with sudden sweeping runs. This he often used not only in his overtures but also in the body of his operas and oratorios.

There can be no question that the Italian and Italian-oriented opera seria owes much to the *tragédie lyrique,* and French dramaturgy contributed basic ideas to the various "reforms" that began with Apostolo Zeno. The mature Gluck is unthinkable without Rameau, and in our opinion Handel was also indebted to him and to French music in general, though of course to a much lesser degree than was Gluck.

XXV

Handel's instrumental music—Strong Italian influence—Motivic unity—
Euphony as main condition—German sources—French and English
elements—Chamber music—Orchestral works—"Oboe" concertos, Opus 3
—Mixture of old and new—*Twelve Grand Concertos*, Opus 6—Other
concertos and suites—Organ concertos—Harpsichord works

O NE WOULD EXPECT HANDEL'S INSTRUMENTAL MUSIC TO
constitute a relatively small and not particularly significant part of his
enormous output, no matter how fine much of it might be; for it would seem
that this music could only be incidental to the dramatic works, which held
his interest all his life. The external circumstances appear at first to support this view, because most of the chamber music originated in Handel's
early years, as did most of the keyboard works and some of the concertos,
their dates of publication notwithstanding. The only instrumental works
of a later date are the *Twelve Grand Concertos*, Opus 6, and some of the
organ concertos. In addition, there are many transcriptions and arrangements among the instrumental compositions, and some give the impression of having been hastily composed to counter piracy.

We see the same recipe that Handel, when threatened with competition, followed with success in the theatrical works: against the pirated
version he offered a "correct" text and "additional" numbers, a tactical
move that immediately reduced the value of the competitive offering. Had
it not been for his usually prompt and angry retaliation to piracy, perhaps
even those few of the harpsichord works we now possess would not have
been composed. The circumstances were not unlike those surrounding the
beginnings of oratorio and pastoral, when *Esther* and *Acis and Galatea,*
almost forgotten by Handel, were pirated by a theatrical company. This is
clear from the preface to his *Suites de pièces de clavecin* (1720). "I have
been obliged to publish some of the following Lessons, because surrepti-

cious and incorrect Copies of them had got Abroad. I have added several new ones to make the Work more usefull, which if it meets with a favourable Reception; I will still proceed to publish more, reckoning it my duty, with my Small Talent, to serve a Nation from which I have receiv'd so Generous a protection." But the promised sequel did not appear until 1733, and then only because of Walsh's insistence. The material it contains does not redound to Handel's fame. The first set of organ concertos, Opus 4, appeared in 1738 with the following notice: "These Six Concerto's were publish'd by Mr. Walsh from my own Copy corrected by my self, and to him only I have given my Right therein." At that, some of the instrumental music was published by Walsh without Handel's knowledge and to his intense annoyance.

But all this is deceptive. The supposed insignificance of Handel's instrumental music is not even relatively so, for we are dealing with some fifty chamber-music compositions, dozens of concertos, various orchestral suites, and harpsichord music. Moreover, much of this music was composed for Handel's own use with the pressure of commission or competition absent. Indeed, instrumental music was not Handel's *petite luxe.* He combines the primal delight in music making with the sensitivity of an old and noble musical civilization, the Italian, to create sonatas, trios, and suites. This chamber music is not modern for its day, and in this respect Handel shows a kinship with Bach. Both carried the old style to its culmination, though each in his own way, at a time when everything around them was beginning to change; and together they represent the apex of Baroque chamber music. Handel's instrumental compositions are not *pièces d'occasion,* the asides, as it were, of the dramatic composer: they are genuine, independent, legitimate, idiomatic, and solid. In them speaks a master who forms an integral link in the chain that begins with Corelli, and the musical values are absolute. As to the orchestral works, notably the *Twelve Grand Concertos,* Opus 6, they are among the most powerful and significant works of their kind of the entire Baroque era. As a composer for orchestra, Handel was bold and forward-looking; nevertheless, the opinion that all this is of small significance, that Handel "hardly goes beyond Corelli," is still held by some. So early an admirer as Burney had to defend Handel against those who considered the latter's concertos inferior to those of the Italians, but his colleague, Hawkins, sided with the critics. He was convinced that Handel's concertos "will stand no comparison with the concertos of Corelli, Geminiani, and Martini," adding flatly that "in general they are destitute of art and contrivance." Curiously, Hawkins endorsed the harpsichord pieces, among which there are few comparable to the concertos, as "the most masterly productions of their kind that we know in the world."

Behind these views is the circumstance that by the time Handel came upon the scene the forms of instrumental music had become rather stereotyped; they were standardized parts to be assembled by any skilled craftsman. Handel accepted the conventional forms and stayed within the spirit of tradition, but the letter he did not observe. "No great music has been more derivative," says Basil Lam, "yet none bears more firmly the impression of personality." We should complement this succinct characterization with a statement by Mainwaring, which, though it concerns Handel's playing, is equally valid applied to the composer: "Handel had an uncommon brilliancy and command of finger; but what distinguished him from all other players who possessed the same qualities, was that amazing fulness, force, and energy, which he joined with them." Even if many of the ideas in Handel's sonatas and concertos are the stock formulas of the period, their manipulation and the elasticity of form and procedure are altogether and unmistakably personal.

The Italian influence is strong so far as style and idiom are concerned; everywhere one feels the overwhelming desire for bright, sensuous sound, the glorious sound of the Italian violin school. Yet Handel's music also differs from that of Corelli and the older Italians because, especially in the mature concertos, it no longer reflects their serenity within a well-defined and, for the Italians, inviolate framework. Handel is adventurous, like Vivaldi, though in a different way, and, as we have remarked earlier, it is puzzling that Vivaldi exerted so small an influence on him. One would think that Vivaldi's boldness, capriciousness, his ready exploitation of stray ideas and impressions, would have struck an echo in Handel, the great improviser. Handel's abiding sense for the organic even in the improvisatory must have made him a life-long worshipper of the "classic" Corelli, whose influence is ever present. Like Corelli he likes to stay within the general outlines of the genre, and, unlike Vivaldi's, his conception is cyclic.

While in the slow movements his instruments sing, in the dances and fugues the writing becomes entirely instrumental, the whole apparatus, technique, proportions, stylistic turns exude the spirit of instrumental music. The most characteristic trait of his construction is motivic unity; the stylized turns of melody have as much formal significance as the simplest melodic idea. In technical ability Handel matches anything the period offers; the harmony is well planned, and there is a readiness for polyphonic configurations, though this tendency is often tantalizingly felt rather than executed, giving piquancy to the music. The dance pieces are flexible, colorful, of many shades, and with their warm tones, frequent asymmetry, and unconventional rhythms, are sharply differentiated from the formality of the actual dances. In matters of polyphony—there are many fugal movements in this music—Handel is not amenable to any restriction either. Even the traditional place of the fugue in suites or concertos is ignored; the fugal movement can be the first, second, third, or fourth.

As we have said, Corelli remained Handel's model throughout his life, but one important statute in the code was ignored. Corelli separated the instrumental genres into solo sonata, the two varieties of trio sonata, and concerto, which nevertheless were united in comprehensive *opera*. Handel accepted the distinctions, but within the individual species he went his own way with remarkable freedom. What attracted him most in the music he heard in Italy was the Italians' concentrated power in shaping plastic thematic material in their sonatas and concertos. This is also what attracted Bach, who liked to borrow such themes from Italian composers. Handel, to whom this ability was native, only requiring release, could immediately plunge into the Italian style with kindred and even more concentrated ideas, but while this concentration is generally relaxed by the Italians once the thematic subject has been launched, it is seldom dissolved with Handel, no matter how improvisatory the process.

Though his treatment of the instruments is highly idiomatic and the spirit of string music is dominant, Handel's mode of composition, with some exceptions in his keyboard music, was not governed by the requirements and possibilities of the instruments, as was the music of Locatelli or Geminiani. Double stopping and all the other violinistic techniques so adroitly exploited by Corelli's disciples did not interest him. Nor did he care for the German variety of violin technique, with its dense polyphonic writing, scordatura, and other devices, or for the mysticism of such composers as Biber. This brings us to the unavoidable comparison with Bach.

In Bach's chamber music the dominating thought is the multilinear and, paradoxically, it is even more so when the medium of performance is reduced to a single unaccompanied string instrument. The unaccompanied sonatas and partitas are the last outposts of the musically feasible, a region congenial to Bach, but incomprehensible to Handel. It would never have occurred to him to compose a four-part fugue for a solo violin; he would not have put up with the severe restrictions such writing places on the composer. Hans Mersmann expressed this well when he characterized older German instrumental music as being an art in which "the idea is stronger than the need for effect, and is carried out without any concessions, even at the cost of the shape of things." Bach seeks even in the dances a polyphonic-spiritual core, where Handel finds motion, euphony, and function. They differ fundamentally from each other precisely because of Handel's unwillingness to tax the musical ear with more than it can naturally take in. This once more testifies to the absence of any form of mysticism in Handel; he composes only what he perceives, what sounds well, what can stand by itself. Euphony was a *conditio sine qua non* for him, influencing even the turn of his counterpoint. Both composers wrote concertos and both used the same Italian sources, but upon comparison we see that the only thing they wholeheartedly shared was the love of the genial manipulation of a given musical substance; the execution of this penchant was another matter. Handel kept the substance flowing with little regard for linear logic, whereas Bach sought to develop it according to much more severe principles of musical architecture. Thus once more the two musicians are too different to be comparable.

When Handel went to Italy, he found that because of the strong attraction exerted by the concerto, a recent development in Italy and as yet little known in Germany, the various genres were beginning to be blended. Corelli's concerti grossi, for instance, represent an amalgam of suite and concerto, but the concerto had a more pronouncedly orchestral quality than the suite Handel knew at home. Corelli liked a substantial string body, at times approaching the size of our modern orchestra. Handel witnessed all this while in Rome and Venice, and acquired a taste for the distinctly orchestral as opposed to the enlarged chamber music that was the German suite. While he liked wind instruments and used them with skill, the German wind suite did not interest him at all, even though he appreciated its out-of-doors quality. We have seen that he objected to King George's request to write the *Royal Fireworks Music* for winds alone and at the first opportunity added strings to the suite.

The Germans were by preference keyboard composers; outstanding violinists, like Biber or Pisendel, were few, and their violin playing was specifically German, quite different from the Italian. By the time German instrumental ensemble music began its spectacular rise that eventually was to lead to world hegemony, Handel had long since left the German orbit. Nevertheless, he must have heard a great deal of chamber and orchestral music while still in Germany. Since only one of Zachow's chamber-music compositions survives, a fine trio sonata for flute, bassoon, and thoroughbass, we cannot form a judgment of his influence on Handel in this particular regard, though it must have been a factor. On the other hand, the chamber music of Krieger, Buxtehude, Pachelbel, and others, which he must have heard in the Zachow circle, left no perceptible traces in his music. Curiously, as Handel shied away from Vivaldi, so he did, again unaccountably, from the magnificent romanticism of Buxtehude, though the reason may have been the same: his innate leaning to thematic-formal cohesion. Buxtehude's sonatas were printed in 1696 and thus were available to the young Handel, and he knew Reinken's *Hortus Musicus* of 1687, but all this music was displaced by the Italian experience. The more recent and numerous German concertos of Johann David Heinichen and Christoph Graupner, which are richly orchestrated with woodwinds and brass, or Mattheson's he could not have known, though Telemann's *Musique de table* (1733) he certainly knew because he borrowed themes from it, if for different purposes. This particular score was undoubtedly sent to London by his old friend and correspondent. Thus Arthur Hutchings (as well as a number of German authors) is somewhat off the mark when he names German composers as the primary influences on Handel's instrumental music, though he is right when he mentions French suite music as a source (*The Baroque Concerto*). Kusser's collection of orchestral suites ("suivant la méthode française") was published in 1682, and other collections followed in 1700. The French influence was considerable in Germany and most composers were touched by it, but a particular place must be reserved for Georg Muffat (c. 1645–1704). Muffat was not a "systematic" composer, like Froberger; his suites contain a great variety of dance forms that pay little attention to the order set by either the older German suite or the French variety. This is really theatre music, ballet, and it must have been this quality that drew Handel to Muffat. In addition Muffat was a good melodist, wrote fluent light counterpoint, and though Gallicized in his technique and elegance, could be varied in mood. His *Florilegium* set an example for the newer German orchestral suite. Handel also certainly knew the works of the composers who followed Muffat's lead, such as Philipp Heinrich Erlebach and Johann Kaspar Ferdinand Fischer, for their collections were published while he was under Zachow's tutelage. His almost exclusive interest in the French overture is surely attributable to youthful impressions, because all German composers around the turn of the century were under the influence of Lully, whose ambassador to Germany was Muffat. To this French streak were later added elements from English instrumental music, not only the occasional hornpipe but all manner of other English folk and dance tunes and patterns.

But the overwhelming experience, as we have said, was his acquaintance with Italian instrumental music, and this too antedates his trip to Italy. Torelli's Opus 6, *Concerti musicali,* was published in Germany in 1698. These were the first true orchestral concertos unless Corelli's great set printed in 1712 was really ready in 1682, as Muffat, who studied with Corelli, maintains. While this is unlikely, it is a fact that Corelli's concertos were known a few years before their publication. Since Torelli resided in Germany, and not far from Halle, in Ansbach, he could hardly have escaped the inquisitive Zachow's attention. Albinoni's Opus 2, a set of very attractive concertos, was also available around the turn of the century, together with Vivaldi's first opus, though the latter Handel perhaps did not hear until he visited Venice. Albinoni particularly fascinated Bach, but his popularity in Germany began after Handel's departure.

Despite his acquaintance with most of this music, Handel's instrumental works, especially the concertos, are a highly personal achievement, in which Corelli remained the dominating influence. The hallmarks of Corelli's style, the dynamic contrasts (which Corelli indicated with detailed instructions, unusual for the time and paralleled only by Handel's similarly elaborate superscriptions), the solemnity and grandeur of the slow movements, the rousing vitality of the allegros, and the always magnificent string sound, are all there. The Italian models were pervasively present in London too. Geminiani and Veracini, both exponents of Corelli's art, were resident in London, and there was no dearth of published scores. Albinoni's Opus 2 was published there as early as 1709, Veracini's Opus 3 in about 1714, Corelli's Opus 6 in 1730. Many additional Italian works in Dutch contraband editions circulated freely in London's musical circles. Geminiani in particular interested Handel, for this Italian was a faithful disciple of Corelli, in some aspects surpassing his master, as in his skill in developing his materials and in his somewhat ampler fugal writing. Though in the main "conservative," like Handel, he also liked to step outside the codified style, as when he made the concertino into a full-fledged quartet by the addition of a viola. Perhaps it was Geminiani's example of using wind instruments in some of his concertos that prompted Handel to add oboe parts to his *Twelve Grand Concertos;* but, after reworking the first few, he abandoned the project.

[2]

HANDEL'S chamber music—some fifty compositions—amounts to a far from negligible repertory. He likes the stateliness of the church sonata, but he also likes the dances; the combination is very attractive, especially when the long lines are relieved by little rhapsodic inserts. Euphony and melodic expressivity govern these pieces and there is a fine balance between forward movement and polyphonic manipulation. There are no "problems," yet this kind of music, which appears here as slippered musical prose, easy and cool, there with the decorative briskness of the Italians, may be made to carry a considerable weight of seriousness without any disturbance of its smooth, conversational surface. At times a sonata promises little, then suddenly reveals, not indeed spectacular beauties but glimpses of tranquil loveliness. The pictorial quality so characteristic of Handel's dramatic and pastoral music is not missing, but the main feature is stylistic security and consistency.

As a rule, Handel relied altogether on the thoroughbass practice of his time; only one of these fifty works has a written-out continuo part. In the solo sonatas, treble and bass are carefully set down, but the rest was left to the harpsichordist, whose task was not made easier by the frequent absence of figuring. In the trio sonatas the three obbligato parts, even when elaborately polyphonic, give unequivocal indication of the harmonic procedure. Everywhere one notes the firm, often majestic, bass; constantly on the move and alive, it is not a mere harmonic support, but intimately concerned with the convolutions of the other parts.

The solo sonatas with basso continuo have fine melodies, richly embroidered instrumental arias, and vivacious dance movements. The collection, designated as Opus 1 and first printed in Amsterdam in 1724, was later republished by Walsh, who added a few items. The publication contained twelve sonatas for recorder or transverse flute ("German flute") or violin, and basso continuo. It is impossible to date these works. One or another may be from Handel's early youth, but the elegance, poise, and secure shaping of most of them palpably express the art of a much more mature composer. The trio sonatas for two oboes and thoroughbass Chrysander definitely assigns to the Halle period, but as we have remarked in the chapter dealing with this period, these also must be considered the works of the master musician of later years. If they were originally composed in Halle, which is quite possible, the version we possess is undoubtedly a somewhat later reworking. Opus 2, *Nine Sonatas or Trios for Two Violins, Flutes, or Hoboys with a Thorough Bass for the Harpsichord,* published in 1733, contains what we may safely regard as works of art. The seven trio sonatas in Opus 5, for violins or German flutes and harpsichord, are remarkable too. All of them are outside the German orbit because of their pronounced melodic quality; they have often been converted into vocal pieces. The spirited fugal writing made subsequent transference to oratorio overtures also readily feasible. All of these sonatas reflect the genius of the Italian trio sonata, the upper parts entwined in flowing melody or brisk imitative runs, the bass shepherding them with constant vigilance. From Opus 5 onward Handel combines the sonata with the suite, the gathered gravity and resonance of the one freshened with the lighter dances of the other. The exquisitely turned trios of Opus 5 stand, with Bach's trio sonatas, at the head of Baroque chamber-music literature.

[3]

IN ITALY THE concerto grosso was part of the general scheme of instrumental music. At the same time the concerto grosso was unmistakably orchestral in nature, representing a definite type, a species with well-defined order and characteristics, which reached a plateau in the works of Corelli, who was lavish with one hand while strictly regulating matters with the other. Handel never ceased to admire the intensely felt precision and sinewy tenderness of Corelli's concertos but would not accept the occasional neglect of incidental vitality for the sake of a pervading unity. If Corelli's was largely a genuine orchestral style, Handel's was exclusively so; there is a bracing vigor, a keen saliency in his concertos, their principal asset being a readiness for action. The great difference between Handel's concertos, especially those in Opus 6, and most other Baroque concertos is that they do not represent a type or species; each one of them is different and individual even though it hews to the main lines as established by Corelli's synthesis.

The Italians, especially the generation of Vivaldi and even more that of Geminiani, proceeded from their instrument, the violin; they fiddled as they composed, happily and highly subjectively. This love of the medium can be found in some of the slow movements of Handel's solo sonatas, and in most of his harpsichord music, but not in the orchestral works. Highly ornamented writing he found detrimental to orchestral monumentality, he wanted his contours solid, and creative freedom he always combined with a subtle but binding constructive logic. He reconciled the basis of musical matter with its mechanism, he brought into play the resources of instrumental technique, but everything had to obey the shifting dexterity of construction. The result was an orchestral style far more modern than that of his contemporaries even though in many ways his attitude may be called conservative. "Handel sports with the band," says Burney, "and turns it to innumerable unexpected accounts, of which neither Corelli nor Geminiani had ever the least conception."

Why Handel suddenly decided in 1734 to compose and publish a set
of concertos is not clear, but, since it was in that year that Walsh became
his permanent publisher and since concertos were in demand, it is quite
possible that it was the energetic and piratical publisher who forced the
venture. Handel knew quite well that if he did not agree Walsh might
proceed on his own; this happened more than once. The set, given the
opus number 3, "though called *Hautbois Concertos,* has very few solo
parts for that instrument; most of the divisions, and difficult passages,
being assigned to the principal Violin . . . [these concertos] are admirably calculated for a large and powerful band" (Burney). Opus 3 is an interesting mixture of old and new. Some of its constituent numbers are
much earlier than the date of publication would indicate, though Chrysander's statement that Opus 3, No. 3 was composed in Hanover in
1711–12 is hardly defensible. Handel is "sporting" here as if deliberately
wanting to tease the pedants, for the curious theme in the fugue violates
the codified rules of melodic progression by using augmented and diminished intervals. These concertos are richly orchestrated; Handel uses in
turn recorders, oboes, bassoons, harp, positive organ, and the usual string
body. Nevertheless, the hasty publication project is betrayed by the many
transcriptions; half of the movements are borrowings and reworkings.
Handel called into service some of his keyboard fugues, the overtures to
Amadigi and *Ottone,* the last movement of his harpsichord suite in D
minor (a favorite subject for transcription), the anthem *In the Lord put I
my trust,* and so forth. On the whole, Opus 3 lacks the supple lucidity of
movement that distinguishes Opus 6; the material has not been fully com-
pacted. Yet while inferior to the great Opus 6, it contains many splendid
movements and the colorful orchestration is always interesting.

The *Twelve Grand Concertos,* composed in a few weeks and published by Walsh in 1739, belong fundamentally to the Corelli "school" and
may be called conservative. Compared to them, Locatelli's concertos
Opus 1 (1721) seem more modern in idiom and tone. Grout correctly observes that "the serious, dignified bearing and the prevailingly full contrapuntal texture of this music are less characteristic of the 1730s than of the
earlier part of the century when Handel was forming his style in Italy" (*A
History of Western Music*). The "conservative" attitude is reflected in the
adherence to a number of Corelli's canons. Thus the violin parts are always treated as in the trio sonata; they are equals, the parts freely crossing each other, the second violin often rising far above the first. The slow
movements follow Corelli's similar pieces in his *sonate da chiesa.* The

"modern" quality is evident in the leaning toward the symphonic, in the built-in crescendos, the surprise dynamics, and the dramatic turns and interruptions. However, the most unusual feature of these concertos, neither conservative nor modern but altogether Handelian, is their improvisatory freedom within the established principles of the genre. The almost bewildering variety of ingredients caused serious concern among historians, who were unable to relate Handel's to any known procedure. Some complained that these concertos are so different from one another that "a basic formal concept can hardly be recognized in them." Indeed, there is no regular, schematic alternation between solo and tutti, the concertino may be altogether absent, and no two of them are alike either in form or procedure. Three of the concertos have four movements, eight have five, and one has six. The elements used are a fantastic jumble: French overture, Italian, French, and English dances, *sonata da chiesa*, chamber duet, all freely mixed; then again we hear an aria or an accompanied recitative, theme and variations, fugue, etc. Some movements are entirely in the *concerto a quattro* style, that is, for orchestra alone without solo parts, others tend towards the solo concerto, still others rightfully belong in the domain of the suite, and some are decidedly symphonic. The concertino is usually episodic and can hardly wait to rejoin the tutti. This fantastic variety, seeming to indicate an *ad hoc* garland of movements forced into one set, misled many critics, who failed to appreciate this riot of imagination, its freedom and unpredictability, the immense gusto, élan, creative energy, and surging excitement that went into the making of these concertos. Though the absolute antipode of Bach's *Brandenburg Concertos*, the *Grand Concertos* represent with them the highest achievement of Baroque orchestral music.

[4]

THE FIRST concerto begins "with pride and haughtiness," as Burney says, the opening section followed by one of those imperious allegros whose crispness never falters. Now the muscular eloquence is relieved by lyricism; the adagio is a love duet of pure Mediterranean suavity. After a vigorous fast fugue, whose fine technical achievement is touched with nonchalance, the final allegro tails off somewhat.

The first movement of the second concerto is a happy pastoral piece, though not of the dainty kind; the orchestra is robust, only the concertino is tender. The movement does become pensive, though, towards the end when the bustle subsides in gently drooping sixths in the violins, followed by a halting recollection of the initial happy theme. The second movement is symphonic, carried by a powerful thrust that climaxes in an unusually long insistence on the Neapolitan sixth. The Largo's pathos and expressiveness is almost theatrically vocal, while the final movement, a fugue—but one such as no treatise knows—is equally dramatic. This is an exceptionally fine and imaginative work.

The third concerto opens with a broad quasi ostinato that with its vein of pathos mingled with robust sound makes an irresistible appeal. The Andante, which might be called a sort of double fugue, is moody, with an unusually pregnant theme; the contrapuntal work is superb, and the short piece rises to a magnificent climax. It is followed by what commences as a typical Italian concerto grosso movement, recalling Vivaldi in the sharply accented theme with its octave leaps, but suddenly Handel decides to turn it into a solo concerto by inserting episodes for the first violin of the concertino; and so the piece runs its course from one surprise to another. The Polonaise is not a polonaise at all—unless the Poles used bagpipes and drone basses and shifted the traditional rhythmic pattern of their national dance; but a fine and imaginative piece it is. The brief closing Allegro is a little delicate epigram, though not without one moment of anxiety when a sudden harmonic change makes the listener sit up.

In the A minor concerto, the fourth, Handel strikes passionate tones. The Larghetto affettuoso is an instrumental arioso of an astonishingly modern cut. The broad melody winds its way, at times tortuously, never for a second forgetting the "affettuoso" in the superscription. It is followed by a masterly fugue built upon an unruly, demanding theme. Handel accepts the challenge; the fugue is one of his finest. If the fugue is wild, the subsequent Largo e piano is a *Stabat Mater.* Nothing happens, only bittersweet chains of suspensions in the upper parts over a strolling bass, but the vision hangs there tranquil as the evening star. The piece could be sung without any change. The wildness returns in the Allegro, an extraordinarily dramatic piece the like of which no other composer of the age would—or could—place in a concerto. The bitingly sharp theme is driven mercilessly, but twice Handel interrupts the compelling flow with a mysterious, hesitant, and dark interlude that throws a furtive shadow over the movement.

The opening French overture of the fifth concerto Burney considered the finest of its kind ever composed, one that "seems to require a convulsive, determined, and military cast." It is indeed a most impressive piece, small in compass but great in scale. The fugue is a worthy companion to the one in the fourth concerto, dancing its way effortlessly and abounding with contrapuntal finesse. The third movement is extraordinary even in this collection of extraordinary pieces, and though one would expect its virtually 19th-century tone to appeal instantly to anyone, most commentators completely misread its portent. The movement, entitled Presto, is nothing less than a modern orchestral scherzo, swift, tight, and bold. Surprisingly, not only Burney but even Leichtentritt is cool to it. How Leichtentritt, who always finds correspondences with Beethoven, Brahms —even Wagner—of the most tenuous sort, could have missed such an excellent opportunity to cite a *Vorahnung* of the scherzo in Mendelssohn's *Midsummer Night's Dream* music is difficult to understand. The second Allegro is even more symphonic, at times furiously so, as Handel makes his strings race with tremolo tuttis without permitting the pace to sag. This was too much for Burney. Though he recognized the nature of the movement—"here we have a very early specimen of the symphonic style in Italy"—the style was actually too "late" for his taste. He did not like tremolos and fast repeated tones, and sadly concluded that all this was noise and mere filling. In contradistinction, the concluding Minuet was everyone's favorite. A modest compliment is due to the younger Muffat, who contributed to the first two movements of the work.

The sixth concerto starts with a pensive dramatic scene. The fugue, too, with its contorted theme, is dark, though not without strength. While the hurly-burly of the dynamics of motion associated with the symphonic style had no meaning for Burney, he did appreciate a fine fugue, and for this somber G minor fugue, heavily chromatic in design, he had words of unbounded admiration. "The fugue is remarkably curious in subject; which is so unobvious and difficult to work, that no composer of ordinary abilities, in this learned species of writing, would have ventured to meddle with it, if such an unnatural series of sounds had occurred to him." The Musette is expressive of gentle serenity, of the charm of Neapolitan folk music. Handel's procedure is again in defiance of all tradition. Even though the opening section was borrowed from Leo (so Schering tells us), surely no one in the first half of the 18th century could have made such an uncommonly imaginative compound piece out of the material. The Musette consists of several sections that form a sort of rondo; the first is satisfied with the pleasant bourdon of the bagpipes, while in the second section a totally new, whimsical picture is presented as the rhythm changes to the Scotch snap. There is something reassuring in the way the basses take over the rhythm from the violins, repeating the delicate tune with their awkward, tripping, good-natured grumbling. Now Handel decides that his violins need a workout and makes them concertize, but just as suddenly the whole first complex returns and the delightful piece ends with a gentle cadence that is like a satisfied sigh. The remaining two movements again were found troublesome by many, and defended by others with unconvincing gallantry. Burney, who does not hide his distaste, recommends their omission, saying that even Handel often omitted them in his own performances. If so, the reason must be sought in their bold quality, too advanced for the times. Those who are looking for black and white rhythms and melodies will not find them in this boisterous Allegro. It begins with a sharply Vivaldian subject, but in Handel's hands the typical Baroque theme has a rather grim determination. As we wonder what turn the piece will take, the solo violin embarks upon a seemingly altogether unrelated bit of concerto music with Vivaldian cascades of sequences, but somehow the determined tutti returns with its brisk statements. Presently the interchange becomes more nervously agitated, the solo violin is reduced to short plaintive interpolations that are drowned by the assertive tutti. After a while the orchestra decides that the game is up, a furiously onrushing chromatic run sweeps away the solo, an angry Neapolitan sixth sealing its doom. The piece is ended with an energetic tutti. This is a rousing, powerful, and fantastic movement that apparently was still looked upon with incomprehension a bare half century ago. The final piece, though much calmed down, still shows fight, its energetic triplets opposing the angular theme of the dance tune. It brings to conclusion this concerto put together of a rainbow of forms, themes, and moods.

After a very brief and quiet introduction in the seventh concerto, Handel is again on the rampage, writing a fugue whose theme consists of one tone constantly repeated in ever smaller note values. This is one of the few occasions when Handel permitted the more robust side of his humor to find expression in music. Actually, the fugue is more symphonic than fugal; Handel takes hold of the little figure at the end of the theme, belaboring it with almost Haydnesque gusto. Both following movements, a Largo and an Andante, turn to suite music. Though polyphonic, the Largo is really an instrumental aria, the melody sustained, the harmony rich. The Andante drops all pretense at polyphony and simply spins the garlands of its melody over a simple accompaniment. There is no concertino in this concerto, all the violins sing together. The robust, "symphonic" Handel is back in the last movement, a Hornpipe. Handel is visibly enjoying himself, with insatiable pleasure exploring both the lusty rhythm of the old English dance and the convolutions he can coax out of the wide-ranging treble: a capital piece.

The eighth concerto is really a suite, beginning with a stately, serious Allemande. The initially imitative motif is gradually relegated to the bass, where it seems to defend the original idea against the elaborate figurations in the treble. This is a dramatic piece, full of surprising deceptive cadences, but Handel has no intention of making the whole of the C minor Concerto dramatic, though serious it remains to the end. After a short Grave, an Andante allegro plays elegantly with a little ornament in a subdued fashion; the dissonances are soft, and a slight melancholy floats over the piece. A beautifully flowing Siciliana brings warmth, and the brief final Allegro fascinates with its metrically sophisticated theme.

The Largo of the ninth concerto is palpably theatre music, wherefore some authors call it primitive, but its "indeterminate" mood makes a fine introduction to the bustling Allegro that follows. This is a good piece, but with the following Larghetto it belongs to the less distinguished movements in Opus 6. The "fugue," built on an elaborate theme, is fine, however. Once the exposition is finished, the piece becomes a beehive of activity with scarcely a rest in the four parts and we realize that this Allegro is not a fugue at all.

In the D minor concerto Handel, who was coasting a little in the ninth, is again fully alert. The introductory French overture is floridly ceremonious in tone and gesture—the grand manner—while the three Allegros are all splendid contrapuntal pieces with themes that lend themselves to spirited play. In the last Allegro the countersubject is in genial contrast to the spitting principal theme, and Handel again disturbs the general felicity by some little homophonic-dramatic interludes, the busy piece ending on that enigmatic tone. The Allegros are separated by an aria, again theatre music, sad and pleading.

The eleventh concerto is once more baffling. The opening Andante larghetto Handel wants played staccato; the gestures are large and so are the intervals played by the violins, but after a while he begins to vary the atmosphere by dramatic touches, the tone becomes mysterious, passionate, and pleading. The piece ends as if it had some hidden program. The double fugue with sharply contrasting themes is from the top drawer, and though the Andante is a somewhat overextended dance piece, the final Allegro, again with a metrically piquant theme and bedecked with virtuoso violin solos, is thoroughly enjoyable.

The last of the concertos begins with an unusual French overture, more nearly an expressive orchestral recitative than the customary ceremonial music. It is heavily dotted, the intervals are "wild" (Burney), and the traditional grand pathos is interspersed with fantastic improvisations.

The following Allegro is a superb concerto number, bursting with health, and so is the final Allegro, which with its sharply dotted, impudent theme romps gaily, and when this sharp rhythm is not enough, Handel combines it with triplets. The first Largo between the fast movements is like a quiet stream whose ripples are barely visible, though the second once again tells a tragic story in a few measures.

[5]

IN 1741 WALSH PUBLISHED AN anthology, *Select Harmony,* that contained three further concertos by Handel. One of these, composed for the performance of *Alexander's Feast* in 1736, is a gay and brilliant piece that enjoyed great popularity, though it is not in a class with the master-works in Opus 6. Handel's unorthodoxy shines particularly in the second Allegro, a rondo that must be unique in the literature. The principal theme returns in rondo fashion, but almost always in a different key, while in the episodes the concertino has its own merry time.

There are a number of other concertos we might call unattached, because they do not belong to any collection; since, however, they are little more than echoes of things Handel had done before, or were incorporated in other works such as the *Water Music* and the *Royal Fireworks Music* and became known as integral parts of these compositions, we shall not discuss them. Brief mention should be made of the double concertos (*a due cori*). In reality there are three "choirs," two for winds and one for strings. The first of these works, in B-flat, contains transcriptions from *Messiah,* but the arrangement is so skilful that the piece is well worth performing. The second, in F, is even more richly orchestrated, with oboes, bassoons, and horns in addition to the strings. This is a large work, with many of its nine movements of unusual scope. The brilliance of the concerto is enhanced by the sonorous handling of the wind and string choirs, here antiphonal, there united in massive tuttis. The variety of the movements is also considerable. The other large-scale orchestral works, the *Water Music* and the *Royal Fireworks Music,* have been discussed above, pages 142 and 483.

[6]

THE ONLY species of keyboard and concerted music cultivated by Handel after the 1730s was the organ concerto, which he continued to produce until the end of his creative career, the last work of this kind being dated by the composer January 4, 1757.[1] Like the English oratorios, these concertos represent an original genre, the like of which could be found in neither Italy nor Germany. Its birth was no doubt occasioned by the unique combination of composer, performer, and impresario in one. Handel was famous for his virtuosity on the keyboard, and his legendary ability to improvise amazed Mattheson even after hearing him "hundreds of times." The impresario took cognizance of this asset, employing it as an added attraction by performing between the acts of oratorios. Since the orchestra was there, sitting and waiting for the oratorio to resume, the idea of combining organ with orchestra must have occurred quite naturally.

The first collection of these concertos, the title carefully worded "for Harpsichord or Organ," was published by Walsh in 1738 as Opus 4. Two years later another set of six concertos was issued, without opus number; the third half dozen (Opus 7) however, was not printed until 1760, after Handel's death. While the reference to "harpsichord or organ" served business purposes, the publisher was not stretching a point. These concertos can be played on the harpsichord without any alteration, because the English organ in Handel's time was not that "most excellent—large —plump—lusty—full-speaking" instrument Thomas Mace mentions in his *Musick's Monument* but a one-manual positive without pedal board. It was especially suited for solo playing, or for accompanying a chorus, and it was part of the pit orchestra. Some of these small, bright instruments had a sort of swell box, so the player had a certain control over the expressiveness of his playing. This contrivance, known in England since 1712, first appeared attached to harpsichords, whence it was transferred to the organ. Handel is known to have been interested in it. Nevertheless, in some instances the sustained quality of the organ sound is unquestionably called for. Handel assigns long note values to the solo while the strings continue their melodic convolutions counting on the unfading tone of the solo instrument. Such passages would lose coherence if performed on the harpsichord. In the last set, especially Opus 7, No. 1, we finally have genuine organ music. Even the pedal makes its first appearance: Handel must have had access to one of the few English organs equipped with pedal board.

Though reared among the splendid German organs especially built for polyphonic playing, and all of them equipped with pedal board, Handel never wrote anything for that instrument. In his notebook almost all

---

[1] This final concerto borrows material from Habermann, Handel obviously quoting from memory. But the blind composer's reworking is as masterful as ever.

the keyboard music he copied was by southern German masters or by Italians, such as Poglietti. All these were Catholics in whose repertory the great chorale preludes and paraphrases, the toccatas and fugues, of the North German school are absent, for in the Catholic service the organ was largely restricted to accompanying the choir. Thus the organ, the core of Bach's art, was peripheral in Handel's, even though he loved the instrument and was one of the ablest players of his age. After he heard and played the organs in Italy and then in England, all memory of the great German art of organ music seems to have left him forever; not, however, the born improviser's desire to make use of the instrument for the joy of making music extempore.

These organ concertos demand from the performer sound musicianship, taste, and stylistic insight, for long stretches in the solo parts are mere skeletons of what Handel's audiences heard. Aside from the fact that Handel was his own interpreter, Baroque practice presupposed skill in embellishing and elaborating such a skeletal part. It goes without saying that the prevailingly two-voice writing in the solo part requires filling-out in the sense of the basso continuo practice. Yet while the solo part demands virtuosity, the texture must remain light and transparent, and in the fast-moving, violin-concerto-like figurations and chains of sequences the two-part setting must remain untouched. This is not polyphonic music, it does not even resemble the organ literature of the age, and of course has not even a trace of the "churchly." Handel is usually in an easy and relaxed mood, making the organ and orchestra vie with each other in pleasant, fresh, even jaunty music that has neither great fugues nor even any elaborate structure. This is popular concert music in the best sense of the word.

Hawkins's description of Handel's playing of the concertos (II, 912) is eloquent and particularly valuable because it comes from a musically trained person who was an eye witness.

His amazing command of the instrument, the grandeur and dignity of his style, the copiousness of his imagination, and the fertility of his invention were qualities that absorbed every inferior attainment. When he gave a concerto, his method in general was to introduce it with a voluntary movement on the diapasons, which stole on the ear in a slow and solemn progression; the harmony close wrought, and as full as could possibly be expressed; the passages concatenated with stupendous art, the whole at the same time being perfectly intelligible, and carrying the appearance of great simplicity. This kind of prelude was succeeded by the concerto itself, which he executed with a degree of spirit and firmness that no one ever pretended to equal.

It can be seen that the concerto itself was a continuation of the improvised prelude, and what we have in the printed score is little more than a
sketch that enables the player to stay with the orchestra. In the D minor
Concerto, Opus 7, No. 4, Handel wrote out the whole cadenza, thus giving us a good idea how these works were executed. In some of the later
works the improvisation extends to whole movements, so that a two-
movement concerto would actually consist of three, Handel simply indicating that between the two notated movements one may be played *ad
libitum*. Nevertheless, many of these concertos have a firm formal design,
a sort of amalgam of the concerto grosso and sonata da camera.

The variety is considerable: pompous-pathetic largos, sparkling allegros, delicate dance movements, dialogues with solo instruments, virtuoso passage work, occasionally interspersed with tiny concerted sections
for solo violin or cello, fugatos, ostinatos, and also folksong-like melodies.
Like the *Twelve Grand Concertos,* these compositions are gloriously independent of convention, and no two of them are similar in construction
and procedure. Though they have a generous share of the everyday routine of Baroque instrumental music, in the aggregate they are original and
personal. The melodies are warm and expressive, and in the fast movements one repeatedly notices that the tone is bantering, even saucy—
Handel was having fun. In the last concertos, dating from 1740–50,
though the polyphony increases, the transition from Baroque to pre-
Classic style is in evidence. Here we find a decided trend toward the
sonata, thematic work, and even tonal and thematic dualism. This collection contains the finest and most original specimens of the genre. They are
larger in scale, and while Opus 4 offers enlarged chamber music of a more
intimate character despite the virtuosity of the solo part, Opus 7 is orchestral in nature, frequently approaching the grand style. While only the fifth
and sixth concertos in the first set are transcriptions, all of those in the
second are in this category, the material having been taken from Opus 6.
It appears that these arrangements were made by Walsh's men without
Handel's concurrence.

[7]

OF ALL OF Handel's works it is the many harpsichord pieces
that may provide a glimpse of his creative youth. This is natural, because
keyboard music was the German cantor's native soil. Chrysander published a collection of these pieces, to which he gave the title *Klavierbuch
aus der Jugendzeit.* Here we can find many prototypes and original ver-

sions of some of the pieces reworked and published later. "Reworking" is
the key to the uneven quality to Handel's output in this area, for the keyboard pieces show a wide range in quality, from the slight and insignificant to the magnificent and highly artistic. When an old piece was used in
its original shape—that is, when Walsh or a Continental pirate published
it without Handel's permission—the result was unworthy of the great
composer. When Handel had a chance to "correct" a youthful piece we
are dealing with an altogether different kind of music, and, of course, the
new pieces added to the collection by the mature master are almost all
first-rate Handel. The music is no longer that of a young provincial German composer but of an elegant, experienced, and knowledgeable international composer intimately acquainted with Italian and French music.

The success of these pieces was phenomenal; they were the most
popular compositions of their sort in all Europe. Published by John Cluer
and Walsh as independent volumes of "Lessons," selections often appeared both in London anthologies and in the pirated publications of
Dutch, Swiss, French, and German printers. In sales the harpsichord volumes outdid by far Couperin's, Rameau's, and Bach's similar collections.
As usual when the business methods of the estimable publishing house of
Walsh are combined with Handel's own ways with his musical hoard,
things become hazy as to time, place, and even the identity of the composer. The first volume of suites, of 1720, was not yet within Walsh's
grasp; it was published by John Cluer "for the Author." These suites could
not have been composed before the Italian journey. Perhaps some of
them were written in Hanover, but, at any rate, they surely were thoroughly gone over for the "corrected" edition. The second set, published
by Walsh in 1733, without Handel's permission, also contains eight suites,
but this music is considerably weaker than the 1720 collection, undoubtedly because the material, somehow filched by Walsh, was not subjected
to Handel's usual reconditioning treatment. Among other reasons that indicate an arbitrary collection is the neglect of tonal order. The scheme in
the first book of suites is carefully arranged and contrasted: A major, F
major, D minor, E minor, E major, F-sharp minor, G minor, F minor. In
the second book there is no orderly succession, and it is most unlikely that
Handel would have agreed to pairs of consecutive suites in the same key.
Of the third set, published later, not only the date is uncertain: one wonders whether these "suites" were not put together by the publisher from
single, unrelated pieces. Indeed, we are not even sure that Handel had
anything to do with this largely insignificant music.

The fugues, published in 1735, this time with the composer's consent, are another matter. We have seen how these fine pieces, embodying Handel's conception of fugal procedure, served as a reservoir for later use in choral reincarnations. They were published as *Troisième Ouvrage*, a title that should be interpreted as indicating the "third set" of keyboard music in Walsh's catalogue; Opus 3 had already been allotted to the oboe concertos. The fugues must also have been composed earlier, though probably not before 1720; Mattheson speaks of them in 1721 as "the newest of Handel's fugues." Most of the rest of the harpsichord music is probably spurious, the set of *Fugues faciles* certainly so. Handel's keyboard music was in universal demand, and the factories were busy manufacturing Handeliana all over Europe.

To return to the most substantial of these lessons, the first set: the feeling for and reliance on the technique and sound of the keyboard instrument is so strong as to result in a keyboard sonority par excellence. These pieces can be played on any keyboard instrument, including the modern piano, without any loss of character. As we have observed, the individual numbers are uneven. Thus the fugue in the second suite simply sparkles with wit, whereas the variations in the third suite do not venture beyond the simplest ornamentation. The fourth suite again opens with a fugal allegro that recalls the virtuoso pieces of the North German contrapuntists. The following dances are all delectable, the twenty-measure first statement of the Sarabande being one of those wide-spun Handelian melodies that nothing can stop until it has run its course. The fifth suite, neatly worked, contains the variations that became famous under the title *The Harmonious Blacksmith* (see above, page 141). The sixth suite, in F-sharp minor, is pensive and romantic—Handel is thoroughly engaged. Commentators have found it related to various preludes and fugues in *The Well-Tempered Clavier,* some of which indeed have the same poetic-improvisatory tone. But if the hunt for influences is undertaken it would be advisable to remember that the final version of the first volume of *The Well-Tempered Clavier* dates from 1722, by which time Handel's suites had been in circulation for three years (counting also the pirated edition of 1719). The seventh suite, opening with the grand, sweeping pathos of the French overture, tails off into figuration, but the eighth, in F minor, is, like the fifth, a masterpiece from beginning to end. The melodies are noble, the polyphony wonderfully suited to the keyboard, the fugue brilliant, and the dances enchanting. The second set, printed by Walsh in 1733, is considerably weaker, though there are some fine pieces here and there. Brahms borrowed the theme for his *Handel Variations* from the first suite in this collection. The third volume is even weaker than the second, and, as we have observed, contains either unedited youthful works or spurious compositions; no wonder Handel was angry about its publication.

Quite in another class are the six fugues of 1735, which end Handel's career as composer for the harpsichord. These contrapuntal studies, vigorous, idiomatic, grateful to play, and full of wit and invention, are, *mutatis mutandis,* Handel's *Art of Fugue.* They do not present a searching examination of the final reaches and possibilities of polyphony, but a lively and altogether un-selfconscious demonstration of Handel's conception of freely flowing polyphony that knows no restrictions or rules such as his erstwhile compatriots respected and cherished. The themes are piquant, the harmony solid, the part-writing pure fantasy (some of the three-part fugues have an occasional supernumerary fourth part), and the countersubjects always deftly contrasted. Most of them are double fugues—but in the Handelian sense; no one can tell whether he meant them to be double fugues or whether he just wanted to play with a countersubject. Mattheson, the sharp-eyed "Spectator in Music," was for a long time the only one to see this quality in Handel's counterpoint. Comparing Handel's fugal writing to that of the North German school, he finds in it "an altogether different spirit, in particular one that knows and possesses all reaches of harmony so well that where others give the impression of laboring, Handel appears to be joking and playing."

Handel's harpsichord music may seem relatively inconsequential, but in a sense it occupies a position of central importance in his life work. A number of these compositions serve as proving ground for his dramatic works. In them appear certain basic ideas and models that were to follow Handel throughout his career.

XXVI

TODAY WE ARE USED TO THE HOMOGENEOUS, WELL-BLENDED sound of the Classic-Romantic orchestra, and, though recent music shows a sharp departure from this ideal, both this new sound and that of the Baroque are somewhat strange to most of us. The modern listener hears the Baroque orchestra as a pleasant but undifferentiated sound, the differentiation made more difficult because of the ubiquitous presence of the keyboard continuo, whose "filling-in" lends a certain uniformity to the aural picture. Berlioz, in a letter from Berlin, where in 1843 he was invited to attend a performance of Bach's *St. Matthew Passion,* exasperatedly comments on the "wearisome effect" this "wretched instrument" causes by its "constant strumming" which spreads "a thick layer of monotony over the whole, but that is doubtless one reason for not giving it up. An old custom is so sacred only when it is bad!"

In Handel's time, the character not only of the orchestra as a whole but of the role of the individual instruments was quite different from ours. The oboes, which we find everywhere in these scores, we play in our own manner, that is, discreetly blended with the strings. However, they were the principal melody instruments among the woodwinds, and their presence was meant to be heard, not merely suspected. The bassoons, to us the clowns of the orchestra, were considered sensuous, elegiac, and dramatic instruments. But perhaps the greatest difference—and to modern players the most forbidding—is presented by the "clarin" trumpets, great favorites with the Baroque composer. The playing of the natural trumpet, the low-pitched instrument of the 17th and early 18th centuries, was a special art reserved for trumpeters who played nothing but the highest harmonics. These musicians could play stratospheric runs with the agility of a flute. Though so-called Bach trumpets, short three-valve instruments, are being constructed by modern makers, their tone-quality leaves much to be desired, while when Baroque parts are played on the standard orchestral trumpets the constant threat of misintonation makes the players timid and cautious. As early as the late 1770s, Hiller, in editing the *Utrecht Te Deum,* was compelled to change the trumpet parts in a way that robbed Handel's music of its festive tone; and, ever since, players and conductors have been uneasy about these high trumpet parts, fearful of the constant danger of derailment. While not nearly so florid as the trumpet parts, the horn parts were also relatively high because the diatonic scale was obtainable only in the highest register. When devising such passages for the usual pair of horns Handel could be more free with the open tones obtainable in that register by specially trained players than could Haydn and Mozart. The horn players were trained like the clarin players, the first horn seldom playing below the sixth harmonic, and the second not much lower.

The differences and difficulties, then, are numerous and real, but again it is principally our lack of experience and stylistic insight that hampers us, for while we smile at Berlioz's naive ignorance, our distinguished conductors are not much ahead of the French master when it comes to performing Baroque music. This Baroque orchestra was not "primitive," it was already quite modern under Scarlatti, for the minute the concerto principle was introduced, ensemble playing became lively, precise, colorful, and expressive. By calling on his vast experience with all kinds of techniques, Handel raised orchestral writing to the pinnacle of Baroque music.

"Monotony" and "undifferentiated sound" disappear when we examine and execute this music without attempting to force our own practices upon it. The Baroque opera composer of Handel's time fully recognized the importance of the proper use of instruments for expressive purposes. Charles Avison (*An Essay on Musical Expression,* 1752), a pioneer in authoritative musical criticism, shows that by the middle of the century we are dealing with a long tradition. It was this same tradition that established the principal Baroque orchestral sonority, the string orchestra with harpsichord, with the wind instruments *added* to the ensemble. This statement is basically true even though the oboes and bassoons usually played *colla parte* with the strings unless their participation was expressly disclaimed. This is evident from the frequent instructions *senza oboi* or *senza fagotti* which give the first inkling that they are present in the orchestra. Almost all the overtures and most other independent orchestral numbers should be so interpreted, but within the body of the opera or oratorio Handel liked pure string sound for the accompaniments.

It was the composer's task to find variation within the established sound pattern. Handel possessed a fine sense for the subtleties of the string orchestra and for instrumental timbre in general, in which neither his German nor his Italian colleagues of the day could match him; only Rameau was his peer. In view of the magnificent string compositions of the Italian school such a statement seems exaggerated, for surely Corelli and Vivaldi in their concertos are incomparable masters of the string orchestra. However, in a concerto, no matter how imaginative, the nature of the genre demands a certain uniform continuity. It was in the opera pit that the modern orchestra was born; the dramatic composer lives from word to word, and Handel's acute sense for the smallest dramatic accent is as much present in the orchestra as on the stage. His minutely calculated string writing offers veritable miracles of subtlety and balance—he knew a counterpoint of timbres. This may range from two- or three-part writing in the sonata tradition to the use of divided strings in several parts and finally to a large ensemble of strings and winds. His accompaniments are consistently substantial and interesting. The orchestra is generally employed in the concerto grosso manner, the violin figurations lively, often virtuoso, and the bass a meaningful participant. This is true even when only treble and bass are composed and the rest left to the continuo player. Handel's fine feeling for timbre and mood seldom failed him, especially noteworthy being his use—or deliberate omission—of the lower registers, the skilful employment of the mute, pizzicato, and the combination of these effects with plucked instruments such as lute or harp.

The string orchestra was complemented at one time or another by flutes, recorders, oboes, clarinets, bassoons, trumpets, horns, trombones, timpani, harpsichord, and organ. On special occasions lute, theorbo, mandolin, harp, carillon, "bass flute" (really alto flute), and contrabassoon joined the ensemble. Handel was among the first, with Rameau, to use the early clarinet, the chalumeau (*Tamerlano* and *Riccardo I*). At times the forces he used were considerable; *Rinaldo* calls for four trumpets, *Giulio Cesare* for four horns, and there are indications that he would have used the trombones more often had they been available. Unfortunately, in the revivals they disappeared even from *Saul*, and on the few occasions when he had them at his disposal this was announced as a special treat: "with

the Sackbuts." The orchestral panoply in *Saul,* with its flutes, oboes, bassoons, trumpets, trombones, kettledrums, theorbo, carillon, two organs,
and two harpsichords, was not equalled for a long time to come. This
large *instrumentarium* was, of course, never employed simultaneously.
Since the horns and trumpets, flutes and oboes, and some of the other instruments were often played by the same musicians, they were seldom
used together, but a more important reason for selective use of this rich
orchestra was the organizational functioning of the ensemble.

Handel's opera is prevailingly intimate, not calling on large forces.
The Covent Garden pit was small, and the Haymarket Theatre could not
seat many more than thirty players. This chamber opera was accompanied by an orchestra based on the concerto grosso principle, with wind
instruments added as the occasion required. Modern conductors almost
invariably make the mistake of accompanying the arias with the full orchestra, whereas only the concertino, as a rule, is indicated. The overtures
and ritornels were played by the tutti—ripieno and concertino—but as
soon as the solo voice entered, the concertino, supported by the harpsichord, took over. This was a flexible orchestra, but, with all its liveliness,
always deferring to the voice. Handel avoided complications that would
detract from the singing even in cases, which are frequent, when the accompaniment is concerted and elaborate.

Handel's basso continuo, as always in Baroque music, needs special
attention. There is a great difference between slovenly chord-playing (it
may have been this that provoked Berlioz's contempt) and imaginative—
indeed creative—playing. As a rule Handel employed two harpsichords,
again following the concerto grosso arrangement; both played in the
tuttis, but only the principal instrument, played by Handel himself, accompanied the concertino. The presence of lute, theorbo, mandolin, and
harp does not represent an archaic remnant of the old *ad hoc* orchestra,
dispensable in modern performances. On the contrary, now that we have
excellent modern replicas of these instruments, and musicians trained to
play them, we should restore the aural distinction they lend to the ensemble.[1] This is the more desirable because Handel's basso continuo is
often varied, using bass lute or other chordal instruments or obbligato
organ instead of the harpsichord. The role of the organ presents a special
problem about which more will be said below.

While such works as *Acis and Galatea* or *L'Allegro* demand the same

[1] As recently as 1925 the role of these instruments was completely misunderstood.
Adam Carse, in his *The History of Orchestration,* recommends that these "obsolete
instruments . . . need not be taken into account except as curiosities."

intimacy as the operas, the dramatic oratorios were designed for larger forces, and Handel often commanded a good-sized ensemble. What we may call the standard complement consisted of ten to fifteen violins, three to five violas,[2] three cellos, two or three bass viols, pairs of oboes and bassoons, trumpets, and drums, supported by harpsichords and organ. Horns and recorders were added to this ensemble on occasion. This is a respectable orchestra even by modern standards and can easily be reconstituted, but the roles of wind instruments and of the continuo demand a specific balance that differs from ours. If a fair-sized string orchestra is used, something like 10-10-6-4-3, the oboe and bassoon parts should be doubled in the tuttis. The woodwind parts were also treated as solo and ripieno. Their prominent color is an essential ingredient of the Baroque orchestral sound pattern, because they aerate the string sound.

The old pit harpsichords were relatively powerful instruments, at any rate more so than their average modern replicas; on the other hand, the positive organ had little resemblance to our instruments with their torrent of muddy sound. The indiscriminate and continuous use of the organ in Handel's oratorios is one of the means whereby these works are made "sacred." Handel's organ had a double role: first of all it was an *orchestral* instrument, frequently playing *tasto solo;* secondly it was used as the continuo instrument. The principal continuo instrument was the harpsichord; recitatives and arias were always accompanied by it unless Handel specifically asked for the organ, which happens infrequently. If he does so it is for coloristic or dramatic and certainly not for religious purposes. To replace the harpsichord by the organ is an outright falsification of the aural effect intended by the composer, and of course to use the organ for the accompaniment of the secco recitatives is a contradiction in terms. Our habit of making the fat Romantic organ enthusiastically pump a volume of tone into the ensemble whenever possible is a lamentable mistake that ruins the choral sound.[3] This awkward situation will not be remedied until good replicas of the old choir organ or positive are created for this specific purpose.

Handel's chorus consisted of basses, tenors, falsettists, and boys. This leaves three of the vocal parts unaffected for modern performances, but

[2] Eighteenth-century violas were larger than ours and had an ampler tone.

[3] The unfortunate notion that the presence of the organ is an essential requirement of "sacred" music is not limited to our conception of Baroque music. Masses and oratorios of the Classic era, though composed for a symphonic ensemble that makes the continuo altogether superfluous, are still played with the organ prominently lording it over all. To cite an example, in Mozart's *Requiem,* which does not call for the organ at all, the choral sound is almost always ruined by the unwanted intruder.

the falsetto part has no exact equivalent in our practice, because boy altos
and falsettists could sing lower than the ordinary run of female altos. An
occasional E and F below middle C does create some difficulty for our
altos, and it is therefore advisable to increase their numbers. On ceremonial occasions, or when several church choirs were combined, the chorus
was large, and with the orchestra correspondingly reinforced, we are close
to the modern ensemble. As a rule, however, Handel's chorus numbered
around twenty, and since the soloists joined it when not otherwise employed, four to six good voices were added to this number. All told, the
normal Handelian performance employed forty to sixty participants, including singers and instrumentalists. Although the same ensemble can still
be used with felicitous effect, there can be no question that in our large
concert halls larger forces are needed. It stands to reason that the full-
bodied eight-part choruses in *Israel in Egypt* and other such works cannot
be performed by puny forces for an audience of a couple of thousand, but
neither should they be produced by three hundred bawling larynxes. A
well-drilled—and balanced—chorus of sixty to seventy should be the max-
imum even in a large hall; anything beyond that destroys the quality of
the part-writing that is the glory of this music. Handel did not write
"paper music"; he always gauged the sonorities to the finest point, and a
large chorus, no matter how well managed, cannot do justice to his intentions.

[2]

IF WE ARE TO value Handel's works as expressions of his mind
and imagination, it is important that they should not be divested of their
nature and diluted with ingredients introduced supposedly to increase
their appeal to modern audiences. Before discussing Handel's performance practices something must be said about the various views concerning
the quality of playing in Handel's time. It is generally assumed that Ha-
beneck's orchestra in Paris represents the earliest instance of acceptable
and disciplined orchestral playing. This is based on Wagner's affidavit,
and anything antedating the Conservatoire orchestra of about 1830 is supposed to have been miserable. This distorted view is reinforced by the belief that 18th-century instruments were primitive, ill tuned, and incapable
of being played with accuracy. Some attempts have been made to play on
old woodwind and brass instruments, but it is of course ridiculous to expect modern players accustomed to modern instruments to play correctly
on old instruments without such an inordinate amount of practice as to

make the performers unfit for their own instruments. Such antiquarianism, in any case, is not synonymous with historical accuracy; the point is to play the music on modern instruments in the proper spirit. Valves and keys do not make an instrument, they only make its handling more comfortable; lips and fingers and experience are the deciding factors. Anyone who played a flute or clarinet fifty years ago knows that even without the Boehm system, or with fewer keys, perfect tuning could be obtained by the use of half or three-quarter holes, cross fingering, lip pressure, and other devices.[4] Even the modern horn player, whose work was made immeasurably easier with the introduction of valves, still relies on his lips and his fist in the bell. The old musicians practiced day and night on their "primitive" instruments until they mastered them to the satisfaction of conductors not a whit less exacting than Toscanini. It is sufficient to recall what able musicians reported about Lully's rehearsals and the quality of his orchestra, and we know that Handel, who had a number of first-class virtuosos in his orchestra, was a hard taskmaster. Quantz, a severe and competent critic, who visited London in 1727, thought that the performance he heard under Handel "made an extremely good effect." The superiority we feel toward these poor devils with their ragged instruments is matched only by our ignorance of their capabilities.

Aside from the exaggerated and unbalanced ensembles, perhaps the worst feature of modern Handelian performances is their pace. What Bernard Shaw complained about in 1892, the "insufferable lumbering which is the curse of English Handelian church singing," is still with us. Conductors addicted to solemn dragging should consult Handel's own estimates of the duration of each act; he frequently noted down the timing. Handel's basic *tempo ordinario,* the animated andante-allegro of the late Baroque, is usually slowed to a walk, especially in the choral numbers, which negates what Larsen calls "the fluid basic motion of the baroque." Larsen (*Handel's Messiah*) made a revealing comparison between the metronome indications various editors assign to the aria, "He shall feed his flock." While Chrysander and Seiffert suggest a total of less than four minutes, other editors dilate it to more than twice this duration, to eight and a half minutes, thus completely ruining the flowing siciliana.

Handel took considerably more pains than any of his contemporaries to indicate his wishes as to tempo, dynamics, and mood. Superscriptions such as *un poco più lento, un poco più piano, very slow,* and so on, are unusual for the period, though more customary with dramatic composers

[4] Some of the instruments had adjustable slides, interchangeable joints of different sizes, and screw plugs by which pitch could be regulated.

than with taciturn cantors such as Bach. Handel demanded crescendos and also knew how to forestall unwanted ones by requesting *piano continuando*. In *Agrippina* (1709) we already find such instructions as *piano, poco a poco più forte*. This matter brings us to the myth of "terrace dynamics," supposedly abolished only since the "invention" of the crescendo by the Mannheim orchestra. The sharp contrast of solo and tutti in the concerto was of course characteristic of the era, but the Baroque knew graduated dynamics as well as we do. Such freely changing dynamics are an essential expressive element in dramatic music. The black and white dynamic scheme should be abandoned, together with the conviction that every Baroque figure must be played with the *grand détaché*. We have positive proof in many scores that Handel and his fellow dramatic composers distinguished several grades within the extremes, and the difference between piano and mezzo forte or between piano and pianissimo was well understood; only the deafening fortissimo that defaces so many present-day oratorio performances was unknown. Handel's solicitude for accurate dynamic scale extends to the individual parts in the orchestra, as when he writes *violino 1 sempre forte* while all other parts are marked piano.

The superscriptions in Handel's scores also took care of the continuity. Unfortunately many editors disregard these, assuming that there was an ironclad rule for performing the da capo arias and other set pieces. Even where Handel omits the repeat, obviously wanting a dramatic effect by attacking the next number without a break, Chrysander will arbitrarily call for a repeat or at least will place a pause sign in his edition of the score, at times not even noticing—or ignoring—that this next number is to take the place of the da capo and should follow immediately. But then what would happen to the solemn "oratorio pause" that we expect after each number? Others have simply taken it for granted that Handel forgot the repeat, and have made the unsuspecting performer return to the first part in a mechanical way. While the situation should be clear to any musician from the context, Handel often helps by writing *attacca il coro*. The double bars that appear in the modern printed edition are often spurious; they are absent in the original manuscripts, and obeying them can destroy the intended dramatic effect. Thus at the end of the sinfonia opening the third act of *Semele* there is no halt, as is clear from the tonal arrangement, because the ending of the instrumental piece is inconclusive; it is Juno's recitative that brings the harmonic solution. The double bar placed there ruins the intended dramatic turn as the dreamy atmosphere of nirvana is shattered by the sudden explosion of the orchestra and

Juno's command: "Somnus arise!" Tempo and continuity also are constantly threatened by our practices. In the operas the final cadence of the continuo in a recitative was immediately followed by the next number; indeed, if in the same key, the last and first notes of the two pieces may coincide. There is no reason why in the oratorio, which is a dramatic work composed with the same techniques employed in opera, we should wait for an agonizing devotional cadence followed by a break. Rubato was well known and practiced in the Baroque—how could one sing without it? Evelyn, describing an Italian singer's delivery long before Handel's time, speaks of his "delicateness in extending or losing a note." The asthmatic retards at the end of sections and even phrases, which we consider *de rigueur* in "old music," are an invention of the 19th century. Whenever Handel wanted a perceptible slowing down he almost always indicated it by "adagio." In this connection the worst offenders are the continuo players in the recitatives. There seems to be a basic misunderstanding about the duration of the chords in a recitative, and one is usually painfully aware of the long-held melancholy notes of the continuo cello. Both the cellist and the harpsichordist are supposed to be crisp—note values in the secco are approximate and not binding. The various *regole* and *Anweisungen* are quite clear about that, and once the recitative is finished, any dallying on the final cadence (not to speak of the respectful pause that follows) hurts the continuity and dramatic pace.

[3]

When the Baroque was "rediscovered" by serious musicians, who with the reactivation of the harpsichord did such splendid work in bringing this vast store of great music before the public, the execution of ornamentation and embellishment seemed to be the supreme test—and problem—of Baroque music-making. Those musicians took the elaborate superstructure of ornaments that cover keyboard music, in particular, terribly seriously; scarcely a single note was permitted to remain unadorned. By regarding ornamentation as something primarily expressive of sentiment and fancy, which it was their duty to place in its context, these enthusiastic pioneers of Baroque performance practice promoted the *agréments* into a separate and virtually independent branch of musical design. It is indisputable that the ornaments were an essential part of Baroque music and that they made the da capo aria into something quite different from what it appears when repeated literally. But surely we must distinguish between the lute-descended game of decorative tinkling necessitated by the inability of plucked instruments to nurture tones much beyond their momentary appearance, and the sustained melodic phrases composed for voice, violin, and organ. The little French dance pieces require some sort of ornament on practically every beat, especially in the slow movements; an arching aria melody needs far less. Ornament is justified only in proportion to its formal inherence in the musical line it enhances. At the same time, ornament can give a background from which the melody emerges more significant because its elements are lengthened, minced, repeated, and so on, thereby raising it above its everyday existence. Ornamentation can be routine, but it can also be pure inspiration, and technique can lead to invention just as ornaments can endow a flat architectural surface with meaning. By study of contemporary scores and writings these ornaments can be ascertained and reconstructed; nevertheless the dangers attending their application are numerous. Singers, players, and conductors unfamiliar with the style or not possessed of creative imagination will either go astray or will indulge in little more than mechanical application of the known principles. On the other hand, composing musicologists are insufferably dull and often a menace. The only solution seems to be to entrust the ornamentation to musicologically informed composers or players, a very rare breed.

There is still another obstacle in the way of our understanding: our sense for, and appreciation of, melodic design, which is opposed to the breaking up of a flowing melody by too many ornaments. The highly ornamental Baroque melody already appeared somewhat artificial to Burney: "So changed is the style of Dramatic Music, since Handel's own period, that almost all his songs seem scientific"—i.e. contrived. Clearly, what is called for is a compromise by which a modest rather than extensive use of ornaments should be restored to the arias. We do have a few good examples of the ornamentation Handel expected from his singers and used in his own playing, and there is a large literature on its practice and application. Nevertheless, I do not find it advisable to restore these beyond a certain degree. We must remember that Handel was to some extent a captive of a custom that was largely the result of the virtuosity—and vanity—of the pampered Italian singers. On the other hand, his melodic design is so ample, his use of what Doni and other theorists called the "excessive intervals" gave his melody such expressiveness that it is in little need of emendations. Any elaborate ornamentation, especially the unaccompanied vocal cadenzas, is likely to result in mannerism. We can no longer contribute anything but more or less tasteful clichés, and since clichés abound in any well-settled style, we might leave well enough alone, especially since we have Burney's testimony that Handel was opposed to excessive ornamentation. A modicum of ornamentation is welcome, but only persons with impeccable musicianship and stylistic sense should attempt it. An absence of ornaments is infinitely preferable to poor or mechanical ones.

[4]

THE FIRST requirement for judicious performance is a good score. The task of restoring an old and abused score, to provide an unexceptionable, "definitive" musical text, is always difficult, calling for sound scholarship, a high sense of responsibility and integrity, and profound musicianship. In Handel's case the difficulties dwarf anything an editorial board ordinarily has to face. The historian is dealing with a Bruckner magnified a hundredfold. But while Bruckner patched endlessly, it would not have occurred to him to make a quodlibet of his symphonies, shifting the trio of the scherzo in the Second Symphony to the Seventh or vice versa; yet this is exactly what Handel did in his oratorios. Every revival changed the physiognomy of the work, sometimes radically. The editors must decide where to find a resting place for the eternally peregrinating pieces. It is easy to excise a Chandos Anthem from an oratorio, but what about a chorus that everyone knows, let us say, from *Judas Maccabaeus,* which in reality belongs in *Esther?* What shall be its fate? Another difficulty in preparing artistically correct editions is created by the frequent absence of figuring in the bass. Since Handel was his own performer, he needed only "reminders," which we must interpret and elaborate.

"The concealment of truth is the only indecorum known to scholarship," said Westermarck, but the editors of Handel's works did not honestly try to be decorous. Friedrich Chrysander was a distinguished musical scholar; in his day there were few to equal his learning and none even to approximate his industry and his devotion to the cause. He dedicated his whole life to the collection and publication of Handel's works, and his tenacity, his refusal to bow before superior forces, and his courage in adversity were of Handelian proportions. But he was an autocrat, a law into himself, who often made his selection according to his desires, who altered and revised at will, and who even falsified documents to suit his purposes. The old Händelgesellschaft edition is anything but complete and reliable, as anyone who browses in the British Museum and the Fitzwilliam Museum soon discovers. Chrysander could not, of course, acquire the original manuscripts, which were in the King's Music Library, but he did acquire a set of copies, the so-called conducting scores, later deposited in the Hamburg Library. These are of course very valuable, but only if collated with the originals, the sketches, and other copies (of which there are several), as well as with the various editions of the librettos; for the other sources contain many modifications by Handel himself, and they also contain additional music which, of course, is of exceptional importance. All these sources were available to Chrysander and he consulted many, yet both he and Seiffert relied too much on secondary sources, as have, indeed, even present-day German editors.

The conducting scores in Hamburg convey largely post-Handelian practices fostered by John Christopher Smith, Jr. While Smith undoubtedly acted from authentic first-hand experience, his performances inevitably reflected the conceptions of one a generation removed from the original scene. Larsen, who examined this question thoroughly (*Handel's Messiah*), came to the conclusion that the Hamburg scores, while undeniably copies that served for actual performances, "were not used by Handel himself." One discovers repeatedly that Chrysander, though mentioning autograph scores, proceeded from some later edition without using the manuscript score. In addition, the heroic editor of the hundred-volume Händelgesellschaft set was quite arbitrary in his decisions as to what to accept and what to reject. One of his worst failings was his bland disregard of Handel's own directions. If he did not like an adagio marking he changed it to andante or vice versa, inserting his own directions, furthermore, without distinguishing them from Handel's. Therefore the old collected edition, though a magnificent achievement, and in part of excellent quality, is badly in need of replacement. It is not without irony that this cavalier editor had his own troubles with his sub-editors. The preparation of the first volume of the Händelgesellchaft edition was entrusted to Julius Rietz, a fine cellist and reputable conductor. Chrysander's discovery that Rietz, a stranger to the scholarly process, paid little attention to Handel's instructions, even "considered them worthless," earned Rietz a sour epitaph in the preface to the very first volume of the *Gesamtausgabe*. Chrysander resented any form of criticism but was always ready to upbraid others.

The Novello scores are so lacking in elementary care that they cannot be considered, and as to the vocal scores Oskar Hagen concocted for the Göttingen Handel performances, they are wildly incongruous specimens of German theatrical Expressionism of 1920 vintage. The trouble with Hagen was that, though a distinguished art historian, he was an amateur musicologist and musician, unfamiliar with operatic history and dramaturgy, who approached the Baroque from the point of view of the 20th-century theatre. This led to frightful mangling of the scores; the da capo arias were left hanging in the air, the tonal scheme was dislocated, recitatives were cut to the bone in the mistaken belief that they were insignificant connecting links, and so on. The unfortunate Göttingen "reconstructions" were abandoned as their falsity was recognized, and the initiative passed from the amateurs into the hands of professionals, who are presently engaged in the editing of a new critical collection of Handel's works. It remains to be seen how this new *Hallische Händelausgabe* will cope with the many problems, prejudices, and malpractices that for two hundred years have obscured the life and works of Handel.

[5]

EVEN IF we are to be provided with an excellent critical edition of the scores, the performer is still faced with many grave decisions that no one can solve for him. The editor's duty is to provide the materials in as complete a form as possible. He may make recommendations concerning cuts and other details of performance, but the final responsibility for the presentation of a score rests with the conductor. If we are to enjoy Handel we must definitely reduce the proportions of many a large oratorio or opera. Poe was right: there is a time limit to our capability for being thrilled. Even if we leave aside the well-founded doubt that there ever was in Handel's time a great oratorio performed with all the numbers now associated with it, we must admit that not infrequently in his dramatic works a high exhilaration subsides into a sense of fatigue or unconcern. We have called attention to Handel's tendency to lose interest once the dénouement has taken place, to the often perfunctory mopping-up operations to provide the expected happy ending for which he had a distaste. But selection is very difficult and seldom satisfies all parties. It depends, among other things, on the legitimacy of the additions, for they were often intended to satisfy a popular singer or reward a Handelian favorite or suit a substitute. With a little exaggeration we may say that no two performances of an oratorio were the same; there were external changes, cuts, insertions, transpositions, exchanges, and new numbers. The editors must take into consideration every variant, the conductor can use only one of them.

Even if a judicious choice is made from among the accretions, many of Handel's scores are of a length so excessive as to be no longer bearable for us. He shared with other Baroque composers a propensity for what seems to us disproportionate length; the *St. Matthew Passion* would also gain in dramatic force and plain musical digestibility by the omission of several arias, no matter how beautiful. The palate of the present day is not schooled to so voluminous exercise as a four-hour oratorio or Passion. These *revenants* from the ages must be pruned. Of course such a statement is tantamount to heresy, *lèse majesté*, or, as they might say at court-martials, conduct unbecoming a scholar. But there is a vast difference between participating in a cult and enjoying a great work of art. In the case of both Bach and Handel the large number of arias, especially when given to the same type of voice, creates a feeling of unwarranted length that makes intelligent cutting mandatory. Some of these pieces undoubtedly represent the old Italian custom of the *arie da baule*, the reserve arias the composer always had on hand for unexpected contingencies. These reserves should never be committed in toto. The ideal and musically most profitable way, and one that would preserve all the good music without unduly trying the listener's ability to absorb what he hears, would be to use the good variants on alternate occasions. The very existence of the variants almost dictates this procedure, and no violence is done to those dramatically sprawling works. However, it cannot be done in the manner of Sir Thomas Beecham or Oskar Hagen. Choruses and accompanied recitatives are usually firm constituents of the dramatic plan, few of them can be eliminated this side of the post-dénouement sections of the oratorios. It is in the arias that most of the pruning must be done, with a careful weighing of the tonal relationship. A case in point is afforded by the so-called simile arias. Though they are often very beautiful, as their illustrative purpose usually tempted Handel to compose fine descriptive music, they are also often completely extraneous to the drama. Those who insist on unabridged Passions and oratorios should examine the situation that prevails in the theatre, where scholars accept the necessity of making cuts in classic works to suit their length to present-day performance. Shakespearean plays often need trimming as much as large Baroque scores; their exceptional length presents the same problems and hazards.

[6]

NOTHING IS MORE ILLOGICAL, not to say asinine, than the invoking of the preposterous hypothesis by arrangers of Bach and Handel that "had those composers lived today they would undoubtedly have availed themselves of our modern resources." [5] No question about it, and Pope Gregory the Great, had he lived today, would have composed juicy organ accompaniments to his chants. But they are not living today, history is not retroactive, and one does not copy Giotto in the pointillistic manner. Allied to this anachronistic concept is an even more incredible view: Handel was found wanting in expressiveness, even intelligibility, so the Victorians decided to subject the scores to systematic "clarification" by means of "additional accompaniments." They based their argument on incontrovertible precedents: Mozart also reworked Handel and so did other distinguished composers.

Such reworkings and transcriptions are justified by some on the ground that what matters is the content; only the philologists of music, the musicologists, it is said, would cling rigidly to the antiquated and primitive exterior. And yet it is the artists among all concerned who should cling to the faithful "exterior," for that exterior is the form. They ought to understand these things, they ought to know the importance of form. The musicologist is equally interested in "content," but he believes, as do all cultivated performers, that content cannot be conveyed when taken out of context. All the transcribers and arrangers, from Hiller to Goossens, forget that the composer does not offer content alone but also mood and form, and the three are indivisible. They could learn something from such a poet-scholar as Matthew Arnold (*On Translating Homer*), who eloquently proved that a translation in a different form is no longer a translation but an entirely different elaboration of the same subject. The same is true of the reorchestrated or inflated transcriptions and arrangements, for indeed, these arrangements are like literal translations of poetry into a foreign language; the original rhythms disappear, the verse loses its riverbed, the momentum its impetus. We know how rare a good transcription is, a musical event of a unique and fortuitous quality, which, as in the case of literature, should appear only when there is no other way to present the original work.

Transcriptions can, of course, have their uses; Liszt's piano versions of Schubert's songs and Bach's organ works made them known and appreciated, leading people to the originals. But even the best transcription cannot be used for the establishment of values, for it is an amalgam in which author and arranger are not separable. Davenant and Dryden

---

[5] The Beechams and Stokowskis were not the originators of this quaint idea, even though it is unlikely that they had knowledge of their predecessor. Hiller, speaking of his refurbishing of Handel in 1784, proudly stated that he wrote "an entirely new score, approximating what Handel himself would have written had he lived in our day."

came close to destroying Shakespeare's poetry, yet they were convinced that they had improved *The Tempest.* Equally earnest were the musicians who reconstructed Handel, not realizing that it is a crime to underscore, color, and thus coarsen what Handel wanted only to be divined. The citing of Mozart's arrangements of Handel's scores disregards many facts. In the first place, the reorchestration of these scores was not Mozart's idea, he was commissioned by Baron van Swieten to bring them up to date, and he was paid a fee, which as always he needed badly. In the late 18th century they knew only one style, the contemporary; little if any old music was played, and of course the historical sense and a regard for stylistic propriety had yet to make their appearance. Even decades later, a Mendelssohn and a Schumann found it advisable to add a piano accompaniment to Bach's Chaconne. Needless to say, when Mozart undertook such a commission he always produced something brilliant and worthwhile; he went about his work with skill and seriousness and the Handelian transcriptions appropriately have their own Köchel numbers. But Mozart's version of Handel is like Pope's translation of Homer: an excellent work without being a good translation. Mozart's language is not Handelian, and his personality is far removed from Handel's. As Larsen puts it: "The Valley of the shadow of death [in *Messiah*] has become a well-kept cemetery garden." Beethoven, with all his respect for Mozart, remarked about the restoration that "Handel would have survived without it."

The refurbishings started with Starzer and Hiller, followed by Mozart; then came the Victorians, and the 20th-century virtuoso transcribers. Early in the 19th century the great *Funeral Ode* was converted in Germany to a syrupy "oratorio" called *Feelings at the Tomb of Jesus,* and its tremendous opening number chopped into pieces. Many a Novello score falls into this category. Mendelssohn's organ accompaniments to *Israel in Egypt* were greeted with hosannas by Justus Thibaut, who welcomed the "cleansing" of church music from instruments.

We are tempted to suggest a reactivation of Lycurgus's law which forbade the "cobbling and heeling" of the plays of the great Attic dramatists, but we remember that Handel himself was an arch transcriber and arranger; once more we must guard against absolutes. This is especially important in the operas, for in the 18th century, roles were composed for individual artists and individual theatres. In addition, since in the absence of any agreement on standards, tuning was altogether an arbitrary affair, every theatre had its own pitch. The difference could be considerable. An opera composed for Venice, where the pitch was high, could not be performed in Rome, where it was low, without alterations and transcriptions.

It was the local maestro's task to carry out the changes, and as Telemann and others adjusted Handel's operas for Hamburg, so Handel, in his capacity as music director of the Royal Academy of Music, arranged other composers' scores for his theatre. But he did the same with his own works whenever the cast changed, when other circumstances so required, or when he had second thoughts. Many of these transcriptions were carried out with his wonted skill, though in not a few instances, especially when hurried, he simply transposed, leaving it to the singer to adjust the details to suit the changed situation.

Whenever an editor or conductor finds that a Baroque aria is exceedingly difficult to perform as notated in the score, he must find out for whom it was composed and for what occasion. Obviously the coloratura runs originally devised for a high soprano or castrato will not suit a tenor or bass. When discussing Baroque opera (Chapter VII) we expressed the belief that the greatest single obstacle to its revival is the role of the castrato, because the substitution of female sopranos or altos, or countertenors, only makes a bad situation worse. These roles should be transferred to men's voices; Handel gave us ample precedent to justify the procedure. To cite one example from among many, the role of David in *Saul*, originally for countertenor, was subsequently variously changed to soprano, tenor, and bass. The part of Abner, in the same work, was sometimes for tenor, sometimes for bass. Moreover, Handel has also shown us how a florid aria can be simplified in such a transcription without jeopardizing the original.

[7]

We have seen how the timorous neo-Puritan editors of the 19th century violated Handel's English texts, wilfully changing words and entire passages to give the oratorios a more virtuous and moral cast. In Germany, where woolly-headed and prissy editors were not behind their English colleagues, the texts were further bowdlerized by uniformly bad translations. The rendering of English verse into German is difficult enough without the necessity of regard for the music. Aside from reflecting the nuances of meaning, the problem of turning uninflected into inflected speech, short syllables into long, and so on, is very considerable, and to do all this while observing the musical values would seem an almost impossible task.[6] The translations are virtually re-compositions, *Nachdichtungen*, a fact that of course infuses a psychological element not

[6] It goes without saying that these difficulties apply to almost all translations of musical texts, whatever the language.

present in the original. We have the same difficulty with the Italian texts, for the original Italian lyrics in Handel's operas are carefully arranged for singability. If the texts are translated and the unskilled, unpoetic, and unmusical translator fills the singers' mouths with consonants and sibilants, we hear a sound quite different from what the composer had in mind. Translations are justified and often necessary, but they require the same skill and feeling needed for the carrying out of the ornamentation. To this day German audiences are treated to grotesque misrepresentations, for most of the oratorios are still sung in Chrysander's and Gervinus's often inaccurate and pedestrian translations. A few examples of these inept exercises should suffice.

In *L'Allegro,* "Let the merry bells ring round" is rendered with *Horch wie das Tambourin erklingt;* in *Samson,* Dalila's "With plaintive notes and amorous moan" is turned into *Verlassen weilt in Einsamkeit.* In the final chorus of the *Ode to St. Cecilia,* where Dryden says "The trumpet shall be heard"—and it is heard, because Handel naturally sets the music for the trumpet—the German audiences following the performance with libretto must wonder why the conductor changed the orchestration. Their copy reads "The trombone [*Posaune*] shall be heard." Rudolf Steglich has pointed out innumerable spots where such bad translations not only disfigure the meaning of the text but disregard the music. Many of his suggested changes are felicitous.

XXVII

HANDELIAN BIOGRAPHY IS A DIFFICULT SUBJECT FOR THE
historian, if only because it has become so conventionalized that until recent times it took a special act of the imagination to break out of the rut.
Handel has been imprisoned by the Germans in a ponderous biography
begun by Chrysander and finished by Serauky, from which we have not
yet been able wholly to deliver him. On the English side, until recent
times, Handelian musicography was not based on a scholarly and creative
contemplation of the historical past; it was largely an echo of its own desires, beliefs, and musical-religious order, which it projected into the past.
Neither Englishmen nor Germans were above using such documents as
lent themselves to their purposes while ignoring those that did not, and
what is even worse, falsifying or reconstructing others. We have seen
what happened to Handel's works in both German and English editions.
Chrysander's idea was magnificent, but the execution often faulty because
of his conception of the unlimited powers of the editor. Some of his English editorial colleagues carried the same principles from arbitrariness to
an insensitiveness verging on brutality. The deep humility of the scholar is
allied with a profound sense of the categorical sanctity of original documents. A historical document is sacred, even to its moles and warts; it
must remain intact and must on no account be changed and seldom even
tidied up for publication. In the hands of the unskilled, retouching is perilous, and, it may be added, sometimes also in the hands of the skilled.
If Handel's scores have been distorted, even more unfaithful is the

familiar portrait of the man, the interpretation of his motives, and the exegesis of his music. Musicography is fertile in enigmas, and international music criticism is fruitful in absurdities. It might be said that with few exceptions the attitude of critics toward Handel and his *oeuvre* has been a long absurdity. It is not the purpose of this author to constitute himself a one-man court and jury to pass judgment on scholars who toiled for many years with skill and devotion in the Handelian garden. Nevertheless, certain conclusions and opinions are inescapable, and the reader may rightfully expect them to be enunciated. Far be it from me to belittle the great accomplishments of Handelian research in Germany. It produced the first important scholarly results in biography and stylistic criticism, such as only experienced and painstaking scholarship can provide. Chrysander's devotion and dogged pursuit of his aims are wholly admirable. Nor do I dismiss the valuable contributions of Schering, Leichtentritt, Seiffert, Steglich, and many others. Nevertheless, with few exceptions, these fine scholars also helped in that most unscholarly reclamation project that wrested Handel from England. As an instance of this absurdity and an enigma of Handelian scholarship the case of Friedrich Chrysander is among the strangest.

Doubting Thomas may be the patron saint of historians, but he certainly was never invoked by Chrysander and his colleagues. While there is a deep sincerity and a formidable apparatus of scholarship in their presentations, the view they offer is a self-conscious exposition of German *Weltanschauung*. The aim was the rescuing of the German *Volksgeist* from the depredations of foreign influences. This *Volksgeist* possesses certain attributes whose maintenance and realization are mandatory for most German scholars: they are profundity (*Tiefe*), introspection (*Vergeistigung*), emphasis on a definite conception of the meaning of life and on action for its own sake, as well as the concept of blood and soil. Its particular application in Handel's case had to survive a collision with the hard fact of his nearly half-century of residence and work in England. Out of the clash of these two has developed a considerable body of literature. The Germans saw only through German spectacles, and German blood had for them a quality almost of holiness. They could have learned a lesson from Goethe, intensely interested in the accomplishments of all minds of whatever country, paying tribute to excellence wherever he saw it.

The Germans' point of view is that Handel's inheritance of blood, balanced against the personal experience of a protracted stay within an altogether different environment, decisively outweighed it; that he remained essentially a German in mind, temperament, and outlook, and that his work is altogether rooted, "as is Bach's, in German Baroque music" (Schiedermair). Chrysander even explains Handel's naturalization as merely a convenience to escape the annoyances a foreigner is subjected to. They always emphasize the atmosphere into which Handel was born, never seeing that it was an atmosphere Handel early and consistently tried to escape from. By assuming that he would remain untouched by English life even after decades of intimate contact with it, they show a disconcerting propensity to rewrite history, and they are over-vigorous in their deductions from facts capable of more than one interpretation. The warrant for their attitude is wholly nationalistic and should be recognized as such. The claim to justify it on "scientific" grounds is quite baseless, for this is no more than a convenient but unscholarly device for disposing of what is an awkward situation from a nationalistic point of view. It is perhaps understandable that German historians, looking back upon the long, glorious, and undisputed supremacy of German music, which was theirs until the beginning of our century, should claim the expatriate son for the Fatherland, even though he was spiritually and habitually sundered from Germany. They knew of the stagnation of music in England following Purcell's death, and therefore they assumed that the rekindling of a national music could be ascribed only to the presence of a God-fearing German Lutheran musician who functioned in England exactly as his twin, Bach, did back at home; he just happened to have lived in England.

The German scholars' view of the English was clouded by a conflict within their personal attitude towards the nation and her achievements. On the one hand, they admired England as one of the Germanic nations, though remaining somewhat bewildered by its institutions; on the other, they regarded English culture with a feeling of superiority. Serauky thought that Handel's omission of certain bold and unusual pieces in revivals of the oratorios was due to the fact that "he did not grant the English sufficient musical judgment to cope with the grandeur of his musical conceptions." The bon mot Handel addressed to Gluck about the sensitiveness of English eardrums was accepted and interpreted literally as an authoritative value judgment (though it should be said that some English critics also like to quote it). The narrowness of outlook, the existence of appalling misconceptions, originates not so much in lack of scholarship, and certainly not in lack of industry, as in a biased attitude and a considerable ignorance of English history, music, and letters, and of the age's religious dialectic. In particular, German music historians seem to be unable to understand the extraordinary fluidity, despite the traditional formality, of English institutions. Thus they are often baffled by the primary documents, which they either misinterpret or choose to do without. It is almost unbelievable that the man who completed Chrysander's great biography, duplicating its vast bulk, worked almost exclusively from secondary material, from modern sources such as the studies of Schering, Heuss, Leichtentritt, and others. From English sources, Serauky quotes mostly those that have been translated into German—Mainwaring, Flower, Dent, and so on.[1] Ignorance of English history, even of elementary topography, can be amazing. One author, whose publications form a small library, calls Frederick "the Prince of Wales, the future George III," another refers to Lord Burlington's residence as a "country estate in Piccadilly," while still another cites the Strand as "a community near London."

The work of salvaging Handel for the Fatherland as a good German and staunch Lutheran began early. We might call it the "Battle for the *Umlaut*," for the modification of the "a" in Handel's name became the symbol of this Anglo-German rivalry.[2] Friedrich Gottlieb Klopstock (1724–1803), the creator of the new German lyric poetry and himself the author of an enormously long epic poem, *Messiah,* wrote an ode entitled *Wir und Sie* ("We and They [the English]"), in which he asks, "Whom have they who like Handel can summon the highest flights of sorcery?" The answer is simple: "We are far above them." Klopstock and his supporters tried hard to get Carl Philipp Emanuel Bach to set the ode to music, but that learned and well-informed musician refused even though he was a friend of the poet and set others of his poems. Finally Gluck was persuaded to compose the silly piece.

If 18th-century poets may be forgiven for being naively patriotic, the similar attitude of well-trained and well-equipped scholars is inexcusable. In their eagerness to preserve the *Umlaut* in Handel's name they advance claims that ruin their valuable contribution by swathing it in a mass of wrapping, most of which is irrelevant and indefensible. Serauky, speaking of the first chorus of the *Ode for St. Cecilia's Day,* comes to these conclusions: "Such immersion in the symbol values and symbol possibilities of music makes it clear that Handel always remained conscious of his German being. A chorus such as this proclaims German profundity, a concept

---

[1] A similar and particularly glaring case is afforded by Alfred Heuss's study, *Das Textproblem von Händels "Judas Maccabaeus"* (*Händel Jahrbuch,* I). It is quite obvious that Heuss never read the original text, basing his entire criticism on Chrysander's German translation, which differs from the original in many important details.

[2] American music librarians join the battle on the Germans' side, for to them too a birth certificate is the only and final criterion, which neither naturalization nor Handel's own spelling can alter.

that recent psychology interprets as representing a greater wealth of spiritual potential in the creative German than in any other national." And this is said about one of Handel's most English, most Purcellian works! Indeed, it is even claimed that the pastoral charms of *L'Allegro* are due to "the profundity and force of Handel's feeling for nature, which remained German." Streatfeild's "honest English merryment" is surely the proper description of this work. While one readily acknowledges the reality of *deutsche Gemütstiefe* and *Innigkeit,* surely this cannot be made into an exclusively German characteristic. Pepusch, another German who settled in London, did not have it simply because he was not a great creative musician; Handel had it for the same reason as did a Monteverdi or a Purcell.

When we read the works of the great Romantic biographers, such as Spitta or Jahn, we may smile at their almost poetic effusiveness, but, though in these old-fashioned biographies there is naiveté and special pleading, there is also dignity and cohesion. Their hero may be obscured by clouds of misinformation, but he was not misrepresented or torn apart in the interests of a nationalistic thesis. It is too serious for smiling when Alfred Heuss or Hans Joachim Moser see German characteristics in Handel's heroes, and conversely un-German qualities in the less sympathetic figures. But when an outstanding scholar of Hermann Abert's accomplishments not only shares such views but confidently adds that few if any Englishmen could ever understand the finer points of these disguised German heroes, one is at a loss. Indeed, Abert saw in the victory paean that is *Judas Maccabaeus* a "subtle criticism of the British character." [3] Even the physically impossible is no obstacle: Hans Engel in his otherwise excellent discussion of the instrumental concerto calmly places Handel's concertos composed in London under the heading "The Baroque concerto *in* Germany." The frantic search for the most tenuous evidence of the presence of Lutheran chorale tunes, of similarities to Schütz and Bach, as well as to the entire gallery of 18th- and 19th-century German composers really becomes comical. When discussing *Theodora,* Leichtentritt detects the simultaneous presence of the medieval hocket and Beethoven's Fifth Symphony. A comparison here and there can be apt and enlightening, but

---

[3] These curious aberrations received new political impetus in the 1940s when *Judas Maccabaeus* was converted into *Wilhelm von Nassau* and *Israel in Egypt* into *Mongolensturm.* After the war the pendulum swung in the other direction: the East Germans gave these oratorios a socialist cant which, by the way, had also been done much earlier in England, by the Workers' Music Association. It may have been the English example that gave the idea to the "Democratic" Germans in the East, though not much prompting was needed.

persistent likening of even completely episodic little things to this and that composer, and often in a paternalistic way (*wäre eines Gluck durchaus würdig*), is a painful form of local patriotism.

Serauky reads like a schoolboy's accurate translation of Catullus: everything is there except understanding. The fantastic length of his primitive and commonplace analyses, the aridity of style, the daunting provincialism, and the profusion of quotations of little if any relevance will chill the boldest heart and tire the strongest mind. It is another matter with Chrysander, a man of genuine erudition, whose part of the great biography was written by a scholar. Carrying out his work unflinchingly under the most trying conditions in a workshop in Bergdorf near Hamburg he spent his life and every penny he earned in the pursuit of the great undertaking that was the Händelgesellschaft edition. (For some years the distinguished Heidelberg literary scholar Gottfried Gervinus [1805–1871] was his loyal helper.) The devoted Chrysander quarrels even with those who praise Handel because they do not praise him highly enough, and if he finds a somewhat conventional piece he excuses it on the ground that it hides particularly edifying religious feelings. Chrysander is impatient and cavalier with his English colleagues who dare to set foot in his private enclosure. This extreme jealousy for his hero is a fault of which no generous-minded reader will complain, and Chrysander's immense work entitles him to respectful recognition. But he was a scholar who deliberately took upon himself the role of patriot-preacher; he is largely responsible for the aberrations in the German Handel literature. His precept was followed for a hundred years by all German writers in patient submission and without criticism (only recently, in some of the entries in *MGG*, do we see doubts expressed concerning the accuracy of some of his findings). This is the more surprising because Chrysander mercilessly denigrated the fine German musicians around Handel (not to speak of the Italians), for he did not tolerate the slightest competition with his idol. Still, it is impossible not to admire his courage in tight places, as well as his earnest advocacy of Baroque performance practices in the face of the widespread belief in "modernization."

Happily, this German Handelian literature has been slowly changing. While Serauky only a few years ago still advanced wild claims for Handel's undiluted German nature, Hans Mersmann quietly stated that "the English rightfully place Handel in their own musical history." We have mentioned Friedrich Blume's warning about misconstruing the significance of Handel's music, made at a time when Chrysander's opinions were accepted as final (see p. 359). Blume was quite explicit in stating that Handel's "sacred" music reflects with much eloquence not only a remarkably rich responsiveness to the splendors of life but also the dynastic-national consciousness of his second homeland. Robert Haas also went against the current in declaring that "Handel's church music shows his profound immersion in the particular spirit of his models, especially Purcell." There are some instances of this recognition even earlier: Leichtentritt writes concerning *L'Allegro*'s Purcellian arias, "The orientation of this music is neither German nor French; its bright clarity, its light charm, its racy rhythms are English growths." German musicologists of more recent times, not less erudite, not less penetrating, seem at the same time to be more judicious than their predecessors, and are content to treat musical history as musical history, without imposing preconceived meanings on the documents. Bruno Flögel, the author of a good study of Handel's aria technique, "deplores" the fact that the "strong ties that bind Handel to the musical life of England, a musical life that rests on an ancient culture, have as yet been so little investigated." This we would naturally expect from the English Handelians, who were on home grounds, for only an English mind can apprehend with ease such a synthesis of apparent opposites as was involved in Handel's work, which sought to combine loyalty to the national Establishment with fidelity to the requirements of an ideal theatre.

[2]

THE FIGURE OF Handel is so deeply imbedded in the history of his time in England, and the more so because of his own reserve, that those who would dig him out must themselves go deep into that history. There can be no doubt that there has been a greater expenditure of ink on the 18th century than on any other century in English history. Its personalities, its politics, its court, its social history, its literature, art, and religion, all receive the tribute of a constant flow of books. Alas, the magnificent scholarship of the literary men and the historians has not, until very recent times, been matched by the musicographers. British literature on music of the 18th century, with few exceptions, shows a bias and provincialism that not only equals the German but is allied to a generous lack of musical scholarship.

It cannot often enough be emphasized that when Handel arrived in England he was in the fullness of his powers, an experienced and superbly trained composer and performer far more knowledgeable than a good German cantor twice his age. The exceptionally thorough training he received at the hands of Zachow, the experiences in Hamburg with another fine and neglected master, Keiser, who first roused the dramatic instinct in the journeyman musician, are all glossed over in English studies. And of course the complete assimilation of Italian music, with all that this implies in melody, expression, timing, and general savoir-faire, seldom rates more than a few perfunctory pages. Italy was for Handel—as it was for Goethe and Keats—more than a fascinating country, it was an idea. His Italian sojourn produced impressions of wondrously different landscapes, but the great figures of Scarlatti and Corelli, and the many other musicians studied in their native habitat, constituted the experience. None of them can be missing from the total picture; they became a part of Handel's art, as Handel, with them, became part of the crowning of the Baroque. Moreover, Handel knew a great deal of music, German, Italian, French; and young as he was, he had already reconciled these vast territories in his own way. At twenty-five he was no longer a provincial German musician but a sophisticated European, though not a cosmopolite. This he remained all his life, and deliberately so, as can be seen from his constant, stubborn attempts to acquire the technical and expressive means of all the leading musical nations, eventually applying them to what was to become a national English style.

Of his enormous production, British writers dealt mainly with samples. The lovely Italian cantatas they regarded as preparatory, experimental works, and they did little more than nibble at the operas. They pointed out the musico-technical elements Handel took from Purcell, which are indeed considerable. But like Mozart later in the century, Handel simply reached out and appropriated everything within his grasp, making it his undisputed property. Of far greater importance were the tone and attitude he took from Purcell, although both are more imponderable than aspects of counterpoint, false relations, or literal borrowings. The really intimate and subtle Purcellian traits appear much later, when they become part of Handel's bloodstream. But the most disconcerting activity of the older British Handelians was the treatment of Handel's librettos, the suppression, omission, and yes, falsification of documents, and of scores themselves in order to accommodate the textual changes. The Victorian editors wanted to reconcile the "questionable" elements in the oratorios with their own particular ideals of probity, denaturing the Handelian music drama in the process.

In the older literature the general course of Handel's life was, on the whole, traced in accordance with the external facts, though little light was thrown on his music. We have touched upon contemporary commentators and the great pioneer historians of the end of the 18th century sufficiently to forgo here a discussion of their role and ideas, but the 19th century needs a brief recapitulation.

Victorian musicography suffered from several inhibitions. Having inherited the legend of Handel's conversion to the service of religion, the Victorians not only fostered but substantially enlarged it. It was in the first third of the century that many of Handel's obiter dicta originated, but even had they been authentic, the earnest biographer must always scrutinize his subject's autobiographical statements. Secondly, the Victorians were, almost to a man, wary of Italian opera, uneasily dismissing it as essentially ridiculous and unworthy of attention by serious Englishmen. Until the end of the century they had a way of passing vaguely over the problems of opera, and evinced a tendency to use the subject as a peg for generalizations perhaps stimulating but not always relevant. It is doubtful whether they possessed the temperament of the scholar or the detachment of the historian; theirs was simply an apologia, more or less disguised, for the great religious composer. The moral issues were foremost in their minds, and it was then that the work of cleansing Handel's scores of "frivolity" and "impropriety" began in earnest. While it is doubtful whether there were more cases of private vice covered by the public display of virtue in that age than in any other, there was a special temptation to overemphasize the possession of virtue. The Victorian historians, condemning with Jove-like calm all deflections from the standards of the age, were in effect lecturing the 18th century for failing to conform to 19th-century customs.

English studies of Handel in the third quarter of the century, even after an excellent example of scholarship was given by Victor Schoelcher, add little to our knowledge of the creative mind that produced the operas, oratorios, and concertos. This we must attribute partly to a lack of scholarship but even more to Puritan esthetics—that is, to the absence of esthetics. Victor Schoelcher was a French man of letters and politician who because of his ardent republican sympathies had to spend many years in exile in England. During his stay there he did a prodigious amount of original research on Handel, placing at the disposal of his English colleagues much valuable information, especially in the field where they were most deficient, opera. Apparently his *Life of Handel* (1857), a pioneering work in Handelian research, remained largely unnoticed by the organists and church musicians who dabbled in musicography.

The literature of the *fin de siècle* and the first decade of the 20th century is still square-toed and solemn; sensitive readers will wince at these

writers' wantoning with the Muses. The most popular biography of these
years was William Rockstro's *Handel* (1883). Rockstro, completely taken
by the prevailing literary tendency of romantic idealization, is today un-
readable; one would think that he must have been nearly so in his own
time. As we assess this literature, its oracular gravity, its cloudy and
diffused treatment of events, we see that these writers were inclined to
posture and to repeat historical commonplaces. The line between fact and
fancy is not easy to draw, and the Handel who emerges from these biographies embodies contradictions that remain unresolved. It is true, of
course, that writers and critics of that era who were not scholars could not
be expected to know the extent to which Handel's editors, from a pathetic
sense of duty to the memory of the "sacred composer," had disfigured his
scores, erasing where they could anything that showed sympathy, in
thought or language, with the "grosser" life of humanity, tempering his
pantheistic joy in nature, and striving generally to lay him out in the dignity of his sacerdotal robes. Neither did they realize that the scores they
did know were a mere skimming from an immense amount of music.
Among the better-known writers of the next generation, scholarship was
not wanting, but it was still being mixed with the old prejudices. Even
Donald Tovey is guilty of some regrettable nonsense, but then to these
excellent musicians the Baroque, especially Baroque dramatic music, was
a musical Tibet. A particular position must be assigned to Ernest Walker,
the author of *A History of Music in England* (1907); stand-offish, wildly
unjust and unforgiving, Walker's assertions are so sweeping and extravagant that it would be a waste of space to discuss them. To put it bluntly,
he was an eccentric, continually inconsistent, and often irresponsible. Sir
Jack Westrup, in his new edition (1952), toned down the worst aspects of
the work, but then it is no longer Walker. Yet in the welter of this nondescript literature there appeared in 1909 a fine biography, R. A. Streatfeild's *Handel*. While today it seems gracefully inaccurate, this biography
is the work of a highly literate and sensitive person, many of whose observations can still be read with profit and enjoyment.

This brings us to our times, when Sir Newman Flower has been accepted even abroad as the outstanding Handelian authority, a sort of
latter-day English Chrysander. Flower, whose general attitude reminds
one of Wolsey's practice of beginning his official documents with *Et ego
et rex meus*, did approach his task with a modicum of scholarship, but in
the end the scholarship was transmogrified. It is all the more to be regret-
ted that though he had an evident appreciation of Handel as a person
(though little of his music), he should nevertheless have written about him

in a style that adds a note of caricature. If Serauky's style is crabbed to the verge of obscurity, with a tendency to elaborate parentheses and diffuse digressions, in Flower's *Handel* (1923, revised 1948) the acid of irony and the sugar of sentiment meet all too often in a common insipidity. His eternal and irrelevant harping on the moral issues all but negates the scholarship that went into the preparation of the book. He was more than a moralist; a rigorist we should call him, and a glib one at that. Repeatedly he finds the situations and episodes he has to deal with disgusting and repellent—Hamburg, or Roman, or London society suggests to him mites in the cheese and moles in the earth—but perhaps most trying is his priggish commiseration with Handel in moments of adversity. Flower's personal bias is seldom concealed, and his account of the evils attending the "infatuation" with opera is informed with a generous indignation.

But this biography, and all the others of its kind, were swept away by the present-day Handelian authors ably led by Winton Dean. We have mentioned and cited most of these works repeatedly, but should once more call attention to Dean, that stout assailant of the dominant tradition in Handelian biography and interpretation, because he takes cognizance of facts and inferences other than the purely documentary, though these facts and inferences are not necessarily less historical. He sometimes attains a felicity of intuition that mere learning could scarcely bring about. When reading *Handel's Dramatic Oratorios and Masques* (1959), one delights in the dexterity, concision, and never-flagging verve with which, in rapid succession, he exhibits and explodes erroneous facts and chaotic theories. Often a brief aside is enough. The book is rich in imagination scrupulously fed on facts, rich too in independent judgment, and it is as readable as it is precise in all its references. On the whole, such modern Handelians as Dean, W. C. Smith, Herbage, Abraham, and Lam, though all devoted admirers of their man, are far more level-headed and critical than their German colleagues. There is no breast-beating, no paternity suits, no metaphysics, no excessive hermeneutics, and a gratifying absence of the eternal analogies with Bach, Mozart, Beethoven, and Brahms. Interestingly enough, if in rare instances there is such a comparison, it is usually a reference to Verdi; this writer wholeheartedly agrees with the kinship seen here.

Though making giant strides, present-day British musicology must be censored for an unforgivable lack of enterprise. It is nothing short of a British national disgrace that with so many competent editors available, the critical edition of Handel's works begun in 1955 should have been sur-

rendered to Halle. I do not wish for one moment to question the abilities
of my German colleagues, nor are they in any need of defense, for their
record in publishing the collected works of the great of music is unexampled and unchallengeable. But Handel is a composer whose life work is
inextricably entwined with English history and culture, which, until after
the wars, was the musical and cultural territory least known to Germans.
Italian and French music has always been the preserve of German scholars, who knew a great deal more about it than their French or Italian confrères, but English music was dismissed, and rather contemptuously at
times. As a result few German musicologists, however able, have an adequate knowledge of English thought and institutions—that is, of the environment without which Handel's music is unthinkable. They cannot
possibly understand all the ramifications, and they must work with materials almost wholly preserved in England. To edit Handel's works in Halle
is very much like preparing an edition of Lully's works in Florence. It
should have been the rightful privilege and duty of British musicology to
prepare the new, modern critical edition of the works of their national
composer.

[3]

MARC PINCHERLE, in his fine study of Vivaldi, remarks that
"the habit is firmly formed in historians never to deal with Bach without
immediately invoking the name of Handel." We might add that the reverse of this is equally true, as indeed the two composers are taken for as
natural a pair as Wordsworth and Coleridge. The categorical establishment of this dual German-Baroque monarchy is perhaps the most astounding miscarriage of justice that must be laid at the door of German
musicology. To lump together Bach and Handel is to depend on external
similarities, and even these are limited to little more than their common
Saxon origin. "Bach and Handel; the singers of Christ, neither without the
other and neither against the other." This is the doctrine, and Müller-
Blattau announces it in the very first sentence of his *Händel* (1933):
"Handel and Bach! Both together they constitute the totality of German
Baroque music." Scarcely an essay, or history of music, fails to endorse the
doctrine of the "twin German peaks of the Baroque," the two Lutheran
heroes of Christian music. How is this possible in the face of every known
document, when even a simple perusal of Handel's works will disclose
that he did not sing of Christ but of men, that he saw in the Old Testament a historical-heroic world that he wanted to resurrect, not for the

church, nor even for himself, but for the English public?

One cannot view Bach and Handel with the same eyes; men whose experiences are so different, whose rapport with art, religion, love, and the business of life is so different, cannot be hyphenated and treated as one. For what characterizes the creative artist but his experience? Surely Bach expressed the essence of the land that remained his from birth to death, just as surely as Handel became completely absorbed in the spirit of the land of his adoption and expressed its particular genius; for Handel his England was an idea, for Bach Saxony was simply a fact of existence. Handel united his English consciousness with a very particular biblical flavor drawn from the Old Testament, while Bach concerned himself with the New Testament, which, unlike the Old in Handel's conception, was entirely separated from the secular world. Both Bach and Handel saw perspectives that were tremendous, and both expressed their subjective selves to an extent bordering on the limits of creativity; the great difference between them was basic in content and consequently in form. Bach's subject, the mystery of Christianity, was beyond question and measure; for Handel the subject was man and his predicament, that is, a world full of questions demanding answers.

Ever since Schweitzer's popular book, Bach has been for us the great solitary mystic. Handel, on the other hand, has never appeared as an unworldly contemplative; he fought his battles with all available weapons, subtle or blunt, and he was always ready to take off his gloves. He was practical, an impresario, a businessman, who loathed worldly failures and so always played for big stakes and never followed the sheltered way. Bach, too, was a good businessman who kept his home and office in excellent order, or—as Terry puts it—"Bach's business mind was as orderly as his counterpoint." But Handel was an investor and a speculator who welcomed any odds and played them with zest. Bach supplied models "for young people anxious to learn," in the shape of various *Büchlein* and other didactic collections, which was something that could never have entered Handel's mind; he wanted a paying public of adults. Handel created his music always before a large audience, marshalling all of Europe's musical forces as a spokesman for a single nation. Bach is the German bourgeois musician of the provincial city, unconcerned with a public, composing for the church and for intimate music-making in the home or in the *collegium musicum*. He is the summit of Lutheran art, the repository of all the riches quietly and diligently gathered by generations of Lutheran cantors. It was he, the highest expression of German musical genius, who established the kingdom of German music that was to reign for centuries to come. Handel represents a deliberate and tyrannically imposed cult of himself. He created his own order, he could wait until luck or a shrewd move brought along what he needed, and coolly reject what he did not want. He could fight doggedly but he could also compromise, he faced every danger and trampled upon it, suffered loneliness and made arrangements to remain forever alone. Every resonance that reached him from without was a fortuitous gain, a happy, usable accident, but his own life was a merciless, triumphal, and logical necessity.

While the Enlightenment was changing the entire world around him, Bach remained steadfastly within the bounds of orthodox Lutheranism. Handel did not deny religion; rather, like a good Englishman, he settled with it. But unlike Bach he was a dramatist, who firmly subscribed to the motto, *Totus mundus agit histrionem*. Bach's sacred music calls for a church and "dim religious light"; Handel exhibits a delight in splendor coupled with a recognition of its religious pretensions; he demands a large, bright, festive hall and the out-of-doors.

Bach is the prototype of the solid and honorable German middle-class citizen. Surrounded by a wife and a host of children, he lived an industrious life, creating in quiet, profound security and spiritual conviction one work after another, never venturing forth from his native country. Handel was a man of the world, much travelled, a gentleman, and a public figure, keenly concerned with political, social, and business issues. The events of his own crowded, adventurous life were neither accidents irrelevant to his composing nor hindrances to his self-expression. The strange but harmonious combination of sentiment with hard business acumen, of international savoir-faire with intense national feeling, realism with imagination, modernity with tradition, stand in sharp contrast to Bach's single-minded devotion to duty and métier. But circumstances obliged Handel to waste himself in skirmishing and scavenging, and his life work therefore seems fragmentary beside the great unified façade of Bach. This unfavorable contrast is remarkable, especially when we realize that Handel's rise to the summit of creative power began about the time when Bach's immense productivity ceased. In the last decade of his life Bach concentrated on a few extraordinary works that had nothing to do with his duties.[4]

[4] Recent research indicates that the traditional portrait of Bach is also in need of retouching. It is indisputable that he lived within the old Lutheran middle-class ideal of "service" centered around church and school, but he chafed under it more than once. Still accepting the maxim that the aim of music is *laudatio Dei*, he was nevertheless aware of the inroads made by the Enlightenment on this theocratic Ger-

Handel's character drove him in his early youth away from the narrow circle of orderly petit-bourgeois existence, towards active participation in life on the "outside." He avoided the traditional career of the German Lutheran musician by physically leaving the seat of that tradition and engaging in a different profession in a different country, as far removed from the traditional as possible: the theatre. He propelled himself into the glare of public life, into its calamities and intrigues, which he found congenial, playing his self-selected role to the hilt. Bach remained within the cantors' tradition and was firmly rooted in German middle-class life, except that as he turned more and more inward he put between himself and the surrounding world a distance the extent of which his contemporaries could not understand, not even his inquisitive and knowledgeable son, Emanuel. Nevertheless we can say that it was his vocation that made Bach; Handel made the vocation. Handel chose not to remain untouched by the world, its aims and tendencies; Bach saw in the world only various detours over which man always comes back to himself. His life work was not without considerable internal and artistic struggle, but in the end his serene discipline was usually victorious. Bach the man and the artist could not be subdued, except by himself.

Bach, who set to music the joys of Pentecost and the triumphs of Easter, sings remarkably often of death. In this longing for death, which is a characteristic trait of Bach's cantata music, there is none of the romantic dreamer's sentimentality, for it is entirely saturated with biblical sobriety. In serene reliance he sings, "Man, thou must die," for the invisible world of the hereafter offers peace—death brings Redemption; the Lutheran gains certain salvation by Christ's death. Christianity conceives life as a way station to death, it is eternally immersed in the riddle of suffering and death, in faithful contemplation of their relationship to the death of the Saviour. In Handel's music such contemplation had no place. To him, who absorbed a great deal of the hereditary paganism of the Mediterranean, everything was an affirmation of this life; the only duty to him was creativity; daily he girded himself for new battles, for new conquests. Thus he became the greatest antipode of his fellow Saxon. And who would claim that this esthetic ideal, though entirely of this world, is not elevated, majestic, and entirely worthy of the position assigned to

---

man world. Circumstances bound him to the cantorate, however, and after a while he gave up the struggle with his official superiors, gradually withdrawing into his study, giving his job dutiful attention but no longer bringing to it the creative enthusiasm of the earlier years. The dates of the Leipzig cantatas are now being revised and it is gradually becoming clear that many of them are earlier works while others are parodies.

Handel by posterity on mistaken premises?

Bach, like the older German Protestant masters, wanted to find the content of life in a Christian godliness, submitting himself to this conception. In this confident submission, this freely imposed self-discipline, there is a good deal of the spirit of the Middle Ages, of its highest pathos, the turning away from the external world. Handel's creative force drives him to cling with all his might to the realities of earthly life; the circle of human sentiments is given a new radius from work to work. He avoids anachronisms and he avoids metaphysics, he is always simple and direct in everything, having learned from the Italians the beauty and poetry of simplicity. The brush strokes with which he paints his characters, his soaring imagination, his dramatic violence, are never obscured by a complicated musical fabric, not even in the tremendous eight-part choruses. Handel relies on the intuition of the artist, not the theories of the theologian; he speaks only of what he really experiences, what he has seen. The dramatis personae in Bach are, in a way, more middle-class than heroic. What we see there is infinite sorrow, not the tragedy that dominates Handel's heroic milieu of the Old Testament. There is, then, a considerable difference in expressive climate between the two masters.

Both composers' knowledge of music, German and foreign, was extensive, but while Handel's sole interest was practical, Bach studied theoretical and pedagogical problems with thoroughness. The absorption and assimilation of this music by each of the two was as different as were their personalities. "Whatever Bach learned from Italian and French masters—and he certainly learned a great deal from the Italians—he remained through and through a German composer writing German music" (Abraham). Handel simply inhaled Italian, French, and English music, and with each breath the new material, like oxygen, passed into his bloodstream. There was little scrutiny, and there was no conflict with tradition because he relied largely on his musical instinct. Impulse in Handel was far more immediate and organic than in Bach; to miss an artistic or business opportunity simply irritated him.

Nothing is more characteristic of Bach than his desire for synthesis and unification: *Clavierübung, The Well-Tempered Clavier, The Musical Offering,* and so forth. But he can also give us the living experience and the poetic idea in chains of involved numerological or other symbolism. The religious-moral symbolism can be bizarrely profuse, but at other times he separates everything extraneous from the strictly musical, as if to purify himself. The embodiment of purified musical thought is then conveyed in such great summae as *The Art of Fugue.* There was no composer

in the history of music who could match Bach's ability to coerce his material with an iron determination and discipline into the exact shape he
wanted. The constant turning inward occasionally makes for obscurity, a
momentary failure to achieve communication between his vision and our
more common ears, but we never feel that we are wilfully bemused.

Handel was a dramatist who knew that the analysis of a human soul
demands lyric expression. His music always remains within the realm of
the earthly and sensuous, never approaching Bach's metaphysics. What
for Bach was a clarification of his spirit, for Handel turned into dramatic
action. Far from being abstract and complicated, Handel's music is infused with a caressing sense of nearness to things human and natural,
which grow and fade and are ever renewed. He likes the direct musical
statement, trusting to its distinctiveness to save it from flatness. He is a
composer light of hand and quick of eye, but he can also stab his meaning
into the listener.

Finally, let us compare the "twins" in the field where superficial
agreement is most pronounced, in the German Passion and the English
oratorio, though in reality not only the conceptions but also the idiom and
form are diametrically opposed. The two types, German Passion and English oratorio, are quite different on another score: one rested on long-
standing tradition, the other was Handel's personal achievement. Bach
seems to stand at the church door, like a holy beggar, offering his mind
and heart to the wonders of faith, and at times he appears to have met
God, his great fellow poet. He did not seek in Christ the glory of transfiguration but the thought of Redemption which brings succor, and Christ to
him was not the Pantocrator of the Byzantines clad in purple stole. To the
German Lutheran the Passion of the Lord is the most majestic and forceful subject for musical representation. But this Passion is artistically conceived not as visible or historical; it is contemplative and invisible because
the drama is inward. The Handelian oratorio is a broad historical drama
that takes place in the visible world; it is not the religious significance of
the Old Testament that is glorified here, but human ideals, warm, plausible, and comprehensible. Handel avoided Christ as a subject, he was not
a "singer of Christ," for he found Him unrepresentable; in the only Christian devotional work of his maturity, *Messiah,* he avoided any dramatization. Bach did not find the musical representation of Christ a limiting factor, but neither did he find dramatic-psychological characterization necessary in such a representation, as Handel did in the case of the great and
conflict-torn human figures of the Old Testament. Handel was aware of
the limitations of the German Passion; he knew that the form was reli-

gious story-telling rather than dramatic composition. He had learned this early, when as a young man he had tried his hand at composing a traditional German Passion. His attempt was not successful, he realized it, and he gave it up; "objective lyricism" was incomprehensible to him. His oratorio was pure music drama unencumbered by any theological or churchly or liturgical considerations. What he wanted was to find musical accents capable of characterizing a man or a whole people. He is pagan and yet Christian, sensuous and yet spiritual, his men, though mythical heroes, are entirely human, and his women are both his lovers and his sisters. He is receptive as wax and yet clean and hard as marble, and among Baroque composers he is the most virile and yet also the most capricious. He matched his narrative with that of the Bible.

Bach and Handel and their works represent and express two fundamentally different worlds. They can neither be compared nor joined nor opposed; they complement each other and only thus give the Baroque its "twin peaks."

While most of our German friends have held fast to their conception of their two indivisible "singers of Christ," and while in the English-speaking world *Messiah* has been made the epitome of sacred music, there are also not a few voices who refuse Handel equality with Bach because they see him wrongly as a religious composer, then dismiss him for being not religious enough. Especially the old-line Bach worshippers are unwilling to grant Handel citizenship in their world, for to them Handel is forever saddled with his "frivolous" operatic past. They object to the clear sensuousness of his melodies, to his "lack of problems" (whatever that may mean), to his unwillingness to indulge in profound abstractions, and, ironically enough, to his "lack of religious sincerity." There is nothing in Bach to disturb the picture of the religiously dedicated man; Spitta, whose great Bach biography set the standards for modern times, goes so far as to declare gravely that even Bach's secular cantatas are "not genuinely secular because his only vein was the sacred." Against such views the "Italian" Handel of *Rodelinda, Giulio Cesare, Orlando,* but also the "English" Handel of *Acis and Galatea, L'Allegro, Semele, Susanna,* and all the other vibrant human dramas and amorous pastorals cannot measure up. But such attitudes recall the story of the distinguished German divine who was saddened by Goethe who could have become the St. Augustine of modern times had he not "elected to take the Greeks for his teachers instead of the Apostles." Handel's character and his music would perhaps appear less puzzling if those who see him through the window of St.

Thomas's in Leipzig would instead look into the Haymarket Theatre and St. Paul's Cathedral in London. If Handel is Bach's complement, it is by way of antithesis.

[4]

HANDEL's overwhelming presence on the English scene gave rise to divergent judgments. While one faction proclaimed Handel a direct descendant of Purcell and thus a genuine English composer, another insisted that this German immigrant, as he became an unchallengeable national institution, threatened to extinguish English musical culture, because his enormous prestige made it impossible for anyone else to become an authentic spokesman for English national music. The airing of such opinions, as anyone reading musical history will realize, soon led the foreigner to see nothing else but the towering figure of the Saxon. European opinion, abetted by some Englishmen, completely devalued English music, could not see anything "English" in Handel, and made English musicians into pitiful artistic beggars. It was this blotting out of the view behind Handel's broad back that caused the Germans to call England "the land without music"; they retained Handel as their own by simply extending German musical history across the sea. Perhaps one can understand the Continental point of view; not only Germans but all Europeans had a distorted perspective and never really understood the ways of that peculiar little island, but for Englishmen to regard Handel as the cause of the blight of their music is self-mutilation. The dangers of such an attitude are manifest, and throughout the 19th century Britain suffered from it. Nations with an insignificant musical past entered the scene gathering glory, while Britons in their eagerness to enthrone Mendelssohn as the successor of Handel and Haydn dismissed their own music.[5] Some of the pronouncements of English historians parallel the theory of Louis Reynaud, that French Romanticism was an Anglo-Germanic pollution of the pure national literary tradition. Ernest Walker did not mince words when dealing with this subject, and there were others who branded Handel with the unforgivable sin of "completely extinguishing native talent in England." Curiously enough, these authors at the same time dispute Handel's "Englishness," Dent even declaring him "the classical type of an in-

[5] Even as recently as a generation ago an attempt was made to make Sibelius into an honorary British musical saint, but by that time such sponsors as Cecil Gray were up against a far better informed and articulate musical public, and the grand old Finnish composer remained an ordinary mortal.

ternational eclectic." [6] It is amusing to observe that the very Englishmen who prostrated themselves before the Bayreuth magician, or who saw the Star of Bethlehem shining on Busoni, disavowed Handel as an English composer. A glance into Fielding will show how popular this disputed Englishness had become. Sophia, so middle-class and so unintellectual, plays Handel on the harpsichord for Tom Jones, taking it for granted, not showing off. Others display for English music of the period an undiscerning contempt that still passes for historical knowledge. But the conditions of English music cannot be explained by too zealous denigration of all of Handel's contemporaries and predecessors. If we consider the expanse between Morley and Purcell, we shall find, perhaps to our surprise, that the consensus voiced by Rolland, that when Handel arrived in England "national art was dead," is incorrect.

Neither Burney nor Dent is convincing when he maintains that Handel was contemptuous of the music he found in England. In the first place it was not in character. It is true that he was a composer of Italian opera, and there was little in that line to be found by an English composer. But Handel's was an inquisitive mind, and he examined everything that came within his purview, without, however, expressing opinions about the music so examined. In the second place, it is simply inconceivable that he could have found the English tone so unerringly in the *Birthday Ode for Queen Anne* and the *Utrecht Te Deum,* his very first "English" compositions, without an already respectable familiarity with English music. We are undoubtedly dealing in the early 18th century with an England musically impoverished to a degree, but the views of French, German—and English—writers that Handel arrived in a musical desert are untenable. English musicians for the most part lived and worked with little heed to the world beyond their bailiwick, shielded from the mainstream of contemporary art. Among them, however, were conspicuous exceptions whose history is part of the history of England.

The truth is that "golden ages" are usually followed by gray periods; the spirit is intermittent, and national genius runs on a barter economy.

---

[6] While one may gloss over Walker's naive aberrations, it is not easy to account for Dent's eccentricities, for we are dealing with a distinguished scholar of conspicuous achievements. Yet this author of admirable studies could on occasion unburden himself of statements ill becoming a man of his standing. Deploring the dearth of good English librettos, Dent regrets that Gay, who wrote (really edited) the fine book for *Acis and Galatea,* did not live long enough to write a libretto "on that character of all characters, Falstaff," for which he would have "gladly sacrificed all the oratorios." We must add, though, that one can never tell whether Dent, a whimsical man who liked to play the devil's advocate, is facetious or in earnest.

Every national art has periods when it sags and then with the aid of stimulants, sometimes ancient and national, sometimes modern and foreign, it recuperates. Such stimulants can cause marvelous recovery by bringing out latent energies and creating a new savoir-faire, as has been well demonstrated by Vaughan Williams and the other English composers of the immediate past. They threw off lethargy by discovering their folksong and their great Elizabethan ancestors. Did not English literature begin with importation? Yet no one would doubt Chaucer's Englishness. English music was admittedly stagnating when Handel tried to foist Italian opera upon it. Had he remained a purveyor of Italian opera perhaps he would have been just another Alessandro Scarlatti with a foreign accent, for pitted against certain trends in culture even the most powerful individual is weak. But with his oratorio, ceremonial, and instrumental music he not only created a new flowering, he found connections with a thoroughly English musicality which he made entirely his own. This new music once more established ties with the community, it once more became timely, representative of national cultural aspirations, and was able to become a continuation of English musical culture. If this is unacknowledged by those who still see a "deplorable accident" in the advent of the Italianized Saxon to England, it should nonetheless be evident to them that the results of his presence are anything but accidental.

It was not Handel who crushed music in England, but the moral-religious institution his adopted countrymen mistakenly made of his grand and human music. It was that which killed imagination in the British musical mind, because after the mammoth commemoration concerts every British composer found it obligatory to write pious oratorios and anthems in what they conceived to be a Handelian style, later fortified with Mendelssohn. The entire atmosphere was absolutely alien to Handel; he composed for the theatre and set to music human beings, not plaster statues. A good deal of this sanctimonious nonsense has departed, and English music is once more a modern and independent art, but Handel is not yet rehabilitated. As for the "Handelian style," if one examines the musical supplements in the venerable London *Musical Times,* one is aware of its enduring presence even though the comatose "sacred music" is flanked by excellent and enlightened musicography.

We have discussed the fundamental English opposition to opera and have seen that while Locke's or Lawes's music is well made, it is clearly in the service of the play rather than a conversion of the play into music. Nevertheless, while the vital element of dramatic expressiveness and tension is missing in this song-lyricism, its faithful musical prosody and its tunefulness were not wasted on succeeding generations of musicians. Humphrey, Blow, and Purcell do reach an essentially operatic language, but English opera still failed to materialize, with the exception of Purcell's one authentic masterpiece.

The penchant for the theatrical, for the dramatic, for the stage, is an English quality that appears at all stages of English history, in all walks of English life, and in all English arts. We do not have to hold forth on the English theatre; it is, of course, part of our own, and well enough known in our country. But let us look at their painters, at Hogarth, Gainsborough, and Reynolds. Only in the latter's landscapes, and even there not always, is a mimic quality missing. But the English, ever since Steele and Addison, would not accept theatre without spirited dialogue and a more or less complicated psychological plot. They saw in the lyric stage a positive danger to the spoken theatre and were not willing to accept such an extension of the meaning of "theatre." All they were prepared to admit was incidental music as a form of decoration to the play, indeed, as animated décor. Purcell, though antedating the days when the critique of operatic dramaturgy became articulately formulated by the literary men, shows a reticence entirely in accord with these ideas.

Handel knew Purcell and knew him well; the 17th-century English composer's influence on the 18th-century German was strong. Right from the beginning of the latter's career in England, with the first ceremonial pieces, the Purcellian tone is unmistakable, yet it was much later, in his English dramatic music, that Handel really came to grips with Purcell. Perhaps at first this was no more than self-encouragement, in order to follow his own new path with more security, but there is ample evidence to show that he deliberately tried to solve questions raised by Purcell. Still, when he actually reached the point of grappling with English opera, when he was a stone's throw from achieving it, he turned aside. English opera was "in the air," a number of musicians were working at it, but the titles themselves show that they were still inhibited; obviously, English opera "in the Italian manner" could not lead to a real national genre. There was no operatic tradition in England, and in the century during which the innovation coming from Italy had been rejected only a genius of the stature of Purcell had been able to master the opera, and then only once.

It seems to this writer that Handel, who reacted to stylistic essences like a seismograph, detected something in Purcell that made him hesitate about English opera. *Dido and Aeneas* he admired, for the opera presents genuine human characters, and Handel must have found it to his liking that Dido is a stronger figure than Aeneas—his own heroines are often superior to their lovers or masters. But he knew that this opera was an exception, and Purcell's other theatre music, while congenial to the English, did not suit the Italian-trained, confirmed *operista*. Purcell remained emotionally somewhat remote from his themes, seldom living the life of his figures. Handel is close to them, he learns from his themes, their change and development is his own development, he is more subjective, extrovert, and excitable than is the Apollonian Englishman. The true tragic tone that Purcell can find only exceptionally—he died so young—is second nature with Handel. The center of the work is always kept visible by Purcell; Handel is easily carried away by a developing dramatic situation which will shift the center as individual points attain comprehensive unity of their own. Handel's drama is colorful and lively, while Purcell's is at times a little bare, but both share a feeling for the monumental and for the intimate.

Purcell's dilemma was even greater than Handel's. He came on the scene at a moment when even the choice of a new direction, let alone its realization, was a problem. What he achieved was so entirely a personal artistic feat, so exclusively valid for him only, that it really constituted no solution at all. Handel found Purcell's musical language most attractive but palpably felt the absence of primary thrust, concentration, and tension, which to him was the essence of the music drama. While he gladly accepted the language, he did not follow the form. In addition, the peculiarly English quality of Purcell's music, the gently sensuous melancholy, present even in the ceremonial pieces, initially baffled the German-Italian composer accustomed to the directness of "basic affections." It took him a long time to penetrate to the essence of Purcell's style, and by the time he mastered it the die was cast: the Purcellian qualities went into Handel's English pastorals and oratorios. Though he swung back more than once in the direction of English opera, he could not overcome the earlier impressions. By that time there was no turning back; Handel had absorbed enough of the English psyche to share some of the attitudes and feelings that were native to his adopted countrymen. Opera was Italian and remained so; when the singers sang in English it had to be something else. In the end, neither geography nor anthropology nor racial psychology can entirely explain the reasons for the failure of English opera in the 17th and 18th centuries; national feelings, even national ideals, have their mystic regions.

It cannot, then, be often enough repeated that the course of events did not originate with Handel; he found the tradition fully formed and in reality could neither oppose nor bypass it, not even with many great Italian operas. He did, nevertheless, involuntarily contribute to the throttling of the modest efforts of the elder Arne and others who tried to do something about the English lyric stage. Unfortunately, the way they went about it, by trying to use some of Handel's own works, touched Handel at his most sensitive spot: he would not endure piratical competition. By hurriedly revamping *Esther,* and a month later *Acis and Galatea* (1732), which the freebooting company headed by the senior Arne proposed to produce, and by using a resplendent cast of singers, he defeated them. But he also defeated their hopes of producing English opera. This seems to be an academic question, however; it is doubtful whether they ever could have succeeded. For while England was not really bereft of composers who understood the issues and were willing to deal with them, this was an era of modest talents; the great comprehensive conceptions and the ability to encompass the entire horizon of a drama were missing. The English composer of the early 18th century could compose good music, but he could not create a musical poetry that epitomized the nation's genius; that had passed with Purcell. Otherwise musical life in England in Handel's time was extensive and industrious, and Handel contributed to it materially. Hawkins reports that "Covent-Garden Theatre was an excellent seminary; and by the performances of the oratorios there, the practice of music was greatly improved throughout the kingdom." There were numerous amateur and semi-amateur choral and instrumental societies, not only in London but also in the provinces. They kept alive the ancient English proficiency in choral singing, and many of them took readily to Handel, though of course not to his operas, which they could not perform anyway for lack of the specific type of singers needed for Baroque opera. But the oratorios and anthems, as well as the instrumental music, including many of the overtures, soon became popular.

Those who have found Handel's autocratic reign the chief deterrent to the rekindling of native English music do not seem to have noticed the presence of numerous foreign musicians of eminence. After all, Ariosti, Loeillet, Bononcini, Porpora, Porta, Geminiani, Galuppi, Locatelli, Gluck, and many others lived and worked intermittently in London and had their ardent partisans. As a matter of fact, complaints about the country being overrun by foreign musicians started long before Handel's arrival. John Playford, in *A Briefe Introduction to the Skill of Musicke* (1654), deplores the decline of a pure English style. "Our late and solemn artistic Musicke, both Vocal and Instrumental, is now jostled out of esteem by the new Corants and Jigs of Foreigners, to the grief of all sober and judicious Understanding of that formerly solid and good Musick." A few years later he added, "nor is any Musick rendered acceptable, or esteemed by many but what is presented by Forreigners." Matthew Locke, and others, also showed a measure of xenophobia, from which it can be seen that besides those who admired French and Italian music and endeavored to acclimatize it—Humphrey, or Blow, or Purcell—there were others who deplored its presence.

Hawkins says that Handel "totally extinguished emulation," but surely this is again one of those generalizations that must be qualified. Maurice Greene and William Boyce composed oratorios with very attractive music, and while others, such as Defesch, J. C. Smith, Jr., and Stanley, did not reach this level, their oratorios were not behind the ordinary German or Italian products of the times. Dean calls Greene's *Deborah,* which preceded Handel's oratorio of the same title, "a better work than Handel's." If the statement is surprising, it is borne out by the vocal score published by Schott. Similarly good quality can be found in instrumental music too. Burney reports that Boyce's *Twelve Sonatas or Trios for Two Violins and Base* (1747) "were longer and more generally purchased, performed, and admired, than any production of the kind in this kingdom, except those of Corelli." Among others, Arne, *fils,* in particular deserves to be better known, for in the midst of the Handelian domination this fine composer showed independence and a particularly English quality, which goes to show that real talent cannot be snuffed out, even when toiling in the shadow of an overwhelming genius. The other new genre created by Handel, the organ concerto, also found enthusiastic followers; even Dr. Burney tried his hand at it.

[5]

WHILE IT was not given Handel to found a dynasty of English composers there were good reasons for this. He brought the peculiarly national species he created, the English oratorio, to a peak, from which further development was not possible. This parallels the fate of the Passion in Germany, where with Bach's great works the species reached its unsurpassable end. There was no issue, nor could there be, any more than there was or could be issue to the Wagnerian drama—both were utterly personal and original conceptions and achievements that could not be continued, nor even imitated. The truly creative influence of Handel must be sought among later composers outside of England, in the works of Haydn, Mozart, Mendelssohn, and a few others, but that is a topic that requires an essay by itself and cannot be dealt with here. Suffice it to say that in these composers it is not imitation that we see; the Handelian influence was considerable, but it was completely digested and transformed into a personal style and utterance. Any such living continuation of Handel's legacy was doomed in England by the capital misconception of the nature of his oratorio as sacred music. Handel's imitators tried to follow him for a century and a half, but in their worshipful hands the biblical heroes became provincial church elders whose passion and vigor was lumpish and sententious. Throughout the 19th century every church organist, every music professor considered it his duty to compose "sacred oratorios," and every one of them was convinced that he was following in the master's footsteps. But even so fresh and original a musical mind as Sullivan's had to succumb to the hardness of the oak pew in which he was forced to compose his oratorio. It was Elgar who first broke through the old barriers, rising above this distressing "tradition"; he once more brought life and honest passion to the oratorio.

A contributing factor in this sad situation was the manner in which these worthies were educated for the office of composer. The peculiar conservatism of English music of the 19th century was undoubtedly a byproduct of the unique situation whereby composers were trained in the universities rather than in free conservatories or the opera pit. Hawkins indignantly protests this penchant for academicism, which seems to have been strong in his day and whose beginnings he places in the Handelian era. He praises the quality of the performance of music, but

as to its precepts, the general opinion was that they needed no further cultivation: Dr. Pepusch had prescribed to the students in harmony a set of rules, which no one was hardy enough to transgress; the consequence thereof was a disgusting uniformity of style in the musical productions of the time; while these were adhered to, fancy laboured under the severest restrictions, and all improvement in the science of composition was at a stand.[7]

The situation must have been bad if Hawkins, a confirmed conservative, found it "disgusting." But, it sank still lower in the 19th century. English musicians tried to satisfy the strict and stifling requirements for the Bachelor and Doctor of Music degrees, which had become something quite different since the days of Drs. Bull, Blow, and Greene. This se-

---

[7] A typical example of these doctoral exercises, an eight-part choral composition, can be found in the original edition of Burney's *History of Music*. In the modern reprint of 1935 this piece was omitted as being "very dull," which it assuredly is. But since it earned the doctorate for Burney himself it should have been preserved as an interesting document.

verely formal system of professional education for the creative artist was a strong support for the latter-day "Handelian style," repressing what little imagination the hopeful novice brought to the university. Later in the century this academic isolation was lessened as more and more English musicians journeyed to what was then the Mecca of music for Germans and Englishmen, the Leipzig Conservatory, but the change only resulted in renewed foreign influence as Haydn's mantle was transferred to Mendelssohn's shoulders. The returning English musicians merely grafted German Romanticism upon the existing post- and pseudo-Handelian style, composing "sacred oratorios," anthems, and organ music. But university conservatism would not go along even with the "radicalism" of the hardy Mendelssohnians, and the good Victorian music professors were so shocked by Purcell's almost two-hundred-year-old harmonic and contrapuntal audacities, which defied the guidelines of current academic music theory, that in the early Purcell Society volumes all the "mistakes" were piously corrected. The decisive change came only at the end of the century, but the real renewal of English music is the work of our century. In this new atmosphere Handel is beginning to be seen in his true colors, and perhaps what Oliver Goldsmith wrote in the *British Magazine* in 1760 will now be accepted as the reasoned verdict of Handel's role in musical history. "Handel, in a great measure, found in England those essential differences which characterize his music," said Goldsmith, declaring him, his German origin notwithstanding, "at the head of the English school."

EPILOGUE

ONCLUDING MY HANDELIAN WAYFARING, HOW SHALL I now, at the end of my journey, compose that last ringing sentence? What shall be its principal part, the enriching clauses, the colorful interpolations? I have tried to penetrate beyond what is known of this great life to open a few secret drawers. In its final synthesis, however, the critic-biographer's truth is determined by what he likes. I know how elusive is the giant I have momentarily netted and how difficult it is to avoid disaster with this boundless subject. But I do like him, and I hope that, though perhaps inked in with blots and shaky line, my way of liking him has shown a great man and artist, and not a figure in inferior stained glass.

I trust that the false colors of the composer's commonly accepted picture, as well as its unhistorical distortion, are open to dispassionate contemplation, as analyses of the creative personality are to challenge and change. We know that this picture was different in Handel's time, and we know that some of the greatest musicians of the 18th and early 19th centuries saw Handel the composer free from the amorphous legend that early began to envelop him. When in 1745 he was elected to the *Societät der musikalischen Wissenschaften*, founded by Lorenz Mizler, the learned musicians in the group gave their unanimous vote not to a legendary plaster saint but to the admired worldly maestro. Mizler's "Association for Musical Science" was made up of musicians respected for their "science," i.e. their highly developed skill. Bach, who became a member after Handel (though Mizler was Bach's disciple), submitted a six-part canon and the canonic variations on *Vom Himmel hoch* to qualify for membership. Handel was not even required to compete; he was made an honorary member—the only one—and the Society awarded him its gold medal. Haydn said to William Shield, one of his English musician friends, that before hearing *Joshua* in London "he had long been acquainted with music but never knew half its power." His oratorios composed after the London visits eloquently testify to his indebtedness to Handel, as do Mozart's choral works. Gerhard von Breuning relates the seriously ill Beethoven's delight at receiving the forty volumes of Samuel Arnold's edition of Handel's works, published as the first "complete" edition in 1787–97. This was in December, 1826, after Beethoven's first operation, and his young friend describes how the composer propped up the volumes on his sickbed, saying "I have long wanted them, for Handel is the greatest, the ablest composer that ever lived. I can still learn from him." Nevertheless, Handel's discovery and acceptance in Germany was slow, and his Mendelssohn was an Englishman, Arne, whose performance of *Messiah* in Hamburg (1772) was the first Handelian oratorio heard in Germany. The Handel cult started in earnest with Hiller, who seems to have been inspired by the London commemoration ceremonies. Ironically enough, Hiller's first performance of *Messiah* in Berlin Cathedral (1786) was in Italian!

Today we ask the question, "Can that understanding and admiration be recaptured, shall we attain an intelligent and more durable appreciation?" The opinions of later musicians are by no means as unanimous as those we have just mentioned. Berlioz saw in Handel nothing but "pork and beer," and in our day Stravinsky writes that "Handel's reputation is a puzzle . . . [his] inventions are exterior; he can draw from an extensive reservoir of allegros and largos, but cannot pursue a musical idea through an intensifying degree of development" (*Exposition and Developments*). The palm, however, goes to Cyril Scott (*Philosophy of Modernism*):

The beauty of one age often becomes the banality of the next. Is not the greater part of the work of Handel, for instance, as unbearable nowadays as the greater part of Wordsworth is unbearable; for where is the serious-minded musician to be found who could subject himself to a hearing of *Messiah?* And yet, undoubtedly at one time *Messiah* was a thing of beauty, and possibly also of intellectual complexity.

Handel remains as blandly impervious to such strange animadversions as does the *Kreutzer Sonata* to strictures of a Tolstoyan character.

The saddest fact is that the bicentennial in 1959 found him not so much deprecated as unknown, for even many of his admirers have no glimmering of what his *oeuvre* represents, what achievements it encompasses. The churchmen have had him long enough, the bees in their bonnets have buzzed to a standstill; it is high time for the musicians and the theatre to reclaim their heritage. The task of presenting the music of this most virile and vigorous of men must be seized by hands more virile and vigorous than those of present-day church musicians. We might apply what Joubert said about Chateaubriand's excursions into theology: "Let him stick to his own business, let him entertain us." This is still a difficult prescription. Ortega y Gasset's argument that "the semi-religious character, cultivating pathos of a sublime type has now been completely extirpated" is true perhaps in literature, but certainly not in music. Old Handelians may be unwilling to abandon the churchly atmosphere without which Handel is unthinkable to Anglo-Saxon Protestantism, and will reject the new portrait, refusing to see the greater man and musician. But it seems inconceivable that Handel's profound musical poetry, his sturdiness in composition, his richness in pictorial plasticity, his wondrous dramatic sense, and his refined stylization should have been an indiscretion of history.

The lesson is that the interpretation of Handel can never be ended and that every student may contribute something that even for those who reject it may throw a measure of light on the subject. But to understand how Handel succeeded in building a universal body of work on a national basis and to grasp the quality of the whole man, his music must be better known. A small portion of his enormous output has exclusive currency and obscures the totality, but we must awaken Handel's real lovers from their idyll of religious grandiloquence. And when the truth washed free of bias shall come to pass, it will be as though a living voice, muffled for two centuries by some strange spell, were suddenly to speak to us.

"Perhaps," says Dr. William Hayes in his *Remarks* on Avison's *Essay*,

as I have been so particular in delivering my sentiments concerning the Hero of the Essay, You may expect me to give you a Detail of the various Excellencies, which still remain unmentioned in HANDEL; and to point out wherein he excells *all others* of his Profession . . . I say, perhaps you may expect me to enter into *Particulars*, to *defend* and *characterize* this man:—but the first would be an endless Undertaking;—his Works being almost out of Number.—The second, a needless one, the Works themselves being his best Defense:—And the third, I must acknowledge is above my Capacity; and therefore once more refer you to his works, where only his true character is to be found . . .

BIBLIOGRAPHICAL NOTE

THE HANDELIAN BIBLIOGRAPHY IS VAST AND UNWIELDY; TO reproduce it here in its entirety is patently impossible—and unnecessary. If the reader wants to see its full extent he can consult:

Sasse, Konrad, *Händel Bibliographie*. Leipzig, 1963. (This volume incorporates the earlier extensive bibliography of Kurt Taut.)

It will perhaps be useful to remind the reader that the three great modern dictionaries of music should be consulted when a name or subject must be run down:

Enciclopedia della Musica. Milan, 1964–1965.
Grove's Dictionary of Music and Musicians. Fifth edition, London, 1954.
Die Musik in Geschichte und Gegenwart. Kassel, 1949–
All other compilations of this sort merely present history in shirt sleeves.

As we turn to the Handelian literature proper, it is astounding to see how slow it was in fulfilling its role. In the register of the vaults in Westminster Abbey this notice appears: "At the foot of Handel's coffin, on the left and on the right, there remains place for good graves." Well over a hundred years passed before one of them was assigned—to Dickens. It took much longer for worthy Handelian literature to fill the empty spaces around Handel's artistic monument, and it was considerably after Dickens's time that the vacuous rhapsodies, the ingenious and wayward trifles, and the gravely sanctimonious essays were thrown out with the intellectual pitchfork of unbiased scholarship. Before that time the reader must proceed warily.

The most important bibliographical reference concerns the musical sources. Of the great masters, Handel has been the least well served by editors, and we must still rely on the old Händelgesellschaft volumes edited by Friedrich Chrysander and published between 1859 and 1894. The edition, though an incomparable personal achievement, is antiquated, incomplete, and often incorrect, but it will be some time before the new

Hallische Händelausgabe, now barely past its first offerings, gives us the whole body of Handel's works in a modern critical edition. This will compel anyone seeking to do serious work to turn to the manuscripts and the many early printed editions. Fortunately, there exists an excellent summary of these sources, where information is given concerning the location of the manuscripts as well as of important copies and printed editions:

Abraham, Gerald (ed.), *Handel, a Symposium.* London, 1954. See the chapter entitled "Catalogue of Works," by William C. Smith, pp. 275–310.

For Handel's own writings and for contemporary statements, newspaper notices, extracts from memoirs, correspondence, and so on, nothing can approach the fullness and practical service afforded by:

Deutsch, Otto Erich, *Handel, a Documentary Biography.* New York, 1955.

For general historical and cultural background the selected works listed below are recommended; they will also supply additional bibliographical references:

Gagey, M., *Ballad Opera.* New York, 1937.

George, M., *London Life in the Eighteenth Century.* London, 1945.

McGiffert, A. C., *Protestant Thought Before Kant.* New York, 1915.

Nicoll, Allardyce, *Eighteenth Century Drama, 1700–1750.* Cambridge, 1925.

——*A History of Restoration Drama.* Cambridge, 1928.

Richardson, A. E., *Georgian England.* London, 1931.

Stephen, Sir Leslie, *History of England in the Eighteenth Century.* New York, 1927.

Of the 18th-century literature, the following books are of basic importance:

Avison, Charles, *An Essay on Musical Expression.* Second edition, London, 1753.

Brown, John, *A Discussion on the Rise, Union, and Power, the Progressions, Separations, and Corruptions of Poetry and Music.* London, 1763.

Burney, Charles, *An Account of the Musical Performances in Westminster Abbey. . . .* London, 1785. Reprint, Amsterdam, 1964.

——*A General History of Music.* London, 1776–1789. Modern edition, London, 1935.

Delany, Mary, *Autobiography and Correspondence of Mary Granville, Mrs. Delany,* edited by Lady Llanover. London, 1861.

Hawkins, Sir John, *A General History of the Science and Practice of Music.* London, 1776. Reprint of the 1853 edition, New York, 1963.

Hodgkin MSS (Historical Manuscript Commission). London, 1897.

Mainwaring, John, *Memoirs of the Life of the Late George Frederic Handel.* London, 1760.

Mattheson, Johann, *Der vollkommene Capellmeister.* Hamburg, 1739. Reprint, Kassel, 1964.

——*Grundlagen einer Ehren-Pforte.* Hamburg, 1740. New edition, Berlin, 1910.

In the categories of biographies and essays, we shall omit the various writings published under the heading of "Berühmte Musiker" or "Lives of Great Musicians," and once more remind the reader that works mentioned in this highly selective list will provide further ample bibliographies.

Chrysander, Friedrich, *Georg Friedrich Händel.* Leipzig, 1858–1867. Second ed., Leipzig, 1919.

Leichtentritt, Hugo, *Georg Friedrich Händel.* Stuttgart, 1924.

Rolland, Romain, *Haendel.* Paris (1910), 1951.

Schoelcher, Victor, *The Life of Handel.* London, 1857.

Streatfeild, Richard A., *Handel.* London, 1909. New York, 1964.

Young, Percy M., *Handel.* London, 1947.

Abraham, Gerald (ed.), *Handel, a Symposium.* London, 1954.

Blume, Friedrich, *Die Evangelische Kirchenmusik.* Potsdam, 1931.

Bredenförder, Elisabeth, *Die Texte der Händel-Oratorien.* Leipzig, 1934.

Bukofzer, Manfred F., *Music in the Baroque Era.* New York, 1947.

Cannon, Beekman, *Johann Mattheson, Spectator in Music.* New Haven, 1947.

Clercx, Suzanne, *Le Baroque et la Musique.* Brussels. 1948.

Dean, Winton, *Handel's Dramatic Oratorios and Masques.* London, 1959.

Dent, Edward J., *Alessandro Scarlatti.* London, 1905.

——*Foundations of English Opera.* Cambridge, 1928.

Eisenschmidt, Joachim, *Die szenische Darstellung der Opern G. F. Händels auf der Londoner Bühne seiner Zeit.* Wolfenbüttel, 1940.

Florimo, F., *La scuola musicale di Napoli e i suoi Conservatori.* Naples, 1880.

Händel Jahrbuch. Leipzig, 1928–1933. New series, 1955–

Langley, H., *Dr. Arne.* Cambridge, 1938.

Larsen, Jens Peter, *Handel's Messiah, Origins, Composition, Sources.* New York, 1957.

Myers, Robert Manson, *Handel's Messiah, a Touchstone of Taste.* New York, 1948.

——*Early Moral Criticism of Handelian Oratorio.* Williamsburg, Va., 1947.

Pasquetti, G., *L'Oratorio musicale in Italia.* Florence, 1912.

Pincherle, Marc, *Corelli.* New York, 1956.

Reinecke, H., *Hamburg, ein Abriss der Stadtgeschichte.* . . . Bremen, 1926.

Salvioli, G., *I. Teatri musicali di Venezia del secolo XVII*. Milan, 1879.

Seiffert, Max, Preface to Volumes 21, 22 of *Denkmäler deutscher Tonkunst* (Zachow). Leipzig, 1905.

Serauky, Walter, *Musikgeschichte der Stadt Halle*. Halle, 1935–1943.

Smith, William C., *Concerning Handel*. London, 1948.

Schering, Arnold, *Geschichte des Instrumentalkonzerts*. Leipzig (1905) 1927. Reprint, 1965.

——*Geschichte des Oratoriums*. Leipzig, 1911.

Taylor, Sedley, *The Indebtedness of Handel to Works by Other Composers*. Cambridge, 1906.

Westrup, Sir Jack A., *Purcell*. London, 1947.

Wolff, Hellmuth Christian, *Die Barockoper in Hamburg*. Wolfenbüttel, 1957.

——*Die venezianische Oper*. Berlin, 1957.

INDEX OF HANDEL'S WORKS
DISCUSSED IN THIS BOOK

1. Vocal Music

2. Instrumental Music

GENERAL INDEX

HANDEL, GEORGE FRIDERIC

General:

Elements of Style: